BAHAMAS
19TH EDITION

Where to Stay and Eat
for All Budgets

Must-See Sights
and Local Secrets

Ratings You Can Trust

Fodor's Travel Publications   New York, Toronto, London, Sydney, Auckland
www.fodors.com

FODOR'S BAHAMAS
Editor: Nina Rubin

Editorial Production: Jenna L. Bagnini
Editorial Contributors: Harriet Edleson, Evelyn Kanter, Patricia Rodriguez, Stephen Vletas, Chelle Koster Walton
Maps: David Lindroth *cartographer*; Bob Blake and Rebecca Baer, *map editors*
Design: Fabrizio La Rocca, *creative director*; Guido Caroti, *art director*; Melanie Marin, *senior picture editor*
Production/Manufacturing: Colleen Ziemba
Cover Photo: Stephen Frink/Tony Stone Images

SPECIAL SALES
This book is available for special discounts for bulk purchases for sales promotions or premiums. Special editions, including personalized covers, excerpts of existing books, and corporate imprints, can be created in large quantities for special needs. For more information, write to Special Markets/Premium Sales, 1745 Broadway, MD 6-2, New York, New York 10019, or e-mail specialmarkets@randomhouse.com.

AN IMPORTANT TIP & AN INVITATION
Although all prices, opening times, and other details in this book are based on information supplied to us at press time, changes occur all the time in the travel world, and Fodor's cannot accept responsibility for facts that become outdated or for inadvertent errors or omissions. So **always confirm information when it matters,** especially if you're making a detour to visit a specific place. Your experiences—positive and negative—matter to us. If we have missed or misstated something, **please write to us.** We follow up on all suggestions. Contact the Bahamas editor at editors@fodors.com or c/o Fodor's at 1745 Broadway, New York, New York 10019.

PRINTED IN THE UNITED STATES OF AMERICA

10 9 8 7 6 5 4 3 2

DESTINATION BAHAMAS

The sea is livelihood, attraction, and inspiration for this country of more than 700 islands. The water ranges from pale aqua to deep sapphire, the spectrum changing hourly as the relentless Bahamian sun sweeps across the sky. Stately palms surround silken sand beaches; inland lies a lush world of tropical foliage. Tiny villages known as "settlements," with New England–style cottages dressed up in vibrant tropical hues, dot the landscape. Underwater, you can explore fantasies of frilly fan coral and phantasmagoric sponges on the sea floor below. If you should nap away the day in a hammock overlooking the deserted shores, no one would think it odd—many visitors' favorite activity is no activity at all. Or skip the glorious laziness in favor of snorkeling, diving, and boating—arguably some of the world's best—or try prowling through Nassau's bustling shopping district and hitting the casinos. However you spend your time, have a fabulous trip!

Tim Jarrell, Publisher

CONTENTS

Understanding the Bahamas 247

Index 266

Maps

CloseUps

ABOUT THIS BOOK

There's no doubt that the best source for travel advice is a like-minded friend who's just been where you're headed. But with or without that friend, you'll have a better trip with a Fodor's guide in hand. Once you've learned to find your way around its pages, you'll be in great shape to find your way around your destination.

SELECTION

Our goal is to cover the best properties, sights, and activities in their category, as well as the most interesting communities to visit. We make a point of including local food-lovers' hot spots as well as neighborhood options, and we avoid all that's touristy unless it's really worth your time. You can go on the assumption that everything you read about in this book is recommended wholeheartedly by our writers and editors. Flip to On the Road with Fodor's to learn more about who they are. It goes without saying that no property mentioned in the book has paid to be included.

RATINGS

Orange stars ★ denote sights and properties that our editors and writers consider the very best in the area covered by the entire book. These, the best of the best, are listed in the Fodor's Choice section in the front of the book. Black stars ★ highlight the sights and properties we deem Highly Recommended, the don't-miss sights within any region. Fodor's Choice and Highly Recommended options in each region are usually listed on the title page of the chapter covering that region. Use the index to find complete descriptions. In cities, sights pinpointed with numbered map bullets ❶ in the margins tend to be more important than those without bullets.

SPECIAL SPOTS

Pleasures & Pastimes focuses on types of experiences that reveal the spirit of the destination. Watch for Off the Beaten Path sights. Some are out of the way, some are quirky, and all are worth your while. If the munchies hit while you're exploring, look for Need a Break? suggestions.

TIME IT RIGHT

Wondering when to go? Check On the Calendar up front and chapters' Timing sections for weather and crowd overviews and best days and times to visit.

SEE IT ALL

Use Fodor's exclusive Great Itineraries as a model for your trip. (For a good overview of the entire destination, follow those that begin the book, or mix regional itineraries from several chapters.) In cities, Good Walks guide you to important sights in each neighborhood; ☞ indicates the starting points of walks and itineraries in the text and on the map.

BUDGET WELL	Hotel and restaurant price categories from ¢ to $$$$ are defined in the opening pages of each chapter; expect to find a balanced selection for every budget. For attractions, we always give standard adult admission fees; reductions are usually available for children, students, and senior citizens. Look in Discounts & Deals in Smart Travel Tips for information on destination-wide ticket schemes. Want to pay with plastic? AE, D, DC, MC, V following restaurant and hotel listings indicate whether American Express, Discover, Diners Club, MasterCard, or Visa are accepted.
BASIC INFO	Smart Travel Tips lists travel essentials for the entire area covered by the book; city- and region-specific basics end each chapter. To find the best way to get around, see the transportation section; see individual modes of travel ("Car Travel," "Train Travel") for details. We assume you'll check Web sites or call for particulars.
ON THE MAPS	Maps throughout the book show you what's where and help you find your way around. Black and orange numbered bullets ❶ ❶ in the text correlate to bullets on maps.
BACKGROUND	In general, we give background information within the chapters in the course of explaining sights as well as in CloseUp boxes and in Understanding the Bahamas at the end of the book. To get in the mood, review the suggestions in Books & Movies. The glossary can be invaluable.
FIND IT FAST	Within the book, chapters are divided into small regions, within which towns are covered in logical geographical order; attractive routes and interesting places between towns are flagged as En Route. Heads at the top of each page help you find what you need within a chapter.
DON'T FORGET	Restaurants are open for lunch and dinner daily unless we state otherwise; we mention dress only when there's a specific requirement and reservations only when they're essential or not accepted—it's always best to book ahead. Hotels have private baths, phones, TVs, and air-conditioning and operate on the European Plan (a.k.a. EP, meaning without meals). We always list facilities but not whether you'll be charged extra to use them, so when pricing accommodations, find out what's included.

SYMBOLS

Many Listings

★ Fodor's Choice
★ Highly recommended
⊠ Physical address
✛ Directions
🕮 Mailing address
☎ Telephone
🖷 Fax
⊕ On the Web
✉ E-mail
🎫 Admission fee
🕓 Open/closed times
► Start of walk/itinerary
Ⓜ Metro stations
🖃 Credit cards

Outdoors

⚑ Golf
⚠ Camping

Hotels & Restaurants

🏨 Hotel
🛏 Number of rooms
♨ Facilities
🍽 Meal plans
✕ Restaurant
🍴 Reservations
🎩 Dress code
⊘ Smoking
🍷 BYOB
✕🏨 Hotel with restaurant that warrants a visit

Other

☺ Family-friendly
🔋 Contact information
⇨ See also
⊠ Branch address
☞ Take note

ON THE ROAD WITH FODOR'S

A trip takes you out of yourself. Concerns of life at home completely disappear, driven away by more immediate thoughts—about, say, what marvels will beguile the next day, or where you'll have dinner. That's where Fodor's comes in. We make sure that you know all your options, so that you don't miss something that's around the next bend just because you didn't know it was there. Because the best memories of your trip might well have nothing to do with what you came to the Bahamas to see, we guide you to sights large and small all over the region. You might set out to laze on the beach, but back at home you find yourself unable to forget your ascent to the Hermitage at the top of Mt. Alvernia or the little roadside conch stand that you stumbled upon in Eleuthera. With Fodor's at your side, serendipitous discoveries are never far away.

Our success in showing you every corner of the Bahamas is a credit to our extraordinary writers. Although there's no substitute for travel advice from a good friend who knows your style, our contributors are the next best thing—the kind of people you would poll for travel advice if you knew them.

A native of Tarrytown, New York, **Harriet Edleson** lived in several American cities before moving to Manhattan in 1999. She has been traveling since she was 10, covering parts of North America, the Caribbean, Europe, the Middle East, and Australia. Since graduating from Mount Holyoke College, she has held numerous staff and freelance writing posts, including working at the *Houston Chronicle, Travel Agent,* and *WMAL* radio, the ABC affiliate in Washington, D.C. Her articles have appeared in the *New York Times,* the *Washington Post, Kiplinger's Personal Finance,* and Conde Nast's *Bride's.*

Evelyn Kanter is a New York City–based writer and photographer. After becoming intoxicated with scuba diving while visiting the Bahamas, she became a certified diver. She has returned to the islands repeatedly to indulge her sense of adventure and her desire to capture on film and pixel the beauty of the land and its people. Also a skier, Evelyn has updated *Skiing USA* and *New York City* for Fodor's, and has freelanced for a number of magazines and newspapers.

After working as a Texas-based travel editor for several years, **Patricia Rodriguez Terrell** decided that merely visiting other countries wasn't enough. In 2003, she and her chef husband moved with their infant son to a small cay in the Abacos in the Bahamas, where she lived while contributing to this guide. She now lives in the Dominican Republic, where she writes for various U.S. publications, and vows she will never again reside in any place that receives snow.

Chelle Koster Walton admits she's a "fair-weather writer"—her specialty is travel to Florida and the Caribbean. She has written for such publications as *FamilyFun, Bridal Guide,* the *St. Petersburg Times,* and the *Miami Herald.* A resident of Sanibel Island, Florida, for 25 years, she is the author of several Florida guidebooks, including *Sarasota, Sanibel Island & Naples, Fun with the Family in Florida,* and *Insight Orlando.*

A fly-fishing and powder-skiing junkie, **Stephen F. Vletas** is based in Jackson Hole, Wyoming, where he is at work on a new novel. Vletas was the owner of an international fly-fishing company for 16 years, and is the author of *The Bahamas Fly-Fishing Guide.* He has also written many articles for national publications including *Fly Rod & Reel, Fly Fisherman, Fly Fishing in Salt Waters,* and *Scientific Anglers Quarterly.* Vletas and his wife, Kim, consider Andros Island their second home, though they also can't seem to get enough of Argentina's Mendoza wine country.

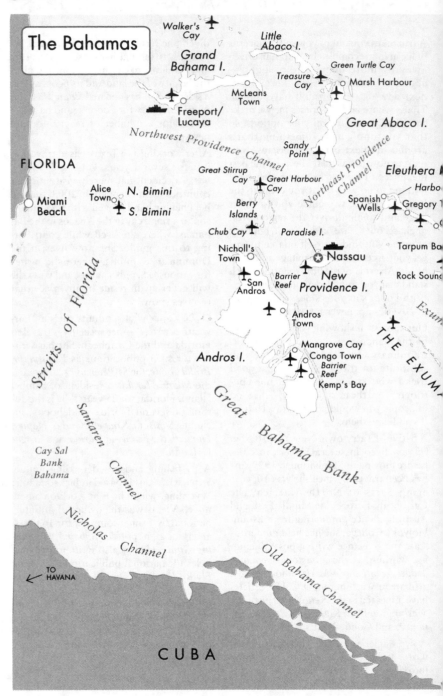

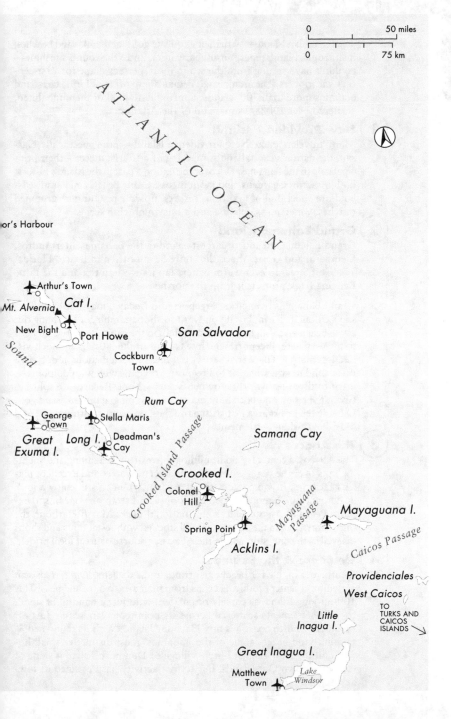

WHAT'S WHERE

The Bahamian Islands—with their exquisite gold- and pink-sand beaches, lush tropical landscapes, unsullied waters, and year-round sunshine—couldn't have sprung from the sea in more perfect shape for 21st-century vacationers. The archipelago begins 55 mi off the Florida coast and contains more than 700 islands, approximately 30 of them inhabited, scattered over 100,000 square mi of the Atlantic.

(1) New Providence Island

Many travelers make New Providence Island—more specifically Nassau, the nation's capital and something of a tourist mecca—their principal stop in the Bahamas. Discover the nation's past in the island's historic buildings, forts, gardens, and monuments. Cable Beach and Paradise Island are chock full of luxurious resorts, upscale restaurants, groomed beaches, watersports aplenty, and a busy nightclub scene.

(2) Grand Bahama Island

Grand Bahama, the fourth-largest island in the Bahamas after Andros, Eleuthera, and Great Abaco, lies only 52 mi off Palm Beach, Florida. The Gulf Stream's ever-warm waters lap its western tip, and the Little Bahama Bank protects it from the northeast.

Grand Bahama's twin cities, Freeport and Lucaya, may not have Nassau's colonial charm, but if you want to shop, gamble, or just hang out at the beach—at a slightly lower cost than in the capital—there's no need to go elsewhere. Freeport, which was built in the '60s, has a much-visited International Bazaar, where you'll find imported goods at duty-free prices. In Lucaya, adjacent to Freeport, you can swim with dolphins or learn to dive at a world-renowned scuba school. Resorts are split between the cities, and both have access to shopping, gambling, and golf. Outside the resort area lie pristine beaches, ecotourism attractions, and old-island fishing settlements.

(3) The Abacos

The Abacos, a center for boatbuilding, have attracted sailing and yachting fans over the years with their translucent waters and excellent marina facilities. If you come without a yacht, you can still enjoy a look at Elbow Cay's famous striped lighthouse and strap on your fins to explore Pelican Cay, an underwater national park. Marsh Harbour, the third-largest city in the country, is well stocked with restaurants and shops (as well as the only stoplight in the Abacos, a source of great local pride).

(4) Eleuthera & the Exumas

Eleuthera, notable for beaches, surfing, and excellent diving, is also an agricultural center producing crops from mangoes to okra and peas. This 100-mi-long island is sparsely populated, with just a handful of small, friendly settlements scattered across its bounteous landscape. Just off Eleuthera's north coast lies tiny Harbour Island. With its renowned 3-mi pink-sand beach, some of the Bahamas' most distinctive small hotels, and the New England–style village of Dunmore Town, it's one of the best-known Out Islands, but tourist activity hasn't ruined its low-key appeal.

The hundreds of little cays that make up the Exumas are prime cruising ground for yachters, but you might also come to enjoy the charms of several attractive towns, welcoming small hotels, Exuma Land and Sea Park (a favorite with snorkelers and bird-watchers), and a 7-mi beach fabled for its seashells.

⑤ The Other Out Islands

To escape New Providence's and Grand Bahama's crowds and glittering modernity, hop a plane, boat, or even a helicopter to one of the Out Islands, where life progresses at a slower pace, and the landscape is still largely unaffected by major development. In fact, many seasoned Bahamas travelers skip the more populated islands altogether and head straight for these unspoiled isles, usually called the Family Islands by locals (it's the rare Bahamian who doesn't have roots here). Wander uncluttered beaches and narrow, sand-strewn streets, or lunch in a village where fishermen's tidy homes are painted in soft pastel shades and shrouded in brilliantly colored vegetation. The Out Islands' common traits—an abundance of natural beauty and small-town atmosphere—should not disguise their differences, however. You may be surprised by the variety of sites and activities the islands have to offer.

⑥ Turks & Caicos Islands

The Turks and Caicos, two groups of islands that lie to the southeast of the Bahamas, are nearly unknown to all but avid divers and seekers of untrod beaches. Although there's talk of developing the islands along the lines of some Bahamian destinations, for now you'll find all of the beauty but very little glitz.

The most important thing to decide is what kind of vacation you want: a quiet getaway or an action-packed excursion. If you want shopping, dining, and nightlife, head straight for Nassau on New Providence or Freeport and Lucaya on Grand Bahama Island, where's there's plenty to do and lots to see. If it's a tranquil trip you're seeking, go to the Out Islands. Below are suggested itineraries for both areas. See the Exploring sections in each chapter for more information about individual sights.

Of course, your interests will determine what will be the right destination for you. If you're a dedicated angler, Bimini or the Berry Islands are where you should head. Bird-watchers should choose Inagua; devotees of island architecture should try Elbow Cay in the Abacos (or, for that matter, Nassau). Divers can head to Andros; fishing types to the Abacos and Bimini. For those who would like a mix of urban and rural experiences without having to leave the island, Grand Bahama provides some of the best of both worlds. And if you're interested in doing nothing at all, consider Cat Island or San Salvador.

New Providence Island

Day 1: If you've opted for a lively three days on New Providence, spend your first morning in **downtown Nassau** visiting historic sights. Have a leisurely lunch and spend the afternoon shopping. Be sure to check out the shopping on Bay Street and its environs. Day or night, you can test your luck in the two **casinos** (one on Cable Beach, one on Paradise Island).

Day 2: Begin by exploring the sights on the island's eastern side, including **The Retreat** and **St. Augustine's Monastery.** Continue west around the island, perhaps taking time to visit the **Bacardi Distillery** or the **Commonwealth Brewery.** Head back toward Nassau and stop by **Arawak Cay,** a nice spot for a quick, local-style lunch. Or, alternatively, visit three nearby sites: **Fort Charlotte,** the **Nassau Botanic Gardens,** and **Ardastra Gardens and Conservation Centre,** home to the famous marching flamingos. If you have any energy left after this, dance the night away in a club or see one of the glittery extravaganzas offered by the resorts.

Day 3: Spend your last day on Paradise Island wandering through the **Atlantis, Paradise Island** resort, visiting **Cabbage Beach** or **Paradise Beach,** and passing a few minutes in the lovely **Versailles Gardens.** If you're still in search of more activity, watersports abound, and, of course, lounging on the beach can occupy the rest of your time.

If you have more time on your hands, spend your fourth day on an excursion to the **Exuma Cays,** reached by powerboat or seaplane. You can also take a day trip via boat or helicopter to quaint **Harbour Island.** In either case you can make it back to Nassau in time for dinner. Spend your last day in the water—swim for a few hours or sign up for a guided tour. With Dolphin Encounters, you can actually swim with dolphins. More experienced underwater types might consider the shark dive available in south New Providence.

The Exumas

If you've decided to head for the Out Islands, **Exuma** is a good choice if your time is limited. You can fly straight into George Town airport, outside Great Exuma's main town.

Day 1: On your first day, wander through the village of **George Town,** stopping to chat with the ladies in the tiny straw market.

Day 2: Pick up some made-to-order seafood or conch salad at Fish Fry, a cluster of beachside shacks just north of town, before catching the ferry to picture-perfect **Stocking Island,** just a few minutes away and good for a half-day's worth of shelling and tanning. If you're feeling adventurous, rent a car and see some of this enticing island, from the tiny settlements of **Barreterre** and **Rolleville** in the north all the way down to **Williams Town** at Little Exuma's southern tip, connected to Great Exuma by a bridge.

Day 3: On your last day, you may want to try bonefishing, diving, or snorkeling. There are operators in town (check with the local tourist office) who will gladly set you up. Another half-day possibility: a bush-medicine tour with a local flora expert, who will show you how various island plants are used medicinally.

If you have two more days to spare, fly to **Marsh Harbour** in the Abacos. Start your explorations in **Elbow Cay**—be sure to visit charming Hope Town with its vibrant Cape Cod–style houses, peppermint-stripe lighthouse, and Wyanie Malone Historical Museum. If you can arrange to rent a boat for the rest of your stay, you'll discover endless possibilities for exploring the cays. But even on the infrequent ferry service, you can manage a day trip to **Man-O-War Cay,** home of the Abacos' boatbuilding industry. Visit **Albury's Sail Shop,** where several generations of women fashion luggage and other products from brightly colored sail canvas, or wander some of the most isolated beaches in the country. Spend your final day on **Green Turtle Cay** (it's a ferry, cab, and ferry ride from Elbow Cay, but doable), relaxing on tranquil **Coco Beach** or the wilder ocean shores, visiting the charming village of **New Plymouth,** or arranging a snorkeling expedition through **Brendal's Dive Shop.** Then, it's time to head home. The best place to fly out from here is Treasure Cay.

If You Have 10 Days or More

See the best of both worlds, spending half your time in Nassau and the rest on one of the Out Islands, just a short flight away. The fast ferry service out of Nassau allows you to make day trips to several destinations in the Eleuthera Islands, and speed boats take you back and forth to Exuma. If you're determined, you could manage to see three destinations. Spend four days in Nassau, and split the rest of your days between, for instance, Exuma and Cat Island. You could fly directly to George Town, Exuma, catch a flight back to Nassau from there, and head out a few days later to Cat, returning home on a flight out of Cat Island International Airport by way of Nassau. But that gets a little complicated. Maybe you're best plunking yourself down on a quiet patch of Exuma, Eleuthera, Cat, Long, Andros, or any of the scores of other islands in the archipelago, and learning to live (for 10 days, at least) on Bahamian time.

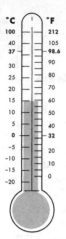

The Bahamas is affected by the refreshing trade-wind flow generated by an area of high atmospheric pressure covering a large part of the subtropical North Atlantic, so the climate varies little during the year. The most pleasant time is from December through May, when the temperature averages 70°F–75°F. It stands to reason that hotel prices during this period are at their highest—around 30% higher than during the less popular times. The rest of the year is hot and humid and prone to tropical storms; the temperature hovers around 80°F–85°F. Hurricane season is from about June 1 through November 30, with greatest risk for a storm from August through October.

Whether you want to join it or avoid it, be advised that Spring Break takes place between the end of February and mid-April. This means a lot of vacationing college students, beach parties, sports events, and entertainment.

Climate

What follows are average daily maximum and minimum temperatures for Nassau. Freeport's temperatures are nearly the same: a degree or two cooler in the spring and fall, and a degree or two warmer in the summer.
🔁 Forecasts **Weather Channel Connection** ⊕ www.weather.com.

NASSAU

Jan.	77F	25C	May	85F	29C	Sept.	88F	31C
	62	17		70	21		74	23
Feb.	78F	26C	June	87F	31C	Oct.	85F	29C
	63	17		73	23		72	22
Mar.	80F	27C	July	89F	32C	Nov.	82F	28C
	64	18		75	24		68	20
Apr.	82F	28C	Aug.	89F	32C	Dec.	79F	26C
	66	19		75	24		64	18

WINTER	
Dec.	The **Authentically Bahamian Christmas Trade Show** showcases crafts, pottery, jewelry, and batiks.
	The **National Junkanoo Competition Finals,** the "Olympics of Junkanoo," is held on Paradise Island.
	Christmas Day and **Boxing Day,** December 25 and 26, are both public holidays. Boxing Day coincides with the first of the **Junkanoo** parades.
	Other annual December doings in Nassau include the **Police Band Beat Retreat, Junior Junkanoo Parade, Night of Christmas Music, New Year's Eve Party,** and **Renaissance Singers Concert.**
Jan.	**Junkanoo** continues its uniquely Bahamian (Mardi Gras–style) festivities welcoming the New Year with the **New Year's Day Junkanoo Parade,** in downtown Nassau. Less extensive celebrations take place in the Out Islands and in the Turks and Caicos—also on January 1, a public holiday.
	The **New Year's Sailing Regatta** at Montagu Bay, Nassau, includes competition among Bahamian-built sloops, whereas the **Staniel Cay Annual New Year's Day Cruising Regatta** in the Exumas marks the finale of a five-day celebration.
	Pomp and pageantry take over when the **Supreme Court** opens in Nassau with the Chief Justice inspecting the Royal Bahamas Police Force Guard-of-Honor, accompanied by the acclaimed Bahamas Police Force Band.
	For cultural types, the repertory season begins at Nassau's **Dundas Centre for the Performing Arts.**
	The **Bahamas Wahoo Tournament** draws great numbers of anglers to the waters around several Out Islands for a series of three competitions beginning in November and running through February.
	The **Breitling Crystal Pro-Am Golf Tournament** is a week of meets on Grand Bahama Island that draws a roster of professional and amateur golfers almost as long as the tourney's name.
	The **Grand Bahama Island Carnival** comes to town the last two weeks of January. Held in Goombay Park, it offers games, food, music, and rides.
Feb.	The **Farmer's Cay Festival** is held the first weekend on this tiny cay in the Exumas. Boat races, treasure hunts, music, and food are highlights.

Nassau Race Week comprises three days of international sailboat championship racing.

Jamz Fest headlines international hip-hop artists at Queen Elizabeth Sports Centre.

The Bahamas Wahoo Tournament has its final installment in the Out Islands.

Also in the Out Islands, Exuma begins its monthlong Annual Cruising Regatta.

Beginning in February and continuing through April, Whalewatching Trips depart from several islands in the Turks and Caicos.

SPRING

Mar.

The annual Red Cross Fair at the Queen Elizabeth Sports Centre rounds off Nassau's winter social season.

In Nassau, Bahamas Heritage Festival takes place at Arawak Cay. `

The weeklong Bacardi Rum Billfish Tournament, which rotates around Grand Bahama and the Out Islands, is one of the most prestigious events of the year for deep-sea sportfishers.

The Andros Annual International Square Celebration is a celebration of Andros residents of all heritages, with flag raising, music, and international cuisines.

A one-man show by one of the islands' foremost painters, the Annual Alton Lowe Art Exhibition takes place at the Nassau Beach hotel.

Apr.

Held at Long Bay Cays Park, the Andros Going Back to the Island Festival is a week of contests, traditional food and music, games, and fun. South Eleuthera holds a similar Eleuthera Homecoming Festival; and there's Mastic Point Homecoming in Andros.

In Grand Bahama, Cricket Festival pays homage to the islands' favorite sport with a weeklong series of matches between local and U.S. teams. Port Lucaya Marina hosts Dolphin/Tuna Classic Tournament on Grand Bahama.

Coconut Festival in Grand Bahama's Pelican Point settlement includes coconut food sampling, coconut tree climbing, and other activities.

Long Island's CornFest consists of competitions, corn product sales, a flea market, and a cultural show.

Good Friday, Easter, and the following Easter Monday are public holidays.

May

There are numerous fishing tournaments in the Out Islands this month, including the Bahamas Billfish Championship, Boat Harbour Billfish

Blast Championship and Green Turtle Club Billfish Tournament in Abaco, and Bimini Festival of Champions and Saltwater Sportsman Fishing Tournament in Bimini.

The Barreterre Festival livens up this settlement on the north end of Great Exuma, while the Cat Island Heritage Festival brings a weekend of performing arts and Bahamian food to Arthur's Town on Cat Island.

The Long Island Sailing Regatta, Salt Pond, Long Island, has sloop races, a yacht parade, and a lot of activity both on and off the water.

SUMMER

June

Labour Day, the first Friday of the month, and Whit Monday are public holidays in the Bahamas.

Yes, more fishing tournaments: Treasure Cay International Billfish Tournament in Abaco, the Inter-Island Fly Fishing Tournament, and the continuation of the Bahamas Billfish Tournament are major ones this month.

The Cat Island Rake and Scrape Festival is a two-day fest of performances of the Bahamas' indigenous rake and scrape music.

Three days of crab races, cook-offs, live rake and scrape music, and a performance by the Bahamas Police Band comprise the Crab Fest.

Nassau's Arawak Cay is transformed into a heritage village every weekend for the cultural festival Junkanoo in June; live performances, crafts, kids' programs, fabulous local dishes, and a costumed Junkanoo Rushout (parading in the streets) occur each night.

Gregory Town is the scene of the four-day Eleuthera Pineapple Festival, with a Junkanoo parade, crafts displays, tours of pineapple farms, games, contests, and sports events—as well as an opportunity to sample what Eleuthera natives proclaim to be the sweetest pineapple in the world.

Sailing sloops from throughout the country meet in the Grand Bahama Sailing Regatta, in the exciting "Championship of the Seas." On-shore festivities take place at Taíno Beach and include Junkanoo Rushout parades, dancing, music, and food.

Grand Turk's Conch Carnival celebrates the Turks and Caicos' favorite culinary icon with four days of music, dancing, kayak races, and conch fritter eating contests.

July

The Bahamas' most important public holiday falls on July 10—Independence Day, which was established in 1973 and marks the end of 300 years of British rule. There is a progression of flag ceremonies on each of the islands, beginning June 30 and culminating in New Providence on July 9. **Independence Week** is celebrated throughout the Bahamas with regattas, boat races, fishing tournaments, and a plethora of parties.

Eleuthera offers three **Homecoming Festivals,** in Savannah Sound, Governor's Harbour, and Bluff; all are great ways to mingle with locals over food, drink, games, and general partying.

The **Annual Racing Time in Abaco** is an eight-day event with races and tons of on-shore festivities.

Goombay Festivals—traditional summertime parties with dance troupes and musical groups—take place in Andros and Abaco.

In the Turks and Caicos, August brings the **Caicos Classic All-Release Fishing Tournament,** which takes place throughout the month. **Provo Summer Festival** spans a week of pageants and cultural shows in Providenciales.

Aug.	**Emancipation Day,** which marks when the English freed Bahamian and Turks and Caicos slaves in 1834, is a public holiday celebrated on the first Monday in August (always August 1 in the Turks and Caicos).
	The Nassau **Fox Hill Festival** is a two-week event that pays tribute to Emancipation with an early morning Junkanoo Rushout, music, cookouts, games, and other festivities.
	The annual **Cat Island Regatta** includes parties, fashion shows, and other entertainment. The **Rolleville Regatta & Homecoming** hits the Exumas with a weekend of native sloop racing.
	Swimming, biking, and running make up the **Great Nassau Triathlon,** which draws more than 200 international competitors.
	Yet another Bimini fishing competition takes place in August: the **Family Fishing Tournament,** which runs for four days.
FALL	
Sept.	More than 200 contestants participate in the grueling **Great Abaco Triathlon,** which includes swimming, running, and biking. The Abaco islands are also the setting for the **All Abaco Sailing Regatta,** a weekend event highlighted by native sloop racing, Junkanoo festivities, and a food fest.
Oct.	The **Annual Kalik Junkanoo Rushout** gives islanders and visitors on Grand Bahama a reason to party without waiting for the Junkanoo holidays on Taíno Beach.
	The **Annual McLean's Town Conch Cracking Contest,** which includes 20 days of conch-cracking competitions, games, entertainment, and good eating, takes place on Grand Bahama Island as it has for

more than 30 years. South Andros holds a smaller version, Conch Fest, with a day's worth of music and conching.

Discovery Day, commemorating the landing of Columbus in the islands in 1492, is observed on October 12, a public holiday. (On Turks and Caicos Islands, it's known simply as Columbus Day.)

The North Eleuthera Sailing Regatta occupies five days of busy sailing.

Nassau comes alive with culture this month, with the Ministry of Foreign Affairs–sponsored International Cultural Weekend at the Botanical Gardens, and the Wine and Art Festival, sponsored by the Bahamas National Trust at its headquarters, The Retreat.

Nov.

At the Chickcharnie Festival, Andros islanders keep alive the legend of the island's eponymous mythical character with storytelling, dancing, and local entertainment at Queen's Park in Fresh Creek.

Christmas Jollification is a monthlong arts-and-crafts fair with Bahamian Christmas crafts, food, and music held at the Retreat in Nassau.

The National Dance Company of the Bahamas performs traditional Bahamian and Caribbean dance throughout the month at Atlantis resort on Paradise Island.

At the Annual One Bahamas Music and Heritage Festival you'll enjoy a day of concerts, food, and games celebrating national unity.

The Bahamas Wahoo Tournament has its first leg of a three-part series that traverses the Out Islands; it ends in February.

On Grand Bahama the annual Conchman Triathlon is a swimming-running-bicycling competition for amateurs that raises funds for local charities.

PLEASURES & PASTIMES

Beaches You're standing in water so clear you can see straight down to your toes; in the distance, the sea becomes the patchwork of emerald, aqua, and sapphire that you thought existed only in postcards. The torrid Bahamian sun beats inexorably down, and golden sands stretch toward infinity. As you look around, you realize there's only one thing you don't see: other people. And that—sun, sea, sand, and seclusion—is the appeal of the Bahamas in a nutshell. Best of all, the concept of private beaches doesn't apply here; all beaches in the Bahamas are public up to the high-water mark. Of course, land access can be restricted, so you may need to boat into that unspoiled Eden. But if you can get there, it's yours—for the afternoon, anyway.

In Nassau, the major Cable Beach and Paradise Island hotels sit right on the water, whereas hotels on the outskirts are always near beaches such as Love Beach and Saunders Beach on New Providence's north shore and Adelaide Beach on the south. On Grand Bahama, only Our Lucaya, Xanadu, Viva Wyndham Fortuna Beach, and a few other properties are beachside, but if you're staying in Freeport you'll have access to public beaches such as Xanadu Beach, Taíno Beach, and the long strip at Williams Town, all local favorites. The Out Islands are similarly brimming with beautiful beaches. One of the most intriguing is the pink-sand beach at Harbour Island, off Eleuthera.

Most islands' calm, leeward, western sides have the safest and most popular swimming beaches. There are no big waves, little undertow, and the buoyant salt water makes staying afloat almost effortless. The islands' windward, or Atlantic, sides are a different story, and even strong, experienced swimmers should exercise caution here. For novices, ocean waves are powerful and can be dangerous, and unseen currents, strong undertows, and uneven, rocky bottoms only make things more perilous. Some beaches post signs or flags to alert swimmers to water conditions, but few—even those at the best hotels—are protected by lifeguards. Swim at your own risk.

Casinos There are three glitzy casinos in the Bahamas: two on New Providence Island, the Crystal Palace Casino at the Nassau Wyndham Resort on Cable Beach and the Paradise Island Casino at Paradise Island's Atlantis resort; and one on Grand Bahama, Freeport's Royal Oasis Casino (formerly the Casino at Bahamia). All have above-average restaurants and lounges, and some have colorfully costumed revues. Although a couple of Out Island resorts have apparently received casino licenses, there are no immediate plans to bring gambling to these low-key locales.

Dining Restaurants on New Providence (Nassau, Paradise Island, and Cable Beach) and Grand Bahama (Freeport and Lucaya) range from Indian and Chinese to upscale French and Italian. Ironically, Bahamian cuisine used to be hard to find in the tourist centers. Yet nowadays the Ministry of Tourism's "Real

Taste of the Bahamas" program, which encourages the use of local ingredients, is thankfully changing the culinary landscape. One night you might
be munching conch fritters and panfried grouper at an out-of-the-way local
spot, and the next you might be savoring a Grand Marnier soufflé in a fancy
French bistro. On the Out Islands, Bahamian food predominates, but international fare is gaining ground, particularly at resorts.

Most Bahamian cuisine looks to the sea, which provides a cornucopia of
fresh products. Meat, on the other hand, is often imported and consequently
expensive. The islands' signature seafood is the conch. This slow-moving creature abounds in the Bahamas' shallow waters, and thus finds its way onto
many a menu. Its widely touted aphrodisiacal qualities don't hurt its popularity either. (Its shell's shiny pink interior appears in pendants, bracelets,
earrings, brooches, and other ornaments, and you can even find the occasional conch pearl.) Conch meat turns up in a variety of incarnations, including cracked conch (pounded until tender and fried in seasoned batter),
conch salad (raw, marinated in lime juice, with onions and peppers), conch
chowder, conch fritters, even conch burgers. You can find stands selling fresh
conch salad throughout the islands, and you might see fishermen on docks
preparing scorched conch, said to cure hangovers, which is eaten straight
from the shell after being flavored with hot peppers, salt, and lime.

Grouper is the headline fish, and you can feast on it and other fish from
dawn to dusk if you so desire. For breakfast, you might try "boil fish," cooked
with salt pork, onions, peppers, and spices, or "stew fish," in a rich brown
gravy—both are usually served with grits or mildly sweet johnnycake. For
lunch you might move on to steamed fish, cooked with a fragrant tomato
base, then sample panfried grouper for dinner. Bahamian lobster, clawless
and somewhat toothier than its cousins from Maine, is another delicious option. Order minced lobster and the meat will come shredded and cooked
with tomatoes, green peppers, and onions.

At lunch and dinner, your entrée will likely be flanked by a generous mound
of peas 'n' rice, potato salad, coleslaw, baked macaroni and cheese, or
fried plantains. Some other local specialties, easier to find in the Out Islands,
include turtle steak, wild boar, mutton, okra soup, "peas soup" and dough
(dumplings), and the morning eye-opener known as souse—pigs' feet,
chicken parts, sheep's tongue, or other bits of meat simmered with onions
and potatoes in a spicy broth. Salads and other greens are scanty on most
local menus, but fruit is abundant. Walk by a neighborhood fruit stand and
you're likely to see such alluring offerings as mangoes, pineapples, breadfruit, sugarplums, hog plums, sapodillas, sea grapes, coco plums, soursops,
avocados, tangerines, tamarinds, and papayas.

For many, beer is the thirst quencher of choice. Be sure to try locally brewed Kalik, a beer named for the sound of the cowbells played in indigenous Junkanoo music. When you're in the mood for a fruity, rum-based concoction, sip a Goombay Smash, a Bahama Mama, or a Yellowbird.

Bring your meal to a sweet close with guava duff, made by slathering guava jelly on a strip of dough, rolling and boiling it, then pouring a cream, rum, and egg–based sauce onto warm slices. Bahamians also love benny cake (created by cooking sesame seeds with sugar) and coconut jimmy (chewy dumplings in coconut sauce).

For the most inexpensive local treats, stop in on one of the fund-raising cookouts or parties periodically hosted on beaches and in Nassau and Freeport churches. The staff at your hotel or local newspapers can provide details.

Fishing

The Bahamas is an angler's dream. Light tackle, heavy tackle, fly-fishing, deep-sea fishing, reef fishing, fishing for blue marlin, bonefishing—you name it. Fishing in the Bahamas starts in the waters of Bimini off the Florida coast and ends at the southernmost island, Inagua, on the Caribbean's northern edge. Tournaments pop up all over the Out Islands during the year.

Golf

Golfers will find some enticing courses, most of them with refreshing sea views. The 18-hole, par-72 championship courses on New Providence and Paradise islands are all spectacularly beautiful and will put your swing to the test. Cable Beach Golf Club is on West Bay Street in Nassau, part of the Radisson Cable Beach Resort and newly upgraded. The South Ocean Golf Club, on the island's south coast, is secluded and scenic. A third course, Paradise Island Golf Course, covers most of the east end of Paradise Island. Atlantis Resort, also on Paradise Island, has plans to build a new 18-hole course on Athol Island to the east, pending environmental approval. All three courses are open to the public and instruction is available. A fourth course, at the Lyford Cay Golf Club, is available only to members and their guests.

There are also four 18-hole and one 9-hole courses and a golf school on Grand Bahama. The 18-hole courses are divided between Royal Oasis Resort (formerly the Princess) in Freeport and Our Lucaya in Lucaya, which also has the Butch Harmon School of Golf. Grand Bahama and Paradise Islands host tournaments annually.

Although your choices for teeing off on the Out Islands are more limited, you'll still find some appealing courses: one in Treasure Cay, Great Abaco; another at the Cotton Bay Club in Rock Sound, Eleuthera, and a third at the Four Seasons Resort Great Exuma at Emerald Bay.

Junkanoo

Nowhere is the Bahamians' zest for life more exuberantly expressed than in the Junkanoo celebrations held yearly on Boxing Day (the day after Christmas) and New Year's Day. Junkanoo can be likened in its uninhibited and frenzied activities to Carnaval in Rio de Janeiro and Mardi Gras in New Orleans. Although festivals occur throughout the islands, the biggest celebrations are in Nassau. Raucous revelers dressed in costumes representing everything from kaleidoscopic dragons to eye-poppingly bright fish carry elaborately adorned floats fashioned from cardboard fastened to aluminum rods and decorated with glitter and crepe paper. The music, too, is distinctly Bahamian and indisputably clamorous, filling the breezy night with the sounds of goatskin drums, clanging cowbells, and shrieking whistles.

Lodging

Beachfront resort hotels—on Cable Beach and Paradise Island on New Providence Island, and in Lucaya on Grand Bahama Island—are among the most expensive. They also have the widest range of sports facilities, including tennis courts and sailboats. High room rates in many hotels in winter season (slightly less on Grand Bahama than on New Providence) are cut by as much as 30% during the slower May–December period, when managements try to outdo one another with attractive three-day or one-week packages. Prices at hotels away from the beach tend to be considerably lower and are often a better deal because accessible beaches are never far away. Many of these hotels provide free shuttle service.

In addition to cottages that have fully equipped kitchens, Out Islands lodging includes numerous furnished apartment rentals, as well as fishing and diving lodges.

People-to-People Programme

The free People-to-People Programme, a popular socializing opportunity in the islands, gives visitors a more intimate glimpse of Bahamian life. The most extensive programs are on New Providence and Grand Bahama islands, where coordinators match visitors with Bahamians who have similar interests. Your hosts may show you around their town, invite you to attend a church service or community event, or even ask you into their home for a meal. People-to-People also sponsors an afternoon tea at Government House on the last Friday of each month (January–August). People-to-People events in the Out Islands consist mainly of monthly teas, fashion shows, barbecues, dances, and other gatherings; check with the local tourist office to see whether anything's been scheduled during your stay.

Coordinators ask that potential participants contact the **People-to-People Programme** (☎ 242/356–0435 ✉ PeopletoPeople@bahamas.com) or a Bahamas tourist office in the United States two to three weeks before their visit. Arrangements can sometimes be made with short notice, however, so if you're already in the islands, go to a Nassau or Freeport Tourist Information Centre or ask at your hotel's events desk.

Sailing & Seafaring

Crystal seas tinted every color from deep sapphire to pale aqua are dotted with tiny, palm-fringed cays that beckon the weary sailor to step ashore for a brief respite. With more than 700 to visit, the best and only way to reach many of the isles is by ship. And with such pleasures as prime-quality diving and snorkeling, it would be a shame not to get off the islands for some exploration. Boat rentals are scattered through the islands, making it easy to procure your own craft for a seafaring adventure (most also offer crews for the sailing-challenged). Sheltered waters, protected by offshore cays and undersea coral reefs, make navigating relatively easy, and plentiful marinas (many Out Island hotels offer facilities to boaters) means you're never far from a spot to tie up for the night.

Scuba

Few places in the world offer a wider variety of diving opportunities than the Bahamas. Wrecks and reefs, blue holes and drop-offs, sea gardens and shallow shoals can all be found here. In fact, one of the most famous scuba centers in the world is UNEXSO (Underwater Explorers Society), in Lucaya, Grand Bahama. For the most stunning peek at the watery underworld, head to the less crowded Out Islands, where many hotels offer economical dive packages.

With hundreds of islands, the Bahamas has literally thousands of dive sites in its crystal-clear waters. Local dive shops can offer regularly scheduled dives or personalized custom diving and are generous in offering correct and precise directions to many dive sites. In some cases, they will even give you the coordinates of a location. Unless you and your navigational equipment are extremely sharp, however, you could miss a site by 100 yards or so, which would still give you a lot of seabed to search. Some sites, of course, are obvious; you won't need a local guide to show you a sunken ship that stands 25 feet out of the water, and drop-offs aren't that hard to spot. Local experts, however, will know the best places to dive, the drop-offs, the safest places to drop an anchor, and even the best time of day to dive.

Weddings

Although perhaps not a "Pleasure and Pastime" for everyone, getting married in the Bahamas is very popular. In fact, there are so many visitors who say "I do" in the Bahamas that the Ministry of Tourism has established a separate Weddings Division, which takes care of all the paperwork necessary to marry in the Bahamas. It can arrange everything from a shipboard service to nuptials in the stunning Versailles Gardens—and it even finds the minister and photographer.

FODOR'S CHOICE

LODGING

$$$$	**Old Bahama Bay**, West End. A genteel nautical flavor permeates this property, which has everything the big resorts do but on a more intimate scale.
$$$$	**One & Only Ocean Club**, Paradise Island. Once the private hideaway of A&P heir Huntington Hartford, this resort, with its 35-acre gardens and imported French cloister, is the ultimate in understated elegance.
$$$–$$$$	**Atlantis, Paradise Island**, Paradise Island. Exotic walk-through aquariums, lagoons, caves, and waterfalls, and a hopping casino ringed by restaurants and a shopping arcade, guarantee nonstop action.
$$–$$$$	**Abaco Beach Resort & Boat Harbour**, Marsh Harbour. If you love to lounge, this oceanfront Marsh Harbour resort provides the utmost in amenities and comforts, while adventurous types can explore small, uninhabited cays located right across the Sea of Abaco.
$–$$$$	**Bluff House Beach Hotel**, Green Turtle Cay. A sense of retro luxury permeates this resort, whose elegant rooms come with a spectacular vista from the hotel's perch on a cliff overlooking the Sea of Abaco.
$$–$$$	**Our Lucaya Beach & Golf Resort**, Lucaya. Grand Bahama Island's ultimate destination resort is equal parts playful and sophisticated, with water, water everywhere.
$–$$$	**Dolphin Beach Resort**, Great Guana Cay. Pine cottages painted in exuberant Junkanoo colors dot the bluff overlooking gorgeous, uninhabited Guana Cay Beach at this upscale, pocket-size haven.
$–$$$	**Guana Seaside Village**, Great Guana Cay. Warm innkeepers, simple yet inviting rooms splashed with handpainted murals, and the chance to stay in a secluded clapboard cottage just steps from the water are the draws at this Guana Cay retreat.
$–$$$	**Hope Town Harbour Lodge**, Hope Town. This lodge combines the best of two worlds: Airy, stylish rooms overlooking the crashing Atlantic surf, and close proximity to the charming shops, restaurants, and historic homes of Hope Town.
$$	**Tiamo Resorts**, Driggs Hill. Experience the pristine nature of the islands in style and comfort at this stunning beachfront eco-haven in the secluded South Bight of Andros.

BUDGET LODGING

$	**The Cove, Eleuthera,** Gregory Town. Guests at this resort atop one of the tallest hills on the island are treated to sweeping panoramic views and the option of viewing both sunrise and sunset from the accommodations and restaurant.
$	**Pelican Bay,** Lucaya. This inn's got European flair, harborside ambience, and impeccable style, all in a cute little package.

RESTAURANTS

$$–$$$$	**Luciano's,** Lucaya. This long-time bastion of fine Continental fare continues to impress diners amid an onslaught of flashy new restaurants popping up nearby.
$–$$$	**Ferry House,** Lucaya. Pure inspiration goes into the crafting of cutting-edge culinary masterpieces at this restaurant on the water's edge.

BUDGET RESTAURANTS

¢	**Queen Conch,** Dunmore Town. Inside a tiny wooden shack on the Eleuthera waterfront, Lavaughn Percentie and her daughter dice and season some of the islands' freshest conch into conch salad so good that many visitors have her package it in dry ice to take back home to the States.

BEACHES

Great Guana Cay. A beautiful, lightly visited stretch of white sand bordered by palm trees, the 7-mi-long western coast of this cay is what you probably envision when you imagine running away to a tropical isle.

Harbour Island Beach, Harbour Island. This 3-mi stretch of talcum-fine pink-sand beach surely ranks as one of the most beautiful in the world. You'll find joggers and dog walkers in the early morning and lovers of memorable sunsets later in the day.

Taíno Beach, Lucaya. Fluffy white sands, inviting blue-green waters, watersports, conch shacks, and lively sunset bonfire parties make this beach the happening spot for families and young partyers alike.

Treasure Cay. Named after the Spanish ships that sunk offshore here in the 17th century, today's treasure is what is considered by many to be the finest beach in the Abacos, if not the entire Bahamas. This narrow peninsula offers a magnificent 3½-mi of pristine white sand bordering a shallow turquoise bay with calm, crystal-clear water.

GOLF

Our Lucaya Lucayan Course, Lucaya. Balancing boulders, Pro-Am tournaments, and a renowned golf school make this well-established course way above par.

Treasure Cay Hotel Resort and Marina, Treasure Cay. Dick Wilson's 18-hole course is the centerpiece of the Treasure Cay Resort and Marina. With 60 strategically placed sand bunkers, it challenges even the best of players.

NATURE

The Dolphin Experience, Lucaya. Hit the open waters and meet some bottle-nosed friends with this well-respected pioneer of interactive dolphin experiences.

Lucayan National Park, Grand Bahama Island. Step into a dark, dank ancient Indian burial cave and then out into the sunlight of a friendly beach.

Thunderball Grotto, Staniel Cay. Beneath a three-story domed curved limestone ceiling, this cave at the northern end of the Exumas chain has some of the best snorkeling and diving in the Family Islands. And James Bond aficionados will recognize it from one of the boat chase scenes in the movie *Thunderball*.

UNEXSO (Underwater Explorers Society), Lucaya. The offerings are vast at this famous outfitter: learn to dive, get certified, check out reefs and wrecks, or swim with dolphins. Top-notch equipment and expert teachers add to the appeal.

SMART TRAVEL TIPS

Finding out about your destination before you leave home means you won't squander time organizing everyday minutiae once you've arrived. You'll be more streetwise when you hit the ground as well, better prepared to explore the aspects of the Bahamas that drew you here in the first place. The organizations in this section can provide information to supplement this guide; contact them for up-to-the-minute details, and consult the A to Z sections that end each chapter for facts on the various topics as they relate to the different regions. Happy landings!

ADDRESSES

"Whimsical" might best describe Bahamas addresses. Streets change name for no apparent reason, and many buildings have no numbers. In more remote locations, such as the Out Islands, street addresses often aren't used. To find your destination, you might have to ask a local. Postal codes aren't used throughout the Bahamas.

AIR TRAVEL

Most international flights to the Bahamas—to Nassau, Freeport, and the Out Islands alike—connect through airports in Florida, New York, Baltimore, Newark, or Atlanta, depending on the airline. Most domestic flights make a quick stop in Miami. If you are flying to the Out Islands, you may have to make a connection in both Florida and Nassau. British Airways flies direct from London to Nassau; Alitalia has a direct route from Milan to Freeport during summer months only.

BOOKING

When you book, look for nonstop flights and remember that "direct" flights stop at least once. Try to avoid connecting flights, which require a change of plane. Two airlines may operate a connecting flight jointly, so ask whether your airline operates every segment of the trip; you may find that the carrier you prefer flies you only part of the way. To find more booking tips and to check prices and make online flight reservations, log on to www.fodors.com.

CARRIERS

A few major U.S. carriers fly into the Bahamas and American Airlines, Bahamasair, Delta, and US Airways fly into Providenciales in Turks and Caicos Islands. British Airways is the only European carrier with flights into Nassau—about three per week. Other European carriers get you as close as Miami.

AirTran flies to Freeport from Atlanta and Baltimore. Continental codeshare partner Gulfstream International Airways has nearly 200 flights per day from Florida (Fort Lauderdale, Miami, Key West, Tampa, Jacksonville, and West Palm Beach) to Providenciales and 19 Bahamas destinations. Delta flies direct to Nassau from New York, Orlando, and Atlanta, and also direct from Atlanta to Freeport and Providenciales (Saturdays during winter season only). US Airways/US Airways Express flies direct from Philadelphia, New York Laguardia, Boston, Washington, D.C., and Charlotte, North Carolina, to Nassau; from Miami to North Eleuthera and Governor's Harbour; and from West Palm Beach to Treasure Cay and Marsh Harbour. From Canada, Air Canada flies from Montréal and Toronto to Nassau.

There are also smaller airlines with service to the Bahamas. Air Sunshine flies out of Fort Lauderdale to Marsh Harbour and Treasure Cay (Abaco), New Bight (Cat Island), Great Inagua, Stella Maris (Long Island), San Salvador, and George Town (Exuma). American/American Eagle flies to Nassau, Freeport, Marsh Harbour, George Town, and Providenciales from Miami. Bahamasair, the national carrier of the Bahamas, flies from Miami, Orlando, and Fort Lauderdale to Nassau, with connections to George Town, Marsh Harbour, Treasure Cay, Acklins, Andros, Cat Island, Eleuthera (North Eleuthera, Governor's Harbour, and Rock Sound), George Town, Inagua, Stella Maris, and San Salvador. There's a direct flight from West Palm Beach to Marsh Harbour. Chalks Ocean Airways flies to Paradise Island and Bimini from Fort Lauderdale and Miami. Comair flies to Nassau from Cincinnati and Orlando. Island Express flies from Fort Lauderdale to Marsh Harbour, Treasure Cay, and North Eleuthera, as well as to Turks and Caicos. Lynx Air International connects Fort Lauderdale to Cat Island. Twin Air flies out of Fort Lauderdale to Treasure Cay and several destinations in Eleuthera (North Eleuthera, Governor's Harbour, and Rock Sound).

To reach the more remote islands, fly Bahamasair or charter a plane at Nassau International Airport through Sky Unlimited or Take Flight Air Charters. Cherokee Air runs charters from Marsh Harbour. Major Air flies out of Freeport. Some Grand Bahama and Out Islands lodgings charter planes for guests, so *see* Chapters 2 through 5 as well. For service throughout the Bahamas and Caribbean, including Jamaica and Puerto Rico, check with LeAir—which, like many charters, offers an air ambulance service as well as normal charters.

To travel interisland within the Turks and Caicos, contact Sky King or other local charters.

🛫 **To & From the Bahamas** 🛫 **Major Airlines from the U.S. & Canada Air Canada** ☎ 888/247-2262 ⊕ www.aircanada.ca. **AirTran** ☎ 800/247-8726 ⊕ www.airtran.com. **Gulfstream International Airways** ☎ 800/231-0856 ⊕ www.gulfstreamair.com. **Delta** ☎ 800/221-1212 or 800/241-4141 ⊕ www.delta.com. **US Airways** ☎ 800/428-4322 ⊕ www.usair.com.

🛫 **Smaller Airlines Air Sunshine** ☎ 800/327-8900 or 954/434-8900 ⊕ www.airsunshine.com. **American Eagle** ☎ 800/433-7300 ⊕ www.aa.com. **Bahamasair** ☎ 800/222-4262 ⊕ www.bahamasair.com. **Chalks Ocean Airways** ☎ 800/424-2557 ⊕ www.flychalks.com. **Cherokee Air** ☎ 242/367-2089. **Comair** ☎ 800/354-9822 ⊕ www.comair.com. **Island Express** ☎ 954/359-0380 ⊕ www.abacotoday.com/islandexpress. **Lynx Air International** ☎ 888/596-9247 ⊕ www.lynxair.com. **Twin Air** ☎ 954/359-8266 ⊕ www.flytwinair.com.

🛫 **Within the Bahamas Bahamasair** ☎ 242/352-8341 ⊕ www.bahamasair.com. **LeAir** ☎ 242/377-2356. **Major Air** ☎ 242/352-5778. **Sky Unlimited** ☎ 242/377-8993 ⊕ www.bahamas.mall.bs/skyunlimited/default.htm. **Take Flight Air Charters** ☎ 242/362-1877 or 242/362-2561 ⊕ www.takeflightcharters.com.

Within the Turks & Caicos Global Airways
649/941-3222. **Interisland Airways** 649/946-4999. **Sky King** 649/941-5170 www.skyking.tc.

CHECK-IN & BOARDING

Always **find out your carrier's check-in policy.** Plan to arrive at the airport about two hours before your scheduled departure time for domestic flights and 2½ to 3 hours before international flights. You may need to arrive earlier if you're flying from one of the busier airports or during peak air-traffic times. To avoid delays at airport-security checkpoints, try not to wear any metal. Jewelry, belt and other buckles, steel-toe shoes, barrettes, and underwire bras are among the items that can set off detectors.

Assuming that not everyone with a ticket will show up, airlines routinely overbook planes. When everyone does, airlines ask for volunteers to give up their seats. (This is a common occurrence in Miami.) In return, these volunteers usually get a several-hundred-dollar flight voucher, which can be used toward the purchase of another ticket, and are rebooked on the next flight out. If there are not enough volunteers, the airline must choose who will be denied boarding. The first to get bumped are passengers who checked in late and those flying on discounted tickets, so get to the gate and check in as early as possible, especially during peak periods.

Always **bring a government-issued photo ID** to the airport; even when it's not required, a passport is best.

CUTTING COSTS

The least expensive airfares to the Bahamas are priced for round-trip travel and must usually be purchased in advance. Airlines generally allow you to change your return date for a fee; most low-fare tickets, however, are nonrefundable. It's smart to call a number of airlines and check the Internet; when you are quoted a good price, book it on the spot—the same fare may not be available the next day, or even the next hour. Always check different routings and look into using alternate airports. Also, price off-peak flights, which may be significantly less expensive than others.

Travel agents, especially low-fare specialists (⇨ Discounts & Deals), are helpful.

Consolidators are another good source. They buy tickets for scheduled flights at reduced rates from the airlines, then sell them at prices that beat the best fare available directly from the airlines. (Many also offer reduced car-rental and hotel rates.) Sometimes you can even get your money back if you need to return the ticket. Carefully read the fine print detailing penalties for changes and cancellations, purchase the ticket with a credit card, and confirm your consolidator reservation with the airline.

When you fly as a courier, you trade your checked-luggage space for a ticket deeply subsidized by a courier service. There are restrictions on when you can book and how long you can stay. Some courier companies list with membership organizations, such as the Air Courier Association and the International Association of Air Travel Couriers; these require you to become a member before you can book a flight.

Many airlines, singly or in collaboration, offer discount air passes that allow foreigners to travel economically in a particular country or region. These visitor passes usually must be reserved and purchased before you leave home. Information about passes often can be found on most airlines' international Web pages, which tend to be aimed at travelers from outside the carrier's home country. Also, try typing the name of the pass into a search engine, or search for "pass" within the carrier's Web site.

Consolidators AirlineConsolidator.com 888/468-5385 www.airlineconsolidator.com; for international tickets. **Best Fares** 800/880-1234 or 800/576-8255 www.bestfares.com; $59.90 annual membership. **Cheap Tickets** 800/377-1000 or 800/652-4327 www.cheaptickets.com. **Expedia** 800/397-3342 or 404/728-8787 www.expedia.com. **Hotwire** 866/468-9473 or 920/330-9418 www.hotwire.com. **Now Voyager Travel** 45 W. 21st St., Suite 5A, New York, NY 10010 212/459-1616 212/243-2711 www.nowvoyagertravel.com. **Onetravel.com** www.onetravel.com. **Orbitz** 888/656-4546 www.orbitz.com. **Priceline.com**

⊕ www.priceline.com. **Travelocity** ☎ 888/709–5983, 877/282–2925 in Canada, 0870/876–3876 in the U.K. ⊕ www.travelocity.com.

⚠ Courier Resources Air Courier Association/Cheaptrips.com ☎ 800/280–5973 or 800/282–1202 ⊕ www.aircourier.org or www.cheaptrips.com; $34 annual membership. **International Association of Air Travel Couriers** ☎ 308/632–3273 ⊕ www.courier.org; $45 annual membership. **Now Voyager Travel** ⊠ 45 W. 21st St., Suite 5A, New York, NY 10010 ☎ 212/459–1616 🖷 212/243–2711 ⊕ www.nowvoyagertravel.com.

⚠ Discount Passes All Asia Pass, Cathay Pacific, ☎ 800/233–2742, 800/268–6868 in Canada ⊕ www.cathay-usa.com or www.cathay.ca. **Boomerang Pass,** Qantas, ☎ 800/227–4500, 0845/774–7767 in the U.K., 131–313 in Australia, 0800/808–767 in New Zealand (outside Auckland), 03/578–900 in Auckland ⊕ www.qantas.com. **Flight-Pass,** EuropebyAir, ☎ 888/387–2479 ⊕ www.europebyair.com. **Pacific Explorer Airpass,** Hideaway Holidays, ☎ 02/9743–0253 in Australia 🖷 02/9743–3568 in Australia, 530/325–4069 in the U.S. ⊕ www.hideawayholidays.com.au. **Polypass,** Polynesian Airlines, ☎ 800/264–0823 or 808/842–7659, 020/8846–0519 in the U.K., 1300/653737 in Australia, 0800/800–993 in New Zealand ⊕ www.polynesianairlines.co.nz. **SAS Air Passes,** Scandinavian Airlines, ☎ 800/221–2350, 0870/6072–7727 in the U.K., 1300/727707 in Australia ⊕ www.scandinavian.net.

ENJOYING THE FLIGHT

State your seat preference when purchasing your ticket, and then repeat it when you confirm and when you check in. For more legroom, you can request one of the few emergency-aisle seats at check-in, if you're capable of moving obstacles comparable in weight to an airplane exit door (usually between 35 pounds and 60 pounds)—a Federal Aviation Administration requirement of passengers in these seats. Seats behind a bulkhead also offer more legroom, but they don't have underseat storage. Don't sit in the row in front of the emergency aisle or in front of a bulkhead, where seats may not recline.

Ask the airline whether a snack or meal is served on the flight. If you have dietary concerns, request special meals when booking. These can be vegetarian, low-cholesterol, or kosher, for example. It's a good idea to pack some healthful snacks and a small (plastic) bottle of water in your carry-on bag. On long flights, try to maintain a normal routine, to help fight jet lag. At night, get some sleep. By day, eat light meals, drink water (not alcohol), and **move around the cabin** to stretch your legs. For additional jet-lag tips consult *Fodor's FYI: Travel Fit & Healthy* (available at bookstores everywhere).

Smoking policies vary from carrier to carrier. Many airlines prohibit smoking on all of their flights; others allow smoking only on certain routes or certain departures. Ask your carrier about its policy.

FLYING TIMES

A direct flight from New York City to Nassau takes approximately three hours. The flight from Charlotte, North Carolina, to Nassau is two hours, and the flight from Miami to Nassau takes about an hour. From Fort Lauderdale to Freeport takes about 35 minutes.

HOW TO COMPLAIN

If your baggage goes astray or your flight goes awry, complain right away. Most carriers require that you **file a claim immediately.** The Aviation Consumer Protection Division of the Department of Transportation publishes *Fly-Rights*, which discusses airlines and consumer issues and is available online. You can also find articles and information on mytravelrights.com, the Web site of the nonprofit Consumer Travel Rights Center.

⚠ Airline Complaints Aviation Consumer Protection Division ⊠ U.S. Department of Transportation, Office of Aviation Enforcement and Proceedings, C-75, Room 4107, 400 7th St. SW, Washington, DC 20590 ☎ 202/366–2220 ⊕ airconsumer.ost.dot.gov. **Federal Aviation Administration Consumer Hotline** ⊠ for inquiries: FAA, 800 Independence Ave. SW, Washington, DC 20591 ☎ 800/322–7873 ⊕ www.faa.gov.

RECONFIRMING

Check the status of your flight before you leave for the airport. You can do this on your carrier's Web site, by linking to a flight-status checker (many Web booking services offer these), or by calling your carrier or travel agent. Always confirm international flights at least 72 hours ahead of the scheduled departure time.

AIRPORTS

The major gateways to the Bahamas include Freeport, on Grand Bahama Island, and Nassau, on New Providence Island. There are also some direct flights from Florida to Out Islands airports such as Marsh Harbour and Treasure Cay in the Abacos. *See* the A to Z sections *in* Chapter 5 for more airports.

🛪 Airport Information **Freeport** ☎ 242/352–6020.**Nassau** ☎ 242/377–7281.

BIKE TRAVEL

Biking in the Bahamas is fairly easy due to the flat island terrain. Some hotels offer bikes as amenities to their guests, or rent them out. So do general stores. In the Out Islands and Turks and Caicos, bikes are often the most logical way to get around on land and match the laid-back pace of life. For the location of bike rental outlets, ⇨ *see* the Biking sections of individual chapters.

BIKES IN FLIGHT

Most airlines accommodate bikes as luggage, provided they are dismantled and boxed; check with individual airlines about packing requirements. Some airlines sell bike boxes, which are often free at bike shops, for about $20 (bike bags can be considerably more expensive). International travelers often can substitute a bike for a piece of checked luggage at no charge; otherwise, the cost is about $100. Most U.S. and Canadian airlines charge $40–$80 each way.

🛪 Bicycling Resources **Bahamas Amateur Cycling Federation** ✑ Box CB–12352, Nassau ⊕ http://members.tripod.com/~xtremesp/races.html has information on upcoming races, and a listing of bike shops and local contacts. **Wolf's Extreme Cycling** ⊕ http://members.tripod.com/~xtremesp/wolf.html has information on triathlons in the Bahamas, as well as cycling.

BOAT & FERRY TRAVEL

If you're of an adventurous frame of mind, and have time to spare, you can revert to the mode of transportation that islanders used before the advent of air travel: ferries and the traditional mailboats, which regularly leave Nassau from Potter's Cay, under the Paradise Island bridge. You may find yourself sharing company with goats and chickens, and making your way on deck through piles of lumber. Fares start at $35 for one-way and range up to $140 for round-trip, depending on the destination. **Don't plan to arrive or depart punctually**; the flexible schedules can be thrown off by bad weather. Remember, too, that they operate on Bahamian time, which is a casual, unpredictable measure. You cannot book ahead, and services are extremely limited. In Nassau, check details with the dockmaster's office at Potter's Cay. You can purchase tickets from the dockmaster or from the captain or mate just before departure.

Within the Bahamas, ferries connect Nassau to Harbour Island and North Eleuthera twice daily. Round-trip fares cost $90, and more expensive excursion rates are available. The trip from Nassau's Harbour Club to Harbour Island takes less than two hours; you can take advantage of the bar and food service on board.

Bahamas Fast Ferry connects Nassau to Harbour Island and Spanish Wells once daily departing at 8 AM, but leaves twice daily on Fridays only, at 8 AM and 1:30 PM. Boats from Nassau to Governor's Harbour (Eleuthera) via Spanish Wells sail twice weekly, on Friday at 7:30 AM and Sunday at 4:45 PM. Boats sail from Harbour Island to Nassau Monday–Thursday and Saturday at 3:55 PM, Friday at 10:25 AM and 3:55 PM, and Sunday at 2 PM. From Governor's Harbour, boats depart Friday at 9:45 PM and Sunday at 7 PM. Travel times from Nassau to Spanish Wells are 1¾ hours; from Nassau to Harbour Island are 2¼ hours; from Nassau to Governor's Harbour, 2 hours. Same-day or next-day ferry service from Nassau also connects on a non-daily basis to Exuma, Andros, Abaco, and North Eleuthera. Daily ferries run between Fort Lauderdale and Grand Bahama Island. For information about mailboat service, contact the Potter's Cay dockmaster.

Local ferries in the Out Islands transport islanders and visitors from the main island to smaller cays.

If you're setting sail yourself, note that cruising boats must clear customs at the nearest port of entry before beginning any diving or fishing. The fee is $150 for boats 35 feet and under and $300 for boats 36 feet and longer, which includes fishing permits and departure tax for up to four persons. Each additional person will be charged the $15 departure tax.

FARES & SCHEDULES
🚢 **Boat & Ferry Information** Bahamas Fast Ferry ☎ 242/323-2166 🖷 242/322-8185 ⊕ www.bahamasferries.com. **Potter's Cay dockmaster** ☎ 242/393-1064.

BUSINESS HOURS
BANKS & OFFICES
Banks are open Monday–Thursday 9:30–3 and Friday 9:30–5. Commonwealth Bank opens at 8:30. Principal banks are Bank of the Bahamas, Bank of Nova Scotia, Barclays Bank, Canadian Imperial Bank of Commerce, Chase Manhattan Bank, Citibank, Commonwealth Bank, and Royal Bank of Canada. Most Bahamian offices observe bank hours.

MUSEUMS & SIGHTS
Hours for attractions vary. Most open between 9 and 10 and close around 5.

PHARMACIES
Though some drugstores typically abide by normal store hours, some stay open 24 hours.

SHOPS
Shops in downtown Nassau are open Monday–Saturday 9–5. Grand Bahama's International Bazaar and Port Lucaya Marketplace are open 10–6. Most stores, with the exception of straw markets and malls, close on Sunday. **Shop in the morning,** when streets are less crowded. Remember that when you're shopping in Nassau, Freeport, and Port Lucaya, you may be competing with the hordes of passengers that pour off cruise ships daily.

BUS TRAVEL
Buses on New Providence Island and Grand Bahama are called jitneys, and are actually vans. Route numbers are clearly marked. Exact change of $1 (around town; more for long-distance travel) is required, and while there are established stops, you can sometimes hail a jitney. Let the driver know where you would like to get off.

CAMERAS & PHOTOGRAPHY
Frothy waves in a turquoise sea and palm-lined crescents of beach are relatively easy to capture on film if you **don't let the brightness of the sun on sand and water fool your light meter.** You'll need to compensate or else work early or late in the day when the light isn't as brilliant and contrast isn't such a problem. Try to **capture expansive views** of waterfront, beach, or village scenes; consider shooting down onto the shore from a clearing on a hillside or from a rock on the beach. Or **zoom in on something colorful,** such as a delicate tropical flower or a craftsman at work. Always **ask permission to take pictures of locals or their property** and **offer a gratuity.** The *Kodak Guide to Shooting Great Travel Pictures* (available at bookstores everywhere) is loaded with tips.
🚩 **Photo Help Kodak Information Center** ☎ 800/242-2424 ⊕ www.kodak.com.

EQUIPMENT PRECAUTIONS
Don't pack film or equipment in checked luggage, where it is much more susceptible to damage. X-ray machines used to view checked luggage are extremely powerful and therefore are likely to ruin your film. Try to ask for hand inspection of film, which becomes clouded after repeated exposure to airport X-ray machines, and keep videotapes and computer disks away from metal detectors. Always keep film, tape, and computer disks out of the sun. Carry an extra supply of batteries, and be prepared to turn on your camera, camcorder, or laptop to prove to airport security personnel that the device is real.

FILM & DEVELOPING

Film is expensive in the Bahamas, so it's best to buy it back home. Popular brands of film are available in Nassau and Freeport, with a more limited selection in the Out Islands. Likewise, you'll find film developing stores (some with one-hour service) in shopping centers in Nassau and Freeport, but developing likely will be pricier and more difficult to find in the Out Islands.

CAR RENTAL

To rent a car, you must be 21 years of age or older in both the Bahamas and the Turks and Caicos, the latter of which charges a flat tax of $10 on all rentals.

🚗 **Major Agencies Alamo** ☎ 800/522-9696 ⊕ www.alamo.com. **Avis** ☎ 800/331-1084, 800/879-2847 in Canada, 0870/606-0100 in the U.K., 02/9353-9000 in Australia, 09/526-2847 in New Zealand ⊕ www.avis.com. **Budget** ☎ 800/527-0700, 0870/156-5656 in the U.K. ⊕ www.budget.com. **Dollar** ☎ 800/800-6000, 0800/085-4578 in the U.K. ⊕ www.dollar.com. **Hertz** ☎ 800/654-3001, 800/263-0600 in Canada, 0870/844-8844 in the U.K., 02/9669-2444 in Australia, 09/256-8690 in New Zealand ⊕ www.hertz.com. **National Car Rental** ☎ 800/227-7368, 0870/600-6666 in the U.K. ⊕ www.nationalcar.com.

CUTTING COSTS

For a good deal, book through a travel agent who will shop around.

🚗 **Local Agencies A J Rent A Car** ✉ Nassau ☎ 242/323-1800. **KSR Car Rental** ✉ Freeport International Airport, Freeport ☎ 242/351-5737.

INSURANCE

When driving a rented car you are generally responsible for any damage to or loss of the vehicle. You also may be liable for any property damage or personal injury that you may cause while driving. Before you rent, see what coverage you already have under the terms of your personal auto-insurance policy and credit cards.

REQUIREMENTS & RESTRICTIONS

In the Bahamas your own driver's license is acceptable for up to three months. An International Driver's Permit is a good idea; it's available from the American or Canadian automobile association, from the Automobile Association or Royal Automobile Club in the United Kingdom, or from a number of Web sites (search for "International Driver's Permit"). These international permits are universally recognized, and having one in your wallet may save you a problem with the local authorities.

SURCHARGES

Before you pick up a car in one city and leave it in another, ask about drop-off charges or one-way service fees, which can be substantial. Also inquire about early-return policies; some rental agencies charge extra if you return the car before the time specified in your contract while others give you a refund for the days not used. To avoid a hefty refueling fee, fill the tank just before you turn in the car, but be aware that gas stations near the rental outlet may overcharge. It's almost never a deal to buy the tank of gas that's in the car when you rent it; the understanding is that you'll return it empty, but some fuel usually remains.

CAR TRAVEL

Your driver's license may not be recognized outside your home country. International driving permits (IDPs) are available from the American and Canadian automobile associations and, in the United Kingdom, from the Automobile Association and Royal Automobile Club. These international permits, valid only in conjunction with your regular driver's license, are universally recognized; having one may save you a problem with local authorities.

EMERGENCY SERVICES

In case of road emergency, **stay in your vehicle with emergency flashers engaged and wait for help,** especially after dark. If someone stops to help, relay information through a small opening in the window. If it's daylight and help does not arrive, walk to the nearest phone and call for help. In the Bahamas, motorists readily stop to help drivers in distress.

ROAD CONDITIONS

In and around Nassau, roads are good, although a bit crowded in peak season.

From 7–10 AM and 3–6 PM, downtown Nassau and most major arteries are congested with cars and pedestrians. When cruise ships are in, pedestrian traffic further stifles the flow. On Grand Bahama Island and the Out Islands, conditions vary from the perfectly paved and manicured boulevards in Freeport to severely pot-holed and winding roads of the countryside. **Make sure you have a spare tire in good condition and necessary tools.**

ROAD MAPS
Bahamas Trailblazer Maps and AT&T Road Maps, which are fairly dependable (some small streets and roads are not included), are distributed for free throughout the islands.

RULES OF THE ROAD
Remember, like the British, islanders **drive on the left side of the road,** which can be confusing because most cars are American with the steering wheel on the left. It is illegal, however, to make a left-hand turn on a red light. Many streets in downtown Nassau are one-way. Roundabouts pose further confusion to Americans. Remember to keep left and yield to oncoming traffic as you enter the roundabout and at GIVE WAY signs.

CHILDREN IN THE BAHAMAS
Be sure to plan ahead and **involve your youngsters** as you outline your trip. Take them to the library and **find children's books about life in the islands** to prepare them for the new culture they will be experiencing. Check out *The Bahamas* from the Enchantment of the World Book Series, by Martin and Stephen Hintz (recommended for ages 8 to 12), to get your kids up to speed. When packing, include things to keep them busy en route. On sightseeing days, try to schedule activities of special interest to your children. Besides beaches, the Bahamas offers a variety of kid-friendly parks, museums, natural attractions, and opportunities to learn how to make local crafts. Many large resorts supervise children's programs. The Out Islands are less accommodating, but even the most remote, with their rich culture and family-centric lifestyles, are intriguing to children. **Make your visit a learning experience for the children** whenever possible. If you are renting a car, don't forget to arrange for a car seat when you reserve. For general advice about traveling with children, consult *Fodor's FYI: Travel with Your Baby* (available in bookstores everywhere).

FLYING TO THE BAHAMAS
If your children are two or older, ask about children's airfares. As a general rule, infants under two not occupying a seat fly at greatly reduced fares or even for free. But if you want to guarantee a seat for an infant, you have to pay full fare. Consider flying during off-peak days and times; most airlines will grant an infant a seat without a ticket if there are available seats. When booking, confirm carry-on allowances if you're traveling with infants. In general, for babies charged 10% to 50% of the adult fare you are allowed one carry-on bag and a collapsible stroller; if the flight is full, the stroller may have to be checked or you may be limited to less.

Experts agree that it's a good idea to use safety seats aloft for children weighing less than 40 pounds. Airlines set their own policies: if you use a safety seat, U.S. carriers usually require that the child be ticketed, even if he or she is young enough to ride free, because the seats must be strapped into regular seats. And even if you pay the full adult fare for the seat, it may be worth it, especially on longer trips. Do **check your airline's policy about using safety seats during takeoff and landing.** Safety seats are not allowed everywhere in the plane, so get your seat assignments as early as possible.

When reserving, request children's meals or a freestanding bassinet (not available at all airlines) if you need them. But note that bulkhead seats, where you must sit to use the bassinet, may lack an overhead bin or storage space on the floor.

FOOD
Nassau and Freeport have all the fast-food chains children love. Try to **introduce them to local cuisine,** which is

entirely palatable to children. Peas 'n' rice, macaroni and cheese, and chicken are common specialties. Adventurous little ones will think it's fun eating conch fritters and johnnycake.

LODGING

Most hotels in the Bahamas allow children under a certain age to stay in their parents' room at no extra charge, but others charge for them as extra adults; be sure to find out the cutoff age for children's discounts. Club Med, Breezes, Sandals, and some small inns discourage or don't permit children. Be sure to ask. Other large resorts are designed around families. Resorts with fine kids' facilities and programs include Atlantis in Paradise Island, Radisson Cable Beach Resort, Nassau Marriott Resort, Royal Oasis Resort and Our Lucaya in Grand Bahama Island, Small Hope Bay in Andros, and Beaches in Providenciales.

PRECAUTIONS

Babies' and children's skin is highly susceptible to the strength of the tropical sun. Child-grade sun protection is available in Nassau, Freeport, and other large towns. If you're staying on an Out Island, **bring your own child-grade sun protection.**

It's also a good idea to check with locals before you head for a swim at a deserted beach—currents can sometimes be too rough for kids, and for many adults.

SIGHTS & ATTRACTIONS

Places that are especially appealing to children are indicated by a rubber-duckie icon (🐤) in the margin.

SUPPLIES & EQUIPMENT

Disposable diapers, baby formula, and other necessities are widely available throughout the Bahamas, though at a higher price than you would pay at home. **Take your own disposable diapers** so you will have the extra space for souvenirs on the trip home. For older children, you can find toys and games at stores throughout the islands, again at up to double what they would cost in the States. Straw markets sell inexpensive maracas and folk dolls.

COMPUTERS ON THE ROAD

If you are carrying a laptop into the Bahamas, you must **fill out a Declaration of Value form** upon arrival, noting make, model, and serial number. **Bring an extra battery.** They're not always readily available in out-of-the-city locations. Bahamian electrical current is compatible with U.S. computers. If you are traveling from abroad, **pack a standard adaptor.**

CONSUMER PROTECTION

Whether you're shopping for gifts or purchasing travel services, **pay with a major credit card** whenever possible, so you can cancel payment or get reimbursed if there's a problem (and you can provide documentation). If you're doing business with a particular company for the first time, contact your local Better Business Bureau and the attorney general's offices in your state and (for U.S. businesses) the company's home state as well. Have any complaints been filed? Finally, if you're buying a package or tour, always consider travel insurance that includes default coverage (⇨ Insurance).

⚏ BBBs Council of Better Business Bureaus ⊠ 4200 Wilson Blvd., Suite 800, Arlington, VA 22203 ☎ 703/276-0100 🖷 703/525-8277 ⊕ www.bbb.org.

CRUISE TRAVEL

A cruise can be one of the most pleasurable ways to see the islands. A multi-island excursion allows for plenty of land-time because of the short travel times between destinations. Be sure to shop around before booking. To learn how to plan, choose, and book a cruise-ship voyage, consult *Fodor's FYI: Plan & Enjoy Your Cruise* (available in bookstores everywhere).

⚏ Cruise Lines Carnival Cruise Lines ⊠ 3655 N. W. 87th Ave., Miami, FL 33178 ☎ 888/227-6482 ⊕ www.carnival.com. Celebrity Cruises ⊠ 5201 Blue Lagoon Dr., Miami, FL 33126 ☎ 800/437-3111, 0800/018-2525 in the U.K. ⊕ www.celebrity-cruises.com. Costa Cruise Lines ⊠ 200 South Park Rd., Hollywood, FL 33021 ☎ 800/462-6782 ⊕ www.costacruises.com. Crystal Cruises ⊠ 555 5th Ave., New York, NY 10017 ☎ 800/446-6620 ⊕ www.cruisecrystal.com. Discovery Cruise Line

⌂ 1775 N.W. 70th Ave., Miami, FL 33126 ☎ 800/
866-8687 ⊕ www.discoverycruiseline.com. **Disney
Cruise Line** ⊠ 210 Celebration Pl., Suite 400, Celebration, FL 34747 ☎ 800/951-3532 ⊕ www.
disneycruise.com. **Holland America** ⌂ 300 Elliott
Ave., West Seattle, WA 98119 ☎ 877/932-4259
⊕ www.hollandamerica.com. **Norwegian Cruise
Line** ⊠ 7665 Corporate Center Dr., Miami, FL 33126
☎ 800/327-7030 ⊕ www.ncl.com. **Radisson
Seven Seas Cruise Line** ⊠ 600 Corporate Dr.,
Suite 410, Fort Lauderdale, FL 33334 ☎ 877/505-
5370 ⊕ www.rssc.com. **Royal Caribbean International** ⊠ 1050 Caribbean Way, Miami, FL 33132
☎ 800/327-6700, 0800/018-2525 in the U.K.
⊕ www.rccl.com. **Silversea Cruises** ⊠ 110 E.
Broward Blvd., 23rd fl., Fort Lauderdale, FL 33301
☎ 800/722-6655 ⊕ www.silversea-cruises.com.

CUSTOMS & DUTIES

When shopping abroad, keep receipts for all purchases. Upon reentering the country, **be ready to show customs officials what you've bought.** Pack purchases together in an easily accessible place. If you think a duty is incorrect, appeal the assessment. If you object to the way your clearance was handled, note the inspector's badge number. In either case, first ask to see a supervisor. If the problem isn't resolved, write to the appropriate authorities, beginning with the port director at your point of entry.

IN AUSTRALIA

Australian residents who are 18 or older may bring home A$400 worth of souvenirs and gifts (including jewelry), 250 cigarettes or 250 grams of cigars or other tobacco products, and 1,125 ml of alcohol (including wine, beer, and spirits). Residents under 18 may bring back A$200 worth of goods. Members of the same family traveling together may pool their allowances. Prohibited items include meat products. Seeds, plants, and fruits need to be declared upon arrival.

🛈 **Australian Customs Service** ⌂ Regional Director, Box 8, Sydney, NSW 2001 ☎ 02/9213-2000 or 1300/363263, 02/9364-7222 or 1800/020-504 quarantine-inquiry line 🖷 02/9213-4043 ⊕ www.customs.gov.au.

IN THE BAHAMAS & TURKS & CAICOS

Customs allows you to bring in 1 liter of wine or liquor and five cartons of cigarettes in addition to personal effects, purchases up to $100, and all the money you wish. But **don't even think of smuggling** in marijuana or any kind of narcotic. Justice is swift and severe in the Bahamas.

You would be well advised to **leave pets at home,** unless you're considering a prolonged stay in the islands. An import permit is required from the Ministry of Agriculture and Fisheries for all animals brought into the Bahamas. The animal must be more than 6 months old. You'll also need a veterinary health certificate issued by a licensed vet. The permit is good for one year from the date of issue, costs $15, and the process must be completed immediately before departure.

🛈 **Ministry of Agriculture and Fisheries** ⊠ Levy Bldg., East Bay St., Nassau ☎ 242/325-7502.

IN CANADA

Canadian residents who have been out of Canada for at least seven days may bring in C$750 worth of goods duty-free. If you've been away fewer than seven days but more than 48 hours, the duty-free allowance drops to C$200. If your trip lasts 24 to 48 hours, the allowance is C$50. You may not pool allowances with family members. Goods claimed under the C$750 exemption may follow you by mail; those claimed under the lesser exemptions must accompany you. Alcohol and tobacco products may be included in the seven-day and 48-hour exemptions but not in the 24-hour exemption. If you meet the age requirements of the province or territory through which you reenter Canada, you may bring in, duty-free, 1.5 liters of wine or 1.14 liters (40 imperial ounces) of liquor or 24 12-ounce cans or bottles of beer or ale. Also, if you meet the local age requirement for tobacco products, you may bring in, duty-free, 200 cigarettes and 50 cigars. Check ahead of time with the Canada Customs and Revenue Agency or the Department of Agriculture for policies regarding meat products, seeds, plants, and fruits.

You may send an unlimited number of gifts (only one gift per recipient, however) worth up to C$60 each duty-free to Canada. Label the package UNSOLICITED GIFT—VALUE UNDER $60. Alcohol and tobacco are excluded.

🚩 **Canada Customs and Revenue Agency** ✉ 2265 St. Laurent Blvd., Ottawa, Ontario K1G 4K3 ☎ 800/461-9999 in Canada, 204/983-3500 or 506/636-5064 ⊕ www.ccra.gc.ca.

IN NEW ZEALAND

All homeward-bound residents may bring back NZ$700 worth of souvenirs and gifts; passengers may not pool their allowances, and children can claim only the concession on goods intended for their own use. For those 17 or older, the duty-free allowance also includes 4.5 liters of wine or beer; one 1,125-ml bottle of spirits; and either 200 cigarettes, 250 grams of tobacco, 50 cigars, *or* a combination of the three up to 250 grams. Meat products, seeds, plants, and fruits must be declared upon arrival to the Agricultural Services Department.

🚩 **New Zealand Customs** ✉ Head office: The Customhouse, 17–21 Whitmore St., Box 2218, Wellington ☎ 09/300-5399 or 0800/428-786 ⊕ www.customs.govt.nz.

IN THE U.K.

From countries outside the European Union, including the Bahamas, you may bring home, duty-free, 200 cigarettes, 100 cigarillos, 50 cigars, or 250 grams of tobacco; 1 liter of spirits or 2 liters of fortified or sparkling wine or liqueurs; 2 liters of still table wine; 60 ml of perfume; 250 ml of toilet water; plus £145 worth of other goods, including gifts and souvenirs. Prohibited items include meat products, seeds, plants, fruits, and dairy products.

🚩 **HM Customs and Excise** ✉ Portcullis House, 21 Cowbridge Rd. E, Cardiff CF11 9SS ☎ 0845/010-9000 or 0208/929-0152 advice service, 0208/929-6731 or 0208/910-3602 complaints ⊕ www.hmce.gov.uk.

IN THE U.S.

U.S. residents who have been out of the country for at least 48 hours may bring home $600 worth of foreign goods duty-free, as long as they have not used the $600 allowance or any part of it in the past 30 days. This allowance, lower than the standard $800 exemption, applies to the 24 countries in the Caribbean Basin Initiative (CBI)—including the Bahamas. If you visit a CBI country and a non-CBI country, you may bring in $800 worth of goods duty-free, but no more than $600 may be from a CBI country. If you're returning from the U.S. Virgin Islands (USVI), a U.S. insular possession, the duty-free allowance is $1,200. If your travel included the USVI and another country—say, the Dominican Republic—the $1,200 allowance still applies, but at least $600 worth of goods has to be from the USVI.

U.S. residents 21 and older may bring back 2 liters of alcohol duty-free, as long as one of the liters was produced in a CBI country. In addition, regardless of your age, you are allowed 200 cigarettes and 100 non-Cuban cigars. Antiques, which U.S. Customs and Border Protection defines as objects more than 100 years old, enter duty-free, as do original works of art done entirely by hand, including paintings, drawings, and sculptures. This doesn't apply to folk art or handicrafts, which are in general dutiable. You may also send packages home duty-free, with a limit of one parcel per addressee per day (except alcohol or tobacco products or perfume worth more than $5). You can mail up to $200 worth of goods for personal use; label the package PERSONAL USE and attach a list of its contents and their retail value. If the package contains your used personal belongings, mark it PERSONAL GOODS RETURNED to avoid paying duties. You may send up to $100 worth of goods as a gift; mark the package UNSOLICITED GIFT. Mailed items do not affect your duty-free allowance on your return.

🚩 **U.S. Customs and Border Protection** ✉ for inquiries and equipment registration, 1300 Pennsylvania Ave. NW, Washington, DC 20229 ⊕ www.cbp.gov ☎ 877/287-8667 or 202/354-1000 ✉ for complaints, Customer Satisfaction Unit, 1300 Pennsylvania Ave. NW, Room 5.2C, Washington, DC 20229.

DISABILITIES & ACCESSIBILITY

Downtown Nassau took into account wheelchair accessibility when it underwent redevelopment in 1995. The Bahamas Association for the Physically Disabled has a van for hire that can pick up people with disabilities from the airport or provide other transportation. Reservations must be made well in advance. The association can also provide temporary ramps and other portable facilities.

⚡ Local Resources **Bahamas Association for the Physically Disabled** ☎ 242/322-2393.

LODGING

Most major hotels throughout the Bahamas have special facilities for people with disabilities, in the way of elevators, ramps, and easy access to rooms and public areas. Here are some suggestions based on a survey conducted by the Bahamas Association for the Physically Disabled:

⚡ Nassau **British Colonial Hilton Nassau** ✉ 1 Bay St. (Box N-7148) ☎ 242/322-3301 ⊕ www.nassau.hilton.com. **Nassau Wyndham Resort & Crystal Palace Casino** ⌂ Box N-8306 ☎ 242/327-6200 ⊕ www.wyndhamnassauresort. com. **Radisson Cable Beach Casino & Golf Resort** ✉ West Bay St. (Box N-4914) ☎ 242/327-6000 ⊕ www.radisson.com.

⚡ Paradise Island **Bay View Village** ⌂ Box SS-6308 ☎ 242/363-2555 or 800/757-1357 ⊕ www. bayviewvillage.com. **Holiday Inn SunSpree Resort** ⌂ Harbour Dr., Box SS-6249 ☎ 242/363-2561 or 800/331-6471 ⊕ www.gbvac.com.

⚡ Grand Bahama **Royal Oasis Golf Resort & Casino** ⌂ Box F 40207, Freeport ☎ 242/350-7000 or 800/227-6963 ⊕ www.theroyaloasis.com.

⚡ Long Island **Stella Maris Resort Club** ⌂ Box LI-30105 ☎ 242/338-2050 or 800/426-0466 ⊕ www.stellamarisresort.com.

RESERVATIONS

When discussing accessibility with an operator or reservations agent, ask hard questions. Are there any stairs, inside *or* out? Are there grab bars next to the toilet *and* in the shower/tub? How wide is the doorway to the room? To the bathroom? For the most extensive facilities meeting the latest legal specifications, opt for newer accommodations. If you reserve through a toll-free number, consider also calling the hotel's local number to confirm the information from the central reservations office. Get confirmation in writing when you can.

SIGHTS & ATTRACTIONS

The beaches of the Bahamas and the Turks and Caicos are generally accessible. In Grand Bahama Island, the two largest shopping malls—International Bazaar and Port Lucaya—have some second-story restaurants not accessible by wheelchair. The Dolphin Experience can make special arrangements for travelers with disabilities. In Nassau, Ardastra Gardens is accessible in most areas, Government House has limited access, and Parliament Square is fully accessible.

TRANSPORTATION

⚡ Complaints **Aviation Consumer Protection Division** (⇨ Air Travel) for airline-related problems. **Departmental Office of Civil Rights** ✉ for general inquiries, U.S. Department of Transportation, S-30, 400 7th St. SW, Room 10215, Washington, DC 20590 ☎ 202/366-4648 🖶 202/366-9371 ⊕ www.dot. gov/ost/docr/index.htm. **Disability Rights Section** ✉ NYAV, U.S. Department of Justice, Civil Rights Division, 950 Pennsylvania Ave. NW, Washington, DC 20530 ☎ ADA information line 202/514-0301, 800/ 514-0301, 202/514-0383 TTY, 800/514-0383 TTY ⊕ www.ada.gov. **U.S. Department of Transportation Hotline** ☎ for disability-related air-travel problems, 800/778-4838 or 800/455-9880 TTY.

TRAVEL AGENCIES

In the United States, the Americans with Disabilities Act requires that travel firms serve the needs of all travelers. Some agencies specialize in working with people with disabilities.

⚡ Travelers with Mobility Problems **Access Adventures/B. Roberts Travel** ✉ 206 Chestnut Ridge Rd., Scottsville, NY 14624 ☎ 585/889-9096 ⊕ www.brobertstravel.com ✍ dltravel@prodigy. net, run by a former physical-rehabilitation counselor. **CareVacations** ✉ No. 5, 5110-50 Ave., Leduc, Alberta, Canada T9E 6V4 ☎ 780/986-6404 or 877/ 478-7827 🖶 780/986-8332 ⊕ www.carevacations. com, for group tours and cruise vacations. **Flying Wheels Travel** ✉ 143 W. Bridge St., Box 382, Owatonna, MN 55060 ☎ 507/451-5005 🖶 507/451-1685 ⊕ www.flyingwheelstravel.com.

☑ Travelers with Developmental Disabilities
Sprout ☒ 893 Amsterdam Ave., New York, NY 10025
☎ 212/222-9575 or 888/222-9575 📠 212/222-9768
⊕ www.gosprout.org.

DISCOUNTS & DEALS

Be a smart shopper and compare all your
options before making decisions. A plane
ticket bought with a promotional coupon
from travel clubs, coupon books, and di-
rect-mail offers or purchased on the Internet may not be cheaper than the least
expensive fare from a discount ticket
agency. And always keep in mind that
what you get is just as important as what
you save.

DISCOUNT RESERVATIONS

To save money, look into discount reservations services with Web sites and toll-free
numbers, which use their buying power to
get a better price on hotels, airline tickets
(⇨ Air Travel), even car rentals. When
booking a room, always **call the hotel's
local toll-free number** (if one is available)
rather than the central reservations number—you'll often get a better price. Always
ask about special packages or corporate
rates.
☑ Airline Tickets Air 4 Less ☎ 800/AIR4LESS;
low-fare specialist.
☑ Hotel Rooms Accommodations Express
☎ 800/444-7666 or 800/277-1064 ⊕ www.acex.
net. **Hotels.com** ☎ 800/246-8357 ⊕ www.hotels.
com. **Quikbook** ☎ 800/789-9887 ⊕ www.
quikbook.com. **Turbotrip.com** ☎ 800/473-7829
⊕ www.turbotrip.com.

PACKAGE DEALS

Don't confuse packages and guided tours.
When you buy a package, you travel on
your own, just as though you had
planned the trip yourself. Fly/drive packages, which combine airfare and car
rental, are often a good deal. In cities, ask
the local visitor's bureau about hotel and
local transportation packages that include tickets to major museum exhibits or
other special events.

EATING & DRINKING

The restaurants we list are the cream of the
crop in each price category. You'll find all

types, from cosmopolitan to the most casual restaurants, serving all types of cuisine.
Price categories are as follows:

CATEGORY	COST*
$$$$	over $40
$$$	$30–$40
$$	$20–$30
$	$10–$20
¢	under $10

*per person for a main course at dinner

MEALS & SPECIALTIES

Dining in the Bahamas reflects its island
location and mixed cultures. While there,
check out fresh seafood and home-grown
vegetables in pan-Caribbean styles such as
fish stew and *souse* (a soup of onion, lime,
celery, peppers, and meat). Touches of the
American South show up in the popular
brunch dish boiled fish and grits and in
such dinner favorites as fried chicken and
macaroni and cheese. Almost every main
course will be accompanied by peas 'n'
rice, and you'll also find the sweet bread
called johnnycake on many a local menu
(and table).

No menu in the Bahamas is complete
without conch. Pronounced "konk," this
ubiquitous "Queen of the Shellfish" (gas-
tropod mollusk) is at the heart of
Caribbean cuisine and has had a place in
local life for centuries, having been used
for jewelry, fishhooks, and religious ornaments. Edible conch, actually the foot of
the sea snail, weighs around 4–12 ounces.
You'll have the chance to try it deep fried
(cracked conch) or in conch salad, which
is prepared raw with lime and spices,
similar to ceviche. It's also used in stews,
soups, and fritters.

RESERVATIONS & DRESS

Reservations are always a good idea; we
mention them only when they're essential
or not accepted. Book as far ahead as you
can, and reconfirm as soon as you arrive.
(Large parties should always call ahead
to check the reservations policy.) We
mention dress only when men are required to wear a jacket or a jacket and
tie. Otherwise you can assume that dining
out is a casual affair.

ECOTOURISM

There are 12 National Parks in the Bahamas, and more areas are slated to join the natural reserve network, all of which are managed by the Bahamas Natural Trust. Included in those areas is the Andros Barrier Reef, the third largest living coral reef in the world, and the 287 square mi Inagua National Park, home to world's largest flock (more than 60,000) of brilliant pink West Indian flamingos. Environmental consciousness has been heightened in the Bahamas, as it has been elsewhere. Tour operators have begun focusing on kayaking, hiking, and biking as well as on the islands' traditional sports of fishing, diving, and boating. Local guides have become more in tune with their environment. The Bahamas offers a full array of adventures in places untainted by civilization. Right outside Freeport are designated wildlife preserves. In the Out Islands, especially Abaco, Andros, and Great Inagua, you'll find rare and endangered animals, pristine "bush," and vital reefs. Near Providenciales (Turks and Caicos), Little Water Cay Nature Trail takes you into the habitat of the rare West Indian rock iguana. You can do your part to keep the Bahamas beautiful—don't purchase products made from endangered species, use care when diving to avoid damage to reefs, don't leave any of your belongings or trash behind (or, in outdoor parlance, pack out what you pack in), and properly dispose of anything you can't remove. Also, be sure your ecotour really is, in fact, eco-friendly.

ECOTOURISM RESOURCES

The Bahamas National Trust (📭 Box N-4105, Nassau ☎ 242/393–1317 ⊕ www.bahamas.gov.bs/bahamasweb/home.nsf). **Ecotourism Association of Grand Bahama** (📭 c/o Kayak Nature Tours, Box F 41230, Freeport ☎ 242/373–2485). **Nila Destinations** (📭 Box 721 Providenciales, Turks and Caicos ☎ 649/941–4375).

ELECTRICITY

Electricity is 120 volts/60 cycles AC, which is compatible with all U.S. appliances.

EMBASSIES

When you're on the road, it's a good idea to get in touch with your country's consulate or embassy officials to let them know you're in the area. This is especially true if you plan to get way off the beaten path (or lost), or think that you might be in harm's way where you're traveling. They are also key in replacing lost passports, or with assistance in emergencies. 🔢 **Embassy Contacts** United States (✉ Mosmar Bldg., Queen St., Nassau ☎ 242/322–1181. **United Kingdom** (✉ 8197 East St., Ansbacher House, 3rd floor, Nassau ☎ 242/325–7471 or 242/325–7472 ⊕ www.britishhighcommission.gov.uk/bahamas.

EMERGENCIES

The emergency telephone number in the Bahamas is **911**.

EMERGENCY AIR SERVICES

Emergency airlifts can be arranged by **Med Evac** (✉ 4th Terrace, Centerville (Box N–3018), Nassau ☎ 242/322–2881).

ETIQUETTE & BEHAVIOR

Bahamians greet people with a proper British "good morning," "good afternoon," or "good evening." When approaching an islander to ask directions or information, **preface your request with such a greeting,** and ask "how are you?" **Smile, and don't rush into a conversation,** even if you're running late.

Humor is a wonderful way to relate to the islanders, but don't force it. Don't try to talk their dialect unless you are adept at it. This takes long exposure to the culture. Church is central in the lives of the Bahamians. They dress up in their fanciest finery; it's a sight to behold on Saturday evening and Sunday morning. To show respect, dress accordingly if you plan to attend religious ceremonies. No doubt, you'll be outdone, but do dress up regardless.

BUSINESS ETIQUETTE

Business in the Bahamas is conducted very much like it is in the United States. Handshakes, business card swapping, and other protocols are the same. Meetings are usually held in office conference rooms, and occasionally at a local restaurant for lunch, in which case either the person who invites pays, or all pay their own tab. Islanders wear suits and typical business attire for work and meetings, so **don't be tempted to wear resort dress** in an office atmosphere.

GAY & LESBIAN TRAVEL

7 Gay- & Lesbian-Friendly Travel Agencies Different Roads Travel ✉ 8383 Wilshire Blvd., Suite 520, Beverly Hills, CA 90211 ☎ 323/651-5557 or 800/429-8747 (Ext. 14 for both) 📠 323/651-5454 ✉ lgernert@tzell.com. **Kennedy Travel** ✉ 130 W. 42nd St., Suite 401, New York, NY 10036 ☎ 212/840-8659 or 800/237-7433 📠 212/730-2269 ⊕ www. kennedytravel.com. **Now, Voyager** ✉ 4406 18th St., San Francisco, CA 94114 ☎ 415/626-1169 or 800/255-6951 📠 415/626-8626 ⊕ www.nowvoyager. com. **Skylink Travel and Tour/Flying Dutchmen Travel** ✉ 1455 N. Dutton Ave., Suite A, Santa Rosa, CA 95401 ☎ 707/546-9888 or 800/225-5759 📠 707/636-0951; serving lesbian travelers.

HEALTH

Hospitals and other health care facilities are readily available in Nassau, Freeport, and Grand Turk. In the Out Islands, facilities range from clinics to private practitioners. You will, however, always be able to find a local bush medicine practitioner. If you're comfortable with alternative treatments, many Bahamians have had herbal remedies passed down to them. For more serious emergencies, an airlift can be arranged from any location.

DIVERS' ALERT
Do not fly within 24 hours of scuba diving.
Always know where your nearest decompression chamber is *before* you embark on a dive expedition, and how you would get there in an emergency.
7 Decompression Chambers Lyford Cay Hospital ✉ Box N-7776, Nassau ☎ 242/362-4400.

FOOD & DRINK
The major health risk in the Bahamas is traveler's diarrhea. This is most often caused by ingesting fruits, shellfish, and drinks to which your body is unaccustomed. **Go easy at first on new foods such as mangoes, conch, and rum punch.**
There are rare cases of contaminated fruit,

vegetables, or drinking water. If you are susceptible to digestive problems, **avoid ice, uncooked food, and unpasteurized milk and milk products,** and **drink bottled water,** or water that has been boiled for several minutes, even when brushing your teeth. Mild digestive treatments might include Imodium (known generically as loperamide) or Pepto-Bismol, both of which can be purchased over the counter. Travelers prone to travel-related stomach disorders who are comfortable with alternative medicine might pick up some *po chai* tablets from a doctor of Oriental medicine or Asian pharmacy—it's a great stomach cure-all. Drink plenty of purified water or tea; chamomile is a good folk remedy. In severe cases, rehydrate yourself with a salt-sugar solution (½ teaspoon salt and 4 tablespoons sugar per quart of water).

Consult a doctor—preferably your own physician, and prior to your trip—before ingesting any medication that's new to you. Pack familiar digestive remedies with your belongings, **but also have them on you** if you're out traveling for the day.

HOSPITALS
Most medical situations can be handled by local area hospitals.
7 Local Hospitals Princess Margaret Hospital ✉ Shirley St., Nassau ☎ 242/352-2861. **Rand Memorial Hospital** ✉ East Atlantic Dr., Freeport ☎ 242/352-6735.

MEDICAL PLANS
No one plans to get sick while traveling, but it happens, so consider signing up with a medical-assistance company. Members get doctor referrals, emergency evacuation or repatriation, hotlines for medical consultation, cash for emergencies, and other assistance.
7 Medical-Assistance Companies International SOS Assistance ⊕ www.internationalsos.com ✉ 8 Neshaminy Interplex, Suite 207, Trevose, PA 19053 ☎ 215/245-4707 or 800/523-6586 📠 215/244-9617 ✉ Landmark House, Hammersmith Bridge Rd., 6th fl., London, W6 9DP ☎ 20/8762-8008 📠 20/8748-7744 ✉ 12 Chemin Riantbosson, 1217 Meyrin 1, Geneva, Switzerland ☎ 22/785-6464 📠 22/785-6424 ✉ 331 N. Bridge Rd., 17-00, Odeon Towers, Singapore 188720 ☎ 6338-7800 📠 6338-7611.

OVER-THE-COUNTER REMEDIES

Pharmacies carry most of the same pain relief products you find in the United States, but often at a higher price, so **pack any over-the-counter medications you regularly use.** They also sell a product called 2-2-2, which is equal parts aspirin, caffeine, and codeine. It's an effective pain killer but can cause stomach upset.

PESTS & OTHER HAZARDS

No-see-ums (sand fleas) and mosquitoes pose the worst bother. Some travelers have allergies to sand-flea bites, and the itching can be extremely bothersome. To prevent the bites, **use a recommended bug repellent.** To ease the itching, **rub alcohol on the bites.** Some Out Island hotels provide sprays or repellents in the room, but it's a good idea to bring your own.

SHOTS & MEDICATIONS

A vaccination against yellow fever is required if you're arriving from Angola, Benin, Bolivia, Brazil, Burkina Faso, Colombia, Cameroon, Democratic Republic of Congo, Ecuador, French Guiana, Gabon, Gambia, Ghana, Guinea, Liberia, Nigeria, Sierra Leone, Peru, and Sudan. Travelers must be vaccinated 10 days prior to entering the Bahamas and must have a valid certificate of vaccination against yellow fever. Otherwise, no special shots are required before visiting the Bahamas.

SUNBATHING

Basking in the sun is one of the great pleasures of a Bahamian vacation, but because the sun is closer to Earth the farther south you go, it will burn your skin more quickly, so take precautions against sunburn and sunstroke. On a sunny day, even people who are not normally bothered by strong sun should **cover up with a long-sleeve shirt, a hat, and pants or a beach wrap** while on a boat or midday at the beach. **Carry UVA/UVB sunblock** (with a sun protection factor, or SPF, of at least 15) for your face and other sensitive areas. If you're engaging in water sports, be sure the sunscreen is waterproof. Wear sunglasses because eyes are particularly vulnerable to direct sun and reflected rays. Be sure to **drink enough liquids—water or fruit juice preferably—** and avoid coffee, tea, and alcohol. Above all, limit your sun time for the first few days until you become accustomed to the rays. Do not be fooled by an overcast day. Quite often you will get the worst sunburns when you least expect them. The safest hours for sunbathing are 4–6 PM, but even then it is wise to limit initial exposure.

⌘ Health Warnings National Centers for Disease Control and Prevention (CDC) ⌧ Office of Health Communication, National Center for Infectious Diseases, Division of Quarantine, Travelers' Health, 1600 Clifton Rd. NE, Atlanta, GA 30333 ☎ 877/394–8747 international travelers' health line, 800/311–3435 other inquiries, 404/498–1600 Division of Quarantine 🖷 888/232–3299 ⊕ www.cdc.gov/travel. **World Health Organization** (WHO) ⊕ www.who.int.

HOLIDAYS

The grandest holiday of all is Junkanoo, a carnival that embraces the Christmas season. **Don't expect to conduct any business during the week of festivities.** During other legal holidays, most offices close. In the Bahamas, they include New Year's Day, Good Friday, Easter, Whit Monday (last Monday in May), Labour Day (first Monday in June), Independence Day (July 10), Emancipation Day (first Monday in August), Discovery Day (Oct. 12), Christmas Day, and Boxing Day (Dec. 26). In Turks and Caicos, islanders also celebrate Commonwealth Day (March), Easter Monday, National Heroes Day (May), The Queen's Birthday (June), National Youth Day (September), and International Human Rights Day (October). They celebrate Emancipation Day (August 1) but do not celebrate Whit Monday, Labour Day, or Independence Day.

INSURANCE

The most useful travel-insurance plan is a comprehensive policy that includes coverage for trip cancellation and interruption, default, trip delay, and medical expenses (with a waiver for preexisting conditions).

Without insurance you'll lose all or most of your money if you cancel your trip, regardless of the reason. Default insurance covers you if your tour operator, airline, or cruise line goes out of business—the chances of which have been increasing. Trip-delay covers expenses that arise because of bad weather or mechanical delays. Study the fine print when comparing policies.

If you're traveling internationally, a key component of travel insurance is coverage for medical bills incurred if you get sick on the road. Such expenses aren't generally covered by Medicare or private policies. U.K. residents can buy a travel-insurance policy valid for most vacations taken during the year in which it's purchased (but check preexisting-condition coverage). British and Australian citizens need extra medical coverage when traveling overseas.

Always **buy travel policies directly from the insurance company**; if you buy them from a cruise line, airline, or tour operator that goes out of business you probably won't be covered for the agency or operator's default, a major risk. Before making any purchase, review your existing health and home-owner's policies to find what they cover away from home.

🚩 Travel Insurers In the U.S.: **Access America** ✉ 2805 N. Parham Rd., Richmond, VA 23294 ☎ 800/284-8300 🖶 804/673-1491 or 800/346-9265 ⊕ www.accessamerica.com. **Travel Guard International** ✉ 1145 Clark St., Stevens Point, WI 54481 ☎ 715/345-0505 or 800/826-1300 🖶 800/955-8785 ⊕ www.travelguard.com.

🚩 Insurance Information In the U.K.: **Association of British Insurers** ✉ 51 Gresham St., London EC2V 7HQ ☎ 020/7600-3333 🖶 020/7696-8999 ⊕ www.abi.org.uk. In Canada: **RBC Insurance** ✉ 6880 Financial Dr., Mississauga, Ontario L5N 7Y5 ☎ 800/668-4342 or 905/816-2400 🖶 905/813-4704 ⊕ www.rbcinsurance.com. In Australia: **Insurance Council of Australia** ✉ Insurance Enquiries and Complaints, Level 12, Box 561, Collins St. W, Melbourne, VIC 8007 ☎ 1300/780808 or 03/9629-4109 🖶 03/9621-2060 ⊕ www.iecltd.com.au. In New Zealand: **Insurance Council of New Zealand** ✉ Level 7, 111-115 Customhouse Quay, Box 474, Wellington ☎ 04/472-5230 🖶 04/473-3011 ⊕ www.icnz.org.nz.

LANGUAGE

Islanders speak English with a lilt influenced by their British and/or African ancestry. When locals talk among themselves in local dialect, it is virtually impossible for the unaccustomed to understand them. They take all sorts of short cuts and pepper the language with words all their own. When islanders speak to visitors, they will use standard English. For a humorous guide to Bahamian speech, look for Patricia Glinton-Meicholas' little book *Talkin' Bahamian,* sold locally.

LODGING

The lodgings we list are the cream of the crop in each price category. We always list the facilities that are available—but we don't specify whether they cost extra: when pricing accommodations, always ask what's included and what costs extra. Properties marked ✕🏠 are lodging establishments whose restaurants warrant a special trip.

Assume that hotels operate on the European Plan (EP, with no meals) unless we specify that they use the Continental Plan (CP, with a Continental breakfast), Breakfast Plan (BP, with a full breakfast), Modified American Plan (MAP, with breakfast and dinner), Full American Plan (FAP, with all meals), or are all-inclusive (including all meals and most activities).

CATEGORY	COST*
$$$$	over $400
$$$	$300-$400
$$	$200-$300
$	$100-$200
¢	under $100

All prices are for a standard double room in high season, excluding 6%–12% tax and 10%–15% service charge. Note that the government hotel tax doesn't apply to guest houses with fewer than four rooms.

APARTMENT & VILLA [OR HOUSE] RENTALS

If you want a home base that's roomy enough for a family and comes with cooking facilities, consider a furnished rental. These can save you money, especially if you're traveling with a group.

Home-exchange directories sometimes list rentals as well as exchanges.

❼ International Agents Hideaways International ✉ 767 Islington St., Portsmouth, NH 03801 ☎ 603/430-4433 or 800/843-4433 🖷 603/430-4444 ⊕ www.hideaways.com, annual membership $145. **Vacation Home Rentals Worldwide** ✉ 235 Kensington Ave., Norwood, NJ 07648 ☎ 201/767-9393 or 800/633-3284 🖷 201/767-5510 ⊕ www.vhrww.com. **Villas International** ✉ 4340 Redwood Hwy., Suite D309, San Rafael, CA 94903 ☎ 415/499-9490 or 800/221-2260 🖷 415/499-9491 ⊕ www.villasintl.com.

❼ Local Agents Bahamas Home Rentals ✉ 2722 Riverview Dr., Melbourne, FL 32901 ☎ 888/881-2867 or 321/725-9790 🖷 321/676-1452 ⊕ www.bahamasweb.com. **Bahamas Vacation Homes** ☌ Box EL 27528, Spanish Wells, Bahamas ☎🖷 242/333-4080. **Hope Town Hideaways** ✉ 1 Purple Porpoise Pl., Hope Town, Abacos ☎ 242/366-0224 🖷 242/366-0434 ✐ inquiries@hopetown.com.

HOME EXCHANGES

If you would like to exchange your home for someone else's, join a home-exchange organization, which will send you its updated listings of available exchanges for a year and will include your own listing in at least one of them. It's up to you to make specific arrangements.

❼ Exchange Clubs HomeLink International ☌ Box 47747, Tampa, FL 33647 ☎ 813/975-9825 or 800/638-3841 🖷 813/910-8144 ⊕ www.homelink.org; $110 yearly for a listing, online access, and catalog; $70 without catalog.

HOSTELS

No matter what your age, you can save on lodging costs by staying at hostels. In some 4,500 locations in more than 70 countries around the world, Hostelling International (HI), the umbrella group for a number of national youth-hostel associations, offers single-sex, dorm-style beds and, at many hostels, rooms for couples and family accommodations. Membership in any HI national hostel association, open to travelers of all ages, allows you to stay in HI-affiliated hostels at member rates; one-year membership is about $28 for adults (C$35 for a two-year minimum membership in Canada, £14 in the U.K., A$52 in Aus-

tralia, and NZ$40 in New Zealand); hostels charge about $10–$30 per night. Members have priority if the hostel is full; they're also eligible for discounts around the world, even on rail and bus travel in some countries.

❼ Organizations Hostelling International–USA ✉ 8401 Colesville Rd., Suite 600, Silver Spring, MD 20910 ☎ 301/495-1240 🖷 301/495-6697 ⊕ www.hiusa.org. **Hostelling International–Canada** ✉ 205 Catherine St., Suite 400, Ottawa, Ontario K2P 1C3 ☎ 613/237-7884 or 800/663-5777 🖷 613/237-7868 ⊕ www.hihostels.ca. **YHA England and Wales** ✉ Trevelyan House, Dimple Rd., Matlock, Derbyshire DE4 3YH, U.K. ☎ 0870/870-8808, 0870/770-8868, or 0162/959-2600 🖷 0870/770-6127 ⊕ www.yha.org.uk. **YHA Australia** ✉ 422 Kent St., Sydney, NSW 2001 ☎ 02/9261-1111 🖷 02/9261-1969 ⊕ www.yha.com.au. **YHA New Zealand** ✉ Level 1, Moorhouse City, 166 Moorhouse Ave., Box 436, Christchurch ☎ 03/379-9970 or 0800/278-299 🖷 03/365-4476 ⊕ www.yha.org.nz.

HOTELS

Many American, European, and Caribbean chains operate in the Bahamas, including Westin, Sheraton, Comfort Suites, Radisson, Sandals, SuperClubs, and Club Med. Their full-service resorts, along with other individual properties, are destinations in themselves. Smaller lodges and resorts offer easier access to local life and are attractive to travelers who want a cultural experience or a sequestered getaway focused on fishing, diving, and other watery pastimes. Many small, family-run hotels throughout the Bahamas, including the occasional B&B, offer low-key, warm accommodations. All hotels listed have private bath unless otherwise noted.

❼ Toll-Free Numbers Best Western ☎ 800/528-1234 ⊕ www.bestwestern.com. **Choice** ☎ 800/424-6423 ⊕ www.choicehotels.com. **Club Méditerranée** ☎ 800/258-2633 ⊕ www.clubmed.com. **Comfort Inn** ☎ 800/424-6423 ⊕ www.choicehotels.com. **Hilton** ☎ 800/445-8667 ⊕ www.hilton.com. **Holiday Inn** ☎ 800/465-4329 ⊕ www.ichotelsgroup.com. **Marriott** ☎ 800/228-9290 ⊕ www.marriott.com. **Quality Inn** ☎ 800/424-6423 ⊕ www.choicehotels.com. **Radisson** ☎ 800/333-3333 ⊕ www.radisson.com. **Sheraton** ☎ 800/325-3535 ⊕ www.starwood.com/sheraton. **Westin Hotels & Resorts** ☎ 800/228-3000 ⊕ www.starwood.com/

westin. **Wyndham Hotels & Resorts** ☎ 800/822–4200 ⊕ www.wyndham.com.

MAIL & SHIPPING

Regardless of whether the term "snail mail" was coined in the Bahamas, you're likely to find that you arrive home long before your postcards do. No postal (zip) codes are used in the Bahamas—all mail is collected from local area PO boxes.

OVERNIGHT SERVICES

FedEx delivers to Nassau, Freeport, Abaco, Andros, Eleuthera, Long Island, Providenciales, and Grand Turk. UPS has service to numerous Bahamas locales and provides incoming delivery only in Turks and Caicos.

🗗 Major Services FedEx ☎ Freeport: 242/352–3402 or 242/352–3403, Nassau: 242/322–5656 or 242/322–5657, Abaco: 242/367–2817, Andros: 242/368–2540, Eleuthera: 242/332–2720, Long Island: 242/337–6786, Grand Turk: 649/946–2542, Providenciales: 649/946–4682, U.S. international customer service: 800/247–4747 ⊕ www.fedex.com. **UPS** ☎ Abaco (Marsh Harbour): 242/367–2333, Freeport: 242/352–6253, Nassau: 242/393–3795, Grand Turk: 649/946–2030.

POSTAL RATES

First-class mail to the United States is 65¢, 70¢ to Europe, and 80¢ to Australia and New Zealand per half-ounce. Airmail postcards to the United States, Canada, the United Kingdom, Europe, Australia, and South America require a 55¢ stamp in the Bahamas; the stamps must be Bahamian. In Turks and Caicos, prices are comparable, about 50¢–80¢.

RECEIVING MAIL

Mailing time to the United States from the Bahamas is five to 10 days, 10–18 days to Canada, and 20 days to the United Kingdom, Australia, and New Zealand.

SHIPPING PARCELS

U.S. citizens may increase their duty-free allowance by mailing home up to $50 worth of gifts. Label the package PERSONAL USE and attach a list of its contents and their retail value.

MEDIA

NEWSPAPERS & MAGAZINES

You'll get all the Bahamian news and a good idea of what's going on internationally in the *Tribune, Bahamas Observer,* and *Nassau Guardian* on New Providence and in the *Freeport News* on Grand Bahama. Local newspapers are available in most Out Islands one day after publication. If you want up-to-date news on what's happening around the world, you can also get the *Miami Herald,* the *Wall Street Journal, USA Today,* and the *New York Times* daily at newsstands.

TELEVISION

Cable brings American television to the Bahamas. The local TV station is ZNS.

MONEY MATTERS

Generally, prices in the Bahamas reflect the exchange rate: they are about the same as in the United States, less expensive than in the United Kingdom. A hotel can cost anywhere from $50 a night (for cottages and apartments in downtown Nassau and in the Out Islands) to $185 and up (at the ritzier resorts on Cable Beach and Paradise Island and in Freeport and Lucaya), depending on the season. Add $35–$50 per person per day for meals. Four-day/three-night and eight-day/seven-night package stays offered by most hotels can cut costs considerably. In the Out Islands, you'll notice that meals and simple goods can be expensive; prices are high due to the remoteness of the islands and the costs of importing. Prices throughout this guide are given for adults. Substantially reduced fees are almost always available for children, students, and senior citizens. For information on taxes, *see* Taxes.

ATMS

There are ATMs at banks and malls throughout the major islands. You'll find an ATM at Nassau International Airport and at many other locations on New Providence, Paradise Island, Grand Bahama Island, and throughout the Out Islands.

🗗 ATM Locations Cirrus ☎ 800/424–7787 for locations in the Bahamas and worldwide. Call **Plus** ☎ 800/843–7587 ⊕ www.visa.com for locations in the United States; visit the Web site for international locations.

CREDIT CARDS

Both credit and debit cards offer excellent, wholesale exchange rates. And both protect you against unauthorized use if the card is lost or stolen. Your liability is limited to $50, as long as you report the card missing. Some smaller hotels in the islands do not accept credit cards.

Throughout this guide, the following abbreviations are used: **AE**, American Express; **D**, Discover; **DC**, Diners Club; **MC**, MasterCard; and **V**, Visa.

CURRENCY

The U.S. dollar is on par with the Bahamian dollar and is accepted all over the Bahamas. The U.K. pound sterling will get you 1.76 Bahamian dollars, and the Canadian dollar about .79 dollars. Bahamian money runs in bills of $1, $5, $10, $20, $50, and $100. The U.S. dollar is the currency of the Turks and Caicos.

CURRENCY EXCHANGE

In the Bahamas, only U.S. cash will be exchanged freely in hotels, stores, or restaurants, and since the U.S. currency is accepted throughout, there really is no need to change to Bahamian. Also, you won't incur any transaction fees for currency exchange, or worry about getting stuck with unspent Bahamian dollars. **Carry small bills when bargaining at straw markets.** For the most favorable rates, **change money through banks.** Although ATM transaction fees may be higher abroad than at home, ATM rates are excellent because they're based on wholesale rates offered only by major banks. You won't do as well at exchange booths in airports or rail and bus stations, in hotels, in restaurants, or in stores. To avoid lines at airport exchange booths, get a bit of local currency before you leave home.

⛶ Exchange Services International Currency Express ✉ 427 N. Camden Dr., Suite F, Beverly Hills, CA 90210 ☎ 888/278-6628 orders 🖷 310/278-6410 ⊕ www.foreignmoney.com. **Travel Ex Currency Services** ☎ 800/287-7362 orders and retail locations ⊕ www.travelex.com.

TRAVELER'S CHECKS

Do you need traveler's checks? It depends on where you're headed. If you're going to rural areas and small towns, go with cash; traveler's checks are best used in cities. Lost or stolen checks can usually be replaced within 24 hours. To ensure a speedy refund, buy your own traveler's checks—don't let someone else pay for them: irregularities like this can cause delays. The person who bought the checks should make the call to request a refund.

PACKING

The reason you're going to the Bahamas is to get away from all of that suit-shirt-and-tie turmoil, so your wardrobe should reflect the informality of the experience. Aside from your bathing suit, which will be your favorite uniform, take lightweight clothing (short-sleeve shirts, T-shirts, cotton slacks, lightweight jackets for evening wear for men; light dresses, shorts, and T-shirts for women). If you're going during the high season, between mid-December and April, toss in a sweater for the occasional cool evening. Cover up in public places for downtown shopping expeditions, and save that skimpy bathing suit for the beach at your hotel.

Some of the more sophisticated hotels require jackets for men and dresses for women at dinner. There is no dress code in any of the Bahamas' casinos.

In your carry-on luggage, pack an extra pair of eyeglasses or contact lenses and enough of any medication you take to last a few days longer than the entire trip. You may also ask your doctor to write a spare prescription using the drug's generic name, as brand names may vary from country to country. In luggage to be checked, **never pack prescription drugs, valuables, or undeveloped film.** And don't forget to carry with you the addresses of offices that handle refunds of lost traveler's checks. Check *Fodor's How to Pack* (available at online retailers and bookstores everywhere) for more tips.

To avoid customs and security delays, carry medications in their original packaging. Don't pack any sharp objects in your carry-on luggage, including knives of any size or material, scissors, nail clippers, and corkscrews, or anything else that might arouse suspicion.

To avoid having your checked luggage chosen for hand inspection, don't cram bags full. The U.S. Transportation Security Administration suggests packing shoes on top and placing personal items you don't want touched in clear plastic bags.

CHECKING LUGGAGE

You're allowed to carry aboard one bag and one personal article, such as a purse or a laptop computer. Make sure what you carry on fits under your seat or in the overhead bin. Get to the gate early, so you can board as soon as possible, before the overhead bins fill up. Short flights between Florida and the islands or between islands are often aboard small planes where you may be required to check even large carry-ons before boarding.

Baggage allowances vary by carrier, destination, and ticket class. On international flights, you're usually allowed to check two bags weighing up to 70 pounds (32 kilograms) each, although a few airlines allow checked bags of up to 88 pounds (40 kilograms) in first class. Some international carriers don't allow more than 66 pounds (30 kilograms) per bag in business class and 44 pounds (20 kilograms) in economy. On domestic flights, the limit is usually 50 to 70 pounds (23 to 32 kilograms) per bag. In general, carry-on bags shouldn't exceed 40 pounds (18 kilograms). Most airlines won't accept bags that weigh more than 100 pounds (45 kilograms) on domestic or international flights. Expect to pay a fee for baggage that exceeds weight limits. Check baggage restrictions with your carrier before you pack.

Airline liability for baggage is limited to $2,500 per person on flights within the United States. On international flights it amounts to $9.07 per pound or $20 per kilogram for checked baggage (roughly $640 per 70-pound bag), with a maximum of $634.90 per piece, and $400 per passenger for unchecked baggage. You can buy additional coverage at check-in for about $10 per $1,000 of coverage, but it often excludes a rather extensive list of items, shown on your airline ticket.

Before departure, itemize your bags' contents and their worth, and label the bags with your name, address, and phone number. (If you use your home address, cover it so potential thieves can't see it readily.) Include a label inside each bag and **pack a copy of your itinerary.** At check-in, make sure each bag is correctly tagged with the destination airport's three-letter code. Because some checked bags will be opened for hand inspection, the U.S. Transportation Security Administration recommends that you leave luggage unlocked or use the plastic locks offered at check-in. TSA screeners place an inspection notice inside searched bags, which are resealed with a special lock.

If your bag has been searched and contents are missing or damaged, file a claim with the TSA Consumer Response Center as soon as possible. If your bags arrive damaged or fail to arrive at all, file a written report with the airline before leaving the airport.

▐ Complaints U.S. Transportation Security Administration Contact Center ☎ 866/289–9673 ⊕ www.tsa.gov.

PASSPORTS & VISAS

When traveling internationally, carry your passport even if you don't need one (it's always the best form of ID) and **make two photocopies of the data page** (one for someone at home and another for you, carried separately from your passport). If you lose your passport, promptly call the nearest embassy or consulate and the local police.

U.S. passport applications for children under age 14 require consent from both parents or legal guardians; both parents must appear together to sign the application. If only one parent appears, he or she must submit a written statement from the other parent authorizing passport issuance for the child. A parent with sole authority must present evidence of it when applying; acceptable documentation includes the child's certified birth certificate listing only the applying parent, a court order specifically permitting this parent's travel with the child, or a death certificate for the nonapplying parent. Application forms and instructions are available on the Web site of the U.S. State Department's Bureau of Consular Affairs (⊕ travel.state.gov).

ENTERING THE BAHAMAS
Residents of the United States or British Commonwealth countries can stay in the Bahamas for up to 8 months. British subjects from the U.K. and colonies may enter the Bahamas as visitors without passports or visas for periods not exceeding three weeks. For longer stays they must present a passport.

Countries whose citizens require a visa include China, Colombia, Egypt, India, Nigeria, Pakistan, Poland, Russia, and Saudi Arabia. For specific entry questions, contact the Bahamas Immigration Department or the nearest consulate.
🔃 **Bahamas Department of Immigration** ✉ Hawkins Hill (Box N–831), Nassau, ☎ 242/322–7530.

ENTERING TURKS & CAICOS
U.S. citizens need some proof of citizenship, such as a birth certificate with a raised seal, plus a photo ID or a current passport. British subjects are required to have a current passport. All visitors must have an ongoing or return ticket.

PASSPORT OFFICES
The best time to apply for a passport or to renew is in fall and winter. Before any trip, check your passport's expiration date, and, if necessary, renew it as soon as possible.
🔃 **Australian Citizens Passports Australia** Australian Department of Foreign Affairs and Trade ☎ 131–232 ⊕ www.passports.gov.au.
🔃 **Canadian Citizens Passport Office** ✉ to mail in applications: 200 Promenade du Portage, Hull, Québec J8X 4B7 ☎ 819/994–3500 or 800/567–6868 ⊕ www.ppt.gc.ca.
🔃 **New Zealand Citizens New Zealand Passports Office** ☎ 0800/22–5050 or 04/474–8100 ⊕ www.passports.govt.nz.
🔃 **U.K. Citizens U.K. Passport Service** ☎ 0870/521–0410 ⊕ www.passport.gov.uk. 🔃 **U.S. Citizens**

National Passport Information Center ☎ 877/487–2778, 888/874–7793 TDD/TTY ⊕ travel.state.gov.

REST ROOMS
Most attractions, restaurants, and shopping areas have reasonably clean, and sometimes attended, public rest rooms. Beaches away from the resorts often have no facilities. **Headquarter your beach escape near a bar or restaurant** for restroom access.

SAFETY
Don't wear a money belt or a waist pack, both of which peg you as a tourist. Distribute your cash and any valuables (including your credit cards and passport) between a deep front pocket, an inside jacket or vest pocket, and a hidden money pouch. Do not reach for the money pouch once you're in public.

Crime against tourists is rare, and, unlike some of the Caribbean countries, the Bahamas has little panhandling. But take the precautions you would in any foreign country: be aware of your wallet or handbag at all times, and keep your jewelry in the hotel safe. **Be especially wary in remote areas, always lock your rental vehicle, and don't keep any valuables in the car, even in the locked trunk.**

WOMEN IN THE BAHAMAS & TURKS & CAICOS
If you carry a purse, choose one with a zipper and a thick strap that you can drape across your body; adjust the length so that the purse sits in front of you at or above hip level. (Don't wear a money belt or a waist pack.) Store only enough money in the purse to cover casual spending. Distribute the rest of your cash and any valuables between deep front pockets, inside jacket or vest pockets, and a concealed money pouch.

Women traveling alone should not go out walking unescorted at night in Nassau or in remote areas. Crime is low, but there's no need to take unnecessary risks. In most other cases, women are safe and treated with respect. To avoid unwanted attention, **dress conservatively and cover up swimsuits off the beach.**

SENIOR-CITIZEN TRAVEL

To qualify for age-related discounts, mention your senior-citizen status up front when booking hotel reservations (not when checking out) and before you're seated in restaurants (not when paying the bill). Be sure to have identification on hand. When renting a car, ask about promotional car-rental discounts, which can be cheaper than senior-citizen rates.

🎓 Educational Programs **Elderhostel** ✉ 11 Ave. de Lafayette, Boston, MA 02111-1746 ☎ 877/426-8056, 978/323-4141 international callers, 877/426-2167 TTY 🖷 877/426-2166 ⊕ www.elderhostel.org.

SHOPPING

There's enough of a savings over U.S. prices (30%–50%, in many cases) to make duty-free shopping profitable on New Providence and Grand Bahama. On all the islands, be sure to visit the straw markets, where you can bargain for low-priced hats, baskets, place mats, T-shirts, and other items. But be aware that most of the straw goods you find in a straw market are actually imported from Taiwan or other places.

KEY DESTINATIONS

In Nassau, Bay Street is the center for duty-free shopping, souvenirs, straw market goods, and art galleries.

Grand Bahama Island has two popular shopping arenas. International Bazaar in Freeport carries items from around the world and is a good place to look for duty-free jewelry, cigars, perfume, and crystal. Newer Port Lucaya carries many of the same goods in charming Bahamian-style stores.

In Providenciales (Turks and Caicos), small shopping malls near the resorts at Ports of Call, and near the airport at the Market Place and Central Square, sell limited duty-free items and a variety of souvenirs.

SMART SOUVENIRS

For authentic souvenirs, check out the art and crafts galleries you will find throughout the Bahamas. Most are concentrated in Nassau. Bahamian artists hold their own in the burgeoning marketplace for Caribbean art.

Trademark products include Junkanoo-inspired art, wood sculpture, painted straw masks, handmade batik, model ships, and hand-plaited straw work. Jackson Burnside is one master of Junkanoo art. His Doongalik Studios in Nassau sells his work and that of other artists.

Long Island is known for its hand-plaiting, which has survived the onslaught of cheap imported goods. The island of Andros is home to the Androsia Batik factory, which produces island-style batik cloth and clothing that is available throughout the islands.

On the island of Green Turtle Cay, the Lowe brothers are famous. Albert Lowe is the official Bahamian artist, whose masterpieces dwell in the four- and five-figure price range. Vertram Lowe assembles realistic models of sailing ships, which start around $700.

In Providenciales in the Turks and Caicos, Bamboo Gallery carries fine local, Haitian, and other Caribbean sculpture and paintings. You can contribute to the well-being of the islands' environment by taking home handmade crafts that don't include such natural items as coral, feathers, and rare shells.

WATCH OUT

U.S. Customs does not allow any product made from black coral or tortoise shell into the country. **Smoke your Cuban cigars in the Bahamas.** They're illegal in the United States, and the fine is stiff.

SPORTS & OUTDOORS

BICYCLING

Companies in Nassau and Freeport offer nature bike tours although biking is most popular on the more remote, less-trafficked islands, especially Abaco, Andros, Eleuthera, and Providenciales. Many resorts in these locations provide bikes for guests. In Grand Bahama, long-distance road and trail biking is a growing sport outside of the Freeport-Lucaya area.

BOATING

The Bahamas and its 700 islands provide 100,000 square mi of seas ideal for sailing, motor-boating, and island-hopping. Every major island has marinas. For inexperienced sailors, charter companies take the helm for sea exploration. Customs and immigration clearance is available at 29 marinas on Abaco, Andros, Berry Islands, Bimini, Cat Cay, Cat Island, Eleuthera, Exuma, and Grand Bahama.

DIVING & SNORKELING

World-class diving has built a reputation for the Bahamas and the Turks and Caicos. The Bahamas claims the world's third longest barrier reef, accounting for 5% of the world's coral. The variety is astounding—caves, walls, ledges, shipwrecks, reefs, and blue holes set the stage for incredible marine life. Diving facilities and tours are available on most of the islands. In Grand Bahama Island, UN-EXSO (Underwater Explorers Society) has carved a niche for dolphin and cave diving. Many resorts rent snorkeling equipment, and tour boats offer snorkeling excursions.

7 **Diving Information** Get information on certified dive shops and courses before you leave home. **PADI International** ⊠ Unit 7, St. Philips Central, Albert Rd., St. Philips, Bristol BS2 OPD, UK ☎ 117/300-7234 or **PADI USA** ⊠ 30151 Tomas St., Rancho Santa Margarita, CA 92688 ☎ 800/729-7234 or 949/858-7234 ⊕ www.padi.com.

FISHING

Most celebrated for their bonefishing flats, the islands of Bahamas and Turks and Caicos have thrilled sports lovers with marlin, tuna, wahoo, grouper, mahimahi, and other deep-sea catches.

GOLF

Golf aficionados steer their vacations in the direction of Grand Bahama Island or Nassau/Paradise Island. Grand Bahama Island has four 18-hole courses; the Nassau area, three. Other resort courses are found on Treasure Cay in the Abacos, Eleuthera, and Exuma. In the Turks and Caicos, Providenciales has one course and Grand Turk another.

HIKING

As ecotourism grows in the islands, so do the opportunities for hiking in the wilds. Grand Bahama Island is supreme in its hiking and nature trails. In the other islands, beach-walking is the favored form of by-foot travel.

KAYAKING & CANOEING

Both sea and inland water kayaking have grown as a popular and intimate means of exploring nature and seeking thrills. Canoe outfitters are found to a lesser extent throughout the islands.

STUDENTS IN THE BAHAMAS

TRAVEL AGENCIES

Students of marine ecology and biology flock to the Bahamas like West Indian flamingos. If you're a student visitor, there are resources to help save money—**look into deals available through student-oriented travel agencies.** To qualify you'll need a bona fide student ID card. Members of international student groups are also eligible.

7 **IDs & Services STA Travel** ⊠ 10 Downing St., New York, NY 10014 ☎ 212/627-3111, 800/777-0112 24-hr service center ☎ 212/627-3387 ⊕ www.sta. com. **Travel Cuts** ⊠ 187 College St., Toronto, Ontario M5T 1P7, Canada ☎ 800/592-2887 in the U.S., 416/979-2406 or 866/246-9762 in Canada ☎ 416/979-8167 ⊕ www.travelcuts.com.

TAXES

There's no sales tax in the Bahamas. There is a $20 departure tax and security fee in the Bahamas. Travelers age 6 and under pay only a $5 security fee. Departure tax from Turks and Caicos is $23 for persons older than age 1. Tax on your hotel room is 6%–12%, a small service charge on your room for maid service and bellman may be about 4%. U.S. visitors can take home $600 worth of duty-free goods. The next $1,000 is taxed at 10% (⇨ Customs and Duties, *above*).

TAXIS

There are taxis waiting at every airport, and in Nassau along Bay Street and outside all of the main hotels and cruise ship docks. Beware of "hackers"—drivers who don't display their license (and may not have one). You can negotiate a fare, but you must do so before you enter the taxi. On Grand Bahama and New Providence, taxi rates are $2.20 for two passengers for

¼ mi, 30¢ for each additional ¼ mi. Third passengers can incur a fee of $3. Cabs can also be hired by the hour for $20, and $10 for every additional half hour. In the Out Islands, rates are negotiated, and you might find that renting a car is more economical. Upon arriving, you're likely to find that Bahamian taxi drivers are more loquacious than their U.S. counterparts, so by the time you've reached your hotel, you will be already familiar with points of interest. Taxi rates from the Nassau airport to Cable Beach are $15; from Paradise Island airport to Cable Beach, $20.

TELEPHONES

BaTelCo (Bahamas Telecommunications Corporation) is the phone company in the Bahamas. Most public phones require BaTelCo phone cards (available at outlets throughout the islands) and also use AT&T calling cards. Check on the surcharge from your calling card provider prior to making calls, and always ask at your hotel desk if there is a charge for making card calls from your room. There is usually a charge for making toll-free calls to the U.S.

AREA & COUNTRY CODES

The area code for the Bahamas is 242. The area code for the Turks and Caicos is 649. You can dial either number from the United States as you would make an interstate call. The country code is 1 for the United States and Canada, 61 for Australia, 64 for New Zealand, and 44 for the United Kingdom.

DIRECTORY & OPERATOR ASSISTANCE

Dial 916 for directory information and 0 for operator assistance.

INTERNATIONAL CALLS

From outside the United States and Canada, the country code for the Bahamas is 1. After dialing the appropriate international access code (00 in the U.K.), dial 1 followed by the 242 Bahamas area code.

LOCAL CALLS

Within the Bahamas, to make a local call from your hotel room, dial 9, then the

number. If your party doesn't answer before the fifth ring, hang up or you'll be charged for the call. Some 800 and 888 numbers—particularly airline and credit card numbers—can be called from the Bahamas. Others can be reached by substituting an 880 prefix and paying for the call.

LONG-DISTANCE SERVICES

AT&T, MCI, and Sprint access codes make calling long-distance relatively convenient, but you may find the local access number blocked in many hotel rooms. First ask the hotel operator to connect you. If the hotel operator balks, ask for an international operator, or dial the international operator yourself. One way to improve your odds of getting connected to your long-distance carrier is to travel with more than one company's calling card (a hotel may block Sprint, for example, but not MCI). If all else fails, call from a pay phone.

🗹 Access Codes Access codes are as numerous as the number of calling plans offered by the major phone carriers. Be sure to write your access number, and your phone and PIN numbers in more than one location before you leave home.

PHONE CARDS

To place a call from a public phone using your own calling card, dial 0 for the operator, who will then place the call using your card number.

PUBLIC PHONES

Pay phones accept BaTelCo phone cards.
🗹 BaTelCo ☎ 242/302–7000.

TIME

The Bahamas and the Turks and Caicos lie within the Eastern Standard Time (EST) Zone, which means that it's 7 AM in the Bahamas (or New York) when it's noon in London and 10 PM in Sydney. During the summer, the islands switch to Eastern Daylight Time (EDT).

TIPPING

The usual tip for service from a taxi driver or waiter is 15% and $1 a bag for porters. Many hotels and restaurants automatically add a 15% gratuity to your bill.

TOURS & PACKAGES

Because everything is prearranged on a prepackaged tour or independent vacation, you spend less time planning—and often get it all at a good price.

Many prearranged tours aren't for those who like to spread their wings. If you get a good enough deal, however, book the tour, but skip the excursions. Many cost extra anyway.

BOOKING WITH AN AGENT

Travel agents are excellent resources. But it's a good idea to collect brochures from several agencies, as some agents' suggestions may be influenced by relationships with tour and package firms that reward them for volume sales. If you have a special interest, find an agent with expertise in that area; the American Society of Travel Agents (ASTA; ⇨ Travel Agencies) has a database of specialists worldwide. You can log on to the group's Web site to find an ASTA travel agent in your neighborhood.

Make sure your travel agent knows the accommodations and other services of the place being recommended. Ask about the hotel's location, room size, beds, and whether it has a pool, room service, or programs for children, if you care about these. Has your agent been there in person or sent others whom you can contact?

Do some homework on your own, too: local tourism boards can provide information about lesser-known and small-niche operators, some of which may sell only direct.

BUYER BEWARE

Each year consumers are stranded or lose their money when tour operators—even large ones with excellent reputations—go out of business. So check out the operator. Ask several travel agents about its reputation, and try to **book with a company that has a consumer-protection program.** (Look for information in the company's brochure.) In the United States, members of the United States Tour Operators Association are required to set aside funds ($1 million) to help eligible customers cover payments and travel ar-

rangements in the event that the company defaults. It's also a good idea to choose a company that participates in the American Society of Travel Agents' Tour Operator Program; ASTA will act as mediator in any disputes between you and your tour operator.

Remember that the more your package or tour includes, the better you can predict the ultimate cost of your vacation. Make sure you know exactly what is covered, and beware of hidden costs. Are taxes, tips, and transfers included? Entertainment and excursions? These can add up.

🎟 Tour-Operator Recommendations American Society of Travel Agents (⇨ Travel Agencies). National Tour Association (NTA) ✉ 546 E. Main St., Lexington, KY 40508 ☎ 859/226-4444 or 800/682-8886 🖷 859/226-4404 ⊕ www.ntaonline.com. United States Tour Operators Association (USTOA) ✉ 275 Madison Ave., Suite 2014, New York, NY 10016 ☎ 212/599-6599 🖷 212/599-6744 ⊕ www.ustoa.com.

TRAVEL AGENCIES

A good travel agent puts your needs first. Look for an agency that has been in business at least five years, emphasizes customer service, and has someone on staff who specializes in your destination. In addition, **make sure the agency belongs to a professional trade organization.** The American Society of Travel Agents (ASTA)—the largest and most influential in the field with more than 20,000 members in some 140 countries—maintains and enforces a strict code of ethics and will step in to help mediate any agent-client disputes involving ASTA members if necessary. ASTA (whose motto is "Without a travel agent, you're on your own") also maintains a Web site that includes a directory of agents. (If a travel agency is also acting as your tour operator, *see* Buyer Beware *in* Tours & Packages.)

🎟 Local Agent Referrals American Society of Travel Agents (ASTA) ✉ 1101 King St., Suite 200, Alexandria, VA 22314 ☎ 703/739-2782 or 800/965-2782 24-hr hotline 🖷 703/684-8319 ⊕ www.astanet.com. Association of British Travel Agents ✉ 68-71 Newman St., London W1T 3AH ☎ 020/7637-2444 🖷 020/7637-0713 ⊕ www.abta.com. Association of Canadian Travel Agencies ✉ 130

Albert St., Suite 1705, Ottawa, Ontario K1P 5G4
☎ 613/237-3657 ⎙ 613/237-7052 ⊕ www.acta.ca.
Australian Federation of Travel Agents ✉ Level 3,
309 Pitt St., Sydney, NSW 2000 ☎ 02/9264-3299 or
1300/363-416 ⎙ 02/9264-1085 ⊕ www.afta.com.
au. **Travel Agents' Association of New Zealand**
✉ Level 5, Tourism and Travel House, 79 Boulcott
St., Box 1888, Wellington 6001 ☎ 04/499-0104
⎙ 04/499-0786 ⊕ www.taanz.org.nz.

VISITOR INFORMATION

Learn more about foreign destinations by
checking government-issued travel advisories and country information. For a
broader picture, consider information
from more than one country.
🛈 Tourist Information **Bahamas Ministry of
Tourism** ☎ 242/322-7500 ⊕ www.bahamas.com
✉ Box N-3701, Nassau ⎙ 242/832-0796 ✉ 150 E.
52nd St., 28th fl. (north), New York, NY 10022
☎ 800/823-3136 or 212/758-2777 ⎙ 212/753-6531
✉ Bahama Out Islands Promotion Board, 1200 Cornerstone, South Pine Island Rd., Suite 700, Plantation, FL 33324 ☎ 954/475-8315 ⎙ 954/236-8354
⊕ www.bahama-out-islands.com/home.php
✉ 3450 Wilshire Blvd., Suite 1204, Los Angeles, CA
90010 ☎ 213/385-0033 ⎙ 213/383-3966 ✉ 121
Bloor St. E, Suite 1101, Toronto M4W 3M5 ☎ 416/
968-2999 ⎙ 416/968-6711 ✉ 3, The Billings, Wal-
nut Tree Close, Guildford, Surrey GU1 4UL, U.K.
☎ 01483/448-900 ⎙ 01483/571-846.

Caribbean Tourism Organization ✉ 80 Broad St.,
32nd fl., New York, NY 10014 ☎ 212/635-9530
⎙ 212/697-4258 ⊕ www.doitcaribbean.com. **Mor-
ris-Kevan International Ltd.** ✉ International
House, 47 Chase Side, Enfield, Middlesex EN2 6NB
☎ 0181/364-5188 ⎙ 0181/367-9949. **Nassau/
Paradise Island Promotion Board** ✉ Hotel's

House, Dean's La., Suite 804, Nassau ☎ 242/322-
8381 ⎙ 242/326-5346.

Turks and Caicos Islands Tourist Board ✉ Front
St., Box 128, Grand Turk, Turks and Caicos Islands
☎ 800/241-0824 or 649/946-2321 ⎙ 649/946-2733
⊕ www.turksandcaicostourism.com.
🛈 Government Advisories **Australian Department
of Foreign Affairs and Trade** ☎ 300/139-281 travel
advice, 02/6261-1299 Consular Travel Advice Faxback
Service ⊕ www.dfat.gov.au.**Consular Affairs Bureau of Canada** ☎ 800/267-6788 or 613/944-6788
⊕ www.voyage.gc.ca. **New Zealand Ministry of
Foreign Affairs and Trade** ☎ 04/439-8000
⊕ www.mft.govt.nz.

U.K. Foreign and Commonwealth Office ✉ Travel
Advice Unit, Consular Division, Old Admiralty Building, London SW1A 2PA ☎ 0870/606-0290 or 020/
7008-1500 ⊕ www.fco.gov.uk/travel. **U.S. Department of State** ✉ Overseas Citizens Services Office,
2100 Pennsylvania Ave. NW, 4th fl., Washington, DC
20520 ☎ 202/647-5225 interactive hotline, 888/
407-4747 ⊕ www.travel.state.gov.

WEB SITES

Do check out the World Wide Web when
planning your trip. You'll find everything
from weather forecasts to virtual tours of
famous cities. Be sure to visit Fodors.com
(⊕ www.fodors.com), a complete travel-
planning site. You can research prices and
book plane tickets, hotel rooms, rental
cars, vacation packages, and more. In addition, you can post your pressing questions in the Travel Talk section. Other
planning tools include a currency con-
verter and weather reports, and there are
loads of links to travel resources.

NEW PROVIDENCE ISLAND

Updated by
Harriet Edleson

NEW PROVIDENCE ISLAND, home to two-thirds of all Bahamians, is a study in contrasts: glitzy casinos and quiet, shady lanes; trendy, up-to-date resorts and tiny settlements that recall a distant, simpler age; land development unrivaled elsewhere in the Bahamas; and vast stretches of untrod territory. In the course of its history, the island has weathered the comings and goings of lawless pirates, Spanish invaders, slave-holding British Loyalists who fled the United States after the Revolutionary War, Civil War–era Confederate blockade runners, and Prohibition rumrunners. Nevertheless, New Providence remains most influenced by England, which sent its first royal governor to the island in 1718. Although Bahamians won government control in 1967 and independence six years later, British influence is felt to this day.

Nassau is the nation's capital and transportation hub, as well as the banking and commercial center. Although businesspeople take advantage of bank secrecy laws that rival Switzerland's and enjoy the absence of inheritance, income, and sales taxes, most visitors need look no farther than Nassau's many duty-free shops for proof of the island's commercial vitality.

The fortuitous combination of tourist-friendly enterprise, tropical weather, and island flavor with a European overlay has not gone unnoticed: Each year more than a million cruise-ship passengers arrive at Nassau's Prince George Wharf, on short trips from Florida or as a stop on Caribbean cruises. In keeping with New Providence's commercial spirit, the welcome center on the wharf offers much more than maps and directions—it was designed to showcase the work of Bahamian artisans, and exhibits the handmade wares of more than 45 vendors. Another joy for hard-bargaining shoppers is Nassau's Bay Street shops. A 2001 fire destroyed the **Straw Market,** a premier Nassau shopping attraction, and it still has not been rebuilt. In the meantime, you can spar with many of the same vendors at a **temporary straw market site** on nearby Bay Street.

A mile or so east of town, under the bridge from Paradise Island, Potter's Cay Dock is another colorful scene: Sloops bring catches of fish and conch, and open-air stalls carry fresh fruit, vegetables, and local foods—freshly made conch salad predominates. If the daytime bustle isn't enough, the nighttime action at the island's nightclubs and casinos can take you into the wee hours of the morning.

Be sure to leave some time for outdoor activities, one of the area's major draws. From shark diving and snorkeling to bicycle tours, horseback riding, tennis, and golf, active pursuits abound in Nassau. Avid watersports fans will find a range of possibilities, including waterskiing, sailing, windsurfing, and deep-sea fishing. Or simply cruise the clear Bahamian waters for a day trip or an evening ride. Although the resorts have a great deal to offer, it would be a shame not to venture into the incredible alfresco world that is the Bahamas' calling card.

Most hotels are either on Cable Beach or Paradise Island; just outside downtown Nassau, these tourist areas offer unfettered beach access and

Numbers in the text correspond to numbers in the margins and on the New Providence Island, and Nassau and Paradise Island maps.

**If you have
3 days**

You can take in most of the markets, gardens, and historic sites of 🏛 **Nassau ❶–⓯** in a single day. A good starting point is ☞ **Rawson Square ❶**, in the heart of the commercial area. Do your shopping in the morning, hitting the **Bay Street** strip and the artisans' marketplace at **Prince George Wharf ❷**. To avoid the afternoon heat, visit the cluster of museums near the **Bahamas Historical Society Museum ⓭**, checking out the colonial architecture along the way. Or sit in the shade at one of Nassau's lush public gardens. For a change of pace, spend the next day relaxing at the beach. Decide whether you'd prefer a secluded stretch of sand or a beach right in the middle of the action, such as **Cable Beach**—New Providence has both. Tour 🏛 **Paradise Island ⓰–⓴** on the following day. Try your luck at the casino, and explore the giant aquariums, shops, and restaurants of the megaresort **Atlantis, Paradise Island ⓰**.

**If you have
5 days**

Follow the suggested three-day itinerary, and on Day 4, head north for lunch and a bit of local flavor at ☞ **Arawak Cay ㉘**. Visit nearby **Potter's Cay ⓴**, where you can find the freshest seafood and produce on the island. On your final day, drive to 🏛 **Western New Providence ㉕–㉞**, stopping in **Adelaide Village ㉝** and taking a tour of **Commonwealth Brewery ㉜** or **Bacardi Distillery ㉞**.

**If you have
7 days**

A week will give you plenty of time to explore most areas of New Providence and 🏛 **Paradise Island ⓰–⓴**. For your first five days, follow the itinerary above. On Day 6, go on a sailing cruise or a guided tour—choose your outfitter and trip based on which area you'd like to see: **Eastern New Providence ㉑–㉔**, or 🏛 **Western New Providence** and the **South Coast ㉕–㉞**. Or, keep it mellow and spend more time at the beach and in the water. For your final evening, splurge at one of New Providence's fancier restaurants or hit the 🏛 **Nassau ❶–⓯** nightclub scene. Spend the next day at a spa, finish up that last-minute shopping, or take in your final rays before the trip home.

---

proximity to casinos. Cable Beach, so named because the Bahamas' first transatlantic telephone cable was laid here, is a crescent-shape stretch of sand west of Nassau, rimmed by resorts and the Crystal Palace Casino. Although by no means secluded—a string of high-profile resorts rub up against each other on the shore—Cable Beach is one of New Providence Island's prettiest stretches.

Paradise Island is connected to downtown Nassau's east end by a pair of bridges, one leading to P.I. (as locals call the island), and the original, just east, heading back to Nassau. Its status as an unspoiled alternative to the glitz of Cable Beach is long gone; Paradise Island has been irrevocably changed by the megaresort Atlantis. The tallest building in the Bahamas is home to a beachfront resort complete with a gamut of dining options, the largest casino in the Caribbean, and some of its fanciest shops. Most memorable, however, are the water-based activities, slides, and aquariums. Love it or despise it, it's today's face of Paradise.

Exploring New Providence

Tourist action is concentrated on New Providence's northeastern side, mostly in the capital city of Nassau and nearby Paradise Island and Cable Beach. You could easily spend your entire trip in those three areas, but if you're staying for more than a few days, you may want to see the rest of this 7- by 21-mi island. This can even be done in a single day, making occasional stops. The terrain is flat, and getting around is easy. Renting a car is your best bet—or pick up a scooter for a more adventurous ride. Wear comfortable shoes, and aim to do most of your walking early in the day, before the Bahamian sun reaches its full midday force.

As competition among Caribbean destinations continues to intensify, the Bahamas government is working toward improving its capital city. A coalition has been established to redesign the downtown area, highlighting the colorful history of the region—including its frequent brushes with pirates and slave traders. In the meantime, Nassau maintains its appeal as a shopping mecca and home to various museums and pink colonial buildings.

About the Restaurants

New Providence's high-caliber dining ranges from Continental fare to ethnic specialties, including Bahamian, Mediterranean, Asian, Latin, and European eats. Dining out is a major activity, especially now that internationally renowned chefs have started moving to the Bahamas to hone their skills.

Fresh fish is the staple for tourists and locals alike. Most popular are grouper, snapper, and mahi-mahi (known locally as dolphin), but tuna, wahoo, and conch are also well-liked. Restaurateurs rely on local fishermen and Nassau wholesalers to stock their kitchens.

About the Hotels

Accommodations in New Providence cater to a myriad of tastes and budgets, from glitzy luxury hotels on Cable Beach to small guesthouses in the western and southern reaches of the island. Consider what type of vacation you want—the ambience, amenities, service and activities—then study the various options to determine which best suits your style and needs.

Do you prefer to be in the action or on a secluded property away from the hubbub? Must the beach be outside your doorstep, or are you willing to drive or take public transportation? Are on-property restaurants and a casino essential to your vacation? If convenience and luxury are your top priorities, an all-inclusive is probably best for you. If you want to mix with the locals and experience a little more of Bahamian culture, choose a hotel in downtown Nassau. Whatever your priorities, you're likely to find what you're looking for in New Providence.

1

Beaches for All Types
Bahamian beaches make an indelible impression: Think warm, blue-green waves lapping up against pink-sand beaches. New Providence beaches, though less secluded and pristine than those on the Out Islands, still tempt travelers with their balmy breezes and aquamarine water. Choose between the more remote beaches of Paradise Island, action-packed strips on Cable Beach, or man-made beaches in downtown Nassau. One of the few peaceful stretches of sand on Cable Beach is the ½-mile strip at the Nassau Beach Hotel. (Many of the big resorts have monopolized the best beaches.) Try Love Beach for snorkeling—40 acres of coral and forests of fern known as the Sea Gardens.

Culinary Playground
New Providence is a playground for seafood lovers, adventurous eaters, gourmands, and meat-and-potatoes people alike. The island has a restaurant for every price range—and most every palate. Fresh seafood abounds, in addition to world-class Continental fare and ethnic eateries, including Bahamian, Indian, Chinese, French, and Greek. The beauty of dining in New Providence is that you can eat at a grungy local dive for one meal, and feast in a four-star restaurant for the next.

A Feast for the Eyes
Downtown Nassau intrigues travelers of all types. Shoppers, history buffs, culture mavens, and strollers all seem to find their niche in the blur of colors and aromas. Wander through the straw market, chat with the vendors, then bargain for a hat to shield yourself from the midday sun. Linger in Parliament Square, where pink, colonnaded national government buildings from the early 1800s and palm trees create an old-world ambience. Immerse yourself in the world of booty and high seas adventures at the Pirates of Nassau interactive museum. Visit Festival Place, adjacent to the Prince George Wharf, to buy hand-crafted souvenirs or designer purses. Or sample local culinary specialties such as conch fritters, and take a nap in one of the lush public gardens.

WHAT IT COSTS				
$$$$	$$$	$$	$	¢
RESTAURANTS over $40	$30–$40	$20–$30	$10–$20	under $10
HOTELS over $400	$300–$400	$200–$300	$100–$200	under $100

Restaurant prices are for a main course at dinner, excluding gratuity, typically 15%, which is often automatically added to the bill. Hotel prices are for two people in a standard double room in high season, excluding service charges and 6%–12% tax.

Timing
With the warm Gulf Stream currents swirling and balmy tradewinds blowing, the Bahamas is an appealing year-round destination. The temperature usually hovers in the 70s and 80s, and rarely gets above 90 degrees

on a midsummer's day or below 60 degrees on a winter's night. June to October tend to be the hottest and wettest months, although rain is often limited to periodic showers.

The best time to visit New Providence, particularly Nassau and Paradise Island, is December through March or April, especially if you are escaping the cold. Be aware that tropical depressions, tropical storms, and hurricanes can plague New Providence during the Atlantic hurricane season from early June to late November.

AROUND THE ISLAND

Life in the Bahamas is not *all* about glorious laziness. Nassau, the country's capital, is a bustling town on New Providence Island with shops, nightclubs, and an enviable array of restaurants, glitzy casinos, and posh hotels. Even in Nassau, though, there are quiet byways and shady lanes where you can escape the main tourist drags' tumult. Shop 'til you drop or wander past buildings that reveal the capital's colonial history. Dine on French cuisine in an elegant restaurant or rub shoulders with Bahamians in a down-home friendly eatery. Drop your dollars in a clangorous casino or escape to Paradise Island's secluded Versailles Gardens. Boogie the night away in a rowdy club or take a nighttime stroll along now-quiet Cable Beach, the daytime hubbub just a memory.

Of course, you can flee the hurly-burly altogether and head straight for the water. You'll be hard-pressed to find yourself alone on a stretch of sand, but take heart—relatively secluded beaches do exist, they're just harder to come by.

Nassau

Nassau's sheltered harbor bustles with cruise-ship hubbub, while a block away, broad, palm-lined Bay Street is alive with commercial activity. Shops angle for tourist dollars with fine imported goods at duty-free prices, yet you will find a handful of shops overflowing with authentic Bahamian crafts, food supplies, and other delights. Most of Nassau's historic sites are centered around downtown.

With its thoroughly revitalized downtown, and the revamped British Colonial Hilton leading the way, Nassau is recapturing some of its past glamour. Nevertheless, modern influence is very apparent: Fancy restaurants, suave clubs, and trendy coffeehouses have popped up everywhere. This trend comes partly in response to the growing number of upper-crust crowds that now supplement the spring-breakers and cruise passengers who have traditionally flocked to Nassau.

Today the seedy air of the town's not-so-distant past is almost unrecognizable. Petty crime is no greater than in other towns of this size, and the streets not only look cleaner but feel safer. Of course, you can still find a wild club or a rowdy bar, but you can also sip cappuccino while viewing contemporary Bahamian art or dine by candlelight beneath prints of old Nassau, serenaded by the soft, island-inspired calypso music. Culture and luxury abound: Coffeehouses advertise art exhibitions and bistro

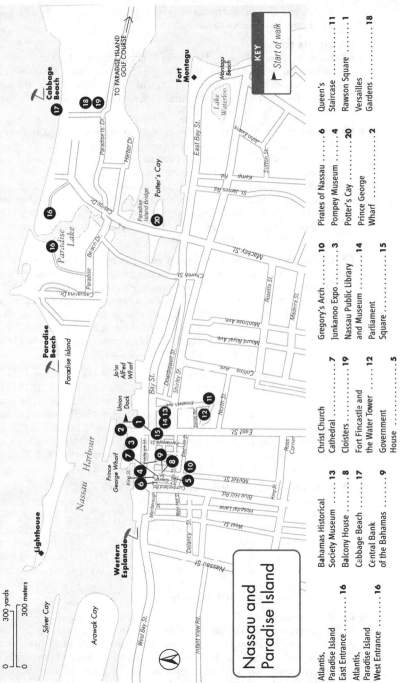

Nassau and Paradise Island

nights, and along the streets you'll find elegant stores that many bigger towns would be lucky to have.

Sights to See

⑬ **Bahamas Historical Society Museum.** For those interested in the country's origins and life before European settlement, this small collection contains a wealth of archaeological, historical, and anthropological artifacts. ✉ *Shirley St. and Elizabeth Ave.* ☎ *242/322–4231* 💲 *$1* ⊘ *Mon. 10–1, Tues.–Fri. 10–4, Sat. 10–noon.*

★ ⑧ **Balcony House.** A charming 18th-century landmark—a pink two-story house named aptly for its overhanging balcony—this is the oldest wooden residential structure in Nassau, and its furnishings and design recapture the elegance of a bygone era. The house was originally built of American cedar. A mahogany staircase, believed to have been salvaged from a ship during the 19th century, is a highlight of the interior. A guided tour through this fascinating building is an hour well spent. ✉ *Market St. and Trinity Pl.* ☎ *242/302–2621* 💲 *Donation recommended* ⊘ *Mon.–Wed., Fri. 10–4:30, Thurs., Sat. 10–1.*

⑨ **Central Bank of the Bahamas.** The Central Bank of the Bahamas monitors and regulates the country's financial institutions. The building's cornerstone was laid by Prince Charles on July 9, 1973, during the country's Independence celebrations, and the bank was opened by Queen Elizabeth II in February 1975 (you can find commemorations of these events at the back of the building). Throughout the year, exhibits on two floors of the lobby display emerging Bahamian artists' work. ✉ *Market St. and Trinity Pl.* ☎ *242/322–2193* ⊘ *Weekdays 9:30–4:30.*

★ ⑦ **Christ Church Cathedral.** It's worth the short walk off the main thoroughfare to see the stained-glass windows of this cathedral, built in 1837. The white pillars of the church's spacious, airy interior support ceilings beamed with dark wood. The crucifixion depicted in the east window's center panel is flanked by depictions of the Empty Tomb and the Ascension. Be sure to spend a few minutes in the small, flower-filled Garden of Remembrance, where stone plaques adorn the walls. ✉ *George and King Sts.* ☎ *242/322–4186* ⊘ *Daily 8:30–6.*

⑫ **Fort Fincastle and the Water Tower.** Shaped like a paddle-wheel steamer and perched near the top of the **Queen's Staircase**, Fort Fincastle—named for Royal Governor Lord Dunmore (Viscount Fincastle)—was completed in 1793 to serve as a lookout post for marauders trying to sneak into the harbor. It served as a lighthouse in the early 19th century. The fort's 126-foot-tall water tower, which is more than 200 feet above sea level, is the island's highest point. From here, the panorama of Nassau and its harbor is spectacular. ✉ *Top of Elizabeth Ave. hill, south of Shirley St.* 💲 *Water Tower 50¢* ⊘ *Daily 8–5.*

★ ⑤ **Government House.** The official residence of the governor-general of the Bahamas since 1801, this imposing pink-and-white building on Duke Street is an excellent example of the mingling of Bahamian-British and American Colonial architecture. Its graceful columns and broad, circular drive recall the styles of Virginia or the Carolinas. But its pink color, distinctive white quoins (cross-laid cornerstones), and louvered wooden shutters (to keep out the tropical sun) are typically Bahamian. Here you can also catch the crisply disciplined but beautifully flamboyant changing of the guard ceremony, which takes place every other Saturday morning at 10. The stars of the pomp and pageantry are members of the Royal Bahamas Police Force Band, who are decked out in white tunics, red-striped navy trousers, and spiked, white pith helmets with red bands. The drummers sport leopard skins. ⊠ *Duke and George Sts.* ☎ *242/322–7500 for changes in ceremony schedule.*

10 Gregory's Arch. Named for John Gregory (royal governor from 1849 to 1854), this arch, at the intersection of Market and Duke streets, separates downtown from the "over-the-hill" neighborhood of **Grant's Town,** where much of Nassau's population lives. Grant's Town was laid out in the 1820s by Governor Lewis Grant as a settlement for freed slaves. Visitors once enjoyed late-night mingling with the locals in the small, dimly lighted bars of Grant's Town. Nowadays, tourists should exhibit the same caution they would if they were visiting impoverished areas of a large city; nevertheless, it's a vibrant section of town. Here you can rub shoulders with Bahamians at a funky take-out food stand or downhome restaurant while catching a glimpse of local life.

3 Junkanoo Expo. Handmade floats and costumes used by revelers during the annual Bahamian Junkanoo celebration are exhibited in an old customs warehouse at the wharf's entrance. Junkanoo, which is celebrated yearly on Boxing Day (the day after Christmas) and New Year's Day, can be likened in its uninhibited and frenzied activities to Carnaval in Rio de Janeiro and Mardi Gras in New Orleans. Visiting the Expo is the next best thing to seeing the festivities in person. The accommodating staff will tell you everything you want to know about Junkanoo, and the colorful displays speak for themselves. ⊠ *Prince George Wharf* ☎ *$1 ◷ Daily 9–5:30.*

14 Nassau Public Library and Museum. The octagonal building near Parliament Square was the Nassau Gaol (the old British spelling for *jail*), circa 1797. You're welcome to pop in and browse. The small prison cells are now lined with books. The museum has an interesting collection of historic prints and old colonial documents. ⊠ *Shirley St. between Parliament St. and Bank La.* ☎ *242/322–4907* ☎ *Free ◷ Mon.–Thurs. 10–8, Fri. 10–5, Sat. 10–4.*

15 Parliament Square. Nassau is the seat of the national government. The Bahamian Parliament comprises two houses—a 16-member Senate (Upper House) and a 40-member House of Assembly (Lower House)—and a ministerial cabinet headed by a prime minister. Parliament Square's pink, colonnaded government buildings were constructed in the early 1800s by Loyalists who came to the Bahamas from North Carolina. The square is dominated by a statue of a slim young Queen Victoria that was erected on her birthday, May 24, in 1905. In the immediate area are a half dozen magistrates' courts (open to the public; obtain a pass at the door to view a session). Behind the House of Assembly is the **Supreme Court.** Its four-times-a-year opening ceremonies (held the first weeks of January, April, July, and October) recall the wigs and mace-bearing pageantry of the Houses of Parliament in London. The Royal

T MIGHT NOT BE AN EXAGGERATION to say that the Bahamas is a playground for children—or anyone else who likes building castles in the sand, searching for the perfect seashell, and playing tag with ocean waves.

While water-related activities are the most obvious enticements, these relaxed and friendly islands also offer a variety of indoor options, particularly in Nassau and on adjacent Paradise Island. Nassau is rich in colonial heritage, with historic **Parliament Square** and the **Bahamas Historical Society Museum,** which has a collection of photographs, documents, military uniforms, weapons, and tools, some items dating back to prehistoric days. For tales of the high seas, **Pirates of Nassau** has artifacts and interactive exhibits of the original pirates of the Caribbean.

Both Nassau and Freeport, on Grand Bahama Island, offer the chance to have close encounters of the dolphin kind. **Blue Lagoon Island Dolphin Encounter,** off Cable Beach, lets you stand waist deep in a protected pool of water and interact with trained dolphins, or put on snorkeling gear and swim with them. In Freeport, **UNEXSO** (formerly known as the Underwater Exploration Society, one of whose founders was Jacques Cousteau) has a similar program at Sanctuary Bay, a refuge for dolphins. After a performance of back flips and other tricks, these intelligent creatures literally snuggle up to be petted. Older children and adults also can spend a day learning how these remarkable creatures are trained.

For watersports enthusiasts, snorkeling, parasailing, and boating opportunities abound. In Exuma, rent a power boat and take the kids to Hog Beach, Big Major Island, to see the famous **swimming pigs.** Rumor has it that about fifty years ago, a farmer brought some pigs to the island to forage in the wild and serve as the food supply for his family. The farmer is long gone, but the pigs remain, swimming into the surf to greet arriving boats and beg for day-old bread.

Back on land, Freeport's **Garden of the Groves,** named for American financier and developer Wallace Groves, is a kid-friendly spot where pink flamingos, snorting pot bellied pigs, and raucous and colorful macaws, parrots, and cockatoos roam free in the lush 12-acre garden.

Much of the most incredible scenery of the Bahamas is underwater. Families with children five and older can walk the sea floor to view the kaleidoscope of colors and textures with **Hartley's Undersea Walk.** Participants don diving helmets configured with a special tube and air pump, allowing them to witness life under the sea at a depth of 10–15 feet. But you don't even have to get wet to get a glimpse of some of the 50,000-odd creatures of the sea. At **Atlantis,** a resort on Paradise Island, purchase a day pass and explore the world-class aquarium. For a dose of action and adrenaline, hit the waterslides or float in a tube through a shark-filled lagoon.

Many large hotels, such as Atlantis and **Four Seasons Emerald Bay Exuma,** offer supervised all-day children's programs, and some resorts are free for kids. Even the most remote of the Out Islands can be intriguing to children, and are rich in family-centered activities. Wherever you bring the kids, you're sure to get a warm welcome.

Bahamas Police Force Band is usually on hand for the event. ✉ *Bay St.* ☎ *242/322–7500 for information on Supreme Court ceremonies* ⛁ *Free* ☉ *Weekdays 10–4.*

  Pirates of Nassau. Take a journey through Nassau's pirate days in this interactive museum devoted to such notorious members of the city's past as Blackbeard, Mary Read, and Anne Bonney. Costumed guides greet you at every turn, some of them offering dialogue straight from a period adventure novel. Board a pirate ship, see dioramas of intrigue on the high seas, hear historical narration, and experience sound effects recreating some of the gruesome highlights. Two children under 12 get in free with an adult admission, and after that kids pay half price, making it a fun (if slightly scary) family outing. Be sure to check out the offbeat souvenirs in the Pirate Shop, and the lively Pirate Pub and Courtyard Grill, next door. ✉ *George and King Sts.* ☎ *242/356–3759* ⊕ *www. pirates-of-nassau.com* ⛁ *$12* ☉ *Mon.–Sat. 9–5.*

Pompey Museum. Damaged in the fire of 2001, this museum is scheduled to reopen during 2004. In a building where slave auctions were held in the 1700s, it is named for a rebel slave who lived on the Out Island of Exuma in 1830. Exhibits focus on the issues of slavery and emancipation and highlight the works of local artists, such as Amos Ferguson, one of the country's best-loved artists; his folk-art canvases depict a wide variety of subject matter, from religious imagery to nature study. ✉ *Bay and George Sts.* ☎ *242/326–2566* ⛁ *$1* ☉ *Weekdays 10–4:30, Sat. 10–1.*

Prince George Wharf. The wharf that leads into Rawson Square is the first view that cruise passengers encounter after they tumble off their ships. Up to a dozen gigantic cruise ships call on Nassau at any one time, and passengers spill out onto downtown, giving Nassau an instant, and constantly replenished, surge of life. ✉ *Waterfront at Rawson Sq.*

Queen's Staircase. These 65 steps are thought to have been carved out of a solid limestone cliff by slaves in the 1790s. The staircase was later named to honor Queen Victoria's 65-year reign. Recent innovations include a waterfall cascading from the top, and an ad hoc straw market along the narrow road that leads to the site. ✉ *Top of Elizabeth Ave. hill, south of Shirley St.*

Rawson Square. Many locals congregate at this square, which connects Bay Street to Prince George Wharf. As you enter off Bay Street, note the statue of Sir Milo Butler, the first post-independence (and first native Bahamian) governor-general. Horse-drawn surreys wait for passengers in Woodes Rogers Walk, which runs down the middle of the square (expect to pay about $10 for a half-hour ride through Nassau's streets). On the Walk's other side, you can look into (or perhaps stop inside) the **hair-braiding pavilion,** where women work their magic at prices ranging from $2 for a single strand to $100 for an elaborate do. An often-overlooked pleasure near the pavilion: Randolph W. Johnston's lovely bronze statue, *Tribute to Bahamian Women.* ✉ *Bay St.*

Paradise Island

The graceful, arched Paradise Island bridges ($1 toll for cars and motorbikes from Nassau to P.I.; free for bicyclists and pedestrians), 1 mi east of Nassau's Rawson Square, lead to and from the extravagant world of Paradise Island.

Until 1962, Paradise Island was largely undeveloped and known as Hog Island. A&P heir Huntington Hartford changed the name when he built the island's first resort complex. Although several huge high-rise resorts have been erected since then—as have many million-dollar houses—you can still find several quiet getaway spots. The north shore is lined with white-sand beaches, and the protected south shore, directly across the harbor from Nassau, is a haven for yachts. Aptly renamed, the island *is* a paradise for beach lovers, boaters, and fun lovers. Casinos abound.

Sights to See

★ ☺ ⑯ **Atlantis, Paradise Island.** The unmistakable sight of this peach fantasia comes into view just as you cross the Paradise Island Bridge. The towering sunstruck visage is actually Royal Towers, the largest and newest wing of the Atlantis resort. With glitzy shopping malls, a cabaret theater, and seemingly unlimited choices for dining and drinks, Atlantis is as much a tourist attraction as a resort hotel. Many of its facilities, including the restaurants and casino, are open to nonguests. For a peek at the rest, take the self-guided "Discover Atlantis" tour, which begins near the main lobby at an exhibition called "The Dig." This wonderful series of walk-through aquariums, themed around the lost continent and its re-created ruins, brings you face to face with sharks, manta rays, and innumerable forms of exotic sea life. The rest of the tour tempts you with a walk through the many water slides and pools inaccessible to nonguests. ⊠ *Casino Dr.* ☏ *242/363–3000* ⊠ *Discover Atlantis tour $25, casino admission free* ☉ *Tours daily 9–5, casino daily 24 hrs.*

⑰ **Cabbage Beach.** The stretch of white sand along the north side is one of the prettiest on New Providence. Although resorts line much of its length, several minutes' stroll to the east will take you to a nearly uninhabited span of beach overlooking emerald waters and tiny offshore cays.

★ ⑲ **Cloisters.** At the top of the **Versailles Gardens** stand the remains of a 14th-century French stone monastery that were imported to the United States in the 1920s by newspaper baron William Randolph Hearst. (The cloister is one of four that have ever been removed from French soil.) Forty years later, grocery-chain heir Hartford bought the Cloisters and had them rebuilt on their present commanding site. At the center is a graceful, contemporary white marble statue called *Silence,* by U.S. sculptor Dick Reid. Nearly every day tourists take or renew wedding vows under the delicately wrought gazebo overlooking Nassau Harbour. The Cloisters are owned by the One & Only Ocean Club, but visitors are welcome to look around. ⊠ *Paradise Island Dr.*

★ ⑳ **Potter's Cay.** From Nassau, walk the road beneath the Paradise Island Bridge to watch sloops bring in and sell loads of fish and conch. Along the road to the cay are dozens of stands where you can watch the conch, straight from the sea, being extracted from its glistening pink shell. If you don't have the know-how to handle the tasty conch's preparation—getting the diffident creature out of its shell requires boring a hole at the right spot to sever the muscle that keeps it entrenched—you can enjoy a conch salad on the spot, as fresh as it comes, and take notes for future attempts. Empty shells are sold as souvenirs. Many locals and hotel chefs come here to purchase the fresh catches; you can also find vegetables, herbs, and such condiments as fiery Bahamian peppers preserved in lime juice, and locally grown pineapples, papayas, and bananas.

⑱ Versailles Gardens. Fountains and statues of luminaries and legends (such as Napoleon and Josephine, Franklin Delano Roosevelt, David Livingstone, Hercules, and Mephistopheles) adorn Versailles Gardens, the terraced lawn at the One & Only Ocean Club, which was once the private hideaway of Huntington Hartford. The Cloisters grace the top of the gardens. Although the property is owned by the One & Only Ocean Club, visitors are welcome. ⊠ *One & Only Ocean Club, Paradise Island Dr.* ☎ *242/363–2501.*

Eastern New Providence

New Providence Island's eastern end is residential, although there are some interesting historic sites and fortifications here. From East Bay Street, just beyond the Paradise Island bridges, it's a short, scenic drive along Eastern Road, which is lined with gracious homes, to Eastern Point (also known as East End Point)—about 20 minutes, depending on traffic.

Sights to See

㉑ Fort Montagu. The oldest of the island's three forts, Montagu was built of local limestone in 1741 to repel Spanish invaders. The only action it saw was when it was occupied for two weeks by rebel American troops—among them a lieutenant named John Paul Jones—seeking arms and ammunition during the Revolutionary War. The small fortification is in disrepair, though you are welcome to go inside. The second level has a number of rusted cannons. A narrow public beach stretching for more than a mile beyond the fort looks out upon Montagu Bay, where many international yacht regattas and Bahamian sloop races are held annually. ⊠ *East of Bay St. on Eastern Rd.* ☜ *Free.*

㉓ Fox Hill. Settled by freed slaves who were given land grants, which they paid for either in cash or labor, this residential area was originally four smaller settlements. Today there's not much here of tourist interest—except on the second Tuesday of August, when the community holds its annual Fox Hill Day celebration. It falls a week after the rest of the island celebrates Emancipation Day (some say that's because back in 1834 it took a week for the news of the emancipation to reach the community here). Festivities include music, home-cooked food, and arts-and-crafts booths. Call the Ministry of Tourism for more information. ☎ *242/322–7500.*

★ **㉒ The Retreat.** Nearly 200 species of exotic palm trees grace the 11 verdant acres appropriately known as The Retreat, which serves as the head-

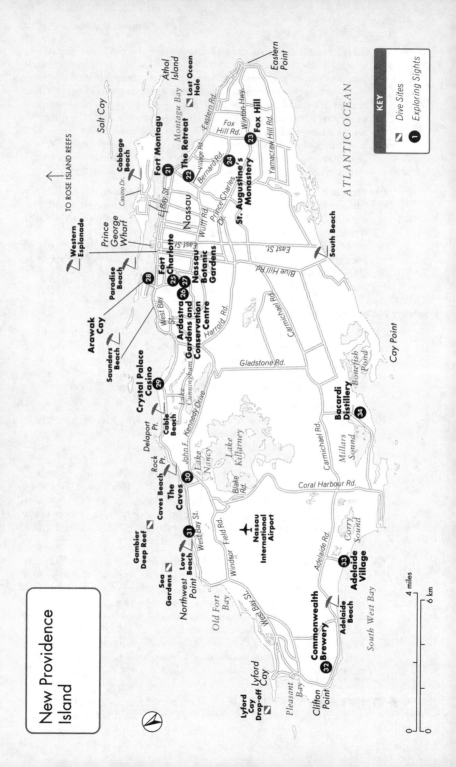

New Providence Island

TO ROSE ISLAND REEFS

Salt Cay

Athol Island

Eastern Point

Lost Ocean Hole

Montagu Bay

Fort Montagu 21

Cabbage Beach

Casino Dr.

Bay St.

East St.

The Retreat 22

Eastern Rd.

Village Rd.

Bernard Rd.

Fox Hill 23

Fox Hill Rd.

Winton Hwy.

Nassau

Prince George Wharf

Western Esplanade

Paradise Beach

Fort Charlotte 25

East St.

Wulff Rd.

Prince Charles Dr.

St. Augustine's Monastery 24

Yamacraw Hill Rd.

ATLANTIC OCEAN

South Beach

East St.

Blue Hill Rd.

Nassau Botanic Gardens 26 27

Ardastra Gardens and Conservation Centre

Arawak Cay

Saunders Beach

West Bay St.

Harrold Rd.

Cunningham Lake

28

Crystal Palace Casino 29

Cable Beach

Delaport Pt.

Rock Pt.

John F. Kennedy Drive

Lake Nancy

Lake Cunningham

Gladstone Rd.

Carmichael Rd.

Cay Point

Caves Beach

The Caves 30

Lake Killarney

Lake Cunningham

Blake Rd.

Coral Harbour Rd.

Millars Sound

Bacardi Distillery 34

Bonefish Pond

Gambier Deep Reef

Sea Gardens

Love Beach 31

Northwest Point

West Bay St.

Field Rd.

Nassau International Airport

Windsor Field Rd.

Carmichael Rd.

Corry Sound

Old Fort Bay

Adelaide Rd.

Adelaide Village 33

Commonwealth Brewery 32

Adelaide Beach

Lyford Cay Drop-off

Lyford Cay

Pleasant Bay

West Bay St.

Clifton Point

South West Bay

KEY

◿ Dive Sites

① Exploring Sights

4 miles

6 km

quarters of the Bahamas National Trust. Stroll in blessed silence through the lush grounds, past smiling Buddhas, and under stone arbors overhung with vines. It's a perfect break on a steamy Nassau day. Guided tours are available, or walk through this sanctuary on your own. ⊠ *Village Rd.* ☎ *242/393–1317* 💷 *$2* ⊙ *Weekdays 9–5.*

㉔ St. Augustine's Monastery. The Romanesque home of the Bahamas' Benedictine brothers was built in 1946 by a monk named Father Jerome, also famed for his carvings of the Stations of the Cross on Cat Island's Mt. Alvernia. The St. Augustine buildings, home to a college as well as the religious complex, overlook beautiful gardens. A truly off-the-beaten-track sight. Call first to see if the monks will give you a tour. ⊠ *Bernard Rd., west of Fox Hill Rd.* ☎ *242/364–1331.*

Western New Providence & South Coast

Starting from downtown Nassau, West Bay Street follows the coast west past the resorts, posh residential neighborhoods, and ever-increasing new developments of Cable Beach, then past popular Love Beach to Northwest Point. Just beyond is Lyford Cay, the island's most exclusive residential area. Old-money pioneers started settling the cay four decades ago, and along with its 200-odd houses there is a private golf course for residents. Your experience of Lyford Cay is likely to be voyeuristic at best—an entrance gate wards off all but residents and friends.

Much of the interior and southwestern coast of New Providence is undeveloped, with pristine coastal scenery and long, low stretches of palmetto and pine forest. The loop around the island's west and south coasts can be done in a couple of hours by car or scooter; however, you may wish to take time out for lunch and a swim along the way.

Sights to See

㉝ Adelaide Village. The small community on New Providence's southwestern coast sits placidly, like a remnant of another era, between busy Adelaide Road and the ocean. It was first settled during the early 1830s by Africans who had been captured and loaded aboard slave ships bound for the New World. They were rescued on the high seas by the British Royal Navy, and the first group of liberated slaves reached Nassau in 1832. Today, only a few dozen families live in Adelaide. They grow vegetables, raise chickens, and inhabit well-worn, pastel-painted wooden houses, sheltered by bougainvillea and other vegetation. The village has a primary school, some little grocery stores, and locally popular **Avery's Restaurant and Bar** (⊠ Adelaide Rd. ☎ 242/362–1547).

㉘ Arawak Cay. Known to Nassau residents as "The Fish Fry," Arawak Cay is one of the best places to knock back a Kalik beer (brewed right on New Providence Island), chat with the locals, or sample traditional Bahamian fare. You can get small noshes or full meals at one of the pastel-color shacks that line the large fairground's perimeter. Order some fried fish or fresh conch salad, a spicy mixture of chopped conch (just watching the expert chopping is a show as good as any in town) mixed with diced onions, cucumbers, tomatoes, and hot peppers in a lime marinade. Goldie's Enterprises, on the cay's western side, is one of the most popular stalls. Try their "crack conch" and Goldie's famous Sky Juice (a potent gin and coconut-water concoction).

To reach Arawak Cay, head west along Bay Street, follow the main road around the British Colonial Hilton hotel, and continue west past Western Esplanade beach. The cay is on the north side of the T-junction of West Bay and Chippingham Road. It's approximately a five-minute drive or 30-minute walk.

㉖ Ardastra Gardens and Conservation Centre. Marching flamingos? These national birds of the Bahamas give a parading performance at Ardastra daily at 11, 2, and 4. The zoo, with more than 5 acres of tropical greenery and flowering shrubs, also has an aviary of rare tropical birds, native Bahamian creatures such as rock iguanas, and a global collection of small animals. ✉ *Chippingham Rd., south of W. Bay St.* ☎ *242/323–5806* ✑ *$12* ☉ *Daily 9–5.*

㉞ Bacardi Distillery. The factory, established in 1962, is open to the public for tours. You can sample a range of its well-known rum products (and, needless to say, purchase some) at the Visitors Pavilion. ✉ *Bacardi and Carmichael Rds.* ☎ *242/362–1412* ✑ *Free* ☉ *Mon.–Thurs. 10–3.*

㉚ The Caves. These large limestone caverns that the waves have sculpted over the aeons are said to have sheltered the early Arawak Indians. An oddity perched right beside the road, they're worth a glance—although in truth, there's not much to see, as the dark interior doesn't lend itself to exploration. Just a short drive beyond the caves, on an island between traffic lanes, is **Conference Corner,** where U.S. president John F. Kennedy, Canadian prime minister John Diefenbaker, and British prime minister Harold Macmillan planted trees on the occasion of their 1962 summit in Nassau. ✉ *W. Bay St. and Blake Rd.*

㉜ Commonwealth Brewery. Kalik, Nassau's very own beer, pale in color but with a full-bodied taste, is brewed here. The local beverage—by far the most popular among Bahamians—is named for the sound of the cowbells used in the Junkanoo Parade. Free tours are given by appointment only. ✉ *Clifton Pier and Southwest Rd.* ☎ *242/362–4789.*

㉙ Crystal Palace Casino. You can try your luck at baccarat, blackjack, roulette, craps, and Caribbean stud poker or simply settle for the slots. There's plenty to keep you entertained, including a sports book for betting on your favorite teams, and games from "pai gow poker" to "let it ride" and "war" tables. ✉ *Nassau Wyndham Resort & Crystal Palace Casino, Cable Beach, Nassau* ☎ *242/327–6200* ☉ *Tables 10 AM–4 AM weekdays, 24 hrs weekends; slots 24 hrs daily.*

★ ㉕ Fort Charlotte. Built in the late 18th century, this imposing fort comes complete with a waterless moat, drawbridge, ramparts, and dungeons. Lord Dunmore, who built it, named the massive structure in honor of George III's wife. At the time, some called it Dunmore's Folly because of the staggering expense of its construction. It cost eight times more than was originally planned. (Dunmore's superiors in London were less than ecstatic with the high costs, but he managed to survive unscathed.) Ironically, no shots were ever fired in battle from the fort. It is about 1 mi west of central Nassau. ✉ *W. Bay St. at Chippingham Rd.* 🖺 *Free* ⊙ *Local guides conduct tours daily 8–4.*

③① **Love Beach.** One of the island's loveliest little beaches is near New Providence's northwestern corner. About 1 mi off Love Beach are 40 acres of coral and sea fan, with forests of fern, known as the Sea Gardens. The clear waters are a favorite with snorkelers.

②⑦ **Nassau Botanic Gardens.** Six hundred species of flowering trees and shrubs, a small cactus garden, and two freshwater ponds with lilies, water plants, and tropical fish cover 18 acres. The many trails that wind through the gardens are perfect for leisurely strolls. The Botanic Gardens are across the street from the **Ardastra Gardens and Conservation Centre,** home of Nassau's zoo. ✉ *Chippingham Rd., south of W. Bay St.* ☎ *242/323–5975* 🖺 *$1* ⊙ *Weekdays 8–4, weekends 9–4.*

BEACHES

New Providence is blessed with stretches of white sand studded with palm and sea-grape trees. Some of the beaches are small and crescent shape, whereas others stretch for miles. Right in downtown Nassau is the **Western Esplanade.** It sweeps west from the British Colonial Hilton on Bay Street and offers public rest rooms. On Paradise Island, **Paradise Beach,** at the island's far western tip, is a nice stretch of sand. Paradise Island's real showpiece is 3-mi-long **Cabbage Beach,** which rims the north coast from the Atlantis lagoon to Snorkeler's Cove. At the east end you can rent jet skis and nonmotorized pedal boats, and go parasailing.

Cable Beach is on New Providence's north shore, about 3 mi west of downtown Nassau. Resorts line much of this beautiful, broad swath of white sand, but there is public access. Jet-skiers and beach vendors abound, so don't expect quiet isolation. Just west of Cable Beach is a rambling pink house on the Rock Point promontory, where much of the 1965 Bond film *Thunderball* was filmed. Tiny, crescent-shape **Caves Beach** is beyond Cable Beach on the north shore, about 7 mi from downtown just before the turnoff on Blake Road that leads to the airport. **Love Beach** is a snorkeler's favorite, on the north shore beyond Caves Beach, about 9 mi from town (about a 20-minute drive). Access technically lies within the domain of Love Beach residents, but they aren't inclined to shoo anyone away. On the south shore, drive down to **Adelaide Beach,** at the end of Adelaide Village, for sand that stretches down to Coral Harbour. The people who live at New Providence's east end flock to **South Beach,** at the foot of Blue Hill Road on the south shore.

WHERE TO EAT

With the escalation of Bahamian tourism, meal preparation at the better dining spots has become as sophisticated as that in any leading U.S. city. European chefs brought in by the top restaurants have trained young Bahamians in the skills of haute cuisine. Chinese, Indian, Mexican, Creole, and Japanese fare have also become available.

However, don't neglect the Bahamian food. Several relatively inexpensive spots serve traditional dishes, which now also appear on the ritzier menus: peas 'n' rice, conch (chowder, fritters, and cracked), Bahamian lobster, "stew" or "boil" fish, grouper fingers, fresh local bread, and, for dessert, guava duff, a warm marriage of boiled Guava dough and sweet sauce. Because meats and some seafood often have to be imported, local fish is usually the most economical entrée.

Coffeehouses have sprung up everywhere. Most serve light fare and desserts plus specialty coffees and teas.

Many all-inclusives also offer meal plans for nonguests.

For general information, *see* Dining *in* Smart Travel Tips A to Z at the front of the book.

WHAT IT COSTS In U.S. dollars				
$$$$	**$$$**	**$$**	**$**	**¢**
AT DINNER	over $40	$30–$40	$20–$30	$10–$20	under $10

Prices are per person for a main course at dinner.

Nassau

Bahamian

¢–$$$ ✕ **Conch Fritters Bar & Grill.** A favorite in downtown Nassau, this lively, tropically themed restaurant is best known for conch. You can sample this Bahamian specialty in chowders, salads, and, of course, fritters. That said, conch-phobes need not worry. You'll find a diverse menu brimming with burgers, sandwiches, and pasta; the selection of steaks includes a serious 24-ounce porterhouse. There's a live band 7 to midnight nightly except Monday and a festive Junkanoo celebration on Saturday from 8 to 11 PM. ✉ *Marlborough St., across from the British Colonial Hilton* ☎ 242/323–8778 ▭ AE, D, MC, V ✣ *Breakfast also served.*

$–$$ ✕ **The Poop Deck.** Just east of the bridge from Paradise Island and a quick cab ride from the center of town is this favorite haunt of locals. You can scan the vista of the Bahamas' largest marina from breezy tables on the large waterfront deck. The restaurant's popularity has resulted in a second Poop Deck on Cable Beach's west end, but for residents, this is still the place. Expect spicy dishes with such names as Mama Mary's steamed fish and Rosie's chicken; there's also an extensive wine list. Save room for guava duff and a calypso coffee spiked with secret ingredients. ✉ *E. Bay St., at Nassau Yacht Haven Marina, east of bridge from Paradise Island* ☎ 242/393–8175 ▭ AE, D, MC, V.

¢–$$ ✕ **Shoal Restaurant and Lounge.** Saturday morning brings hordes of hungry Bahamians digging into boil fish and johnnycake, the restaurant's specialty. A bowl of this peppery local dish, filled with chunks of boiled potatoes, onions, and grouper, may keep you coming back to this dimly lit, basic, out-of-the-way "Ma's kitchen," where Bahamian dishes, including peas 'n' rice and cracked conch, are staples. ✉ *Nassau St., between Meadow St. and Poinciana Dr.* ☎ 242/323–4400 ▭ AE, D, MC, V ✣ *Closed Wed.*

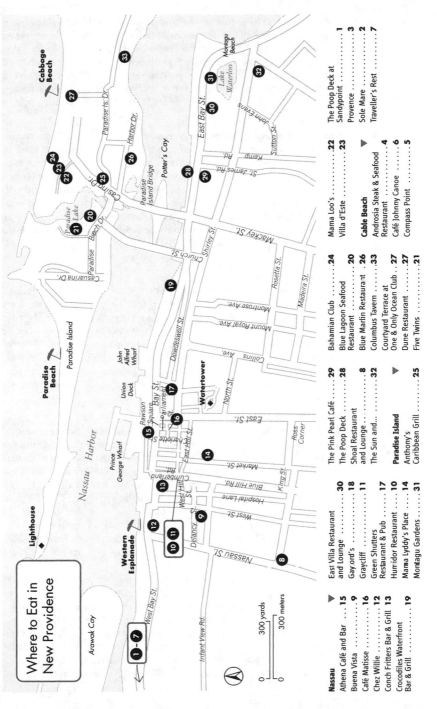

Where to Eat in New Providence

0 |——————| 300 yards
0 |——————| 300 meters

Arawak Cay

Lighthouse

West Bay St.

Infant View Rd.

Western Esplanade

Nassau Harbor

Prince George Wharf

Cumberland Rd.

Union Dock

John Alfred Wharf

Paradise Beach

Paradise Island

Paradise Dr.

Casuarina Dr.

Paradise Beach Dr.

Paradise Lake

Cabbage Beach

Paradise Is. Dr.

Harbor Dr.

Potter's Cay

Paradise Island Bridge

Casino Dr.

Lake Waterloo

Montagu Beach

East Bay St.

John Evans

Sutton St.

Kemp Rd.

St. James Rd.

Shirley St.

Mackey St.

Church St.

Rosetta St.

Madeira St.

Montrose Ave.

Mount Royal Ave.

Collins Ave.

North St.

East St.

Ross Corner

Dowdeswell St.

Watertower

Parliament St.

Bay St.

Rawson Square

Charlotte St.

East Hill St.

Market St.

King St.

Blue Hill Rd.

Hospital Lane

West St.

Delancy St.

Nassau St.

West Hill St.

★ ¢–$ ✕ **Mama Lyddy's Place.** Just off the beaten tourist track, this old house is the place for true Bahamian cooking. Start with a local-style breakfast of souse or "boil fish" and watch Nassau residents stream in for take-out or sit-down meals. For lunch and dinner try fried snapper, cracked conch, minced or broiled crawfish, pork chops, and chicken. All are served with peas 'n' rice or peas 'n' grits and other typical Bahamian side dishes. ⊠ *Market St. at Cockburn St.* ☎ *242/328–6849* ▤ *No credit cards.*

Chinese

¢–$$ ✕ **East Villa Restaurant and Lounge.** Nassau residents declare that this restaurant, set back from the busy street, serves the best Chinese food in town. The Chinese-Continental menu includes such entrées as conch with black bean sauce, *hung shew* (walnut chicken), and steak *kew* (cubed prime fillet served with baby corn, snow peas, water chestnuts, and vegetables). The New York strip steak is nirvana. A short taxi ride from Paradise Island or downtown Nassau, this is the perfect spot if you're seeking something a little different from the typical area restaurants. ⊠ *E. Bay St., near Nassau Yacht Club* ☎ *242/393–3377* ▤ *AE, D, MC, V* ⊘ *No lunch Sat.*

Contemporary

★ $$ ✕ **The Pink Pearl Café.** The Pink Pearl is set in a 1943 mansion made of limestone and local pine. Its inventive menu and impeccable service draw crowds, as does the live jazz that you can listen to on weekends from the breezy side porch. From the moment you arrive, you know you're in for a treat—aromatic bread arrives in a large calabash shell. Entrées might include roasted grouper with a ragout of onion, tomato, thyme, mushrooms, and potatoes, or grilled conch drizzled with tamarind barbecue sauce. ⊠ *E. Bay St., east of bridge from Paradise Island* ☎ *242/ 394–6413* ▤ *AE, D, DC, MC, V* ⊘ *Closed Sun.*

Continental

★ $$$–$$$$ ✕ **Buena Vista.** High on a hill above Nassau Harbour, this serene restaurant sits secure in its reputation as one of the city's dining institutions; it draws a loyal local clientele. Established in 1946, it occupies what was once a rambling private home built in the early 1800s. Tuxedoed waiters whisk about the dining room, where tables are set with china, crystal, and silver. Although jackets aren't absolutely required, you'll find most gentlemen wearing them. Exemplary entrées include grouper and rack of spring lamb. Leave room for Mrs. Hauck's Orange Pancakes, baked in a Grand Marnier sauce—a house specialty for decades. ⊠ *W. Hill and Delancy Sts.* ☎ *242/322–2811* ▤ *AE, D, DC, MC, V* ⊘ *Closed Sun. No lunch.*

$$$–$$$$ ✕ **Graycliff.** A meal at Graycliff begins in the elegant parlor, where, over live piano music, drinks are served and orders taken. When your appetizer is ready, you're escorted into one of several dining rooms. Graycliff's signature dishes include roast rack of lamb and the thermidor-style Lobster Graycliff. Prices are no higher than other top-notch Nassau restaurants except for wine: The cellar contains more than 175,000 bottles that have been handpicked by owner Enrico Garzaroli, some running into the tens of thousands of dollars. ⊠ *W. Hill St. at Cumberland Rd.,*

across from Government House ☎ 242/322–2796 ☐ AE, D, DC, MC, V ⊘ No lunch weekends.

★ **$$$–$$$$** ✕ **The Sun and . . .** If you're hoping to catch sight of international superstars, this is a good place to look (assuming that they—or you—make it past the hostess). Dine in a series of rooms surrounding an enclosed garden area with a rock pool and fountain—as magical a dining setting as Nassau offers. Feast on such creations as salmon mousseline and crayfish tails rolled in grouper fillets, topped with Chardonnay-lobster sauce, or veal with porcini mushrooms and white truffle oil. End your meal divinely with one of Belgian owner-chef Ronny Deryckere's six soufflés, which range from almond amaretto to guava. ☒ *Lakeview Rd. and E. Shirley St.* ☎ 242/393–1205 ☖ Jacket required ☐ AE, D, MC, V ⊘ Closed Mon. and Aug.–Sept. No lunch.

★ **$$–$$$** ✕ **Humidor Restaurant.** Carved-wood statues of pipe smokers, imported from Cuba, set the tone at this relaxed restaurant in the Graycliff hotel's Graycliff Cigar Company wing. This spot is a stogie-lover's delight. Here you can get a set meal including a selection of cigars. The tasty bistro fare includes tuna tartare, lobster cakes, and risotto with porcini mushrooms and lamb. For postprandial indulgence, retire to the lounge or stroll along the hotel's garden terraces and fountains. ☒ *W. Hill St., off Cumberland Rd.* ☎ 242/328–7050 ☐ AE, DC, MC, V ⊘ Closed Sun.

$–$$$ ✕ **Montagu Gardens.** Angus beef and fresh native seafood—flame grilled and seasoned with home-mixed spices—are the specialties at this romantic restaurant in an old Bahamian mansion on Lake Waterloo. The dining room opens to a walled courtyard niched with Roman-style statues and gardens that lead to a waterside balustrade. Besides seafood and steak (carnivores love the filet mignon smothered in mushrooms), menu selections include chicken, lamb, pasta, ribs, and several Bahamian-inspired dishes such as conch fritters and minced crawfish with taco chips. A favorite dessert is Fort Montagu Mud Pie. ☒ *E. Bay St.* ☎ 242/394–6347 ☐ AE, D, MC, V ⊘ Closed Sun.

Eclectic

¢–$$$ ✕ **Crocodiles Waterfront Bar & Grill.** The informal outdoor grill, with deck tables shaded by palms and adorned with signs from a plethora of Nassau establishments, is a good spot to linger under thatched umbrellas and take in harbor views. You can opt for a light bite—conch salad, burgers (standard and conch varieties), calamari, nachos, and sandwiches— or try one of the heartier choices such as the mammoth T-bone steak. The sea breezes, relaxing music, and friendly staff make happy hour at Crocodiles (daily 5 to 7:30) a Nassau classic. ☒ *E. Bay St., west of bridge to Paradise Island* ☎ 242/323–3341 ☐ MC, V.

★ **$–$$** ✕ **Café Matisse.** Low-slung settees, stucco arches, and reproductions of the eponymous artist's works set a casually refined tone at this restaurant, owned by a husband-and-wife team—he's Bahamian, she's northern Italian. Sit in the ground-floor garden under large white umbrellas or dine inside the century-old house. Start with salmon carpaccio, then dive into freshly made pasta such as duck-filled ravioli and lobster cannelloni, or such delights as pizza *frutti di mare* (topped with fresh local seafood). ☒ *Bank La. and Bay St., behind Parliament Sq.* ☎ 242/356–7012 ☐ AE, D, MC, V ⊘ Closed Sun.–Mon.

English

$–$$$ ✕ **Green Shutters Restaurant & Pub.** In a 190-year-old building, this popular watering hole looks and feels like it's tucked away in jolly old England (except for the sight of palm trees through the windows). And it's no wonder: The entire pub area, as well as the restaurant's tables and chairs, were shipped over from Britain and reassembled. Sip a pint of Guinness or Boddingtons while you wait for your steak and kidney pie. The restaurant also offers gourmet Bahamian-inspired dinners like Grouper Marsha (grouper stuffed with minced lobster) and coconut-crusted snapper. ⊠ *48 Parliament St.* ☎ *242/322–3701* ▭ *AE, D, MC, V.*

French

$$$ ✕ **Chez Willie.** Elegant and romantic, this restaurant specializes in French cuisine with a Bahamian twist. Dine by candlelight in the intimate dining room or alfresco on the patio overlooking the lush gardens. Start with caviar or goose liver pâté, then try the signature grouper served in a puff pastry with crabmeat and coconut cream sauce. Or go with someone you love and share the chateaubriand for two. ⊠ *W. Bay St.* ☎ *242/322–5364 or 242/322–5366* ⌘ *Reservations essential* ▭ *AE, MC, V* ☾ *Dinner only.*

Greek

$–$$ ✕ **Athena Café and Bar.** A mainstay since 1960, this Greek restaurant is a break from the Nassau culinary routine. Sit on the second floor among Grecian statuary, or the balcony overlooking the action below. Enjoy souvlaki, moussaka, and spanakopita, among other specialties, along with Greek beer in a relaxed and friendly atmosphere. Gregarious owner Peter Mousis and his family serve tasty fare at moderate prices. ⊠ *Bay St. at Charlotte St.* ☎ *242/322–8833* ▭ *AE, D, MC, V* ☾ *Closed Sun.*

Indian

$–$$ ✕ **Gaylord's.** A handsome historic building that dates from the 1870s is home to this restaurant. Plates, plaques, and other Indian works of art decorate the walls of the two dining areas. Draped silk adorns the ceilings. Begin with a *samosa* (a savory vegetable or meat filling enveloped in pastry and then deep fried). Next try one of the tandoori dishes cooked in a special clay oven, including nan bread (plain, or stuffed with chicken, cheese, garlic, or lamb) and mild *korma* (lamb or chicken in a rich cream sauce) or fiery vindaloo. ⊠ *Dowdeswell St. near Victoria Ave.* ☎ *242/356–3004* ▭ *AE, D, MC, V* ☾ *No lunch weekends.*

Paradise Island

Caribbean

$–$$$ ✕ **Anthony's Caribbean Grill.** Color is the standout feature of Anthony's: bright red, yellow, and blue tablecloths spiked with multihued squiggles; yellow-and-green walls with jaunty cloths hanging from the ceilings; booths printed with bright sea themes; and buoyant striped curtains. The lively spirit is reflected in the bouncy, often live music, and cheery service. The food is standard Caribbean fare: jerk chicken, rib eye seasoned with "Rasta" spices, or ribs served a multitude of ways—jerk, barbecue, or coconut-mango style. There's also a good selection of burgers, pasta, and salads. ⊠ *Paradise Village Shopping Centre* ☎ *242/363–3152* ▤ *AE, D, MC, V.*

Chinese

$$–$$$ ✕ **Mama Loo's.** This dinner-only restaurant in Atlantis serves Chinese fare amidst tropical-Chinese decor enhanced with huge porcelain urns, carved wood ceilings, lush floral arrangements, and black-lacquer chairs. Pick grouper stir-fry, braised duck, cashew chicken, or beef with oyster sauce. ⊠ *Atlantis, Paradise Island* ☎ *242/363–3000* ▤ *AE, D, DC, MC, V* ☉ *Closed Mon. No lunch.*

Continental

★ $$$$ ✕ **Courtyard Terrace at One & Only Ocean Club.** An elite clientele congregates here to indulge in refined dining under the stars, accompanied by the music of a calypso combo. With its Wedgwood china, Irish-linen napery, lighted fountains, and towering palms, this garden setting is one of the most romantic in the Bahamas. The carefully orchestrated menu emphasizes the lighter side of Continental cuisine, with a distinct island touch. Sample the duck breast with brandied cherry sauce, lobster tail with crab fried rice, or sweet and tart grouper. Alfresco dining begins at twilight. Service is superb. ⊠ *Ocean Club Dr.* ☎ *242/363–2501* ⌚ *Reservations essential* 🏛 *Jacket required* ▤ *AE, D, DC, MC, V* ☉ *No lunch.*

$$$–$$$$ ✕ **Bahamian Club.** Reminiscent of a British country club, this handsome restaurant has walls lined with dark oak, overstuffed chairs, and leather banquettes. Meat is the house specialty—grilled T-bone steak, veal chop, roast prime rib, and chateaubriand for two—but grilled swordfish steak, Bahamian lobster, salmon fillet, and other fresh seafood dishes are all prepared with finesse. Dinner is accompanied by soft piano music; between courses, couples can waltz on the small dance floor. ⊠ *Atlantis, Paradise Island* ☎ *242/363–3000* ▤ *AE, D, DC, MC, V* ☉ *No lunch.*

★ $–$$$$ ✕🏠 **Dune Restaurant.** At Dune you'll feast on intricately prepared dishes while overlooking Cabbage Beach at the renowned One & Only Ocean Club. Go for breakfast or lunch for the most reasonable prices. For breakfast, try the smoked salmon with potato pancake and chive sour cream or the egg-white omelet with fresh herbs. Dinner entrées include roasted grouper, rack of lamb, and sirloin steak. It's a great place to unwind amid ocean breezes. ⊠ *Ocean Club Dr.* ☎ *242/363–3000 Ext. 64739* ▤ *AE, D, MC, V.*

Eclectic

$$$–$$$$ ✕ **Five Twins.** The only one of Atlantis's fine-dining restaurants that's in the casino dining complex, Five Twins offers a menu with pan-Asian flair. Choices include sushi, Indonesian *sates* (marinated pieces of chicken or beef on skewers), Indian-spiced squab, and Szechuan duck breast. Imbibers may want to visit the Rum Bar at the restaurant's entrance. ⊠ *Atlantis, Paradise Island* ☎ *242/363–3000* 🏛 *Jacket required* ▤ *AE, D, DC, MC, V* ☉ *No lunch.*

Italian

$$$–$$$$ ✕ **Villa d'Este.** Upscale Northern Italian cuisine is served in an Italianate room with dark wood, upholstered chairs, statuary, and an impressive fresco on the ceiling. The antipasti display whets the appetite for such dishes as veal in Madeira and asparagus sauce or spaghetti *alla carbonara* (pasta with a rich sauce made of cream, Parmesan cheese, eggs, and bacon). The dessert pastries are delectable. ⊠ *Atlantis, Paradise Island* ☎ *242/363–3000* ▤ *AE, D, DC, MC, V* ⊗ *No lunch.*

Seafood

$$–$$$ ✕ **Blue Lagoon Seafood Restaurant.** The decor tends toward the nautical, with hurricane lamps and brass rails, in this narrow third-floor dining room looking out to Nassau on one side and Atlantis to the other. Choose from simply prepared dishes such as broiled Bahamian lobster tail or grouper, or fancier selections such as almond-fried shrimp and stuffed grouper au gratin. ⊠ *Club Land'Or* ☎ *242/363–2400* ▤ *AE, DC, MC, V* ⊗ *No lunch.*

$$–$$$ ✕ **Columbus Tavern.** Overlooking Nassau Harbour, this casual restaurant has a nautical feel—from the enormous open windows and deck-like floors to the blue and white accents throughout. Watch the boats sail by as you dine on lobster, grouper, and conch. Or set aside your seafaring ways and try the steak Diane flambé—it's served flaming, as the name implies. The tavern serves three meals a day, every day. ⊠ *Paradise Island Dr.* ☎ *242/363–2534* ▤ *D, MC, V.*

$–$$ ✕ **Blue Marlin Restaurant.** A longtime favorite in the Hurricane Hole Plaza, Blue Marlin is (no surprise) known for seafood—try seafood linguine, lobster thermidor, or the ever-popular cracked conch—although such dishes as Eleuthera Coconut Chicken and Guava Ribs will also please. Limbo and steel-pan band shows, as well as reasonably priced lunch and dinner specials, keep the place hopping. The restaurant upstairs, Bahama Mama's, uses the same kitchen but adds some Italian dishes. ⊠ *Hurricane Hole Plaza* ☎ *242/363–2660* ▤ *AE, D, MC, V.*

Cable Beach

Bahamian

$–$$ ✕ **Café Johnny Canoe.** Johnny Canoe is said to have been a wild-living African chieftain from whose name, most believe, the word *Junkanoo* is derived. A mini-Junkanoo show winds among this crowded restaurant's tables on Friday night. With spacious outdoor seating and a menu of traditional Bahamian fare—cracked conch and grouper fillet— as well as burgers, chicken, ribs, and tropical drinks, this has become a favorite casual tourist hangout. Desserts include guava duff and Bacardi rum cake. ⊠ *W. Bay St., next to the Nassau Beach Hotel* ☎ *242/ 327–3373* ⊗ *Breakfast also served* ▤ *AE, D, MC, V.*

Continental

$$$–$$$$ ✕ **Androsia Steak & Seafood Restaurant.** The specialty here is Peppersteak au Paris, a New York sirloin served with Dijon mustard, cracked peppercorns, cream, and brandy. But you'll find a wide seafood selection as well at this comfortably upscale restaurant, where rich striped curtains add elegance, and starfish and lanterns on the wall lend a nautical flavor. ⊠ *W. Bay St., in the Shoppers Haven Plaza* ☎ *242/327–7805 or 242/327–6430* ▤ *AE, D, MC, V* ⊗ *Closed Sun. No lunch.*

Italian

★ **$$-$$$** ✕ **Sole Mare.** The elegant ocean-view setting, excellent service, and expertly prepared entrées make this one of the best Italian restaurants on the island. Start off with imported meats and cheeses for your antipasti, and follow it up with lobster fra diavolo or chicken with white wine and artichokes. End the meal with a Marsala-strawberry or chocolate-ricotta soufflé. ✉ *Nassau Wyndham Resort & Crystal Palace Casino* ☎ *242/327–6200 Ext. 6861* ▤ *AE, D, DC, MC, V* ☉ *Closed Mon. No lunch.*

Mediterranean

★ **$$-$$$$** ✕ **Provence.** Provence draws the well-to-do and Hollywood set. The chef bills his fare as "Cuisine Du Soleil"—you can see why with the fiery grilled rib-eye steak in peppercorn sauce, and the oven-roasted Atlantic salmon with citrus butter. At dinner, try the Mediterranean bouillabaisse, braised osso bucco, or pan-seared sea bass and black grouper fillets. ✉ *Old Town Sandyport* ☎ *242/327–0985* ▤ *AE, D, MC, V* ☉ *Closed Sun.*

Seafood

$$-$$$$ ✕ **The Poop Deck at Sandyport.** A more upscale version of the other Poop Deck, this waterside restaurant has soaring ceilings, a cool pink and aqua color scheme, and a dazzling view of Cable Beach. Start with sweet-potato fish cakes or grilled shrimp and Brie before diving into the fresh seafood, paired with a selection from the extensive wine list. There are also a smattering of choices for the seafood-phobic. ✉ *W. Bay St.* ☎ *242/327–3325* ▤ *AE, D, DC, MC, V* ☉ *Closed Mon.*

Western New Providence & South Coast

Bahamian

$-$$ ✕ **Traveller's Rest.** Across the street from Compass Point, this relaxed family restaurant with a great ocean view opened in the early 1970s. The fresh seafood dinner served just steps from the beach is a real treat—conch, grouper, and crawfish are the big hitters. Try the "smudder fish"—a tasty local fish literally smothered in onions, peppers, and other vegetables. Dine outside or in, and toast the sunset with a fresh-fruit banana daiquiri—a house specialty. ✉ *W. Bay St., Gambier* ☎ *242/327–7633* ▤ *AE, D, MC, V.*

Contemporary

★ **$$-$$$** ✕ **Compass Point.** Like the hotel in which it's housed, the Compass Point restaurant is New Providence's hippest spot. The indoor section has a mix of cracked tile and colorful wall decorations, a look that's carried outside to the ocean-view terrace and the small but comfy bar. The glorious setting is matched by an elegant, dynamic menu where Bahamian, European, and Asian cuisines collide. It features standbys such as Bahamian conch sushi rolls with bits of cucumber and mango, and local lobster. Is that a fashion model or recording star next to you? No matter—everyone's treated like a celebrity at this customer-friendly spot. ✉ *Compass Point Resort, W. Bay St., Gambier* ☎ *242/327–4500* ▤ *AE, MC, V.*

WHERE TO STAY

New Providence Island is fortunate to have an extensive range of hotels, from quaint, family-owned guesthouses to the megaresorts at Cable Beach and on Paradise Island. Downtown Nassau's beaches are not beautiful; if you want to be beachfront on a gorgeous white strand, stay on Cable Beach or Paradise Island's Cabbage Beach. Reasons to stay in Nassau include proximity to shopping, and affordability (although the cost of taxis to and from the better beaches can add up). Nassau's British Colonial Hilton, for instance, is a top-rate hotel; but its manmade beach, although pretty, can't compare to Cabbage Beach or Cable Beach.

The homey, friendly little spots will probably not be on the beach—and you'll have to go out to eat unless you have access to a kitchen (although some inns will prepare meals for you on request). On the flip side, your stay is likely to be relaxing, low-key, and less removed from everyday Bahamian life. The plush resorts are big and beautiful, glittering and splashy, but they can be overwhelming. In any case, these big, top-dollar properties generally have more amenities than you could possibly make use of, a selection of dining options, and a full roster of sports and entertainment. The battle for the tourist dollar rages ceaselessly between Cable Beach and Paradise Island. The competition encourages agents to put forth an endless stream of travel deals, with enticements such as free snorkeling gear, free scuba lessons, and free admission to Las Vegas–style revues.

Paradise Island was once the quieter alternative to more active resorts on Cable Beach. With the spread of the Atlantis Resort, however, all that has changed. There are still a few peaceful retreats on P.I., but the boisterous megaresort has eliminated most of the quiet strolling lanes and brought its own brand of flash to the island. However, Cable Beach probably still tilts younger in its orientation. Some prefer the lineup of resorts along the Cable Beach strip, others like the look of P.I., which has hotels scattered around every corner (and which is, unlike Cable Beach, walkable from downtown).

A tax ranging from 8% to 10%, representing resort and government levies, is added to your hotel bill. Some hotels also add a gratuity charge of between $2.50 and $4 (or higher) per person, per day, for the housekeeping or pool staff.

The prices below are based on high-season (winter) rates, generally in effect from December through March. Expect to pay between 15% and 30% less off-season at most resorts. In general, the best rates are available through packages, which almost every hotel offers. Call the hotel directly or ask your travel agent.

WHAT IT COSTS In U.S. dollars					
	$$$$	**$$$**	**$$**	**$**	**¢**
FOR 2 PEOPLE	over $400	$300–$400	$200–$300	$100–$200	under $100

All prices are for a standard double room in high season, excluding 9% tax and 10%–15% service charge. Note that the government hotel tax doesn't apply to guesthouses with fewer than four rooms.

Nassau

★ **$$–$$$** ✕⊞ **Graycliff.** The old-world flavor of this Georgian Colonial landmark has made it a perennial favorite with an upscale crowd. The Duke and Duchess of Windsor, Winston Churchill, Aristotle Onassis, and the Beatles—not to mention its original owner, pirate Captain John Howard Graysmith—have sojourned here. Thick foliage envelops a series of garden villas and cottages, amid limestone courtyards with ponds and fountains. It's easy to forget that you're steps from downtown Nassau. For refined Continental fare, the hotel's original restaurant, Graycliff, is one of the island's premier places to dine. ⊠ *W. Hill St.* ☎ *Box N-10246* ☎ *242/322–2796 or 800/688–0076* 🖷 *242/326–6110 or 242/326–6188* 🌐 *www.graycliff.com* 📞 *7 rooms, 13 suites* ☖ *2 restaurants, in-room hot tubs, 3 pools, hair salon, health club, massage, sauna, 3 bars, business services* ▤ *AE, D, MC, V.*

★ **$$** ⊞ **British Colonial Hilton Nassau.** From a lustrous saffron facade to gleaming marble floors and arched, skylighted ceiling, this landmark building, first opened in 1900 as the Hotel Colonial, is the sharpest and most elegant in all of Nassau. Its rooms have sleek wood furniture and most have good views. A small man-made beach adjacent to lushly landscaped grounds overlooks the cruise ships at Prince George Wharf. Live Bahamian, Caribbean, jazz, and R&B music wafts from the lounges most evenings. With the Nassau Stock Exchange in an adjacent wing, this hotel is the best business choice in the Bahamas. ⊠ *1 Bay St.* ☎ *Box N-7148* ☎ *242/322–3301* 🖷 *242/302–9009* 🌐 *www.hiltoncaribbean.com/nassau* 📞 *270 rooms, 21 suites* ☖ *2 restaurants, room service, in-room data ports, in-room safes, cable TV, pool, hair salon, health club, massage, spa, beach, dive shop, snorkeling, volleyball, lounge, shops, babysitting, laundry service, concierge floor, Internet, business services, convention center, meeting rooms, car rental* ▤ *AE, D, DC, MC, V.*

$ ⊞ **Buena Vista Hotel.** Surrounded by a beautiful 3-acre garden, this 19th-century plantation house is ½ mi from downtown Nassau. The two-story building is better known for its restaurant, but the spacious, simple, and rather imposingly dark rooms, surprisingly affordable in this elegant setting, are individually decorated with solid-wood furniture. Climb the aqua-hued staircase from the low-key, tasteful lobby, which is filled with tropical greenery, to a long hallway where the rooms are all but invisible to the restaurant guests. The public beach is just a 10-minute walk away. ⊠ *Delancy St.* ☎ *Box N-564* ☎ *242/322–2811* 🖷 *242/322–5881* 📞 *5 rooms* ☖ *Restaurant, refrigerators, cable TV, bar* ▤ *AE, D, MC, V.*

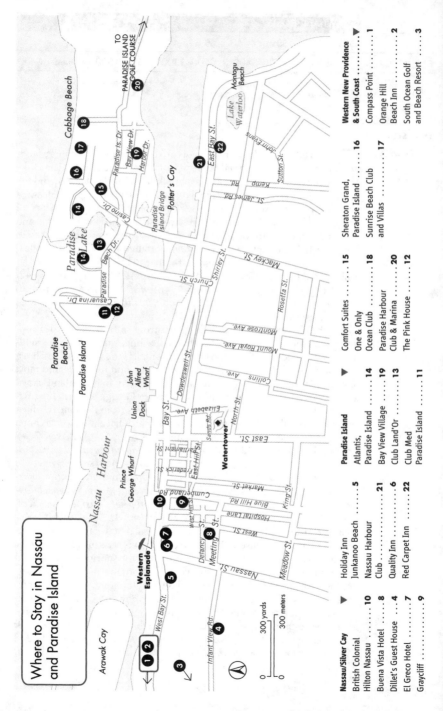

Where to Stay in Nassau and Paradise Island

★ $ ▦ **Dillet's Guest House.** You're in for something special the minute you enter the lounge of this family-run guesthouse—the arched entry, ceiling fans, wicker furniture, caged birds, and massive flower arrangements exude old Nassau charm. Crisp and clean, the place is furnished with true island flair. Rooms are named for island fruits, marked by hand-painted pieces of driftwood on the doors. Situated a few miles from downtown Nassau, this place is ideal for those who prefer Bahamian style to a standard hotel room. ⊠ *Dunmore Ave. and Strachan St.* ⬧ *Box N-204* ☎ *242/325-1133* 🖶 *242/325-7183* ⊕ *www.islandeaze.com/dillets/index.html* ⬧ *7 rooms* ⬧ *Dining room, some kitchenettes, minibars, microwaves, pool, bicycles, library, Internet* ☰ *AE, MC, V* ⦿| *CP.*

$ ▦ **El Greco Hotel.** Pleasant Greek owners and friendly staff create an ambience more in keeping with a cozy guesthouse than a hotel. Although the decorations are not elaborate, the rooms are large, quiet, and have soothing earth tones. They surround a small pool tucked within a bougainvillea-filled courtyard. The hotel appeals primarily to a European crowd. The El Greco is a few minutes walk from Bay Street and downtown and is directly across the street from the public Western Esplanade beach. For those on a budget who want to be in Nassau, El Greco is a pleasant find. ⊠ *W. Bay St.* ⬧ *Box N-4187* ☎ *242/325-1121* 🖶 *242/325-1124* ⊕ *www.bahamasnet.com/elgrecohotel* ⬧ *26 rooms* ⬧ *Restaurant, cable TV, pool, bar, baby-sitting* ☰ *AE, D, MC, V.*

$ ▦ **Holiday Inn Junkanoo Beach.** The salmon-colored, five-story chain hotel is a moderately priced option a few minutes west of downtown, across the street from little Western Esplanade beach. The hotel is modern and well managed: An activities desk in the lobby will help coordinate your island activities. Some suites come with hot tubs and/or bunk beds. ⊠ *W. Bay St.* ⬧ *Box SS-19055* ☎ *242/356-0000 or 800/465-4329* 🖶 *242/323-1408* ⊕ *www.nassau-hotel.com* ⬧ *183 rooms, 12 suites* ⬧ *Restaurant, room service, in-room data ports, in-room safes, cable TV, 2 pools, health club, hot tub, bar, shop, laundry service, business services, meeting rooms* ☰ *AE, D, DC, MC, V.*

$ ▦ **Red Carpet Inn.** Cleanliness and quiet are stressed here—it's one of the few area hotels in its price category not geared toward spring-breakers. The owners live on premises, which explains the devotion to spotlessness and the agreeable atmosphere, and the hotel is far enough off the beaten path to provide a sense of island solitude. Rooms are simple, but come with microwaves and full-size refrigerators. Downtown Nassau is a 15- to 20-minute walk away. ⊠ *E. Bay St.* ⬧ *Box SS-6233* ☎ *242/393-7981* 🖶 *242/393-9055* ⊕ *www.redcarpetinnbahamas.com* ⬧ *30 rooms, 10 suites* ⬧ *Restaurant, in-room safes, microwaves, refrigerators, pool, laundry facilities* ☰ *AE, D, MC, V.*

¢–$ ▦ **Nassau Harbour Club.** The Harbour Club is popular with international sailing aficionados and hordes of students on spring break, which, along with its location a mile down the main road into town, does not make it an oasis of peace and quiet. Locals and tourists gather at the downstairs Dockside Bar and Grill to watch televised sports or sit outside on the deck overlooking the harbor. On the hotel's main floor, up a spiral wooden staircase from the bar, is Chiban Sushi restaurant. ⊠ *E. Bay St.* ⬧ *Box SS-5755* ☎ *242/393-0771* 🖶 *242/393-5393* ⬧ *50 rooms* ⬧ *Restaurant, pool, dock, bar* ☰ *AE, D, MC, V.*

¢–$ 🏨 **Quality Inn.** This beachfront hotel is a welcome addition to the Providence Island budget lodging market. It is clean and well-kept, with pleasantly decorated rooms. Ask for a room with an ocean view, as many rooms have only a partial view or none at all. Be aware that each guest must pay a daily service charge of $11.50. ⊠ *West Bay St. and Nassau St.* ⬧ *Box N-1836, Suite A081* ☏ *242/322–1515* 🖷 *242/322–1514* ⊕ *www.qualityinn.com* ⇝ *63 rooms* ⚷ *Restaurant, in-room data ports, bar, lounge, business services* ▭ *AE, D, DC, MC, V.*

Paradise Island

$$$$ 🏨 **One & Only Ocean Club.** Once the private hideaway of A&P heir Hun-
Fodor's Choice tington Hartford, this ultra-expensive resort on magnificent Cabbage
★ Beach's quietest stretch provides the ultimate in understated—and decidedly posh—elegance. Its Versailles Gardens includes 35 acres of terraced serenity and an imported French cloister. Set amid private gardens, the spacious colonial-style rooms have intricately carved furniture and marble bathrooms. The open-air restaurant, Dune, is perched over the beach. ⊠ *Ocean Club Dr.* ⬧ *Box N-4777, Nassau* ☏ *242/363–2501 or 800/321–3000* 🖷 *242/363–2424* ⊕ *www.oneandonlyresorts.com* ⇝ *87 rooms, 14 suites, 5 cottages* ⚷ *3 restaurants, room service, cable TV, golf privileges, 9 tennis courts, pool, health club, spa, beach, snorkeling, windsurfing, boating, waterskiing, bicycles, 2 bars, baby-sitting, laundry service* ▭ *AE, D, DC, MC, V.*

☉ $$$–$$$$ 🏨 **Atlantis, Paradise Island.** A bustling fantasy world—part water park,
Fodor's Choice entertainment complex, megaresort, and beach oasis—this is by far the
★ biggest and boldest resort in the country. The overriding theme here is water—for swimming, snorkeling, and observing marine life, as well as for mood and effect, in lagoons, caves, waterfalls, and several walk-through aquariums (touted as the largest marine habitat in the world). The public areas are lavish, with fountains, glass sculptures, and gleaming shopping arcades. Numerous sporting activities are available, and there is plenty of nightlife on the premises; the casino, ringed by restaurants, is the largest in the Bahamas and the Caribbean. ⊠ *Casino Dr.* ⬧ *Box N-4777, Nassau* ☏ *242/363–3000 or 800/321–3000* 🖷 *242/363–3524* ⊕ *www.atlantis.com* ⇝ *2,097 rooms, 230 suites* ⚷ *20 restaurants, room service, in-room data ports, in-room safes, cable TV, golf privileges, 10 tennis courts, 11 pools, hair salon, health club, spa, beach, dock, snorkeling, windsurfing, boating, basketball, volleyball, 13 bars, casino, comedy club, nightclub, shops, baby-sitting, children's programs (ages 4–12), concierge floor, Internet, business services, convention center, meeting rooms, car rental, travel services* ▭ *AE, D, DC, MC, V* ⊺◯⊺ *MAP.*

$$$–$$$$ 🏨 **Club Med Paradise Island.** Club Med was permitted to develop this stunning setting on the condition that the original private estate gardens be preserved; thus the meandering paths bordered by swaying casuarina trees and graceful palms, an Olympic-size swimming pool surrounded by a garden of more than 100 species of plants, and long stretches of green lawn. Guests are likely to be parents traveling without their kids, honeymooners (especially in the secluded "House in the Woods"), and other romantic sorts. The closely guarded gate ensures

privacy and security but tends to keep the guests in a world far removed from Bahamian culture and its people. ⊠ *Casuarina Dr.* ⌂ *Box N-7137, Nassau* ☎ *242/363–2640 or 800/258–2633* 🖷 *242/363–5855* ⊕ *www. clubmed.com* ➫ *314 rooms* ⚭ *2 restaurants, miniature golf, 18 tennis courts, 2 saltwater pools, gym, beach, snorkeling, windsurfing, archery, billiards, boccie, 3 bars, nightclub* ▤ *AE, D, MC, V* ⦿⬤ *All-inclusive.*

★ **$$$** 🏨 **Sunrise Beach Club and Villas.** Lushly landscaped with crotons, coconut palms, bougainvillea, and hibiscus, this low-rise, family-run resort on Cabbage Beach has a tropical wonderland feel. Two pools sustain the ambience with statuary and tropical plantings, and the beach is accessible via a long flight of wooden stairs built right into the cliff. Paths wind through the floral arcadia, past trickling fountains, archways, and terra-cotta tiles with color insets. Choose from one-bedroom town houses with spiral staircases that lead to an upstairs bedroom, two-bedroom apartments, or three-bedroom villas. All have fully equipped kitchens, king-size beds, and patios. ⊠ *Casino Dr.* ⌂ *Box SS-6519, Nassau* ☎ *242/363–2234* 🖷 *242/363–2308* ⊕ *www.sunrisebeachvillas. com* ➫ *18 1-, 2-, and 3-bedroom units* ⚭ *Kitchens, microwaves, cable TV, 2 pools, beach, bar, baby-sitting, laundry facilities, Internet access* ▤ *AE, D, MC, V.*

$$–$$$ 🏨 **Club Land'Or.** In Atlantis's shadow just over the bridge from Nassau, this friendly time-share property has one-bedroom villas with full kitchens, bathrooms, living rooms, desks, and patios or balconies that overlook the lagoon, the gardens, or the pool. The units are described as accommodating four people, but they seem better suited to couples. The Blue Lagoon Seafood Restaurant is a favorite of locals and guests. Many activities are planned throughout the week. ⊠ *Paradise Beach Dr.* ⌂ *Box SS-6429, Nassau* ☎ *242/363–2400* 🖷 *242/363–3403* ⊕ *www.clublandor.com* ➫ *72 villas* ⚭ *Restaurant, kitchens, microwaves, cable TV, pool, bicycles, 2 bars, shops, baby-sitting, laundry facilities* ▤ *AE, D, MC, V* ⦿⬤ *EP, MAP.*

$$–$$$ 🏨 **Paradise Harbour Club & Marina.** With a marina and an enviable location, this collection of oversize, comfortable apartments is a great choice for those who want the freedom of a private residence with the facilities of a large resort. Full kitchens (complete with refrigerator, minibar, and dishwasher) lend a homey feeling to these somewhat characterless but very cushy lodgings. Commodious closet and sink space are among the extras. If you prefer a view, opt for the top-floor digs. ⊠ *Paradise Island Dr.* ⌂ *Box SS-5804, Nassau* ☎ *242/363–2992* 🖷 *242/363–2840* ⊕ *www.phclub.com* ➫ *22 units* ⚭ *Restaurant, kitchenettes, tennis court, pool, hot tub, boating, bicycles, bar* ▤ *AE, MC, V.*

$$–$$$ 🏨 **Sheraton Grand, Paradise Island.** A soaring lobby and pleasant rooms containing Sheraton's usual amenities make this one of the island's top hotels. Although not as grand as Atlantis next door, the Sheraton is not far from its neighbor's casino, and shares a quieter bit of the same lovely beach. Every room overlooks the water from at least a small side balcony. The activities desk is among the busiest in town. Note the fine print: Some guests are displeased at checkout by daily energy and housekeeping surcharges; and, odd for a hotel of its caliber, there's no Internet access. ⊠ *Casino Dr.* ⌂ *Box SS-6307, Nassau* ☎ *242/363–3500 or 800/ 325–3535* 🖷 *242/363–3900* ⊕ *www.sheratongrand.com/sheraton.htm*

⊋ *340 rooms* ⚲ *4 restaurants, room service, in-room safes, minibars, cable TV, tennis court, pool, health club, beach, dive shop, snorkeling, windsurfing, boating, parasailing, waterskiing, bicycles, volleyball, 3 bars, nightclub, baby-sitting, meeting rooms, travel services* ▤ *AE, D, DC, MC, V.*

$$ ▦ **Bay View Village.** This four-acre condominium resort has a lush, intimate feel. Guests socialize around three pools (two for general use, one reserved for the villas) that are surrounded by tropical plants, including several hibiscus and bougainvillea varieties. Choose between one- and two-bedroom apartments and two- and three-bedroom villas, all of which are spacious, clean, comfortable, and decorated in bright island style. All rooms have private balconies or garden terraces. Cabbage Beach is a 10-minute walk away. ⊠ *Bay View Dr.* ⌂ *Box SS-6308, Nassau* ☎ *242/363–2555 or 800/757–1357* 🖷 *242/363–2370* ⊕ *www.bayviewvillage.com* ⊋ *72 units and villas* ⚲ *Snack bar, fans, kitchens, microwaves, cable TV, tennis court, 3 pools, bar, baby-sitting, laundry facilities* ▤ *AE, D, MC, V.*

$$ ▦ **Comfort Suites.** The all-suites, three-story pink-and-white hotel has an arrangement with Atlantis that allows guests to use that resort's facilities. Kids can also enroll at Atlantis's Discovery Channel Camp. For many, that's reason enough to stay here, in the middle of the Paradise Island action. For those who want to stay on the grounds, try a poolside lunch and a drink at the swim-up bar. Rooms share a cozy feel and have sitting areas with sofa beds. Cabbage Beach is just a hop, skip, and a jump away. ⊠ *Paradise Island Dr.* ⌂ *Box SS-6202 Nassau* ☎ *242/363–3680 or 800/228–5150* 🖷 *242/363–2588* ⊕ *www.choicehotels.com* ⊋ *228 junior suites* ⚲ *Restaurant, in-room safes, minibars, cable TV, pool, bar, baby-sitting* ▤ *AE, D, MC, V* ⦿ *CP.*

★ $ ▦ **The Pink House.** A former Sears family estate, this charming guesthouse appears through a thicket of bamboo and palm trees in the middle of a wonderful tropical garden. A throwback to colonial times, it sits placidly on its own plot of land within Club Med's gates, and guests can take advantage of that resort's private beach and gardens. You're also just steps from Atlantis: the combination of location and price are unbeatable on New Providence. Owner Minnie Winn's personal attention will make you feel like a resident or treasured family member. Not for those craving luxury or anonymity. ⊠ *Casuarina Dr.* ⌂ *Box SS-19157, Nassau* ☎ *242/363–3363* 🖷 *242/363–1136* ⊋ *4 rooms* ⚲ *Cable TV, pond* ▤ *D* ⦿ *CP.*

Cable Beach

$$$$ ▦ **Guanahani Village.** The substantial, well-furnished time-share and rental accommodations are perfect for young families or groups of friends traveling together. Stucco units are spread across landscaped grounds. The tiled three-bedroom luxury villas, oceanfront or garden side, sleep six comfortably, up to eight using roll-aways (so the price, although in the top category, is really quite reasonable when shared by several people). Each unit has oversize rooms, a delightful secluded patio, a fully equipped kitchen, a washer and dryer, and a dishwasher. The pool overlooks the ocean, although beaches are a bit of a walk. ⊠ *W. Bay St.* ⌂ *Box CB-*

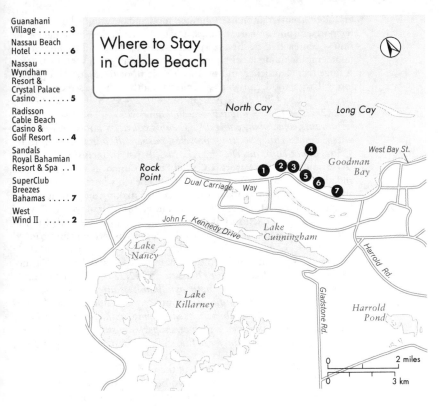

**Where to Stay
in Cable Beach**

North Cay   Long Cay

West Bay St.

Goodman
Bay

Rock
Point

Dual Carriage   Way

John F. Kennedy Drive

Lake
Cunningham

Lake
Nancy

Gladstone Rd.

Harrold Rd.

Harrold
Pond

Lake
Killarney

0   2 miles

0   3 km

13317, Nassau ☎ *242/327–7568 or 242/327–4254* 🖷 *242/327–8311*
🌐 *www.guanahanivillage.com* 📼 *35 units* 🕭 *Snack bar, kitchens, cable
TV, pool, tennis court* ☰ *AE, D, MC, V.*

$$$$ 🏨 **Sandals Royal Bahamian Resort & Spa.** Cable Beach's most expensive
spot presents elegantly furnished rooms with views of the ocean, pool,
or grounds replete with pillars and faux Roman statuary. There's a state-
of-the-art fitness club, and a multilingual concierge service that assists
foreign guests. Eight restaurants offer cuisines ranging from Caribbean
to Japanese (make reservations well in advance), and nightly entertainment takes place in the resort's amphitheater. Sandals caters to hetero-
sexual couples only—it will turn away gay and lesbian couples who try
to reserve. ⊠ *W. Bay St.* 🕭 *Box CB-13005, Nassau* ☎ *242/327–6400
or 800/726–3257* 🖷 *242/327–6961* 🌐 *www.sandals.com* 📼 *77 rooms,
327 suites* 🕭 *8 restaurants, room service, cable TV, 2 tennis courts, 5
pools, gym, health club, spa, beach, dive shop, snorkeling, windsurfing, boating, waterskiing, basketball, croquet, shuffleboard, volleyball,
7 bars, dance club, recreation room, Internet, meeting rooms* ☰ *AE,
D, MC, V* ⦿ *All-inclusive.*

$$$–$$$$ 🏨 **SuperClub Breezes Bahamas.** Right on Cable Beach, this property of-
fers couples and singles (age 16 or older) an all-inclusive rate that cov-

ers lodging, entertainment, unlimited food and beverages, land and watersports, airport transfers, taxes, and gratuities. Take advantage of the fitness center, five freshwater pools, swim-up bar, and nightly entertainment, including local bands, toga or pajama parties, and karaoke. A huge fish chandelier and multicolor tile floor decorate the open-air lobby. Large, modern rooms are pleasant although not striking. ⊠ *W. Bay St.* ⊕ *Box CB-13049, Nassau* ☎ *242/327–5356 or 800/859–7873* 🖷 *242/327–5155* ⊕ *www.breezesbahamas.com* ↪ *400 rooms* ⚲ *5 restaurants, snack bar, cable TV, 3 tennis courts, 5 pools, health club, beach, windsurfing, boating, bicycles, basketball, billiards, volleyball, 4 bars, dance club, Internet* ☰ *AE, MC, V* ⦿ *All-inclusive.*

$$　🏨 **Nassau Wyndham Resort & Crystal Palace Casino.** If you prefer glitz and glitter, stay at the Wyndham on Cable Beach where the five towers are illuminated with bands of varying colors, making the hotel look like a giant rainbow reflecting off the ocean. High-rollers love the Crystal Club, three concierge floors at the top of the Casino Tower with 30 spectacularly decorated executive suites. The resort has its own palm-fringed beach and lagoon, a health club with top-notch equipment and daily aerobics classes, and the 35,000-square-foot Crystal Palace Casino. ⊠ *W. Bay St.* ⊕ *Box N-8306, Nassau* ☎ *242/327–6200 or 800/222–7466* 🖷 *242/327–6459* ⊕ *www.wyndhamnassauresort.com* ↪ *743 rooms, 124 suites* ⚲ *6 restaurants, room service, cable TV, pool, aerobics, hair salon, health club, beach, snorkeling, windsurfing, boating, 5 bars, casino, recreation room, theater, shops, baby-sitting, children's programs (ages 4 and up), concierge floors, Internet, meeting room* ☰ *AE, D, DC, MC, V* ⦿ *FAP, MAP.*

$$　🏨 **West Wind II.** Privacy is the lure of these cozy villas on Cable Beach's west end, 6 mi from downtown. Two-bedroom, two-bath condominiums have fully stocked kitchens and balconies or patios overlooking the ocean or pools. The reasonable prices and relaxed atmosphere are ideal for families or groups on a budget, and the pleasant, quiet location—off the road amid manicured lawns and pruned gardens—gives children the freedom to play outdoors. The spectacular sea view somewhat compensates for the tiny and very windy beach. A bus stop and taxi stand are right outside. ⊠ *W. Bay St.* ⊕ *Box CB-11006, Nassau* ☎ *242/327–7211 or 242/327–7019* 🖷 *242/327–7529* ↪ *54 villas* ⚲ *Snack bar, kitchenettes, cable TV, 2 tennis courts, 2 pools, beach, snorkeling, boating, baby-sitting, laundry service, travel services* ☰ *MC, V.*

$-$$　🏨 **Nassau Beach Hotel.** For a low-key atmosphere, try this Cable Beach mainstay, built in the 1940s on a ½-mi sandy beach. Be sure to ask for one of the refurbished rooms, decorated in colonial style. All rooms have balconies, but views vary. Guests have use of all nonmotorized watersports equipment. Tennis on the six courts (three lighted) is free before 5 PM, $7 per person hourly during "prime time" (5–9). The hotel has indoor and outdoor restaurants on-site, as well as a shopping arcade. The Crystal Palace Casino is next door, and the Cable Beach Golf Club is across the street. ⊠ *W. Bay St.* ⊕ *Box N-7756, Nassau* ☎ *242/327–7711 or 888/627–7282* 🖷 *242/327–8829* ⊕ *www.nassaubeachhotel.com* ↪ *400 rooms* ⚲ *5 restaurants, cable TV, 6 tennis courts, 2 pools, gym, beach, snorkeling, windsurfing, boating, 3 bars, shops, baby-sitting, meeting rooms* ☰ *AE, D, MC, V* ⦿ *BP, EP, FAP, MAP.*

$–$$ ⊞ **Radisson Cable Beach Casino & Golf Resort.** This high-rise property is smack in the middle of Cable Beach action. Connected by a shopping arcade to Crystal Palace Casino, the hotel buzzes with activity. Daytime options include dance lessons by the pool, beach volleyball, free scuba lessons, and plenty of children's activities. Guests get special rates at the hotel's challenging 18-hole Cable Beach Golf Club. At night, select from a slew of dining possibilities, beach parties, revues, and—of course—gambling. All rooms have balconies and face either the beach and pool or gardens. ⊠ *W. Bay St.* ☎ *Box N-4914, Nassau* ☎ *242/327–6000* 🖷 *242/327–6907* ⊕ *www.radisson-cablebeach.com* 🛏 *669 rooms, 31 suites* ⚬ *6 restaurants, room service, cable TV, 18-hole golf course, 5 tennis courts, 3 pools, hair salon, health club, beach, snorkeling, boating, bicycles, racquetball, squash, volleyball, 2 bars, casino, shops, baby-sitting, children's programs (ages 4–11), Internet, meeting room* 🖃 *AE, D, DC, MC, V* ⦿ *All-inclusive, EP.*

Western New Providence & South Coast

★ **$$–$$$** ⊞ **Compass Point.** Hotelier and recording-studio mogul Chris Blackwell has scored a hit with this beachfront property 20 minutes west of downtown Nassau. Designer Barbara Hulanicki's brilliant Junkanoo colors are a feast for the eyes. The hotel attracts a trendy crowd of celebrities and wannabes, but the staff treats everyone with the same down-to-earth, welcoming helpfulness. Cottages, huts, and cabanas appear through dense foliage like vibrant parrots. Some are duplexes on stilts, some are octagonal, some directly face the ocean. Compass Point has a small beach, and Love Beach—which is great for snorkelers—is next door. ⊠ *W. Bay St., Gambier* ☎ *Box CB-13842, Nassau* ☎ *242/327-1500 or 800/688–7678* 🖷 *242/327–3299* 🛏 *5 cabanas, 9 cottages, 4 huts* ⚬ *Restaurant, room service, fans, in-room fax, kitchenettes, in-room VCRs, tennis court, pool, beach, snorkeling, fishing, bar* 🖃 *AE, MC, V.*

$ ⊞ **South Ocean Golf and Beach Resort.** Imposing oceanfront villas with cool Mexican tile floors, four-poster beds, whirlpool baths, 25-inch TVs, and sea-view balconies make this a great choice. Owing to a massive renovation project, more than 100 rooms were closed at this writing. Facilities on-site or nearby include an 18-hole golf course at which resort guests receive reduced rates, and Stuart Cove's Dive South Ocean facility, one of the town's best dive operations. ⊠ *S. Ocean Dr.* ☎ *Box N-8191, Nassau* ☎ *242/362–4391 or 877/766–2326* 🖷 *242/362–4810* ⊕ *www.southoceanbahamas.com* 🛏 *130 rooms* ⚬ *2 restaurants, cable TV, 18-hole golf course, 4 tennis courts, 2 pools, beach, dive shop, snorkeling, boating, 2 bars, baby-sitting* 🖃 *AE, D, MC, V.*

$ ⊞ **Orange Hill Beach Inn.** If you prefer down-home coziness over slick glamour, then this charming inn—on the site of a former orange plantation perched on a hilltop overlooking the ocean—is the place to stay. Guests are treated like family, and the homey feel extends to the comfortably eclectic living room and daytime honor bar. Orange Hill has a reputation as an inexpensive alternative for honeymooners and scuba divers. It's a half-hour drive from town, 15 minutes from the casino, and 300 feet from a pleasant roadside beach. Rooms and apartments vary considerably in size. ⊠ *W. Bay St.* ☎ *Box N-8583, Nassau* ☎ *242/*

327-7157 🖷 *242/327-5186* ⊕ *www.orangehill.com* ⮂ *30 rooms* ⚙ *Restaurant, some kitchenettes, cable TV, pool, basketball, bar, laundry facilities* ⊟ *D, MC, V.*

NIGHTLIFE & THE ARTS

Nightlife

Cable Beach and Paradise Island resorts have their own flashy clubs where residents and visitors alike come to enjoy late-night entertainment. The attire for attending these soirees is typically as casual as the atmosphere, although some clubs require dressier duds. The casinos also are casual, so leave your black tie at home. You have to be at least 18 years old to gamble; Bahamians and permanent residents are not permitted to indulge. Most coffeehouses are open late into the evening, but note that a few close around 6.

Cable Beach

CASINOS **Crystal Palace Casino.** Slots, craps, baccarat, blackjack, roulette, Big Six, and face-up 21 are among the games in this 35,000-square-foot space. There's a Sports Book facility for sports betting, equipped with big-screen TVs, which air live sporting events. Both VIPs and low-limit bettors have their own areas. Casino gaming lessons are available for beginners. Tables and slots are open 24 hours daily. ⊠ *Nassau Wyndham Resort & Crystal Palace Casino, Cable Beach* ☎ *242/327-6200* ⊕ *www. wyndhamnassauresort.com.*

NIGHTCLUBS **Zoo Nightclub.** Nassau's largest indoor nightclub, Zoo has five regular bars, a sports bar, and a VIP lounge where the drinks keep coming while party animals dance the night away to top chart hits. Its café is open from noon until the wee hours. ⊠ *W. Bay St., across from Saunders Beach* ☎ *242/322-7195.*

Nassau

COFFEEHOUSES **Café Paradiso.** On Bay Street's eastern end, this pleasant coffeehouse serves up sandwiches and salads—try the chicken Caesar or spicy mango shrimp. Tasty desserts include Grandma's homemade brownies and a chocolate-apricot torte. ⊠ *E. Bay St., between Elizabeth St. and Victoria Ave.* ☎ *242/356-5282* ⊙ *Closed Sun.*

Caffè Caribe. In the Logos Bookstore, this tiny spot has a simple, modern look with high tables and stools. Salads, quiches, and sandwiches supplement the coffee selection; there's a long list of fruity- and nutty-flavored espressos. It closes at 6 PM. ⊠ *Harbour Bay Shopping Centre, E. Bay St.* ☎ *242/394-7040* ⊙ *Closed Sun.*

Cappuccino Café and Specialty Shop. Although a bit out of the way, and only open until 6 PM, this little upscale deli and coffeehouse has a bright, appealing look. There's an extensive gourmet food selection as well as coffeehouse standards. ⊠ *Royal Palm Mall, Mackey St.* ☎ *242/394-6332* ⊙ *Closed Sun.*

Flamingo Cigars and Gourmet Café. This simple shop is a refuge from Bay Street's shopping frenzy. The smoker's lounge upstairs is a hidden wood-paneled nook in which to savor the Cohibas and Montecristos for sale.

✉ *1 Bay St., east side of Colonial Hilton Hotel* ☎ *242/325–8510* ☉ *Closed Sun.*

Le Bistro. A two-story European-style bistro in the heart of downtown Nassau, Le Bistro serves coffee, wine, bar drinks, and pastries, as well as Edy's ice cream. Early birds and late-nighters love the long hours, 9 AM–midnight (2 AM on Saturday). ✉ *Charlotte St., north of Bay St.* ☎ *242/ 326–0206* ☉ *Closed Sun.*

NIGHTCLUBS **Club Waterloo.** Claiming to be Nassau's largest indoor-outdoor nightclub, the club has five bars and nonstop dancing Monday through Saturday until 4 AM (live bands weekends). Try the spring break special Waterloo Hurricane, a tropical mixture of rums and punches. ✉ *E. Bay St.* ☎ *242/393–7324.*

The Drop Off. In the heart of downtown's Bay Street, this downstairs pub has live entertainment in a sporty, noisy atmosphere. ✉ *Bay St.* ☎ *242/ 322–3444.*

Mangoes. On the second floor of the 18th-century Seamen's Chapel, this perch above Bay Street is perhaps the most centrally located Nassau nightspot. A live DJ spins on the wooden dance floor beneath a high peaked roof. The restaurant here serves food 11 AM–10 PM. It's a fine place to have a drink on a terrace overlooking Bay Street. ✉ *Bay St., just east of British Colonial Hilton Hotel* ✍ *$10 men, $5 women for nightclub.*

601 Nightclub. The most upscale club in town, 601 recaptures the feel of old Nassau in its elegance and formality. The dress code, considerably relaxed from former days, now forbids shorts and tennis shoes. Bands Visage and Spank keep things hopping. This club is open Friday through Sunday nights only; happy hour is 6 to 9. ✉ *E. Bay St.* ☎ *242/322–3041.*

Paradise Island

CASINOS **Paradise Island Casino.** At 50,000 square feet (100,000 if you include the dining and drinking areas), this is the Caribbean/Bahamian area's largest facility. Ringed with restaurants, it offers more than 1,100 slot machines, baccarat, blackjack, roulette, craps tables, and such local specialties as Caribbean stud poker. There's a high-limit table area, additional games at most of the eateries, and a spectacularly open and airy design. Tables are open from 10 AM to 4 AM daily; slots, 24 hours. ✉ *Atlantis, Paradise Island* ☎ *242/363–3000.*

COFFEEHOUSES **News Café.** In Paradise Island's Hurricane Hole Plaza, this is the perfect place to refuel with a light, inexpensive lunch or just a delicious milk shake before heading into town or indulging in some P.I. shopping. Enjoy coffee, muffins, and excellent $5–$6 sandwiches served on your choice of fresh bread. Use the Internet, or choose from their collection of foreign magazines and newspapers. ✉ *Hurricane Hole Plaza, Paradise Island* ☎ *242/363–4684* ☉ *7:30 AM–10 PM.*

NIGHTCLUBS **Dragons Lounge and Dance Club.** Part of Atlantis's casino dining/ entertainment complex, Dragons offers music and dancing just steps away from the high-rolling action. ✉ *Atlantis Resort* ☎ *242/363–3000.*

Oasis Lounge. There's live piano or vocal music here nightly from 7:30 to midnight. ✉ *Club Land'Or* ☎ *242/363–2400.*

CloseUp

JUNKANOO

I T'S AFTER MIDNIGHT, and the streets of Nassau are crowded but hushed; the only sound is a steady buzz of anticipation. Everyone is waiting. Suddenly the streets erupt in a kaleidoscope of sight and sound—the Junkanoo groups are rushing down Bay Street. Their vibrant costumes sparkle in the light of the street lamps, and the crowd shouts with delight. Best of all is the music. The revelers bang on goatskin drums, clang cowbells, and blow on conch-shell horns, hammering out a steady beat of celebration. It's Junkanoo time again.

Junkanoo holds an important place in the history of the Bahamas, but the origin of the word Junkanoo remains a mystery. Many believe it comes from John Canoe, an African tribal chief who was brought to the West Indies in the slave trade and then fought for the right to celebrate with his people. Others believe the word stems from the French gens inconnus, which means "the unknown people"—significant because Junkanoo revelers wear costumes that make them unrecognizable.

The origin of the festival itself is more certain. Though its roots can be traced back to West Africa, it began in the Bahamas during the 16th or 17th century when Bahamian slaves were given a few days off around Christmas to celebrate with their families. They left the plantations and had elaborate costume parties where they danced and played homemade musical instruments. They wore large, often scary-looking masks, which gave them the freedom of anonymity, so they could let loose without fear of being recognized. After slavery was abolished, Junkanoo almost vanished, but a few former slaves kept the tradition alive, and over time it grew into the massively popular celebration you'll see today.

Junkanoo is an important part of the Christmas season in the Bahamas.

Parades are held in the wee hours of the morning (1 or 2 AM until dawn) on Boxing Day (December 26) and again on New Year's Day. Surprisingly, what appears to be a random, wild expression of joy is actually a very well organized and planned event. Family and friends gather in large groups (often as many as 500–1,000) and perform together in the parade.

Competition is heated among the groups, who choose a different theme each year and keep it a closely guarded secret until Junkanoo day, when their efforts are revealed. Most groups spend months preparing for the big day at what they call their "base camp" or "shack." They choreograph dance steps, choose music, and design intricate costumes. Then it's time to practice, practice, practice. Among the regular groups are the "Saxons," "Valley Boys," "Roots," and "One Family." Judges watch the event closely and award prizes for best music, best costumes, and best overall group presentation. With thousands of dollars of prize money up for grabs, people go to extremes to please the crowd and put on the best show.

If you're lucky enough to be in the Bahamas around Christmas, don't miss this spectacular sight. The grandest Junkanoo celebration is in Nassau, where the best views are upstairs on Bay Street, or on the benches that line the streets. Plan ahead and arrive early to secure a good spot. You can also experience Junkanoo on Grand Bahama Island, Eleuthera, Bimini, and Abaco. If you miss the festivities, be sure to stop by the **Junkanoo Expo** in downtown Nassau to see some of the most memorable costumes and floats from years past.

The Arts

Cable Beach

THEATER **Rainforest Theatre.** The redesigned theater, which now has an atmosphere true to its name, presents lavish shows. Check with the resort for the latest offerings (and the weather report). ⊠ *Nassau Wyndham Resort & Crystal Palace Casino, Cable Beach* ☎ *242/327–6200 Ext. 6861.*

Nassau

THEATER **Dundas Centre for the Performing Arts.** Plays and musicals by local and out-of-town artists are staged throughout the year. ⊠ *Mackey St.* ☎ *242/ 393–3728.*

SPORTS & THE OUTDOORS

For all the dining, shopping, and nightlife possibilities, Nassau's draw—as with all of the Bahamas—remains its outdoor life; with flawless weather nearly year-round, it's a rare visitor to New Providence who doesn't experience some of the natural delights that remain, even among the frenzied construction. Many of these pleasures revolve around the water, and everyone from experienced boaters and divers to novice snorkelers can enjoy seeing (in the words of one local promotion) "how the other two-thirds live." You can participate in sports activities or lie back and enjoy a cruise, often with snorkeling or other water-based fun involved.

Boating

From Chub Cay—one of the Berry Islands 35 mi north of New Providence—to Nassau, the sailing route goes across the mile-deep Tongue of the Ocean. The Paradise Island Lighthouse welcomes yachters to Nassau Harbour, which is open at both ends. The harbor can handle the world's largest cruise liners; sometimes as many as eight tie up at one time. Two looming bridges bisect the harbor connecting Paradise Island to Nassau. Sailboats with masts taller than the high-water clearance of 72 feet must enter the harbor from the east end to reach marinas east of the bridges. On the Nassau side of the harbor, **Nassau Yacht Haven** (☎ 242/393–8173 ⊕ www.nassauyachthaven.com) is a 150-berth marina—the largest in the Bahamas—that also arranges fishing charters. **Brown's Boat Basin** (☎ 242/393–3331), on the Nassau side, offers a place to tie up your boat, as well as on-site engine repairs. **Nassau Harbour Club** (☎ 242/393–0771) is a hotel and marina on the Nassau side with 50 slips. Sixty-five-slip **Hurricane Hole Marina** (☎ 242/363–3600) is on the Paradise Island side of the harbor. The marina at **Atlantis, Paradise Island** (☎ 242/363–3000) has 63 "mega-yacht slips." At the western end of New Providence, **Lyford Cay** (☎ 242/362–4131), a posh development for the rich and famous, has an excellent marina, but there is limited availability for the humble masses.

If your children would enjoy sitting in a row on a rubber banana and bouncing along behind a motorboat, ride the big banana at **Premier Wa-**

tersports (☎ 242/324–1475, 242/427–0939 cellular), at the beach at the Sheraton Grand and Atlantis.

Fishing

The waters here are generally smooth and alive with many species of game fish, which is one of the reasons why the Bahamas has more than 20 fishing tournaments open to visitors every year. A favorite spot just west of Nassau is the Tongue of the Ocean, so called because it looks like that part of the body when viewed from the air. The channel stretches for 100 mi. For boat rental, parties of two to six will pay $300 or so for a half day, $600 for a full day.

The **Charter Boat Association** (☎ 242/393–3739) has 15 boats available for fishing charters. **Born Free Charters** (☎ 242/393–4144) has three boats and guarantees a catch on full-day charters—if you don't get a fish, you don't pay. **Brown's Charters** (☎ 242/324–1215) specializes in 24-hour shark fishing trips, as well as reef and deep-sea fishing. **Chubasco Charters** (☎ 242/324–3474 ⊕ www.chubascocharters.com) has two boats for sportfishing and shark fishing charters. **Nassau Yacht Haven** (☎ 242/393–8173 ⊕ www.nassauyachthaven.com) runs fishing charters out of its 150-slip marina.

Fitness Clubs & Spas

Nassau has a number of health clubs and gyms for those in the mood for an indoor workout or some spa pampering—an energizing alternative to shopping on an overcast day. Most are stocked with the latest high-tech machinery, including stair climbers, treadmills, and exercise bikes, and offer aerobics and other fitness classes. If you plan to stay in the area for a stretch, check into the package rates available at many clubs.

Azure Spa (✉ British Colonial Hilton, Bay St. ☎ 242/325–8497) offers quality à la carte services including facials (50-minute steam, massage, and mask is $70), body scrubs and wraps, hydrotherapy ($45 for 25 minutes), and numerous types of massages (hour-long aromatherapy is $80).
Gold's Gym (✉ Bridge Plaza, just over the eastern Paradise Island bridge ☎ 242/394–4653) has aerobics, step, and cardio-funk classes, as well as top-of-the-line fitness equipment, a juice bar, and a nursery. A full-access day pass is $8.
Palace Spa (☎ 242/327–6200), in the Wyndham Crystal Palace complex and adjoining the Radisson Cable Beach, is a full-service gym with all the amenities and aerobics classes. Exercise bikes face the water, and the spa has stair machines and excellent showers. Pamper yourself at the relaxing hot tub and sauna. Fees are $10 daily and $35 weekly (discounts for Nassau Wyndham Resort and Nassau Beach Hotel guests).
Forever Young (✉ E. Bay St. ☎ 242/393–0033 or 242/393–8788) offers a variety of ultramodern spa treatments such as hydrotherapy and salt glows as well as top-quality facials, massages, manicures, and pedicures. There is also a small, exclusive training center. Daily rates for training equipment and steam, sauna, and shower facilities are $10 ($40/month); spa treatments start at $35 (a 1-hour massage is $60).

Golf

Guests at affiliated hotels receive discounts at the following courses; prices quoted are for nonguests.

Cable Beach Golf Club (7,040 yards, par 72), the oldest golf course in the Bahamas, was undergoing renovation at this writing, though you can play 9 holes until the new course opens. The links are owned by the Radisson Cable Beach Casino & Golf Resort, whose guests get discount rates. ⌂ *Box N-4914, Nassau* ☎ *242/327–6000 Ext. 6189* ⛳ *18 holes $95, 9 holes $70; carts included. Clubs $25* ⊙ *Daily 7–5:30, last tee-off at 5:15.*

Golf Course (6,805 yards, par 72), formerly the Paradise Island Golf Club, had a major face-lift, care of Tom Weiskopf. The championship course is surrounded by the ocean on three sides, which means that winds can get stiff. Call to check on current availability and up-to-date prices (those not staying at Atlantis or the One & Only Ocean Club may find themselves shut out completely). ⊠ *Paradise Island Dr., next to airport* ⌂ *Box N-4777, Nassau* ☎ *242/363–3925, 800/321–3000 in the U.S.* ⛳ *18 holes $225. Clubs $35* ⊙ *Daily 7–6.*

South Ocean Golf Club (6,707 yards, par 72), in western New Providence, past Cable Beach, is the newest course to surrender its divots to visiting players. Narrow fairways are a notable feature. The course was designed by Joe Lee and built in 1969. ⌂ *Box N-8191, Nassau* ☎ *242/362–4391 Ext. 23* ⛳ *18 holes $90, 9 holes $50; carts included. Clubs $20. Reductions for South Ocean Golf and Beach Resort guests* ⊙ *Daily 7–6.*

Horseback Riding

Happy Trails Stables gives guided 90-minute trail rides, including basic riding instruction, through remote wooded areas and beaches on New Providence's southwestern coast. Courtesy round-trip bus transportation from hotels is provided (about an hour each way). Tours are limited to eight persons. There is a 200-pound weight limit, and children must be at least nine years old. Reservations are required. ⊠ *Coral Harbour* ☎ *242/362–1820 or 242/323–5613* ⛳ *$85 per person* ⊟ *MC, V* ⊙ *Mon.–Sat.*

Jet Skiing

A number of outfitters rent jet skis in front of Atlantis and the Sheraton Grand on Cabbage Beach. **Premier Watersports** (☎ 242/324–1475, 242/427–0939 cellular) is the most reliable, and charges $55 for 30 minutes.

Parasailing

Premier Watersports (☎ 242/324–1475, 242/427–0939 cellular) gives you the chance to be lifted off a platform and into the skies for five to eight minutes—at $45 a pop. Ask for Captain Tim or his crew on Cabbage Beach in front of the large hotels.

Sailing

Nassau Beach Hotel (☎ 242/327–7711 Ext. 6590) rents Sunfish sail-boats for $35 per hour and 16-foot catamarans for $50 per hour.

Scuba Diving & Snorkeling

Diving operations are plentiful in Nassau. Most hotels have diving in-structors who teach short courses, followed the next day by a reef trip. Many small operations have sprung up in which experienced divers with their own boats run custom dives for one to five people; these are often one-person efforts. In many cases, the custom dive will include a picnic lunch with freshly speared lobster or fish cooked over an open fire on a private island beach.

Dive Sites

New Providence Island has several popular dive sites and a number of dive operators who offer regular trips. The elusive (and thus exclusive) hole, **Lost Ocean Hole** (east of Nassau, 40–195 feet), is aptly named be-cause it is difficult to find. The rim of the 80-foot opening in 40 feet of water is dotted with coral heads and teeming with small fish—grunts, margate, and jacks—as well as larger pompano, amberjack, and some-times nurse sharks. Divers will find a thermocline at 80 feet, a large cave at 100 feet, and a sand ledge at 185 feet that slopes down to 195 feet. The series of shallow reefs along the 14 mi of Rose Island is known as **Rose Island Reefs** (Nassau, 5–35 feet). The coral is varied, although the reefs are showing the effects of the heavy traffic. Plenty of tropical fish make these reefs home. The wreck of the steel-hulled ship *Mahoney* is just outside the harbor.

Gambier Deep Reef, off Gambier Village about 15 minutes west of Cable Beach, goes to a depth of 80 feet. **Sea Gardens** is off Love Beach on the northwestern shore beyond Gambier. **Lyford Cay Drop-Off** (west of Nas-sau, 40–200+ feet) is a cliff that plummets from a 40-foot plateau al-most straight into the inky blue mile-deep Tongue of the Ocean. The wall has endless varieties of sponges, black coral, and wire coral. Along the wall, grunts, grouper, hogfish, snapper, and rockfish abound. Off the wall are pelagic game fish such as tuna, bonito, wahoo, and king-fish. The south-side reefs are great for snorkelers as well as divers be-cause of the reefs' shallowness.

Operators

All dive shops listed below are PADI facilities. Expect to pay about $65–$70 for a two-tank dive or beginner's course. Shark dives run $100–$125, and certification, $400 and up.

Bahama Divers Ltd. (☎ 242/393–1466 or 800/398–3483 ⊕ www. bahamadivers.com), the largest and most experienced dive operation in the country, offers twice-a-day dive safaris daily as well as half-day snorkel-ing trips. PADI certification courses are available, and there's a full line of scuba equipment. Destinations are drop-off sites, wrecks, coral reefs and gardens, and an ocean blue hole. For Paradise Island guests, Bahama Divers has opened a small dive operation (which also carries snorkel equipment for rent) in the Sheraton Grand.

Dive Dive Dive, Ltd. (☎ 242/362–1143, 242/362–1401, or 800/368–3480 ⊕ www.divedivedive.com) specializes in small groups. Dives include trips to walls and reefs, night dives, and shark dives. Transportation is provided.

Diver's Haven (☎ 242/394–8960), part of Nassau Island Cruises, offers three daily dives, equipment rental, classes at several area hotels, and a four-day scuba certification course. Two-tank dives are available, or, for the more adventurous, dive trips to the Out Islands can be arranged.

Nassau Scuba Centre (☎ 242/362–1964 or 800/805–5485 ⊕ www.nassau-scuba-center.com) provides trips to some of Nassau's prime sites, including the James Bond Wrecks and the walls near Tongue of the Ocean. With two state-of-the-art dive boats, it's well equipped to handle beginners and experts alike.

Stuart Cove's Dive South Ocean (☎ 242/362–4171 or 800/879–9832), at South Ocean Golf and Beach Resort on the island's south shore, is considered by aficionados to be the island's leading dive shop. Although they're pros at teaching beginners (scuba instruction and guided snorkel tours are available), experienced thrill-seekers flock to Stuart Cove's for the famous shark dives (Cove is one of the world's leading shark handlers). Also popular are his Out Island "Wilderness Safaris," and "Wall Flying Adventures," in which you ride an underwater scooter across the ocean wall. Check out the collection of celebrity photos. The shop runs dive trips to the south-shore reefs twice a day.

Spectator Sports

Among other imperishable traditions, the British handed down to the Bahamians such sports as soccer, rugby, and cricket. The latter, somewhat confusing sport (bring an expert with you, or you'll never know what's going on), is played at Haynes Oval. Baseball games are at Queen Elizabeth Sports Center, rugby at Winton Estates, and softball at Clifford Park. For information on spectator sports, call the **Ministry of Tourism** (☎ 242/322–7500), or check the local papers for sports updates and calendars.

Tennis

Most people play at the hotel where they're staying. Fees below are for nonguests.

The **Nassau Beach Hotel** (☎ 242/327–8410) tennis shop charges $5 per person from 9–6 and $7 per person until 9 PM. Three of the six courts are lighted, and rackets can be rented at $6 per person hourly. Monday evenings are reserved for members.

Waterskiing

You'd be hard-pressed to find anyone waterskiing these days (most prefer jet skiing), but if the desire strikes, Captain Tim at **Premier Watersports** (☎ 242/324–1475, 242/427–0939 cellular) can make it happen.

Windsurfing

Nassau Beach Hotel (☎ 242/327–7711 Ext. 6590) rents sailboards for $20 per hour, with more advanced boards costing $30 per hour.

SHOPPING

For many, shopping is one of Nassau's greatest delights. Bargains abound between Bay Street and the waterfront. For more upscale items, don't forget to look in the hotel arcades. You can return home with a suitcase full of handmade Bahamian goods or splurge at duty-free shops that offer such savings you simply have to load up. You'll find duty-free prices—generally 25%–50% less than U.S. prices—on imported items such as crystal, linens, watches, cameras, sweaters, leather goods, and perfumes. Prices here rival those in other duty-free destinations.

Most of Nassau's shops are on Bay Street between Rawson Square and the British Colonial Hotel, and on the side streets leading off Bay Street. Some stores, however, are beginning to pop up on the main shopping thoroughfare's eastern end. Be aware that prices in shops are fixed, and do observe the local dress customs when you go shopping: Shorts are acceptable, but beachwear is not.

Although a few shops will be happy to mail bulky or fragile items home for you, most won't even deliver purchases to your hotel, plane, or cruise ship.

Markets & Arcades

The **International Bazaar,** a collection of shops under a huge, spreading bougainvillea, sells linens, souvenirs, and offbeat items. This funky shopping row is on Bay Street at Charlotte Street. **Prince George Plaza,** which leads from Bay Street to Woodes Rogers Walk near the dock, just east of the International Bazaar, has about two dozen shops with varied wares. The **Nassau Arcade** (☎ 242/325–0338), on Bay Street between East Street and Elizabeth Avenue, just east of Parliament Square, houses a few small stores, including the Bahamas' Anglo-American bookstore, a tiny storefront with a smattering of interesting reading material.

Specialty Shops

Antiques, Arts & Crafts

Bahamacraft Centre (⊠ Paradise Island Dr., across from Hurricane Hole Plaza ☎ No phone) offers some top-level Bahamian crafts, including a selection of authentic straw work. Dozens of vendors hawk everything from baskets to shell collages inside this vibrantly colored building, designed by noted architect Jackson Burnside of Doongalik Studios. You can catch a shuttle bus from Atlantis to the center.
Balmain Antiques and Gallery (⊠ Bay St. ☎ 242/323–7421) collects Bahamian artwork as well as antique maps, prints, and bottles.
Doongalik Studios (⊠ 18 Village Rd. ☎ 242/394–1886 ⊕ www.doongalikstudios.com) offers dynamic canvases inspired by Junkanoo

celebrations, vibrantly painted furniture, Junkanoo masks, and kaleidoscopic sculpture. Don't miss the sculpture garden or the re-creation of a traditional Bahamian home that serves as a display room for handmade Christmas ornaments, art cards, and other inexpensive and unique gifts. You can watch a Junkanoo video while you shop.

Kennedy Gallery (⊠ Parliament St. ☎ 242/325–7662 ⊕ www.kennedygallerybahamas.com) sells watercolors, oils, sculpture, and other artwork by Bahamian artists, from the best-known to emerging young talent.

Marlborough Antiques (⊠ Marlborough St. ☎ 242/328–0502) specializes in English furniture and bric-a-brac. You can also find Bahamian art, rare books, European glassware, and Victorian jewelry.

Soft Touch Productions (⊠ Market St. ☎ 242/323–2128), known for its wire-sculpted dolls depicting local characters and scenes, also sells wicker and straw baskets and other souvenirs.

Baked Goods

The Bread Shop (⊠ Shirley St., east of Mackey St. ☎ 242/393–7973) is, as the sign proclaims, "The home of Rosie's Raisin Bread." Cinnamon rolls, pound and banana cakes, and other sweet delights are also offered in this amiable spot in Nassau's east end.

Kelly's Bakery (⊠ Market St. ☎ 242/325–0616) is a convenient place to stop for muffins, cakes, and other goodies.

Model Bakery (⊠ Dowdeswell St. ☎ 242/322–2595), in Nassau's east end, is another great local bakery. Be sure to try the cinnamon twists.

China, Crystal, Linens & Silver

Linen Shop (⊠ Bay St. ☎ 242/322–4266) sells fine embroidered Irish linens and lace.

Solomon's Mines (⊠ Several Bay St. locations, Hurricane Hole Plaza, and Atlantis on Paradise Island ☎ 242/322–8324) sells, among other names, Waterford, Hummel, Lladró, Wedgwood, Lenox, Lalique, Baccarat, Bally of Switzerland, Hermes, and Salvatore Ferragamo.

Cigars

The expansive displays of Cuban cigars, imported by Bahamian merchants, lure aficionados to the Bahamas for cigar sprees. Be aware, however, that some merchants on Bay Street and elsewhere in the islands are selling counterfeits—sometimes unwittingly. If the price seems too good to be true, chances are it is. Check the wrappers and feel to ensure that there is a consistent fill before you purchase. A number of stores along the main shopping strip do stock only the best authentic Cuban stogies.

The Cigar Box (⊠ Bay St. ☎ 242/326–7352), next to Planet Hollywood, offers all the well-known Cuban brands as well as a small selection of humidors.

Graycliff (⊠ West Hill St. ☎ 242/322–7050 ⊕ www.graycliff.com) carries one of Nassau's finest selections of hand-rolled cigars, overseen by the prestigious Avelino Lara, who created some of Cuba's best-known cigars. In fact, Graycliff's operation is so popular that it has expanded the hotel to include an entire cigar factory, open to the public for tours and purchases. Rolling the cigars are a dozen Cuban men and women who live on the lovely premises, and work here through a special arrangement with the Cuban government. True cigar buffs will seek out the Graycliff's owner, Enrico Garzaroli.

Havana Humidor (✉ Crystal Court at Atlantis, Paradise Island ☎ 242/363–5809) has the largest selection of authentic Cuban cigars in the Bahamas. Watch cigars being made, or browse through the cigar and pipe accessories.

Pipe of Peace (✉ Bay St. ☎ 242/322–3908) has a wide selection of cigars, pipes, and cigarettes, including all major Cuban cigars. Although the cigar counter occupies just a small portion of the eclectic souvenir shop, it's well known as a good source.

Tropique International Smoke Shop (✉ Nassau Wyndham Resort & Crystal Palace Casino ☎ 242/327–7292) has well-stocked atmosphere-controlled humidors; the well-trained staff provides knowledgeable guidance.

Eclectic

Far East Traders (✉ Prince George's Plaza, Bay St. ☎ 242/325–7095) has embroidered linens from Asia, silk nighties and kimonos, and handwoven blouses and vests.

Green Lizard (✉ Bay St. ☎ 242/323–8076) is home to a cornucopia of native and imported gifts, including a specialty item you might be tempted to use during your stay: string hammocks.

House of Music (✉ Mackey St. ☎ 242/393–0331) has the best selection of island calypso, soca, reggae, and Junkanoo music.

The Island Shop and Island Bookstore (✉ Bay St. ☎ 242/322–4183) has two floors of travel guides, novels, paperbacks, gift books, and international magazines, as well as clothing, swimwear, and souvenirs. Take a peek at the Bahamian section, which has books on everything from history to cookery.

Island Tings (✉ Bay St. ☎ 242/326–1024) carries a variety of items, some Bahamian, some not (look carefully before assuming you're buying local work). Art includes prints by Eleutheran artist Eddie Minnis, wood carvings, and Androsia fabric—produced on the island of Andros. There's also a sizable food section.

Royal Palm Trading Co. (✉ Bay St. ☎ 242/322–5131) is an upscale store carrying designer clothing lines such as Tommy Bahama and Androsia. It also sells Fashion Fair cosmetics, placemats, and other gift items.

Fashion

Clothing is no great bargain in Nassau, but many stores sell fine imports. Perhaps the best local buy is brightly batiked Androsia fabric—available by the yard or sewn into sarongs, dresses, and blouses.

Brass and Leather (✉ Charlotte St., off Bay St. ☎ 242/322–3806) sells leather goods for men and women, including bags, shoes, and belts.

Cole's of Nassau (✉ Parliament St. ☎ 242/322–8393 ✉ Crystal Court at Atlantis, Paradise Island ☎ 242/363–4161 ✉ Bay Street, next to John Bull ☎ 242/356–2498) is a top choice for designer fashions, sportswear, bathing suits, shoes, and accessories.

Fendi (✉ Bay St. at Charlotte St. ☎ 242/322–6300) occupies a magnificent old building and carries the Italian house's luxury line of handbags, luggage, watches, jewelry, and shoes.

Tempo Paris (✉ Bay St. ☎ 242/323–6112) offers men's clothing by major designers, including Ralph Lauren, Calvin Klein, and Gianni Versace.

Jewelry, Watches & Clocks

Coin of the Realm (✉ Charlotte St. off Bay St. ☎ 242/322–4862 or 242/322–4497) has Bahamian coins, stamps, native conch pearls, tanzanite, and semi-precious stone jewelry.

Colombian Emeralds International (✉ Bay St. ☎ 242/322–2230 ✉ Atlantis, Paradise Island ☎ 242/322–3020) is the local branch of this well-known jeweler, carrying not only its signature gem but a variety of other fine jewelry.

The Jewelry Box (✉ Bay St. ☎ 242/322–4098) specializes in tanzanite jewelry. It's the largest Bahamian supplier of this gem, mined in the foothills of Mt. Kilimanjaro, but it also sells other precious and semiprecious stones and 14-karat gold jewelry.

The Jewelry Mart (✉ Bay St. ☎ 242/328–8869) offers Movado, Bulova, and other watches as well as gold jewelry and pieces fashioned from tanzanite, rubies, and emeralds, among other gems.

John Bull (✉ 284 Bay St. ☎ 242/322–4252 ✉ Crystal Court at Atlantis, Paradise Island ☎ 242/363–3956), established in 1929 and magnificently decorated in its Bay Street incarnation behind a Georgian-style facade, fills its complex with wares from Tiffany & Co., Cartier, Mikimoto, Nina Ricci, and Yves Saint Laurent.

Solomon's Mines (✉ Three Bay St. locations, Hurricane Hole Plaza, and Atlantis on Paradise Island ☎ 242/322–8324 or 877/765–6463) is the place to buy duty-free watches by Tag-Heuer, Omega, Borel, Swiss Army, and other makers. It also carries African diamonds, as well as Spanish pieces of eight in settings.

Perfumes

The Body Shop (✉ Bay St. ☎ 242/356–2431) sells the company's internationally acclaimed line of all-natural body lotions, shampoos and conditioners, and makeup.

John Bull (✉ 284 Bay St. ☎ 242/322–4252 ✉ Crystal Court at Atlantis, Paradise Island ☎ 242/363–3956) has fragrances by Chanel, Yves Saint Laurent, and Estée Lauder.

Perfume Bar (✉ Bay St. ☎ 242/325–1258) carries the best-selling French fragrance Boucheron and the Clarins line of skin-care products, as well as scents by Givenchy, Fendi, and other well-known designers.

The Perfume Shop (✉ Bay and Frederick Sts. ☎ 242/322–2375) is a landmark perfumery that has the broadest selection of imported perfumes and fragrances in the Bahamas.

Solomon's Mines (✉ Three Bay St. locations, Hurricane Hole Plaza, and Atlantis on Paradise Island ☎ 242/356–6920 or 877/765–6463), one of the Caribbean's largest duty-free retailers, stocks French, Italian, and U.S. fragrances, skin-care products, and bath lines.

NEW PROVIDENCE ISLAND A TO Z

To research prices, get advice from other travelers, and book travel arrangements, visit ⊕ www.fodors.com

AIR TRAVEL

Flights listed below originate in the United States and Canada. If you are arriving from the United Kingdom, the best option is to fly to Miami and transfer to one of the numerous carriers listed below for the hour-long final leg to Nassau.

CARRIERS Air Canada flies from Montréal and Toronto. American Eagle, an American Airlines subsidiary, flies into Nassau daily from Miami and Fort Lauderdale and also serves the Abacos, Exumas, and other destinations in the Out Islands. Bahamasair, the national carrier, has daily flights from Miami and Fort Lauderdale, as well as five flights weekly from Orlando. The airline also flies to all of the Out Islands. Continental flies in daily from Newark under service operated by Nassau–Paradise Island Express, and daily from West Palm Beach, Fort Lauderdale, and Miami on Continental's partner, Gulf Stream International. Delta is one of the busier carriers, with daily flights from Atlanta, New York City, Cincinnati, Charleston, and Orlando. Trans World Airlines flies to Nassau daily from New York's John F. Kennedy airport. US Airways flies in daily from Charlotte, NC, and offers seasonal services from Philadelphia.

🛪 **Airlines & Contacts Air Canada** ☎ 800/776-3000. **American Eagle** ☎ 800/433-7300. **Bahamasair** ☎ 242/377-5505 or 800/222-4262. **Continental** ☎ 242/377-2050 or 800/722-4262. **Delta** ☎ 800/221-1212. **Gulf Stream International** ☎ 242/377-4314 or 800/231-0856. **Trans World Airlines** ☎ 800/221-2000. **US Airways** ☎ 242/377-8887 or 800/622-1015.

AIRPORTS & TRANSFERS

Nassau International Airport, 8 mi west of Nassau by Lake Killarney, is served by an increasing number of airlines. With the closure of the Paradise Island Airport, it's the only game in town now.

🛪 **Airport Information Nassau International Airport** ☎ 242/377-7281.

TRANSFERS No bus service is available from Nassau International Airport to New Providence hotels, except for guests on package tours. (Breezes, Sandals, and Atlantis have promotional booths at the airport.) A taxi ride from the airport to Cable Beach costs $15; to Nassau, $22; and to Paradise Island, $28 (this includes the $1 causeway toll). These are fixed costs for two passengers; each additional passenger is $3. In addition, drivers expect a 15% tip. Some resorts offer airport shuttle service.

BOAT & FERRY TRAVEL

Nassau is a port of call for a number of cruise lines, including Carnival Cruise Lines, Celebrity Cruises, Costa Cruise Line, Disney Cruise Line, Premier Cruise Lines, Regal Cruises, Royal Caribbean International, and Silversea Cruises. Ships dock at Prince George Wharf, in downtown Nassau.

Ferries operate during daylight hours (usually 9–5:30) at half-hour intervals between Prince George Wharf and Paradise Island. The one-way cost is $3 per person.

BUS TRAVEL

For the adventuresome, consider jitney (bus) service to get around Nassau and its environs. Rides in these buses, which career along with windows open and music blaring, range from smooth sailing to hair-raising. If you want to join locals on a jitney, hail one at a bus stop, hotel, public beach, or in a residential area. Most carry their owner's name in boldly painted letters, so they're easy to spot, and with downtown's main streets being one-way, it's not hard to tell where they're going. If you're not sure of the jitney's direction, ask your concierge on which side of the street to stand, or check with the friendly drivers. The fare is $1, exact change required. Call out to the driver as your stop approaches.

In downtown Nassau, jitneys wait on Frederick Street between Bay Street and Woodes Rogers Walk. Bus service runs throughout the day until 7.

BUSINESS HOURS

Banks are open on New Providence Island Monday–Thursday 9:30–3 and Friday 9:30–5. They are closed on weekends. Principal banks on the island are Bank of the Bahamas, Bank of Nova Scotia, Barclays Bank, Canadian Imperial Bank of Commerce, Citibank, and Royal Bank of Canada.

Shops are generally open Monday–Saturday 9–5 (many stay open later). Bay Street shops are legally permitted to open on Sunday, but the main thoroughfare remains all but deserted.

CAR RENTAL

Avis Rent-A-Car has branches at the Nassau International Airport, on Paradise Island in the Paradise Village Shopping Centre, and downtown, just west of the British Colonial Hotel. Budget has branches at the Nassau International Airport and on Paradise Island. Dollar Rent-a-Car, which often has the lowest rates (there are frequent $39 rentals), can be found at Nassau International Airport and downtown, at the base of the British Colonial Hotel. Hertz has branches at Nassau International Airport and on East Bay Street, a block east of the bridge from Paradise Island. Thrifty has a branch at the airport.

🚗 **Major Agencies Avis Rent-A-Car** ☎ 242/377-7121, 242/363-2061, or 242/326-6380. **Budget** ☎ 242/377-9000 or 242/363-3095. **Dollar Rent-a-Car** ☎ 242/377-7301 or 242/325-3716. **Hertz** ☎ 242/377-6231 or 242/393-0871. **Thrifty** ☎ 242/377-0355.

CAR TRAVEL

For exploring at your leisure, it's best to have a car. Rentals are available at Nassau International Airport, downtown, on Paradise Island, and at some resorts. Plan to pay $80–$120, depending on the type of car. Gasoline costs around $3.00 a gallon. Remember to drive on the left.

The current price of gas varies from dealer to dealer. The present range is $2.89, $2.91, and $3.03. Rental car rates also vary: $81.95 for a compact, $94.95 medium, and $119.95 full size.

CARRIAGES

Beautifully painted horse-drawn carriages will take as many as four people around Nassau at a rate of $10 per adult and $5 per child for a 30-minute ride; don't hesitate to bargain. Most drivers give a comprehensive tour of the Bay Street area, including an extensive history lesson. Look for the carriages on Woodes Rogers Walk, in the center of Rawson Square.

CONSULATES & EMBASSIES

British High Commission ⊠ Bitco Bldg., East and Shirley Sts. ☎ 242/325-7471 ⎙ 242/323-3871. **Canadian Consulate** ⊠ Shirley Street Shopping Plaza, Shirley St. ☎ 242/393-2123 ⎙ 242/393-1305. **U.S. Embassy** ⊠ Queen St., across from British Colonial Hilton ☎ 242/322-1181 ⎙ 242/328-7838.

EMERGENCIES

In an emergency dial 911. Princess Margaret Hospital is government operated, and Doctors Hospital is private.

Ambulance ☎ 911 or 242/322-2221. **Police** ☎ 911 or 242/322-4444.

Hospitals Doctors Hospital ⊠ Collins Ave. and Shirley St. ☎ 242/322-8411. **Princess Margaret Hospital** ⊠ Shirley St. ☎ 242/322-2861.

SCOOTERS

Two people can ride around the island on a motor scooter for about $40 for a half day, $50 for a full day. Helmets and insurance for both driver and passenger are mandatory and are included in the rental price. Many hotels have scooters on the premises. You can also try Knowles, on West Bay Street, in the British Colonial Hilton parking lot, or check out the stands in Rawson Square. Remember to drive on the left.

Knowles ☎ 242/356-0741.

SIGHTSEEING TOURS

More than a dozen local operators provide tours of New Providence Island's natural and commercial attractions. Some of the many possibilities include sightseeing tours of Nassau and the island, glass-bottom boat tours to Sea Gardens, and cruises to offshore cays, all starting at $12. A full day of ocean sailing will cost around $60. In the evening, there are sunset and moonlight cruises with dinner and drinks ($35–$50) and nightlife tours to casino cabaret shows and nightclubs ($28–$45). Tours may be booked at hotel desks in Nassau, Cable Beach, and Paradise Island or directly through one of the tour operators listed below, all of which have knowledgeable guides and a selection of tours in air-conditioned cars, vans, or buses.

TAXIS

Taxis are generally the best and most convenient way to get around New Providence. Fares are determined by zone. For airport fares, *see* Airports and Transfers, *above.* The fare is $6 for trips within downtown Nassau and on Paradise Island (which includes the bridge toll), $9 from Paradise Island to downtown, and $18 from Cable Beach to Paradise Island (including toll). Fares are for two passengers; each additional passenger is $3, regardless of the destination. It is customary to tip taxi drivers 15%. You also can hire a car or small van for about $50 per hour.

Bahamas Transport has radio-dispatched taxis. You can call the Taxi Cab Union directly for a cab. There are also stands at major hotels, or the front desk can call you a cab.

⚹ Taxi Companies Bahamas Transport ☎ 242/323-5111, 242/323-5112, 242/323-5113, or 242/323-5114. **Taxi Cab Union** ☎ 242/323-4555 or 242/323-5818.

TOURS & PACKAGES

CRUISE TRIPS One of the best ways to enjoy Nassau's seafaring pleasures is to sign up with one of the many day or evening cruise operators, typically on a catamaran or similar sailboat. These offerings range from three-hour snorkeling trips to romantic sunset cruises or full-day excursions. Prices are fairly standard among the operators: A half-day snorkeling cruise will run about $45, and a full day $60, usually including a drink and snacks; prices for a sunset sail, with drinks and hors d'oeuvres, are around the same. Full-day or dinner cruises, both with meals, cost around $50. Hotel transportation is generally included.

Barefoot Sailing Cruises transports you to a secluded Rose Island beach for snorkeling and sunbathing on a half-day sail or snorkel cruise; other options include an all-day island barbecue and champagne sunset cruise. Feeling luxurious? Arrange a private dinner cruise.

Flying Cloud runs half-day catamaran cruises at 9:30 and 2, as well as sunset "sail-and-a-dinner" cruises on which you can enjoy a candlelight meal in a secluded cove. A five-hour Sunday cruise departs at 10 AM.

Island Tours offers a half-day catamaran excursion to Rose Island beach for beach volleyball and snorkeling. Snacks and an open bar are included as are bus transfers to and from your hotel.

Sea Island Adventures runs half- and full-day trips to Rose Island for snorkeling and a tropical lunch, as well as sunset cruises. Private charters can also be arranged.

⚹ Cruise Lines Barefoot Sailing Cruises ☎ 242/393-0820 or 242/393-581 ⊕ www. barefootsailingcruises.com. **Flying Cloud** ☎ 242/363-4430 ⊕ www.bahamasnet.com/ flyingcloud. **Island Tours** ☎ 242/327-8653. **Sea Island Adventures** ☎ 242/325-3910 ⊕ www.bahamasnet.com/seaislandadventure.

OUT ISLANDS Several options exist for getaways to the less-frequented Out Islands. TRIPS Expect to pay from $90 for no-frills ferry service to several hundred dollars for full-day excursions with meals, snorkeling, and sightseeing.

Bahamas Fast Ferries provides a wonderful way to escape to Harbour Island—possibly the most charming island in the Bahamas—Spanish Wells, or unspoiled Eleuthera; the high-speed, colorful, and extremely safe *Bo Hengy* catamaran whisks you from Nassau to Out Island getaways in two hours. Book just transport or, better yet, the Bo Hengy Harbour Island package ($159 for adults, $99 for children) that includes a historic walking tour of Harbour Island, a great lunch, and beach time at the famous pink sands—Fast Ferries has its own fully equipped cabana on the beach with complimentary refreshments. Horseback riding is usually available on the beach. You'll be back in Nassau by nightfall.

Exuma Powerboat Adventures offers full-day excursions to the Exuma Cays. After zipping over via one of three speed boats, feed iguanas at Allan's Cay, participate in a nature walk, and do some snorkeling in the Exumas' Land and Sea Park. There are also shallow-water shark feeds. It's a great way to experience some of the beauty of the less-developed islands outside Nassau. Lunch is included.

Island World Adventures offers full-day excursions to Saddleback Cay in the Exumas on a high-speed powerboat. You can take a guided trek and learn about Bahamian flora and fauna or just snorkel and sunbathe the day away. Lunch, soft drinks, beer, and rum punch are included.

Seaplane Safaris utilize low-flying craft for the Exuma Cays trip, allowing you to glide right over the water's surface. You can swim right off the seaplane into Thunderball Grotto, an eerie natural formation (scenes from the James Bond movie bearing its name were filmed here), and enjoy some snorkeling, explore nature trails, or simply loll on the beach on Warderick Wells, the headquarters of the Land and Sea Park. Lunch is included, and the trip takes a full day.

🚢 **Bahamas Fast Ferries** ☎ 242/323-2166 ⊕ www.bahamasferries.com. **Exuma Powerboat Adventures** ☎ 242/393-7116 ⊕ www.powerboatadventures.com. **Island World Adventures** ☎ 242/363-3333 ⊕ www.islandworldadventures.com. **Seaplane Safaris** ☎ 242/393-2522 or 242/393-1179.

SPECIAL-INTEREST TOURS During the Close Encounter ($75 per person) arranged by Dolphin Encounters on Blue Lagoon Island (Salt Cay), just east of Paradise Island, you stand in waist-deep water while dolphins play around you. The two-hour program consists of an educational session as well as the encounter. Trainers are available to answer questions. Swim-with-the-Dolphins ($145 per person) actually allows you to swim with these friendly creatures for about 30 minutes. For more complete involvement, try the Assistant Trainer for a Day program ($195 per person, 16 years old minimum), where you learn about care and training by helping with feeding, cleaning, and food preparation. Programs are available daily 8–5:30, and the cost includes transfers from your hotel and the boat ride to the island. Make reservations as early as possible.

Hartley's Undersea Walk takes you for a stroll on the ocean floor. Special helmets protect hair, eyeglasses, and contacts while allowing you to see the fish and flora. Hartley's yacht, the *Pied Piper*, departs daily at 9:30 and 1:30 from the Nassau Yacht Haven on East Bay Street. Reserve in advance to guarantee a spot.

Pedal & Paddle Ecoventures is a unique, full-day ecotourism adventure that combines all-terrain bicycle rides through forests and along coastlines with kayaking tours through mangrove creeks and sheltered waters. Lunch is included in the full-day tours, which can be booked at most hotel desks. Half-day tours are also available.

Seaworld Explorer is a "semi-submarine" that cruises through the harbor as it makes its way to Sea Gardens Marine Park; you can sit above water on the deck or descend to view the ocean life firsthand through undersea windows.

Stingray City, on Blue Lagoon Island, takes you snorkeling and even allows you to feed a surprisingly friendly stingray or two.

🄵 Dolphin Encounters ☎ 242/363-1003 ⊕ www.dolphinencounters.com. **Hartley's Undersea Walk** ☎ 242/393-8234 ⊕ www.underseawalk.com. **Pedal & Paddle Ecoventures** ☎ 242/362-2772. **Seaworld Explorer** ☎ 242/356-2548. **Stingray City** ☎ 242/363-3333 ⊕ www.nassaucruisesbahamas.com.

WALKING TOURS A walking tour around Historic Nassau, arranged by the Tourist Information Office at Rawson Square, is offered daily. The cost is $10. Call ahead for information and reservations.

🄵 Historic Nassau ☎ 242/302-2055.

VISITOR INFORMATION

The Ministry of Tourism's Help Line is an information source that operates from 8 AM to midnight daily. The ministry also operates tourist information booths at Nassau International Airport, open daily from 8:30 AM to 11:30 PM, and at the Welcome Center (Festival Place), open daily from 9 AM to 5 PM, adjacent to Prince George Wharf. The telephone numbers are 242/323–3182, 242/323–3183, and 242/356–0435 for the weddings division. Ask about Bahamahosts, specially trained tour guides who will tell you about island history and culture and pass on their individual and imaginative knowledge of Bahamian folklore.

The Ministry of Tourism's People-to-People Programme is designed to let a Bahamian personally introduce you to the Bahamas. By prearrangement through the ministry, you can spend a day with a Bahamian family with similar interests to learn local culture firsthand or enjoy a family meal. It's best if you make arrangements—through your travel agent or by calling direct—prior to your trip. (This is not a dating service!) People-to-People also holds teas at Government House (call for details) and sponsors activities for spouses of conference attendees, student exchanges, and pen pal programs.

🄵 Tourist Information Ministry of Tourism 🖃 Box N-3701, Nassau ☎ 242/322-7500 or 242/302-2000 🖷 242/302-2098 ⊕ www.bahamas.com ☎ 242/326-4357 Help Line ✉ Nassau International Airport booths ☎ 242/377-6833, 242/377-8606, or 242/377-6782 ☎ 242/326-9772 Rawson Square. **People-to-People Programme** ☎ 242/326-5371 or 242/356-0435.

WEDDINGS

Fallen in love? The Ministry of Tourism's Wedding Division arranges weddings for visiting couples. Formerly run by People-to-People, the weddings have proven so popular that the ministry has established a separate department to handle them. Ministry staff will take care of all the paperwork and set up ceremonies ranging from a simple seaside "I do" to more outrageous nuptials. Underwater vows, anyone?

🄵 Wedding Division ☎ 242/302-2034.

GRAND BAHAMA ISLAND

UTTER ELEGANCE AWAITS
at Luciano's candlelit restaurant ⇨*p.71*

MAKE FLIPPERED FRIENDS
in a swim-with-the-dolphins program ⇨*p.63*

HUMMINGBIRDS SIP NECTAR
alongside trails with 130 plant types ⇨*p.61*

THE BARGAINS ARE ENDLESS
at the International Bazaar ⇨*p.63*

GET YOUR TAN ON
at Taíno ⇨*p.65*

SWING WITH THE BEST
at four championship courses ⇨*p.84*

Updated by
Chelle Koster
Walton

GRAND BAHAMA, the fourth-largest island in the Bahamas after Andros, Eleuthera, and Great Abaco, lies only 52 mi off Palm Beach, Florida. The Gulf Stream's ever-warm waters lap its western tip, and the Little Bahama Bank protects it from the northeast.

In 1492, when Columbus set foot on the Bahamian island of San Salvador, Grand Bahama was already populated. Skulls found in caves here attest to the existence of the peaceable Lucayans, who were constantly fleeing the more bellicose Caribs. The skulls show that the parents flattened their babies' foreheads with boards to strengthen them, making them less vulnerable to the cudgels of the Caribs, who were reputedly cannibalistic.

Spanish conquistadors visited the island briefly in the early 16th century. They used it as a watering hole but dismissed it as having no commercial value and went on their way. In the 18th century, Loyalists settled on Grand Bahama to escape the wrath of American Revolutionaries who had just won the War of Independence. Remnants of that colonial exodus crop up around the settlement of Eight Mile Rock, just west of Freeport Harbour, including 150-year-old St. Peter's Anglican Church and rock walls built by the early colonists. When Britain abolished the slave trade early in the 19th century, many of the Loyalists' former slaves settled here as farmers and fishermen.

Grand Bahama took on new prominence in the Roaring '20s, when the island's western end and Bimini to the south became convenient jumping-off points for rumrunners ferrying booze to Florida during Prohibition. But it was not until the 1950s, when the harvesting of Caribbean yellow pine trees (now protected by Bahamian environmental law) was the island's major industry, that American financier Wallace Groves envisioned Grand Bahama's grandiose future. Groves dreamed of establishing a tax-free port for the shipment of goods to the United States, a plan that involved building a city.

On August 5, 1955, largely due to Groves's efforts and those of British industrialist Sir Charles Hayward, the government signed an agreement that set in motion the development of a planned city and established the Grand Bahama Port Authority to administer a 200-square-mi area near the island's center. Settlers received tax concessions and other benefits. In return, the developers built a port, an airport, a power plant, roads, waterways, and utilities. They also promoted tourism and industrial development.

From that agreement, the city of Freeport and later Lucaya evolved. They are separated by a 4-mi stretch of East Sunrise Highway (a.k.a. Churches Row for all the houses of worship that line it), although few can tell you where one community ends and the other begins. A modern industrial park has developed west of Freeport close to the harbor. Major companies were drawn here because there are no corporate, property, or income taxes and no customs duties or excise taxes on materials used for export manufacturing. In return, the companies hire local workers and have become involved in community activities and charities.

Most of Grand Bahama's commercial activity is concentrated in Freeport, the Bahamas's second-largest city. On average, about 15 percent of the roughly 4 million people who come to the Bahamas each year visit Freeport and neighboring waterfront Lucaya. Cruise-ship passengers arrive at Lucayan Harbour mostly from the Florida ports of Fort Lauderdale and Cape Canaveral. The harbor has undergone a $10.9 million renovation and expansion with a clever Bahamian-style look, expanded cruise-passenger terminal facilities, and two entertainment-shopping villages. Still more expansion is underway for cruise and container shipping.

Lucaya, with the debut of the grand and sprawling Our Lucaya Beach & Golf Resort, stepped up to the role of island tourism capital. With its modern shopping complex, as well as a 19,500-square-foot casino, it raised the bar for the island. In Freeport and the West End, Our Lucaya's challenge was met with the restructuring of Royal Oasis Golf Resort & Casino and the opening and expansion of deluxe Old Bahama Bay.

Despite the bustle of business and the influx of tourists, Grand Bahama offers many opportunities to enjoy solitude and nature. For decades, tourism forces have shifted the emphasis away from Freeport to Grand Bahama Island to raise awareness of what lies beyond shopping and gambling. As far as nature-lovers are concerned, three spots in and around Freeport shouldn't be missed: Parrot Jungle's Garden of the Groves, the Bahamas National Trust's (BNT) Lucayan National Park, and the BNT Rand Nature Centre.

Eco-sensitivity has spawned stimulating ecotourism adventures, including kayak trips through the national park, adventure tours to the island's East End, bird-watching excursions to spot species not found elsewhere in North America, snorkeling tours of coral reefs, and horseback rides through pine forests and along ocean beaches.

Grand Bahama Island also affords a plenitude of opportunities for heritage tourism. The friendly local population is accessible in daily interaction and through the People-to-People Programme (call ☎ 242/352–8044 or 800/448–3386 for more information), which can hook you and your family up with hospitable locals of like interests. Most restaurants outside the large resorts serve Bahamian cuisine, and many attractions and tours explore the island's history and culture. For a potent taste of island tradition, plan your visit during Junkanoo celebrations at Christmas and in the summer. A throwback to slavery days, Junkanoo colorfully showcases the song, dance, and spirit of Grand Bahama Island with bright and extravagant costumery, horns, bells, drums, and whistles.

Exploring Grand Bahama

Shopping, golfing, and gambling initially drew many of Grand Bahama's first tourists, but today, beach-going, kayaking, and exploring the island's old fishing settlements are also popular on visitors' to-do lists. Freeport is the hub of the gambling and commercial scenes, but long before it arose as an exotic playground for high-rollers and shoppers, settlements clustered around coastal areas where islanders made their living from the sea. That way of life remains intact in the island's

Numbers in the text correspond to numbers in the margins and on the Grand Bahama Island and Freeport-Lucaya maps.

If you have
3 days

Begin in the morning with a shopping binge at ☞ **Port Lucaya Marketplace ❹**. Stop at **UNEXSO ❺** next door to make reservations for tomorrow's swim with dolphins, resort dive course, or excursion. Have lunch at the marketplace before heading to the beach across the street for an afternoon of sunning and watersports. Hit the restaurants and bars at the marketplace for the evening's entertainment. The next day, after your trip, explore the ▦ **Freeport** area, beginning at **International Bazaar ❷** for more shopping. Get a quick taste of Bahamian nature at **Bahamas National Trust Rand Nature Centre ❼**. Finish the day with a visit to **Water World** for family entertainment or **Royal Oasis Casino ❶** for gambling and partying. On Day 3, head west to **Parrot Jungle's Garden of the Groves ❽** in the morning, then take a break at **Taíno Beach** for great beach action, lunch, watersports, and sunning. Catch an evening dinner cruise and show with **Bahama Mama Cruises.**

2

If you have
5 days

With an extra two days, follow the three-day itinerary above and spend Day 4 on an all-day eco- or heritage tour. The next day, catch a bus to **Paradise Cove** for snorkeling, kayaking, and lunch. Have dinner in Freeport and prowl the nightclubs around International Bazaar for after-dark fun.

If you have
7 days

A week allows you to explore in greater depth the island's environmental treasures. For the first five days use the itinerary above, and on Day 6 visit ☞ **Lucayan National Park ❾** and its beach—either on your own or with a tour group. In the afternoon, visit **Pirates of the Bahamas** and stay for the bonfire party. Spend your last morning horseback riding down the beach. In the afternoon, either go on a fishing or glass-bottom boat tour or, if you prefer to stay landbound, drive or take a bus to West End for an eyeful of local culture. Have dinner on your way back to town at **Pier One** and watch the shark-feeding.

---

far-reaching areas on the West End and East End, especially in the offshore island of Sweeting's Cay. Driving to these out-flung areas is a cinch, as traffic is practically nonexistent, especially out toward East End. Roads are good and the billboards entertaining, if instructive: "Undertakers love overtakers" (i.e., people who pass), and "Littering is stupid; don't do it" (how's that for straightforward?).

Back in the hub and hum of things, the best way to taste local culture is in the restaurants and natural areas. Even in the middle of town, environmental attractions introduce visitors to the curly-tailed lizards, Bahamian parrot, pink flamingos, and "flutterbys" (the Bahamian word for butterflies) that make their home in the islands. Of course, fine shops, greens, and the casino scene still remain prominent to round out the Grand Bahama experience to its multidimensional proportion.

About the Restaurants

For the true Bahamian dining experience, look for restaurants named after the owner or cook—such as Becky's, Geneva's Place, and Georgie's. Conch, grouper, and Bahamian lobster are the specialties, fresh from local waters. Go to the colorful conch beach shacks at Taíno Beach and at Lucaya, just west of Our Lucaya Beach & Golf Resort. Equally colorful are the owners of such places, such as radio personality Tony Macaroni and the inventor of roasted conch, Joe Billy.

The Grand Bahama dining scene stretches far beyond traditional Bahamian cuisine. The resorts and shopping centers have eateries that rate with Nassau's finest, serving up everything from Italian and English fare to fine Continental and creative Pacific Rim specialties.

About the Hotels

Accommodations took a step up when Our Lucaya Beach & Golf Resort opened its doors in 2000. It had a rejuvenating effect on an island whose resorts had grown dated and faded. Royal Oasis Resort & Casino, after undergoing a series of name changes, debuted a new look revolving around its million-gallon beach pool, a gargantuan effort that involved detouring the island's main boulevard. Other smaller hotels around the island have taken the cue to spruce up. Old Bahama Bay opened at floundering West End to inject new life into the old capital, and continues to thrive and grow.

Despite all the money that's recently been poured into renovations, Grand Bahama Island accommodations remain some of the Bahamas' most affordable, especially those away from the beach. The majority are located near the two major shopping centers and provide free shuttle service to the nearest stretch of sand.

WHAT IT COSTS					
	$$$$	**$$$**	**$$**	**$**	**¢**
RESTAURANTS	over $40	$30–$40	$20–$30	$10–$20	under $10
HOTELS	over $400	$300–$400	$200–$300	$100–$200	under $100

Restaurant prices are for a main course at dinner, excluding gratuity, typically 15%, which is often automatically added to the bill. Hotel prices are for two people in a standard double room in high season, excluding service charges and 6%–12% tax.

Timing

Anytime is a good time to take advantage of Grand Bahama Island's sunny skies and Gulf Stream–warmed waters. Summers can get oppressively hot (into the mid- and high 90s) and muggy, however, so unless you're planning on doing a lot of snorkeling, diving, and other watersports, you may want to schedule your trip for cooler months. Afternoon thunderstorms and occasional tropical storms and hurricanes also make summer less attractive weather-wise. June through September average around 20 days of rain a month. The good news is that hotel rates plummet and diving and fishing are great.

2

Hitting the Sand
What Bahamas vacation is complete without a beach? And Grand Bahama Island has more than its share fringing its length of 96 mi. All dusted with platinum sands, some are bustling with watersports activity while others lie so far off the beaten path it takes a four-wheel-drive vehicle and local knowledge to find them. Taíno Beach is the most accessible to the general public. Restaurants and bars provide visitors an anchor and offer watersports rentals and tours. Many resorts off the beach provide free shuttles and some beach bars have vans that will pick you up at your hotel.

Golf
Golf was a big deal on the island long before it became fashionable in the late 1990s. This means that many of the golf courses have a classic design, though most have been renovated in recent years. With plenty of room to build, early designers made the fairways long and scenic, while challenging golfers with lots of water. Today's courses retain those characteristics, but have been renovated and improved upon, one notable addition being the first-class golf academy at Our Lucaya's Lucayan Course.

Shopping Close to Home
Savvy shoppers head directly to the duty-free shops for great buys on liquor, jewelry, china, perfume, and other luxury items. If you're an experienced Caribbean duty-free buyer, however, you will quickly realize that these aren't the best deals to be had in the islands—but they are the closest to the U.S. At the other end of the scale, the straw markets are fun, colorful, and sell cheap souvenirs that make good gifts. Do realize that most of the items are made in Taiwan or Japan. Look in the galleries for more authentic island craftsmanship.

Snorkeling & Scuba Diving
Between the shipwrecks, caves, and coral reefs, Grand Bahama Island offers some of the Bahamas' most varied and vivid underwater scenery. Snorkeling can be anything but tame with blue holes and teeming marine life to discover. Most resorts have snorkeling and scuba facilities. A pioneer in diving, Underwater Explorers Society (UNEXSO) has set a high standard for scuba charters. It is particularly famous for its dolphin dives.

Exploring Nature
Rare birds and stretches of undisturbed wilderness attract nature-lovers to the island's "bush," as the native call it. Explore by foot, bike, kayak, or jeep safari to discover not only the island's natural wonders but its intriguing past. Geological features range from gorgeous sandy beach to limestone caves and pine forests. With the right guide, you'll learn how social and natural history intertwine on the island, where bush medicine and fishing are only two of the ways man still depends on nature.

As one of the northernmost Bahamas, Grand Bahama experiences temperatures dipping into the high 60s and low 70s in January and February, which may require jackets and wet suits. On the upside, the migrant bird population swells and diversifies during that time of year. The other timing consideration is seasonal crowds and the subsequent increase in room rates. High tourist season runs Christmas to Easter, peaking during spring break (late February to mid-April), when the weather is the most agreeable. To avoid the crowds, high prices, heat, and cold, October through mid-December is ideal.

AROUND THE ISLAND

Grand Bahama's appeal lies in its combination of commercial vitality and natural beauty. In the two main towns, Freeport and Lucaya, visitors can find just about everything that bustling Nassau has to offer: resort hotels, fine restaurants, golfing, duty-free shopping complexes, and gambling. But on Grand Bahama, unlike New Providence, the touristy spots take up only a small portion of an island that, on the whole, consists of uninhabited stretches of sand and patches of forest.

Just steps from the action, outdoor opportunities abound, particularly water-related. The island is a mecca for scuba divers and is home of the world-famous Underwater Explorers Society (UNEXSO). Surrounding waters lure anglers from around the world to compete in big game and bonefishing tournaments, such as the Bahamas Wahoo Championship, part of which is held in Grand Bahama each November. For many landlubbers, the island's golf courses—known for their long fairways and water challenges—guarantee year-round entertainment and challenge. A surge in eco-sensitivity has generated an increase in ecotourism opportunities, both land- and water-based. And then there's swimming and snorkeling, perhaps two of the most popular vacation activities in the Bahamas.

Freeport

Freeport is an attractive, planned city of modern shopping centers, resorts, and other convenient tourist facilities. The airport is just a few minutes from downtown, and the harbor is about the same distance.

Sights to See

★ ❼ **Bahamas National Trust Rand Nature Centre.** On 100 acres just minutes from downtown Freeport, ½ mi of trails shows off 130 types of native plants, including many orchid species. The center is the island's birding hot spot, where you might spy a red-tailed hawk or a Cuban emerald hummingbird sipping hibiscus nectar. Don't miss the Flamingo Pond. From its observation deck you can see graceful pink flamingos from the Bahamian island of Inagua. The reserve is named for philanthropist James H. Rand, the former president of Remington Rand, who donated a hospital and library to the island. ⊠ *E. Settlers Way, Freeport* ☎ *242/ 352–5438* 🖙 *$5* ☉ *Weekdays 9–4; guided nature walk by advance reservation* ☉ *Closed Sat.–Sun.*

MOVING TOWARD ECOTOURISM

TO EXPAND TOURISM BEYOND the island's traditional gambling and shopping attractions, Freeport-Lucaya is now marketed as Grand Bahama Island. It makes sense. For beyond the 6-mi strip that comprises the island's metropolis lies another 90 mi of unadulterated wilderness. The balance of the island is given to natural and uncrowded beaches, old-island settlements, and untamed "bush," as the locals call the wilds.

The emphasis on the island's natural attributes began below the water line with **UNEXSO** diving and **The Dolphin Experience.** UNEXSO's preoccupation with extreme diving led to the exploration of the island's unique cave system and the opening of **Lucayan National Park,** a portal to the underground labyrinth accessible to the public. One of the caves holds a cemetery of the island's aboriginals, the Lucayans. The Smithsonian Institution dated the skeletons found there and returned them to their resting place. The park also gives intrepid visitors a taste of the beauty and seclusion of out-of-town beaches. When it opened, the park marked the end of civilization. Rutted dirt roads led to rarely visited time-stilled settlements without electricity and telephones, and long stretches of pine and palmetto forest edged in white sand. In the mid-1990s, as paved roads and telephone wires reached the remote East End, tours began to transport visitors to this other world.

Today, kayaking, biking, snorkeling, boating, jeeping, and cultural safaris help share Grand Bahama Island's most precious treasures with visitors. **East End Adventures,** one of the best, bumps along off-road to the island's past, to the ruins of Old Freetown, the first settlement, and its pristine beach. Along the way, safari participants peer into a blue hole, learn about bush medicine, and hear old-island tales. At McLean's Town, they jump into a boat for a conch-cracking demonstration at remote Sweeting's Cay, followed by home-cooked Bahamian lunch on an uninhabited island beach and blue-hole snorkeling. **Kayak Nature Tours,** another top-notch operation, follows backwater trails to Lucayan National Park and other off-the-beaten-path destinations. Knowledgeable native guides give lessons on island ecology along the way. The company also hosts full-day kayak trips to outer islands.

Parrot Jungle's Garden of the Groves was among the first to capitalize on the natural outdoor beauty of Grand Bahama Island, with lushly landscaped grounds, waterfalls, and a replica of one of the island's first churches. Right in downtown Freeport, the **Bahamas National Trust Rand Nature Centre** was also precursor to ecotourism on Grand Bahama Island. It still provides an oasis for rare birds as well as residents and visitors.

On the island's other extreme, close to West End, **Paradise Cove** also takes you below the waves. Here you can rent snorkeling equipment or kayak to experience the island's best swim-to reef—Deadman's Reef. Its duck pond teems with opportunities for the binoculars crowd.

Ecotourism promises to be a fixture on Grand Bahama Island, attracting a new brand of island vacationer, one more adventurous and ready to experience the less-touted and richer offerings of Grand Bahama's great outback. For more information, contact the **Ecotourism Association of Grand Bahama** (call ☎ 242/373–2485).

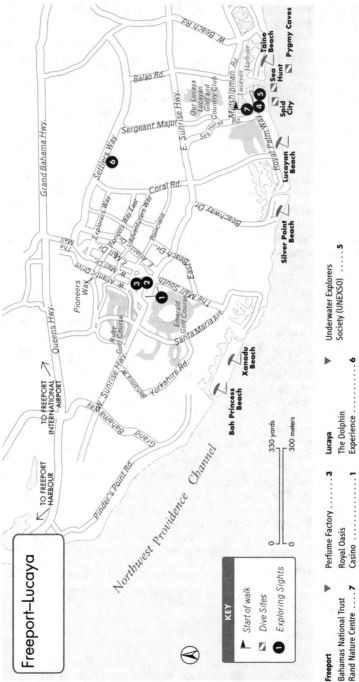

Freeport–Lucaya

KEY

▶ Start of walk

◪ Dive Sites

① Exploring Sights

330 yards

300 meters

Freeport

▶ Bahamas National Trust
Rand Nature Centre **7**

International
Bazaar **2**

▶ Perfume Factory **3**

Royal Oasis
Casino **1**

Lucaya

The Dolphin
Experience **6**

Port Lucaya
Marketplace **4**

▶ Underwater Explorers
Society (UNEXSO) **5**

★ ❷ **International Bazaar.** If the cobbled lanes and jumble of shops and restaurants in this 10-acre complex look like something from a Hollywood soundstage, that's not surprising: It was designed by special-effects artist Charles Perrin in 1967. Having undergone a recent face-lift, it once again exudes the energy and exotica it did when it opened. Sections themed Africa, Greece, China, France, and beyond sell clothing, T-shirts, and tacky souvenirs, along with the island's widest selection of duty-free goods. A new straw market sits behind the stores complex and at the entrance stands a 35-foot *torii* arch, a red-lacquered gate that is a traditional symbol of welcome in Japan. ✉ *W. Sunrise Hwy. and Mall Dr.* ☎ *No phone* 💲 *Free* ☉ *Mon.–Sat. 10–6.*

❸ **Perfume Factory.** The quiet and elegant Perfume Factory is in a replica 19th-century Bahamian mansion—the kind built by Loyalists who settled in the Bahamas after the American Revolution. The interior resembles a tasteful drawing room. This is the home of Fragrance of the Bahamas, a company that produces perfumes, colognes, and lotions using the scents of jasmine, cinnamon, gardenia, spice, and ginger. Take a free five-minute tour of the mixology laboratory. For $30 an ounce, you can blend your own perfume using any of the 35 scents ($15 for 1.5 ounces of blend-it-yourself body lotion). Sniff mixtures until they hit the right combination, then bottle, name, and take home the personalized potion. ✉ *Behind International Bazaar, on access road* ☎ *242/352–9391* ⊕ *www. perfumefactory.com* 💲 *Free* ☉ *Weekdays 10–5:30, Sat. 11–3.*

★ ❶ **Royal Oasis Casino.** Completely renovated with new games and contemporary entertainment, this longstanding Freeport landmark now has a Mediterranean look and feel, with a bell tower replacing the erstwhile trademark onion domes. Gamblers come in droves to try their hand at about 700 slot machines, blackjack, and other gambling temptations. Place a bet on your favorite NFL, NBA, NHL, and NCAA contenders at the digitized Sports Book, surrounded by 18 sports-tuned TVs. The casino is part of the Royal Oasis Golf Resort and adjacent to the International Bazaar. ✉ *W. Sunrise Hwy.* ☎ *242/350–7000, 800/422–2294 in the U.S.* ☉ *Daily 8:30 AM–3 AM.*

Lucaya

Lucaya, on Grand Bahama's southern coast and just east of Freeport, was developed as the island's resort center. These days, it's booming with a megaresort complex, a fine sandy beach, championship golf courses, a first-class dive operation, and Port Lucaya's marina facilities. There's promise of a new casino opening "any day now," which translates into "once the red tape has been unraveled."

Sights to See

❻ **The Dolphin Experience.** Encounter Atlantic bottle-nosed dolphins in Sanctuary Bay at one of the world's first and largest dolphin facilities, about 2 mi east of Port Lucaya. A ferry takes you from Port Lucaya to the bay to observe and photograph the animals. If you don't mind getting wet, you can sit on a partially submerged dock or stand waist deep in the water, and one of these friendly creatures will swim up and touch

Fodor's Choice
★

you. You can also engage in one of several swim-with-the-dolphins programs. The Dolphin Experience began in 1987, when it trained five dolphins to interact with people. Later, the animals learned to head out to sea and swim with scuba divers on the open reef. A two-hour dive program is available. Buy tickets for The Dolphin Experience at the Underwater Explorers Society (UNEXSO) in Port Lucaya. Make reservations as early as possible. ⊠ *The Dolphin Experience, Port Lucaya* ☎ *242/373–1250, 242/373–1244, or 800/992–3483* ☏ *242/373–8956* ⊕ *www.unexso.com* ⊠ *2-hr interaction program $69, 2-hr swim program $159, ultimate experience $259* ☉ *Daily 9–5.*

★ ➍ **Port Lucaya Marketplace.** Lucaya's capacious and lively shopping complex—a dozen low-rise, pastel-painted colonial buildings whose style was influenced by traditional island homes—is on the waterfront 4 mi east of Freeport and across the street from a massive resort complex. The shopping center, whose walkways are lined with hibiscus, bougainvillea, and croton, has about 100 well-kept establishments, among them waterfront restaurants and bars, and shops that sell clothes, crystal and china, watches, jewelry, and perfumes. Vendors display crafts in small, brightly painted wooden stalls. The marketplace's centerpiece is **Count Basie Square,** where live bands often perform Bahamian music, jazz, and gospel in the gazebo bandstand. Lively outdoor watering holes line the square. ⊠ *Sea Horse Rd.* ☎ *242/373–8446* ⊕ *www.portlucaya.com* ☉ *Mon.–Sat. 10–6.*

➎ **Underwater Explorers Society (UNEXSO).** One of the world's most respected diving facilities, UNEXSO welcomes more than 50,000 individuals each year and trains hundreds of them in scuba diving. UNEXSO's facilities include an 18-foot-deep training pool with windows that look out on the harbor, changing rooms and showers, docks, equipment rental, and an air-tank filling station. Beginners can take one-day or complete certification courses, and experienced divers can receive specialized training. Vacation packages are available. ⊠ *On the wharf at Port Lucaya Marketplace* ☎ *242/373–1244 or 800/992–3483* ⊕ *www.unexso.com* ⊠ *Dives from $25, resort dives $99, night dives $35, dolphin dives $169* ☉ *Daily 8–5.*

FodorśChoice ★

Beyond Freeport-Lucaya

Grand Bahama Island narrows at picturesque West End, once Grand Bahama's capital and still home to descendants of the island's early settlers.

Little seaside villages, with concrete block houses painted in bright blue and pastel yellow, fill in the landscape between Freeport and West End. Many of these settlements are more than 100 years old. Their names derive from geographical features or the original homesteaders' surnames, and most residents are descendants of these founders. On your way back east, veer left at the Eight Mile Rock settlement intersection to drive along the town's colonial structures. The seaside backroad eventually returns you to the main road.

The East End is Grand Bahama's "back-to-nature" side. The road east from Lucaya is long, flat, and mostly straight. It cuts through vast pine forest to reach McLean's Town, the end of the road. Curly-tailed lizards, raccoons, pelicans, and other native creatures populate this part of the island.

Sights to See

❾ Lucayan National Park. In this 40-acre seaside land preserve, trails and
Fodor'sChoice elevated walkways wind through a natural forest of wild tamarind and
★ gumbo-limbo trees, past an observation platform, a mangrove swamp, sheltered pools containing rare marine species, and what is believed to be the largest explored underwater cave system in the world (7 mi long). You can enter the caves at two access points. One is closed during bat nursing season (June and July). Just 20 mi east of Lucaya, the park contains examples of the island's five ecosystems: beach, sandy or whiteland coppice (hardwood forest), mangroves, rocky coppice, and pine forest. Across the road, trails and boardwalks lead through pine forest and mangrove swamp to Gold Rock Beach, a beautiful, lightly populated strand of white sand, aquamarine sea, and coral reef. Signs along the trail detail the park's distinctive features. ⊠ *Grand Bahama Hwy.* ☎ *242/352–5438* ✉ *$3 (tickets must be purchased in advance at Rand Nature Centre)* ☉ *Daily 8:30–4:30.*

★ ℭ ❽ Parrot Jungle's Garden of the Groves. Some 10,000 varieties of tropical flora, including fruit trees, ferns, bougainvillea, oleander, and chenille plant, flourish at this 12-acre botanical paradise. Birds, alligators, Bahamian raccoons, a playground, and a petting zoo add family appeal. Follow the Main Waterfall Trail to a picture-perfect church on a hill. It is a full-size replica of the chapel at Pine Ridge, one of Grand Bahama's earliest settlements. A small café serves breakfast and dinner daily. ⊠ *Midshipman Rd. and Magellan Dr.* ☎ *242/373–5668* ⊕ *www.gardenofthegroves.com* ✉ *$9.95 adults, $6.95 children* ☉ *Daily 9–4.*

BEACHES

Some 60 mi of magnificent, pristine stretches of sand extend between Freeport-Lucaya and McLean's Town, the island's isolated eastern end. Most are used only by people who live in adjacent settlements along the way. The outlying beaches have no public facilities, so beachgoers often headquarter at one of the local beach bars. Lucaya hotels have their own beaches and watersports activities, and guests at Freeport hotels are shuttled free to nearby beaches. **Xanadu** is a mile-long strip of white sand
Fodor'sChoice with an outdoor bar and watersports concessions. **Taíno** appeals to fam-
★ ilies, watersports enthusiasts, and partyers alike. Its powdery, white sands stretch long and wide, and the beach bars, conch shacks, and watersports concessions provide the makings for a perfect activity-oriented day at the beach.

Local residents prefer the beach at **William's Town,** south of Freeport (off East Sunrise Highway and down Beachway Drive) and east of Xanadu Beach, where sandy solitude is broken only by the occasional passing of horseback riders from Pinetree Stables at the water's edge.

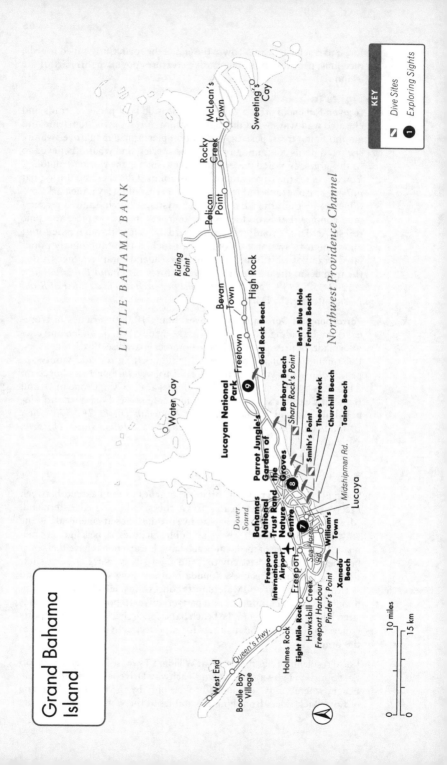

Grand Bahama Island

LITTLE BAHAMA BANK

West End
Boole Bay Village
Queen's Hwy.
Holmes Rock
Eight Mile Rock
Hawksbill Creek
Freeport
Freeport Harbour
Pinder's Point
Freeport International Airport
Xanadu Beach
Sea Horse Rd.
William's Town
Bahamas National Trust Rand Nature Centre 7
Dover Sound
Parrot Jungle's Garden of the Groves 8
Lucaya
Midshipman Rd.
Barbary Beach
Sharp Rock's Point
Smith's Point
Theo's Wreck
Churchill Beach
Taino Beach
Water Cay
Lucayan National Park 9
Freetown
Gold Rock Beach
Bevan Town
Riding Point
High Rock
Ben's Blue Hole
Fortune Beach
Pelican Point
Rocky Creek
McLean's Town
Sweeting's Cay

Northwest Providence Channel

KEY	
⚑	Dive Sites
①	Exploring Sights

0 10 miles

0 15 km

East of Port Lucaya, several delightful beaches run along the **South Shore—Churchill Beach, Smith's Point, Fortune Beach,** and lesser-known **Barbary Beach.** Farther east, at the end of the trail from the Lucayan National Park, you'll find **Gold Rock Beach,** which is only a 20-mi drive from the Lucaya hotels. On the West End, snorkeling beachgoers escape by tour to **Paradise Cove.**

WHERE TO EAT

Grand Bahama Island's restaurants afford rich opportunities for sampling native cuisine. Practically every restaurant has something conch on the menu, for that is both a Bahamian icon and a staple. In the scheme of the Bahamian islands, Grand Bahama ranks slightly below Nassau in both sophistication and price, but well above many of the Out Islands in variety and creativity.

You will find many options in Freeport and Lucaya, from elegant hotel dining rooms and charming waterside cafés to local hangouts and familiar fast-food chains. Menus often combine Continental, American, and Bahamian fare. A native fish fry takes place on Wednesday evening at Smith's Point, east of Lucaya (taxi drivers know the way). Here you can sample fresh fish, sweet-potato bread, conch salad, and all the fixings cooked outdoors at the beach. It's a great opportunity to meet local residents and taste the real thing in Bahamian cuisine–and in what better setting than seaside under the pines and palms. On Friday nights, locals hit Churchill Garden Bar next to the International Bazaar for its well-loved "Mini Crab Fest," featuring land crab dishes indigenous to Andros Island and Gully Wash—a local libation consisting of green coconut juice, sweetened condensed milk, and gin. An automatic 15% gratuity is added to most dining tabs. For general information and price categories, *see* Dining *in* Smart Travel Tips A to Z at the front of the book.

WHAT IT COSTS In U.S. dollars				
$$$$	**$$$**	**$$**	**$**	**¢**
AT DINNER	over $40	$30–$40	$20–$30	$10–$20	under $10

Prices are per person for a main course at dinner.

Freeport

American

¢–$$ ✕**Café Michel's.** Stop by this unpretentious bistro for a light meal or snack. Whereas the alfresco tables, with red umbrellas and tablecloths, place you in an ideal people-watching location just off the Bazaar's main promenade, the café's cozy interior is more intimate. The menu has American and Bahamian dishes such as cracked conch, hamburger, fried chicken, and lobster tail. ⊠ *International Bazaar* ☎ *242/352–2191* ▭ *AE, MC, V.*

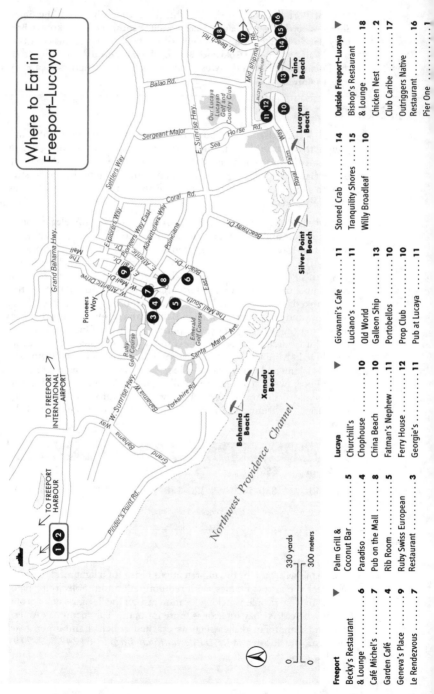

Where to Eat in Freeport-Lucaya

330 yards
300 meters

Freeport ▶

Becky's Restaurant
& Lounge **6**
Café Michel's **7**
Garden Café **4**
Geneva's Place **9**
Le Rendezvous **7**
Palm Grill &
Coconut Bar **5**
Paradiso **4**
Pub on the Mall **8**
Rib Room **5**
Ruby Swiss European
Restaurant **3**

Lucaya ▶

Churchill's **11**
Chophouse **10**
China Beach **10**
Fatman's Nephew **11**
Ferry House **12**
Georgie's **11**
Giovanni's Cafe **11**
Luciano's **11**
Old World **13**
Galleon Ship **13**
Portobellos **10**
Prop Club **10**
Pub at Lucaya **11**
Stoned Crab **14**
Tranquility Shores **15**
Willy Broadleaf **10**

Outside Freeport-Lucaya ▶

Bishop's Restaurant
& Lounge **18**
Chicken Nest **2**
Club Caribe **17**
Outriggers Native
Restaurant **16**
Pier One **1**

Bahamian

★ ¢-$$ ✕ **Becky's Restaurant & Lounge.** This popular eatery opens at 7 AM and may be the best place in town to fuel up before a full day of gambling or shopping. Its diner-style booths provide a comfortable backdrop for the inexpensive menu of traditional Bahamian and American food, from conch salad and steamed mutton to steak or a BLT. Pancakes, eggs, and special Bahamian breakfasts—"stew" fish, "boil" fish, or chicken souse (the latter two are both lime-seasoned soups), with johnnycake or grits—are served all day. ⊠ *E. Beach Dr. and E. Sunrise Hwy.* ☎ *242/352–5247* ⊟ *D, MC, V.*

★ ¢-$ ✕ **Geneva's Place.** Geneva's sets the standard for home-cooked Bahamian food. The interior is nothing fancy: a former-life Italian restaurant whose brick walls have been painted light blue, a canal-scene mural, wrought-iron grating, and grape leaves. Cook and owner Geneva Munroe will prepare your grouper broiled, steamed, or fried; your pork chops fried or steamed; your conch cracked, or, for breakfast, stewed. Everything comes with a big plate of side dishes. The peas 'n' rice are fantastic. ⊠ *E. Mall Dr. and Kipling La.* ☎ *242/352–5085* ⊟ *D, MC, V.*

Continental

$$-$$$ ✕ **Rib Room.** In a handsome wood-trimmed setting brightened by banks of windows, enjoy prime rib, juicy porterhouse, chateaubriand for two, or seafood dishes such as lobster bisque and salmon. Resort guests and outsiders alike come here for the some of the best beef on the island. ⊠ *Crowne Plaza Country Club at Royal Oasis Golf Resort & Casino* ☎ *242/350–7000* ⌘ *Reservations essential* ⊟ *AE, D, DC, MC, V* ☾ *No lunch.*

$-$$ ✕ **Paradiso.** Royal Oasis Resort's newest signature restaurant excels at gourmet Italian cuisine. Cozy up in one of the tall booths and choose from such creations as veal saltimbocca, osso buco, fettucine *pescatore* (with lobster, shrimp, conch, scallops, and fish), and filet wrapped in pancetta. ⊠ *Crowne Plaza Tower at Royal Oasis* ☎ *242/352–7000* ⌘ *Reservations essential* ⊟ *AE, D, DC, MC, V* ☾ *Closed Sun. No lunch.*

$-$$ ✕ **Ruby Swiss European Restaurant.** The extensive Continental menu has seafood, steak, veal, and an all-you-can-eat spaghetti bar. Specialties include steak Dianne (flamed with cognac), Wiener schnitzel, lobster thermidor, and desserts flambéed tableside. The wine list's 50-odd varieties represent six countries. Dinnertime guitar music adds a romantic touch to the bustling dining hall scene. Snacks are served into the wee hours, making this a good place to come after hitting the Royal Oasis Casino, nearby. ⊠ *W. Sunrise Hwy., across from Crowne Plaza Tower at Royal Oasis* ☎ *242/352–8507* ⊟ *AE, D, DC, MC, V.*

Eclectic

¢-$$$ ✕ **Pub on the Mall.** You have four options at this spot across from International Bazaar called Ranfurly Circus, which is actually four restaurants clustered together. **The Prince of Wales Lounge** (☎ *242/352–2700*), an authentic English-style pub, serves fish-and-chips, sandwiches, steaks, sweet-and-sour baby back ribs, and draft ale in a medieval setting. **Islander's Roost Steak House** (☎ *242/352–5110*) offers a meat-lover's menu of steak *au poivre,* T-bones, porterhouse for two, and veal cutlets in a relaxed setting festooned with colorful Junkanoo masks and costumes. A third restaurant, **Silvano's** (☎ 242/352–5111), serves a wide selection of Italian-style fish, pasta, and meat in a circular sunshine-yellow dining room. Specialties include table-flamed filet mignon, veal scallopine, vegetable lasagna, and linguine al pesto. **The Red Dog Sports Bar** (☎ 242/352–2700) has a friendly if sometimes boisterous atmosphere and four TV screens, including a 96-inch monster screen. Most people go for the pizza. ⊠ *Ranfurly Circus, opposite International Bazaar* ▤ *AE, D, MC, V* ☉ *Islander's Roost is closed Sun.; the summer schedule varies from year to year.*

$$ ✕ **Garden Café.** Opening onto the Royal Oasis Resort Casino for a view of the action, it serves buffet-style meals all day. The dinner buffet includes hot, fresh-made Bahamian and international entrées, along with carved prime rib, salad and dessert bars, cold cuts, and soups. ⊠ *Casino at Royal Oasis Resort & Casino* ☎ 242/350–7000 ▤ *AE, D, DC, MC, V.*

$ ✕ **Le Rendezvous.** This sidewalk café epitomizes the International Bazaar's cosmopolitan flair, covering all of the ethnic bases—Italian, Mexican, East Indian, Caribbean, Thai, Indonesian, and Bahamian. Try curried veg-rolls or Bangkok stuffed shrimp for an appetizer; grouper piccata or Thai stir-fry for the main course. End your meal with a shot of flavored rum. ⊠ *International Bazaar* ☎ 242/352–9610 ▤ *AE, D, MC, V.*

Seafood

$–$$ ✕ **Palm Grill and Coconut Bar.** Off the lobby at Royal Oasis Golf Resort & Casino, this stylish bistro offers seating outdoors at teak tables or inside looking out at the pool through floor-to-ceiling windows. The focus is on seafood of all types, like crab cakes, cracked conch, and snapper. Its all-day (11:30–11) menu runs the gamut from sandwiches and pizza to New York strip steak and seafood crepes Newburg. ⊠*Crowne Plaza Tower at Royal Oasis Golf Resort & Casino* ☎ 242/350–7000 ▤ *AE, MC, V.*

Lucaya

American

$$–$$$$ ✕ **Churchill's Chophouse.** Walk through the handsome wood piano bar to a dining room that evokes the plantation era with white wainscoting and French windows. The atrium ceiling over the circular room illuminates Bahamian life with mural scenes and heavy chandeliers. As elegant as the setting, the menu focuses on beef, but escapes single-mindedness with herb-crusted rack of lamb, potato-crusted sea bass with cranberry port reduction, a lobster surf-and-turf, and other dishes of equal sophistication. ⊠ *Westin Lighthouse Pointe, Our Lucaya Beach & Golf Resort* ☎ 242/373–1333 ▤ *AE, D, DC, MC, V* ☉ *No lunch.*

$–$$ ✕ **Prop Club.** Spare bits of recovered aircraft wreckage and brightly painted chairs accent this casual resort hangout, which becomes a lively dance floor by night. Giant glass-paned garage doors open to make this an indoor-outdoor place to dine and party on the beach. The menu is reasonably casual, with offerings like pizza, Cajun chicken sandwich, blackened grouper, and baby back ribs. ⊠ *Westin Breakers Cay, Our Lucaya Beach & Golf Resort* ☎ 242/373–1333 ▤ *AE, D, DC, MC, V.*

¢–$$ ✕ **Tranquility Shores.** Opened in 2003 where Kaptain Kenny's closed a couple of years prior, it serves the same primary purpose—a place for visitors staying off the beach to come and station their day of fun in the sand. Besides a complete menu of watersports activities, it serves a well-rounded selection of American and Bahamian culinary favorites such as Philly cheese steak sandwich, conch fritters, grilled grouper, drunken wahoo (local fish fried with Bahamian-brewed Kalik beer batter), and lamb chops. Go for Friday's happy hour party 5–9 and enjoy free hors d'oeuvres and drink specials. ⊠ *Taíno Beach, 5 Jolly Roger Dr.* ☎ *242/374–4460* ⊕ *www.tranquilityshores.com* ⊟ *AE, D, MC, V* ⊗ *Mon.*

¢–$ ✕ **Old World Galleon Ship.** Eat at the ship-shaped bar or at wooden tables looking out at the beach. Fare is beach-style American, including hamburgers, conch burgers, Cajun shrimp, barbecue ribs, and panfried grouper. Call ahead for reservations and free transportation. Sunday through Friday nights, a bonfire feast with chicken, ribs, and all the fixings, live music, and drinks costs $50 per adult, $40 for children. ⊠ *Pirates of the Bahamas Theme Park, 5 Jolly Roger Dr.* ☎ *242/373–8456* ⊟ *AE, D, MC, V.*

Bahamian

★ ¢–$$ ✕ **Fatman's Nephew.** Owner Stanley Simmons named his restaurant for the two rotund uncles who taught him the trade. One of the better spots to dine in Port Lucaya, this place serves substantial Bahamian fare. The regular menu is somewhat limited, featuring local dishes such as Bahamian turtle, cracked conch, and curried mutton. A blackboard listing a full complement of daily seafood specials widens the offerings. The best seating is on the L-shape outdoor terrace overlooking the waterway and marina. ⊠ *Port Lucaya Marketplace* ☎ *242/373–8520* ⊟ *AE, D, MC, V.*

★ ¢–$$ ✕ **Georgie's.** Sit alfresco at this pleasant, casual spot on the harbor at Port Lucaya Marketplace; it's open for breakfast, happy hour and snacks, lunch, and dinner. Local favorites such as barbecue chicken, conch fritters, lobster, and grouper come with delicious cole slaw and peas 'n' rice. Georgie's cracked conch is the real thing. Inside, the decor is plain, but refreshingly air-conditioned. ⊠ *Port Lucaya Marketplace* ☎ *242/ 373–8513* ⊟ *AE, D, MC, V.*

Contemporary

$–$$$ ✕ **Ferry House.** The windowed dining room of this bright restaurant hangs
Fodor'sChoice over the water just outside the Port Lucaya Marketplace. Its changing
★ menu, always well executed, leans toward the experimental with dishes like grilled grouper with cardamom carrot purée, rack of lamb with herbed goat cheese, and roasted squab breast. A daily tasting menu includes seven courses for $75. Inside Bell Channel, Ferry House serves as the main restaurant for the nearby Pelican Bay at Lucaya resort. ⊠ *Port Lucaya* ☎ *242/373–1595* ⊟ *AE, MC, V* ⊗ *No lunch Sat. and Sun.*

Continental

$$–$$$$ ✕ **Luciano's.** Linens, soft candlelight, and a twinkling view of the har-
Fodor'sChoice bor add to the glamour and romance of this sophisticated, second-story
★ Port Lucaya restaurant. Classic Continental specialties include *filet au poivre* (fillet with peppercorn sauce), grouper almondine, stuffed quail, and chateaubriand for two, served in the formal, subdued dining room or on the veranda overlooking the marina. For a big finish, order the

flamed crêpes suzette. ⊠ *Port Lucaya Marketplace* ☎ *242/373–9100* 🖃 *AE, D, MC, V* ⊗ *Closed Sun.*

Eclectic

★ **$$$$** ✕ **Willy Broadleaf.** For an adventure in dining, graze the multicultural buffet line here. Dine in a Mediterranean marketplace, African village, maharajah's dining hall, Mexican courtyard, or Egyptian market. Sample global dishes such as wild boar sausage, tandoori chicken, Greek stew, pork dumplings, and marvelous desserts. Friday and Saturday is seafood buffet night. The restaurant is open for all meals. ⊠ *Westin Breaker's Cay, Our Lucaya Beach & Golf Resort* ☎ *242/373–1333* 🖃 *AE, DC, MC, V.*

English

¢–**$$** ✕ **Pub at Lucaya.** On the Port Lucaya waterfront, this amiable pub has a reputation for dependable English fare, such as bangers 'n' mash and shepherd's and steak-and-ale pies. You also can't go wrong with the frenched lamb chops, Bahamian lobster tail, or strip sirloin. Lunchtime brings burgers, pasta, and sandwiches. The nautical decor incorporates antiques, heavy rustic tables, and ersatz Tiffany lamps suspended from a wood-beam ceiling. Ask for a table on the outside terrace. ⊠ *Port Lucaya Marketplace* ☎ *242/373–8450* 🖃 *AE, DC, MC, V.*

Italian

$–$$ ✕ **Giovanni's Cafe.** Tucked away under the bougainvillea at Port Lucaya Marketplace, this corner café evokes a bit of Italy. As you relax on the patio or study the giant mural of an Italian waterway inside the café, treat yourself to local seafood such as lobster in white wine cream sauce and pan-fried grouper in lemon-wine sauce. Full-flavored, classic Italian dishes include spaghetti carbonara and chicken marsala. ⊠ *Port Lucaya Marketplace* ☎ *242/373–9107* 🖃 *AE, MC, V* ⊗ *Closed Sun.*

★ **$–$$** ✕ **Portobellos.** The house specialty, seafood spaghetti, unites the best of the Bahamian seas with Mediterranean flair. Other imaginative dishes, all served on colorful dishware, include lobster and asparagus ravioli, grilled marinated veal, and penne with veal and spinach. Sit indoors among classic stone arches or outdoors with a view of the ocean. ⊠ *Westin Breakers Cay, Our Lucaya Beach & Golf Resort* ☎ *242/373–1333* 🖃 *AE, D, DC, MC, V.*

Pan-Asian

★ **$–$$** ✕ **China Beach.** Food in this elegant dining room with its exhibition kitchen extends far beyond Chinese, incorporating elements of Vietnamese, Korean, Thai, Indonesian, Malaysian, and other Pacific Rim styles. From the monthly changing menu, sample sushi, Japanese dumplings, seafood teppanyaki, Thai chicken, and other Asian specialties. ⊠ *Westin Breakers Cay, Our Lucaya Beach & Golf Resort* ☎ *242/373–1333* 🖃 *AE, D, DC, MC, V.*

Seafood

$$ ✕ **Stoned Crab.** This long-standing, pyramidal-roof restaurant faces one of the island's loveliest stretches of sand, Taíno Beach. Don't miss the scrumptiously sweet stone crab claws and lobsters, both locally caught.

Crabs of all varieties are the specialty; try stone and snow crab, stuffed crab, and crab cake in the crab sampler. Other specialties include swordfish, grouper, and yellowfin tuna. The sound of the waves beckons you onto the patio. ⊠ *Taíno Beach* ☎ *242/373–1442* ▭ *AE, D, MC, V* ⊘ *No lunch.*

Outside Freeport-Lucaya

Get out of town for a taste of true Bahamian cooking. Many of the island's far-flung restaurants provide courtesy shuttles from hotels.

Bahamian

★ ¢–$ ✕ **Bishop's Restaurant & Lounge.** A longtime favorite of locals and visitors who venture out into the East End's settlements, it serves all the Bahamian favorites with homemade goodness and a view of the sea. The cracked conch is light and crunchy; the peas 'n' rice full-flavored. ⓕ *Box F 42029, High Rock* ☎ *242/353–4515* ▭ *D.*

¢–$ ✕ **Outriggers Native Restaurant.** For Bahamian food fixed by Bahamians, head east to the generational property of an old island family, just beyond Taíno Beach. Stop at Gretchen Wilson's place for cracked conch, lobster tail, and barbecue chicken down-home style. You'll feel as though you're dining in someone's spotlessly clean home. Wednesday night the quiet little settlement comes to life when Outriggers throws its famous weekly fish fry. In winter, the Outriggers Beach Club, across the street, serves light lunch. ⊠ *Smith's Point* ☎ *242/373–4811* ▭ *No credit cards* ⊘ *Closed Sun. and for lunch in off-season.*

¢ ✕ **Chicken Nest.** At West End, this simple, home-style spot has the nononsense menu of cousins Lovie and Rosie Nixon, including fish, fritters, conch salad, and homemade sweet-potato bread. You can shoot pool while you wait for your order or sit at the bar, where, if you order a hard drink, you get the bottle. ⊠ *Bayshore Rd., West End* ☎ *242/346–6440* ▭ *No credit cards* ⊘ *Closed Mon.*

Seafood

★ $–$$ ✕ **Pier One.** Observe Lucayan Harbour's cruise-ship activity over lunch, sunset over cocktails, or the frenzied feeding of sharks over dinner. Shark—prepared blackened, curried with bananas, panfried, and in spicy fritters—is the specialty of the house. Steak, grouper, and lobster also star on the extensive menu. In season, call ahead to reserve an outdoor table, or dine inside, surrounded by aquariums and nautical paraphernalia. Swarms of fish and sharks frenzy for handouts at 7, 8, and 9 PM. ⊠ *Lucayan Harbour* ☎ *242/352–6674* ▭ *AE, D, MC, V* ⊘ *No lunch Sun.*

¢–$ ✕ **Club Caribe.** Small and very casual, this beachside haunt is an ideal place to headquarter your day at the beach. Unwind with a Bahama Mama and try the local fare, such as conch fritters, grilled grouper, or barbecued ribs. You can also get American burgers and sandwiches. Free transportation is provided to and from your hotel (reservations are essential). ⊠ *Mather Town, off Doubloon Rd. on Spanish Main Dr.* ☎ *242/373–6866* ▭ *AE, D, MC, V* ⊘ *Closed Mon.*

WHERE TO STAY

Once a leader in exotic, glamourous resort-casino complexes, Grand Bahama is rising again to set standards with complete makeovers in Freeport, Lucaya, and West End. You can choose from among Grand Bahama's approximately 4,000 rooms and suites, ranging from attractive one- and two-bedroom units in sprawling resort complexes to practical apartments with kitchenettes to comfortable rooms in economy-oriented establishments. The more extravagant hotels in Freeport and Lucaya include the Royal Oasis Golf Resort & Casino (formerly Bahamia and Bahamas Princess); the sprawling, three-pronged Our Lucaya and nearby Pelican Bay Viva Wyndham Fortuna Beach, an all-inclusive east of Lucaya; and the West End's elegant Old Bahama Bay. The latter, like many Grand Bahama resorts, caters to the boating crowd.

Small apartment complexes and time-share rentals are economical alternatives, especially if you're planning to stay for more than a few days. If you value proximity to the beach, stay at Old Bahama Bay, Xanadu, Our Lucaya, Island Seas, or Viva Wyndham Fortuna Beach, which are right on the beach. The Royal Oasis Resort & Casino built its own beach at a zero-entry pool with a sand bottom. UNEXSO, Grand Bahama Island's scuba central, and Port Lucaya Marketplace are within easy walking distance of Lucaya's hotels.

The larger hotels offer honeymoon, golfing, gambling, scuba, and other packages. Families will find that many hotels offer baby-sitting services and children's programs. Some lodgings allow children under 12 to stay in your room for free and may not charge you for a crib or roll-away bed.

A 6%–12% tax is added to your hotel bill, representing resort and government levies. Rates from April 15 through December 14 tend to be 25%–30% lower than during the rest of the year. For general information and price categories, *see* Lodging *in* Smart Travel Tips A to Z at the front of the book.

WHAT IT COSTS In U.S. dollars				
$$$$	**$$$**	**$$**	**$**	**¢**
FOR 2 PEOPLE over $400	$300–$400	$200–$300	$100–$200	under $100

All prices are for a standard double room in high season, excluding 6%–12% tax and 10%–15% service charge. Note that the government hotel tax doesn't apply to guesthouses with fewer than four rooms.

Freeport

$$ 🎌 **Island Seas Resort.** If you're looking for fun on the beach away from urban bustle, this time-share property accommodates nonmembers. Balconies overlook the flowery courtyard, where thatched-roofed Co-CoNuts Grog & Grub and a free-form pool with waterfalls and swim-up bar create the centerpiece. The beach, used by guests from other non-beachside resorts, is busy with watersports activity. One- and two-bedroom rooms are done in bright modern island style. The property has 117 rooms, but not all are included in the open rental plan. ⬠ *Box F 44735, William's Town, Freeport* ☎ *242/373–1271* 🖷 *242/373–1275* ⊕ *www.islandseas.com* ↦ *50 rooms* ⚸ *Restaurant, pool, beach, boating, parasailing, bicycles, basketball, horseback riding, volleyball, bar* ▭ *D, MC, V.*

★ $ 🏨 **Best Western Castaways.** Near the action in Freeport, this property was gutted and re-created as a much nicer version of its former self. The prettily coral rock–accented lobby introduces four stories of rooms in bamboo and earth and floral tones. Family friendliness is underscored by a playground next to the pool, and beach shuttle is provided. The restaurant is open only for its famous breakfast but there is a wide selection of other dining options within easy walking distance. ⬠ *Box F 42629, Freeport* ☎ *242/352–6682 or 800/700–4752* 🖷 *242/352–5087* ⊕ *www.castaways-resort.com* ↦ *97 rooms, 21 suites* ⚸ *Restaurant, pool, 2 bars, nightclub, baby-sitting, playground, laundry facilities* ▭ *AE, D, MC, V.*

$ 🏨 **Royal Islander.** All the amenities without the sticker shock: this two-story, tin-roof, motel-style property is near the International Bazaar and Royal Oasis Casino and provides free scheduled shuttle service to Xanadu Beach. The rooms have light-wood and rattan furnishings, lively tropical fabrics, framed pastel prints, and tile floors on the lower level. You'll find carpeted floors upstairs, where no-smoking rooms are available. An inviting white-and-floral lobby faces the spacious pool area. ⬠ *Box F 42549, East Mall Dr., Freeport* ☎ *242/351–6000* 🖷 *242/351–3546* ↦ *100 rooms* ⚸ *Dining room, snack bar, pool, Ping-Pong, bar, shop, travel services, no-smoking rooms* ▭ *AE, D, MC, V.*

★ $ 🏨 **Royal Oasis Golf Resort & Casino.** Two sister resorts make up this 1,000-acre complex with an impressive selection of amenities—two 18-hole championship golf courses, a fitness center and spa, a children's club with a kids-only restaurant, and a massive casino. The sand beach–entry pool with sand bottom and slides brings the beach to the middle of town. If you prefer the ocean beach, hop on the free shuttle to a nearby beach club.

Crowne Plaza Tower. Next door to the casino and close to International Bazaar, this 400-room, 10-story building is the more elegant of the two properties, geared toward couples and high-rolling gamblers. A dramatic fountain-dominated lobby and rooms dressed in fall tones and old plantation style infuse this hotel with good taste.

Crowne Plaza Country Club. More conducive to families and golfers, this 565-room property is home to its own waterpark. Man-made rock formations frame the second pool with a swim-up bar and hot tub. Two- and three-story guest-room wings radiate outward like the spokes of a wheel from the circular deck around the pool area. Decorated much like Crowne Plaza Tower's rooms, but smaller, they represent one of the island's greatest values. ⬠ *Box F 2623, Freeport* ☎ *242/350–7000 or 800/227–6963* 🖷 *242/350–7002* ⊕ *www.theroyaloasis.com* ↦ *914 rooms, 49 suites* ⚸ *6 restaurants, pizzeria, room service, in-room safes, some kitchens, refrigerators, 2 18-hole golf courses, 9 tennis courts, 3 pools, gym, 2 hair*

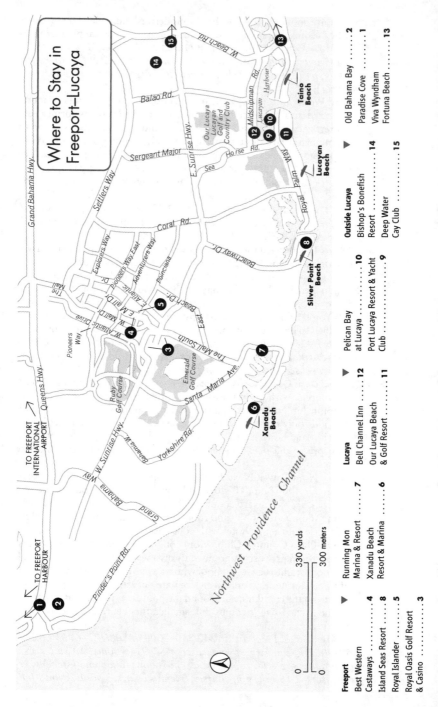

Where to Stay in Freeport–Lucaya

Freeport

Best Western
Castaways **4**
Island Seas Resort **8**
Royal Islander **5**
Royal Oasis Golf Resort
& Casino **3**

Running Mon
Marina & Resort **7**
Xanadu Beach
Resort & Marina **6**

Lucaya

Bell Channel Inn **12**
Our Lucaya Beach
& Golf Resort **11**

Pelican Bay
at Lucaya **10**
Port Lucaya Resort & Yacht
Club **9**

Outside Lucaya

Bishop's Bonefish
Resort **14**
Deep Water
Cay Club **15**

Old Bahama Bay **2**
Paradise Cove **1**
Viva Wyndham
Fortuna Beach **13**

330 yards
300 meters

salons, 2 outdoor hot tubs, spa, snorkeling, boating, parasailing, waterskiing, billiards, Ping-Pong, volleyball, 6 bars, casino, dance club, showroom, children's programs (ages 12 and under), playground, Internet, convention center, travel services ▤ AE, D, DC, MC, V.

$ ▦ **Xanadu Beach Resort & Marina.** Only a few minutes from town, the property's tower, pool wing, and villas overlook the oval pool and fountain, marina, parking lot, or beach. Rooms show their age but have been spruced up with a new designer look. Coconut palms sway at the wide, gorgeous beach, a three-minute walk from the hotel. Come here for watersports and beach volleyball. An on-site watersports concession has all the wet stuff your vacation needs. ⬡ *Box F 2438, Sunken Treasure Dr., Freeport* ☎ *242/352–6782* 🖷 *242/352–6299* ⊕ *www.xanadubeachhotelandmarina.com* ⇆ *137 rooms, 49 suites* ⌂ *2 restaurants, 3 tennis courts, pool, massage, beach, dive shop, dock, snorkeling, boating, jet skiing, parasailing, fishing, Ping-Pong, volleyball, 3 bars, shop, baby-sitting, laundry facilities, meeting rooms* ▤ AE, D, MC, V.

¢ ▦ **Running Mon Marina & Resort.** If boating is your thing, this pumpkin orange stucco hotel with natural-wood decking is ideal. Each room in this waterfront resort has a view of the 70-slip marina. Boat owners will appreciate the haul-and-launch facility, on-site mechanics, and repair services. Ask the dockmaster to arrange a deep-sea fishing charter, or take a dip in the small pool framed by oleanders and a harbor view. A white baby grand piano is the elegant centerpiece of Mainsail, the resort's restaurant and lounge. ⬡ *208 Kelly Ct. (Box F 42663), Freeport* ☎ *242/352–6834 or 800/932–4959* 🖷 *242/352–6835* ⊕ *www.running-mon-bahamas.com* ⇆ *31 rooms, 1 suite* ⌂ *Restaurant, in-room safes, refrigerators, cable TV, pool, boating, jet skiing, marina, fishing, bicycles, bar, video game room, shops, playground, laundry facilities, meeting rooms, travel services, no-smoking rooms* ▤ AE, D, MC, V.

Lucaya

$$–$$$ ▦ **Our Lucaya Beach & Golf Resort.** Grand Bahama's grandest resort
Fodor's Choice spreads three hotels along 7½ acres of soft-sand beach. The accent here
★ is on dramatic play-area water features and golf. The property has a 19,500-square-foot casino, twelve restaurants, lounges, a children's camp, a first-rate spa, and a shopping complex.

Sheraton. Geared toward family vacationers, this resort focuses on a water park with a sugar-mill ruin theme, complete with a zero-entry pool and water slide. The headquarters for children's programs is nearby: a bright, circular building with peekaboo windows for undetected parental spying. The resort's public areas and 511 rooms have a tropical Miami Beach flair. Sheraton offers an all-inclusive plan including alcoholic beverages year-round.

Westin Breakers Cay. The 10-floor high-rise resort curves like a wavy cruise ship between the other two, with rooms and suites, restaurants, a long lap pool, and a small half-moon infinity pool encasing a swim-up bar on the beach.

Westin Lighthouse Pointe. The property's all-water-view rooms and suites are in two-story structures built to replicate a Caribbean-style plantation manor. The 21 lanai suites come with a butler. A half-moon infinity pool clasps the property and visually blends into the ocean beyond. Stay here if you want to be farther from the bustle. ⊠ *Sea Horse La., Lucaya* ☎ *242/373–1333, 877/687–5822 in the U.S.* 🖷 *242/373–8804* ⊕ *www.westin.com/ourlucaya or www.sheraton.com/ ourlucaya* ➷ *1,371 rooms and suites* ⚿ *14 restaurants, coffee shop, room service, in-room data ports, in-room safes, refrigerators, 2 18-hole golf courses, 4 tennis courts, pro shop, 9 pools, gym, spa, beach, snorkeling, boating, waterskiing, basketball, horseshoes, volleyball, 8 bars, casino, shops, children's programs (ages 2½–12), concierge floor, business services, meeting rooms, travel services* ▤ *AE, D, DC, MC, V.*

$
FodorśChoice
★

🏨 **Pelican Bay at Lucaya.** Experience the romance of the Caribbean with European design. A step above typical small-inn Bahamian accommodations, Pelican Bay has a clean, modern appeal and accommodations that overflow with character, with decorative elements collected from around the world. Town houses are fancifully trimmed in West Indian gingerbread and latticework. Smartly furnished rooms and suites overlook the pool and whirlpool, the channel, and the marina. The newest suites have extras like rain showers, espresso machines, and DVD players. Pelican Bay is next door to UNEXSO, which makes it popular with divers. Only steps away from Port Lucaya Marketplace, the resort also has its own marina nearby and a ferry shuttle to Taíno Beach. Deluxe rooms include Continental breakfast at a higher rate. ⌂ *Box F 42654, Royal Palm Way, Freeport* ☎ *242/373–9550 or 800/600–9192* 🖷 *242/ 373–9551* ⊕ *www.pelicanbayhotel.com* ➷ *90 rooms, 96 suites* ⚿ *2 restaurants, in-room safes, some microwaves, refrigerators, 3 pools, outdoor hot tub, marina, bar, library, laundry facilities, meeting room, no-smoking rooms* ▤ *AE, D, MC, V.*

$ 🏨 **Port Lucaya Resort & Yacht Club.** Members can dock at the 50-slip marina; others pull in next door at Port Lucaya Marina. Golf carts transport guests to 10 brightly painted buildings around the Olympic-size swimming pool, hot tub, and restaurant. The rooms have garden, pool, or marina views, punctuated sparingly with rattan furniture, tile floors, large wall mirrors, and tropical floral patterns. The walk to the beach takes less than 10 minutes. At night, Port Lucaya Marketplace's celebratory sounds spill into buildings 7, 8, 9, and 10, and guests can enjoy the festivities from their balconies. ⌂ *Box F 42452, Bell Channel Bay Rd., Freeport* ☎ *242/373–6618 or 800/582–2921* 🖷 *242/373–6652* ⊕*www.portlucayaresort.com* ➷*157 rooms, 3 suites* ⚿ *Restaurant, pool, outdoor hot tub, dock, marina, 2 bars, playground, laundry service, no-smoking floors* ▤ *AE, D, MC, V.*

¢ 🏨 **Bell Channel Inn** The location is perfect for the scuba-oriented—right on the water near Port Lucaya with easy access to the island's best downunder sites. The inn has its own dive shop and lodging-dive packages. The dive boat conveniently leaves from behind the hotel and the shop is full-service with equipment rentals and certification courses. Most of the simply furnished rooms are equipped with a small refrigerator; all have a view of the channel and Port Lucaya. The convivial restaurant-bar on property serves seafood and good spirit come happy hour each day. A small pool sits on a wood deck along the water, and the hotel provides free shuttle service to the beach. ⌂*Box F 43817, Freeport* ☎*242/373–1053* 🖷*242/*

373–2886 ⊕ *www.bellchannelinn.com* ⤴ *32 rooms* ⟁ *Restaurant, some refrigerators, pool, dive shop, dock, bar* ⊟ *AE, D, MC, V.*

Outside Freeport-Lucaya

★ **$$$$** ▦ ⑂ **Deep Water Cay Club.** Ideal if you want to get away from it all and angle for bonefish, this private island has Bahamian-style one- and two-bedroom cottages. Activities center around a main lodge with a dining room, self-service bar, and tackle shop. Diversions include beaching, boating, and some of the best bonefishing in the Bahamas. Accommodations are available in three-, four-, or seven-night packages only, including meals, and daily guided fishing excursions. The resort can arrange a charter flight from Florida, which lands at the property's own airstrip. ⊠ *Deep Water Cay* ⌑ *Box 280, Richmond Hill, GA 31324* ☎ *912/756–7071* 🖷 *912/756–3559* ⊕ *www.deepwatercay.com* ⤴ *9 units* ⟁ *Dining room, fans, refrigerators, pool, snorkeling, boating, fishing, bar* ⊟ *No credit cards* ⑂ *All-inclusive.*

$$$$ ▦ **Old Bahama Bay.** Relax and luxuriate in relative seclusion at this hotel
Fodor'sChoice designed principally for boating vacationers. Waterfront suites, one- and
★ two-bedroom, treat you to heavy wood furnishings and a view of the beach through French doors. The suites contain a wet bar, bathrobes, cooking utensils, and a DVD-CD player (with a complimentary library). While endearingly intimate and individual, Old Bahama Bay has all the amenities of a full-grown, self-contained resort, making it one of the Bahamas' top small, marina properties. ⊠ *Box F 42546, West End* ☎ *242/350–6500 or 800/444–9469* 🖷 *242/346–6546* ⊕ *www.oldbahamabay. com* ⤴ *43 junior suites, 4 2-bedroom suites* ⟁ *3 restaurants, in-room safes, microwaves, refrigerators, tennis court, pool, gym, spa, snorkeling, boating, marina, fishing, bicycles, 2 bars, shop* ⊟ *AE, D, MC, V.*

★ **$$$** ▦ ⑂ **Viva Wyndham Fortuna Beach.** Popular with couples and families, this secluded resort provides a casual, low-stress, all-inclusive getaway. One price covers meals, drinks, tips, nonmotorized watersports, nightly entertainment, and other activities. A 1,200-foot private beach bustles with activity. Meals are served buffet style in the huge, gazebo-like dining pavilion or tableside at La Trattoria. Simple rooms in two-story buildings have light-wood furniture, tile floors, and balconies or porches. Kids under age 12 stay free with adults. ⊠ *Churchill Dr. and Doubloon Rd. (Box F 42398), Freeport* ☎ *242/373–4000, 800/996–3426 in the U.S.* 🖷 *242/373–5555* ⊕ *www.vivaresorts.com* ⤴ *276 rooms* ⟁ *2 restaurants, snack bar, in-room safes, 2 tennis courts, pool, aerobics, gym, beach, dive shop, snorkeling, windsurfing, boating, bicycles, archery, boccie, Ping-Pong, bar, dance club, theater, shops, children's programs (ages 4 and up), playground, laundry service, meeting rooms, travel services* ⊟ *AE, D, MC, V* ⑂ *All-inclusive.*

★ **$** ▦ **Bishop's Bonefish Resort.** Stay on the beach in a small community east of Lucaya, without the hefty price tags and bustle of Lucaya. Owned by Bahamian Ruben "Bishop" Roberts, the property comprises eight white-tiled, spacious rooms. Bishop will arrange bonefishing excursions to the East End, feed you at his landmark restaurant, and talk politics with you at the bar. Meal packages are available. ⌑ *Box F 42029, High Rock* ☎ *242/353–4515* 🖷 *242/353–4417* ⊕ *www.gbweekly.com/*

bishopsbonefish ⤴ *7 rooms* ♦ *Restaurant, refrigerators, beach, fishing, bar* ⊟ *AE, MC.*

$ 🖼 **Paradise Cove.** Owned by a local family, Paradise Cove owns a handful of two-bedroom cottages and one-bedroom apartments on the island's best reef. It's the only lodging on Deadman's Reef, quiet and far removed from the resort world. By day, activity mounts as snorkelers arrive by bus. The comfortable, unpretentious accommodations have kitchens. There's a protected stretch of beach, and snorkeling gear is available for a fee. Kayaks are available for guests' use. Staff can arrange spear fishing and other fishing excursions. ⊠ *Deadman's Reef (Box F 42771) Freeport* ☎ *242/349–2677* 🖷 *242/352–5471* ⊕ *www.deadmansreef. com* ⤴ *5 apartments and cottages* ♦ *Snack bar, kitchenettes, in-room VCRs, beach, snorkeling, boating, volleyball, bar* ⊟ *AE, D, MC, V.*

Time-Sharing

Contact any of the following for information about rentals. For information about other time-share houses, apartments, and condominiums, check with the Grand Bahama Island Tourism Board.

Freeport Beach Resort & Club (🖅 Box F 2514, Freeport ☎ 242/352–5371 ⊕ www.freeportresort.com). The 50 suites are in a garden setting close to the International Bazaar and the Royal Oasis Casino. Owners have golf privileges at Royal Oasis courses.

Lakeview Manor Club (🖅 Box F 42699, Freeport ☎ 242/352–9789). The club's 52 studio and one-bedroom units are adjacent to the fairway of the fifth hole of the Ruby Golf Course.

Mayfield Beach and Tennis Club (🖅 Box F 458, Freeport ☎242/352–9776). The rentals here consist of apartments that share a pool, small beach, and tennis court on Port-of-Call Drive at Xanadu Beach.

Ocean Reef Resort and Yacht Club (🖅 Box F 42639, Freeport ☎ 242/373–4661 ⊕ www.oryc.com). These 63 one- to three-bedroom apartments are midway between the International Bazaar and the Lucayan Beach hotels. The resort has a marina and pools.

Vacation Club at Royal Oasis (🖅 Box F 684, Freeport ☎ 242/350–7060). On the grounds of the Crowne Plaza Country Club at Royal Oasis Golf Resort & Casino, efficiencies and one- and two-bedroom apartments allow guests resort privileges.

NIGHTLIFE & THE ARTS

Nightlife

The casino at Royal Oasis Golf Resort is among the island's top attractions. Try your luck with state-of-the-art slot machines, craps and blackjack tables, roulette, and baccarat. Beginners can request a gaming guide, which explains each game's rules (also consult the gambling primer in this book). There's usually weekend entertainment with live music, and drinks are free to table or slots players. Tables open at 10 AM. There's no specific dress code, although bathing suits and bare feet are not permitted. You must be at least 18 years old to go into the casino, and residents of the Bahamas are not permitted to gamble. Photography is prohibited.

For noncasino evening and late-night entertainment, Grand Bahama delivers calypso music, discos, bonfire beach parties, sunset party boats, and live bands for dancing. Nightclubs are generally open from 8 or 9 until 3. Many hotels organize their own nighttime entertainment.

Casinos

★ **Isle of Capri Casino** (✉ Our Lucaya Beach & Golf Resort, Sea Horse La. ☎ 888/687–4753 in the U.S.), a 19,500-square-foot casino opened at the end of 2003, has 400 slot machines, sports betting, and 21 game tables consisting of mini-baccarat, Caribbean stud and three-card poker, craps, blackjack, and roulette. There is also a special "Jewel of The Isle" room, featuring high-limit table games and slot machines. The Cove restaurant serves bistro-style fare. The casino is open from 10 AM until 2 AM daily; slot machines are open 24 hours on weekends.

★ **Royal Oasis Casino** (✉ Royal Oasis Golf Resort & Casino, W. Sunrise Hwy. ☎ 242/350–7000) packs its 28,000 square feet with around 700 slot machines, 27 blackjack tables, 5 craps tables, 4 roulette wheels, 4 Caribbean poker games, and a table each for baccarat and mini-baccarat. In the 360° Tonic bar, 18 sports TVs and a digital Sports Book for betting on games charge the atmosphere. The bar also hosts tournaments and local bands on weekends. An adjacent restaurant offers a view of the gambling. Slots are open daily 8:30 AM–3:30 AM; tables 10 AM–3:30 AM.

Nightclubs

★ **Bahama Mama Cruises** (✉ Superior Watersports ☎ 242/373–7863) has some of the best nightlife in Grand Bahama. In addition to sunset "booze cruises," Bahama Mama offers a surf-and-turf dinner with a colorful "native" show (a local term used to indicate entertainment with a traditional cultural flair); $59 for adults, $39 for children (ages 2–12). The Sunset Cruise and Show is $35. Reservations are essential. The dinner cruise is offered Monday, Wednesday, and Friday 6–9 (October–March) and 6:30–9:30 (April–September); Sunset Cruise and Show runs Monday, Wednesday, and Friday on the same time schedule.

Club Amnesia (✉ Across from International Bazaar on East Mall Dr. ☎ 242/351–2582) is one of the hot spots around International Bazaar that rocks weekend nights with live entertainment and a youthful crowd.

Prop Club Sports Bar & Dance Club (✉ Our Lucaya Beach & Golf Resort ☎ 242/373–1333) hosts live music that propels guests out to the giant dance floor, plus karaoke on Tuesday, sumo wrestling on Wednesday, and a traditional music show every Thursday at 9 PM. Seating is indoors as well as outdoors on the beach. Open daily for lunch and dinner and nightly entertainment.

The Arts

Theater

Freeport Players' Guild (☎ 242/362–8194), a nonprofit repertory company, produces Bahamian and American comedies, musicals, and dramas in the 450-seat Regency Theatre during its September–June season.

CloseUp

SHAKING AND SCRAPING TO THE SOUNDS OF BAHAMIAN MUSIC

THE RADIO CRACKLES, the DJ puts the needle to the vinyl, or the band begins to play. The upbeat pulse of Bahamian music circulates through the room. Suddenly you find yourself moving in place, and then across the floor. At the very least, your toes start tapping, your head begins bouncing side to side, and a smile spreads across your face.

Caribbean music seems to create an undeniably contagious urge to dance. Perhaps it's the strong underlying rhythm, common to most island musics of this region, including the immensely popular *calypso,* originally from Trinidad, and *reggae,* which spread to nearby islands from Jamaica. Both have roots in the drum beats of Africa, which were brought by slaves and spiked with French, British, Spanish, and Portuguese flavors from shipmasters and plantation owners. In the Bahamas, though, the dominant sound is home-grown *soca,* a dance music with a driving percussion and a lilting and gentle quality reminiscent or calypso or Latin meringue.

The fundamental component of soca, calypso, and reggae is the ¼ beat, the base upon which the melody is built. Whereas calypso and reggae emphasize the downbeat, soca music accentuates all four beats evenly—creating tunes that are catchy and easy to dance to. A good Bahamian band can play all three rhythms, often combining them to create a hybrid effect. It's not uncommon to hear a cover of a Bob Marley reggae song in soca style, or a soca-inspired rendition of Harry Belafonte's well-known calypso tune "Maryann," which was written in the Bahamas.

Soca music has many faces. In some cases its closest relative is calypso, other times it's reggae, dub, ragga, or even hip hop. A single keyboard can create soca, or a full symphony orchestra. The formula for most contemporary soca songs is a simple melodic line played on a keyboard or an electric guitar, aggressively rapped lyrics, and that characteristic driving rhythm, played on either a beat machine or a drum.

The drums that are so crucial to Bahamian and Caribbean music come in a myriad of forms. Popular with Caribbean bands are the steel pan, originally constructed out of 55-gallon oil drums, and the conga, often associated with Latin music but played throughout the world. The traditional Bahamian drum is a handmade goatskin-covered instrument. It is the mainstay of another well-known Bahamian sound, **rake and scrape** music.

Rake and scrape is typically made using recycled objects. With a little innovation, household items and even refuse are transformed into percussive tools. An ordinary saw held in a musician's lap, then bent and scraped, becomes an instrument. Plastic juice bottles are filled with pigeon peas, painted in bright colors and turned into maracas. Add a goatskin drum, and you have all you need for a rake and scrape ensemble, although many bands now add a guitar, saxophone, or both.

There's a **Rake and Scrape Festival** each June on Cat Island, in which dozens of bands from all over the Caribbean perform. Some people view the festival as an extremely important event, given that rake and scrape is often seen as a dying art—most young Bahamian musicians seem to prefer electric guitars or keyboards to saws and jugs. To counter this trend, many of the old-time players teach at local schools to keep the tradition alive for the next generation of Bahamians—and future tourists, too.

Grand Bahama Players (☎ 242/373–2299) perform at Regency Theatre, staging cultural productions by Bahamian, West Indian, and North American playwrights.

Port Lucaya Marketplace (⊠ Sea Horse Rd. ☎ 242/373–8446), which opens daily at 10, has a stage that becomes lively after dark, with calypso music and other performances at Count Basie Square (ringed by three popular hangouts: The Corner Bar, The Daiquiri Bar, and The Pub at Port Lucaya).

SPORTS & THE OUTDOORS

Amusement Parks

★ ⓒ **Pirates of the Bahamas** offers watersport rentals, miniature golf (two 18-hole courses), horseshoes, basketball, Ping-Pong, and beach parties Sunday through Friday with live entertainment. There's a playground for the kids. ⊠ *5 Jolly Roger Dr.* ☎ *242/373–8456* ⊘ *Tues., Thurs., Sun. 8:30 AM–9 PM; Mon., Wed., Fri., Sat. 9–5:30.*

ⓒ **Water World** has two scenic, well-maintained 18-hole courses of miniature golf set among waterfalls and water holes, plus a restaurant, 24-lane bowling alley, sports TV room, and ice cream parlor. Planned enhancements include a rollerblading rink, batting cages, and a pool room. ⊠ *E. Sunrise Hwy. and Britannia Blvd.* ☎ *242/373–2197* ⊘ *Daily 10 AM–11 PM.*

Boating & Fishing

Charters

Private boat charters for up to four people cost $250–$500 for a half day and $350 and up for all day. Bahamian law limits the catching of game fish to six dolphinfish, kingfish, or wahoo per person per day.

★ **Capt. Phil & Mel's Bonefishing Guide Services** (⊠ McLean's Town ☎ 242/353–3960 or 877/613–2454 ⊕ www.bahamasbonefishing.net) provides a colorful and expert foray into the specialized world of bonefishing. Cost for a whole day (8 hours) for up to 2 people is $350, transportation included; a half day is $250.

Lucaya Watersports (⊠ Jolly Roger Dr., Lucaya ☎ 242/373–6375 or 242/373–8456 ⊠ Seashore Dr. at Port Lucaya) takes you straight to the big fish aboard an air-conditioned 42-foot fishing yacht. The four-hour Big Game excursion costs $80 per person; the three-hour Bottom Fishing charter costs $45. Four-hour private charters are priced at $500, plus night and shark fishing are available.

Reef Tours Ltd. (⊠ Port Lucaya Marketplace ☎ 242/373–5880) offers sport-fishing for four to six people on custom boats. Equipment and bait are provided free. All vessels are licensed, inspected, and insured. Trips run from 8:30 to 12:30 and from 1 to 5, weather permitting ($85 per angler, $45 per spectator). Full-day trips are also available, as are bottom fishing excursions, glass-bottom boat tours, snorkeling trips, and booze cruises. Reservations are essential.

Marinas

Lucayan Marina Village (⊠ Midshipman Rd., Port Lucaya ☎ 242/373–8888 ⊕ www.lucayanmarinavillage.com) offers complimentary ferry service to Port Lucaya; the marina has 150 slips accommodating boats up to 200 feet long, a fuel dock, customs and immigrations offices, swimming pools, and a bar and grill.

Old Bahama Bay (⊠ West End ☎ 242/350–6500) has 72 slips to accommodate yachts up to 120 feet long. Facilities include a customs and immigration office, fuel, showers, laundry, and electric, cable, and water hookups.

Port Lucaya Marina (⊠ Port Lucaya Marketplace ☎ 242/373–9090) offers a broad range of watersports and has more than 100 slips for vessels no longer than 170 feet.

Running Mon Marina (⊠ Kelly Ct., Freeport ☎ 242/352–6834) has 70 slips for boats up to 130 feet. Marina facilities include port of entry, gas and diesel fuel service, boatyard and on-site mechanics, floating and fixed docks, a 40-ton travel lift (the only one on the island), water and power hookups, a marina store, customs office, charters, laundry facilities, showers, and rest rooms. The boatyard operates weekdays from 7 to 6 and Saturday from 7 to noon. The marina is open daily from 7 to 7.

Xanadu Marina and Beach Resort (⊠ Sunken Treasure Dr., Freeport ☎ 242/352–6783 Ext. 1333) has 400 feet of dockage and 77 slips and is an official port of entry.

Cricket

For a taste of true Bahamian sports, visit the **Lucaya Cricket Club** (⊠ Baloa Rd., Lucaya ☎ 242/373–1460). If you feel like joining in, go to training sessions on Tues., Thurs., or Sun. The clubhouse has a bar, gym, and changing rooms. Tournaments take place in April and November.

Fitness Centers

Grand Bahama Fitness Centre (⊠ E. Atlantic Dr. off E. Sunrise Hwy., Freeport ☎ 242/352–7867) offers weight and cardio machines, aerobic and yoga classes, and a free nursery. Fee is $7 per day, $20 per week.

Olympic Fitness Center (⊠ Coral Beach Hotel, Lucaya ☎ 242/373–8181) has Universal machines, weights, and aerobics classes overlooking the hotel's pool. The fee is $5 per day, $15 per week.

Royal Oasis Golf Resort & Casino (⊠ W. Sunrise Hwy., Freeport ☎ 242/350–7000) has a fitness facility at its poolside spa. Nonguests pay a $20 fee to use the gym and pool facilities.

★ **Senses Spa** (⊠ Our Lucaya Beach & Golf Resort, Lucaya ☎ 242/350–5281) has state-of-the-art cardio and exercise equipment, including free weights, a spinning studio, and fitness classes. The fee is $10 for guests and $15 for nonguests per day, which includes use of sauna facilities.

Golf

Because Grand Bahama is such a large island, it can afford long fairways puddled with lots of water and fraught with challenge. Four championship golf courses (two are at the Royal Oasis Golf Resort, two are at Our Lucaya) and one 9-hole course constitute a major attraction on the island. The Butch Harmon School of Golf at Our Lucaya is one of two of its kind in the world. At Our Lucaya Lucayan Course, the Breitling Crystal Pro-Am takes place in January. The Royal Oasis Golf Resort hosts the Bogey Bash Golf Tournament and the Nat Moore Invitational Golf Tournament. Note that prices tend to be lower in the off-season (mid-May–mid-December).

Fortune Hills Golf & Country Club is a 3,453-yard, 9-hole, par-36 course—a Dick Wilson and Joe Lee design—with a restaurant, bar, and pro shop. ⊠ *E. Sunrise Hwy., Lucaya* ☎ *242/373–2222* ✆ *$48 for 9 holes, $65 for 18 holes (cart included). Club rental, $12 for 9 holes, $17 for 18 holes.*

Fodor'sChoice **Our Lucaya Lucayan Course,** designed by Dick Wilson, is a dramatic ★ 6,824-yard, par-72, 18-hole course. The 18th hole has a double lake and a dramatic Balancing Boulders feature. The property is home to Butch Harmon School of Golf, one of only two schools in the world started by and named for the trainer of students such as Tiger Woods, Greg Norman, and Davis Love III. There is also a restaurant, a cocktail lounge, and a pro shop. A shared electric cart is included in the rates. ⊠ *Our Lucaya Beach & Golf Resort, Lucaya* ☎ *242/373–1066 or 242/373–1333, 877/687–2474 for Butch Harmon golf school* ✆ *In season, $110 weekdays, $120 weekends; off-season, $120 weekdays, $130 weekends. Club rental is $45.*

Our Lucaya Reef Course is a par-72, 6,920-yard course designed by Robert Trent Jones, Jr., with lots of water and a tricky dog-leg left on the 18th hole. ⊠ *Our Lucaya Beach & Golf Resort, Lucaya* ☎ *242/ 373–2002* ✆ *In season $105 weekdays, $115 weekends for guests; $115 weekdays, $125 weekends for nonguests. Club rental is $45.*

★ **Royal Oasis Golf Resort** has two 18-hole, par-72 championship courses redesigned by the Fazio Design Group: the 6,884-yard Ruby, and the 6,679-yard Emerald. The resort also has a pro shop. ⊠ *W. Sunrise Hwy., Freeport* ☎ *242/350–7000* ⊕ *www.theroyaloasis.com* ✆ *$85 for 18 holes, $65 for 9 (shared cart and club rentals included).*

Horseback Riding

★ **Pinetree Stables** runs trail and beach rides Tuesday–Sunday twice a day. All two-hour trail rides are accompanied by a guide—no previous riding experience is necessary. Reservations are essential. ⊠ *Beachway Dr., Freeport* ☎ *242/373–3600* ⊕ *www.bahamasvg.com/pinetree.html* ✆ *$75 for a 2-hr beach ride* ☉ *Closed Mon.*

Kayaking

★ Many resorts rent kayaks for playing in the waves, or can hook you up with an outfitter for more serious adventures. **Kayak Nature Tours** (⊠ Queen's Cove, Freeport ☎ 242/373–2485 or 866/440–4542 ⊕ www.bahamasvg. com/kayak.html) leads group kayaking tours of Lucayan National Park and other custom tours. See the Ecotours section for more information.

Paradise Cove (⊠ Deadman's Reef ☎ 242/349–2677 ⊕ www. deadmansreef.com) is known for its great snorkeling, but it also rents kayaks for day users, starting at $15 for a single.

Parasailing

Lucaya Watersports (✉ Jolly Roger Dr., Lucaya ☎ 242/373–6375 ✉ Seashore Dr. at Port Lucaya ☎ 242/373–8456) charges $50 for parasailing and also offers banana boat rides, waverunner rentals, water-skiing, kayaks, and more.

Paradise Watersports (✉ Xanadu Beach, Freeport ☎ 242/352–2887) has parasailing tow boats and offers five-minute flights for $50.

Reef Tours Ltd. (✉ Port Lucaya Marketplace ☎ 242/373–5880 ⊕ www.bahamasvacationguide.com/reeftours/) will lift parasailers up to 300 feet. It's $50 per person.

Personal Watercraft

Lucaya Watersports (✉ Jolly Roger Dr., Lucaya ☎ 242/373–6375 ✉ Seashore Dr. at Port Lucaya ☎ 242/373–8456) rents waverunners at $60 for 30 minutes.

★ **Tranquility Shores** (✉ Taíno Beach ☎ 242/374–4460 ⊕ tranquilityshores. com) has taken over where Kaptain Kenny's closed a few years back, and offers some of the same watersports rental concessions, including jet skis (tours available), paddleboats, water bikes, kayaks, and snorkel equipment. Lunch and happy hour specials are also offered.

Scuba Diving

An extensive reef system runs along Little Bahama Bank's edge; sea gardens, caves, and colorful reefs rim the bank all the way from the West End to Freeport-Lucaya and beyond. The variety of dive sites suits everyone from the novice to the advanced diver. The island is home to UNEXSO, considered one of the finest diving schools and marine research facilities in the world. It once made shark diving synonymous with Grand Bahama Island, but has discontinued its shark dives in recent years due to lack of interest.

Grand Bahama Island offers dive sites from 10 to 100-plus feet deep. **Sea Hunt** site is a shallow dive and is named for the *Sea Hunt* television show, portions of which were filmed here. **Ben's Blue Hole** is a horseshoe-shape ledge overlooking a blue hole in 40 to 60 feet of water. **Spid City** has an aircraft wreck, dramatic coral formations, blue parrotfish, and an occasional shark. You'll dive about 40 to 60 feet down. For divers with some experience, **Theo's Wreck**, a 228-foot cement hauler, was sunk in 1982 in 100 feet of water. **Pygmy Caves,** for moderately experienced divers, provides a formation of overgrown ledges that cut into the reef. One of Grand Bahama Island's signature dive sites, made famous by the UNEXSO dive operation, **Shark Junction** is a 45-foot dive where 4- to 6-foot reef sharks hang out, along with moray eels, stingrays, nurse sharks, and grouper. UNEXSO provides orientation and a shark feeding with its dives here.

Caribbean Divers (✉ Bell Channel Inn, opposite Port Lucaya ☎ 242/373–9111 ⊕ www.bellchannelinn.com) offers guided tours, NAUI instruction, and equipment rental. A resort course allows you to use equipment in a pool and then in a closely supervised open dive for $89. A one-tank dive costs $35. Shark (two-tank) dives are $65. You get a discount for reserving in advance.

Fodor'sChoice **UNEXSO (Underwater Explorers Society)** (✉ Box F 2433, Port Lucaya Mar-
★ ketplace ☎ 242/373–1244 or 800/992–3483 ⊕ www.unexso.com), a world-renowned scuba-diving facility with its own 18-foot dive pool, provides rental equipment, 15 guides, seven boats, and NAUI, PADI, and SSI certification. Underwater cameras are available for rent, or you can have your dive videotaped. A wide variety of dives are available for beginners and experienced divers, starting at $25. UNEXSO and its sister company, The Dolphin Experience, are known for their work with Atlantic bottle-nosed dolphins.

Xanadu Undersea Adventures (✉ Xanadu Beach Resort ☎ 242/352–3811 or 800/327–8150) offers a resort course for $79, single dives for $37, shark dives for $72, and night dives for $52.

Snorkeling

Aside from dive shops, a number of tour operators offer snorkeling trips to nearby reefs.

★ **East End Adventures** (✉ Freeport ☎ 242/373–6662 ⊕ www. bahamasecotours.com) takes you on a Blue Hole Snorkeling Safari that includes a 55-mi jeep ride and a powerboat jaunt. Guests dive for conch to prepare as part of a Bahamian-style barbecue. The daylong (8–5:30) excursion is $85 for adults, $35 for children.

Lucaya Watersports (✉ Jolly Roger Dr., Lucaya ☎ 242/373–6375 ✉ Seashore Dr. at Port Lucaya ☎ 242/373–8456) departs from two convenient locations three times daily—10 AM, noon, and 2 PM—for a 90-minute adventure that costs $35 for adults, $18 for kids; equipment and instruction included.

Old Bahama Bay (✉ West End ☎ 242/350–6500) rents snorkel equipment and has mapped out a series of seven snorkeling trails to reefs and wrecks in waters 5–15 feet deep.

★ ℭ **Paradise Cove** (✉ Deadman's Reef ⊕ www.deadmansreef.com ☎ 242/349–2677) allows you to snorkel right offshore at Deadman's Reef, a two-system reef with water ranging from very shallow to 35 feet deep. It's considered the island's best spot for snorkeling off the beach— you're likely to see lots of angelfish, barracudas, rays, and the occasional sea turtle. There is an access fee of $3 per person; snorkel equipment rentals are available for $10 a day, $5 an hour extra for wet suits or floatation belts. For $35, a snorkel tour includes briefing, narrated transportation, equipment, and lunch. It's a great deal, especially if you go early and stay late.

Paradise Watersports (✉ Xanadu Beach ☎ 242/352–2887) offers a 90-minute Reef 'N' Wreck snorkeling cruise ($30), during which you'll explore coral reefs and a 40-foot wreck.

★ ℭ **Pat & Diane Fantasia Tours** (✉ Port Lucaya Resort ☎ 242/373–8681 ⊕ www.snorkelingbahamas.com) takes snorkelers to a shallow reef three times a day on cruises aboard a fun-boat catamaran with a 30-foot rock climbing wall and slides into the water. The fee is $30 for the 2¼-hour trip.

Tennis

The island has more than 50 courts, many lighted for night play.

Our Lucaya has four lighted courts: natural grass, artificial grass, clay, and hard. Racquet rental, lessons, and clinics are available. ⊠ *Our Lucaya Beach & Golf Resort* ☎ *242/373–1333* ⊠ *$10–$18 per hr, $32 per hr for the natural grass court; evenings (after 4:30): $20–28, $42 for the grass court.*

Royal Oasis Golf Resort & Casino has nine hard courts between the two resorts, five of which are lighted. ⊠ *W. Sunrise Hwy., Freeport* ☎ *242/352–6721 Ext. 6560* ⊠ *$10 per hr for guests, $12 per hr for nonguests.*

Xanadu Beach Resort has two hard courts. ⊠ *Sunken Treasure Dr., Freeport* ☎ *242/352–6782* ⊠ *Guests free, nonguests $5 per hr.*

Waterskiing

Paradise Watersports (⊠ Xanadu Beach, Freeport ☎ 242/352–2887) lets you ski roughly 1½ mi of waves for $20; a half-hour lesson is $40.

SHOPPING

In the hundreds of stores, shops, and boutiques in Freeport's International Bazaar and at the Port Lucaya Marketplace, you can find duty-free goods costing up to 40% less than what you might pay back home. At the numerous perfume shops, fragrances are often sold at a sweet-smelling 25% below U.S. prices. Be sure to limit your haggling to the straw markets.

Shops in Freeport and Lucaya are open Monday–Saturday from 9 or 10 to 6. Stores may stay open later in Port Lucaya.

Markets & Arcades

Goombay Marketplace (⊠ West of International Bazaar ☎ No phone) is slightly less commercial than the other markets. It has a collection of arts and crafts vendors, set up in small colorful sheds and tucked away from the main flow of shoppers. You can easily walk there from International Bazaar.

International Arcade (⊠ Between the International Bazaar and the Royal Oasis Casino ☎ No phone) has a varied collection of shops, primarily branches of stores found at the adjacent International Bazaar.

★ **International Bazaar** (⊠ W. Sunrise Hwy. and E. Mall Dr. ☎ 242/352–2828) carries imported goods, exotic items, and the island's largest selection of duty-free merchandise. A sprightly straw market gathers on one side.

★ **Port Lucaya Marketplace** (⊠ Sea Horse Dr. ☎ 242/373–8446) has about 80 boutiques and restaurants in 12 pastel-color buildings in a harborside setting. Local musicians often perform at the bandstand in the afternoons and evenings. Artisans sell paintings, carvings, and jewelry from kiosks.

★ **Port Lucaya Straw Market** (⊠ Sea Horse Dr. ☎ No phone) is a collection of wooden stalls at the Port Lucaya complex's east and west ends. Vendors will expect you to bargain for straw goods, T-shirts, and souvenirs.

Specialty Shops

Antiques
Ye Olde Pirate Bottle House (⊠ Port Lucaya Marketplace ☎ 242/373–2000) is a well-stocked souvenir shop, and the adjoining museum, dedicated to the history of bottles, is worth the $3 admission. On display are 250 bottles, some dating from the 17th century.

Art
Art & Nature (⊠ Port Lucaya Marketplace ☎ 242/373–8326) sells a higher quality of handicrafts than the straw markets and souvenir shops. Look for painted canvases and handbags, and quality wood carvings.

★ **Bahamian Tings** (⊠ 15B Poplar Crescent St., Freeport ☎ 242/352–9550) carries well-made Bahamian crafts.

Flovin Gallery (⊠ International Bazaar and Port Lucaya ☎ 242/352–7564 or 242/373–8388) stocks original paintings in addition to T-shirts and other souvenirs.

Leo's Art Gallery (⊠ Port Lucaya ☎ 242/373–1758) showcases the expressive Haitian-style paintings of local artist Leo Brown.

China & Crystal
Island Galleria (⊠ International Bazaar and Port Lucaya Marketplace ☎ 242/352–8194 or 242/373–8404) carries china and crystal by Waterford, Wedgwood, Aynsley, Swarovski, and Coalport, as well as Lladró figurines.

Cigars
Note: It's illegal to bring Cuban cigars into the United States.

Smoker's World (⊠ International Bazaar ☎ 242/351–6899) is a tiny shop that carries Cuban cigars exclusively.

Fashion
★ **Androsia** (⊠ Port Lucaya Marketplace ☎ 242/373–8912) specializes in hand-batiked, nature-inspired fashions made on the Bahamian island of Andros—from bikinis to shirts and dresses.

Animale (⊠ International Bazaar and Port Lucaya Marketplace ☎ 242/351–7197 and 242/374–2066) is known for the wild appeal of its fine ladies' clothing and jewelry.

Bandolera (⊠ Port Lucaya Marketplace ☎ 242/373–7691) sells European-style women's fashions, bags, and jewelry.

Caribbean Cargo (⊠ International Bazaar ☎ 242/352–2929) has swimwear, beachwear, sarongs, quality souvenir T-shirts, and sea-inspired jewelry.

Today's Men (⊠ Port Lucaya Marketplace ☎ 242/373–8912) carries Tommy Hilfiger fashions for men and women.

Jewelry & Watches
The Colombian (⊠ Port Lucaya Marketplace ☎ 242/373–2974) purveys a line of Colombia's famed emeralds plus other jewelry and crystal.

Colombian Emeralds International (⊠ International Bazaar, International Arcade, and Port Lucaya Marketplace ☎ 242/352–5464, 242/352–7138, 242/373–8400, or 800/666–3889) is *the* place to find emeralds, diamonds, rubies, sapphires, and gold jewelry. The best brands in watches, including Tag Heuer, Breitling, and Omega, are also available here.

Leather Goods

Leather Shop (✉ International Arcade ☎ 242/352–5491 ✉ Port Lucaya Marketplace ☎ 242/373–2323) sells HCL, Vitello, Land, and Fendi handbags, shoes, and briefcases.

Unusual Centre (✉ International Bazaar and Port Lucaya Marketplace ☎ 242/352–3994) carries eel-skin leather, peacock-feather goods, and jewelry.

Perfumes

Les Parisiens Perfumes (✉ International Bazaar ☎ 242/352–5380) stocks Giorgio products and the latest French perfumes.

Parfum de Paris (✉ International Arcade, International Bazaar, and Port Lucaya Marketplace ☎ 242/352–8164 or 242/373–8403) offers the most comprehensive range of French fragrances on the island, including Lancome, Fendi, and Tommy.

★ **Perfume Factory** (✉ International Bazaar ☎ 242/352–9391) sells a large variety of perfumes, lotions, and colognes by Fragrance of the Bahamas. Pink Pearl cologne actually contains conch pearls, and Sand cologne for men has a little island sand in each bottle. You can also create your own scent and brand name and register it.

Miscellaneous

Hit Factory (✉ International Arcade ☎ 242/352–6004) has the island's best selection of CDs, tapes, even LPs. Buy reggae, rap, and mainstream American music plus video games.

Intercity Music (✉ International Bazaar and Port Lucaya Marketplace ☎ 242/352–8820) is the place to buy records, tapes, and CDs of Junkanoo, reggae, and soca music. It also burns its own hit collections.

Photo Specialist (✉ Port Lucaya Marketplace ☎ 242/373–7858) repairs cameras and carries photo and video equipment.

UNEXSO Dive Shop (✉ UNEXSO, Port Lucaya Marketplace ☎ 242/373–1244) sells everything water-related, from swimsuits, marine animal T-shirts, dolphin jewelry, and sarongs to snorkeling equipment.

GRAND BAHAMA ISLAND A TO Z

To research prices, get advice from other travelers, and book travel arrangements, visit ⊕ www.fodors.com

AIR TRAVEL

Several United States airlines fly to the Grand Bahama International Airport from cities on the east coast, including Atlanta, Chicago, New York City, Miami, and Fort Lauderdale. Interisland flights to and from Nassau and other destinations are also available.

CARRIERS AirTran flies from Atlanta nonstop daily, with connections to major U.S. cities, and from Baltimore Thursday through Monday. American Eagle serves Freeport from Miami, with American Airlines connections from many U.S. cities. ATA charters provides service January through April from Detroit. Bahamasair serves Grand Bahama International Airport with flights from Miami, as well as via Nassau. Continental/Continental Connection (Gulfstream) travels daily from Newark, New Jersey, and several cities in Florida (Miami, Fort Lauderdale, West Palm Beach, and Tampa) as well as once weekly from Orlando. Delta Connection flies twice daily out of Atlanta. L.B. Ltd. (formerly Laker) flies daily from Fort Lauderdale. US Airways provides daily nonstop service from New York, Philadelphia, and Charlotte, North Carolina. TNT Vacations provides nonstop charter service from Boston February through May.

Grand Bahama Vacations has airfare packages from ten American cities with accommodations at ten Grand Bahama Island resorts. Add-on ground and water tours are also available.

Major's Air Services offers interisland flights from Freeport to Abaco, Bimini, Eleuthera, and Andros.

🛪 Airlines & Contacts **AirTran** ☎ 800/247-8726. **American Eagle** ☎ 800/433-7300. **ATA** ☎ 800/435-9282. **Bahamasair** ☎ 242/352-8341 or 800/222-4262. **Delta Connection** ☎ 800/221-1212. **Grand Bahama Vacations** ☎ 800/545-1300. **GulfStream Continental Connection** ☎ 242/352-6447 or 800/231-0856. **L.B. Ltd.** ☎ 242/352-8881, 800/545-1300. **Major's Air Services** ✈ Box F 41282 ☎ 242/352-5778 📠 242/352-5788. **TNT Vacations** ☎ 800/498-5586. **US Airways** ☎ 800/428-4322.

AIRPORTS & TRANSFERS

Grand Bahama International Airport is just off Grand Bahama Highway, about six minutes from downtown Freeport and about 10 minutes from Port Lucaya.

🛪 Airport Information **Grand Bahama International Airport** ☎ 242/352-6020.

TRANSFERS No bus service is available between the airport and hotels. Metered taxis meet all incoming flights. Rides cost about $11 for two to Freeport, $19 to Lucaya.

BIKE TRAVEL

By virtue of its flat terrain, broad avenues, and long, straight stretches of highway, Grand Bahama is perfect for bicycling. In November, the island hosts the annual Conchman Triathlon, comprising a 1K swim, 25K bike ride, and a 5K run. When biking, wear sunblock, carry a bottle of water, and look left. Inexpensive bicycle rentals (about $20 a day plus deposit) are available from some resorts. Royal Oasis Golf Resort, Old Bahama Bay, and Running Mon Resort have bikes for rent. Viva Wyndham Fortuna Beach allows guests free use of bicycles. For a biking nature tour from Taíno Beach to Garden of the Groves, contact Kayak Nature Tours. The five-hour tour rides along 20 mi of beach and road for $79 per person, including a restaurant lunch.

🚲 Bike Rentals **Royal Oasis Golf Resort** ✉ W. Sunrise Hwy. ☎ 242/350-7000. **Kayak Nature Tours** ✉ Queen's Cove ☎ 242/373-2485 or 866/440-4542 ⊕ www.bahamasvg.com/kayak.html.

BOAT & FERRY TRAVEL

Freeport and Lucaya are the ports of call for several cruise lines, including Carnival Cruise Line, Discovery Cruises, and Disney Cruise Lines (⇨ Cruise Travel *in* Smart Travel Tips A to Z, at the beginning of the book). Discovery Cruises provides daily ferry service from Fort Lauderdale, a five-hour trip each way. Bahama Florida Express (☎ 866/313-3779) zips passengers from Fort Lauderdale in two hours.

Taxis meet all cruise ships. Passengers are charged $16 for trips to Freeport and $24 to Lucaya. The price per person drops with larger groups.

A free government ferry runs between McLean's Town, at the East End, to Sweeting's Cay. It departs from Sweeting's Cay at 7:10 AM and 4 PM; and from McLean's Town at 8:30 AM and 5 PM.

BUS TRAVEL

Buses are an inexpensive way to travel the 4 mi between downtown Freeport and Port Lucaya Marketplace daily until about 10 PM. The fare is $1. Fare from Freeport to Garden of the Groves is $3; $2 from Port Lucaya. Buses from Freeport to West End cost $4; to East End, $8. Exact change is required. Some resorts provide free shuttle service to shopping and beaches.

BUSINESS HOURS

BANKS Banks are generally open Monday–Thursday 9:30–3 and Friday 9:30–5. Some of the major banks on the island include Bank of the Bahamas, Bank of Nova Scotia, Barclays Bank, and Royal Bank of Canada.

SHOPS Shops are usually open Monday–Saturday 9 or 10 to 5 or 6. Straw markets, grocery stores, and drugstores are open on Sunday.

CAR RENTAL

If you plan to drive around the island, it's cheaper to rent a car than to hire a taxi. Automobiles, jeeps, and vans can be rented at the Grand Bahama International Airport. Cars run $50–$100 per day. Some agencies provide free pickup and delivery service to Freeport and Lucaya resorts.

🚗 Major Agencies **Avis Rent-A-Car** ☎ 242/352–7666, 888/897–8448 in the U.S. **Dollar Rent-A-Car** ☎ 242/352–9325, 800/800–4000 in the U.S. **Hertz** ☎ 242/352–9277, 800/654–3131 in the U.S. **Thrifty** ☎ 242/352–9308, 800/367–2277 in the U.S. 🚗 Local Agencies **Bahama Buggies** ☎ 242/352–8750.

Cartwright's Rent-A-Car ☎ 242/351–3002.

KSR Car Rental ☎ 242/351–5737.

EMERGENCIES

Dial 911 to reach the police in case of an emergency. Ambulance service and the fire department have separate numbers.
🚑 **Ambulance** ☎ 242/352–2689. **Bahamas Air Sea Rescue** ☎ 242/325–2628. **Fire Department** ☎ 242/352–8888 or 911. **Police** ☎ 911. **Rand Memorial Hospital** ✉ E. Atlantic Dr. ☎ 242/352–6735.

SCOOTER TRAVEL

Grand Bahama's flat, well-paved roads make for good, safe scooter riding. Rentals run about $35 a day with a $200 deposit (about $15 an hour). Helmets are required and provided. Look for rentals at Port Lucaya Marketplace and Pirates of the Bahamas.

SIGHTSEEING TOURS

Tours can be booked through the tour desk in your hotel lobby, at tourist information booths, or by calling one of the tour operators listed below.

A three-hour sightseeing tour of the Freeport/Lucaya area, including Garden of the Groves, costs $25–$35. A glass-bottom-boat tour to offshore reefs starts at $25. A tour of Lucayan National Park runs about $40.

For evening entertainment, a dinner cruise will cost around $60, with a show. Sunset "booze cruises" run about $30 each, transportation included ($35 with show).

A host of tour operators on Grand Bahama offer a combination of the tours described above. Executive Tours, H. Forbes Charter & Tours, and Sun World Travel have sightseeing land tours that can be booked through the major resorts. H. Forbes Charter & Tours also offers trips to Nassau, nightlife bar-hopping excursions, and other adventures. For on-the-water fun, contact Reef Tours Ltd.

▪ Fees & Schedules Sunworld Travel & Tours ✆ Box F 42631, Freeport ☎ 242/352–3717. **Executive Tours** ✆ Box F 40837, Freeport ☎ 242/373–7863. **Grand Bahama Vacations** ✆ 1170 Lee Wagner Blvd., Suite 200, Ft. Lauderdale, FL 33315 ☎ 800/422–7466 or 800/545–1300 ⊕ www.gbvac.com. **H. Forbes Charter & Tours** ✆ Box F 41315, Freeport ☎ 242/352–9311 ⊕ www.forbescharter.com. **Reef Tours Ltd.** ✆ Box F 42609, Freeport ☎ 242/373–5880 ⊕ www.bahamasvg.com/reeftours.

BOAT TOUR If you don't want to go too far underwater, try an excursion on the Seaworld Explorer semisubmarine, which never fully submerges. Descend into the hull of the boat and observe sea life in air-conditioned comfort from a vantage point 5 feet below the surface. The vessel departs from Port Lucaya and travels to Treasure Reef daily at 9:30, 11:30, and 1:30. The two-hour voyage with transportation and snorkeling costs $39, $20 for children.

▪ Seaworld Explorer ✉ Port Lucaya Marina, Port Lucaya ☎ 242/373–7863.

BREWERY TOUR A one-hour tour sloshes through the Grand Bahama Brewing Company, the island's only microbrewery, fountainhead of Hammerhead beers, weekdays at 10, 12:30, and 4:40, and Saturday at 10:30 (call ahead on Saturday). Samplings of its four types of beer are available, and the $5 tour price can be credited toward a purchase.

▪ Grand Bahama Brewing Company ✉ Logwood Rd., Freeport ☎ 242/351–5191.

ECOTOURS Land-and-sea East End Adventures' guided ecotours include a jeep ride along pristine beaches and through dense pine forests to the site of a now-gone early settlement, and a 6-mi boat trip to Sweeting's Cay and Lightbourne Cay, remote islands off Grand Bahama's eastern extreme. Snorkeling a blue hole, nature and bush medicine lessons, a short wilderness hike, and a home-cooked Bahamian lunch on the beach are all included in this truly worthwhile experience, which is run by native Bahamians. Trips cost $110 per adult, begin at 8 AM, and last until 5:30 PM.

Kayak Nature Tours' eco-excursions explore pristine wilderness by kayak, van, snorkel, and foot. The six-hour tour includes 1½ hours of kayaking through Grand Bahama's mangrove environment for a look at bird and marine habitats, a guided nature hike through Lucayan National Park and its caves, swimming on Gold Rock Beach, and lunch. A five-hour excursion combines kayaking and snorkeling at Peterson Cay. The guides are extremely knowledgeable, particularly about flora and fauna. Air-conditioned transport is provided to and from your hotel. West End kayak and snorkel tours are also offered, as well as a 5-mi heritage hike that takes you to the ruins of the island's original settlement and teaches about bush medicine and local lore. The tours to Lucayan National Park and to Peterson Cay for snorkeling each cost $69.

🛈 **East End Adventures** ✉ Freeport ☎ 242/373-6662 ⊕ www.bahamasecotours. com. **Kayak Nature Tours** ✉ Queen's Cove, Freeport ☎ 242/373-2485 or 866/440-4542 ⊕ www.bahamasvg.com/kayak.html.

TAXIS

Taxi fares are fixed by the government (but generally you are charged a flat fee for routine trips, and these rates can vary slightly) at $3 for the first ¼ mi and 40¢ for each additional ¼ mi, regardless of whether the taxi is a regular-size cab, van, or stretch limo. Additional passengers over two are $3 each. Grand Bahama Taxi Union can provide service for visitors arriving by air. There is a taxi waiting area outside the Royal Oasis Golf Resort & Casino and Our Lucaya Beach & Golf Resort.

🛈 Taxi Companies **Grand Bahama Taxi Union** ✉ Grand Bahama International Airport ☎ 242/352-7101.

VISITOR INFORMATION

Grand Bahama Island Tourism Board has its main office and a separate tourist information center at International Bazaar in Freeport. Branch offices are located at the Grand Bahama International Airport and at the southeast entrance to the Port Lucaya Marketplace. Ask about Bahamahosts, specially trained tour guides who will talk to you about island history and culture and pass on their knowledge of Bahamian folklore. Tourist offices are open weekdays 9–5; information centers, Monday–Saturday 9–5. The airport office is also open on Sunday.

🛈 Tourist Information **Grand Bahama Island Tourism Board** ☎ 242/352-8356, 800/ 448-3386 in the U.S. 🖷 242/352-7840 ⊕ www.grand-bahama.com ☎ 242/352-6909 Freeport ☎ 242/352-2052 Grand Bahama International Airport ☎ 242/373-8988 Port Lucaya.

THE ABACOS

3

EMPTY BEACHES AND GRASSY DUNES
are yours for the taking ⇨*p.113*

GET HOOKED ON BONEFISHING
with some of the Bahamas' best guides ⇨*p.111*

BOATBUILDING HISTORY IS MADE
at Man-O-War Cay ⇨*p.112*

CRUISE IN A GOLF CART
around tiny Green Turtle Cay ⇨*p.118*

DRINK A TOAST TO RUM-RUNNING
at the birthplace of the Goombay Smash ⇨*p.121*

SWIM WITH SEA TURTLES
at a marine park bustling with sea life ⇨*p.107*

HUNT FOR TREASURES
in an underwater shipwreck ⇨*p.112*

SLIP INTO A BAHAMIAN SUNSET
at a hotel perched on a seaside cliff ⇨*p.104*

Updated by
Patricia
Rodriguez
Terrell

THE ATTITUDE OF THE ABACOS might best be expressed by the sign posted in the window of a Hope Town shop: IF YOU'RE LOOKING FOR WAL-MART—IT'S 200 MILES TO THE RIGHT. In other words, the residents of this chain of more than 100 islands know that there's another world out there, but don't necessarily care to abandon theirs, which is a little more traditional, slow-paced, and out of the way than most alternatives.

The Abacos' calm, naturally protected waters, long admired for their beauty, have helped the area become the Bahamas' sailing capital. The islands' resorts are particularly popular with yachting and fishing enthusiasts because of the fine boating facilities available, among the best in the Bahamas. Man-O-War Cay remains the Bahamas' boatbuilding center; its residents turn out traditionally crafted wood dinghies as well as high-tech fiberglass craft. The Abacos play host annually to internationally famous regattas and to a half dozen game-fish tournaments. Outside the resorts, the oceanside villages of Hope Town and New Plymouth also appeal to tourists for their charming New England ambience.

Many of the ten or so inhabited cays of the Abacos were first settled more than 200 years ago by New England Loyalists, who in 1783 began fleeing the upstart United States to what they perceived as a safe haven for those loyal to the crown. Joined by plantation owners and their slaves from Virginia and the Carolinas, the newcomers found it hard going on the rocky, infertile land, and soon turned to the sea. Some began fishing and boatbuilding, a way of making a living that some of their descendants still practice today. Others took advantage of the occasional shipwreck.

At the end of the 18th century, Bahamian waters weren't charted, and lighthouses wouldn't be built in the area until 1836. The "wreckers" of the Abacos worked at night, luring unsuspecting ships onto rocks and shoals by shining misleading lights, then plundering the cargo. Of course, not all these wrecks were caused by unscrupulous islanders. Some ships were lost in storms and foundered on hidden reefs as they passed through the Bahamas. Nevertheless, by means fair or foul, wrecking remained a thriving industry in the Abacos until the mid-1800s.

Today the legacy of the British settlers remains intact. Many of the Abacos' 10,000 residents have accents reminiscent of their ancestors—a charming combination of an island cadence with a vaguely Scottish or English lilt. Seafaring is still a major source of income, especially boatbuilding, fishing, and guided fishing trips. Because the Abacos are one of the Out Islands' most visited destinations, an increasing number of residents work in the tourist industry.

Exploring The Abacos

The Abacos, a boomerang-shape cluster of cays in the northeastern Bahamas, stretch from tiny Walker's Cay in the north to Hole-in-the-Wall, more than 130 mi to the southwest. Many of these cays are very small, providing exquisitely desolate settings for private picnics. The Abacos have their fair share of lagoons, tranquil bays and inlets, and pine forests where wild boar roam, but they also are home to the Bahamas' third-largest community, the commercial center of Marsh Harbour, with all

Numbers in the text correspond to numbers in the margin and on The Abacos map.

If you have 3 days

Make your base in ⌐ ▦ **Marsh Harbour ❶**, the biggest city in the Abacos, and spend the first day getting settled in your hotel, exploring the city or a nearby beach, and having a leisurely dinner on Restaurant Row, overlooking the busy marina. On Day 2, get up early and take the ferry to **Hope Town ❺**, the **Elbow Cay** settlement often considered the most picturesque in the Abacos, with its candy-stripe lighthouse, rows of neat clapboard cottages painted in pastel hues, and plenty of restaurants, shops, and historic sites. Day 3 brings a choice: For another dose of Loyalist history, take the ferry again, this time to **Man-O-War Cay ❻**, the boatbuilding capital of the region; or stay put and book a diving or fishing trip out of one of the Marsh Harbour marinas.

3

If you have 5 days

Follow the suggested three-day itinerary, and on Day 4 go to **Treasure Cay ❽** and catch the first ferry to ▦ **Green Turtle Cay ❾**, your base for the next two days. Stroll through **New Plymouth** for the remainder of your morning, stopping to wander through the sculpture garden, which memorializes accomplished Bahamians, and the **Albert Lowe Museum,** getting a dose of island history, as well as learning about shipbuilding and hurricane survival. After a lunch of locally caught conch or grouper, spend the afternoon at **Ocean Beach** or on calmer **Gillam Bay,** then dress up for a fancy dinner at one of the two fine resorts on **White Sound.** On your last day, if you're a golfer, you'll want to hit the links at nearby Treasure Cay, where the 18-hole course is considered one of the finest in the Caribbean, yet is so blissfully uncrowded that tee times aren't necessary. Otherwise, rent a small boat and visit some of the uninhabited nearby cays, such as **Munjack, No Name,** and **Crab,** where the snorkeling and deserted white-sand beaches are first-rate.

If you have 7 days

Add two days to the ▦ **Marsh Harbour** portion of the five-day itinerary above. On the first additional day, take a ferry to **Great Guana Cay ❼**, with some of the most beautiful beaches in the Abacos and one of the best party-scene restaurants, **Nippers.** On the second, rent a car and explore the southern reaches of **Great Abaco Island,** perhaps searching for the endangered Bahamian parrot at the **Bahamas National Trust Sanctuary ❹**, or checking out the bronze sculptures at **Pete Johnson's Foundry** in **Little Harbour ❷**. Another alternative, if you're a boater, is to rent a boat your first day in Marsh Harbour and spend the week island-hopping; you'll probably want to spend a day or two at anchor in ▦ **Hope Town ❺**, ▦ **Man-O-War ❻**, ▦ **Great Guana ❼**, and ▦ **Green Turtle ❾**. If all that sounds like too much work, consider experiencing life like a local: Bring some books, sunblock, and a few swimsuits; rent a cottage, a dinghy, and a golf cart, perhaps on ▦ **Elbow Cay** or ▦ **Great Guana Cay ❼**; and learn to practice the fine art of relaxation.

the amenities of a small town, including shops, restaurants, and hotels, and the largest marina in the Bahamas. The two main islands, Great Abaco and Little Abaco, are fringed on their windward shore by an emerald necklace of cays that forms a barrier reef against the broad Atlantic.

Aside from the renowned marinas, there are countless other attractions to lure visitors to the Abacos, which are among the most-visited of the Out Islands. The main island of Great Abaco is most people's first stop, and home to the thriving town of Marsh Harbour. Green Turtle Cay, another former Loyalist outpost, is popular for its handful of fine resorts and marinas, as well as its excellent fishing and snorkeling. A more recently developed resort area is Treasure Cay, which has a large hotel, beachside condos, and the only 18-hole golf course in the region. Man-O-War Cay, the Bahamas' boatbuilding capital, was made famous by the Albury family, who built the cay's boats for many generations. Tourists tend to either hole up on one of these islands, or rent a sailboat or yacht and explore several of them. If seclusion is what you're after, head for the tiny resorts at Walker's Cay or Spanish Cay, at the northern tip of the Abacos, or the fishing hot spot of Sandy Cay, at the southern extreme.

About the Restaurants

Fish, conch, and lobster—called crawfish by the locals—have long been the bedrock of local cuisine. Although a few menus, mostly in upscale resorts, feature dishes with Italian, Asian, or Continental influences, most restaurants in the Abacos still serve simple Bahamian fare, with a few nods to American tastes. (It's rare to find a place that still serves sheep's-tongue souse, a stew made from the tongue of a sheep and a handful of other ingredients.)

The Abacos are not particularly dieter-friendly. Breakfasts tend toward the hearty, eggs-bacon-and-pancakes variety. At lunch, even in the trendiest spots, you'll likely find variations on a few standards: fresh grouper "burgers," or breaded, fried fish fillets served on slightly sweet Bahamian buns; cracked conch, which is tenderized, deep-fried conch meat; and hamburgers and sandwiches, all usually sided with french fries, cole slaw, or local favorites like peas 'n' rice.

Dinner provides more options. You might eat local favorites like pork chops, fried chicken, or minced lobster cooked with tomatoes, garlic, and onions at a barebones diner; or head for a fancier restaurant and choose from an ever-changing array of seafood dishes with international flair, such as lobster risotto, sesame-crusted ahi tuna with wasabi sauce, or monkfish wrapped in pancetta.

Remember that almost nothing is grown locally, so high-quality fruits and vegetables are a rarity, especially right before the weekly boat bearing provisions arrives. (By the same token, don't be surprised if all dishes on the menu aren't available every day.) The remoteness also means meals aren't cheap, even in the humblest spot. Lunch usually costs at least $10 per person, and you can easily spend upwards of $30 apiece at dinner, even without drinks.

Snorkeling & Diving

With clear, shallow waters and a series of colorful coral reefs extending for miles, the Abacos provide both the novice and the experienced underwater explorer plenty to see. The reefs, often within swimming distance of shore, are teeming with trigger fish, grouper, parrot fish, green moray eels, angelfish, jacks, damsel fish, sergeant majors, sting rays, sea turtles, dolphins, and even the occasional reef or nurse shark. Dive operators are available in the most heavily touristed areas, but you can also venture out on your own, especially with a rented boat. Good places to start include the reefs near Guana Cay; Fowl Cay National Reserve between Man-O-War and Scotland cays; Pelican Cays National Park, just south of Marsh Harbour; and the reefs around Green Turtle Cay, where a Key West organization called Reef Relief has helped islanders install a series of 18 mooring buoys where you can safely anchor your boat without fear of damaging the fragile reef.

3

Maps of the buoys, which stretch from uninhabited Munjack Cay in the north to No Name Cay in the south, can be picked up at many Green Turtle Cay businesses. Visibility is generally high year-round, but the clear water turns cloudy after heavy storms and high seas. The relatively northern location of the Abacos means you may need a wetsuit from December through March. But no matter what the time of year, the sheer number of good sites and relatively low visitor traffic translate to a fantastic view of life under the sea that you rarely have to share with other snorkelers and divers.

A Living History

Though the Abacos may be most famous for beaches, sailing, and fishing, you'd be missing the boat, so to speak, if you didn't explore the area's rich history. And that doesn't mean spending all those sunny days inside a museum, although there are fine, small museums in Hope Town and New Plymouth, each worth a visit to learn about the boatbuilding and seafaring traditions of the Loyalists who settled these islands.

Because the original settlements have been so well preserved, it's possible to absorb history just by wandering through them. In Hope Town, look for the gingerbread cottages with white picket fences, built 100 or more years ago but still lived in today. In New Plymouth, check out the sculpture garden depicting the accomplishments of famous Bahamians. While you're there, observe the architecture: the neat clapboard homes, shops, and churches, many with carefully tended flower boxes and airy front porches, have survived hurricanes and tropical storms and still look much like they must have when they were built a century ago. On Man-0-War Cay, witness boat-building as it's been done for generations, or see women carefully crafting modern bags out of the same cloth their ancestors used for sails. And everywhere in the Abacos, simply try engaging the local residents in conversation. Nearly all of them, but especially those over 60, have some great tales to tell of what it's like to live on an island where many grew up without cars, TVs, telephones, or daily mail service.

About the Hotels

Small, intimate resorts are the rule in the Abacos. There are a few full-scale resorts, with multiple restaurants, bars, pools, and features like tennis courts, but most accommodations are beachside condos or cottages, or hotels with just a handful of rooms and a single small restaurant. What you may give up in modern amenities and bells-and-whistles additions like spas or 24-hour room service, you'll gain in privacy and beauty. Many hotels have water views, and with a cottage you may even get your own stretch of beach. Although rooms tend to be simple, air-conditioning has become a standard feature, and more places are adding previously unheard-of luxuries like satellite TV, in-room phones, VCRs, and Internet access. Again, small and remote doesn't equate with inexpensive; it's just about impossible to find lodging for under $100.

WHAT IT COSTS				
$$$$	**$$$**	**$$**	**$**	**¢**
RESTAURANTS over $40	$30–$40	$20–$30	$10–$20	under $10
HOTELS over $400	$300–$400	$200–$300	$100–$200	under $100

Restaurant prices are for a main course at dinner, excluding gratuity, typically 15%, which is often automatically added to the bill. Hotel prices are for two people in a standard double room in high season, excluding service charges and 6%–12% tax.

Timing

Unlike the rest of the Bahamas, which are busiest from December through April, the peak months for the Abacos are in June, July, and early August. That's the best time for sailing, boating, and swimming, the season of the most popular regatta and fishing tournaments, and the time you're likely to pay a premium for hotels, boats, and car—if you can book them at all. December through May is a pleasant time to visit, though most locals refuse to get in the water during those months. With average high temperatures in the 70s and low 80s, you might disagree, although in January and February, those highs can sometimes dip as low as 50 degrees when a norther drifts through.

In September and October, typically the peak of hurricane season, the number of visitors drops to a trickle, and many hotels and restaurants shut down for two weeks to two months. If you're willing to take a chance on getting hit by a storm, this can still be a great time to explore, with discounts of as much as 50 percent at the hotels that remain open.

THE ABACOS

Numbers in the margin correspond to points of interest on the Abacos map.

Great Abaco Island

Most visitors to the Abacos make their first stop on Great Abaco Island's east coast at **Marsh Harbour,** the Bahamas' third-largest city and the Abacos' commercial center. Besides having the biggest international airport in the Abacos, Marsh Harbour is considered by boaters to be one of the easiest harbors to enter. It has several full-service marinas, including the 200-slip Boat Harbour Marina and the 80-slip Conch Inn Marina.

Stock up on groceries and supplies here on the way to other islands. The downtown area has several supermarkets with a better selection than the sometimes-limited supplies on the smaller islands, as well as a few department and hardware stores. Most of the gift shops are on the main street, which has the island's only traffic light. If you need cash, this is the place to get it as well; the banks here are open every day and have ATMs, neither of which you will find true on the smaller, more remote cays. There are also gas stations, doctors, government offices, and a few good, moderately priced restaurants. For the ultimate in local fare, however, keep an eye out for "Rolling Kitchens," cars from which women sell island-style food. You might nab a huge plate of lamb, conch, pork chops, or other treats for about $5. The kitchens roll through Marsh Harbour and other locations such as Treasure Cay around lunchtime.

On a hilltop overlooking Marsh Harbour stands **Seaview Castle,** built by "Doctor" Evans Cottman (d. 1976), a high-school biology teacher from Madison, Indiana, who became the islands' official "unqualified practitioner" in the 1940s (i.e., he wasn't really a doctor, but he played one in the Bahamas). Cottman wrote of his experiences in a fascinating book, *Out Island Doctor.* The castle is not open to the public, but you can walk around its grounds.

❷ About 30 mi south of Marsh Harbour lies the small, eclectic artist's colony of **Little Harbour** settled by the Johnston family more than 50 years ago. The centerpiece is **Pete Johnston's Foundry** (☎ 242/367–2720), the only bronze foundry in the Bahamas, out of which sculptor Johnston and his sons and acolytes cast magnificent lifelike bronze figures using the age-old lost-wax method. No trip to Little Harbour would be complete without a stop at Gilligan's Islandesque **Pete's Pub and Gallery** (☎ 242/367–2720 ⊕ www.petespubandgallery.com), which has an Abacos-wide reputation for its laid-back attitude and decor.

About 20 mi south of Marsh Harbour is the little settlement of **Cherokee Sound,** home to fewer than 100 families, most of whom make their living crawfishing. The deserted Atlantic beaches and serene salt marshes in this area are breathtaking, but that seclusion may soon be a thing of the past. A new 18-hole golf course and vacation home community is under construction off stunning Winding Bay, developed by the same entrepreneur who refurbished Skibo Castle, the Scottish estate where Madonna married British director Guy Ritchie. The course and other additions, including a spa and equestrian center, are expected to open in December 2004.

❸ **Sandy Point,** a rustic fishing village with a lovely beach that attracts shell collectors and a growing number of fishing enthusiasts, is slightly more than 50 mi southwest of Marsh Harbour. There are no communities to visit south of Sandy Point, but a major navigational lighthouse

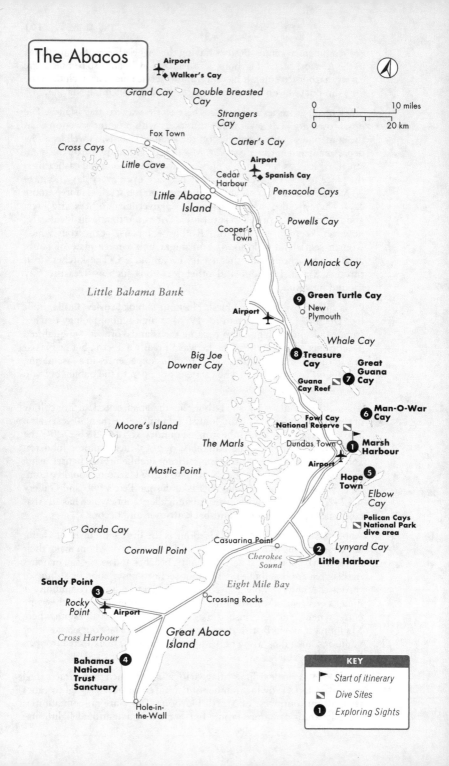

The Abacos

Airport
◆ Walker's Cay

Grand Cay   Double Breasted
                   Cay

                   Strangers
                   Cay

Cross Cays   Carter's Cay

Fox Town

Little Cave   Airport
                   ◆ Spanish Cay
Cedar
Harbour   Pensacola Cays

*Little Abaco
Island*

                   Powells Cay
Cooper's
Town

Little Bahama Bank   Manjack Cay

                         9 Green Turtle Cay
          Airport   New
                               Plymouth

                               Whale Cay

Big Joe   **8** Treasure   Great
Downer Cay   Cay   Guana
                                             Cay
                         Guana   **7**
                         Cay Reef

                                        6 Man-O-War
                                             Cay
Moore's Island   Fowl Cay
                         National Reserve
                         Dundas Town
The Marls   Marsh
                         1 Harbour
                         Airport
Mastic Point
                         5 Hope
                             Town
                                        *Elbow
                                         Cay*

                         Pelican Cays
                         National Park
                         dive area

Gorda Cay   Casuarina Point
                                        2 Lynyard Cay
Cornwall Point   *Cherokee*   Little Harbour
                    Sound

                    Eight Mile Bay

Sandy Point   Crossing Rocks
3
Rocky   Airport
Point
                    Great Abaco
Cross Harbour   *Island*

Bahamas
National   **4**
Trust
Sanctuary

                    Hole-in-
                    the-Wall

0 _____ 10 miles
0 _____ 20 km

KEY	
▶	*Start of itinerary*
◩	*Dive Sites*
1	*Exploring Sights*

stands at **Hole-in-the-Wall,** on Great Abaco's southern tip. It's not open to visitors.

A rugged winding road leads off the Great Abaco Highway, about 40 mi south of Marsh Harbour, passing through the dense pine woodlands

❹ of the **Bahamas National Trust Sanctuary** (☎ 242/393–1317), a reserve for the endangered Bahamian parrot. Your best chance of seeing that bird is at dawn. More than 100 other species have been sighted in this area.

Where to Stay & Eat

★ **\$\$** ✕ **Wally's.** Across the road from the water is a pink two-story building resembling a small mansion. This is one of the Bahamas' best-looking— and most popular—restaurants. Inside are Haitian-style paintings and white wicker chairs on terra-cotta tiles. A well-dressed crowd flocks here at lunch for the large selection of salads, including Greek, Caesar, and greens topped with grilled grouper or chicken. Dinner is served Friday and Saturday only, when the menu includes wild boar, turtle sautéed in onions and mushrooms, grilled wahoo, and duck breast, not to mention a killer key lime pie. ⊠ *E. Bay St., Marsh Harbour* ☎ *242/367– 2074* ▭ *AE, D, MC, V* ☉ *Closed Sun. Closed early Sept.–Oct.*

\$–\$\$ ✕ **Hummingbird Restaurant and Bar.** At this unassuming diner tucked inside a small strip mall, locals trade gossip over heaping plates of pancakes and cheese-stuffed omelets at breakfast, then move on to hearty lunches of cracked conch, burgers, and salads. At dinner, the dress code and the vibe remain casual, but the food presentation gets kicked up a notch; try the stuffed pork chops or, if you want a taste of an old-school Bahamian delicacy, a grilled turtle steak. ⊠ *Memorial Plaza, Marsh Harbour* ☎ *242/367–2922* ▭ *MC, V.*

\$–\$\$ ✕ **Jib Room.** Expect casual lunches of hot wings, conch burgers, fish nuggets, and nachos in this harbor-view restaurant and bar, inside the Marsh Harbour Marina. The twice-weekly barbecue nights are especially popular; on Wednesday it's baby back ribs and on Saturday it's grilled steak, featuring New York strip. ⊠ *Pelican Shores, Marsh Harbour* ☎ *242/367–2700* ▭ *MC, V* ☉ *Closed Sun.–Tues.*

★ **\$–\$\$** ✕ **Mangoes.** European-trained chef Nick Doyle is behind the menu at this waterside favorite, where the open-air deck is a prime place to enjoy typical Bahamian fare (cracked conch, grouper burgers). Or, better yet, branch out and try one of the house specialties, such as Thai beef salad, fried grouper with mango salsa, or grilled pork loin with sweet potato fritters and papaya-tomatillo salsa. An after-dinner highlight is the bread pudding, made with bananas, coconut, and sweet, doughy Bahamian bread. The restaurant is part of a complex containing a boutique selling resort wear and a 29-slip marina. ⊠ *Queen Elizabeth Dr., Marsh Harbour* ☎ *242/367–2366* ▭ *AE, D, MC, V* ☉ *Closed Oct.*

\$–\$\$ ✕ **Sapodilly's.** The colorful bi-level patios will grab your eye—Sapodilly's wooden beams are painted lime green, hot pink, and bright yellow— but the flavorful dishes will hold your attention. Among the best choices are pastas, the grilled grouper kebab, and Marsh Harbour's best burger, topped with blue cheese, bacon, and mushrooms. Or simply go for the drinks and an extensive appetizer menu, including hot wings, conch fritters, escargot, fried shrimp, and onion rings, served with a side of live music on Saturday nights. ⊠ *Queen Elizabeth Dr., Marsh Harbour* ☎ *242/367–3498* ▤ *AE, D, MC, V* ☾ *Closed Sun.*

¢–$ ✕ **Jamie's Place.** There's nothing fancy about this clean, bright diner-style eatery, but the welcome is warm, the Bahamian dishes well-executed, and the prices are right, with most meals clocking in at $10 or under. Choose fried chicken, cracked conch, or fresh-caught dolphin, with a side of mashed or roasted potatoes, peas 'n' rice, macaroni and cheese, or cole slaw. Jamie's is also an ice cream parlor, with a dozen flavors. ⊠ *Queen Elizabeth Dr., Marsh Harbour* ☎ *242/367–2880* ▤ *No credit cards* ☾ *Closed Sun.*

¢ ✕ **Bahamas Family Market.** At lunchtime, the best bargains in town are at the lunch counter inside this small grocery. Jamaican meat pies stuffed with curried beef or chicken go for $3. A sub sandwich full of Italian salami and cheese, plus chips and a soft drink, is just $5. At breakfast, snag a fresh-baked pastry and coffee for two bucks. There's no eating area, but they'll heat up your order if you'd like. ⊠ *Queen Elizabeth Dr., at the stoplight* ☎ *242/367–3714* ▤ *No credit cards.*

¢ ✕ **Show-Boo's Conch Salad Stand.** JUST BE NICE implores the hand-lettered sign on this ramshackle stand, across from Sapodilly's restaurant. Follow the instructions and you'll be rewarded with what the proprietor claims to be "the world's best conch salad," often diced and mixed while you watch. Hours are erratic, especially during the September–November off-season. To find out if Show-Boo showed up for business, just swing by around lunchtime and see if there's a line forming in front of his stand. ⊠ *Queen Elizabeth Dr., Marsh Harbour* ☎ *No phone* ▤ *No credit cards.*

$$$$ ▥ **Rickmon Bonefish Lodge.** Well-regarded fishing guide Ricardo Burrows and his wife Monique opened this small hotel to serve the increasing numbers of anglers attracted to bonefishing in the "flats," or shallow areas, near Sandy Point. The whitewashed, plantation-style building has 11 modern rooms, each with air-conditioning and satellite TV; five overlook the ocean through sliding French doors. Fishing packages, which include private guides, are the most popular option here, but non-fishing guests can fill their time beachcombing, bird-watching, snorkeling, and boating. ⊠ *General delivery, Sandy Point* ☎ *242/366–4477* 🖷 *242/366–4478* ⊕ *www.rickmonbonefishlodge.com* ⇆ *11 rooms* ⌕ *Restaurant, beach, lounge; no room phones* ▤ *No credit cards* ⦿⧠ *All-inclusive.*

$$–$$$$ ✕▥ **Abaco Beach Resort & Boat Harbour.** The spacious rooms have natural-stone floors and antique-white wicker furnishings set against salmon or rich blue walls. Bold, artistic textiles, marble wet bars, built-in hair dryers, and in-room satellite TVs round out the accommodations. Dine on filet mignon topped with sautéed onions and mushrooms or a broiled lobster tail at Angler's Restaurant ($–$$), which overlooks yachts moored at the Marina. The resort's full-service dive shop will arrange fishing charters and boat rentals; use of small sailboats and kayaks is complimentary. Lounge poolside and enjoy umbrella drinks from the swim-up bar while your kids explore the playground. ⌖ *Box AB 20511, Marsh Harbour, Abaco* ☎ *242/367–2158, 242/367–2736, or 800/468–4799* 🖷 *242/367–2819* ⊕ *www.abacoresort.com* ⇆ *52 rooms, 6 villas* ⌕ *Restaurant, refrigerators, 2 tennis courts, 2 pools, dive shop, dock, windsurfing,*

Fodor's Choice ★

boating, fishing, mountain bikes, fitness center, 200-slip marina, 2 bars, lounge, laundry facilities ☰ *AE, D, MC, V* ⓌⓄⓁ *FAP, MAP.*

$–$$ ⚏ **Pelican Beach Villas.** On a quiet, private peninsula opposite the main settlement of Marsh Harbour sit these waterfront clapboard cottages, cheerily painted in pale pink, yellow, blue, and green. Inside the air-conditioned rooms are rattan furnishings with pastel cushions and porcelain tile floors. A small sand beach is out front and the cottages are right near Mermaid Reef, a top pick among snorkelers. There's no restaurant on-site, but there's food within walking distance at the Marsh Harbour Marina; for other options, you'll need to rent a car or, better yet, a dinghy, which you can tie up for free at the 100-foot dock. ⌂ *Box AB 20304, Marsh Harbour, Abaco* ☎ *800/642–7268 or 242/367–3600* 🖷 *912/654–3303* ⊕ *www.pelicanbeachvillas.com* ⇥ *7 cottages* ♨ *Kitchenettes, beach, dock, boating, laundry facilities* ☰ *AE, D, MC, V.*

$ ⚏ **Conch Inn Resort & Marina.** A low-key, one-level marina hotel, this is a good choice for budget travelers. Each simple room has two double beds, white-tile floors, white-rattan furniture, and color-splashed bedspreads. Its Conch Crawl restaurant serves the best breakfast in town, with cheesy omelets and thick, sweet pancakes. The full-service 80-slip marina is one of Marsh Harbour's busiest and is the Bahamas' headquarters for the Moorings sailboatcharter service and Nautic Blue Power Yacht Vacations. Small beaches are within walking distance. ⌂ *Box AB 20469, Marsh Harbour, Abaco* ☎ *242/367–4000* 🖷 *242/367–4004* ⊕ *www.conchinn.com* ⇥ *10 rooms* ♨ *Restaurant, refrigerators, pool, dive shop, dock, marina, bar, shop, laundry facilities* ☰ *AE, MC, V.*

$ ⚏ **Lofty Fig Villas.** Owned by the same family for years, this tiny, tidy compound has six spacious villas that overlook the sparkling pool or harbor; restaurants, marinas, bars, and a dive shop are nearby. The villa kitchens are fully equipped, and the supermarket is within about a 10-minute walk. For families or groups on a budget, this is a super option. ✉ *Across from Mangoes Restaurant* ⌂ *Box AB 20437, Marsh Harbour, Abaco* ☎ *242/367–2681* 🖷 *242/267–3385* ⇥ *6 villas* ♨ *Kitchenettes, pool* ☰ *D, MC, V.*

$ ⚏ **Nettie's Different of Abaco.** In the undeveloped land south of Marsh Harbour, owner Nettie Symonette, a longtime Bahamian restaurateur and hotelier, has created a serene eco-resort that embraces the area's natural habitat, alive with wild boars, peacocks, herons, and flamingos. The airy, colonial-style rooms have wooden floors, vaulted open-beamed ceilings, and handcrafted furniture. Some have air-conditioning, although others depend on fans and gentle sea breezes to keep things cool. Most popular here are fishing and birding packages; more than 75 species of birds have been identified on the property, including the rare Bahamian parrot. ✉ *Casuarina Point, Box AB 20092, Marsh Harbour, Abaco* ☎ *242/366–2150 or 877/505–1850* 🖷 *242/327–8152* ⊕ *www.differentofabaco.com* ⇥ *20 rooms* ♨ *Restaurant, some microwaves, refrigerators, pool, lake, outdoor hot tub, beach, snorkeling, boating, fishing, bicycles, billiards, bar, laundry facilities; no room phones, no room TVs* ☰ *MC, V.*

Sports & the Outdoors

BICYCLING **Rental Wheels of Abaco** (☎ 242/367–4643) rents bicycles for $10 a day, and also has Suzuki and Yamaha mopeds.

BOATING You can get around Marsh Harbour, Great Abaco Island, and most of the nearby settled cays by car or ferry, but it's more fun to have your own boat. Marsh Harbour has the biggest selection of rental boats and the largest marinas in the Abacos, so even if you're staying on another cay, you may want to reserve your boat here. You can rent anything from a small dinghy to a 46-foot yacht or catamaran that will sleep six or more. Most rentals are available on a daily, three-day, or weekly basis. Count on spending at least $100 a day for a small boat and $180 for a larger one; the sky's the limit for a deluxe yacht with crew. Reserving your boat in advance is recommended, and remember that rates don't include fuel, which can cost nearly $4 per gallon in the Bahamas. Sailboats can be chartered by the week or longer, with or without crew.

In Marsh Harbour, **Boat Harbour Marina** (☎ 242/367–2158) has 200 fully protected slips and a slew of amenities. **Conch Inn Marina** (☎ 242/367–4000) is one of the busiest in Marsh Harbour and has 80 slips. **Mangoes Marina** (☎ 242/367–4255) has 29 slips and a full range of amenities, including on-shore showers, pool and a popular restaurant of the same name. **Marsh Harbour Marina** (☎ 242/367–2700) has 68 slips and is the only full-service marina on the left side of the harbor, a 10-minute drive from most shops and restaurants.

Florida Yacht Charters (☎ 242/367–4853 or 800/537–0050 ⊕ www.floridayacht.com), at the Boat Harbour Marina, offers air-conditioning and other amenities on its sailboats, power yachts, and catamarans. **The Moorings** (☎ 242/367–4000 or 888/952–8420 ⊕ www.moorings.com) rents 36- to 47-foot sailboats from its base at the Conch Inn Resort & Marina in Marsh Harbour. **Nautic Blue Power Yacht Vacations** (☎ 242/367–4000 or 800/416–0224 ⊕ www.nauticblue.com) has 34- to 46-foot powerboats. **Sail Abaco** (☎ 242/367–5115 or 800/649–3528 ⊕ www.sailabaco.net) rents sleep-aboard catamarans, with captains or instructors available for an extra fee.

Laysue Rentals (☎ 242/367–4414) is a good option for renting a catamaran in Marsh Harbour. **Rainbow Rentals** (☎ 242/367–4602) has custom-built 22-foot catamarans complete with freshwater showers, as well as powerboats. **Rich's Rentals** (☎ 242/367–2742 ⊕ www.richsrentals.com) is the place for 21- to 26-foot Paramount powerboats, all fully equipped for diving and fishing. **Sea Horse Boat Rentals** (☎ 242/367–2513 ⊕ www.seahorseboatrentals.com) has a variety of boats, from 26-foot Paramounts to 18-foot Boston Whalers.

EVENTS Several sporting events are held annually in the Abacos. The **Boat Harbour Billfish Championship** is held in June. Each July, **Regatta Time in Abaco,** a series of five sailboat races, takes place in five cays, with the party scene attracting even more participants than the races. In September there's a spectator event titled the **All Abaco Regatta** with native Bahamian sloops competing in races, plus nightly festivals with food stands and live music. For information about Abacos events, call Marsh Harbour's **Abaco Tourist Office** (☎ 242/367–3067). The **Out Island Promotion Board** (☎ 954/475–8315 ⊕ www.bahama-out-islands.com) has information on everything from special events to art galleries.

FISHING You can find bonefish in the flats, yellowtail on the reefs, or marlin in the deeps of the Abacos. The **Heritage Bonefishing Club** (☎ 242/366–2150) lures the fishing crowd to Casuarina Point at Different of Abaco—an angler's paradise. **Capt. Creswell Archer** (☎ 242/367–4000) will seek out marlin and bonefishing spots during a half day or full day of deep-sea fishing. Brothers Buddy and Christopher Pinder have a combined 30 years of experience in the local waters, and their **Pinder's Bone Fishing** (☎ 242/366–2163) offers year-round bonefishing on the Marls, a maze of mangroves and flats on the western side of Abaco.

SCUBA DIVING & There's excellent diving throughout the Abacos. Many sites are clustered
SNORKELING around Marsh Harbour, including the reef behind **Guana Cay,** which is filled with little cavelike catacombs, and **Fowl Cay National Reserve,** which contains wide tunnels and a variety of fish.

Pelican Cays National Park is a popular dive and snorkeling area south of Marsh Harbour. This shallow, 25-foot dive is filled with sea life; turtles are often sighted, as are spotted eagle rays and tarpons. The park is a 2,000-acre land and marine park protected and maintained by the Bahamas National Trust. Hook up your own boat to one of the three moorings, or check with the local dive shops to see when trips to the park arc scheduled. Snorkelers will want to visit Mermaid Beach, just off Pelican Shores Road in Marsh Harbour, where live reefs and green moray eels make for some of the Abacos' best snorkeling.

Dive Abaco (☎ 242/367–2787 or 800/247–5338 ⊕ www.diveabaco.com), at the Conch Inn in Marsh Harbour, offers scuba and snorkeling trips on their custom dive boats. Sites explored include reefs, tunnels, caverns, and wreck dives. DiveAbaco also maintains a boat and office at Abaco Beach resort. **Rainbow Rentals** (☎ 242/367–4602) rents catamarans and snorkeling gear. **Sea Horse Boat Rentals** (☎ 242/367–2513) rents snorkeling gear.

TENNIS **Abaco Beach Resort** (☎ 242/367–2158) opens its two lighted courts to visitors. A tennis pro is on hand for clinics and private lessons for adults and children, and there are regular round-robin tournaments for guests.

TOURS The only ecotourism company in the Abacos is **Abaco Outback** (☎ 242/367–5358 ⊕ www.abacooutback.com). Experienced guides lead birding tours to the southern part of Great Abaco Island, home to the native Bahama parrot. Half- and full-day kayak trips take you past inland mangrove creeks while searching for native heron and sea turtles, and also include snorkeling stops. **Abaco Island Tours** (☎ 242/367–2936 ⊕ www.abacoislandtours.com) arranges tours of Marsh Harbour and nearby Hope Town, and also can help arrange diving, sailing, fishing, and dolphin encounter tours through local guides.

WINDSURFING Windsurfing equipment and sea kayaks are offered free of charge to hotel and marina guests at the **Abaco Beach Resort** (☎ 242/367–2158).

Shopping
At Marsh Harbour's traffic light, look for the turquoise-and-white stripe awnings of **Abaco Treasures** (☎ 242/367–3460), purveyors of fine china, crystal, perfumes, and gifts.

Iggy Biggy (⊠ Queen's Hwy., Marsh Harbour ☎ 242/367–3596), inside a couple of bright-pink cottages, is your best bet for hats, sandals, tropical jewelry, sportswear, and souvenirs.

Nassau straw hats and baskets, shell-encrusted coasters and candlesticks, and pillows and linens made in the Abacos are the best choices at **Island-Style Gifts** (⊠ Royal Harbour Village ☎ 242/367–5861).

Sip an iced latte or a strong mug of joe while perusing the ceramics, quilts, pillows, carved wooden boats, and other locally produced artwork at **Java in Abaco** (⊠ Royal Harbour Village ☎ 242/367–5523). There's also a book exchange where you can replenish your supply of paperbacks.

John Bull (⊠ Queen's Hwy., Marsh Harbour ☎ 242/367–2473), near the harbor, is a branch of a leading Nassau shop selling Rolex watches, jewelry by such designers as David Yurman, and makeup and perfume lines that include Iman and Lancome.

Johnston Studios Art Gallery (⊠ Little Harbour ☎ 242/367–2720), 45 minutes south of Marsh Harbor, displays original bronzes by the Johnstons, as well as prints and gifts.

Sand Dollar Shoppe (⊠ Royal Harbour Village ☎ 242/367–4405) sells resort wear, including a decent children's selection, and jewelry, featuring locally made Abaco Gold necklaces and earrings.

Solomon's Mines (⊠ Queen Elizabeth Dr., Marsh Harbour ☎ 242/367–3191) sells upscale watches (think Tag Heuer and Patek Philippe), plus high-quality perfumes, cosmetics, and china, all duty-free. It's at the Abaco Beach Resort's entrance.

Elbow Cay

★ ❺ In the charming village of **Hope Town,** most of the families of the 300-odd residents have lived there for at least several generations, in some cases as many as 10. Hope Town lies southeast of Marsh Harbour on Elbow Cay. A ferry from Marsh Harbour arrives here several times a day. You'll find few cars here, and although modern conveniences like high-speed Internet and satellite TV are becoming more common, they are a relatively new development. In fact, most residents remember well the day the island first got telephone service—back in 1988. Before that, everyone called each other the way many still do here and in other Out Islands: by VHF, the party line for boaters.

This laid-back community enthusiastically welcomes visitors. Upon arrival you'll first see a much-photographed Bahamas landmark, a 120-foot-tall, peppermint-stripe lighthouse built in 1838. The light's construction was delayed for several years by acts of vandalism; then-residents feared it would end their profitable wrecking practice. Today, the **Hope Town lighthouse** is one of the Bahamas' last three hand-turned, kerosene-fueled beacons. Weekdays 10–4 the lighthouse keeper will welcome you at the top for a superb view of the sea and the nearby cays. There's no road between the lighthouse and the town proper. You can take your own boat here, or use the ferry, assuming you want to spend at least an hour here.

For an interesting walking or bicycle tour of Hope Town, follow the two narrow lanes that circle the village and harbor. (Most of the village is closed to cars and golf carts.) The saltbox cottages—painted in brilliant blues, purples, pinks, and yellows—with their white picket fences, flowering gardens, and porches and sills decorated with conch shells, will remind you of a New England seaside community—Bahamian style. Some have fanciful names, like Summer Magic or Valentines, while others are charmingly practical. Your walk will take you past **Hope Town School,** the original 110-year-old, one-room schoolhouse, painted red and white. The hand-carved corners made by Loyalist shipwrights are still in evidence.

Stop by the **Cholera Cemetery,** a deceptively peaceful graveyard that contains the bodies of more than 100 victims of an outbreak of the deadly disease in the 1850s. The cemetery was closed after the outbreak, in hopes of further containing the disease. You may want to stop at the **Wyannie Malone Historical Museum** (☎ 242/366–0293) on Queen's Highway, the main street. It contains Hope Town memorabilia and photographs. Admission is $3, but because the museum is staffed by volunteers, hours vary, and the museum closes completely in September and October. Many descendants of Mrs. Malone, who settled here with her children in 1875, still live on Elbow Cay.

Smack in the town's center stands an old, turquoise municipal building with offices clearly labeled "Commissioner," "Post Office," and "Visitor Information." Forget about the first two—they've long since relocated—but Hope Town's Visitor Information "office" is a cement room with a few well-papered bulletin boards on which everything from current happenings to restaurant menus is posted.

There are several churches in this tiny town. On Sunday morning, you'll hear sermons floating through open windows. Don't be surprised if you come upon an alfresco Catholic service in the dockside park. Residents joke that the priest has to stand in the hot sun while the congregation enjoys the shade of sprawling trees "so he won't talk so long."

Where to Stay & Eat

$–$$ ✕ **Rudy's Place.** In a renovated house standing by itself in the middle of the island, Rudy's makes up for its lack of ambience with its excellent renditions of Bahamian favorites, along with a few other dishes. Rave reviews go to the crawfish baked with Parmesan cheese, and the lobster, prepared any way you choose it. Complimentary delivery is available to most anywhere on the island; call ahead to make arrangements. ✉ *Center Line Rd., Hope Town* ☎ *242/366–0062* ⌕ *Reservations essential* ▤ *MC, V* ⊗ *Closed Sun.*

¢–$$ ✕ **Harbour's Edge.** Hope Town's premier hangout, this bar and restaurant has an inviting deck that allows you to watch the goings-on in the busy harbor. Live bands occasionally play on weekends. If you're looking for a place for an after-dinner drink, this is the one most likely to have a crowd. Try the tender conch burgers, grilled grouper, or lobster salad for lunch or dinner. Authentic Bahamian breakfasts are served on Sunday. Rent bikes here for $8 a day. ✉ *Lower Rd., Hope Town* ☎ *242/ 366–0292* ▤ *MC, V* ⊗ *Closed Tues.*

¢–$ ✕ **Cap'n Jack's.** There are a handful of booths and a small bar, but most of this casual eatery's seating is out on the pink-and-white-striped dock-patio. The menu is nothing fancy, but provides reliable grouper burgers, pork chops, and cracked conch. When it's in season, there's sometimes a lobster special, a good deal at $22. Cap'n Jack's serves three meals a day, offers a full bar, and has live music Wednesday and a DJ Friday nights mid-December through August. ⊠ *Hope Town* ☎ *242/366–0247* ⊟ *MC, V.*

¢–$ ✕ **On the Beach Bar and Grill.** Burgers, fries, conch, and fish are served up with a terrific Atlantic view at this open-air bar and grill, perched high on the beach across the street from the small Turtle Hill resort. It's open only until sunset, and because all seating is open to the elements, a gullywasher of a storm closes the place down. ⊠ *Queens Highway, between Hope Town and White Sound, Hope Town* ☎ *242/366–0557* ⌂ *Reservations not accepted* ⊟ *AE, MC, V* ☉ *Closed Mon.*

$–$$$ ✕▥ **Hope Town Harbour Lodge.** Just steps from town, yet overlooking
Fodor's Choice the rugged Atlantic beach, this resort has one of the best settings in the
★ Abacos, and its rooms and amenities are of equally high quality. All rooms are tastefully decorated, but choose one of the ocean-view or oceanfront cottages, with light pine paneling, terra-cotta tile floors, full kitchenettes, and French doors opening onto private decks. Lunch is poolside, with views of the ocean. At dinner, ($$–$$$) warm up with a key-lime martini, rimmed in graham-cracker crumbs, before tackling a steak or the grilled tuna with creamy wasabi sauce. ⊠ *Upper Rd., Hope Town* ☎ *242/366–0095* ⌨ *242/366–0286* ⊕ *www.hopetownlodge.com* ⌘ *12 rooms, 12 suites, 1 cottage* ⌂ *2 restaurants, some microwaves, pool, beach, dock, boating, bar; no room phones, no room TVs* ⌂ *Reservations essential* ⊟ *D, MC, V.*

$–$$$$ ▥ **Elbow Cay Properties.** Besides being the most cost-efficient way to stay on Elbow Cay, a private house or villa is also likely to be the most comfortable. This longstanding rental agency handles a variety of properties, from cozy two-bedroom, one-bath cottages to a six-bedroom, six-bath villa better described as a mansion. Many of the rental homes are on the water, with a dock or a sandy beach right out front. The owners are set on finding you a place to match your wishes and budget. ⊠ *Western Harborfront, Hope Town* ☎☎ *242/366–0569* ⊕ *www.elbowcayrentals.com* ⌘ *50 units* ⊟ *MC, V.*

$–$$$$ ▥ **Hope Town Hideaways.** This collection of rental homes is located in a secluded spot on the far side of the harbor. The owners also run a large property-management company offering more than 75 private villas and cottages for rent, most of them sleeping four or more. Though some smaller, more modest accommodations are available, the emphasis is on upscale homes, with listings including four-bedroom villas with Vulcan ranges and Sub-Zero refrigerators. The modern villas have airy cathedral ceilings; large, well-stocked kitchens; satellite TV and Internet access; and French doors opening onto decks with harbor views. The patio area in front of the villas has a grill for guests' use, a freshwater pool, and a dock for tying up your dinghy. ⊠ *1 Purple Porpoise Pl., Hope Town* ☎ *242/366–0224* ⌨ *242/366–0434* ⊕ *www.hopetown.com* ⌘ *75 units* ⊟ *AE, D, MC, V.*

$$$ ⊡ **Turtle Hill Vacation Villas.** Bougainvillea- and hibiscus-lined walkways encircle the central swimming pool of this cluster of six villas, each with its own private patio. Inside, villas have light-wood paneling, tile floors, and rattan furnishings, as well as sleeper sofas. The lovely beach, the setting for the resort's bar and grill, is a two-minute walk away. Each villa comes with a golf cart for jaunts into town. Choose an upper villa for distant views of the sea. ⊠ *Off Queens Hwy. between Hope Town and White Sound, Hope Town* ☎ *508/540–2519 or 800/339–2124* 🖷🖷 *242/366–0557* ⊕ *www.turtlehill.com* 🔊 *4 2-bedroom villas, 2 3-bedroom villas* ♻ *Restaurant, fans, kitchenettes, microwaves, in-room VCRs, pool* ⊟ *D, MC, V.*

$–$$$ ⊡ **Sea Spray Resort and Villas.** Consider this resort if you're planning to catch any waves, as the villas are just off Garbanzo Beach, a favorite with surfers. The villas have full kitchens, outdoor grills, and decks. Each is spacious and clean. You can rent motorboats, bikes, and snorkeling gear. The on-site store sells everything from charcoal to surfboard wax. There's also a 60-slip full-service marina, a tiki bar, and a restaurant where you can enjoy your lobster or grilled, fresh-caught grouper while gazing upon the ocean. ⊠ *South end of White Sound* ☎ *242/366–0065* 🖷 *242/366–0383* ⊕ *www.seasprayresort.com* 🔊 *7 villas* ♻ *Restaurant, kitchenettes, pool, dock, snorkeling, boating, marina, fishing, bicycles, bar* ⊟ *D, MC, V* ☉ *Closed Sept., Oct.*

$–$$ ⊡ **Abaco Inn.** Upscale couples favor this beachfront resort, quiet even by Abacos standards. The cozy rooms—seven ocean- and seven harbor-view—have simple, comfortable furnishings and individual hammocks. The luxury villa suites have kitchenettes, a small living area, and both sunrise and sunset water views. After your complimentary pickup in Hope Town, consider renting your own boat so you can zoom into town or to one of the smaller islets around Elbow Cay. You can tie up at the resort. Excellent reefs for snorkeling and diving are nearby. The lounge has a satellite TV and live music several nights a week. ⊠ *2 mi south of Hope Town* ☎ *242/366–0133 or 800/468–8799* 🖷 *242/366–0113* ⊕ *www.abacoinn.com* 🔊 *14 rooms, 8 villas* ♻ *Restaurant, pool, beach, boating, fishing, bicycles, bar, lounge, laundry facilities, airport shuttle; no room phones, no room TVs* ⊟ *AE, D, MC, V.*

Sports & the Outdoors

BOATING **Abaco Multihull Charters** (☎ 242/366–0552) charters 30-foot catamarans for seven days or longer and also offers captained sailing, snorkeling, and sightseeing trips by the day or half-day. **Hope Town Hideaways** (☎ 242/366–0224) has 12 slips. **Island Marine** (☎ 242/366–0282) has 17- to 23-foot boats available for rent from $90 to $135 a day. **Sea Horse Boat Rentals** (☎ 242/367–2513) has Bimini-top boats ranging in length from 18 to 26 feet. It is located in Hope Town. **Sea Spray Resort** (☎ 242/366–0065) has a full-service marina with 60 slips.

FISHING Abaco bonefishing champion **Bonefish Dundee** (☎ 242/366–0478) offers bonefishing, reef fishing, and bottom fishing. **Day's Catch** (☎ 242/366–0059) books charter fishing excursions on the nearby reefs with Will Key, who will even clean your fish afterward. Key is especially patient with children, who will enjoy learning about the fish as much as they'll enjoy landing one. **Seagull Charters** (☎ 242/366–0266) sets up guided deep-sea excursions with Captain Robert Lowe, who has more than 35 years' experience in the local waters.

SCUBA DIVING &
SNORKELING
Day's Catch (☎ 242/366–0059) takes out small groups of snorkelers and divers in a 21-foot offshore boat. **Froggies Out Island Adventures** (☎ 242/366–0431) has snorkel and dive trips, scuba and resort courses, full-day adventure tours, island excursions, and dolphin encounters. You can also rent snorkel and diving gear here.

WINDSURFING
Sea Spray Resort (☎ 242/366–0065) attracts windsurfers to the choice waters just off Garbanzo Beach.

Shopping

Ebbtide (☎ 242/366–0088) is on the upper path road in a renovated Loyalist home. Come here for such Bahamian gifts as batik clothes, original driftwood carvings and prints, and nautical jewelry. Browse through the extensive Bahamian book collection or pick up a magazine.

Fantasy Boutique (✉ Queen's Hwy. ☎ 242/366–0537) has a nice selection of souvenirs, beach wraps, T-shirts, arts and crafts, and Cuban cigars.

Iggy Biggy (✉ Queen's Hwy. ☎ 242/366–0354) is the only shop in Hope Town that carries the lovely Abaco ceramics handmade in Treasure Cay. It also sells wind chimes, sandals, resort wear, jewelry, and island music.

Man-O-War Cay

⑥ Many residents of **Man-O-War Cay** are descendants of early Loyalist settlers named Albury, who started the tradition of handcrafting boats more than two centuries ago. They remain proud of their heritage and continue to build their famous fiberglass boats today. This shipwrighting center of the Abacos lies south of Green Turtle and Great Guana cays, an easy 45-minute ride from Marsh Harbour by water taxi or aboard a small rented outboard dinghy. Man-O-War Cay also has a 28-slip marina, three churches, a one-room schoolhouse, and several shops and restaurants that cater largely to visitors.

A mile north of the island, you can dive to the wreck of the USS *Adirondack,* which sank after hitting a reef in 1862. It lies among a host of cannons in 20 feet of water. The cay is also a marvelous place to walk or to take a rented golf cart for a spin. Two main roads, Queen's Highway and Sea Road, are often shaded with arching sea grape trees interspersed with palms and pines. The island is secluded, but it has kept up-to-date with satellite television and full phone and Internet service. Still, the old-fashioned, family-oriented roots show in the local policy toward liquor: None is sold anywhere on the island. (But most folks won't mind if you bring your own.)

Where to Stay & Eat

$–$$ ✕ **Hibiscus Cafe.** This local favorite isn't fancy, but it turns out dependable Bahamian cooking. Lunchtime is casual, with burgers, grouper, and conch. Dinner, served Thursday through Saturday, is slightly more formal, with rack of lamb among the specialties. ⊠ *Waterfront* ☎ *242/ 365–6380* ⊟ *No credit cards* ⊙ *Closed Sun.*

$–$$ ✕ **Man-O-War Marina Pavilion.** Try the grouper fingers for lunch, when you'll get a good view of the sheltered harbor. Locals and tourists alike come for Friday- and Saturday-night dinners of steak, chicken, ribs, or lamb, served with the expected Bahamian sides of baked macaroni and cheese and peas 'n' rice. ⊠ *Waterfront* ☎ *242/365–6185* ⊟ *No credit cards* ⊙ *Closed Sun. Closed mid-Aug., Sept.*

$$ ▥ **Schooner's Landing.** Perched on a rocky promontory overlooking a long, isolated beach, this small, Mediterranean-style resort has five two-bedroom town-house condos. Enjoy ocean views from each condo or from the wraparound deck of the freshwater swimming pool. Rooms are airy with wicker furniture and ceramic tile floors and include fully equipped kitchens, ceiling fans, TVs, and stereos with CD players. There's no restaurant, but within walking distance is almost every establishment, eating or otherwise, on the cay. There's a barbecue and wet bar in the gazebo, and nearby grocery stores deliver. ⊠ *Man-O-War Cay, Abaco* ☎*242/365–6072* 🖷*242/365–6285* ⊕*schoonerslanding.com* ⟿*5 condominiums* ♿ *In-room VCRs, pool, beach, boating, fishing, laundry service* ⊟ *AE, MC, V.*

Sports & the Outdoors

BOATING **Man-O-War Marina** (☎ 242/365–6008) has 28 slips and rents 26-foot boats, and, for landlubbers, golf carts.

SCUBA DIVING **Man-O-War Dive Shop** (⊠ Man-O-War Marina ☎ 242/365–6013) rents tanks and snorkeling equipment.

Shopping

★ **Albury's Sail Shop** (☎ 242/365–6014) is popular with boaters, who stock up on duffle bags, briefcases, jackets, hats, and purses, all made from colorful, sturdy canvas fabric called duck, traditionally used for sails.

Island Treasures (☎ 242/365–6072) has a wide selection of T-shirts, souvenirs, resort wear, candles, and ceramics.

Joe's Studio (☎ 242/365–6082) sells paintings by local artists, books, clothing, and other nautically oriented gifts, but the most interesting souvenirs are the half-models of sailing dinghies. These mahogany models are cut in half, mounted on boards, and are meant to be displayed as wall hangings. Artist Joe Albury, one of the store's owners, also crafts full, 3-D boat models, which go for as much as $1,800.

Great Guana Cay

❼ The essence of **Great Guana Cay** can be summed up by its unofficial motto,
Fodor'sChoice painted on a hand-lettered sign: IT'S BETTER IN THE BAHAMAS, BUT . . . IT'S
★ GOODER IN GUANA. This narrow island just off Great Abaco Island, reached by ferry from Marsh Harbour or by private boat, is the kind of place people picture when they dream of running off to live on an exotic island, complete with beautiful empty beaches and grassy dunes. Only 100 full-time residents live on 7 mi long Great Guana Cay, where you're more likely to run into a rooster than a car during your stroll around the

drowsy village. Still, there are just enough luxuries here to make your stay comfortable, including a couple of small, laid-back resorts and a restaurant-bar with one of the best party scenes in the entire Abacos.

Where to Stay & Eat

$–$$$ ✕ **Nipper's Beach Bar & Grill.** With awesome ocean views and a snorkeling reef just 10 yards offshore, this set of brightly striped, split-level gazebos is where nearly every visitor to Guana ends up eventually. Linger over a lunch of burgers and sandwiches or a dinner of steak and lobster, then chill out in the solar-heated double pool, one for children and one with a swim-up pool bar for adults. The Sunday lunchtime pig roasts attract revelers from all over the Abacos. Nurse a "Nipper Tripper"—a frozen concoction of five rums and two juices. More than one or two of those, and you'll be happy to take advantage of the Nippermobile, which provides free transport to and from the cay's public dock. ⊠ *Great Guana Cay* ☎ *242/365–5143* ⊕ *www.nippersbar.com* ☰ *AE, D, MC, V.*

$–$$$
Fodor'sChoice
★
✕⌂ **Dolphin Beach Resort.** Upscale and pocket-size, this haven has cozy cottages and a two-story wood-frame main building handcrafted of Abaco pine by Guana Cay shipwrights. Three cottages have two stories with private oceanfront decks—ideal for several couples or families. Each cottage is individually furnished and includes modern kitchen appliances. Outside, secluded showers are surrounded by bougainvillea and sea-grape trees. Boardwalk nature trails winding through the carefully tended 15-acre property lead to uninhabited Guana Cay Beach. The Blue Water Grill ($–$$$), new in 2003, shines at dinner, with specialties including prime rib and a surprisingly sophisticated list of wines and specialty martinis. ⊠ *Great Guana Cay* ☎ *800/222–2646* ☎☎ *242/365–5163* ⊕ *www.dolphinbeachresort.com* ⤳ *9 cottages, 4 rooms* ⚭ *Restaurant, bar, kitchenettes, pool, beach, dive shop, dock, snorkeling, windsurfing, boating, bicycles, shops* ☰ *AE, MC, V.*

$–$$$
Fodor'sChoice
★
✕⌂ **Guana Seaside Village.** An American couple visited Guana and liked it so much, they took over this small resort with eight homey rooms, some with hand-painted murals, arranged around a tropical courtyard. An additional seven cottages, with porches and decks, are just steps from the beach. The cottages have at least two bedrooms, two baths, and a full kitchen, and some have washers and dryers—great for families. Guests can play with complimentary kayaks, snorkeling equipment, and paddleboats, or arrange fishing or diving trips through the helpful staff. Three meals daily are served at Hibiscus ($–$$), where specialties include coconut shrimp, stuffed pork chops, lobster salad, and pastas of all kinds. The two-story restaurant is air-conditioned, but on breezy nights sit in the landscaped courtyard, a romantic option for dinners alfresco. ⊠ *Near Crossing Bay, Great Guana Cay* ☎ *877/681–3091 or 242/365–5106* ☎ *242/365–5146* ⊕ *www.guanaseaside.com* ⤳ *8 rooms, 7 cottages* ⚭ *Restaurant, in-room VCRs, pool, beach, lounge; no phones in some rooms* ☰ *D, MC, V* ☽ *Closed mid-Sept.–Oct.*

Sports & the Outdoors

SCUBA DIVING **Dive Guana** (☎ *242/365–5178*), on the grounds of Dolphin Beach Resort, organizes scuba and snorkeling trips or island tours. The shop also rents boats, kayaks, and bicycles.

Treasure Cay

Running through large pine forests that are still home to wild horses and boars, the wide, paved Sherben A. Boothe Highway leads north from Marsh Harbour for 20 mi to **Treasure Cay**, which is technically not an island but a large peninsula connected to Great Abaco by a narrow spit of land. Here you'll find a small community of mostly winter residents, a 3,000-acre farm that grows winter vegetables and fruit for export, and a spectacular 3½-mi-long beach, often called the best in the Abacos.

❽ Fodor'sChoice ★

Treasure Cay is a large-scale real-estate development project. The centerpiece is the Treasure Cay Hotel Resort & Marina, with its Dick Wilson–designed golf course and 150-slip marina. Unlike the rest of the Abacos, Treasure Cay was largely unpopulated until it was created primarily as a tourist destination, and therefore lacks any sense of history or community. Those seeking local color and an authentic Bahamian experience will find Treasure Cay rather sterile. Fortunately, historic Elbow Cay, Man-O-War Cay, and Green Turtle Cay are all easily accessible by boat.

Treasure Cay's commercial center consists of two rows of shops near the resort with a post office, laundromat, ice-cream parlor, a couple of grocery stores, and the BATELCO. You'll also find car-, scooter-, and bicycle-rental offices here.

Where to Stay & Eat

$-$$ ✕ **Touch of Class.** Ten minutes north of Treasure Cay, this favorite dinner spot serves delicious traditional Bahamian dishes such as grilled fresh-caught grouper and minced local lobster, stewed with tomatoes, onions, and spices. Reasonably priced appetizers, such as conch chowder and conch fritters, and a full bar make this a nice option for a night out away from your hotel or condo. ⊠ *Queen's Hwy. at Treasure Cay Rd.* ☎ *242/365–8195* ☐ *MC, V.*

¢-$ ✕ **Café La Florence.** Stop into this bakery-café in the main shopping strip at Treasure Cay resort for breakfast treats such as just-made muffins and cinnamon rolls. Or go for a light lunch of lobster quiche, conch chowder, or a spicy, Jamaican-style meat patty. You can also arrange for the chef to cater private dinners of lobster, steak, and the like in your rented condo. Florence's ice-cream parlor next door is your answer for treats à la mode. ⊠ *Treasure Cay* ☎ *242/365–8354* ☐ *No credit cards.*

$-$$$ **Fodor'sChoice ★** ✕🛏 **Treasure Cay Hotel Resort & Marina.** Treasure Cay is best known for its 18-hole golf course, which *Golf Digest* has frequently rated as the Bahamas' number one course. The property has rooms and town house–style accommodations forming a long pastel row facing a 150-slip marina. Rooms come with a mini-refrigerator, toaster oven, and small dining counter; suites have vaulted ceilings, pine headboards and armoires, and full modern kitchens. The Spinnaker restaurant ($$–$$$) can seat up to 350 in indoor and outdoor dining areas, and serves both Bahamian and Continental cuisine. A more casual, kid-friendly option is Thursday night pizza at the Tipsy Seagull, the poolside bar and grill that is also a popular drinking and dancing spot. ⊠ *On marina* ✉ *2301 S. Federal Hwy., Fort Lauderdale, FL 33316* ☎ *242/365–8801 or 954/525–7711, 800/327–1584 for reservations* 🖷 *954/525–1699* ⊕ *www.treasurecay.com* ⇆ *54 rooms, 33 suites*

&*Restaurant, dining room, kitchenettes, 18-hole golf course, 4 tennis courts, pool, beach, dive shop, dock, snorkeling, windsurfing, boating, marina, fishing, 2 bars, lounge, baby-sitting ☰AE, D, MC, V ⚏EP, FAP, MAP.*

$$$ ▦ **Bahama Beach Club.** Ideal for families, these two-, three- and four-bedroom condos are right off the famous Treasure Cay beach. Decor varies, but each unit has ceramic floor tiles and stylish rattan furniture with colorful accents, as well as a fully equipped kitchen and a large living room. The condos have a patio or balcony overlooking the water and the grounds, which are landscaped with tropical palms. ✑ *Box AB 22275, Treasure Cay,* ☎ *800/563–0014 or 242/365–8500* 🖷 *242/365–8501* ⊕ *www.bahamabeachclub.com* ⇦ *44 condos* & *Kitchens, pool, beach, laundry facilities ☰AE, D, MC, V.*

$$$ ▦ **Treasure Houses.** Around a courtyard of interconnected swimming pools, footbridges, and burbling waterfalls, these octagonal houses are perched on stilts for lovely beach views. Each two-bedroom guesthouse can sleep six and has airy, exposed-beam ceilings, plush carpeting, and muted tropical-print textiles. Bedrooms open onto narrow private patios. Queen-size sleeper sofas, TVs with VCRs, and fully equipped kitchens are standard. Rent a golf cart or ride one of the gratis bicycles that accompany each unit. The Treasure Houses are 1 mi from the main resort and stores of the Treasure Cay development. ✉ *Treasure Cay beach* ☎ *242/365–8507 or 242/365–8777* 🖷 *242/365–8508* ⊕ *www.islandtreasurehouse.com* ⇦ *2 2-bedroom houses* & *BBQs, kitchenettes, pool, beach, snorkeling, bicycles, laundry facilities; no room phones ☰MC, V.*

$–$$$ ▦ **Banyan Beach Club.** Directly on Treasure Cay's breathtaking beach, these one-, two-, and three-bedroom Mediterranean-style condos are attractive and well situated. Units have high, whitewashed-beam ceilings, terra-cotta tile floors, and vast ocean views from private balconies or patios. Handsome pine furnishings, TVs with VCRs, and full-size modern kitchens round out the digs. The resort's Sandbar serves up burgers, hot dogs, and frosty drinks from 11 AM to 7 PM. On-site golf carts can be rented for exploring the cay. ✉ *¼ mi from village of Treasure Cay* ✑ *Box AB 22158, Treasure Cay* ☎ *242/365–8111 or 888/625–3060* 🖷 *561/625–5301* ⊕ *www.banyanbeach.com* ⇦ *21 condos* & *Kitchenettes, pool, wading pool, beach, snorkeling, bar ☰AE, D, MC, V.*

Sports & the Outdoors

BICYCLING **Wendell's Bicycle Rentals** (☎ 242/365–8687) rents mountain bikes by the half-day, day, or week.

BOATING **J. I. C. Boat Rentals** (☎ 242/365–8465) rents center-console fishing boats; one-, three- and seven-day rates are available. Try to reserve your boat at least two to three weeks in advance. **Rich's Rentals** (☎ 242/365–8582) rents boats by the day, three days, or week. Daily rentals range from $130 to $160 for 21- to 26-foot Bimini-top fishing boats, perfect for island-hopping.

EVENTS A popular sportfishing destination, Treasure Cay hosts several fishing tournaments annually, including a leg of the **Bahamas Billfish Championship** in May. June brings the annual **Treasure Cay International Billfish Tournament.** Call **Treasure Cay Services** (☎ 954/525–7711 or 800/327–1584) for information about fishing and golf tournaments, regattas, and other special events.

FISHING Arrange for local deep-sea fishing or bonefishing guides through **Treasure Cay Hotel Resort & Marina** (☎ 242/365–8250).

GOLF A half mile from the **Treasure Cay Hotel Resort & Marina** (☎ 800/327–
★ 1584 or 954/525–7711 ⊕ www.golfbahamas.com) is the property's par-72, Dick Wilson–designed course, with carts available. There's no need to reserve tee times, and the course is usually delightfully uncrowded, ideal for a leisurely round. A driving range, putting green, and small pro shop are also on-site.

SCUBA DIVING & No Name Cay and Whale Cay are popular marine-life sites. The 1865
SNORKELING wreck of the steamship freighter **San Jacinto** also affords scenic diving and chances to feed the resident green moray eel. **Treasure Divers** (☎ 242/365–8465) rents equipment and takes divers and snorkelers out to a variety of sites.

TENNIS **Treasure Cay Hotel Resort & Marina** (☎ 800/327–1584 or 242/365–8801) has six of the best courts in the Abacos, four of which are lighted for night play.

WINDSURFING Windsurfers and a complete line of nonmotorized water craft are available for rent at the **Treasure Cay Hotel Resort & Marina** (☎ 242/365–8250).

Shopping
Near Treasure Cay resort is **Abaco Ceramics** (☎ 242/365–8489 ⊙ Closed Sat. and Sun.), which offers its signature white clay pottery with blue fish designs.

Green Turtle Cay

❾ A 10-minute ferry ride from a Treasure Cay dock will take you to **Green Turtle Cay.** The tiny island is steeped in Loyalist history. Some residents can trace their heritage back to their ancestors' arrival from the U.S. colonies more than 200 years ago. The cay is surrounded by several deep bays, sounds, and a nearly continuous strip of fine beach.

New Plymouth, first settled in 1783, is Green Turtle's main community. Many of its approximately 550 residents eke out a living by diving for conch or exporting lobster and fish through the Abaco Seafood Company, but an increasing number depend on businesses catering to tourists and vacation-home owners. On some summer days during the height of Green Turtle's tourist season, the visitors on the island can outnumber the native residents.

There are a few grocery and hardware stores, several gift shops, a post office, a bank, a handful of restaurants, and several offices—not to mention the homes that have been owned, in some cases, by the same families for generations. Narrow streets flanked by wild-growing flora (such as amaryllis, hibiscus, and poinciana) wind between rows of New England–style white-clapboard cottages with brightly colored shutters. During the Civil War, New Plymouth provided a safe haven for Confederate blockade runners. One Union ship, the USS *Adirondack,* was pursuing a gunrunner and wrecked on a reef in 1862 at nearby Man-O-War Cay. One of the ship's cannons now sits at the town harbor.

If your accommodations aren't in New Plymouth proper, you'll need transportation into town. Many hotels provide an occasional shuttle, and there is one taxi on the island, but most people travel via golf cart or boat. Your hotel can help to arrange a boat rental through one of several rental companies on the island. Don't worry, you won't miss having a car; even in the slowest golf cart, you can get from one end of the island to the other in 20 minutes or less.

New Plymouth's most frequently visited attraction is the **Albert Lowe Museum,** on the main thoroughfare, Parliament Street. The Bahamas' oldest historical museum, it's dedicated to a model-ship builder and direct descendant of the island's original European-American settlers. You can learn island history through local memorabilia from the 1700s, Lowe's model schooners, and old photographs, including one of the aftermath of the 1932 hurricane that nearly flattened New Plymouth. One of the galleries displays paintings of typical Out Island scenes by acclaimed artist Alton Lowe, Albert's son. Mrs. Ivy Roberts, the museum's director, enjoys showing visitors around and sharing stories of life in the Out Islands before the days of high-speed Internet and daily airline flights. She is often assisted by her husband, a survivor of the '32 hurricane and seaman in the days of wooden schooners. ⊠ *Parliament St.* ☎ *242/365–4094* ⊠ *$5* ☉ *Mon.–Sat. 9–11:45 and 1–4.*

Just a few blocks from the Albert Lowe Museum, on Victoria Street, is **Miss Emily's Blue Bee Bar** (☎ 242/365–4181), which stands next to the old gaol (jail), a tiny stone building thought to be more than 100 years old and, happily, no longer in use. Mrs. Emily Cooper, creator of the popular drink Goombay Smash, passed away in 1997, but her daughter Violet continues to serve up the famous rum, pineapple juice, and apricot brandy concoction. Mementos of customers—business cards, expired credit cards, T-shirts, and autographed dollar bills—and Junkanoo masks cover the walls.

The past is present in the **Memorial Sculpture Garden,** across the street from the New Plymouth Inn. Note that it is laid out in the pattern of the British flag. Immortalized in busts perched on pedestals are local residents who have made important contributions to the Bahamas. Plaques detail the accomplishments of British Loyalists, their descendants, and the descendants of those brought as slaves, such as Jeanne I. Thompson, a contemporary playwright and the country's second woman to practice law.

Where to Stay & Eat

$–$$ ✕ **McIntosh Restaurant and Bakery.** At this simple, diner-style restaurant, lunch means excellent renditions of local favorites, such as fried grouper and cracked conch, and sandwiches made with thick slices of slightly sweet Bahamian bread. At dinner, large portions of pork chops, lobster, fish, and shrimp are served with rib-sticking sides like baked macaroni and cheese, peas 'n' rice, and coleslaw. Save room for a piece of pound cake or coconut cream pie, baked fresh daily and displayed in the glass case up front. Or, on a hot day, step next door to the attached Three Sisters' Ice Cream Shop for a scoop of homemade cookies 'n' cream or coconut ice cream. ✉ *Parliament St.* ☎ *242/365–4625* ▭ *D, MC, V.*

¢–$$ ✕ **Jolly Roger.** This casual bar-bistro at the Bluff House Marina offers lively lunches and in the evening, a less formal alternative to the reservation-only dinners at the island's three hotels. Sit under a canvas umbrella on the deck admiring the handsome yachts and sailboats moored at the marina or inside the wood-paneled, airy dining room. Choices range from standard Bahamian (conch fritters and burgers) to new American (roasted pork tenderloin with salsa, salads with goat cheese and roasted vegetables, and even, on occasion, sushi). It's open weekends only from August to early December. ✉ *Between Abaco Sea and White Sound, at the Bluff House Beach Hotel marina* ✉ *Box AB 22886, Green Turtle Cay* ☎ *242/365–4247* ▭ *AE, MC, V.*

$ ✕ **The Wrecking Tree.** The casual restaurant's wooden deck was built around the wrecking tree, a place where 19th-century wrecking vessels brought their salvage. Today it's a pleasant place to linger over a Bahamian-brewed Kalik and a hearty lunch of cracked conch, fish-and-chips, or fresh-made conch salad. Dinners may include turtle steak or local lobster—if you order by 5 PM; otherwise, choose from dishes like fresh-caught grouper and fried chicken. ✉ *Bay St.* ☎ *242/365–4263* ▭ *No credit cards* ⏲ *Closed Sun.*

$–$$$$ **Fodor'sChoice ★** ✕🏨 **Bluff House Beach Hotel.** From its perch on a rocky bluff overlooking White Sound, this romantic hilltop hideaway provides sweeping views of the sheltered harbor or the Sea of Abaco. Established in 1954 by wealthy Americans who loved to entertain, this elegant resort has grown and improved with age. Formal dinners are still served by reservation only in the dining room ($$$), adjoining the open-air, natural pine cocktail lounge–library. The split-level suites have tropical-style wicker furniture, parquet-inlay floors, and double doors opening onto balconies with sensational ocean vistas. Even more spacious are the two-bedroom marine villas, with huge screened-in verandahs overlooking the marina. ✉ *Between Abaco Sea and White Sound* ✉ *Box AB 22886, Green Turtle Cay, Abaco* ☎ *242/365–4247 or 800/745–4911* 📠 *242/365–4248* 🌐 *www.BluffHouse.com* 🛏 *4 rooms, 8 suites, 9 villas* 👍 *2 restaurants, refrigerators, tennis court, 2 pools, beach, dock, snorkeling, boating, marina, fishing, 2 bars, lounge, laundry service; no room phones, no room TVs* ▭ *AE, D, MC, V* 🍽 *EP, MAP.*

★ $–$$$$ ✕🏨 **Green Turtle Club.** The vibe is simultaneously refined and easygoing at this well-known resort. The cheerful yellow cottages are scattered amid lush trees and shrubs. Villa accommodations have decks overlooking the water and have docks for rental boats; poolside rooms are more formal, furnished with mahogany Queen Anne–style furniture, gleaming hardwood floors, and Oriental rugs. Breakfasts and lunches are served on a screened, terra-cotta tile porch, but it's the dinner seating under the harbor-view dining room's chandeliers—giving the aura of the 1920s—that makes the inn come alive. Choose from an ever-changing menu ($$–$$$) that might include lobster risotto, shrimp in a Thai curry sauce, or filet mignon smothered in blue cheese. At this writing, the resort was in the process of being sold by the family of the original British owners to an

American family. ⊠ *North end of White Sound, Green Turtle Cay* ⌂ *Box AB 22792, Green Turtle Cay* ☎ *242/365–4271 or 800/688–4752* 🖷 *242/365–4272* ⊕ *www.greenturtleclub.com* ⇆ *24 rooms, 2 suites, 8 villas* ⚒ *Restaurant, dining room, fans, refrigerators, some in-room VCRs, pool, beach, dock, snorkeling, boating, 40-slip marina, fishing, bar, laundry facilities; no room phones* ▤ *AE, D, MC, V* ⦿ *EP, MAP.*

$ ✕⊡ **New Plymouth Club & Inn.** The charming, two-story historic hostelry with white balconies is in New Plymouth's center. Built in 1830, it was a French mercantile exchange, a warehouse, and a private residence before it opened as a hotel in 1946. Present owner Wally Davies built the charming patio pool and expanded the tropical gardens. The cozy rooms have canopy beds and terra-cotta tile baths, and are among the most affordable options on the cay. Room rates include breakfast. The dining room was once popular for its formal dinners of lobster and grouper Bahamian-style, but has been closed more often than not lately. ⊠ *Parliament St.* ☎ *242/365–4161* 🖷 *242/365–4138* ⇆ *9 rooms* ⚒ *Restaurant, fans, pool, bar, lounge* ▤ *D, MC, V.*

$–$$$$ ⊡ **Island Property Management.** A five-bedroom, oceanfront mansion with wraparound verandah, fulltime staff, and a marble fireplace could be yours. Or rent a two-bedroom cottage in the heart of New Plymouth. This agency will find you a property to match your budget and needs, and can help arrange excursions and boat and golf cart rentals. Most homes have water views, and some have docks for your rental boat. ⌂ *Box AB 22758, Green Turtle Cay, Abaco* ☎ *242/365–4047 or 561/ 202–8333* 🖷 *561/202–8478* ⊕ *www.go-abacos.com/ipm/* ⇆ *27 units* ▤ *D.*

$$ ⊡ **Coco Bay Cottages.** Sandwiched between one beach on the Atlantic and another calmer sandy stretch on the bay, these homey cottages all have views of the water. Each has attractive rattan furniture, a telephone, a modern kitchen, and linens. Snorkeling and diving are excellent around the reef that protects the Atlantic beach. The bay, where sunset views are fabulous, is prime territory for shell collecting and bonefishing. A separate building holds a library with games and books, satellite TV, and exercise equipment. ⊠ *North of New Plymouth* ☎ *242/365–5464 or 800/752– 0166* 🖷 *242/365–5465* ⊕ *www.cocobaycottages.com* ⇆ *4 cottages* ⚒ *Kitchenettes, gym, beach, dock, snorkeling, library* ▤ *D, MC, V.*

$$ ⊡ **Linton's Cottages.** These two snug cottages were built after the Second World War by Winston Churchill's private pilot, Captain Stephen Cliff. On a rise overlooking an isolated beach, the lovely cottages attract families, groups of friends, and couples looking for an escape. Each has two comfortable bedrooms, a screened-in porch, a combination living and dining room with built-in settees, a well-stocked library, and a fully equipped kitchen. ⊠ *S. Loyalist Rd.* ⌂ *Box 158601, Nashville, TN 37215* ☎ *615/269–5682* ⇆ *2 cottages* ⚒ *Fans, kitchenettes, boating, bicycles, library* ▤ *No credit cards.*

Nightlife

At night, Green Turtle can be deader than dead or surprisingly lively. Bet on the latter if local favorites, the **Gully Roosters,** are playing anywhere on the island. Known locally as just the Roosters, the reggae-calypso band is the most popular in the Abacos. Its mix of original tunes

and covers can coax even the most reluctant revele...
The band's home base is **Rooster's Rest** (☎ 242/36...
restaurant in a bright blue building just at the entrance...
The band's schedule there is erratic; ask at your hot...
one of their haunts on a Friday or Saturday night to...
pening. In addition to Rooster's Rest, try **Bluff Hous...**
(☎ 242/365–4247) and **Green Turtle Club** (☎ 242/365–...) of
which also sell Rooster CDs, a good souvenir of your vis...

★ Other nighttime options include a visit to **Miss Emily's Blue Bee Bar**
(☎ 242/365–4181), where you might find a singing, carousing crowd
knocking back the world famous Goombay Smash. (Or not—many
Goombay novices underestimate the drink's potency, and end up making it an early night.) Locals hang out at **Sundowner's** (☎ 242/365–4060),
a waterside bar and grill where attractions include a pool table and, on
weekend nights, a DJ spinning dance music on the deck under the stars.

Sports & the Outdoors

BICYCLING   The flat roads of Green Turtle Cay are perfect for getting around by bicycle. **D&P Rentals** (☎ 242/365–4655) rents mountain bikes for $10 per day.

BOATING   If you're unable to rent a boat on Green Turtle Cay, try nearby Treasure Cay.

Bluff House Beach Hotel (☎ 242/365–4247) has a marina with 45 slips.
Green Turtle Club (☎ 242/365–4271) has 40 slips.

Donny's Boat Rentals (☎ 242/365–4119) rents boats ranging from 14-
foot Whalers to 23-foot Makos. **Reef Rentals** (☎ 242/365–4145) has fishing boats and pleasure crafts ranging from 19 to 21 feet.

EVENTS   The **Bluff House Fishing Tournament** is held in May. In the beginning of
July, the **Bahamas Cup** boat race, part of **Regatta Time in Abaco,** circum-
navigates Green Turtle Cay. **All Abaco Regatta,** the work-boat race between Green Turtle and Treasure Cay, is held at the end of October. For
information on special events, call the **Abaco Tourist Office** (☎ 242/367–
3067). The **Out Island Promotion Board** (☎ 954/475–8315) has details
on island tournaments and other seasonal events.

FISHING   **Ronnie Sawyer** (☎ 242/365–4070) is one of the Bahamas' premier bonefishing guides. Call **Joe Sawyer** (☎ 242/365–4173) for a morning of reef
fishing in his 29-foot boat. **Rick Sawyer** (☎ 242/365–4261) offers deep-
sea and bonefishing aboard his 27-foot Alben or 17-foot Whaler.

SCUBA DIVING & **Brendal's Dive Shop** (☎ 242/365–4411 or 800/780–9941) leads snorkel-
SNORKELING   ing and scuba trips, plus wild dolphin encounters, glass-bottom boat
cruises, and more. Personable owner Brendal Stevens has been featured
on the Discovery Channel and CNN, and knows the surrounding reefs
so well that he's named some of the groupers, stingrays, and moray eels
that you'll have a chance to hand-feed. Trips can include a seafood lunch,
grilled on the beach, and complimentary rum punch.

Rent some snorkel gear or bring your own, and call **Lincoln Jones** (☎ 242/
365–4223), known affectionately as "the Daniel Boone of the Bahamas," for an unforgettable snorkeling adventure. Lincoln will dive

for conch and lobster (in season) or catch fish, then grill a sumptuous lunch on a deserted beach.

TENNIS   **Bluff House Beach Hotel** (☎ 242/365–4247) has one hard-surface court; rackets and balls are provided.

Shopping

Golden Reef (✉ Parliament St. ☎ 242/365–4511) sells jewelry, including Abaco Gold jewelry made in Marsh Harbour, plus resort wear, kids' clothing, swimwear, and gifts.

Colorful Abaco Ceramics, handmade in Treasure Cay, are the best bet at **Native Creations** (✉ Parliament St. ☎ 242/365–4206). The shop also sells beaded jewelry, picture frames, candles, postcards, and books.

Annexed to Plymouth Rock Liquors and Café, **Ocean Blue Gallery** (✉ Parliament St. ☎ 242/365–4234) is a small gallery with framed and unframed paintings, sculptures, and other works by more than 50 local artists. The adjoining liquor store sells Cuban cigars and more than 60 kinds of rum.

Sid's Grocery (☎ 242/365–4055) has the most complete line of groceries on the island, plus a gift section that includes books on local Bahamian subjects—great for souvenirs or for replenishing your stock of reading material.

Vert's Model Ship Shop (✉ Corner of Bay St. and Gully Alley ☎ 242/365–4170) has Vert Lowe's handcrafted two-mast schooners and sloops. Model prices range anywhere from $100 to $1,200. If Vert's shop door is locked—and it often is—knock at the white house with bright pink shutters next door. If you're still unsuccessful, inquire at the Green Turtle Club, where Vert has worked for more than 30 years.

Spanish Cay

Only 3 mi long, this privately owned island was once the exclusive retreat of millionaires, and many visitors still arrive by yacht or by landing a private plane on the 5,000-foot airstrip. Now, although several private upscale homes dot the coast, a small resort also rents rooms and condos. A well-equipped marina, great fishing, and some fine beaches are among the attractions here.

Where to Stay & Eat

$$ ✕▦ **Spanish Cay Resort.** The two-room hotel suites here are tucked away on a hill overlooking the marina and the Sea of Abaco. Each room has tile floors, pretty pastel drapery and bedspreads, a private porch, a king or double bed, and a desk. The Pointe House ($$–$$$$) serves three meals daily, with locally caught fish the best bet for dinner. The Wrecker's Bar, perched on stilts overlooking the water, is perfect for sipping a cold Kalik and munching on conch fritters or other Bahamian snacks. An 82-slip marina is on-site; boat rentals are available. ⌂ *Cay Resorts Limited, 1110 N.E. 7th Ave., Dania, FL 33004* ☎ *242/365–0083* ☎ *242/365–0453* ⊕ *www.spanishcay.com* ⇆ *18 rooms, 5 condos, 12 villas*

⛳ *Restaurant, refrigerators, microwaves, 4 tennis courts, pool, hot tub, marina, bar; no room phones* ◫ *MC, V.*

Walker's Cay

Fishing enthusiasts have been returning to this privately owned islet for years, and the lone hotel caters to anglers and divers. With few of the wispy casuarina trees that abound on most Out Islands, Walker's Cay, the Bahamas' northernmost island, sprouts more of the gnarled, thick-trunked trees common in cooler regions. Walker's Cay isn't known for its beaches. Most visitors sail off to sandy shores on neighboring islands.

Where to Stay & Eat

$–$$$ ✕▣ **Walker's Cay Hotel and Marina.** The 100 acres of Walker's Cay is under the auspices of this resort, a favorite with anglers because of the spectacular fishing in the surrounding waters. The resort hosts three tournaments annually, including the Bahamas Billfish Tournament in early April. Sportsmen gather at the Lobster Trap restaurant ($–$$$) in the marina at lunch to swap fishing stories; breakfast and dinner are served in the Conch Pearl ($–$$$). Rooms are cheerfully decorated with tropical-style rattan furniture and private patios. For non-fishers, diving options include an exciting shark dive, cavernous coral reefs, and sunken tugboats. The excellent marina attracts many yachters. ⌂ *700 S.W. 34th St., Fort Lauderdale, FL 33315* ☎ *954/359–1400 or 800/925–5377* 🖷 *954/359–1414* ⊕ *www. walkerscay.com* ⟿ *62 rooms, 3 villas* ⛳ *2 restaurants, 2 tennis courts, pool, saltwater pool, dive shop, dock, boating, marina, fishing, 2 bars, laundry service* ◫ *AE, DC, MC, V* ⏱ *EP, MAP.*

Sports & the Outdoors

BOATING **Walker's Cay Hotel and Marina** (☎ 954/359–1400 or 800/925–5377) has a full-service 75-slip marina and some of the Bahamas' best yachting facilities.

EVENTS Spring brings the Walker's Cay leg of the **Bahamas Billfish Championship** (☎ 800/925–5377 or 888/303–2242 ⊕ www.bahamasbillfish.com). One of the most prestigious tournaments in the Caribbean, it attracts up to 40 boats, with teams competing to catch marlin and sailfish.

SCUBA DIVING The living reefs here grow atop a fossil coral reef that forms a limestone buttress. The resulting formations have names such as "Flower Garden" and "Spiral Cavern Reef." The Shark Rodeo dive allows you to safely float among 100-plus blacktip and Caribbean reef sharks as they feed.

All the diving off the cay can be booked through Walker Cay's only hotel, which has two dive boats that can carry a total of up to 42 divers.

ABACOS A TO Z

AIR TRAVEL

There are two major public airports in the Abacos. Most flights land at the international airports in Marsh Harbour or Treasure Cay. Some private planes and charter carriers use the very small, private airstrips at Walker's Cay and Spanish Cay. There is also a small public airstrip in Sandy Cay.

CARRIERS Many carriers operate seasonal schedules to the Abacos. Some routes are flown daily from December through August, and three times a week from September through November. In addition, many airlines serving the Abacos are very small and change schedules frequently, even in season.

Air Florida flies charters to Marsh Harbour from Fort Lauderdale. Air Sunshine flies from Fort Lauderdale to Marsh Harbour and Treasure Cay. American Eagle has a daily flight to Marsh Harbour from Miami. Bahamasair flies daily from Nassau to Marsh Harbour and Treasure Cay. Cherokee Air is the charter-plane service of choice for island hopping to or from the Abacos. Continental Connection flies into both Marsh Harbour and Treasure Cay from Miami and Fort Lauderdale. Island Express Airways has daily flights to Marsh Harbour and Treasure Cay from Fort Lauderdale. Twin Air has several flights per week to Treasure Cay from Fort Lauderdale, and flies to other parts of the Abacos by charter. Vintage Props and Jets flies into Marsh Harbour and Treasure Cay from four airports in Florida: Daytona Beach, Melbourne, Orlando, and New Smyrna Beach. Yellow Air Taxi has scheduled charters into Marsh Harbour and Treasure Cay from Fort Lauderdale and West Palm Beach.

🛂Airlines & Contacts **Air Florida** ☎954/359-7897 or 800/373-9593 ⊕www.air-florida. com. **Air Sunshine** ☎ 954/434-8900 or 800/327-8900 ⊕ www.airsunshine.com. **American Eagle** ☎ 242/367-2231 or 800/433-7300 ⊕ www.aa.com. **Bahamasair** ☎242/367-2095 in Marsh Harbour, 242/365-8601 in Treasure Cay ⊕ www.bahamasair. com. **Cherokee Air** ☎ 242/367-2089 ⊕ www.cherokeeair.com. **Continental Connection** ☎242/367-3415 in Marsh Harbour, 242/365-8615 in Treasure Cay, 800/231-0856 ⊕ www.continental.com. **Island Express Airways** ☎ 954/359-0380 ⊕ http://oii.net/ islandexpress/. **Twin Air** ☎ 954/359-8266 ⊕ www.flytwinair.com. **Vintage Props and Jets** ☎ 800/852-0275 ⊕ www.vpj.com. **Yellow Air Taxi** ☎ 888/935-5694 ⊕ www. flyyellowairtaxi.com.

BOAT & FERRY TRAVEL

Boats are a key method of transportation among the many islands of the Abacos. A good system of public ferries and boat rental agencies allows you to reach the most remote cays. Assuming you have plenty of time and a sense of adventure, you can even arrive in the Abacos by mail boat.

MAIL BOATS A mail boat is scheduled to depart every Tuesday from Potter's Cay, Nassau, for Marsh Harbour and Green Turtle Cay, returning to Nassau on Thursday. Another boat is supposed to depart Nassau each Friday for Sandy Point, at the southern tip of Great Abaco, and return to Nassau on Friday. However, the schedule is often affected by wind, rain, tides, mechanical problems, and other issues. Each one-way journey takes about six hours. For details, call the Dockmaster's Office at Potter's Cay.

FERRIES In contrast to the mail boats, the two major ferry services serving the Abacos are very punctual. Every day except Sunday and holidays, Albury's Ferry Service leaves Marsh Harbour for the 20-minute ride to

BOATING IN THE ABACOS

THE ABACOS PROVIDE SUPERB CRUISING grounds. Marinas and services for yachters range from rugged and rustic to high-tech facilities, but are mostly the latter. Walker's Cay, at the top of the Abacos, is about 55 mi northeast of West End at the tip of Grand Bahama Island, and it's also a 55-mi crossing from Palm Beach. Many yachters coming from the north opt for the 110-mi route from Florida's Fort Pierce–Vero Beach area to Walker's Cay.

Walker's Cay and its neighbor, Grand Cay, represent the contrasts in facilities available. Walker's Cay has a high-class 75-slip, full-service marina; a paved airstrip; and extravagant hotel comforts. Grand Cay is a ramshackle settlement of about 200 people and four times that many dogs of mixed breed, called Bahamian potcakes. Yachters will find the anchorage off the community dock adequate. Double anchors are advised to handle the harbor's tidal current.

Heading south from Walker's Cay and Grand Cay, you will pass (and maybe want to explore by dinghy) a clutch of tiny cays and islets, such as Double Breasted Cays, Roder Rocks, Barracuda Rocks, Miss Romer Cay, Little Sale Cay, and Great Sale Cay. Great Sale Harbour provides excellent shelter. Snorkeling in the shallows along the mangroves, you might spot manta rays and eagle rays, sand sharks, and perhaps a school of small barracuda. Other small islands in the area are Carter Cay, Moraine Cay, Umbrella Cay, Guineaman Cay, Pensacola and Allen's cays (which are now virtually one island since a hurricane filled in the gap between them), and the Hawksbill Cays. Most offer varying degrees of lee anchorage. Fox Town, due south of Hawksbill Cay on Little Abaco's western tip, is the first refueling stop for powerboats traveling east from West End.

A narrow causeway joins Little Abaco to Great Abaco, where the largest community at the north end is Cooper's Town. Stock up here on groceries, hardware, marine parts, liquor, and beer. There are also a coin laundry, a telephone station, a few restaurants, bakeries, and a resident doctor. Green Turtle Cay has excellent yachting facilities at White Sound to the north and Black Sound to the south. The Green Turtle Club dominates White Sound's northern end, whereas Bluff House, halfway up the sound, has docks on the inside and a dinghy dock below the club on the bank side.

South of New Plymouth on Great Abaco's mainland stands the Treasure Cay Hotel Resort & Marina, with one of the area's finest and longest beaches. A New England–style charmer lies a little to the south: Man-O-War Cay, a boatbuilding settlement. This island, with the 28-slip Man-O-War Marina, is devoid of cars and liquor.

The Bahamas' most photogenic lighthouse sits atop Elbow Cay, signaling the harbor opening to Hope Town. Boats also make their way to two less-developed neighboring islands: Guana Cay, with a 22-slip marina, and Spanish Cay, with an 81-slip full-service marina.

Back on Great Abaco, you'll find the Abacos' most populous settlement at Marsh Harbour, which has plenty of facilities for boaters. These include the modern (and growing) 200-slip Boat Harbour Marina, a full-service operation on the island's east side. The other side of town has additional marinas, including the 80-slip Conch Inn Marina, Marsh Harbour Marina and its 68 slips, and a couple of smaller facilities.

Hope Town at 7:15, 9, 10:30, 12:15, 2, 4, and 5:45; ferries make the return trip at 8, 9:45, 11:30, 1:30, 3, 4, and 5. A same-day round-trip costs $15. One-way costs $10. Albury's also provides service between Marsh Harbour and Man-O-War Cay or Guana Cay. Charter excursions can also be booked.

Green Turtle Cay Ferry leaves the Treasure Cay airport dock at 8:30, 10:30, 11:30, 1:30, 2:30, 3:30, 4:30, and 5 (except Sunday) and returns from Green Turtle Cay at 8, 9, 11, 12:15, 1:30, 3, and 4:30. One-way fares are $8, and a same-day round-trip fare is $14. The ferry makes several stops in Green Turtle, including New Plymouth, the Green Turtle Club, and the Bluff House Beach Hotel.

🛈 Ferry Information **Albury's Ferry Service** ☎ 242/367-3147 or 242/365-6010 ⊕ www. oii.net/alburysferry. **Dockmaster's Office** ☎242/393-1064. **Green Turtle Cay Ferry** ☎242/ 365-4032.

BOAT RENTAL   If you don't want to be bound by the somewhat limited schedule of the ferries, rent a small boat. Having your own boat also allows you the freedom to explore uninhabited cays, find your own favorite fishing and snorkeling spots, and picnic on secluded beaches. Most hotels and many rental cottages have docking facilities that allow you to keep your boat in easy reach. Boats can be rented on most islands with tourist facilities, but the best selections are at the main visitor destinations, including Marsh Harbour, Treasure Cay, Hope Town, and Green Turtle Cay.

In Marsh Harbour, Rich's Rentals has 21- and 26-foot Paramount powerboats. The boats at Rainbow Rentals in Marsh Harbour include custom-built 22-foot center-console powerboats. Sea Horse Boat Rentals has a large selection at its two offices in Marsh Harbour and Hope Town. In Treasure Cay, check out J. I. C. Boat Rentals, which rents boats on a daily, three-day, or weekly basis. In Green Turtle Cay, Donny's Boat Rentals and Reef Rentals both offer fishing boats that comfortably carry up to six passengers.

🛈 Boat Rental Information **Donny's Boat Rentals** ☎ 242/365-4119. **J. I. C. Boat Rentals** ☎ 242/365-8465. **Rainbow Rentals** ☎ 242/367-4602. **Reef Rentals** ☎ 242/ 365-4145. **Rich's Rentals** ☎ 242/367-2742. **Sea Horse Boat Rentals** ☎ 242/367-2513.

CAR RENTAL

Cars are not necessary on most of the smaller cays in the Abacos; in fact, rental cars aren't even available in most locations. On Great Abaco, however, you'll need a car if you want to venture beyond Marsh Harbour or Treasure Cay. Rentals are expensive, at about $75 a day and up, and gasoline costs at least $3.50 per gallon. You might negotiate a better rate if you rent for a week or longer. In Marsh Harbour, you can rent automobiles from H & L Car Rentals, A & P Rentals, or Rental Wheels of Abaco. Just outside Treasure Cay Airport, Cornish Car Rentals has a large rental fleet.

🛈 Local Agencies **A & P Rentals** ☎ 242/367-2655. **Cornish Car Rentals** ☎ 242/365-8623. **H & L Car Rentals** ✉ Shell Gas Station ☎ 242/367-2854. **Rental Wheels of Abaco** ☎ 242/367-4643.

EMERGENCIES

The Marsh Harbour Clinic has a resident doctor and a nurse. There are also small government clinics staffed by nurses in Hope Town and New Plymouth, but hours are limited and change frequently. There are several private doctors in Marsh Harbour, and hotels will contact medical personnel upon request. Serious medical emergencies will require evacuation by plane to Nassau or Florida. It's a good idea to buy travel insurance that includes medical evacuation coverage.

⌗ Marsh Harbour Clinic ☎ 242/367-2510. **Police or Fire Emergencies** ☎ 919.

GOLF CART TRAVEL

Golf carts are the vehicle of choice on the majority of the smaller cays, including Elbow Cay, Green Turtle Cay, and Man-O-War Cay. Each can carry four adults comfortably, if slowly. The standard rates are $45 to $50 per day for a gas cart, or $240 per week. Electric-powered carts, which usually must be recharged nightly, are slightly cheaper. Big-wheel carts, which provide a smoother ride on the bumpy, pothole-filled roads common in the islands, cost a little more and are not available at all locations. Reservations are always recommended, but are essential in the busiest travel months of June and July.

In Hope Town, try Hope Town Cart Rentals, Island Cart Rentals, or T&N Cart Rentals. In Treasure Cay, you can rent carts from Cash's Resort Carts or Blue Marlin Rentals. On Green Turtle, Bay Street Rentals is on the grounds of the Bluff House Beach Hotel. D & P Rentals rents carts from an office at the Green Turtle Club. In New Plymouth, try Seaside Carts. On Man-O-War, the Man-O-War Marina has golf carts.

⌗ Bay Street Rentals ☎ 242/365-4070. **Blue Marlin Rentals** ☎ 242/365-8687. **Cash's Resort Carts** ☎ 242/365-8771. **D & P Rentals** ☎ 242/365-4655. **Hope Town Cart Rentals** ☎ 242/366-0064. **Island Cart Rentals** ☎ 242/366-0448. **Man-O-War Marina** ☎ 242/365-6008. **Seaside Carts** ☎ 242/477-5497. **T&N Cart Rentals** ☎ 242/366-0069.

SIGHTSEEING TOURS

In Marsh Harbour, Abaco Island Tours books island tours, diving and sailing excursions, and customized trips. Also in Marsh Harbour, Abaco Outback leads eco-centered kayaking and birding tours. From Green Turtle, Brendal's Dive Center offers fully catered and captained sunset "booze cruises," and glass-bottom boat excursions where dolphin sightings are often a highlight. Froggies Out Island Adventures is the choice on Elbow Cay for sunset cruises and tours of the nearby cays.

⌗ Abaco Island Tours ☎ 242/367-2936 ⊕ www.abacoislandtours.com. **Abaco Outback** ☎ 242/367-5358 ⊕ www.abacooutback.com. **Brendal's Dive Center** ☎ 242/365-4411 or 800/780-9941 ⊕ www.brendals.com. **Froggies Out Island Adventures** ☎ 242/366-0431 ⊕ www.froggiesabaco.com.

TAXIS

Only a few islands have taxi service, including Great Abaco, Green Turtle Cay, and Elbow Cay, but there are plenty of taxis in Treasure Cay and Marsh Harbour. Taxi services meet arriving planes at the airports to take you to your hotel or to a ferry dock, where you can catch a water taxi to neighboring islands such as Green Turtle Cay, Great Guana, or Elbow Cay. Hotels will arrange for taxis to take you on short trips and back to the airport. Fares are generally $1.50 per mi. A 15% tip is customary.

VISITOR INFORMATION

Visit, call, or write Marsh Harbour's Abaco Tourist Office. It is open 9 AM to 5:30 PM, Monday through Friday.

🔟 Tourist Information **Abaco Tourist Office** ✉ Memorial Plaza, Queen Elizabeth Drive, Marsh Harbour 📬 Box AB 20663, Marsh Harbour, Abaco ☎ 242/367–3067 📠 242/367–3068.

ELEUTHERA &
THE EXUMAS

Updated by
Evelyn Kanter

ELEUTHERA AND THE EXUMAS are known for their miles of unspoiled and secluded sand beaches, turquoise water, and deep green forests populated by gnarled pine trees. Hotels and inns are painted in the shades of a Caribbean sunset and decorated with colorful tropical flowers. The laid-back, easy-going pace of the islands, not uncommon in the rest of the Caribbean, guarantees a restful respite. The residents welcome visitors warmly; most will be happy to let you know where to find bargains at a little tucked-away straw market or recommend the best restaurant for conch chowder. People here are serious about fishing, and can show you where to find the best spots—while the other Out Islands attract deep sea fishermen seeking marlin and tarpon, the lure here is bonefish, the elusive and feisty breed that prefers shallow, sandy flats that punctuate these islands.

Eleuthera was named in 1648 by a group from Britain fleeing religious persecution; the name is taken from the Greek word for freedom. These settlers, who called themselves the Eleutheran Adventurers, gave the Bahamas its first written constitution. In the late 1800s, Eleuthera dominated the world's pineapple market, and these small, intensely sweet fruits are still grown in small family farms dotting the island. On the Exumas, you'll still find wild cotton, leftover from plantations established by Loyalists after the Revolutionary War. Breadfruit trees are also in abundance, which a local preacher bought from Captain William Bligh in the late 18th century. The Exumas are now known as the Bahamas' onion capital, although many of the 3,600-odd residents earn a living by fishing as well as farming. Your first impression of the people of the Exumas may be that almost all of them have the surname Rolle. Lord John Rolle, who imported the first cotton seeds to these islands, had more than 300 slaves, to whom he bequeathed not only his name but also the 2,300 acres of land that were bestowed on him by the British government in the late 18th century.

Exploring Eleuthera & the Exumas

Eleuthera is shaped like a praying mantis, 110 mi long and just a few miles wide. It lies 200 mi southeast of Florida and 60 mi east of Nassau. One of the most picturesque parts of Eleuthera is Harbour Island, often compared with Nantucket, and reachable by a three-minute ferry ride from North Eleuthera. Harbour Island is famous worldwide for its 3-mi stretch of powdery pink-sand beach, usually included in lists of the most beautiful beaches on the planet. The Exumas begin less than 35 mi southeast of Nassau and stretch south for about 90 mi, flanked by the Great Bahama Bank and Exuma Sound. They are made up largely of some 365 fragmented little cays, mostly uninhabited. The two main islands, Great Exuma and Little Exuma, lie in the south, connected by a bridge. The islands' capital, George Town, on Great Exuma, is the site of one of the Bahamas' most prestigious and popular sailing events, the Family Islands Regatta, in which locally built wooden work boats compete. During the winter, George Town's Elizabeth Harbour is a haven for yachts. The surrounding waters are legendary for their desolate islands, coves, bays, and harbors.

4

Numbers in the text correspond to numbers in the margins and on the Eleuthera and The Exumas maps.

If you have
3 days

Fly into **North Eleuthera** and stay at a hotel along the famous 3-mi pink-sand beach on ► 🖼 **Harbour Island** ⑬, a taxi and boat ride from the airport. Leave your windows open so you can hear the free-roaming roosters wake you up in time to see the incredible pink and mauve sunrise. Take a morning walk on the beach, then veg out with a good book, interrupted only by lunch at an oceanside restaurant. Stroll through **Dunmore Town** in the afternoon, stopping at the craft stands and visiting the centuries-old churches. The next day, go scuba diving or snorkeling, or hire a guide and try to snag at least one of the elusive and feisty bonefish for which Eleuthera is famous. End the day with dinner in Dunmore Town. Take the ferry to **Spanish Wells** on your last day. Rent a golf cart and enjoy this prosperous lobster fishing island, with its neat, upscale homes and tiny alcove beaches. Be sure to try some fresh lobster before leaving.

If you have
5 days

Follow the suggested three-day itinerary, and on Day 4, take the ferry to "the mainland," what Harbour Island's residents call the main island of ► **Eleuthera** ①–⑭. Drive south past **Glass Window** ⑫, where you can stand in one spot and see the Atlantic Ocean on one side and the Caribbean Sea on the other. Check out the cathedral-like cavern called **The Cave** ⑧ to prowl the stalagmites and hunt for bats and pirates' booty. In the afternoon, drive to **Hidden Beach** off **James Point** for some private sunbathing or snorkeling. Continue south to 🖼 **Governor's Harbour** ⑥, the island's largest town, and grab dinner at one of the seaside restaurants overlooking the harbor. The next morning, drive to **Rock Sound** ① and then head either to **Ocean Hole** ②, a large inland saltwater lake, or to the challenging **Robert Trent Jones golf course** at **Cotton Bay Club** ③.

If you have
7 days

The only way to fly to Eleuthera and the Exumas is through ► 🖼 **Nassau** (unless you charter your own plane, which is exorbitantly expensive), and that means an eight-hour layover. Instead of sitting in the airport, you might as well spend a day exploring, shopping, eating, and gambling. When you've had enough of the neon, noise, and crowds, continue on to 🖼 **Exuma** ⑮–㉓ and the comparative serenity of its beaches and smaller hotels. Camp out on the beach for a day, go golfing, or treat yourself to a massage. On Day 3, go diving at **Angel Fish Blue Hole** or snorkeling at **Stocking Island Mystery Cave,** a blue hole grotto filled with technicolor fish, accessible via a short ferry ride from **George Town** ⑰. Watch the sunset over dinner at an oceanside restaurant.

Spend the next two days based in 🖼 **Staniel Cay** ㉒. Visit **Thunderball Grotto,** site of the famous James Bond movie, where you can snorkel and swim, and check out **Exuma Cays Land and Sea Park** ㉓, a string of uninhabited islands housing some of the Bahamas' most dramatic aboveground scenery and underwater coral reefs. Finish the week at one of the beachfront hotels in 🖼 **George Town** ⑰, preferably including a Friday night so you can join in the festivities at **Palm Bay Beach Club,** where an outdoor barbecue and live band attract most of the island's inhabitants for a friendly evening of dancing.

Eleuthera and the Exumas are a quick flight from Miami or Nassau, or a ferry ride from Nassau, the trip taking just a few scenic hours. It's easy to explore the islands by rented car, bicycle, or golf cart, although you'll need to rent a motorboat to explore some of the smaller and uninhabited islands.

About the Restaurants

Although the ambiance is usually casual, food is taken seriously here, especially such island specialties as conch salad and fritters, the huge and succulent Bahamian lobster most "locals" call crawfish, and barbecued pork or chicken. Fresh fish and seafood, usually pulled that morning from the waters just beyond the restaurant kitchen, is the star of most menus. If you've never had fresh conch, these two islands are the place to indulge, especially at one of the conch shacks favored by island residents. The conch is often so fresh that it may be sitting in a tank outside until you place your order. It is then diced, mixed with chopped red and green peppers and tomatoes, seasoned with each chef's own secret recipe of lemon, lime, and sour orange juices, and topped with a tangy dash of hot pepper sauce.

Most restaurants serve Bahamian food, but there are enough Italian, French, and Asian menu items for those who don't want to venture a taste of island fare. Several newer restaurants feature experimental and fusion cuisine, a trend that is becoming increasingly popular. Many dining establishments are closed two days a week, including Sunday, which is family day on these deeply religious and family-oriented islands.

About the Hotels

Accommodations run the gamut from quaint, family-run guest houses in historic Colonial-era buildings to modern beachfront resorts with as many as several dozen cottages. There is an undeniable appeal to staying at a place that treats you like one of the family, and this is not hard to come by in these parts. Most hotels have their own restaurants, and often have several different meal plans from which to choose. Many of the hotels are busy repainting and remodeling in response to the opening of the luxurious Four Seasons Resort Great Exuma at Emerald Bay, the largest and most upscale resort on the two islands. It also has the only full service spa on either island and the only golf course on Exuma.

WHAT IT COSTS				
$$$$	**$$$**	**$$**	**$**	**¢**
RESTAURANTS over $40	$30–$40	$20–$30	$10–$20	under $10
HOTELS over $400	$300–$400	$200–$300	$100–$200	under $100

Restaurant prices are for a main course at dinner, excluding gratuity, typically 15%, which is often automatically added to the bill. Hotel prices are for two people in a standard double room in high season, excluding service charges and 6%–12% tax.

Timing

All the Out Islands share similar weather, including a steamy late summer hurricane season, and wintertime low temperatures that dip into

Conch Salad

This Bahamian staple is akin to ceviche. Fresh caught conch is removed from its shell, diced, and mixed with chopped onions and red or green peppers. The mix is drizzled with fresh lime and sour orange juices, and spiced with either homemade hot sauce or finely minced local hot peppers, or both. Often the best places to try conch salad are one-room shacks at the water's edge, such as the cluster of shacks called **Fish Fry** just north of George Town in Exuma, or at **Queen Conch** on Harbour Island, Eleuthera, where the salad is made right in front of you. In restaurants, conch salad can be an appetizer or a main course. Conch also is chopped and fried in fritters, stewed with potatoes as chowder, and steamed like lobster.

Pink Sands and Secluded Havens

Go to Eleuthera or the Exumas to sink your toes into soft sand and be lulled into a happy stupor by the sounds of gentle waves. The slightly curved 3-mi pink-sand beach on Harbour Island, Eleuthera, usually rates in the world's top 10 beaches, and deservedly so. Its sand is of such a fine consistency that it's almost as soft as talcum powder, and the gentle slope of the shore makes small waves break hundreds of yards offshore; you have to walk out quite a distance to get past your waist. On moonlit nights, the waves seem lit from underneath. On Exuma, head a few miles north or south from George Town, the island's main city, to find isolated spots of wide sand.

Snorkelers' Paradise

This 176-square-mi park is a favorite of divers and snorkelers attracted by rare pillar coral and huge schools of multicolored fish, and sightseers who just want to enjoy the isolated and pristine eco-system that flourishes here under the watchful eye of park rangers. They patrol in motorized boats to ensure that nobody damages the precious coral reefs, poaches any fish, or bothers the dolphins and porpoises that play here. Stretching some 22 mi between Compass Cay and Norman's Cay along the string of islands at the far northern end of the Exumas, this park is reachable only by seaplane or boat. That's part of its charm. The nearest "civilization" is Staniel Cay, one hour or more away depending on the speed of your boat, which has a marina, restaurant, and tiny airport.

A Warm Bahamian Welcome

Most of the people you'll meet on Exuma and Eleuthera have lived here for their entire lives, except maybe for a few years of college or work, or a brief visit to the United States. Their ties to their homeland and extended families tend to be strong and secure— perhaps this is why the local residents seem to be exceptionally friendly and have an uncanny openness about them. Everybody says "good morning" or "good afternoon" with a smile when they see you. Express the smallest interest in the history, food, or culture of the islands, and you'll probably be rewarded with an instant friendship, or at least a bit of interest and a brief conversation. Good manners are important here, and making guests feel welcome is at the top of the list.

the 60s. The high season for tourism is in December through April, when residents of cold weather climates head to the Caribbean to defrost and soak up some rays. For the cheapest hotel rates and some of the best deals on watersports packages, visit during early summer or fall. For those who want to catch some action and don't mind crowds, the best times to visit Eleuthera and the Exumas are during the annual Junkanoo celebration of music and dance, and the annual Family Islands Regatta in April, when the harbor of George Town, Exuma, is filled with hundreds of multimillion dollar yachts.

ELEUTHERA ISLAND

Numbers in the margin correspond to points of interest on the Eleuthera map.

Rock Sound

❶ One of Eleuthera's largest settlements, the village of **Rock Sound** has a small airport serving the island's southern part. **Front Street,** the main thoroughfare, runs along the seashore, where fishing boats are tied up. If you walk down the street, you'll eventually come to the pretty, white-washed **St. Luke's Anglican Church,** a contrast to the deep blue and green houses nearby, with their colorful gardens full of poinsettia, hibiscus, and marigolds. If you pass the church on a Sunday, you'll surely hear fervent hymn singing through the open windows. Rock Sound has the island's largest supermarket shopping center, where locals stock up on groceries and supplies. Buy fresh fruit—citrus in the winter and luscious papayas and avocados in the spring and summer—from **Rock Sound Farms** (✉ Queen's Hwy. ☎ 242/334–2489) or one of the town's other roadside fruit vendors.

❷ **Ocean Hole,** a large inland saltwater lake a mile southeast of Rock Sound, is connected by tunnels to the sea. Steps have been cut into the coral on the shore so visitors can climb down to the lake's edge. Bring a piece of bread or some fries and watch the fish emerge for their hors d'oeuvres, swimming their way in from the sea. The hole had been estimated to be more than 100 fathoms (600 feet) deep, but, in fact, its depth was measured by a local diver at about 75 feet. He reports a couple of cars at the bottom, too.

❸ Ten miles south of Rock Sound, the now defunct **Cotton Bay Club** hotel is where you'll find the well-known Robert Trent Jones golf course (it's only a golf club now), studded with tree groves and nestled against the sea. Cotton Bay was once an exclusive club, the domain of Pan Am's founder, Juan Trippe, who would fly his friends to the island on a 727 Yankee Clipper for a weekend of golf.

❹ The tiny settlement of **Bannerman Town** (population 40) is at the island's southern tip. From Eleuthera's north end (near Preacher's Cave), it is about a three-hour drive down the Queen's Highway. The beach here is gorgeous, and on a clear day you can see the Bahamas' highest point, Mt. Alvernia (elevation 206 feet), on distant Cat Island. The town lies

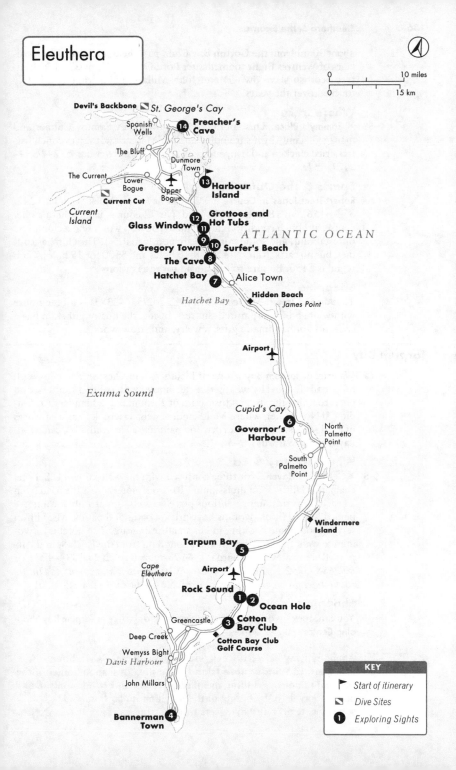

Eleuthera

0 ——————————— 10 miles

0 ——————————— 15 km

Devil's Backbone *St. George's Cay*

Spanish Wells

(14) Preacher's Cave

The Bluff

Dunmore Town

The Current

Lower Bogue

Upper Bogue

Current Cut

Current Island

(13) Harbour Island

Grottoes and Hot Tubs

(12)

Glass Window (11)

(9)(10) Surfer's Beach

Gregory Town

ATLANTIC OCEAN

The Cave (8)

Hatchet Bay (7) Alice Town

Hatchet Bay

Hidden Beach

James Point

Airport

Exuma Sound

Cupid's Cay

(6)

Governor's Harbour

North Palmetto Point

South Palmetto Point

Windermere Island

Tarpum Bay

(5)

Airport

Cape Eleuthera

Rock Sound

(1)(2) Ocean Hole

Greencastle

(3) Cotton Bay Club

Deep Creek

Cotton Bay Club Golf Course

Wemyss Bight

Davis Harbour

John Millars

Bannerman Town (4)

KEY
⚑ *Start of itinerary*
◺ *Dive Sites*
① *Exploring Sights*

about 30 mi from the **Cotton Bay Club,** past the quiet, little fishing villages of **Wemyss Bight** (named after Lord Gordon Wemyss, a 17th-century Scottish slave owner) and **John Millars** (population 15), barely touched over the years.

Where to Eat

¢–$$ ✕ **Sammy's Place.** This spotless stop is owned by Sammy Culmer and managed mainly by his friendly daughter Margarita. It serves conch fritters, fried chicken and fish, and peas 'n' rice. ⊠ *Albury La.* ☎ *242/334–2121* ⊟ *D.*

Sports & the Outdoors

GOLF **Robert Trent Jones Jr. Course** (⊠ Cotton Bay Club, Rock Sound ☎ 242/334–6156), an 18-hole, 7,068-yard, par-72 course, is Eleuthera's only course, although conditions aren't up to par. You won't find a clubhouse or restaurant, and some fairways are poorly marked. The club has caddies, but no carts. Rates are $70 for 9 holes and $100 for 18 holes. Club rental is $150. Be sure to call ahead for reservations.

Shopping

The **Almond Tree** (⊠ Queen's Hwy. ☎ 242/334–2385) is a blue house with white hibiscus–painted shutters. Inside, the quaint gift shop has a collection of handmade gifts, jewelry, and straw work.

Tarpum Bay

❺ Waterfront **Tarpum Bay** is one of Eleuthera's loveliest settlements, with hilly roads flanked by weather-beaten homes with colored shutters, and goats roaming the streets. Just south of Tarpum Bay is **Flanders Art Studio** (☎ No phone), where Mal Flanders sells watercolors and canvases of local scenes, as well as driftwood paintings. The studio is open Monday through Saturday 9–5.

Where to Stay & Eat

¢–$ ✕⌂ **Hilton's Haven.** Not to be confused with the well-known U.S. hotel chain, this Hilton is an unassuming 10-room motel across the road from a beach. This tidy, unpretentious place is run by a matronly local nurse named Mary Hilton. Rooms have private baths and patios. Ms. Hilton serves good home cooking in her small restaurant. The hotel is a two-minute walk from the beach and about 8 mi from the Rock Sound Airport. Room rates are a bargain. ⊠ *Tarpum Bay* ☎ *242/334–4231 or 800/688–4752* ⊟ *242/334–4020* 🛏 *10 rooms, 1 apartment* ⌂ *Dining room, bar; no a/c in some rooms* ⊟ *No credit cards* ⍟ *EP, MAP.*

Shopping

You can stock up on groceries, souvenirs, and the like at **Tarpum Bay Shopping Centre** (☎ 242/334–4022).

en route About halfway between Rock Sound and Governor's Harbour, distinguished **Windermere Island** is the site of vacation homes of the rich and famous, including members of the British royal family. Don't plan on any drive-by ogling of these million-dollar homes. The security gate prevents sightseers from passing.

Governor's Harbour

❻ Governor's Harbour is where the intrepid Eleuthera Adventurers landed. The drive between Governor's Harbour and Rock Sound takes about 35 minutes. If you're here when the mail boats M/V *Bahamas Daybreak III* and M/V *Eleuthera Express* chug in, you'll witness the sight of residents unloading mattresses, lumber, mail, stacks of vegetables, and other household necessities. You might also see the same Eleutherans loading their own vegetables for export to Nassau. While they're here, they'll stop in at their mailboxes at the small post office in the town's pink government building.

If you're cooking during your stay, note that the Governor's Harbour waterfront is a great place to procure fresh fish and conch.

Where to Stay & Eat

$-$$ ✕ **Mate & Jenny's.** A few miles south of Governor's Harbour, this neighborhood restaurant specializes in pizza. Try one topped with conch. Sandwiches, Bahamian specialties, and ice-cream sundaes are also served. The walls are painted with tropical sunset scenes and decorated with photos, and the jukebox and pool table add to the joint's local color. Pizza pie prices are $10, $15, and $24. ⊠ *S. Palmetto Point* ☎ *242/332–1504* 🖃 *MC, V* ⊗ *Closed Tues. No lunch Sun.*

$ ✕ **Tippy's.** Despite its barefoot-casual atmosphere, the menu at this charming beachside restaurant-bar is sophisticated, with Cajun grouper, lobster tempura, seared sushi-grade tuna and sushi, plus pizza. Try to grab a table at the outdoor deck, with its fantastic view of the beach. ⊠ *S. Palmetto Pt.* ☎ *242/332–3331* 🖃 *No credit cards* ⊗ *Closed Wed.*

$ ✕🏠 **Buccaneer Club.** On a hillside overlooking the town and the harbor, this mid-19th-century farmhouse has been transformed into a family-run inn. Bougainvillea, hibiscus, and coconut palms flourish on the grounds. The guest rooms, with two double beds and full baths, are decorated with rattan furniture. The spacious third-floor room has a wonderful view of Governor's Harbour and the water. The beach is a leisurely five-minute stroll away, and the harbor, where you can also swim, is within shouting distance. Local artwork graces the walls at the Buccaneer Club, where you can sample such native specialties as grouper, conch, and crawfish. ⓓ *Box 86, Governor's Harbour* ☎ *242/332–2000* 🖷 *242/332–2888* ⊕ *www.buccaneerclub.com* 🛏 *5 rooms* ⚱ *Restaurant, bar, shop* 🖃 *D, MC, V.*

$ ✕🏠 **Cocodimama Charming Resort.** If decompressing in a hammock is your thing, you're in luck—you'll find one on the private patios of all 12 rooms at this sedate hotel, nestled on the Caribbean side of the island, 6 mi north of Governor's Harbour. Rooms are accented with teak furniture imported from Indonesia as well as Italian tiles, which reflect the taste of the married Italian ex-pats who own and manage the property. Their influence also pervades the menu of the restaurant's Italian-Bahamian menu: buffalo mozzarella and other delicacies are flown in to complement the local fare. Snorkeling equipment and catamaran and kayak rentals are included in the rates. ⊠ *Alabaster Bay, Governor's Harbour* ☎ *242/332–3150* 🖷 *242/332–3155* ⊕ *www.*

cocodimama.com ⇆ *12 rooms* ⬧ *Restaurant, Internet* ▤ *MC, V* ⊙ *Closed Sept.–Nov.*

$ ✕▦ **Unique Village.** Just south of Governor's Harbour near North Palmetto Point, this resort has large, tile-floor rooms. The round restaurant, with its pagoda-style natural-wood ceiling, wraparound covered deck, and panoramic view of the beach makes this village unique. Try the Caesar salad or any of the seafood specialties, especially the substantial lobster salad. The small bar has satellite TV, high captain's chairs, and views from second-story windows. The resort organizes deep sea fishing trips. ⬠ *Box EL 25187, Governor's Harbour* ☎ *242/332–1830* 🖶 *242/332–1838* ⊕ *www.bahamasvg.com/uniquevil.html* ⇆ *10 rooms, 4 villas* ⬧ *Restaurant, beach, snorkeling, fishing, bar* ▤ *MC, V* ⦿ *EP, FAP, MAP.*

$$ ▦ **Best Western Cigatoo Resort.** Surrounded by a white picket fence, this resort sits high on a hill overlooking Governor's Harbour. It has crisp white buildings trimmed in vibrant hues with indoor and outdoor tropical gardens. Rooms have bright, sunny decor; modern furnishings; and private patios or balconies. The resort is just minutes from a pink-sand beach. The Cigatoo Room restaurant specializes in Bahamian cuisine. The guest services department arranges bonefishing or deep-sea fishing trips, day trips to other islands, and car or bike rentals. Note that the resort is for guests 16 and up. ⬠ *Queen's Hwy.* ☎ *242/332–3060* 🖶 *242/332–3061* ⊕ *www.cigatooresort.com* ⇆ *22 rooms* ⬧ *Restaurant, cable TV, 2 tennis courts, pool, bar, recreation room, Internet, meeting room* ▤ *MC, V* ⊙ *Closed Oct.–Nov.*

$ ▦ **Duck Inn and Orchid Garden.** Facing west into the sunset, overlooking beautiful Governor's Harbour, two colonial cottages and a home built in the 1850s nestle into a tropical hillside garden surrounded by a world-class orchid collection. John and Kay Duckworth bought the compound from a Canadian timber baron and restyled the houses. With one bedroom each, the cottages are perfect for couples, whereas the four-bedroom house can sleep eight. Each dwelling has a full kitchen (there are grocery stores just a block away) and a verandah. A full-time gardener tends to tropical fruit trees; guests are welcome to pick and eat—even the apples. ⬠ *Queen's Hwy.* ☎ *242/332–2608* 🖶 *242/332–2160* ⊕ *www.theduckinn.com* ⇆ *2 cottages, 1 house* ⬧ *Kitchenettes, fishing* ▤ *MC, V.*

¢–$ ▦ **Laughing Bird Apartments.** English architect Dan Davies (designer of Windermere Island Club and Jacques Cousteau's villa) and his wife, Jean, own these four tidy apartments on an acre of land at the water's edge. Linens and crockery (including an English teapot and china cups) are furnished. You can stock your kitchen with produce from local stores or dine in any of the four restaurants within walking distance. This is a quiet, on-your-own kind of place, where relaxing and fishing are the name of the game. ⬠ *Box EL 25076, Governor's Harbour* ☎ *242/332–2012* 🖶 *242/332–2358* ⇆ *4 apartments* ⬧ *Kitchens, beach, fishing, Internet* ▤ *D, MC, V.*

Sports & the Outdoors

SNORKELING If you have a four-wheel-drive vehicle, take the road east at the settlement of James Cistern to reach James Point, a beautiful beach with snorkeling and 3- to 10-foot waves for surfers. About 4 mi north of James Cistern on the Atlantic side, take the rough-hewn steps down to **Hidden Beach,** a sandy little hideaway sheltered by a rock-formation canopy, affording maximum privacy and a great spot for novice snorkelers.

Hatchet Bay & Environs

❼ Hatchet Bay has mid-Eleuthera's only marina. Be sure to notice the names of the town's side roads, which have such colorful designations as Lazy Road, Happy Hill Road, and Smile Lane. Just south of town, the Rainbow Inn and Restaurant is the hub of activity for this stretch of Eleuthera.

❽ North of Hatchet Bay lies **The Cave,** a subterranean, bat-populated tunnel complete with stalagmites and stalactites. It was supposedly once used by pirates to hide their loot. An underground path leads for more than a mile to the sea, ending in a lofty, cathedral-like cavern. Within its depths fish swim in total darkness. The adventurous may wish to explore this area with a flashlight (follow the length of guide string along the cavern's floor), but it's best to inquire first at one of the local stores or the Rainbow Inn for a guide. To find the cave, drive north from Hatchet Bay and watch for the vine-covered silo on Queen's Highway's north side. Take the left turn soon thereafter, marked by a white stripe down the center of Queen's Highway. En route to the Cave is Sweeting's Pond, the focus of all sorts of local myths. Some claim that there are Loch Ness–like creatures living in it. Others believe that a wrecked plane lies on the bottom.

Where to Stay & Eat

★ $ ✕🍴 **Rainbow Inn.** Immaculate, generously sized cabins—all with large private porches—dot the waterfront grounds. The restaurant is one of the island's best, with a classy but no-fuss atmosphere and exhibition windows that face gorgeous sunsets. Islanders drive great distances for a meal here, especially when the famed Dr. Seabreeze strums away, on rib night (Wednesday) and steak night (Friday). The Nautical Bar, hung with authentic ship's wheels salvaged from wrecks, drips with local color. Nurse those Goombay Smashes as long as you like; cantankerous co-owner "Krabby" Ken won't be bashful about letting you know when it's time to leave. ✉ *2½ mi south of Hatchet Bay* 🏠 *Governor's Harbour* ☎🖨 *242/335–0294* ☎ *800/688–0047* ⊕ *www.rainbowinn.com* 🛏 *4 apartments, 2 2-bedroom villas, 1 3-bedroom villa* ⚹ *Restaurant, kitchenettes, microwaves, tennis court, pool, fishing, bicycles, bar* ▭ *D, MC, V* ⦿ *EP, MAP* ⊗ *Closed Sept. 1–Nov. 15.*

Gregory Town & Environs

❾ Gregory Town sits on top of a hill, with many of its charming pastel homes dotting the hillside. The town's annual Pineapple Festival begins on the Thursday evening of the Bahamian Labor Day weekend, at the beginning of June. With live music, juicy ripe pineapple (served every possible way), and settlement-wide merriment continuing into the wee hours, this is Gregory Town's liveliest happening.

Gregory Town's claim to fame lies about 2½ mi south of town, where **❿ Surfer's Beach,** a site of the 1960s "Beach Bum" culture, still packs wave-catchers from December through May. If you don't have a jeep, you can walk the ¾ mi to this Atlantic-side beach—follow rough-and-bumpy Ocean Boulevard at Eleuthera Island Shores just south of town.

If you're too lulled by the ebb and flow of lapping waves and prefer your shores crashing with dramatic white sprays, perhaps a visit to Eleuthera's **Grottoes and Hot Tubs** will revive you. The sun warms these tidal pools— which the locals call "moon pools"—making them a markedly more temperate soak than the sometimes-chilly ocean. On most days, refreshing sprays and rivulets tumble into the tubs, but on some it can turn dangerous; if the waves are crashing over the top of the cove's centerpiece mesa, pick another day to stop here. If you're driving from Gregory Town, the entrance is approximately 5 mi north on the right (Atlantic) side of the Queen's Highway, across the road from two thin tree stumps. If you reach the one-lane Glass Window Bridge, you've gone too far.

At a very narrow point of the island a few miles north of Gregory Town is a slender concrete bridge, called the Glass Bridge, linking two sea-battered bluffs that separate the Governor's Harbour and North Eleuthera districts. Sailors going south in the waters between New Providence and Eleuthera supposedly named this area the **Glass Window** because they could see through the narrow cavity to the Atlantic on the other side. Stop to watch the northeasterly deep-azure Atlantic swirl together under the bridge with the southwesterly turquoise Great Bahama Bank, producing a brilliant aquamarine froth. Artist Winslow Homer found the site stunning, too. He painted *Glass Window* in 1885. It's thought that the bridge was a natural span until the early 1900s, when rough currents finally washed it away. A 1991 storm lifted up the just-completed two-lane bridge, setting it down some 7 feet to the south.

Where to Stay & Eat

¢–$ ✕ **Elvina's Bar and Restaurant.** Shoot some pool and enjoy some West Indian specialties like curry chicken at this local favorite that used to double as a laundromat. Walls are covered with license plates and bumper stickers, and the surfboards hanging from the ceiling have been stowed there by surfer-regulars. Elvina's husband, known around these parts as "Chicken Ed," is from Louisiana, and the jambalaya here is the real thing. Be sure to call ahead, as Elvina and Ed don't open every night. ⊠ *Queens Hwy., Governor's Harbour* ☎ *242/335–5032* ▤ *No credit cards.*

¢ ✕ **Thompson Bakery.** Located appropriately on Sugar Hill St., Daisy Thompson bakes the island's best banana muffins, cinnamon rolls, pineapple bread, and pineapple, coconut, and lemon tarts, in a tiny hilltop enclave. Her family reputedly developed the recipe for pineapple rum. ⊠ *Sugar Hill St., Gregory Town* ☎ *242/335–5053* ☉ *Weekends* ▤ *No credit cards.*

✿ $ ✕▥ **The Cove, Eleuthera.** Thirty secluded acres set the tone for this re-
Fodor$Choice laxing seaside inn. A rocky promontory separates two coves: one has a
★ small sandy beach with palapas, lounge chairs, and kayaks, the other is rocky and ideal for snorkeling. The poolside patio is a good place for breakfast or relaxing cocktails. Clustered rooms have tile floors, high slanted ceilings, and white rattan furnishings. There's also a honeymoon suite built on the promontory with a 180° view of the coves and the

sea, from which you can see both sunrise and sunset. The window-lined dining room is spacious and bright, serving three meals a day. The menu includes green salads—hard to find in the Bahamas—and conch fritters and chowder. ⊠ *3 mi south of Glass Window Bridge and 1½ mi north of Gregory Town* ☐ *Box 1548, Gregory Town* ☏ *242/335–5142 or 800/552–5960* ☐ *242/335–5338* ⊕ *www.thecoveeleuthera. com* ☞ *24 rooms, 2 suites* ↻ *Restaurant, 2 tennis courts, pool, snorkeling, fishing, bicycles, bar, lounge* ☐ *D, MC, V* ⑩ *EP, MAP.*

Nightlife

The debonair **Dr. Seabreeze** strums his acoustic guitar while singing native songs that are nothing short of precious oral history. He plays Wednesday and Friday nights at the Rainbow Inn and Thursday night at Unique Village. A local musician, often a buddy of rocker Lenny Kravitz, who lives nearby, plays Tuesday and Friday nights at **Elvina's Bar and Restaurant.**

Sports & the Outdoors

SURFING In Gregory Town, stop by **Rebecca's** (☏ 242/335–5436), a general store and crafts shop, where local surf guru "Ponytail Pete" stocks a few supplies and posts a chalkboard listing surf conditions and tidal reports.

Shopping

Island Made Shop (⊠ Queen's Hwy. ☏ 242/335–5369), run by Pam and Greg Thompson, is a good place to shop for Bahamian arts and crafts, including Androsia batik (made on Andros Island), driftwood paintings, Abaco ceramics, and prints.

en route | Snorkelers and divers will want to spend some time at **Gaulding's Cay** beach, 3 mi north of Gregory town. Swim out to the tiny offshore island to witness a concentration of sea anemones—as if someone had laid carpet—so spectacular it dazzled even Jacques Cousteau's biologists. Gaulding's Cay is also a nice 1,500-foot shelling stretch for beachcombers.

Harbour Island

★ ⑬ **Harbour Island** has often been called the Nantucket of the Caribbean and the prettiest of the Out Islands because of its 3 mi of powdery pink-sand beach and its pastel-color clapboard houses with dormer windows, set among white picket fences, narrow lanes, quaint shops, and tropical flowers. The residents have long called it Briland, their faster way of pronouncing "Harbour Island." The best way to get around is to rent a golf cart or bike; or hire a taxi, since climbing the island's hills can be quite strenuous in midday heat. Within its 2 square mi are tucked some of the Bahamas' most attractive small hotels, each strikingly distinct. At several that are perched on a bluff above the shore, you can fall asleep with the windows open and listen to the waves lapping the beach. Harbour Island is reached via a five-minute ferry ride from the North Eleuthera dock. Fares are $8 per person, $4 per person in a boat of two or more, plus an extra dollar to be dropped off at the private docks of Valentine's or Romora Bay Club. The ferry also occasionally charges more for nighttime rides.

Old trees line the narrow streets of **Dunmore Town,** named after the 18th-century royal governor of the Bahamas, Lord Dunmore, who built a summer home here and laid out the town. The community was once second in the country to Nassau in terms of its prosperity. It's the only town on Harbour Island, and you can take in all its attractions during a 20-minute stroll. Stop first at the **Harbour Island Tourist Office** (☎ 242/333–2621), in the yellow building opposite the ferry dock. Get a map and ask about current events. Across the street is a row of straw-work stands, including Dorothea's, Pat's, and Sarah's, where you'll find straw bags, hats, accessories, T-shirts, and tourist bric-a-brac. Food stands sell conch and other local fare.

On Dunmore Street, you can visit the Bahamas' oldest Anglican church, **St. John's,** built in 1768, and the distinguished 1848 **Wesley Methodist Church.** Both hold services. On Bay Street, **Loyalist Cottage,** one of the original settlers' homes (circa 1797), has also survived. Many other old houses in the area, with gingerbread trim and picket fences, have such amusing names as "Beside the Point," "Up Yonder," and "The Royal Termite." Off the eastern, Atlantic shore lies a long coral reef, which protects the beach and has excellent snorkeling. You can see multicolored fish and a few old wrecks.

Where to Stay & Eat

Note that most Harbour Island hotels and restaurants are closed from September through mid- to late October.

★ **$–$$$$** ✕ **Romora Bay Club.** Thomas Chiarelli, probably the Bahamas' only French chef, expertly prepares nightly dinner menus at this enchanting location. The waterfront alfresco bar, Sloppy Joe's, has Fernand Léger drawings and Andy Warhol prints adorning the brightly painted walls. It's also one of the best places to enjoy a cocktail and views of the Harbour Island sunset. Arrive with plenty of time to secure your seat on the deck. Come nightfall, stroll through the gardens to the main hotel complex for fine post-dusk dining in an intimate dining room overlooking the infinity pool. Also make time for a drink in the jungle-hip Parrot Bar. ⊠ *South end of Dunmore St., Dunmore Town* ☎ *242/333–2325* ⌣ *Reservations essential* ☐ *AE, D, MC, V.*

$–$$ ✕ **Harbour Lounge.** The popular former owners of the Picadilly restaurant—a longtime Nassau favorite—now own this pink building with green shutters across from the government dock. Arrive early if you want good seats on the front deck for watching the sunset over cocktails. The lunch and dinner fare might include smoked dolphinfish dip with garlic pita chips or grouper cake salad. ⊠ *Bay St., Dunmore Town* ☎ *242/333–2031* ☐ *D, MC, V* ☉ *Closed Mon.*

★ **$–$$** ✕ **Sip Sip.** You can't miss this building—it's bright lime green with cobalt shutters—at the end of the block past the elementary school. Sit inside and enjoy the paintings by local artists, or dine on the shaded deck overlooking the beach. The menu is eclectic, with local fish dishes using Mediterranean and Asian ingredients. The food selection changes daily, so check out the blackboard to see what's cooking. ⊠ *Court St., Dunmore Town* ☎ *242/333–3316* ☐ *MC, V* ☉ *Closed Tues.*

¢–$ ✗**Arthur's Bakery and Cafe.** M*A*S*H screenwriter Robert Arthur and his Trinidadian wife, Anna, bake sensational bread every morning. Try the four-herb or jalapeño loaf. Anna coordinates and caters weddings as well. ⊠ *Corner of Crown St. and Dunmore St., Dunmore Town* ☎*242/ 333–2285* ⊟ *No credit cards* ☉ *Closed Sun. No dinner.*

¢ ✗**Dunmore Deli.** Under a green-and-white stripe awning shading a wooden deck, this exceptional deli serves alfresco breakfasts and lunches. It stocks a superb variety of international coffee, imported cheese, and other gourmet items you won't find anywhere else on the island. ⊠ *King St., Dunmore Town* ☎ *242/333–2644* ⊟ *MC, V* ☉ *Closed Sun. No dinner.*

¢ ✗**Queen Conch.** A block and a half from the ferry dock on Bay Street,
Fodor'sChoice Lavaughn and Richard Percentie's colorful snack stand overlooking
★ the harbor is renowned for its freshly caught conch salad ($7), which is diced in front of you, mixed with fresh vegetables, and served in deep bowls. Visitors from the world over place large orders to take home. ⊠*Bay St., Dunmore Town* ☎*No phone* ⊟*No credit cards* ☉ *Closed Sun.*

★ **$$$$** ✗▣**Dunmore Beach Club.** The Dunmore is proud of its guest-to-staff ratio (almost one-to-one) and the length of service of its employees (10 years is not considered a long time here). Accommodations are private New England–style cottages with exquisite interiors, including gorgeous marble bathrooms with two-person whirlpool tubs, enormous stand-alone showers, and separate sink-vanity areas. In the cozy clubhouse you'll find a Villeroy & Boch–tiled ocean-view honor bar, comfy settees, a working fireplace, and a well-stocked library. This is the most formal place to stay or dine on the island. The restaurant serves a four-course international menu at 8 PM. The club's clientele consists predominantly of the yachting crowd. ⊡ *Box EL 27122, Harbour Island* ☎ *242/333– 2200 or 877/891–3100* ⊟ *242/333–2429* ⊕ *www.dunmorebeach.com* ⌁ *16 units in 8 cottages* ⚇ *Restaurant, refrigerators, tennis court, beach, bar, library, laundry service, Internet* ⊟ *D, MC, V* ⑩ *FAP.*

$$$$ ✗▣ **Pink Sands.** Island Records founder Chris Blackwell transformed this old Harbour Island property—on the edge of the famous rosy-hued sands—into a luxury resort. Private, colorful one- or two-bedroom cottages, scattered across the lush, 25-acre property, include such frills as Aveda Spa-Bath toiletries, a cordless phone, a DVD player, and a king-size bed with dual-controlled heater. The main house has a hand-carved bar and imported Indian and Indonesian furniture and antiques. The richness extends to the library, which has a working fireplace and plump, comfy couches. Euro-Bahamian fare is served during lunch in the striking ocean-view Blue Bar, and in the evenings there is a four-course "Chef Recommends" menu. ⊡ *Box 87, Harbour Island* ☎ *242/333– 2030* ⊟ *242/333–2060* ⊕ *www.pinksandsresort.com* ⌁ *25 1- and 2-bedroom cottages* ⚇ *2 restaurants, dining room, in-room safes, mini-bars, in-room VCRs, 3 tennis courts, pool, gym, beach, snorkeling, billiards, 2 bars, library, shop, baby-sitting, laundry service, Internet* ⊟*AE, D, MC, V* ⑩ *MAP* ☉ *Closed two weeks in mid-Oct.*

♻ $$ ✗▣**Coral Sands Hotel.** The resort sits on 9 hilly acres right above its namesake, the world-famous, 3-mi-long pink beach. The bright, individually decorated guest rooms have British Colonial–style furnishings. Upstairs rooms—reached by curving steps—have access to expansive rooftop terraces. Some rooms have child-size futons and adjoining bedrooms; all have small private balconies overlooking the ocean or lushly planted gardens through French doors. The restaurant offers an eclectic mix of Bahamian favorites and Italian classics, served on a balcony with open arches framing breathtaking views of the ocean. Lunch is served at a beach bar high above the rosy sand. ⊠ *Chapel St., Harbour Island* ☎ *242/333–2350, 242/333–2320, or 800/468–2799* 🖷 *242/333–2368* ⊕ *www.coralsands.com* ⮐ *39 rooms and suites* �б *Restaurant, tennis court, pool, beach, snorkeling, boating, fishing, billiards, 2 bars, library, laundry service, Internet; no room TVs* ⊟ *AE, D, MC, V* ⦿ *EP, MAP.*

★ $$ ✕🏠 **The Landing.** Built by uniting two early-19th-century homes, this lovely inn facing the harbor embodies an understated contemporary-rustic chicness. All seven plantation-style bedrooms have harbor views, pastel walls, hand-carved four-poster beds, and large, tiled bathrooms. The management, a former Miss Bahamas queen and her family, use the original parlor with highly polished Abaco pine floors as an intimate restaurant, one of the island's finest. The menu is an elegantly prepared blend of Bahamian and Continental cuisines. You can also dine on the porch overlooking the harbor, and in a lovely garden. The bar is fabulous, offering premium libations you can't find elsewhere on the island. A hearty breakfast is included in the rate. ⊠ *Bay St.* ⚈ *Box 190* ☎ *242/333–2707 or 242/333–2740* 🖷 *242/333–2650* ⊕ *www.harbourislandlanding.com* ⮐ *7 rooms* �б *Restaurant, bar, library, Internet, business services; no room phones, no room TVs* ⊟ *D, MC, V* ⦿ *CP* ☉ *Closed Sept. 10–Nov. 1.*

★ $ ✕🏠 **Rock House.** This complex of historic harborside buildings—including a 19th-century jail and a schoolhouse—has been lavishly renovated by the architectural design team that created Gianni Versace's Miami mansion. The owner's attention to detail is evident at every turn, from the constant tweaking of floral arrangements, to the moonlight-like blue lights in the private cabanas ringing the heated pool (each room has its own cabana). Guest rooms each have a different name and accessory motif, and come with luxurious items like a picnic basket for beach forays and a custom-designed extra-padded mattress. Rock House has Harbour Island's only fully outfitted gym—one of the owners is a fitness nut. The restaurant serves gourmet fare in the front parlor and on the open porch. Try the seafood roll appetizer, a mix of lobster, crab, and tiger prawn in an Asian-style roll; don't miss the homemade ice cream for dessert. ⊠ *Bay St., Harbour Island* ☎ *242/333–2053* 🖷 *242/333–3173* ⊕ *www.rockhousebahamas.com* ⮐ *9 rooms, 2 suites* �б *Restaurant, bar, in-room safes, minibars, in-room VCRs, library, Internet* ⊟ *AE, MC, V* ⦿ *CP.*

$ ✕🏠 **Valentine's Resort and Marina.** Island-hopping Yachties like to tie up at Valentine's modern, fully equipped 39-slip marina. The club hosts the North Eleuthera Regatta on Columbus Day. Valentine's has a complex of time-share and rentable villas with British Colonial dark wood furnishings. A complete dive shop offers a variety of dives, including trips to Current Cut, Sink Hole, and Bat Cavern. The resort shuttles guests to the pink-sand beach and arranges deep-sea and bonefishing excursions. There is a pagoda-shape dockside restaurant-bar with an outside deck, serving solid Bahamian-American fare. ⊠ *Northeast Harbour Island, ¼ mi from Dunmore Town* ☎ *242/333–2142 or 800/323–5655*

☎ 242/333–2135 ⊕ www.valentinesresort.com ➥ 10 rooms ⚪ Restaurant, tennis court, pool, dive shop, marina, fishing, bicycles, bar, Internet, business services ⊟ AE, D, MC, V ⦿ EP, MAP.

¢–$ ✕⊞ **Tingum Village.** These rustic cottages have high pine ceilings, sea-colored furnishings, netting above the king-size beds, and two-person whirlpool tubs overlooking the yard's gardens out of floor-to-ceiling corner windows. In front of the hotel is Ma Ruby's Restaurant, home of Jimmy Buffet's original "Cheeseburger in Paradise," where you can sample Bahamian food on a breezy covered patio three times daily. Leave room for Ma Precentie's home-baked bread, coconut tarts, key lime pie, or pound cake. Tingum Village is on the town's south end and a short walk from Harbour Island's famous pink-sand beach. ⊠ Next to the Harbour Island Library, Harbour Island ☎☎ 242/333–2161 ➥ 12 rooms, 5 1-bedroom and 2 2-bedroom suites, 1 3-bedroom cottage ⚪ Restaurant, bar ⊟ D, MC, V ⦿ EP, MAP.

★ $$$ ⊞ **Romora Bay Club.** Clusters of cottages are scattered about the grounds at this eclectic and artsy resort on Harbour Island's bay side. Each guest room, suite, or villa is decorated with unique artwork and furnishings (including a custom-made bedspread) and has a private patio, TV/VCR, and CD player. Although the hotel is not on the famous pink beach, it's just a short golf-cart ride away. If you'd rather stay on the property, you won't be bored: Watersports galore are yours for the taking; the library has hundreds of movies, CDs, and books for you to borrow; and the lovely pool deck has stunning bay views. ⊠ South End of Dunmore St., Dunmore Town ☎ 242/333–2325 or 800/688–0425 ☎ 242/333–2500 ⊕ www.romorabay.com ➥ 30 rooms, suites, and villas ⚪ 2 restaurants, in-room VCRs, tennis court, pool, dock, waterskiing, fishing, billiards, 2 bars, library, Internet ⊟ AE, D, MC, V ⦿ MAP.

★ $$ ⊞ **Runaway Hill Club.** What was once a private seaside mansion is now an enchanting inn perched on a bluff above Harbour Island's fabled beach. Most rooms face the sea; the rest overlook the gardens. All are individually decorated with antiques, original island artwork, lovely bed linens, and coordinating draperies. The newer hilltop villa has larger, more uniform rooms with colorful patchwork quilts and bookshelves with an array of titles. Stairs lead down to the freshwater pool near the beach. Be sure to make reservations early to check out the club's inventive menu, which focuses on fresh, local ingredients. ⬡ Box EL 27031, Dunmore Town ☎ 242/333–2150 ☎ 242/333–2420 ⊕ www.runawayhill.com ➥ 10 rooms ⚪ Restaurant, pool, beach, bar, lounge; no kids ⊟ AE, D, MC, V ⦿ EP, MAP ⊙ Closed Labor Day–Nov. 15.

★ $ ⊞ **Bahama House Inn.** This upscale bed-and-breakfast was originally deeded in 1796 and built by Thomas W. Johnson, Briland's first justice of the peace. Set in a garden filled with bougainvillea, royal poincianas, and roses, this lovely five-bedroom house thrives thanks to the loving preservation work done by genial owner-hosts John and Joni Hersch. Each guest room has local artwork, four-poster beds with decorative netting, a comfy sofa, and gracious Queen Anne–style writing desks. Enjoy Continental breakfast each morning on deck. ⊠ Dunmore St. ☎ 242/333–2201 ☎ 242/333–2850 ⊕ www.bahamahouseinn.com ➥ 5 rooms, 1 1-bedroom suite ⚪ Library; no room TVs ⊟ MC, V ⦿ CP ⊙ Closed Oct.

Nightlife

Enjoy a brew on the wraparound patio of **Gusty's** (☎ 242/333–2165), on Harbour Island's northern point. This lively hot spot has sand floors, a few tables covered in orange-batiked cloths, and patrons shooting pool or watching sports on satellite TV. On weekends, holidays, and in high season, it's a very crowded and happening dance spot with a DJ.

Enter through the marine life–muraled hallway at **Seagrapes** (✉ Colebrook and Gibson Sts. ☎ 242/333–2389) to a large nightclub with a raised stage that's home to the local Funk Gang band.

Valentine's Resort and Marina (☎ 242/333–2142) is particularly lively on weekend nights. The waterfront Reach Grill and the second-story Reach Up deck make wonderful vantage points for sunset-watching or imbibing.

Vic-Hum Club (✉ Barrack St. ☎ 242/333–2161) occasionally hosts live Bahamian bands in a room decorated with classic record album covers; otherwise, you'll find locals playing Ping-Pong and listening and dancing to loud recorded music, from calypso to American pop and R&B.

Sports & the Outdoors

BOATING &
FISHING
There are abundant spots around the island to angle for bonefish (at a cost of around $75 a half day), bottom fish ($75 a half day), reef fish ($20 an hour), and deep-sea fish ($250–$600 a full day). And there is great bonefishing right off Dunmore Town at Girl Bay. The Harbour Island Tourist Office can help to organize bone- and bottom-fishing excursions, as can all the major hotels.

Valentine's Resort and Marina (☎ 242/333–2142) can arrange various types of fishing trips and has small boats for rent. **Big Red Rentals** (☎ 242/333–2045) offers Boston Whalers (13 foot–21 foot) and banana-boat rides.

SCUBA DIVING &
SNORKELING
Current Cut, the narrow passage between North Eleuthera and Current Island, is loaded with marine life and provides a roller-coaster ride on the currents. **Devil's Backbone,** in North Eleuthera, offers a tricky reef area with a nearly infinite number of dive sites and a large number of wrecks. **Fox Divers** (☎ 242/333–2323) rents scuba equipment and offers instruction, certification, dive packages, and daily dive trips. **Valentine's Dive Center** (☎ 242/333–2309) rents and sells equipment and provides all levels of instruction, certification, dive packages, and daily group and custom dives. **Big Red Rentals** (☎ 242/333–2045) rents snorkeling equipment and offers snorkeling excursions.

Shopping

Blue Rooster (✉ Dunmore St. ☎ 242/333–2240) has a wonderful selection of Bahama Hand Prints clothing, bags, and elegant gift items from around the world. Closed Sunday.

Briland Brushstrokes (✉ Bay St. ☎ 242/333–2085) is a gallery owned by Harvey Roberts, Briland's politician-artist son. Many of Roberts' original acrylics and prints may be viewed and purchased in his office–art gallery. Artwork and sculptures by other local artists are also on display.

Briland's Androsia (⊠ Bay St. ☎ 242/333–2342) has a good selection of bathing suits, bags, and other items made from the bright batik fabric created on the island of Andros.

Dilly Dally (⊠ Dunmore St. ☎ 242/333–3109) sells Bahamian-made jewelry, maps, decorations, and other fun souvenirs.

John Bull (⊠ Bay St. ☎ 242/333–2950), a duty-free shop near the dock, sells watches, fine jewelry, perfume, cigars, and sunglasses. Closed Sunday.

The Landing (⊠ Bay St. ☎ 242/333–2707) has an elegant and eclectic mix of beaded jewelry, sequined and embroidered caftans and shirts, and gift items. Closed Wednesday.

Princess Street Gallery (⊠ Princess St. ☎ 242/333–2788) features original oil and watercolor paintings, hand-loomed throws, painted linens, and wooden bowls by local artists. Closed Sunday.

Sugar Mill (⊠ Bay St. ☎ 242/333–2173) sells prints by local artists, Bahamian coin jewelry, picture frames decorated with Eleutheran shells, and wooden puzzles from the nearby island of Spanish Wells. Closed Sunday.

North Eleuthera

⑭ At the island's tip, **Preacher's Cave** is where the Eleutheran Adventurers took refuge and held services when their ship hit a reef more than three centuries ago. Note the original stone altar inside the cave. The last 2 mi of the road to Preacher's Cave is rough, but passable if you go slowly. Across from the cave is a long succession of deserted pink-sand beaches.

Spanish Wells

Off Eleuthera's northern tip lies St. George's Cay, the site of Spanish Wells. The Spaniards used this as a safe harbor during the 17th century while they transferred their riches from the New World to the Old. Supposedly they dug wells from which they drew water during their frequent visits. Today, water comes from the mainland. Residents—the few surnames go back generations—live on the island's eastern end in clapboard houses that look as if they've been transported from a New England fishing village. Descendants of the Eleutheran Adventurers continue to sail these waters and bring back to shore fish and lobster (most of the Bahamas' langoustes are caught in these waters), which are prepared and boxed for export in a factory at the dock. So lucrative is the trade in crawfish, the local term for Bahamian lobsters, that the 700 inhabitants may be the most prosperous Out Islanders in the Bahamas. Those who don't fish here grow tomatoes, onions, and pineapples. You reach Spanish Wells by taking a five-minute ferry ride ($2) from the Three-Island Dock at North Eleuthera (same dock as ferries to Harbour Island).

Tourists have little to do here but hang out on the beach, dive, and dine on fresh seafood at **Jack's Out Back** (☎ 242/333–4219).

♻ $ ▣ **Abner's Rentals.** Abner Pinder's wife, Ruth, keeps these two attached two-bedroom houses as spotless as her own. A tiny, private sand beach overlooking Harbour Island is just steps from the patio. The house rental includes use of a golf cart so you can explore the island and pick up groceries at one of the local shops. ⊠ *First St., Spanish Wells* ☎ *242/ 333–4890* ⊟ *242/333–4895* ⋟ *2 houses* ♻ *TV, kitchens* ▭ *MC, V.*

Eleuthera A to Z

To research prices, get advice from other travelers, and book travel arrangements, visit ⊕ *www.fodors.com.*

AIR TRAVEL

Eleuthera has three airports—Governor's Harbour, North Eleuthera, and Rock Sound. Head for the one closest to your hotel. Fly into Governor's Harbour if you are staying south of Gregory Town, and into North Eleuthera if you are staying in Gregory Town or to the north. Several North American carriers and national airlines fly to each of the airports.

CARRIERS   Bahamasair has daily service from Nassau to all three airports. Cherokee Air is an on-demand charter service based in Marsh Harbour. It flies all over the Bahamas and serves Palm Beach and Fort Lauderdale as well. Continental Connection has daily flights to North Eleuthera from Miami and Fort Lauderdale. GHL Travel Agency charters two inexpensive daily flights from Nassau to North Eleuthera, and depending on demand flights also stop at Governor's Harbour. Major Air has service from Freeport to Governor's Harbour and North Eleuthera. Twin Air flies from Fort Lauderdale four times a week to Governor's Harbour, Rock Sound, and North Eleuthera. US Airways Express flies daily from Miami to Governor's Harbour and North Eleuthera. Tom Jones Air Charters, owned by the former publisher/editor of the *Pilot's Guide to the Bahamas,* flies all over the Bahamas.

🚪 Airlines & Contacts **Bahamasair** ☎ 800/222-4262. **Cherokee Air** ☎ 242/367-2089 or 242/367-2613. **Continental Connection** ☎ 800/231-0856. **GHL Travel Agency** ☎ 242/323-7217 in Nassau, 242/335-1574 in North Eleuthera. **Major Air** ☎ 242/352-5778. **Tom Jones Air Charters** ☎ 305/931-6612 or 242/335-1353. **Twin Air** ☎ 954/359-8266. **US Airways Express** ☎ 800/622-1015.

AIRPORTS & TRANSFERS

Eleuthera has three airports: North Eleuthera; Governor's Harbour, near the center of the island; and Rock Sound, in the southern part of the island.

🚪 Airport Information **Governor's Harbour** ☎ 242/332-2321. **North Eleuthera** ☎ 242/ 335-1242. **Rock Sound** ☎ 242/334-2177.

TRANSFERS   Taxis wait for incoming flights at all three airports. Call a taxi prior to departing your resort or hotel; on Eleuthera you should allow a half hour for your cab to arrive; on Harbour Island, taxis come a few minutes after you call. If you land at North Eleuthera and need to get to Harbour Island, off Eleuthera's north coast, take a taxi ($4) to the ferry dock (Three Island Dock) on Eleuthera, a water taxi ($4) to Harbour Island, and, on the other side, another taxi ($3 to Coral Sands, for example). You follow a similar procedure to get to Spanish Wells, also off Eleuthera's north shore. Taxi service from Governor's Harbour Airport to the Cove Eleuthera is $42 for two people, though the taxi fare from North Eleuthera to the Cove is only $33 for two people. The fare from Governor's Harbour to Rainbow Inn is $24.

7 Taxi Information **Governor's Harbour Taxi Stand** ☏ 242/332-2568.

BIKE TRAVEL

Bicycles are a popular way to explore Harbour Island. You can rent them at Big Red Rentals or Michael's Cycles.

7 Bike Rentals **Big Red Rentals** ✉ Harbour Island ☏ 242/333-2045. **Michael's Cycles** ✉ Harbour Island ☏ 242/333-2384.

BOAT & FERRY TRAVEL

The following mail boats leave from Nassau at Potter's Cay; for schedules, contact the Dockmaster's Office at Potter's Cay, Nassau.

M/V *Current Pride* sails to the Current, Lower Bogue, Upper Bogue, and Hatchet Bay on Thursday, returning Tuesday. M/V *Bahamas Daybreak III* leaves on Monday for South Eleuthera, stopping at Rock Sound, and returns on Tuesday. It then leaves Thursday from Nassau for the Bluff and Harbour Island, returning on Sunday. The *Eleuthera Express* sails for Governor's Harbour and Spanish Wells on Monday and Thursday, returning to Nassau on Tuesday and Sunday, respectively. The fare is $20 for all Eleutheran destinations.

Bahamas Fast Ferries connects Nassau to Harbour Island, North Eleuthera, and Spanish Wells daily. A round-trip fare costs $100; excursion rates (including a tour, lunch, and a trip to the beach) are somewhat higher. The trip from Fast Ferries terminal on Potter's Cay, Nassau to Harbour Island, with a stop on Spanish Wells, takes two hours. Ferries leave Nassau at 8 AM (and also at 1:30 PM on Fridays and busier weekends) and return at 3:55 (and 6:25 on Fridays on busy weekends). Call to confirm departure times and rates. Make reservations well in advance for trips around Columbus Day, the weekend of the annual North Eleuthera Regatta.

7 Boat & Ferry Information **Bahamas Fast Ferry** ☏ 242/323-2166 🖷 242/322-8185 ⊕ www.bahamasferries.com. **Dockmaster's Office** ☏ 242/393-1064.

BUSINESS HOURS

Most small businesses on Harbour Island close for a lunch break between 1 and 3, a practice unique in the Bahamas. Banks on Eleuthera and its islands are open weekdays from 9:30 to 3, Friday until 5. First Caribbean Bank has a branch in Governor's Harbour. Royal Bank of Canada runs Harbour Island's only bank, in addition to branches in Governor's Harbour and Spanish Wells. Scotia Bank has branches in North Eleuthera and Rock Sound.

BANKS & OFFICES The Scotia Bank in George Town is open weekdays 9:30–3 and Fridays until 5.

7 First Caribbean Bank ☏ 242/332-2300. **Royal Bank of Canada** ☏ 242/333-2250 Harbour Island, 242/332-2856 Governor's Harbour, 242/333-2620 Spanish Wells. **Sco-**

tia Bank ☎ 242/335-1400, 242/335-1406, or 242/334-2620 North Eleuthera, 242/335-1400, 242/335-1406, or 242/334-2620 Rock Sound.

CAR RENTAL

Arranging a car rental through your hotel will most likely be your least complicated option. You can usually have a vehicle delivered to you at the airport. Request a four-wheel-drive if you plan to visit Preacher's Cave or Surfer's Beach. Johnson's Rentals, Arthur Nixon, Hilton's Car Rentals, and Cecil Cooper all rent cars from Governor's Harbour—call to discuss delivery of your automobile. In Rock Sound, Dingle Motor Service rents cars. Baretta's has cars and minivans. On Harbour Island and Spanish Wells, you're better off renting a golf cart.

⚑ Local Agencies Arthur Nixon ☎ 242/332-1006 or 242/332-2568. **Baretta's** ✉ Harbour Island ☎ 242/333-2361. **Cecil Cooper** ☎ 242/359-7007 or 242/332-2568. **Dingle Motor Service** ☎ 242/334-2031. **Hilton's Car Rentals** ☎ 242/335-6241 or 242/332-2568. **Johnson's Rentals** ☎ 242/332-2226.

EMERGENCIES

Governor's Harbour, Harbour Island, Rock Sound, and Spanish Wells each has its own police and medical emergency numbers.

⚑ Medical Clinics ☎ 242/332-2001, 242/332-2774 Governor's Harbour, 242/333-2222 Harbour Island, 242/334-2226 Rock Sound, 242/333-4064 Spanish Wells. **Police** ☎ 242/332-2111 Governor's Harbour, 242/333-2111 Harbour Island, 242/334-2244 Rock Sound, 242/333-4030 Spanish Wells.

GOLF CART TRAVEL

Even if you're a big walker, you'll want a golf cart if you spend more than a couple of days on Harbour Island; there are several golf-cart rental companies there. Cart rates start at $35 for a two-seater and go up according to size (a six-seater is the largest); definitely negotiate if you'll be renting for longer. On Spanish Wells, you'll be able to rent a cart directly at the dock.

⚑ Abner's Rentals ☎ 242/333-4890. **Baretta's** ☎ 242/333-2361. **Big Red Rentals** ☎ 242/333-3128. **Dunmore Rentals** ☎ 242/333-2372. **Grant's** ☎ 242/333-2157. **Johnson's Garage** ☎ 242/333-2376. **Ross's Garage** ☎ 242/333-2122. **R&J Golf Carts** ☎ 242/333-2116. **Sunshine Carts** ☎ 242/333-2509.

SIGHTSEEING GUIDES

Arthur Nixon is probably the most knowledgeable authority on Eleuthera. His presentation will make you want to stand up and applaud. Tell him how much time you have and where you want to go, and he'll take you there, telling stories en route.

⚑ Arthur Nixon ☎ 242/332-1006, 242/332-2568, or 242/359-7879.

TAXIS

To explore Eleuthera, you'd best rent a car, which is cheaper than hiring a taxi, unless you consider having a driver who can double as your tour guide worth the expense. Taxis are available through your hotel. On Eleuthera, have your hotel call for a taxi about a half hour before you need it. On Harbour Island, taxis generally arrive a few minutes after being called. Taxis are almost always waiting at the North Eleuthera and Harbour Island water taxi docks.

TRANSPORTATION
Harbour Island is easily explored on foot—it takes only 30 minutes to walk the length of the island—although you'll be wise to rent a golf cart if you're staying for a few days. Visiting Eleuthera's main sights will require renting a car. North to south is about a three-hour drive. Governor's Harbour, which lies approximately at Eleuthera's midpoint, is a 40-minute drive from Glass Window in the north, and a 35-minute drive from Rock Sound in the south. You can also rent a bike or scooter to explore the island.

VISITOR INFORMATION
Contact the Eleuthera Tourist Office in Governor's Harbour or the Harbour Island Tourist Office on Bay Street right off the dock for brochures and information about the islands. Both are open weekdays 9–5.
🛈 Tourist Information **Eleuthera Tourist Office** ✉ Governor's Harbour ☎ 242/332–2142 🖷 242/332–2480. **Harbour Island Tourist Office** ✉ Bay St. ☎ 242/333–2621 🖷 242/333–2622.

THE EXUMAS

Numbers in the margin correspond to points of interest on The Exumas map.

Little Exuma & Great Exuma

⑮ The old village of **Williams Town** lies at Little Exuma Island's southern tip. Wild cotton still grows out in these parts, along the way to the **Hermitage,** a former plantation house with ruins of slave cottages nearby.

⑯ Five miles south of George Town lies **Rolle Town,** a typical Exuma village—without the tourist trappings. Residents grow onions, mangoes, bananas, and other crops.

⑰ Although **George Town** is the island's hive of activity, it's still on the no-need-for-a-traffic-light scale. The most imposing structure here is in the town center—the white-pillared, sandy pink, colonial-style **Government Administration Building,** modeled on Nassau's Government House and containing the commissioner's office, police headquarters, courts, and a jail. Atop a hill across from the government building is the whitewashed **St. Andrew's Anglican Church,** originally built around 1802 and renovated in 1991. Behind the church is the small Lake Victoria. A leisurely stroll around town will take you past a straw market and a few shops. You can buy fruit and vegetables and bargain with fishermen for some of the day's catch at the **Government Wharf,** where the mail boat comes in. The wharf is close to **Regatta Point** (☎242/336–2206), an attractive guest house named after the annual Family Islands Regatta that curls around Kidd Cove, where the 18th-century pirate Captain Kidd supposedly tied up.

Fish Fry is the name given to a jumble of one-room beachside structures about 2 mi north of George Town, favored by locals for made-to-order fish and barbecue; there's even a sports bar with TVs in each corner. Some shacks are open weekends only, but most are open nightly until 11 PM or midnight.

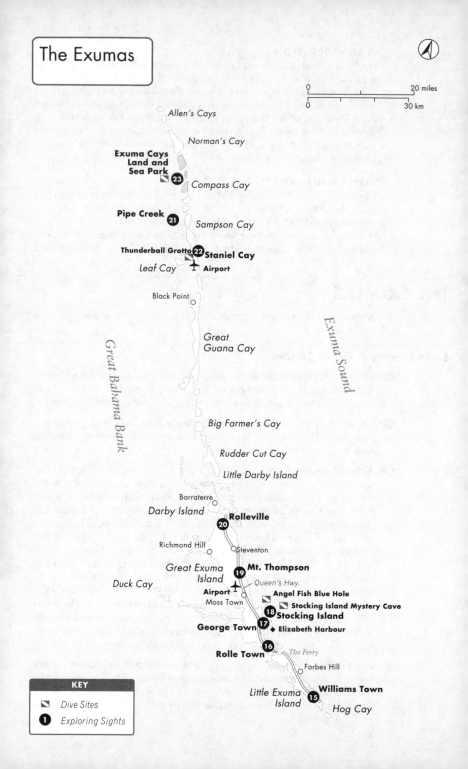

★ **⑱** Slightly more than a mile off George Town's shore lies **Stocking Island.** The 7-mi-long island has only seven inhabitants, a gorgeous white beach rich in seashells, and plenty of good snorkeling sites. Jacques Cousteau's team is said to have traveled a length of some 1,700 feet into **Mystery Cave,** a blue-hole grotto 70 feet beneath the island. Club Peace & Plenty's ferry runs over to Stocking Island twice daily at 10 AM and 1 PM and charges $8 for nonguests. Near the Stocking Island pier, Peace & Plenty Beach Club rents a variety of watersports gear, provides changing rooms (with plumbing), and operates a lunch spot where Dora's "heavenly burgers and dreamful dogs" are the eats of choice. To enjoy the setting sun from Stocking Island, head for the **Chat & Chill,** a lively open-air restaurant and bar right on the point.

⑲ From the top of **Mt. Thompson,** rising from the beach, there is a pleasing view of the **Three Sisters Rocks** jutting above the water just offshore. During your walks, you may glimpse a flock of roaming peacocks on Great Exuma. Originally, a peacock and a peahen were brought to the island as pets by a man named Shorty Johnson, but when he left to work in Nassau, he abandoned the birds, who gradually proliferated into a colony. Some locals hunt these birds because they eat crops, but they are difficult to catch. Mt. Thompson is about 12 mi north of George Town, past Moss Town.

⑳ The town of **Rolleville** sits on a hill above a harbor, 20 mi north of George Town. Its old slave quarters have been transformed into livable cottages. The town's most prominent citizen, Kermit Rolle, runs the **Hilltop Tavern** (☎ 242/336–6038), a seafood restaurant and bar guarded by an ancient cannon.

Where to Stay & Eat

$–$$ ✕ **Eddie's Edgewater.** The specialty at this popular spot is turtle steak, but the menu also offers low-fat steamed chicken (call ahead, or wait the 40 minutes' preparation time). Don't miss the rake 'n' scrape band on Monday; rakes and saws serve as instruments. ⊠ *Charlotte St., George Town* ☎ *242/336–2050* ▤ *D, MC, V* ⊗ *Closed Sun.*

★ **¢–$** ✕ **Chat & Chill.** Yacht folks, locals, and visitors alike rub shoulders at Kenneth Bowe's very hip and upscale—yet still casual—eatery on the point at Stocking Island. All of the incredible edibles are grilled over an open fire. Awesome conch burgers with secret spices and grilled fish with onions and potatoes are not to be missed. The Sunday pig roasts are fabulous. ⊠ *Stocking Island, George Town* ☎ *No phone* ▤ *No credit cards.*

¢–$ ✕ **Iva Bowe's Central Highway Inn.** About 10 mi from George Town, close to the airport, this casual lunch and dinner spot has an island-wide reputation for the best native food. Try one of the delectable shrimp dishes—coconut beer shrimp, spicy Cajun shrimp, or scampi, all for around $10. ⊠ *Queen's Hwy.* ☎ *242/345–7014* ▤ *No credit cards* ⊗ *Closed weekends.*

¢–$ ✕ **Towne Café.** George Town's bakery serves breakfast—consider trying the "stew" fish or chicken souse—and lunch—seafood sandwiches with three sides, or grilled fish. Towne Café is open until 5 PM. ⊠ *Marshall Complex, George Town* ☎ *242/336–2194* ▤ *No credit cards* ⊗ *Closed Sun.*

¢ ✕ **Big D's Conch Shack.** For the freshest conch salad and the coldest beer, look for the splatter-painted seaside shack a stone's throw from the Four Seasons Emerald Bay resort. Daron Tucker does the fishing, wife Dianne heads the kitchen. ⊠ *Queen's Hwy., Steventon* ☎ *242/358–0059* ▤ *No credit cards* ⊘ *Closed Mon.*

★ ¢ ✕ **Jean's Dog House.** A bright-yellow former school bus is now a tiny, spotless kitchen on wheels. Noted for her 'dogs, divine lobster burger, and the "MacJean," a hearty breakfast sandwich with sausage or bacon and sometimes cheese on homemade Bahama bread, Jean cooks them all in her unique "dry-fry" method (no oil). The minibus is parked every weekday from 7 to around 3 at the bottom of schoolhouse hill (a well-known landmark). Jean has an effervescent personality and is a treasure trove of Exuma history. She is also a daughter of the famous "Shark Lady," who spent years going out regularly in her 13-foot Boston Whaler to catch sharks with a 150-foot-long hand line. ⊠ *Queen's Hwy., George Town* ☎ *No phone* ▤ *No credit cards* ⊘ *Closed weekends.*

⏱ $$$–$$$$ ✕▦ **Four Seasons Resort Great Exuma at Emerald Bay.** The luxurious Four Seasons is the only full-service resort on Great Exuma Island. The 470 acres of pristine grounds lie adjacent to a mile-long strip of beach. There is an elaborate spa with two-person treatment rooms for couples, as well as watersports, tennis courts, the island's only 18-hole golf course, and a children's area with its own pool. Guests stay in lemon yellow Colonial-style villas clustered on landscaped grounds. Rooms are decorated in rich, dark woods and rattan offset by pastel walls and sunny artwork. Each room has its own patio or balcony facing the bay. The resort's two restaurants have both Bahamian and Continental dishes, with a heavy emphasis on seafood. Delicious thin-crust pizza baked in a wood-fired oven is another specialty. ⌂ *Box EX 29005, Emerald Bay* ☎ *242/336–6800* 🖷 *242/336–6801* ⊕ *www.fourseasons.com* ⇌ *183 rooms, 43 suites* ⅃ *Two restaurants, in-room data ports, in-room safes, in-room VCRs, 4 pools, watersports, snorkeling, windsurfing, boating, fishing, bar, laundry service, business services, car rental* ▤ *AE, D, MC, V.*

⏱ $$–$$$$ ✕▦ **Palm Bay Beach Club.** Palm Bay is all about light and color. The bungalows have brightly painted exteriors (like turquoise with hibiscus pink trim) and cheerfully sunny interiors. They are clustered on boardwalk paths along a pretty sand beach. Each unit has a patio and a kitchenette with an electric grill and a blender. The huge, open circular poolside bar and patio area attracts what seems like everybody on the island for the Friday night outdoor barbecue with dancing and live music. The Canadian owners have 300 acres across the road and additional units and town houses are due to open there in 2004 or 2005. ⌂ *Box EX 9137, George Town* ☎ *888/396–0606 or 242/336–2787* 🖷 *242/336–2770* ⊕ *www. palmbaybeachclub.com* ⇌ *31 cottages* ⅃ *Restaurant, cable TV, in-room VCRs, pool, snorkeling, windsurfing, boating, waterskiing, fishing, bar, laundry service, business services* ▤ *D, MC, V.*

★ $$$ ✕▦ **Hotel Higgins Landing.** The only resort on undeveloped Stocking Island is this eco hotel, which is 100% solar powered—though everything still works when the weather's overcast. Wood cottages have screen windows with dark-green shutters and private, spacious decks with ocean views. Interiors have antiques, queen-size beds, tile floors, and folksy Americana decor. By day, the bar is an alfresco living room where you can play checkers or darts, or read books from the hotel's library. Colorful blossoms and tropical birds abound. Rates include full breakfasts and gourmet dinners, though be aware that the kitchen cannot accommodate *any* special dietary requests. No children under 16 during the winter season. ⬧ *Box EX 29146, Stocking Island, George Town* ☎ *800/688–4752 Ext. 457* 🖷 *242/336–2460 or 242/357–0008* ⊕ *www.higginslanding.com* ↯ *5 cottages* ⬧ *Restaurant, beach, dock, snorkeling, boating, fishing, bar, library* ☞ *No smoking* ▭ *D, MC, V* ⦿ *MAP.*

$ ✕⬚ **Club Peace & Plenty.** The granddaddy of Exuma's omnipresent Peace & Plenty empire, this pink, two-story hotel is near the heart of George Town. Rooms have private balconies—most overlooking the pool, with ocean views to the side, although some have full ocean vistas. In high season, the hotel is known for its Saturday-night parties on the pool patio, where Lermon "Doc" Rolle has been holding court at the bar since the '70s. The indoor bar, which was once a slave kitchen, attracts locals and a yachting crowd, especially during the Family Islands Regatta. The hotel's restaurant serves some of the best breakfasts in town. ⬧ *Box EX 29055, George Town* ☎ *242/336–2551 or 800/525–2210* 🖷 *242/336–2093* ⊕ *www.peaceandplenty.com* ↯ *35 rooms* ⬧ *Restaurant, pool, beach, dock, boating, fishing, 2 bars, dive shop* ▭ *AE, D, MC, V* ⦿ *EP, MAP.*

$ ✕⬚ **Coconut Cove Hotel.** The Paradise Suite at this intimate hotel has its own private terrace hot tub, a king-size bed, walk-in closet, and an immense bathroom with a black-marble Jacuzzi. Other rooms have queen-size beds, tile floors, and scenic views from private terraces. Bathrobes and fresh-daily floral arrangements add an elegant touch. The restaurant menu includes Angus beef, fresh pastas, and gourmet pizzas served outside on the deck or inside by the fireplace. ⬧ *Box EX 29299, George Town* ☎ *242/336–2659* 🖷 *242/336–2658* ⊕ *www. exumabahamas.com* ↯ *12 rooms, 1 cottage* ⬧ *Restaurant, minibars, pool, dive shop, fishing, bar, laundry service* ▭ *AE, D, MC, V.*

☾ $ ✕⬚ **Peace & Plenty Beach Inn.** The 16-room resort on 300 feet of beach is a mile west of its big brother, the Club Peace & Plenty; a shuttle runs between the two four times daily. The units have white-tile floors, simple tropical-print accents, and French doors opening onto private patios or balconies that overlook the pool and the ocean. Once in the restaurant, marvel at the tiered, stained-pine cathedral ceiling and feast on blackened mahimahi, New York–cut Angus steak, or the delicious chicken breast Alfredo, baked in a crispy puff dough with sun-dried tomatoes. Reservations are required. ⬧ *Box EX 29055, George Town* ☎ *242/336–2250 or 800/525–2210* 🖷 *242/336–2253* ⊕ *www. peaceandplenty.com* ↯ *16 rooms* ⬧ *Restaurant, refrigerators, pool, beach, fishing, 2 bars* ▭ *AE, D, MC, V* ⦿ *EP, MAP.*

★ $ ✕⬚ **Peace & Plenty Bonefish Lodge.** The Out Islands' swankiest bonefishing lodge is on a peninsula 10 mi south of George Town. Dark wood and handsome hunter-green accents lend a gentleman's-club feel to the bar and dining room, where photos of anglers and their catches grace the walls alongside signed jerseys from Mickey Mantle and Duke Snider. The large rooms have white rattan furnishings, louvered wooden doors, and private balconies overlooking the water. Guests will find contemplative, restful spots on the large deck, upstairs veranda, or in a hammock on the sandy point that juts out beyond the lodge's fish pond. In the dining room, Chef Robert prepares serves hearty fare—from 16-ounce New York strip steaks to vegetarian dishes. ✒ *Box EX 29173, George Town* ☎ *242/345–5555 or 800/525–2210* 🖷 *242/345–5556* ⊕ *www. peaceandplenty.com* ⇨ *8 rooms* ♻ *Dining room, fans, snorkeling, boating, fishing, bicycles, 2 bars, library* ▤ *D, MC, V* ⦿⦵ *FAP.*

$$–$$$ ▥ **Bahama Houseboats.** Brightly decorated floating accommodations offer all the comforts of home. There are five houseboats to choose from: three 35-foot boats with one bedroom and two 43-foot boats with two bedrooms. All have water slides that descend from the top deck. No special license or experience is required to rent the houseboats, and you'll be instructed on cruising parameters and safe operation before leaving the dock. The owners are always a radio call away to answer questions and provide peace of mind. Right out your "front door" you can fish, collect shells, snorkel, and cruise Elizabeth Harbour's multihued, incandescent waters. A three-day minimum stay is required. ✒ *Box EX 29031, Government Dock, George Town* ☎ *242/336–2628* 🖷 *242/336–2645* ⊕ *www. bahamahouseboats.com* ⇨ *5 boats* ♻ *Kitchenettes* ▤ *MC, V.*

$–$$ ▥ **Regatta Point.** Soft pink with hunter green shutters, this handsome two-story guest house overlooks Kidd Cove from its own petite island. Connected to George Town by a short causeway, the property is only a five-minute walk from town but far enough from the fray to have a secret hideaway's charm. Rooms have picturesque views of Elizabeth Harbour, a large vaulted ceiling, and porches. Leave the louvered windows open to be lulled to sleep by the waves. The hotel has no restaurant, but units come with modern kitchens, and maid service is included. Sailboats and bicycles are available free to guests. ⊠ *Regatta Point across from George Town* ✒ *Box EX 29006* ☎ *242/336–2206 or 800/ 688–0309* 🖷 *242/336–2046* ⊕ *www.exumabahamas.com* ⇨ *1 1-bedroom unit, 1 2-bedroom unit, 3 suites, 1 cottage* ♻ *Fans, kitchenettes, beach, dock, boating, fishing, bicycles, laundry service* ▤ *MC, V.*

Nightlife

On Monday, head to **Eddie's Edgewater** (☎ 242/336–2050) for the rousing rake 'n' scrape music. In season, the poolside bashes at **Club Peace & Plenty** (☎ 242/336–2551), with its resident band, George Willey and the Inn Crowd, keep Bahamians and vacationers on the dance floor Wednesday and Saturday nights. On Fridays, the live band and outdoor barbecue pack the outdoor patio at **Palm Bay Beach Club.**

Sports & the Outdoors

BOATING   Renting a boat provides opportunity for unforgettable explorations of the cays near George Town and beyond. A number of area hotels allow guests to tie up rental boats at their docks. For those who want to take a water jaunt through Stocking Island's hurricane holes, paddleboats and Sunfish sailboats are ideal options. **Minns Water Sports** (☎ 242/ 336–3483) rents 16-foot Carolina Skiffs, Boston Whalers ranging from 16- to 22-feet, and 20-foot Cats.

On Stocking Island, **Peace & Plenty Beach Club** (☎ 242/336–2551) rents paddleboats ($15 per half day) and Sunfish sailboats ($20 per half day).

EVENTS The **Annual New Year's Day Cruising Regatta** is held at the Staniel Cay Yacht Club, with international yachts taking part in a series of races. At the beginning of March, the **Cruiser's Regatta** hosts visiting boats for a week of races, cookouts, and partying in George Town. The **Family Islands Regatta** is the Bahamas' most important yachting event of the year. It takes place in April. Starting the race in Elizabeth Harbour in George Town, island-made wooden sailing boats compete for trophies. Onshore, the town is a three-day riot of Junkanoo parades, Goombay music, arts-and-crafts fairs, and continuous merriment.

FISHING Most hotels can arrange for local guides, and a list is available from the **Exuma Tourist Office** (☎ 242/336–2430). **Cooper's Charter Service** (☎ 242/336–2711) will take you out for a day of deep-sea fishing, $300 per half day, $500 per full day. **Reno Rolle** (☎ 242/345–5003) is a highly recommended bonefishing guide. **Cely Smith** (☎ 242/345–2341) is both a bonefishing and fly-fishing guide. Fisherman and boat owner **Gus Thompson** (☎ 242/345–5062) will help you hook the big game as well as the feisty bonefish. **Peace & Plenty Bonefish Lodge** (☎ 242/345–5555) has excellent bonefishing guides.

GOLF Golf legend Greg Norman designed the 18-hole, par-72 championship course, featuring six oceanside holes, at **Four Seasons Resort Great Exuma at Emerald Bay** (☎ 242/336–6800), the island's only golf course. There are preferred tee times for hotel guests, who pay $175, including golf cart; the fee for nonguests is $215.

KAYAKING **Exuma Adventure Center** (☎ 242/336–3033) has guided half-day kayak trips to Crab Cay and Moriah Cay National Park in sturdy flat-bottom ocean-going kayaks. Adults pay $60; children pay $45. Kayak lessons are $45 per hour.

SCUBA DIVING **Angel Fish Blue Hole,** minutes from George Town, is a popular dive site filled with angel fish, spotted rays, snapper, and the occasional reef shark. **Exuma Scuba Adventures** (☎ 242/336–2893) offers dive instruction, certification courses, and scuba trips. One-tank dives are $55; night dives are $60. **Stocking Island Mystery Cave** is full of mesmerizing schools of colorful fish but is for experienced divers only.

SNORKELING On Stocking Island, **Peace & Plenty Beach Club** (☎ 242/336–2551) rents snorkel gear for $10 a day. **Exuma Scuba Adventures** (☎ 242/336–2893) offers daily snorkeling trips for $15.

TENNIS Four Har-Tru tennis courts, which are lit for night play, are available to nonguests at **Four Seasons Resort Great Exuma at Emerald Bay** (☎ 242/336–6800), depending on availability, for $25 per hour.

WINDSURFING On Stocking Island, **Peace & Plenty Beach Club** (☎ 242/336–2551) rents Windsurfers for $15 per half day and $30 per full day.

Shopping

In the Exumas, George Town is the place to shop. **Exuma Market** (✉ Across from Scotia Bank, George Town ☎ 242/336–2033) is the island's largest grocery and is considered by many to be the Out Islands' finest. Yachties tie up at the skiff docks in the rear, on Lake Victoria. FedEx, emergency e-mail, and faxes for visitors are accepted here as well.

Exuma Master Tailor Shop (✉ Across street from Exuma Market, George Town ☎ 242/336–2930), with one- to two-day service at very reasonable prices, will duplicate a favorite designer dress or suit while you are out sunning. Bring your own material, buttons, and zippers.

Peace & Plenty Boutique (✉ Opposite Club Peace & Plenty ☎ 242/336–2551) has a good selection of Androsia shirts and dresses.

Sandpiper Boutique (✉ Queen's Hwy. ☎ 242/336–2084) has upscale souvenirs, from high-quality cards and books to batik clothing and art.

Cays of the Exumas

A band of cays—with names like Rudder Cut, Big Farmer's, Great Guana, and Leaf—stretches north from Great Exuma.

㉑ Boaters will want to explore the waterways known as **Pipe Creek**, a winding passage through the tiny islands between Staniel and Compass cays. There are great spots for shelling, snorkeling, diving, and bonefishing. The **Samson Cay Yacht Club** (☎ 242/355–2034), at the creek's halfway point, is a good place for lunch or dinner.

㉒ **Staniel Cay** is a favorite destination of yachters and makes the perfect home base for visiting the Exuma Cays Land and Sea Park. The island has an airstrip, two hotels, and one paved road. Virtually everything is within walking distance. Oddly enough, as you stroll past brightly painted houses and sandy shores, you are as likely to see a satellite dish as a woman pulling a bucket of water from a roadside well. At one of three grocery stores, boat owners can replenish their supplies. The friendly village also has a small red-roof church, a post office, and a straw vendor.

Fodor's Choice
★
Just across the water from the Staniel Cay Yacht Club is one of the Bahamas' most unforgettable attractions: **Thunderball Grotto**, a beautiful marine cave that snorkelers (at low tide) and experienced scuba divers can explore. In the central cavern, shimmering shafts of sunlight pour through holes in the soaring ceiling and illuminate the glass-clear water. You'll see right away why this cave was chosen as an exotic setting for such movies as 007's *Thunderball* and *Never Say Never Again,* and the mermaid tale *Splash.*

㉓ Above Staniel Cay, near the Exumas' northern end, lies the 176-square-mi **Exuma Cays Land and Sea Park,** which spans 22 mi between Conch Cut and Wax Cay Cut. You must charter a small boat or seaplane to reach the park, which has more than 20 mi of petite cays. Hawksbill Cay and Warderick Wells (both with remains of 18th-century Loyalist settlements) have marked hiking trails, as does Hall's Pond. At Shroud Cay, jump into "Camp Driftwood," where the strong current creates a natural whirlpool that whips you around a rocky outcropping to a powdery beach. Part of the Bahamas National Trust, the park appeals to divers, who appreciate the vast underworld of limestone, reefs, drop-offs, blue holes of freshwater springs, caves, and a multitude of exotic marine life, including one of the Bahamas' most impressive stands of rare pillar coral. Strict laws prohibit fishing and removing coral, plants, or even shells as souvenirs. A list of park rules is available at the headquarters on Warderick Wells.

ISLANDS OF THE STARS

THE BAHAMAS HAS SERVED *as a source of inspiration for countless artists, writers, and directors. Just about any day of the year, there's a film crew somewhere in the islands shooting scenes for a movie, music video, or television commercial.*

The Bahamian movie legacy dates back to the era of silent films, including the now-legendary original black-and-white version of Jules Verne's 20,000 Leagues Under the Sea, which was filmed here in 1907. Since the birth of color film, the draw has only increased—directors are lured by the possibility of using the islands' characteristic white sands and luminous turquoise waters as a backdrop. Among the more famous movies shot in the Bahamas are Jaws, the cult favorite whose killer shark has terrified viewers for two decades; Flipper, the family classic about a boy and a porpoise; Splash, whose main character is a mermaid who becomes human; and Cocoon, about a group of elderly friends who discover an extra-terrestrial secret to immortality.

Another memorable film, Thunderball, gave Great Exuma Island the distinction of being the only island in the Caribbean where, not one, but two James Bond movies were filmed. Thunderball and Never Say Never Again were both shot on location in Staniel Cay, one of the northernmost islands of the Exumas chain.

*You can swim and snorkel in **Thunderball Cave**, site of the pivotal chase scene in the 1965 Sean Connery film. The ceiling of this huge, dome-shape cave is about 30 feet above the water, which is filled with yellowtails, parrots, blue chromes, and yellow and black striped sergeant majors. Swimming into the cave is the easy part—the tide draws you in—but paddling back out can be strenuous, especially because if you stop moving the tide will pull you back toward the cave.*

*Well before Connery gave the cave its name, Ian Fleming, the creator of agent Bond, set his book Dr. No on Great Inagua. **Ernest Hemingway** wrote about the Bahamas as well. Hemingway may have been as celebrated for his big game hunting and fishing exploits as he was for his writing. He visited Bimini regularly in the 1930s, coining it the "Sportsfishing Capital of the World." His hangout was the Compleat Angler, a bar which now houses a small Hemingway museum with photos and other mementos. Among the items on display are his drawings for the book Old Man and the Sea—rumor has it that the protagonist looks suspiciously like the bartender at the Angler.*

*The Bahamas not only seem to spark the imaginations of artists, but have also become a playground for the rich and famous in recent years. The stars of Cocoon, the late **Hume Cronyn** and **Jessica Tandy,** were regular visitors to Goat Cay, a private island just offshore from Georgetown, Exuma. Many world-famous celebrities and athletes hide out at **Musha Cay,** an exclusive retreat in the northern part of the Exumas, where a week's stay can set you back five figures. Although the cay won't name its guests, the all-knowing taxi drivers at the Georgetown airport mention **Oprah Winfrey** and **Michael Jordan** as a few of the esteemed guests.*

North of the park is **Norman's Cay,** an island with 10 mi of rarely trod white beaches, which attracts an occasional yachter. It was once the private domain of Colombian drug smuggler Carlos Lehder. It's now owned by the Bahamian government. **Allen's Cays** are at the Exumas' northernmost tip and are home to the rare Bahamian iguana.

Where to Stay & Eat

$–$$ ✕▥ **Staniel Cay Yacht Club.** The club once drew such luminaries as Malcolm Forbes and Robert Mitchum. It's now a low-key getaway for yachties and escapists. The cottages, perched on stilts along a rocky bank, have broad ocean vistas and dramatic sunsets, which you can treasure from a chaise longue on your spacious private balcony. Take a tour of the cay in one of the club's golf carts. ⊠ *Staniel Cay* ☐ *2233 S. Andrews Ave., Fort Lauderdale, FL 33316* ☎ *242/355–2024 or 954/467–8920* 🖷 *954/522–3248 or 242/355–2044* ⊕ *www.stanielcay.com* ➠ *4 1-bedroom cottages, 1 2-bedroom cottage, 1 3-bedroom cottage* ⚮ *Restaurant, fans, boating, fishing, bar, piano, airstrip* 🖃 *AE, MC, V* ⦿ *MAP.*

¢–$ ✕▥ **Happy People Marina.** You may find this casual hotel a bit isolated if you're not interested in yachting. The property is close to Staniel Cay, but it's a long way from the George Town social scene. A local band, however, plays at the Royal Entertainer Lounge, and a small restaurant serves meals. The simple motel-style rooms are on the beach. ⊠ *Staniel Cay* ☎ *242/355–2008* ➠ *8 rooms, 1 2-bedroom apartment* ⚮ *Restaurant, dining room, beach, dock, bar* 🖃 *No credit cards.*

Nightlife

Royal Entertainer Lounge (⊠ Happy People Marina ☎ 242/355–2008) has live Bahamian bands performing on special occasions. **Club Thunderball** (⊠ East of Thunderball Grotto ☎ 242/355–2012) is a sports bar–dance club built on a bluff overlooking the water. It serves lunch everyday and has Friday evening barbecues. It is run by a local pilot.

Sports & the Outdoors

BOATING & FISHING **Staniel Cay Yacht Club** (☎ 242/355–2024) rents 13-foot Whalers and arranges for fishing guides.

SCUBA DIVING & SNORKELING **Exuma Cays Land and Sea Park** and **Thunderball Grotto** are excellent snorkeling and dive sites. **Staniel Cay Yacht Club** (☎ 242/355–2024) rents masks and fins for snorkeling, and fills tanks from its compressor. Call ahead or plan to bring your own scuba gear. **Pink Pearl Market** (☎ 242/355–2040) sells snorkel equipment and is open Monday through Saturday.

Exumas A to Z

AIR TRAVEL

You can fly from Fort Lauderdale, St. Petersburg, Sarasota, or Miami to Exuma International Airport, or to the Staniel Cay airstrip.

CARRIERS Air Sunshine flies from Ft. Lauderdale to George Town on Monday and Thursday; the return trip is on Tuesday and Friday. American Eagle has daily service from Miami. Call for summer scheduling. Bahamasair has daily flights from Nassau and twice-weekly flights from Fort

Lauderdale and Miami to George Town. Executive Air Travel offers charters from Fort Lauderdale Executive Airport to Staniel Cay Yacht Club. Lynx Air International flies from Fort Lauderdale to George Town on Friday, Saturday, and Sunday. Stella Maris is available for charter flights to or from the Exumas as is Chalk's Ocean Airways, which flies seaplanes.

🛪 Airlines & Contacts **Air Sunshine** ☎ 954/435-8900 or 800/327-8900. **American Eagle** ☎ 800/433-7300. **Bahamasair** ☎ 800/222-4262. **Chalk's Ocean Airways** ☎ 305/371-8628 or 800/424-2557. **Executive Air Travel** ☎ 954/979-6162 or 954/224-6022. **Lynx Air International** ☎ 888/596-9247. **Stella Maris** ☎ 954/359-8236, 242/336-2106, or 800/426-0466.

AIRPORTS & TRANSFERS

Exuma International Airport, 9 mi from George Town, is the Exumas' official airport and the official port of entry. It's also one of the Bahamas' tidiest airports. Staniel Cay, near the top of the chain, has a 3,000-foot airstrip that accepts charter flights and private planes, but you must clear customs at the Andros, Nassau, or Exuma airport first.

TRANSFERS Taxis wait at the airport for incoming flights. The cost of a ride from the airport to George Town is about $22 for two people.

BIKE TRAVEL

In George Town's Scotia Bank building, Thompson's Rentals has bicycles. Exuma Adventure Center rents bicycles with helmets and maps for $20 a day, $100 a week. Contact Chamberlain Rentals if you want to pedal around Staniel Cay.

🚲 Bike Rentals **Exuma Adventure Center** ☎ 242/336-3033. **Chamberlain Rentals** ☎ 242/355-2020. **Thompson's Rentals** ☎ 242/336-2442.

BOAT & FERRY TRAVEL

M/V *Grand Master* travels from Nassau to George Town on Tuesday and returns to Nassau on Friday. Travel time is 12 hours, and fares range from $35 to $40 depending on your destination. M/V *Ettienne & Cephas* leaves Nassau on Tuesday for Staniel Cay, Big Farmer's Cay, Black Point, and Barraterre, returning to Nassau on Saturday. The full trip takes 21 hours. Call for fares to specific destinations. For further information, contact the Dockmaster's Office at Potter's Cay, Nassau.

To reach Stocking Island from George Town, the Club Peace & Plenty Ferry leaves from the hotel's dock twice daily at 10 and 1. The ferry departs from the Stocking Island dock at 10:30 and 1:30. The fare is $8 round-trip for non–Peace & Plenty guests.

🚢 Boat & Ferry Information **Club Peace & Plenty Ferry** ☎ 242/336-2551. **Dockmaster's Office** ☎ 242/393-1064.

BUSINESS HOURS

BANKS The Scotia Bank in George Town is open weekdays 9:30–3 and Fridays until 5.

CAR RENTAL

Thompson's Rentals rents cars. Exuma Transport is a car-rental establishment in George Town. Hotels can also arrange car rentals.

🗐 Local Agencies Airport Rent a Car ☎ 242/345-0090. Exuma Transport ☎ 242/336-2101. Raquel's Car Rental ☎ 242/358-5011. Thompson's Rentals ☎ 242/336-2442. Uptown Car Rentals ☎ 242/336-2822.

EMERGENCIES

🗐 In George Town: Police ☎ 242/336-2666 or 919. Medical Clinic ☎ 242/336-2220. In Staniel Cay: Police ☎ 242/355-2042. St. Luke's Medical Clinic ☎ 242/355-2010.

GOLF CART TRAVEL

Staniel Cay Yacht Club rents golf carts for exploring Staniel Cay.

🗐 Staniel Cay Yacht Club ☎ 242/355-2024.

SCOOTER TRAVEL

In George Town, Prestige Scooter Rental rents motor scooters for $60 a day.

🗐 Prestige Scooter Rental ☎ 242/357-0066.

SIGHTSEEING TOURS

From George Town, Captain Cole arranges overnight trips up to the Exuma Cays Land and Sea Park. Luther Rolle will take you on an informative tour of Little and Great Exuma.

🗐 Captain Cole ☎ 242/345-0074. Luther Rolle ☎ 242/345-5003.

TAXIS

Your George Town hotel will arrange for a taxi if you wish to go exploring or need to return to the airport. Kermit Rolle or Luther Rolle Taxi Service will take you where you need to go.

🗐 Kermit Rolle ☎ 242/345-6038. Luther Rolle Taxi Service ☎ 242/345-5003.

TRANSPORTATION

You can stay in George Town proper and enjoy touring Great Exuma by car, but if you want a closer look at any of the hundreds of deserted Exuma cays nearby, you'll appreciate the greater freedom of a boat. If you want to go to Staniel Cay, through Pipe Creek, or to the Exuma Cays Land and Sea Park, water passage via the Exuma Sound or Great Bahama Bank is the only route.

VISITOR INFORMATION

The Exuma Tourist Office is in George Town, across the street from the Exuma Market, one block from the Government Administration Building.

🗐 Tourist Information Exuma Tourist Office ☎ 242/336-2430 🖨 242/336-2431.

THE OTHER OUT ISLANDS

5

MEET HEMINGWAY'S GHOST
at his old haunt, the Complete Angler ⇨*p.187*

TRAVEL THROUGH TIME
to explore crumbling colonial mansions ⇨*p.194*

DIVE INTO THE DEEP BLUE
at the world's third-largest reef ⇨*p.170*

A SEA OF FLAMINGOS
greets you at Inagua National Park ⇨*p.202*

SEE THE LOST CITY OF ATLANTIS
at an ancient underwater rock formation ⇨*p.188*

A WILD URGE TO DANCE
is fiercely contagious at
the rake 'n' scrape festival ⇨*p.191*

Updated by
Stephen F.
Vletas

THE QUIET, SIMPLER WAY OF LIFE of the Bahama Out Islands, sometimes referred to as the Family Islands, is startlingly different from Nassau's and Freeport's fast-paced glitz and glitter. Outside New Providence and Grand Bahama, on the dozen or so islands that are equipped to handle tourists, you leave the sophisticated resorts, nightclubs, casinos, and shopping malls behind. If you love the outdoors, however, you'll be in fine shape: Virtually all the Out Islands have good to excellent fishing, boating, and diving, and you'll often have endless stretches of beach all to yourself.

For the most part, you won't find hotels that provide the costly creature comforts taken for granted in Nassau and Freeport, with the exception of Kamalame Cay on Andros, and Club Med–Columbus Isle on San Salvador. Out Islands accommodations are generally modest lodges, rustic cottages, and small inns—many without telephones and TV (inquire when making reservations if these are important to you). Making a phone call, or receiving one, will sometimes require a trip to the local BATELCO (Bahamas Telecommunications Corporation) telephone station.

Along with the utter lack of stress of an Out Islands holiday, you'll find largely unspoiled environments. Roughing it in Inagua, for example, is a small price to pay for the glorious spectacle of 60,000 pink flamingos taking off into the sky. And a day of sightseeing can mean little more than a stroll down narrow, sand-strewn streets in fishing villages, past small, pastel homes where orange, pink, and bright-red bougainvillea spill over the walls. Meals, even those served in hotels, almost always incorporate local specialties, from conch and fresh-caught fish to chicken with peas 'n' rice. Island taverns are tiny and usually noisy with chatter. You can make friends with locals over a beer and a game of pool or darts much more quickly than you would in the average stateside cocktail lounge. Nightlife may involve listening to a piano player or a small village rake 'n' scrape combo in a clubhouse bar, or joining the crowds at a local disco playing everything from R&B to calypso.

The Out Islands were once mostly the purview of private plane and yacht owners. The tourist who discovered a hideaway on Andros, Eleuthera, or in the Exumas would cherish it and return year after year to find the same faces as before. But the islands are now becoming more and more popular, largely because of increased airline activity. Most islands are served from Nassau or Florida daily. Others may only have a couple of incoming and outgoing flights a week. If you want to partake of simple island life without feeling completely cut off, choose a slightly busier spot that is closer to the mainland United States, such as Bimini or Great Abaco Island. If you go farther away from the mainland, to a place like Cat Island or San Salvador, you'll feel much more like you're getting away from it all.

Exploring the Out Islands

The Out Islands span a sweeping area of shallow seas and deep ocean—from the Biminis, just off southern Florida, to Great Inagua, northeast of Cuba. The northern islands of the Biminis, the Berries, and Andros

Out Island vacations can be adventure-packed explorations or nothing more than laying on an isolated beach surrounded by sand, sea, and blue sky. You can find quiet romance, or happening local bars with live music and dancing. It's easy to put together trips with a combination of action and relaxation to sample the natural wonders and local hospitality of the islands.

Numbers in the text correspond to numbers in the margins and on the Andros, The Biminis, Cat Island, Long Island, and San Salvador maps.

5

If you have 3 days

If you've decided to sample the natural treasures of the Out Islands, the ▶ 🏝 **South Bight** of **Andros** is a clear-cut choice. Fly to **Congo Town airport,** then take your first day to relax on the beach; or jump right in with a kayaking tour of the nearby cays and **Lisbon Creek.** On your second day, sign up for a guided snorkeling exploration of the area's vivid blues holes and the black-coral barrier reef swarming with sea life. In the afternoon go on a nature hike in a pine forest in search of wild orchids and exotic birds. Enjoy sunset cocktails on the beach. For your last day, set out on a boating adventure to the secluded **West Side** for fishing, exploring, and picnicking. Here, the aquamarine water melds with the sky in a dreamy purple haze that creates a dazzling portrait of tranquility.

If you're a bonefishing enthusiast, spend your three days in 🏝 **Cargill Creek.** Fish for the elusive grey ghost with top professional guides in the **North and Middle Bights** and along the white-sand beaches of **Big Wood Cay.** The lodges in the area can also arrange diving and snorkeling excursions, and island sightseeing tours.

If you have 5 days

Follow the suggested three-day itinerary, then transfer to 🏝 **Fresh Creek ❷**. On the way you can stop at the **Androsia Batik Works Factory** in 🏝 **Andros Town ❸**, and shop for the colorful island-made fabrics and other gifts at the **Androsia Outlet Store.** After settling in, get the adrenaline flowing with an "over the wall" dive in the **Tongue of the Ocean.** If you're not certified, you can take the **Small Hope Bay Lodge** resort course, and begin diving around the nearby reef in the afternoon. Or lounge on the beach, swim, and snorkel over shallow-water coral heads. Sip sunset cocktails and relax in the evening. Your last day can be filled with other watersports and activities—windsurfing, snorkeling, fishing, or exploring from Fresh Creek to **Captain Bill's Blue Hole** for a leisurely picnic and a cooling swim. If you're looking for some serious exercise, make this trip on a bicycle, about 6 mi one-way from **Fresh Creek.**

Dedicated anglers don't need to move anywhere else. A continued stay at 🏝 **Cargill Creek** will mean fishing more of the countless flats throughout the Bights. Venture to the **West Side,** where you can pursue tarpon and permit along with bonefish.

If you have

7 days

Add on to the five-day itinerary above by flying to 🚢 **Bimini** for your last two days. Charter a deep-sea fishing boat or dive over the famous ☞ **Atlantis** lost city site. On your final day, hop the ferry to South Bimini to wander the white-sand beaches, snorkel and swim, shop in the **Native Straw and Craft Market,** or visit the **Bimini Museum.** Drinks and dancing at the **Compleat Angler Hotel** is a nightly ritual on Bimini, and a lively way to put an exclamation point on your trip.

With seven days, you can comfortably make the longer trip to San Salvador, Crooked, Acklins, or Great Inagua islands. Or split the week between Long Island and Cat Island, deciding what you want to do a day at a time. Keep in mind that travel between most of the Out Islands takes time, and unless you spend the money to charter a private flight, it can take a full day to go from one island to the next. Whatever you decide, remember the old Out Island saying, "You make your own sunshine, mon."

---

are quick and easy to reach from Florida via scheduled and chartered flight service. Dominated by the Great Bahama Bank, these islands are prime for sportfishing, diving, snorkeling, swimming, and boating. Bimini receives more boaters than any other island and is a weekend party spot. Great Harbour, the largest of the Berry Islands, is sedate, self-contained, and oriented toward family beach and watersport vacationing. Andros is vast, an ultimate retreat for bonefishing and diving. The northern islands are mostly flat, lush with mangroves, rimmed with white-sand beaches, and laced with miles of creeks and lakes. People walk between settlements, or ride bikes or golf carts. Exploring is best done by boat, not car, though taxis are available to cover longer distances.

The southern islands are more remote, exposed to the open Atlantic, and ruggedly dramatic. They are usually reached by air from Nassau. Good roads on Cat and Long Islands allow for convenient exploration by car. Miles of pink sand beaches and aquamarine bays await. Settlements are spread out, and services, including gas stations, are not always available. The weather is a few degrees warmer and more consistent south of the Tropic of Cancer, which slices through the center of Long Island. Club Med on San Salvador, designed for pampered relaxation, is the essence of quiet luxury. Crooked and Acklins Islands, with populations of about 400 people each, are outposts for the self-sufficient adventurer. The same is true for Great Inagua, where the best way to explore is with a local guide.

About the Restaurants

Dining is a casual "get together" experience, and rarely involves anything fancy. Restaurants, lodges, and inns serve traditional Bahamian fare—fresh seafood, grilled chicken, johnnycakes, and barbecued pork with all the fixings (potato salad, cole slaw, peas 'n' rice, and baked macaroni and cheese). Most islands have restaurants that are open during normal mealtime hours, but there are exceptions. Call ahead whenever possible, especially on Crooked, Acklins, and Great Inagua islands.

Beachside restaurants are often small with simple wooden tables and casual dress. Sunset cocktails are standard. Thatched conch stands and colorful roadside bars are a treat and a great way to mingle with local residents. During regatta season, life on the Out Islands gets merrily crazy, and pig roasts are big events.

About the Hotels

Accommodations to suit most tastes can be found, from a handful of luxury properties on private cays and remote beaches to simple fishing lodges and funky hotels with swinging nightlife. You need to have a good idea of what you want—the overall experience, service, amenities, activities—then do your homework before making a reservation. Many resorts and lodges don't have air-conditioning, or only have it in certain rooms. If this is important to you, be sure to ask at the time of your booking. A number of lodges cater specifically to anglers and divers and are not well suited to overall vacationing.

Comfortable motel-style accommodations are most common, and these lodges usually have a restaurant and bar. Places located on the water are better cooled by ocean breezes, which are a huge help in keeping down the bugs—mosquitoes, sand flies, and doctor flies. Family-owned and operated properties tend to be exceptionally warm and friendly, though generally wherever you go, expect a welcoming reception. Off-season rates usually begin in May, with some of the best discounted package deals available in October, November, and early December. Club Med–Columbus Isle offers early-bird booking bonuses and runs pricing promotions year-round.

WHAT IT COSTS				
$$$$	**$$$**	**$$**	**$**	**¢**
RESTAURANTS over $40	$30–$40	$20–$30	$10–$20	under $10
HOTELS over $400	$300–$400	$200–$300	$100–$200	under $100

Restaurant prices are for a main course at dinner, excluding gratuity, typically 15%, which is often automatically added to the bill. Hotel prices are for two people in a standard double room in high season, excluding service charges and 6%–12% tax.

Timing

The peak tourist season is mid-December through April for visitors in the sun-sea-and-sand vacation mode. From the beginning of May, and on through the fall, room rates tend to drop by as much as a third. May, June, July, October, and November are good months for diving, snorkeling, boating, and beach activities at discount prices. Hurricane season technically runs from June through November, though June, July and November are rarely a concern. August and September (the most likely months for hurricanes) can be hot and steamy, and many resorts and restaurants are closed.

Off-season discount rates often won't include lodges focused on fishing, as April through June are prime months for flats and offshore anglers. This is also the perfect time to combine fishing with diving, snorkeling, and beach exploring. October and November are excellent fishing months as well, and the winter period of December through March is good when the weather cooperates. Winter cold fronts—a relative term, with temperatures dropping into the high-60s to low-70s—move down from Florida and can bring wind and clouds for several days that make swimming, sunning, and fishing less appealing. To play the weather odds your best bet is to go to the southern islands (Long Island, San Salvador, Crooked, Acklins, and Great Inagua) December through March. Cold fronts often stall out before reaching these southern islands, and daily temperatures average about five degrees warmer than on the northern islands.

You'll rarely have to worry about crowds in the Out Islands. However, sailing regattas on Andros, Long, and Cat Islands and fishing tournaments in the Biminis and Berries are popular events, and bring out the partying spirit in locals and visitors alike.

ANDROS

The Bahamas' largest island (100 mi long and 40 mi wide), and one of the least explored, Andros's land mass is carved up by myriad channels, creeks, lakes, and mangrove-covered cays. The North, Middle, and South Bights cut through the width of the island, creating boating access to both coasts. Andros is best-known for its bonefishing and diving, and is also a glorious ecotourism spot with snorkeling, blue hole exploration, sea kayaking, and nature hikes. More than a dozen small lodges on the eastern shore cater to sun and sea revelers.

The Spaniards who came here in the 16th century called it *La Isla del Espíritu Santo*—the Island of the Holy Spirit—and it has retained its eerie mystique to this day. In fact, the descendants of a group of Seminole Indians and runaway slaves who left the Florida Everglades in the mid-19th century settled in Andros and remained hidden until a few decades ago. They continue to live as a tribal society. Their village, near the island's northern tip, is called Red Bay, and they make a living by weaving straw goods. The Seminoles are credited with originating the myth of the island's legendary (and elusive) chickcharnies—red-eyed, bearded, green-feathered creatures with three fingers and three toes that hang upside down by their tails from pine trees. These mythical characters supposedly wait deep in the forests to wish good luck to the friendly passerby and vent their mischief on the hostile trespasser.

Andros's undeveloped West Side adjoins the Great Bahama Bank, a vast shallow-water haven for gamefish, including tarpon, and for lobster. Shifting shoals and sandbars, and flats that go dry during low tides, create hazards for boaters. Immense bays, tiny sloughs, and mangrove swamps snake in and out of the chalk-colored shoreline. The island's lush green interior is covered with wild orchids and dense pine and mahogany forests. The forests provide nesting grounds for parrots, partridges, quail, white-crowned pigeons, and whistling ducks, and hunters come to Andros from September through March in search of game.

5

Out Islands Cuisine

Out Islands restaurants are often family-run and focus on home-style dishes. They typically serve a combination of Bahamian, Continental, and American fare. Instead of the menu, it is the ingredients and individual flare of the chef that set one place apart from the next. While fried food, especially seafood, is a staple, more chefs are experimenting with alternate cooking methods, especially baking and grilling. If you see grilled or blackened hog snapper on a menu, give it a try, as this is one of the most popular island dishes, and will probably be well made. Lobster chunks marinated in wine and sautéed is another specialty.

To get a sense of what the locals eat at home, try ordering any fish prepared "Bahamian style," meaning baked and smothered in tomatoes and spices. For a true taste of Out Islands food, don't go home without sampling conch salad with lemon and hot peppers. If you're on the hunt for the freshest conch salad, look for one of the out-of-the-way stands where the commercial fishermen clean their catch. Another worthy culinary challenge is the quest for the best key lime pie, a local dessert favorite.

Your Own Private Paradise

Aside from the large resorts, most hotels on the Out Islands are small and owner-operated, which ensures a personal touch. Some accommodations use an honor-bar system—mix your own and sign for it—so you really feel at home. These are the places that people return to year after year to visit the locals who have become their friends. Although such hotels may not be any cheaper than the big, plush resorts, many visitors feel that it's hard to put a price on the total escape that the more low-key accommodations have to offer. What would you pay for a powdery pink beach that stretches for miles with no footprints but your own? Or water so clear that snorkeling makes you feel like you're flying? You might not have air-conditioning or an in-room phone, but a lot of people find that these conveniences are low priorities in paradise.

The Age-Old Sport of Fishing

Fishing is believed to have been an integral part of Bahamian culture for as long as people have inhabited the islands. The majority of settlements in the Out Islands were established for subsistence fishing and sponging. Commercial fishing, focused on lobster, grouper, and snapper, is what drives the economies of many of these communities today. Sportfishing began with an emphasis on offshore angling—trolling an assortment of lures, rigged baits, and teasers on conventional tackle rods and reels to entice deepwater gamefish into striking distance—for marlin, tuna, wahoo, and dolphin. Bonefishing—stalking bonefish on foot or in a poled boat across clear shallow-water flats, and then sight-casting your bait, jig, lure, or fly to specific fish that you spot—entered the mix in the 1920s and 1930s. Now, big-game blue water fishing and fly-fishing the flats are ingrained in the local fabric. Fishing guides are often second- or third-generation professionals with a contagious enthusiasm for their sport and an encyclopedic knowledge of the best spots, from remote creeks and wide mangrove-lined bays to startling ocean banks and drops loaded with gamefish.

The island's roughly 8,000 residents live in about a dozen settlements on the eastern shore from Morgan's Bluff in the north to Mars Bay in the south. Farming and commercial fishing are the mainstays of the economy, and the island is the country's largest source of fresh water.

The Andros Barrier Reef—the world's third-largest reef—is within a mile of the east shore and runs for 140 mi. It has an enchanting variety of marine life and is easily accessible to divers. Sheltered waters within the reef average 6–15 feet, but on the other side of the reef ("over the wall") lie the depths (more than 6,000 feet) of the Tongue of the Ocean, which is used for testing submarines and underwater weapons by the U.S. and British navies. They operate under the acronym AUTEC (Atlantic Underwater Test and Evaluation Center), and their base is near Andros Town.

Numbers in the margin correspond to points of interest on the Andros map.

Nicholl's Town

❶ **Nicholl's Town**, at Andros's northeastern corner, is the island's largest village, with a population of about 600. This friendly community has stores for supplies and groceries, a few hotels, a public medical clinic, a telephone station, and small restaurants. A few miles north of Nicholl's Town is a crescent beach and a headland known as **Morgan's Bluff**, named after the 17th-century pirate Henry Morgan, who allegedly dropped off some of his stolen loot in the area. Morgan's Bluff is the site of the All Andros Crabfest in June, an annual party with a craft fair, sailboat races, live music, and plenty of Bahamian food and drink.

Several miles south of Nicholl's Town, **Conch Sound** is a wide protected bay with long strands of white sand and tranquil waters. Swimmers and bonefishers can wade on their own on the easily accessible flats.

Where to Stay & Eat

¢–$ ✕🏠 **Conch Sound Resort Inn.** The inn has six simple and spacious rooms with carpeting, mahogany furniture, handmade quilts, soft-cushioned chairs, and satellite TV. There are also four two-bedroom suites with kitchenettes. If you'd prefer not to cook, go to the restaurant for basic Bahamian fare. The inn is on the road between Nicholl's Town and Conch Sound. The beach is a 10-minute walk away, but the hotel will provide transportation. Bonefishing and diving can be arranged. ⬦ *Box 23029, Conch Sound Hwy.* ☎ *242/329–2060* 🖷 *242/329–2338* 🛏 *6 rooms, 4 suites* ⚭ *Restaurant, kitchenettes, pool, bar; no room phones* 🚫 *No credit cards.*

Staniard Creek

Sand banks that turn gold at low tide lie off the northern tip of **Staniard Creek,** a small island settlement 9 mi north of Fresh Creek, accessed by a bridge off the main highway. Coconut palms and casuarinas shade the oceanside beaches. Offshore breezes are pleasantly cooling. **Kamalame Cove** and its nearby private cay are at the northern end of the settlement. Three

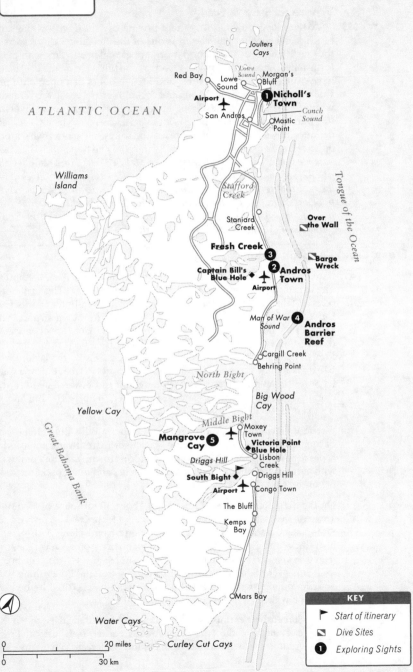

Andros

Joulters Cays

Red Bay
Lowe Sound
Lowe Sound
Morgan's Bluff
Airport
San Andros
1 **Nicholl's Town**
Conch Sound
Mastic Point

Williams Island

Stafford Creek

Staniard Creek

Over the Wall

Tongue of the Ocean

Fresh Creek **3**
Barge Wreck
2 **Andros Town**
Captain Bill's Blue Hole
Airport

Man of War Sound
4 **Andros Barrier Reef**

Cargill Creek
Behring Point

North Bight

Big Wood Cay

Yellow Cay

Middle Bight

Moxey Town
Mangrove Cay **5**
Victoria Point Blue Hole
Lisbon Creek
Driggs Hill
Driggs Hill
South Bight
Congo Town
Airport

Great Bahama Bank

The Bluff

Kemps Bay

Mars Bay

Water Cays
Curley Cut Cays

KEY	
▶	*Start of itinerary*
◣	*Dive Sites*
1	*Exploring Sights*

0   20 miles
0   30 km

creeks snake into the mainland, forming extensive mangrove-lined back bays and flats. The surrounding areas are good for wading and bonefishing.

Where to Stay & Eat

★ **$$$$**   ✕⌹ **Kamalame Cay.** On a 96-acre private cay lined with white-sand beaches and coconut palms, this is one of the most luxurious resorts in the Out Islands. All accommodations are gleaming and airy with plush furnishings, linens, and towels. Cottages and villas are on the beach and have sitting areas, soaking tubs, and French doors that open onto private terraces and gardens. Meals and cocktails are served in the veranda-wrapped plantation-style Great House adorned with cushy oversize furniture and antiques. Dining is an experience—fresh fruits, beef tenderloin sandwiches, homemade breads and soups, and innovative seafood dishes. Fish, dive, snorkel, or lounge by the pool and be pampered. ⌂ *Kamalame Cay, Staniard Creek, Andros* ☎ *800/688–7678 or 242/368–6281* ⓕ *242/368–6279* ⊕ *www.kamalame.com* ⇨ *4 rooms, 5 cottages, 2 villas* ⚒ *2 dining rooms, fans, some minibars, refrigerators, tennis court, pool, massage, beach, dive shop, dock, snorkeling, boating, marina, fishing, bicycles, bar, lounge, library, laundry service, Internet; no room phones, no room TVs* ▤ *MC, V* ⍩ *All-inclusive.*

Fresh Creek–Andros Town

❷ Batik fabric called Androsia is made in **Andros Town,** a small community in central Andros on the south side of Fresh Creek. This brilliantly colored fabric is designed and dyed at the **Androsia Batik Works Factory** (☎ 242/368–2080), a 3-mi drive from Andros Town airport. You can visit the factory and see how the material is made. It's open weekdays 8–4 and Saturday 9–5. The batik fabric is turned into wall hangings and clothing for men and women, which are sold throughout the Bahamas and the Caribbean. Adjacent to the factory is the **Androsia Outlet Store** (⊕ www.androsia.com), where you can buy original fabrics, clothing, Bahamian carvings and straw baskets, maps, CDs, and books. It's open 9–5 everyday except Sunday.

Five miles inland from Andros Town is **Captain Bill's Blue Hole**—one of countless blue holes on the island—a delightful freshwater spring with ropes for swinging across. Also near Andros Town, you can commune with nature by strolling along deserted beaches and forest paths and taking in the wild orchids.

❸ On the north side of Fresh Creek (and about 30 mi south of Nicholl's Town on the east coast) is the small hamlet of **Fresh Creek.** A few restaurants, including **Hank's Place,** line the waterfront, along with several boat docks and a small hotel with a convenience store. A few blocks in from the creek are a couple of markets, shops, and offices. The creek itself cuts over 16 mi into the island, creating tranquil bonefishing flats and welcoming mangrove-lined bays that can be explored by boaters and sea kayakers.

❹ Andros lures fishing enthusiasts to its fabulous bonefishing flats, and divers can't get enough of the sprawling **Andros Barrier Reef,** just off Fresh Creek–Andros Town. Snorkelers can explore such reefs as the Three Sisters, where visibility is clear 15 feet to the sandy floor and jungles of elkhorn coral snake up to the surface. Divers can delve into the 60-foot-deep coral caves of the Petrified Forest, beyond which the wall slopes down to depths of 9,000 feet. Anglers can charter boats to fish offshore or over the reef, and bonefishers can wade the flats on their own in Fresh Creek.

Where to Stay & Eat

★ ¢–$$ ✗ **Hank's Place Restaurant and Bar.** On the north side of Fresh Creek, a block or so east of the bridge, this restaurant and bar is shaded by coconut palms and graced with clear views of the water. Bahamian specialties—panfried grouper, baked hog snapper, and fresh conch salad—make it a favorite gathering place for locals and visitors. Fresh lobster, prepared to your liking, is available in season (August–March). Hank's signature cocktail, aptly named "Hanky Panky," is a dynamite frozen rum and fruit juice concoction. ⊠ *Fresh Creek, Andros* ☎ *242/368–2447* ⌨ *Reservations not accepted* ☐ *MC, V* ⊗ *Closing hours are erratic—call before going.*

$ ✗▢ **Andros Lighthouse Yacht Club and Marina.** The yachting crowd favors this spot, so you're sure to meet an ever-changing parade of people in the cocktail lounge and restaurant. The spacious rooms and villas have tropical fabrics, and private patios. The restaurant ($–$$) serves a sumptuous Bahamian buffet lunch on Sundays. Boat rentals and fishing guides can be arranged. It's a five-minute walk across the bridge to Hank's Place Restaurant and Bar and to convenience stores in the main settlement area. ⊠ *Andros Town, Andros* ☎ *242/368–2305* ⊟ *242/368–2300* ⊕ *www.androslighthouse.com* ⌨ *12 rooms, 8 villas* ⌂ *Restaurant, fans, refrigerators, pool, beach, snorkeling, dock, boating, marina, fishing, bicycles, bar, lounge* ☐ *AE, D, MC, V.*

★ ♨ $ ✗▢ **Small Hope Bay Lodge.** This casual, palm-shaded oceanfront property attracts divers, snorkelers, eco-adventurers, and anglers, and is popular with families. Rooms with Androsia batik prints and straw work are in beachside cottages made of coral rock and Andros pine. The homey main lodge is the center of activity—dining room, bar-lounge, game room, and reading area. Tasty Bahamian meals include lavish seafood buffets and pig roast barbecues. For an additional charge you can select bonefishing and specialty diving packages such as guided explorations of blue holes, diving instruction and certification, and "over-the-wall" dives. Rates include meals, taxes, service charges, and airport transfers. ⊠ *Small Hope Bay, Fresh Creek* ⌨ *Box 21667, Fort Lauderdale, FL 33335* ☎ *242/368–2014 or 800/223–6961* ⊟ *242/368–2015* ⊕ *www.smallhope.com* ⌨ *20 cottages* ⌂ *Dining room, fans, hot tub, massage, beach, dive shop, dock, snorkeling, windsurfing, boating, fishing, bicycles, 2 bars, lounge, library, recreation room, laundry service, baby-sitting, Internet; no a/c, no room phones, no room TVs* ☐ *AE, D, MC, V* ⧖ *All-inclusive.*

$$ ▢ **Coakley House, Private Rental Villa.** This three-bedroom villa has creekside decks and a private dock right on the entrance to Fresh Creek. Each bedroom has air-conditioning and a private bath. There are views of both the ocean and the creek from picture windows in the large living room and dining room. The house has everything you need for a self-sufficient vacation: a fully equipped kitchen, washer/dryer, entertainment system, and linens and towels. Car and boat rentals, and maid

and cook services can be arranged at an additional cost. Fishing guides can be hired who will pick you up at your private dock. The walk into Fresh Creek takes five minutes. The villa is owned by Small Hope Bay Lodge, so all of the resort's activities and facilities are available to villa guests. ⊠ *Coakley House, Small Hope Bay, Fresh Creek* ☐ *Box 21667, Fort Lauderdale, FL 33335* ☎ *242/368–2014 or 800/223–6961* ☐ *242/ 368–2015* ⊕ *www.coakleyhouse.com* ⟟ *1 3-bedroom villa* ☖ *Dining room, fans, hot tub, massage, beach, dive shop, dock, snorkeling, windsurfing, boating, fishing, bicycles, 2 bars, lounge, library, recreation room, laundry service, baby-sitting, Internet* ⊟ *AE, D, MC, V.*

Sports & the Outdoors

BOATING & **Small Hope Bay Lodge** (☎ 242/368–2014 or 800/223–6961) has bone-,
FISHING deep-sea, fly-, reef, and seasonal tarpon fishing, as well as a "west side overnight"—a two-night camping, bone- and tarpon-fishing trip to the island's uninhabited western end. Rates run $250–$300 for a half day and $375–$500 for a full day (full-day trips include all gear and lunch).

Cargill Creek

Fishing—bonefishing in particular—is this quiet area's principal appeal, with wadeable flats winding along the shoreline all the way to Behring Point. Cargill Creek is approximately 20 mi south of Andros Town (30 minutes by taxi). Taxi fare is about $40 one-way for two passengers. Bonefishing packages run $350 to $450 per person per day at the half dozen lodges in the area.

Where to Stay & Eat

$$–$$$$ ✕🖃 **Andros Island Bonefishing Club.** Hard-core bonefishers are drawn to this down-home establishment. Guests have access to 100 square mi of lightly fished flats. Owner Captain Rupert Leadon is a warm, commanding presence with many a story of the elusive bonefish. Captain Leadon purchased the adjacent Creekside Lodge in spring 2003, and joined it with AIBC. Rooms are comfortable, with two queen-size beds, minirefrigerators, and ceiling fans. The dining room–lounges have satellite TV and fly-tying tables. Meals are hearty, with Bahamian fare such as seafood and peas 'n' rice served up family style. Rates include room, meals, and airport transfers. ⊠ *Cargill Creek, Andros* ☎ *242/368–5167* ☐ *242/ 368–5397* ⊕ *www.androsbonefishing.com* ⟟ *30 rooms* ☖ *2 dining rooms, fans, refrigerators, pool, dive shop, dock, snorkeling, boating, fishing, billiards, 2 bars, lounge, recreation room, laundry service; no room phones, no room TVs* ⊟ *AE, D, MC, V* ⊙ *All-inclusive.*

Sports & the Outdoors

FISHING Some of the best private bonefishing guides in the Bahamas work out of Cargill Creek and Behring Point. **Andy Smith** (☎ 242/368–4261 or 242/368–4044) is highly recommended for guiding anglers through the Bights and on the West Side. **Charlie Neymour** is also highly regarded. Contact **Nottages Cottages** (☎ 242/368–4293) to hire Charlie. Call **Tranquility Hill Fishing Lodge** (☎☐ 242/368–4132) at Behring Point to book Barry Neymour, Frankie Neymour, Deon Neymour, Ivan Neymour, Dwain Neymour, Ray Mackey, and Ricardo Mackey, all recommended

UNDERSEA ADVENTURES IN ANDROS

ANDROS PROBABLY HAS the largest number of dive sites in the country. With the third-longest barrier reef in the world (behind those of Australia and Belize), the island offers about 100 mi of drop-off diving into the Tongue of the Ocean. Uncounted numbers of **blue holes** are forming in the area. In some places, these constitute vast submarine networks that can extend more than 200 feet down into the coral (Fresh Creek, 40–100 feet; North Andros, 40–200+ feet; South Bight, 40–200 feet). Blue holes are named for their inky-blue aura when viewed from above and for the light-blue filtered sunlight that is visible from many feet below. Some of the holes have vast cathedral-like interior chambers with stalactites and stalagmites, offshoot tunnels, and seemingly endless corridors. Others have distinct thermoclines (temperature changes) between layers of water or are subject to tidal flow. The dramatic Fresh Creek site provides an insight into the complex Andros cave system. There isn't much coral growth but there are plenty of midnight parrot fish, big southern stingrays, and some blacktip sharks. Similar blue holes are found all along the barrier reef, including several at Mastic Point in the north and the ones explored and filmed off South Bight.

Undersea adventurers also have the opportunity to investigate wrecks such as the Potomac, a steel-hulled freighter that sank in 1952 and lies in 40 feet of water off Nicholl's Town. And off the waters of Fresh Creek, at 70 feet, lies the 56-foot-long World War II LCM (landing craft mechanized) known only as the **Barge Wreck,** which was sunk in 1963 to create an artificial reef. Now encrusted with coral, it has become home to a school of groupers and a blizzard of tiny silverfish. There is a fish-cleaning station where miniature cleaning shrimp and yellow gobies clean grouper and rockfish by swimming into their mouths and out their gills, picking up food particles. It's excellent subject matter for close-up photography.

The split-level **Over the Wall** dive at Fresh Creek takes novices to the 80-foot ledge and experienced divers to a pre–Ice Age beach at 185 feet. The wall is covered with black coral and all kinds of tube sponges. **Small Hope Bay Lodge** is the most respected dive resort on Andros. It's a friendly, informal place where the only thing taken seriously is diving. There's a fully equipped dive center with a wide variety of specialty dives, including customized family-dive trips with a private dive boat and dive master. If you're not certified, check out the lodge's morning "resort course" and be ready to explore the depths by afternoon.

guides. Rooms and all-inclusive fishing packages are available at Tranquility Hill.

Mangrove Cay

⑤ Remote **Mangrove Cay** is sandwiched between two sea-green bights, separating it from north and south Andros and creating an island of black coral shorelines, gleaming deserted beaches, and dense pine forests. **Moxey Town,** known locally as Little Harbour, rests on the northeast corner in a coconut grove. Pink piles of conch shells and mounds of porous sponges dot the small harbor of this commercial fishing and sponging community. Anglers come on a mission, in search of giant bonefish on flats called "the promised land" and "land of the giants." A five-minute boat ride takes fly-fishers to Gibson Cay to wade hard sand flats sprinkled with starfish. The bar at **Moxey's Guest House and Bonefish Lodge** (☎ 242/362–2080), across the road from the harbor, is the place for an après fishing Kalik, or a piece of Pearl Moxey's legendary johnnycake. The **Victoria Point Blue Hole** is good for snorkeling and diving, and there are a number of pristine spots sure to please naturalists looking for birds or wild orchids. The cay's main road runs south from Moxey Town, past the airport, then along coconut-tree shaded beaches to the settlement of Lisbon Creek. From here, a free government ferry (☎ 242/369–0331) makes trips twice daily (usually at 8 and 4) across the South Bight to Driggs Hill, South Andros.

Where to Stay & Eat

$–$$ ✕ **Dianne Cash's Ultimate Delight.** What's on the menu? "Nothing," says Dianne. "What do you want?" Dianne cooks three meals a day to order. Just call a day in advance, to give her enough time to procure the ingredients. Ask for pork chops, lobster, conch salad, or Dianne's specialty—stuffed baked crabs. That's it: just four tables with white rattan chairs, a couple of spots at the counter, and your own personal chef. ⊠ *Queen's Highway* ☎ *242/369–0430* ▤ *No credit cards.*

$–$$ ✕▣ **Mangrove Cay Inn.** Set in a coconut grove, with wild orchid and hibiscus gardens, the inn caters to those who want to get away from it all. The rooms are decorated in peach and green with light Andros pine walls. Relax in the restaurant ($–$$) and bar to enjoy your favorite fresh seafood dish or a cold Kalik. Rent a bicycle to explore the cay, roam miles of nearby beach, or hire a fishing guide. A three-bedroom cottage with full kitchen, overlooking a saltwater lake filled with baby tarpon and snappers, is also available for rent. Rates include taxes and gratuity. ⌂ *General Post Office, Mangrove Cay, Andros* ☎ *242/369–0069* 🖷 *242/369–0014* ⊕ *www.mangrovecayinn.com* ⤴ *12 rooms* ♿ *Restaurant, fans, fishing, bicycles, bar; no room phones, no room TVs* ▤ *No credit cards.*

★ **$** ✕▣ **Seascape Inn.** Five individual cottages with private decks overlook the glass-clear ocean. Owners Mickey and Joan McGowan have decorated each one with handcrafted wooden furniture and original art. The elevated restaurant ($–$$) and bar is the place to relax, swap stories, and enjoy cocktails with the locals. Grilled steaks, coconut grouper, and chicken in white wine sauce are dinner highlights. The hearty breakfasts (included in the rate) are also delicious. Joan bakes killer banana bread and an assortment of yummy muffins. Mickey leads the diving program and can arrange for a fishing guide. ⊠ *Mangrove Cay, Andros* ☎☎ *242/ 369–0342* ⊕ *www.seascapeinn.com* ⤷ *4 1-bedroom cottages, 1 cottage suite* ⚭ *Restaurant, fans, beach, dive shop, snorkeling, boating, fishing, bicycles, bar, library, Internet; no a/c, no room phones, no room TV* ⊟ *AE, MC, V* ⍾ *BP.*

Sports & the Outdoors

SCUBA DIVING & SNORKELING The dive shop at **Seascape Inn** (☎ 242/369–0342) offers snorkeling and diving excursions, and rents dive equipment and kayaks. A minimum of four people is required per group, and you need to call a day in advance.

South Andros–Driggs Hill

Driggs Hill, on South Andros, is a small settlement of pastel houses, a tiny church, a grocery store, the government dock, and the Emerald Palms Resort of South Andros (formerly the Ritz Beach Resort). A mile south is the Congo Town airport. Eight miles farther south, The Bluff settlement sprawls atop a hill overlooking miles of golden beaches, lush cays, and the Tongue of the Ocean. Here skeletons of Arawak natives were found huddled together. A local resident attests that another skeleton was found—this one of a 4-foot-tall, one-eyed owl, which may have given rise to the legend of the mythical, elflike chickcharnie.

Where to Stay & Eat

$–$$$$ ✕⌷ **Emerald Palms Resort of South Andros.** Completely renovated in November 2003, this upscale property added 20 luxurious one- and two-bedroom cottages with individual gardens and private decks surrounded by palm trees. The elegant cottages have marble floors, mahogany furniture, and king-size beds. The spacious clubhouse rooms run along the blue-tile pool and out to the glimmering beach. Ask for one of the beachfront rooms or cottages. A cabana bar overlooks the gin-clear sea. Chef Hall creates hearty Bahamian breakfasts, light zesty lunches, and theme-night four-course dinners. Grilled seafood, steaks, and whole lobsters are specialties, served in the casually elegant poolside restaurant ($–$$$). ⌕ *Box 800, Driggs Hill, Andros* ☎ *242/369–2661 or 242/ 369–2713* 🖷 *242/369–2711* ⤷ *20 rooms, 20 suites* ⚭ *Restaurant, in-room hot tubs, kitchenettes, refrigerators, pool, outdoor hot tub, beach, snorkeling, windsurfing, boating, fishing, bicycles, bar, lounge, laundry service, Internet, car rental; no room phones* ⊟ *AE, D, DC, MC, V.*

$$ ✕⌷ **Tiamo Resorts.** You arrive at this low-key yet sophisticated South
Fodor'sChoice Bight eco-resort via private ferry. There are no phones or TVs. A cold
★ drink awaits in the lodge—an expansive gathering place with wood-beamed ceilings that naturally combine bar, lounge, library, and dining room. Individual bungalows with wraparound porches are strung out along the powdery beach shaded by coconut palms. Commodious bedrooms with soft linens are positioned to receive the cooling ocean breeze. Leisurely meals include seafood delights, homemade breads, and luscious desserts. To explore the wilds of sea and land, guided snorkeling, sea kayaking, nature hikes, and fishing excursions can be arranged at your whim. ⌕ *General Delivery, Driggs Hill, South Andros Island* ☎ *242/ 357–2489* 🖷 *305/768–7707* ⊕ *www.tiamoresorts.com* ⤷ *11 bunga-*

lows ⟡ *Dining room, fans, beach, dive shop, dock, snorkeling, boating, fishing, bar, lounge, library, laundry service; no a/c, no room phones, no room TVs* ⊟ *AE, D, DC, MC, V* ⦿ *All-inclusive.*

Sports & the Outdoors

FISHING   **Emerald Palms Resort of South Andros** (☎ 242/369–2661) can arrange boat rentals, and schedule guides for bonefishing, reef fishing, or deep-sea fishing.

Andros A to Z

AIR TRAVEL

There are four airports on Andros (San Andros, Fresh Creek/Andros Town, Mangrove Cay, and Congo Town). Several small airlines and charter companies have flights from Nassau. Daily charter service is also available from Fort Lauderdale and Freeport. Check with your hotel for the closest airport. Taxis meet incoming planes at the airports, but they can also be booked ahead of time.

CARRIERS   Bahamasair does not offer consistent service to Andros. Western Air has two flights per day from Nassau to each of the four Andros airports. It offers the best and cheapest service by far to Andros. Lynx Air International flies from Fort Lauderdale to Congo Town three days a week. Major Air has charter service from Freeport to all four airports, and regular service Friday and Sunday. Small Hope Bay Lodge offers flights from Fort Lauderdale to Andros Town for a minimum of two passengers and can arrange charter flights for island hopping.

🛪 **Airlines & Contacts Western Air** ☎ 242/377–2222 Nassau, 242/329–4000 San Andros, 242/368–2759 Andros Town, 242/369–0003 Mangrove Cay, 242/369–2222 Congo Town. **Bahamasair** ☎ 242/339–4415 or 800/222–4262. **Lynx Air International** ☎ 888/596–9247. **Major Air** ☎ 242/352–5778. **Small Hope Bay Lodge** ☎ 242/368–2014 or 800/223–6961.

AIRPORTS & TRANSFERS

The San Andros airport is in North Andros. Andros Town airport is in Central Andros. There's also an airport on Mangrove Cay. South Andros airport is in Congo Town. Check with your hotel for the closest airport.
🛪 **Airport Information Andros Town** ☎ 242/368–2030. **Congo Town** ☎ 242/369–2640. **Mangrove Cay** ☎ 242/369–0083. **San Andros** ☎ 242/329–4224.

TRANSFERS   Taxis meet incoming planes at the airports, and they can also be arranged through the hotels. Rates are around $1.50 a mile.

BIKE TRAVEL

Bicycles are available at Andros Lighthouse Yacht Club and Marina. You can rent bicycles at Small Hope Bay Lodge. Seascape Inn rents bicycles.
🛪 **Bike Rentals Andros Lighthouse Yacht Club and Marina** ⊠ Andros Town ☎ 242/368–2305. **Small Hope Bay Lodge** ⊠ Fresh Creek ☎ 242/368–2014.

BOAT & FERRY TRAVEL

A free government ferry makes the half-hour trip between Mangrove Cay and South Andros twice daily. It departs South Andros at 8 AM and 4 PM and departs Mangrove Cay at 8:30 AM and 4:30 PM, but schedules are subject to change. Call the Commissioner's Office for more information.

From Potter's Cay Dock in Nassau, the M/V *Lisa J III* sails to Morgan's Bluff and Nicholl's Town in the north of the island every Wednesday, returning to Nassau the following Tuesday. The trip takes six hours and costs $30. The M/V *Lady D* leaves Nassau on Tuesday for Fresh Creek (with stops at Stafford Creek, Blanket Sound, and Behring Point) and returns to Nassau on Sunday. The trip takes 5½ hours, and the fare is $35. The M/V *Mangrove Cay Express* leaves Nassau on Thursday evening for Driggs Hill, Mangrove Cay, and Cargill Creek and returns on Tuesday afternoon; the trip takes 5½ hours and costs $30. The M/V *Captain Moxey* leaves Nassau on Monday and calls at Kemp's Bay, Long Bay Cays, and the Bluff on South Andros. It returns to Nassau on Wednesday. The trip takes 7½ hours; the fare is $35. Schedules are subject to change due to weather conditions or occasional dry-docking. For more information, contact the Dockmaster's Office at Potter's Cay.

ⓘ Boat & Ferry Information Commissioner's Office ☎ 242/369-0331. Dockmaster's Office ☎ 242/393-1064.

CAR TRAVEL

The main roads are in generally good shape, but watch out for potholes, and remember to drive on the left. Cab drivers will charge $80–$120 for a half-day tour of the island. Even a short taxi ride is usually $10. Many visitors opt to get around by bicycle. If you need a rental car, your best bet is to have your hotel make arrangements. It's smart to book a week in advance during high season as the number of vehicles is limited.

EMERGENCIES

Telephone service is available only through the front desk at Andros hotels, so emergencies should be reported to the management. A doctor lives in San Andros. Medical clinics are in Mastic Point, Nicholl's Town, and Lowe Sound, each with a resident nurse. A health center at Fresh Creek has both a doctor and a nurse. A clinic at Mangrove Cay has a nurse.

ⓘ Police ☎ 919 North Andros, 242/368-2626 Fresh Creek/Central Andros, 242/369-4733 Kemp's Bay/South Andros. **Medical Clinics** ☎ 242/329-2055 Nicholl's Town/North Andros, 242/368-2038 Fresh Creek, 242/369-0089 Mangrove Cay, 242/369-4849 Kemp's Bay/South Andros.

VISITOR INFORMATION

BANKS & OFFICES The Canadian Imperial Bank of Commerce in San Andros is open Wednesday from 10:30 to 2:30. There are also banks in Fresh Creek and on Mangrove Cay that are open two to three days a week, usually Monday and Wednesday, and sometimes Friday.

ⓘ Bank Information Canadian Imperial Bank of Commerce ☎ 242/329-2382.

THE BERRY ISLANDS

The Berry Islands consist of more than two dozen small islands and close to a hundred tiny cays stretching in a curve like a new moon north of Andros and New Providence Island. Although a few of the islands are privately owned, most of them are uninhabited—except by rare birds using the territory as their nesting grounds or by visiting yachters dropping anchor in secluded havens. The Berry Islands start in the north at Great Stirrup Cay, where a lighthouse guides passing ships, and they end in the south at Chub Cay, only 35 mi north of Nassau.

Most of the islands' 700 residents live on Great Harbour Cay, which is 10 mi long and 1½ mi wide. Its main settlement, Bullock's Harbour, has a couple of small restaurants and a grocery store. The Great Harbour Cay resort, a few miles away from Bullock's Harbour, was developed in the early 1970s. It is geared toward fishing enthusiasts. Both Chub and Great Harbour cays are close to the Tongue of the Ocean, where big game fish roam. Remote flats south of Great Harbour, from Anderson Cay to Money Cay, are excellent bonefish habitat, as are the flats around Chub Cay. Deeper water flats hold permit and tarpon.

The Berry Islands appear just north of Andros Island on the Bahamas map at the front of the book.

Chub Cay

Where to Stay & Eat

$–$$$$ ✕🏨 **Chub Cay Resort & Marina.** The resort's huge marina can handle more than 96 oceangoing craft and offers charter boats with guides for big-game and flats fishing, the main pursuits here. The cay claims to be the "fish bowl" of the Bahamas with the Tongue of the Ocean at its doorstep and the Great Bahama Bank bending around to the Joulters Cays. The resort's rooms overlook the ocean or are clustered next to a freshwater pool; two-, three-, and four-bedroom villas are on the horseshoe-shape beach facing west. The Harbour House Restaurant ($–$$$) serves Bahamian and Continental dishes, with fresh seafood the specialty. ⊠ *Chub Cay Resort & Marina, Chub Cay, Berry Islands* ☎ *242/325–1490 or 800/662–8555* 🖷 *242/322–5199* ⊕ *www.chubcay.com* 🛏 *26 rooms, 9 villas* ⚛ *Restaurant, dining room, grocery, refrigerators, 2 tennis courts, 2 pools, beach, dock, snorkeling, waterskiing, boating, marina, fishing, bicycles, 3 bars, shops, laundry facilities; no room phones* ▭ *AE, MC, V.*

Sports & the Outdoors

BOATING The clarity of Bahamian waters is particularly evident when you cross the Great Bahama Bank from the Bimini area, then cruise along the Berry Islands on the way to Nassau. The water's depth is seldom more than 20 feet here. Grass patches and an occasional coral head or flat coral patch dot the light sand bottom. Starfish abound, and you can often catch a glimpse of a gliding stingray or eagle ray. You might spot the odd turtle, and if you care to jump over the boat's side with a mask, you might also pick up a conch or two in the grass. Especially good snorkeling and bonefishing, and peaceful anchorages, can be found on the lee shores of the Hoffmans and Little Harbour Cays. When it's open, **Flo's Conch Bar,** at the southern end of Little Harbour Cay, serves fresh conch prepared every way you can imagine.

Great Harbour Cay

Where to Stay & Eat

$–$$$$ ✕⌂ **Tropical Diversions Resort.** The resort rents privately owned homes, beach villas, and marina town houses with docks on a daily or weekly basis. The furnishings and layouts differ, but all have sundecks, daily maid service, and coffeemakers. Most units have full kitchens. The management meets you at the airport and can help you find fishing guides. Have a light lunch at the Beach Club ($–$$) or sit down for a full meal at the Wharf Restaurant ($–$$) in the marina. A more expensive fish-and-seafood buffet is served a couple of nights each week at the **Tamboo Club** ($–$$$) (☎ 242/367–8203). ⌂ *3512 N. Ocean Dr., Hollywood, FL 33019* ☎ *242/367–8838, 954/921–9084, or 800/ 343–7256* 🖨 *242/367–8115 or 954/921–9089* ⊕ *www. tropicaldiversions.com* ⇨ *13 beach villas and homes, 4 town houses* ⌃ *3 restaurants, beach, dock, snorkeling, boating, fishing; no room phones* ▭ *AE, MC, V.*

Sports & the Outdoors

BOATING In the upper Berry Islands, the full-service **Great Harbour Cay Marina** (☎ 242/367–8005 ⊕ www.greatharbourmarina.com) has 70 slips that can handle boats up to 150 feet. Accessible through an 80-foot-wide channel from the bank side, the marina has one of the Bahamas' most pristine beaches running along its east side.

FISHING The man to see about bonefishing is **Percy Darville** (☎ 242/367–8005), who knows the flats of the Berrys better than anyone. He can arrange for guides, or point you in the right direction to fish on your own. You should call him as far in advance as possible to book a guide or rent a boat. He can also be reached through the Great Harbour Cay Marina.

Berry Islands A to Z

AIR TRAVEL

Tropical Diversions Air flies to Great Harbour Cay and Chub Cay from Fort Lauderdale. Flights are chartered to your schedule, although the company will attempt to group you with other passengers if possible. A number of charter air companies fly to Great Harbour and Chub Cay from Nassau.

🛦 Airlines & Contacts **Tropical Diversions Air** ☎ 954/629–9977 or 800/343–7256.

BOAT & FERRY TRAVEL

Captain Gurth Dean leaves Potter's Cay, Nassau, Friday evening for Bullock Harbour, with stops in Sandy Point and Moore's Island, Abaco. The trip takes about seven hours, and costs $40 one-way. Return is Sunday morning. For schedules and specific destinations, call the Dockmaster's Office at Potter's Cay.

Bimini Mack leaves Potter's Cay, Nassau, Thursday afternoon for Chub Cay, with stops in Bimini and Cat Cay, which is just south of Bimini. The trip takes about 12 hours, and costs $45 one-way. Return is

Monday morning. For schedules and specific destinations, call the Dockmaster's Office at Potter's Cay.

ℹ **Boat & Ferry Information Dockmaster's Office** ☎ 242/393-1064.

EMERGENCIES

Immediately contact the police or a doctor in case of an emergency.

ℹ **Great Harbour Cay Medical Clinic** ☎ 242/367-8400. **Police** ✉ Bullock's Harbour, Great Harbour Cay ☎ 242/367-8344.

TRANSPORTATION AROUND THE BERRY ISLANDS

Happy People's has rental bikes, jeeps, and boats available for exploring the island.

ℹ **Happy People's** ☎ 242/367-8117.

THE BIMINIS

The Biminis have long been known as the Bahamas' big-game-fishing capital. The nearest of the Bahamian islands to the U.S. mainland, they consist of a handful of islands and cays just 50 mi east of Miami, across the Gulf Stream that sweeps the area's western shores. Most visitors spend their time on North Bimini. Throughout the year, more than a dozen billfish tournaments draw anglers to the Gulf Stream and the Great Bahama Bank from the United States, Canada, Britain, and the rest of Europe. Marinas such as Weech's Bimini Dock, the Bimini Big Game Marina, and Blue Water Marina, all on skinny North Bimini's eastern side, provide more than 150 slips for oceangoing craft, many of them belonging to weekend visitors who make the short trip from Florida ports. South Bimini now has a 35-slip marina complete with a customs and immigration center at the Bimini Sands resort complex. North Bimini's western side, along Queen's Highway, is one long stretch of beautiful beach.

Most of the hotels, restaurants, churches, and stores in the Biminis are along North Bimini's King's and Queen's highways, which run parallel to each other. Everything on North Bimini, where most of the islands' 1,600 inhabitants reside, is so close together you do not need a car to get around. Sparsely populated South Bimini, separated from its big brother by a narrow ocean passage, is where Juan Ponce de León allegedly looked for the Fountain of Youth in 1513. Tourists have easy access to the Fountain of Youth site, by way of a very good road, close to South Bimini's little airstrip.

Ernest Hemingway did battle with his share of game fish around North Bimini, which he visited for the first time in 1935 from his home in Key West. He made frequent visits here, where he wrote much of *To Have and Have Not* and *Islands in the Stream*. He is remembered in the area as a picaresque hero, not only for his graphic descriptions of fishing exploits, but for his drinking and brawling, including a fistfight he had with his brother Leicester on the Bimini dock.

Other notables lured to the island have included Howard Hughes and Richard Nixon. The American with the strongest ties to the Biminis was

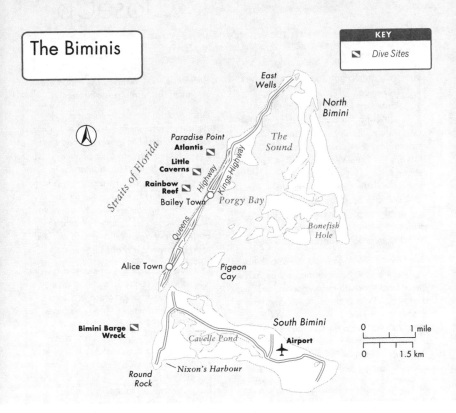

The Biminis

KEY

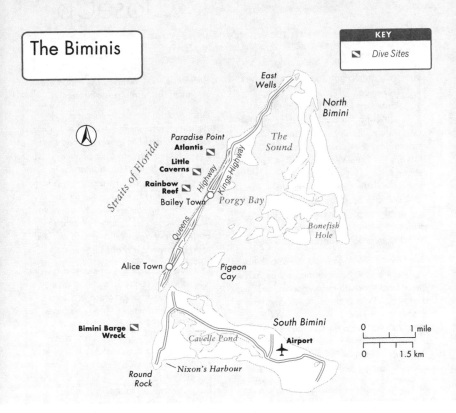 Dive Sites

East Wells

North Bimini

Paradise Point
Atlantis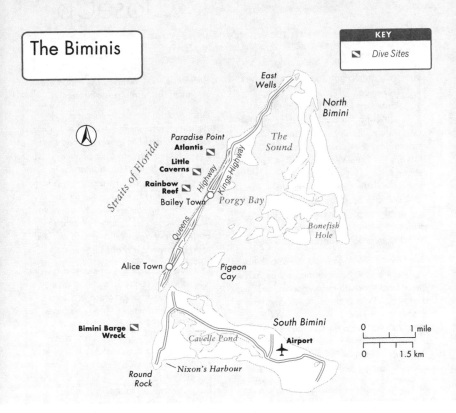

The Sound

Straits of Florida

Little Caverns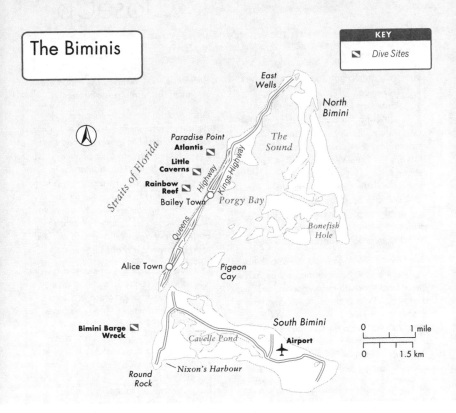

Rainbow Reef

Bailey Town

Queens Highway   Kings Highway

Porgy Bay

Bonefish Hole

Alice Town

Pigeon Cay

Bimini Barge Wreck

South Bimini

Cavelle Pond

Airport

0   1 mile
0   1.5 km

Round Rock   *Nixon's Harbour*

entrepreneur Michael Lerner. He discovered Bimini years before Hemingway and is the man credited with teaching him how to catch giant tuna. Lerner was a great friend to the Biminis and established, among other things, the Lerner Marine Research Laboratory, which conducted research on dolphins and sharks from 1947 to 1974.

The Biminis also have a notorious history as a jumping-off place for illicit dealings; first during the Civil War, when it was a refuge for profiteers bringing in war supplies from Europe, and then during Prohibition, when it was a haven for rumrunners. Today things are pretty quiet—rumrunners have been replaced by fishermen and Floridians. Spring break brings hordes of students who cruise over from Fort Lauderdale for wild nights at what was Papa Hemingway's favorite watering hole, the Compleat Angler. Unlike the rest of the Out Islands, Bimini experiences its busy season in the summer owing to the invasion of vacationing boaters from Florida.

Alice Town

Bimini's main community, Alice Town, is at North Bimini's southern end. It is neat and tidy, and painted in happy Caribbean pastels. In a prominent location stand the ruins of the **Bimini Bay Rod and Gun Club,**

CloseUp

RUNNING FOR RUM

FOLLOWING BRITAIN'S DEFEAT in the American Revolutionary War, Southern loyalists brought their slaves to the Bahamas. They grew cotton under the Crown's protection, maintaining the "cotton connection" through the Civil War, when Bahamians got rich running Confederate cotton to English mills and sending military equipment to Southern rebels. A century later, Bahamians grew wealthy once again, this time smuggling a precious liquid from Britain—liquor.

After the Civil War, temperance took hold in America, and soon made its way across the water. Although many Bahamians "took the pledge" not to drink, their government did not follow the U.S. path to **Prohibition.** With alcohol legal and certain islands less than 60 mi from American shores, the Bahamas once again became an important trans-shipping point for contraband.

British and Scottish whiskey, rum, and gin distillers began transporting large quantities of liquor to the Bahamas. Their ships were too large to dock at Nassau harbor, so they anchored offshore, out of view of the American Consul and revenue agents. The goods were off-loaded onto smaller vessels and stored in a network of warehouses on shore, which became known as **"rum row."** Some supplies were taken to the Out Islands for further transport. U.S. ships, often sailing under another flag to avoid detection, smuggled the bootleg booze to thirsty Americans, carrying the cargo through international waters, and ending up at drop-off points from Florida to New Jersey. But first, smugglers had to avoid U.S. Coast Guard ships that were prowling close to the

Bahamas, which may have been the origin of the term **"rum-running."**

After Prohibition was repealed, the Bahamas lapsed into economic stagnation, but the United States maintained its interest in the islands due to their proximity. During **World War II,** the U.S. military set up camp, establishing an air and sea station in the Bahamas. Though the station is no longer in use, the islands still house military communications facilities, plus drug enforcement agents that guard against today's generation of smugglers.

In 1962, **Bacardi & Company,** the world's largest rum producer, opened a distillery in Nassau. Although there is also a Bahamian brewery, which produces the ever-popular **Kalik** beer, rum is the alcoholic beverage of choice in the Bahamas. The basic cocktail formula is simple: one or more types of rum plus fruit juice. You can order these drinks at every bar. This trio is the most popular:

Bahama Mama—light rum, coconut rum, Nassau Royale (vanilla flavored rum), orange and pineapple juices.

Rum Punch—dark rum, orange and pineapple juices, grenadine, a dash of bitters.

Goombay Smash—light rum, coconut rum, pineapple juice, a dash of Galiano.

The islands' most famous bartender is Lerman Rolle, whose "Doctor of Libation" degree hangs behind the bar at Club Peace and Plenty, in George Town, Great Exuma Island. Like most expert mixologists, he measures by eye, accurate to the last drop whether he is making an single drink or a party-size bowl of punch.

a resort and casino built in the early 1920s and destroyed by a hurricane in 1926. A short walk away is the **Bimini Native Straw and Craft Market,** which bustles on weekends and during fishing tournaments. **Chalks-Ocean** seaplanes splash down in the harbor a block south of town, lumber ashore, and park adjacent to the pink customs and immigration office building. Taxis, passenger vans, and a bus meet all arriving flights, though they're not necessary unless you have a lot of luggage.

The **Compleat Angler Hotel** (✉ King's Hwy. ☎ 242/347–3122) was Ernest Hemingway's hideaway in the '30s, and the legend is perpetuated with a room full of memorabilia related to the writer, including pictures of gigantic fish and framed excerpts from his writings, most of them concerning battles with sharks. A photo of Cuban fisherman and captain of Hemingway's boat *Pilar,* Carlos Fuentes, the supposed model for the hero of *The Old Man and the Sea,* also hangs in the bar. The Angler is where former Colorado senator Gary Hart destroyed his hopes for the 1988 Democratic presidential nomination. He and Donna Rice were photographed in full color whooping it up on the bandstand in the hotel bar. The infamous picture now hangs in a place of honor.

The back door of the small, noisy **End of the World Bar** is always open to the harbor. This place—with a sandy floor and visitors' graffiti, business cards, and other surprises on every surface—is a good spot to meet local folks over a beer and a backgammon board. In the late '60s, the bar became a hangout of the late New York congressman Adam Clayton Powell, who retreated to North Bimini while Congress investigated his alleged misdemeanors. A marble plaque in his honor is displayed in the bar. The bar is 100 yards from the Bimini Bay Rod and Gun Club ruins. ☎ *No phone* ☉ *Daily 9 AM–3 AM.*

Where to Stay & Eat

$–$$ ✕ **Red Lion Pub.** Venture through twin doors emblazoned with the red Tudor lions for fresh seafood and Bahamian dishes in this no-smoking restaurant, which is uncommon in the Bahamas. There's a view out the back sliding-glass doors onto a small bay between the marinas. ✉ *King's Hwy.* ☎ *242/347–3259* ▭ *D.*

¢–$$ ✕ **Opal's Restaurant.** This diminutive, 12-seat dining room delivers huge helpings of ribs and seafood and is noted for its green turtle steaks. It is on the hill across from the Bimini Big Game Resort & Marina. ✉ *Sherman La.* ☎ *242/347–3082* ▭ *No credit cards* ☉ *Closed Sun.*

¢–$ ✕ **Big Game Sports Bar.** Part of the Bimini Big Game Resort & Marina, this is a popular anglers' hangout. The menu has pub fare like burgers and sandwiches along with fritters, chowder, and conch pizza. The bar overlooks the marina. ✉ *King's Hwy.* ☎ *242/347–3391* ▭ *AE, MC, V.*

¢–$ ✕ **Big John's.** For a hearty breakfast or lunch, this cheerful dining room with bright tablecloths and friendly staff is a favorite. Boiled fish and peas 'n' rice are specialties. ✉ *King's Hwy., across from Gateway Gallery* ☎ *242/347–3117* ▭ *No credit cards* ☉ *No dinner.*

★ $–$$$ ✕▦ **Bimini Big Game Resort & Marina.** This resort is a favorite among the fishing and yachting crowd who take advantage of the full-service 74-slip marina. Anglers might prefer the spacious cottages, each with a built-in wet bar, refrigerator, and outdoor grill. First-floor rooms have views of the lush gardens or pool, while second-floor rooms have superb bayfront views. The beach is only a five-minute walk away. The Clubhouse Restaurant ($–$$$) presents the island's most upscale dining, with cuisine ranging from grilled tuna with pineapple to T-bone steaks. If you plan to stay during one of the major fishing tournaments, reserve well in advance. ⊠ *King's Hwy., at pink wall* ☎ *Box 699* ☏ *242/347–3391 or 800/737–1007* 📠 *242/347–3392* ⊕ *www.biminibiggame.com* 📨 *35 rooms, 12 cottages, 4 penthouses* ♺ *2 restaurants, tennis court, pool, boating, marina, fishing, 3 bars, shops, baby-sitting, laundry service; no room phones* ▤ *AE, D, MC, V.*

★ **$–$$$** ✕▥ **Bimini Sands Condos & Marina.** Overlooking the Straits of Florida, this luxury property rents one- or two-bedroom condominiums. The bright, high-ceiling houses have balconies and patios with views of the tropical surroundings, the marina, or the beach. The Petite Conch ($–$$) serves three meals a day, blending Bahamian staples with American favorites. There is a 42-slip marina and a convenient customs office, so guests with boats can tie up and clear their paperwork without venturing to North Bimini customs. An all-night water taxi shuttles you to North Bimini to shop, dine, and party. ⊠ *Bimini Sands, South Bimini* ☎ *242/347–3500* 📠 *242/347–3501* ⊕ *www.biminisands.com* 📨 *21 1- or 2-bedroom condominiums* ♺ *2 restaurants, kitchenettes, tennis court, pool, beach, marina, fishing, bar, volleyball, laundry facilities* ▤ *AE, MC, V.*

$–$$ ✕▥ **Bimini Sands Beach Club.** Adjacent to Bimini's southern tip, the Beach Club is the sister property to the Bimini Sands Condos. Ocean- and marina-view rooms have light-colored interiors and thoughtful touches, like good lighting, flowers, and throw rugs on gleaming terrazzo tile floors. The beach club offers a reception-lounge area with large couches placed in front of a working fireplace, a billiard room, a tiny bar that overlooks the sparkling pool, and a restaurant ($–$$) with superb Bahamian cuisine and unparalleled views of the surrounding waters. ⊠ *Bimini Sands Beach Club, South Bimini* ☎ *242/357–3500* 📠 *242/347–3501* ⊕ *www.biminibeachclub.com* 📨 *38 rooms, 2 suites* ♺ *Restaurant, pool, beach, marina, billiards, volleyball, bar* ▤ *AE, D, MC, V.*

¢–$$ ✕▥ **Bimini Blue Water Resort.** One of Hemingway's hideaways, this resort sits atop a 20-foot hill. You can still rent Marlin Cottage, the place where he wrote some of *Islands in the Steam*. Spotless rooms have dark wood-paneled walls and private balconies. The Anchorage restaurant ($–$$), overlooking the ocean, takes pride in its fresh seafood. The 32-slip full-service marina and dockside pool are across the road on the lee side of the island. ⊠ *King's Hwy.* ☎ *Box 601* ☏ *242/347–3166* 📠 *242/347–3293* 📨 *9 rooms, 1 3-bedroom cottage* ♺ *Restaurant, pool, beach, marina, fishing, bar* ▤ *AE, D, MC, V.*

¢–$$ ▥ **Sea Crest Hotel and Marina.** The yellow, three-story hotel has comfortable, simply furnished rooms with tile floors, refrigerators, cable TV, balconies, and one of the island's friendliest owner-management teams. Pick a room or suite on the third floor; they have lofty, open-beam ceilings and lovely views from either side of the building—sea or marina. The beach is a two-minute walk away. As the name implies, there is a marina, across the street (King's Highway) from the hotel. There is a 5% surcharge for credit cards. ⊠ *King's Hwy.* ☎ *Box 654* ☏ *242/347–*

3071 🖨 242/347–3495 ⊕ *www.seacrestbimini.com* 📞 *11 rooms, 1 2-bedroom suite, 1 3-bedroom suite & Refrigerators, cable TV, marina; no room phones* ⊟ *D, MC, V.*

★ ¢–$ ⊞ **Compleat Angler Hotel.** Dating from the early '30s, this laid-back hotel will forever be associated with Hemingway, who often drank here after a day on the water and almost always stayed in Room 1. Funky and fun, the three-story wood-sided establishment exudes an unforgettable sense of place, making it Bimini's most charismatic accommodation. Ask for an upper floor room with a view of the water. The bar is the island's liveliest night spot, with live music on weekends, a drawback if you're trying to sleep. Guests have access to the pool and marina at Bimini Blue Water Resort. ✉ *3 blocks from Chalks-Ocean, King's Hwy.* 📪 *Box 601* ☎ *242/347–3122* 🖨 *242/347–3293* 📞 *12 rooms & 3 bars, lounge* ⊟ *AE, D, MC, V.*

Sports & the Outdoors

BOATING &
FISHING

Bimini Big Game Resort & Marina (☎ 242/347–3391 or 800/737–1007 ⊕ www.biminibiggame.com), a 74-slip marina, charges $800–$900 a day, and $475–$500 for a half day of deep-sea fishing. **Blue Water Marina** (☎ 242/347–3166), with 32 modern slips, charges from $750 a day, and from $450 a half day, with captain, mate, and gear included. **Bimini Sands Marina** (☎ 242/347–3500), on South Bimini, is a top-notch 35-slip marina offering accommodation to vessels up to 100 feet. Convenient customs clearance for guests is at the marina. Rent a 15-foot Whaler for $140 per day or a Wave Runner for $50 per half hour. Rental fishing gear (flats and blue water) is also available. **Weech's Bimini Dock** (☎ 242/347–3028), with 15 slips, has four Boston Whalers, which it rents for $135 a day or $75 a half day.

The following are highly recommended bonefish guides: **Bonefish Ansil** (☎ 242/347–2178 or 242/347–3098). **Bonefish Ebbie** (☎ 242/347–2053). **Bonefish Ray** (☎ 242/347–2269). **Bonefish Tommy** (☎ 242/347–3234).

EVENTS

The Biminis host a series of fishing tournaments and boating events throughout the year, including the **Mid-Winter Wahoo Tournament** (February), the **Annual Bacardi Rum Billfish Tournament** (March), the **Bimini Break and Blue Marlin Tournament** (April), the **Bimini Festival of Champions** (May), the **Annual Bimini Native Tournament** (August), the **Bimini Family Fishing Tournament** (August), the **Small BOAT—Bimini Open Angling Tournament** (September), and the **Wahoo Championship Tournament** (November). The island also hosts an annual **Bimini Regatta**, which takes place in the spring. For information on dates, tournament regulations, and recommended guides, call the **Bahamas Tourist Office** in Florida and ask for the sportfishing section. (☎ 800/327–7678).

SCUBA DIVING

The Biminis offer excellent diving opportunities, particularly for watching marine life. The **Bimini Barge Wreck** (a World War II landing craft) rests in 100 feet of water. **Little Caverns** is a medium-depth dive with scattered coral heads, small tunnels, and swim-throughs. **Rainbow Reef** is a shallow dive popular for fish gazing. And, of course, there's **Atlantis**, thought to be the famous "lost city." Dive packages are available through most Bimini hotels.

Bimini Undersea (☎ 242/347–3089 or 800/348–4644 ⊕ www. biminiundersea.com), headquartered at Bimini Big Game Resort & Marina, lets you snorkel near a delightful pod of Atlantic spotted dolphins for $119 per person. You can also rent or buy snorkel and diving gear. One-, two-, and three-tank dives cost $49, $89, and $119 per person, respectively.

The **Scuba Bimini Dive Center** (☎ 242/347–4444 or 800/848–4073 ⊕ www.scubabimini.com), at the rustic South Bimini Yacht Club, is a Neal Watson Undersea affiliate offering specialty wreck dives and a sensational blacktip- and reef shark–feeding one-tank dive experience for $75. (The dive masters feed them while you watch.) Call for package rates.

Shopping

Upstairs in the Burns House Building, the **Gateway Gallery** (✉ King's Hwy. ☎ 242/347–3131) sells top-quality Bahamian arts and crafts, original artwork by Biminites, hand-sculpted figures depicting daily Bahamian life, and Bahamian music.

Pritchard's Grocery (✉ Queen's Hwy., next to Baptist church ☎ No phone) is known as the home of the sweet Bimini native bread. Consider placing an order to take home.

Bimini Native Straw and Craft Market (✉ Next door to the Bahamas Customs building) has about 20 vendors, including Nathalie's Native Bread stand.

Elsewhere on North Bimini

Toward King's Highway's north end, you'll see bars, grocery shops, clothing stores, the pink medical center, and a group of colorful fruit stalls. The island's northwestern part bears the ruins of an unrealized luxury development—Bimini Bay—that was to include a marina, private homes, and a hotel. The original developers ran out of money and abandoned the project.

The **Bimini Museum,** sheltered in the restored (1920) two-story original post office and jail—a three-minute walk from the seaplane ramp—showcases varied artifacts, including Adam Clayton Powell's domino set, Prohibition photos, rum kegs, Martin Luther King Jr.'s immigration card from 1964, and a fishing log and rare fishing films of Papa Hemingway. The exhibit includes film shot on the island as early as 1922. ✉ King's Hwy. ☎ 242/347–3038 🖃 $2 🕙 Mon.–Sat. 9–9, Sun. noon–9.

Atlantis, a curious rock formation under about 20 feet of water, 500 yards offshore at Bimini Bay, is shaped like a backward letter J, some 600 feet long at the longest end. It's the shorter 300-foot extension that piques the interest of scientists and visitors. The precision patchwork of large, curved-edge stones form a perfect rectangle measuring about 30 feet across. A few of the stones are 16 feet square. It is purported to be the "lost city" whose discovery was predicted by Edgar Cayce (1877–1945), a psychic with an interest in prehistoric civilizations. Archaeologists estimate the formation to be between 5,000 and 10,000 years old. Carvings in the rock appear to some scientists to resemble a network of highways. Skeptics have pooh-poohed the theory, conjecturing that they are merely turtle pens built considerably more recently.

Most of the island's residents live in **Bailey Town** in small, pastel-color concrete houses. Bailey Town lies on King's Highway, north of the Bimini Big Game Resort & Marina Hotel. Check out Kim's Fruit Stand for a good selection of fresh fruit.

off the beaten path

HEALING HOLE – Locals recommend a trip here for curing what ails you—gout and rheumatism are among the supposedly treatable afflictions. Ask your hotel to arrange a trip out to this natural clearing in North Bimini's mangrove flats. You can take a leap of faith into the water and, if nothing else, enjoy a refreshing dip.

The Biminis A to Z

AIR TRAVEL
The two U.S. gateways to the Biminis are Fort Lauderdale and Miami. If you've just arrived at Miami International Airport, the taxi ride (about $15) to the Watson Island terminal for Chalks-Ocean Airway, across from the Port of Miami, will take about the same time it takes to get to North Bimini. You can also fly to Bimini from Nassau.

CARRIERS Island Air offers charter flights from Fort Lauderdale's Jet Center to South Bimini aboard a seven-passenger Islander. Chalks-Ocean Airway has several 25-minute flights daily into Alice Town, North Bimini, from Miami's terminal at Watson Island on the MacArthur Causeway, and from Fort Lauderdale International Airport (40 minutes). North Bimini is also served from Chalks-Ocean Airway base in Nassau–Paradise Island. Chalks-Ocean Airway uses 17-passenger turbo Mallard amphibians, with takeoffs and landings on water. Baggage allowance is 30 pounds per passenger. Western Air flies to Bimini from Nassau's domestic air terminal.
🛪 Airlines & Contacts **Chalks-Ocean Airway** ☎ 800/424-2557 or 242/347-3024 ⊕www.flychalks.com. **Island Air** ☎954/359-9942 or 800/444-9904. **Western Air** ☎242/347-4100 or 242/377-2222 ⊕ www.westernairbahamas.com.

TRANSFERS If you don't have heavy luggage, you might decide to walk to your hotel from the seaplane terminal in Alice Town, North Bimini's main settlement. Sam Brown's Taxi 1 & 2 (☎ No phone) meets planes and takes incoming passengers to Alice Town in 12-passenger vans. The cost is $3. A $5 taxi-and-ferry ride takes visitors from the South Bimini airport to Alice Town.

BIKE TRAVEL
🛪 Bike Rentals **Bimini Undersea** ☎ 242/347-3089 rents bikes for $7 per hour or $20 per day.

BOAT & FERRY TRAVEL
M/V *Bimini Mack* sails from Potter's Cay, Nassau, to Bimini, Cat Cay, and Chub Cay on Thursday afternoon. Return is Monday morning. The trip takes 12 hours and costs $45 one-way. For information, call the Dockmaster's Office at Potter's Cay.

Boaters often travel from Florida to Bimini, mostly from West Palm Beach, Ft. Lauderdale, and Miami. Crossing the Gulf Stream, however, should only be done by skippers who can plot a course using charts for that purpose. There are a half dozen or so routes that are most commonly used to cross the Stream from Florida to the Bahamas, with the route from Ft. Lauderdale to Bimini being the most popular for sailboats and power craft. The distance is 48 nautical mi. The time to make the crossing depends on the type of craft and the boat's speed. Sailors often like to make an evening departure, and arrive in the morning. Speed boaters sometimes zip over to Bimini for lunch or dinner and then return home. It is important for boaters to consult official government charts for obstructions, sands banks, and other impediments, and to be familiar with harbor entrances and procedures. If using proper safety, the crossing is a delight, and the fishing to and from can be sensational.

❼ Boat & Ferry Information Dockmaster's Office ☎ 242/393-1064.

BUS TRAVEL

Taxi 1 & 2, operated by Sam Brown, has minibuses available for a tour of the island. Arrangements can be made through your hotel.

BUSINESS HOURS

BANKS & OFFICES   The Royal Bank of Canada is open Monday, Wednesday, and Friday from 9:30 to 3. Cash advances are given on MasterCard and Visa only. Note that most stores are closed Sunday.

❼ Bank Information Royal Bank of Canada ☎ 242/347-3030.

CAR RENTAL

Visitors do not need a car on North Bimini and usually walk wherever they go; there are no car-rental agencies.

EMERGENCIES

To reach the police and fire department in an emergency, call ☎ 919. North Bimini Medical Clinic has a resident doctor and a nurse.

❼ North Bimini Medical Clinic ☎ 242/347-2210.

GOLF CART TRAVEL

Rental golf carts are available at the Sea Crest Hotel Marina and Bimini Blue Water Marina from Capt. Pat's for $60 a day or $20 for the first hour and $10 for each additional hour.

❼ Capt. Pat's ☎ 242/347-3477.

VISITOR INFORMATION

The Biminis Tourist Office is open weekdays from 9 to 5:30 and also has a booth at the straw market. The building it occupies was the site of the Lerner Marine Laboratory.

❼ Tourist Information Biminis Tourist Office ✉ Government Bldg., Alice Town ☎ 242/347-3529 🖷 242/347-3530.

TELEPHONES   Pay phones, which accept coins only, are scattered along King's Highway. If you have trouble placing your call, the Bimini Big Game Resort & Marina's office will place a call for you for about $2.50.

CAT ISLAND

Cat Island is 130 mi southeast of Nassau and is a close neighbor of San Salvador, the reputed landing place of Christopher Columbus. Many Cat Islanders maintain, however, that Columbus landed here instead and that Cat Island was once known as San Salvador. Sir Sidney Poitier is a famous local, who left as a youth before becoming a famed movie actor and director. His daughter Ann lives here and spearheads the annual Rake 'N' Scrape Festival held in June.

The island was named after a frequent notorious visitor, Arthur Catt, a piratical contemporary of Edward "Blackbeard" Teach. Slender Cat Island is about 50 mi long and boot shaped, with high cliffs and dense forest. The Cat, as it's often called, is living history with semiruined, vine-covered mansions and crumbling remnants of slave villages that are perfect for exploring. Mrs. Francis Armbrister, the elegant matriarch of the pioneer family that runs Fernandez Bay Village Resort, is the island's unofficial biographer. "Mrs. A," as she is known, has many spellbinding stories about the island, including the practice of obeah, which is a type of voodoo that incorporates bush medicine and witchcraft.

Good roads stretch from Orange Creek in the north to Port Howe and Hawk's Nest in the south. You'll rarely see another car, but watch out for local kids using the highway as a basketball court. The Cat's shores are ringed with mile upon mile of exquisite, untrammeled beaches edged with casuarina trees. Some of the original inhabitants' descendants, who migrated long ago to the United States, are slowly returning here. Large new homes have started to appear throughout the island. The population is about 2,000.

Residents fish, farm, and live a peaceful existence. The biggest event of the year is the Annual Cat Island Regatta in August.

Numbers in the margin correspond to points of interest on the Cat Island map.

Arthur's Town & Bennett's Harbour

6 The claim to fame of **Arthur's Town** is that it was the boyhood home of actor Sidney Poitier, who has written about growing up here in his autobiography. His parents and relatives were farmers. The village has a BATELCO station, a few stores, and Pat Rolle's **Cookie House Bakery** (☎ 242/354–2027)—a lunch or dinner spot and an island institution. When you drive south from Arthur's Town, which is nearly at the island's northernmost tip, you'll wind along a road that passes through small villages and past bays where fishing boats are tied up.

One of the island's oldest settlements of small, weather-beaten houses, **7** **Bennett's Harbour** is some 15 mi south of Arthur's Town. Fresh baked breads and fruit are available at makeshift stands at the government dock. There is good bonefishing in the creek.

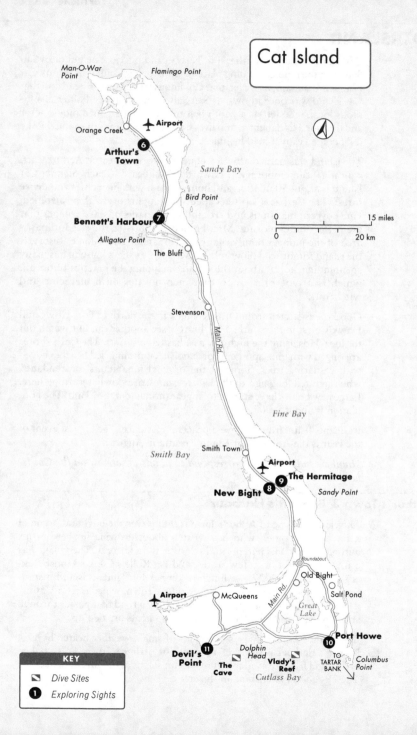

Cat Island

Man-O-War Point
Flamingo Point

Orange Creek ✈ **Airport**
6
Arthur's Town

Sandy Bay

Bird Point

Bennett's Harbour **7**

Alligator Point

The Bluff

Stevenson

Main Rd.

Fine Bay

Smith Bay

Smith Town

✈ **Airport**
8 **9** **The Hermitage**
New Bight

Sandy Point

Roundabout
Old Bight

✈ **Airport**
McQueens
Main Rd.
Salt Pond

Great Lake

Port Howe
10

Devil's Point **11**
The Cave
Dolphin Head
Vlady's Reef
Cutlass Bay

TO TARTAR BANK
Columbus Point

KEY
◥ *Dive Sites*
❶ *Exploring Sights*

0   15 miles
0   20 km

Where to Stay

$–$$$ Pigeon Cay Beach Club. Set in a wide bay a mile off the main road just south of Alligator Point, the club has seven deluxe cottages perched steps away from a 3-mi stretch of sugary white beach. The native stone and stucco cottages have wood and tile floors, colorful island furniture, complete kitchenware, and ceiling fans. You can cook yourself, or the club will provide a cook, and they will stock your cottage before your arrival. Just send your grocery list. Snorkel, kayak, canoe, sail a Hobie cat, fish, swim, or just lay on the beach. The beach bar serves breakfast every morning. ☒ *Pigeon Cay, Cat Island* 🕾 *242/354–5084* ⊕ *www. pigeoncay-bahamas.com* ⤷ *7 cottages* ⚪ *Picnic area, kitchens, refrigerators, beach, snorkeling, fishing, bicycles, bar; no a/c, no room phones, no room TVs* ⊟ *AE, MC, V.*

New Bight

❽ The settlement of **New Bight,** where you'll find a small grocery store, a bakery, and the Bridge Inn, is near the New Bight (also called "The Bight") airport and is south of Fernandez Bay Village. The Village is actually a resort on a bay and is where most Cat Island visitors stay.

Between the airport and the town is the small blue **First and Last Chance Bar,** run by Iva Thompson. This is a good place to have a beer with the locals, play dominoes, and check out Miss Iva's straw work, which is some of the Bahamas' best.

New Bight is the home of the **Twin Palms** (🕾 242/342–3108), a bar perched right on the ocean, where on Saturday night, you could be fortunate to hear the famous Blind Blake play guitar and rake 'n' scrape.

❾ At the top of 206-foot Mt. Alvernia, **The Hermitage** is the final resting place of Father Jerome. Above the tomb's entrance, carved in stone, is the epitaph BLESSED ARE THE DEAD WHO DIE IN THE LORD, and inside, past the wooden gate that hangs on its hinges, his body lies interred. He died in 1956 at the age of 80 and was supposedly buried with his arms outstretched, in a pose resembling that of the crucified Christ.

Father Jerome, born John Hawes, traveled the world and eventually settled in the Bahamas. An Anglican who converted to Roman Catholicism, he built two churches, St. Paul's and St. Peter's, in Clarence Town, Long Island, as well as the St. Augustine Monastery in Nassau. He retired to Cat Island to live out his last dozen years as a hermit, and his final, supreme act of religious dedication was to carve the steps up to the top of Mt. Alvernia. Along the way, he also carved the 12 Stations of the Cross. At the summit, he built a child-size abbey with a small chapel, a conical bell tower, and living quarters comprising three closet-size rooms.

The pilgrimage to the Hermitage begins next to the commissioner's office at New Bight, at a dirt path that leads to the foot of Mt. Alvernia. Try not to miss the slightly laborious experience of climbing to the top. The Hermitage provides a perfect, inspired place to pause for quiet contemplation. It also has glorious views of the ocean on both sides of the island. A caretaker clears the weeds around the tomb, which islanders regard as a shrine, and lights a candle in Father Jerome's memory.

Where to Stay & Eat

★ $–$$ ✕▦ **Fernandez Bay Village.** Brick-and-stone villas and cottages are spread along a dazzling, horseshoe-shape white-sand beach shaded by casuarina pines and colorful hibiscus. Villas are equipped with kitchens, terraces facing the sea, private gardens, and accommodations for four to six persons. Cottages are for two people, and have private patios and garden baths. Canoes, Sunfish sailboats, and kayaks are free to use. Boats and guides can be hired for fishing or snorkeling expeditions. Delicious native dishes are served in the lodge dining room (¢–$$) and on the beachside patio. Nightlife involves conversation around the honor bar or a bonfire. The owners and managers work hard to accommodate your every whim. ⊠ *1 mi west of New Bight airport* ✑ *7744 Peters Rd., Suite 310, Plantation, FL 33324* ☎ *242/342–3043 or 800/940–1905* 🖷 *954/474–4864* ⊕ *www.fernandezbayvillage.com* ⌨ *6 villas, 9 cottages* ⚒ *Dining room, grocery, kitchenettes, beach, snorkeling, boating, waterskiing, fishing, bicycles, bar, laundry service; no room phones, no room TVs* ▭ *AE, D, MC, V.*

¢ ✕▦ **Bridge Inn.** Run by Cat Islanders Mr. and Mrs. Russell (with the help of their large family), this motel-style property is about 300 yards from a beach. A more isolated stretch of sand is about a mile down a back road. The wood-paneled, high-ceilinged rooms have private baths and cable TV. Hot breakfasts, from French toast to stew fish and grits, are served in the hotel's dining room (¢–$$), and picnic lunches can be prepared. Rooms with air-conditioning cost extra. ⊠ *New Bight* ☎ *242/342–3013 or 800/688–4752* 🖷 *242/342–3041* ⌨ *12 rooms* ⚒ *Dining room, beach, snorkeling, boating, bicycles, billiards, bar, baby-sitting; no a/c in some rooms* ▭ *MC, V.*

Port Howe

⑩ At the conch shell–lined traffic roundabout, head east out toward **Port Howe,** believed by many to be Cat Island's oldest settlement. Nearby lie the ruins of the **Deveaux Mansion,** a stark two-story, whitewashed building overrun with wild vegetation. Once it was a grand house on a cotton plantation, home of Captain Andrew Deveaux of the British Navy, who was given thousands of acres of Cat Island property as a reward for his daring raid that recaptured Nassau from the Spaniards in 1783. Just beyond the mansion ruin is the entrance road to the Greenwood Beach Resort, which sits on an 8-mi stretch of umblemished velvet-sand beach.

Where to Stay & Eat

★ ¢ ✕▦ **Greenwood Beach Resort.** Set on an 8-mi stretch of pink shell-strewn sand, the remote resort is about 45 minutes from the New Bight airport. The large clubhouse, with its purple-and-white walls and vivid tropical paintings, is the center of activity. You can relax at the attractive bar or on the stone veranda with open vistas of the violet-blue Atlantic; or catch rays at the pool or beach. Rooms are bright and cheerfully decorated with colorful fish stencils. Dinner (¢–$$) is served family-style:

Don't miss the European-Bahamian bread, baked daily. Picnic lunches are prepared for day excursions. ⊠ *Port Howe* ☎ *242/342–3053* 🖷 *242/342–3053* ⊕ *www.greenwoodbeachresort.com* 🖘 *20 rooms* ⚫ *Dining room, fans, pool, hot tub, beach, dive shop, snorkeling, boating, fishing, bicycles, billiards, bar, laundry service, Internet, car rental; no a/c in some rooms, no room phones, no room TVs* ⊟ *AE, MC, V.*

Sports & the Outdoors

SCUBA DIVING, SNORKELING & FISHING **Cat Island Dive Centre** (⊠ Greenwood Beach Resort, Port Howe ☎ 242/342–3053) is the island's premier dive facility, with a 30-foot dive boat and great snorkeling right off the beach. Beginners can take the $80 crash course, and seasoned divers can plunge deep with spectacular wall-diving just offshore. Take a half-day guided snorkeling trip, or rent snorkeling gear and head off on your own. Boat rentals are available for reef fishing and island exploring. Bonefishing guides can be arranged for fishing the numerous creeks.

Devil's Point

⓫ The small village of **Devil's Point,** with its pastel-color, thatch-roof houses, lies about 10 mi west of Columbus Point. Beachcombers will find great shelling on the pristine beach. You'll also come across the ruins of the **Richman Hill–Newfield plantation.**

Where to Stay

$ ✕🛏 **Hawk's Nest Resort & Marina.** At Cat Island's southwestern tip, this waterfront resort, just yards from a long sandy beach, has its own runway and a 28-slip marina. The patios of the guest rooms, the dining room, and the lounge overlook the expansive Exuma Sound. With cheerful peach walls and bright bedspreads, rooms have either one king-size or two queen-size beds with baths that have both tubs and showers. A hearty breakfast is included in the daily rate. Fresh grilled wahoo, mahimahi, and roasted rack of lamb are dinner specialties ($–$$). The marina can arrange fishing and diving adventures. ⊠ *Devil's Point, Cat Island* ☎ *242/342–7050* 🖷 *242/342–7051* ⊕ *www.hawks-nest.com* 🖘 *10 rooms, 1 2-bedroom house* ⚫ *Restaurant, in-room VCRs, pool, beach, dive shop, snorkeling, boating, marina, fishing, bicycles, 2 bars, lounge; no room phones, no room TVs* ⊟ *MC, V* ⦿| *BP.*

Sports & the Outdoors

SCUBA DIVING & FISHING Contact your hotel, the Cat Island Dive Centre, or Dive Cat Island for more information on any of these sites, or to arrange a dive.

Tartar Bank is an offshore site known for its abundant sea life, including sharks, triggerfish, turtles, eagle rays, and barracuda. **The Cave** has a big channel with several exits to deeper ocean. Reef sharks, barracudas, and other tropical fish are frequently seen here. **Vlady's Reef,** also known as "The Chimney," is near the Guana Cays. Coral heads have created numerous canyons, chimneys, and swim-throughs. You're likely to catch a glimpse of large stingrays.

Dive Cat Island (☎ 242/342–7050) at Hawk's Nest Marina, conducts daily guided diving adventures, rents diving and snorkeling gear, and has equipment and sundries for sale. The running time to dive sites off the southern tip of the island is 15 to 30 minutes in the shop's 27-foot Panga, outfitted with VHF and GPS.

Charter a boat from **Hawk's Nest Marina** (☎ 242/342–7050) and experience dynamite offshore fishing. Look for wahoo, yellowfin tuna, dolphin, and white and blue marlin along the Exuma Sound drop-offs, Devil's Point, Tartar Bank, and Columbus Point. March through July is prime time.

Cat Island A to Z

AIR TRAVEL
Cat Island Air flies daily to New Bight from Nassau and is the best and cheapest service to the southern part of the island. Southern Air flies from Nassau to Arthur's Town and is the best service for the northern portion of the island. Bahamasair flies from Nassau to Arthur's Town or New Bight twice weekly. Lynx Air and Gulfstream (Continental's commuter) fly into New Bight from Fort Lauderdale. Tom Jones Charters offers a six-seat Piper Aztec from Fort Lauderdale into New Bight or Arthur's Town. Lynx Air flies into New Bight from Fort Lauderdale three times a week. Flight time from Nassau to Cat Island is approximately one hour.

Fernandez Bay Village, Greenwood Beach Resort, and Hawk's Nest Resort & Marina offer charter flights from Nassau.

🛫 Airlines & Contacts **Bahamasair** ☎ 800/222–4262. **Cat Island Air** ☎ 242/377–3318. **Fernandez Bay Village** ☎ 800/940–1905. **Greenwood Beach Resort** ☎ 242/342–3053. **Hawk's Nest Resort & Marina** ☎ 800/688–4752. **Lynx Air** ☎ 954/772–9808 or 888/596–9247. **Southern Air** ☎ 242/377–2014. **Tom Jones Charters** ☎ 242/335–1353 or 954/359–8099.

AIRPORTS & TRANSFERS
TRANSFERS Fernandez Bay Village meets guests at New Bight airport, and the transfer is complimentary. If you are going to Greenwood Beach Resort or Hawk's Nest Resort fly into New Bight, unless you can charter directly into Hawk's Nest. Check with your destination for the most convenient airport. If you miss your ride or no taxis are available, just ask around the parking lot for a lift. Anyone going in your direction (there's only one road) will be happy to drop you off.

BOAT & FERRY TRAVEL
The *Lady Rosalind* leaves Potter's Cay, Nassau, every Thursday for Bennett's Harbour and Orange Creek, returning on Saturday. The trip takes 14 hours and costs $40 one-way. *Sea Hauler* leaves Potter's Cay on Tuesday for Smith Bay, and Old and New Bight, returning on Monday. The trip is 12 hours, and the fare is $40 one-way. For information, call the Dockmaster's Office at Potter's Cay.

🛥 Boat & Ferry Information **Dockmaster's Office** ☎ 242/393–1064.

CAR RENTAL
The New Bight Service Station rents cars and can pick you up from New Bight airport. You can rent a car from Candy's Market, which also picks up from the airport. Greenwood Beach Resort arranges car rentals for

guests. Rates depend on the number of days you're renting, but $75 per day is average.

🎵 **Candy's Market** ☎ 242/342-3011. **New Bight Service Station** ☎ 242/342-3014.

EMERGENCIES

Cat Island has three medical clinics—at Smith Town, Old Bight, and Arthur's Town. There are few telephones on the island, but your hotel's front desk will be able to contact the nearest clinic in case of an emergency.

CROOKED & ACKLINS ISLANDS

Historians of the Bahamas tell us that as Columbus sailed down the lee of Crooked Island and its southern neighbor, Acklins Island (the two are separated by a short water passage), he was riveted by the aroma of native herbs wafting out to his ship. Soon after, Crooked Island, which lies 225 mi southeast of Nassau, became known as one of the "Fragrant Islands." The first known settlers didn't arrive until the late 18th century, when Loyalists brought their slaves from the United States and established cotton plantations. It was a doomed venture because of the island's poor soil, and those who stayed made a living of sorts by farming and fishing. A salt and sponge industry flourished for a while on Fortune Island, now called Long Cay. The cay, across the cut of French Well off the southwestern corner of Crooked Island, is the proposed home of a large new marina and resort development near the mostly abandoned settlement of Albert Town. The cay is also home to a flock of over 500 flamingos.

Today, Crooked and Acklins islands inhabitants, about 400 people on each island, continue to survive by farming and fishing. The islands are best known for splendid diving and bone-, tarpon, and offshore fishing—and not much else. They are about as remote as populated islands in the Bahamas get. A number of residents rely on generators for electricity. Phone service, where available, often goes out for days at a time.

Although the plantations have long crumbled, two relics of that era are preserved by the Bahamas National Trust on Crooked Island's northern part, which overlooks the Crooked Island Passage separating the cay from Long Island. Spanish guns have been discovered at one ruin, **Marine Farm,** which may have been used as a fortification. An old structure, **Hope Great House** has orchards and gardens that are still tended by the Bahamas National Trust.

Crooked Island is 30 mi long and surrounded by 45 mi of barrier reefs that are ideal for diving. They slope from 4 feet to 50 feet, then plunge to 3,600 feet in the Crooked Island Passage, once one of the most important sea roads for ships following the southerly route from the West Indies to the Old World. The one-room airport is in **Colonel Hill,** across the main road from a wide bay and white-sand bonefish flat. If you drive up to the settlement, you get an uninterrupted view of the region all the way to the narrow passage at Lovely Bay between Crooked Island and Acklins Island. There are two landmark lighthouses. The sparkling-white **Bird Rock Lighthouse** (built in 1872) in the north once guarded the

Crooked Island Passage. The rotating flash from its 115-foot tower still welcomes pilots and sailors to the Pittstown Point Landings resort, currently the islands' best lodging facility.

The **Castle Island** lighthouse (built in 1867), at Acklins Island's southern tip, formerly served as a beacon for pirates who used to retreat there after attacking ships.

Crooked and Acklins islands appear southeast of Long Island on the Bahamas map at the front of this guide.

Where to Stay & Eat

$ ✕🏨 **Pittstown Point Landings.** Shaded by coconut palms, this remote property on Crooked Island's northwestern tip has miles of open beach on its doorstep and unobstructed views of the emerald water surrounding Bird Rock Lighthouse. Rooms are motel-style units with double beds. Ask for an ocean view and air-conditioning. The main lodge—restaurant, bar, library—once housed the Bahamas' first post office. Fresh grilled wahoo and hog snapper are sure winners on the dinner menu (¢–$$). Bartender Reggie Moss mixes a potent Goombay Smash. Captain Robbie Gibson leads snorkeling, diving, and reef and offshore fishing adventures. All-inclusive bonefishing packages are available with top guides. ⌂ *9274 SE Hawk's Nest Ct., Hobe Sound, FL 33455* ☎ *242/344–2507, 800/752–2322, or 772/546–8299* 🖷 *772/ 546–6092* ⊕ *www.pittstownpointlandings.com* 🛏 *12 rooms* ⌂ *Restaurant, beach, snorkeling, fishing, bicycles, shuffleboard, volleyball, bar, lounge, library, shop, Internet, airstrip; no a/c in some rooms, no room phones, no room TVs* ⊟ *AE, D, MC, V.*

¢–$ 🏨 **Casuarina Villas.** The four modern cottages sit on a half-mi stretch of white-sand beach between Landrail Point and Pittstown Point Landings. Each has a full kitchen, satellite TV, and western facing decks. A local market, gas station, and restaurant are 2 mi away in Landrail Point, or you can eat at Pittstown Point. A rental car and fishing guide can be arranged. Diving excursions are led by owner Ellis Moss. ✉ *Landrail Point, Crooked Island* ☎ *242/344–2197, 242/344–2036, or 242/636– 4056* 🛏 *4 cottages* ⌂ *Kitchens, beach, snorkeling, fishing, laundry facilities; no room phones* ⊟ *No credit cards.*

Sports & the Outdoors

FISHING   Crooked Island has a number of highly regarded bonefishing guides with quality boats and fly-fishing tackle. Most can be booked through Pittstown Point Landings, but the guides also take direct bookings. Be aware that telephone service to and from Crooked and Acklins islands is not always operational.

Michael Carroll (☎ 242/636–7020), **Clinton Scavalla** (☎ 242/422– 3596 or 242/344–2197), **Elton "Bonefish Shakey" McKinney** (☎ 242/ 344–2507), **Jeff Moss** (☎ 242/457–0621), **Randy McKinney** (☎ 242/ 422–3276), and **Derrick Ingraham** (☎ 242/556–8769) are all knowledgeable professional guides.

Captain Robbie Gibson (☎ 242/344–2507) can be contacted through Pittstown Point Landings. He is the most experienced reef and offshore fishing captain on Crooked Island, where astounding fishing in virgin waters is the rule. Many wahoo over 100 pounds are landed each season with his assistance. Robbie's personal best wahoo is a whopping 180 pounds. He is also a skilled guide for anglers pursuing tuna, marlin, sharks, barracuda, jacks, snapper, and grouper.

SCUBA DIVING **The Wall** starts at around 45 feet deep and goes down thousands more. It's about 50 yards off Crooked Island's coast and follows the shoreline for many miles. For more information, contact the Pittstown Point Landings hotel.

Crooked & Acklins Islands A to Z

AIR TRAVEL

Bahamasair flies from Nassau to Crooked and Acklins islands twice a week. Airports are in Colonel Hill on Crooked Island and at Spring Point on Acklins Island. Pittstown Point Landings can pick up its guests flying into Colonel Hill by prior arrangement. The private airstrip at Pittstown Point Landings is complimentary for hotel guests. Nonguests pay landing and parking fees. This airstrip is recommended for private and charter flights.

⚏ Airlines & Contacts Bahamasair ☎ 800/222-4262.

BOAT & FERRY TRAVEL

M/V *United Star* sails from Potter's Cay in Nassau to Acklins Island, Crooked Island, and Long Cay once a week on a varying schedule. Call the Dockmaster's Office in Potter's Cay for schedule information. The fare is $70 one-way, and the trip takes 18 hours. Ferry service between Cove Landing, Crooked Island, and Lovely Bay, Acklins Island, usually operates twice daily on varying schedules between 9 and 4.

⚏ Boat & Ferry Information Dockmaster's Office ☎ 242/393-1064.

CAR RENTAL

Cars are hard to come by. You should reserve a car prior to your arrival with your hotel, but even with a reservation, be prepared for the possibility of not having one. Gas is also not always available on the island, as it is dependent on mail boat deliveries, which are sometimes delayed. Fortunately, it's easy to get a ride to most places with the locals.

EMERGENCIES

The police and commissioner are on Crooked Island. The two government medical clinics on Acklins Island are at Spring Point and Chesters Bay. Crooked Island's clinic is at Landrail Point. The resident doctor and nurse for the area live in Spring Point. Nurses are also available at Colonel Hill on Crooked Island, and Masons Bay on Acklins. You can contact these medical professionals through your hotel.

⚏ Commissioner ☎ 242/344-2197. **Police** ☎ 242/344-2599.

INAGUA

Great Inagua, the Bahamas' third-largest island, is 25 mi wide and 45 mi long. The terrain is mostly flat and covered with scrub. The island's unusual climate of little rainfall and continual trade winds created rich salt ponds, which have brought prosperity to the island over the years. The Morton Salt Company harvests a million tons of salt annually at its Matthew Town factory. About a fourth of the Inaguan population earns its living by working for the company. Inagua is best known for the huge flocks of shy pink flamingos that reside in the island's vast national park and on the property belonging to the salt company. In addition to the famous flamingos, the island is home to one of the largest populations of the rare Bahamian parrot, as well as to herons, egrets, owls, cormorants, and more than a hundred other species of birds.

Although the birds have moved in wholeheartedly, the island remains virtually undiscovered by outsiders. Avid bird-watchers make up the majority of the tourists who undertake the long trip to this most southerly of the Out Islands, about 300 mi southeast of Nassau and 50 mi off the coast of Cuba. Lack of exposure means that people are still friendly and curious about each new face in town. You won't feel like just another tourist. And since crowds and traffic are nonexistent, there's nothing to bother you but the rather persistent mosquito population (be sure to bring strong insect repellent). On the other hand, tourist facilities are very few and far between. There's no official visitor information office on the island. The only inhabited settlement on Inagua is Matthew Town, a small, dusty grid of workers' homes and essential services. The "hotels" are functional at best, and are often difficult to contact.

If you're a beach lover, Inagua is not for you. Although there are a couple of small swimming areas near Matthew Town and a few longer stretches farther north, no perfect combination of hotel and beach has yet been built. However, the virgin reefs off the island have caused a stir among intrepid divers who bring in their own equipment. The buzz is that Inagua could become a hot dive destination. Adventurous self-sufficient bonefishers have also discovered untouched flats with large bones on the northwest and southwest shorelines.

Great Inagua Island appears in the southeast corner of the Bahamas map at the front of this guide.

Matthew Town

About 1,000 people live on Inagua, whose capital, Matthew Town, is on the west coast. The "town" is about a block long. The large, pink, run-down government building (with the commissioner's office, post office, and customs office) is the dominant structure, along with a power plant and several Morton Salt Company machine shops. There is a grocery and liquor store, a bank, a clinic with a resident doctor, a small cinema, several guesthouses, a few restaurants and bars that keep irregular hours, and the small Kiwanis park that has a bench for sunset-gazing. Huge, no longer functional satellite dishes are prominently displayed in the yards of many houses, attesting to the money that flowed through the island in the heady drug-smuggling days of the 1980s. With smuggling on the rise again, the Royal Bahamas Defense Force has established a Southern Satellite Base here as part of a revised drug interdiction program in cooperation with the United States DEA.

The **Erickson Museum and Library** is a welcome part of the community, particularly the surprisingly well-stocked, well-equipped library. The Morton company built the complex in the former home of the Erickson family, who came to Inagua in 1934 to run the salt giant. The museum displays the island's history, to which the company is inextricably tied. ⊠ *Gregory St., on the northern edge of town across from the police station* ☎ *242/339–1863* 🎫 *Free* ⊙ *Weekdays 9–1 and 3–6, Sat. 9–1.*

The desire to marvel at the salt process lures few visitors to Inagua, but the **Morton Salt Company** (☎ 242/339–1300) is omnipresent on the island: It has more than 2,000 acres of crystallizing ponds and more than 34,000 acres of reservoirs. More than a million tons of salt are produced every year for such industrial uses as salting icy streets. (More is produced when the Northeast has a bad winter.) Even if you decide not to tour the facility, you can see the mountains of salt glistening in the sun from the plane. In an unusual case of industry assisting its environment, the crystallizers provide a feeding ground for the flamingos. As the water evaporates, the concentration of brine shrimp in the ponds increases, and the flamingos feed on these animals. Tours are available.

Where to Stay & Eat

¢–$ ✕ **Cozy Corner.** Cheerful and loud, this lunch spot—locals just call it Cozy's—is the best on the island. It has a pool table and a large seating area with a bar. Stop in for a chat with locals over a Kalik and Bahamian conch burger. Cozy's also serves excellent island-style dinners on request—steamed crawfish, grilled snapper, baked chicken and fries, homemade slaw, macaroni and cheese, and fresh johnnycake. ⊠ *Matthew Town* ☎ *242/339–1440* 🍴 *D.*

$ 🏨 **Sunset Apartments.** A good bet for accommodations on Inagua, these apartments sit right along the water on Matthew Town's southern side. The cement units all have modern Caribbean-style terra-cotta tile floors, rattan furniture, small terraces, a picnic area, and a gas grill. About a five-minute walk away is a small, secluded beach called the Swimming Hole. ⊕ *C/o Ezzard Cartwright, Matthew Town, Great Inagua* ☎ *242/ 339–1362* 🛏 *2 apartments* ⚐ *Fans, cable TV, kitchenettes, boating; no room phones* 🍴 *No credit cards.*

¢ 🏨 **The Main House.** The Morton Salt Company operates this small, affordable guesthouse. On the second of two floors, air-conditioned rooms share a sitting area with couches and a telephone. Rooms are spotless and spacious with dark-wood furnishings, Masonite-paneled walls, and floral-print drapes and spreads. The green-and-white hotel is right in Matthew Town, behind the grocery store and directly across the street from the island's noisy power plant. ⊠ *Matthew Town, Great Inagua* ☎ *242/339–1266 or 242/339–1267* 🛏 *5 rooms* ⚐ *Cable TV, refrigerators; no room phones* 🍴 *No credit cards.*

¢ 🏨 **Walkine's Guest House.** On the main drag, and in the mix of the residential community, this cinder block duplex has five motel-style air-conditioned rooms with cable TV. All rooms are bright and comfortable, with two twin beds. Three rooms have private baths, and two share a bath. The owner, Eleanor Walkine, lives in the duplex next door, and will prepare meals on request. ⊠ *Matthew Town, Great Inagua* ☎ *242/ 339–1612* 📞 *5 rooms* ⚲ *Fans, cable TV; no room phones* ▤ *No credit cards.*

Elsewhere on the Island

Although you'll spot them in salt ponds throughout the island, birds and other wildlife also reside in the **Inagua National Park,** managed by **The Bahamas National Trust,** which spreads over 287 square mi and occupies most of the island's western half. Nature lovers, ornithologists, and photographers are drawn to the area and to Lake Windsor (a 12-mi-long brackish body of water in the island's center) to view the spectacle of more than 60,000 flamingos feeding, mating, or flying (although you will rarely see all those birds together in the same place). When planning your trip, keep in mind that November through June is the best time to see the birds, with March through May the breeding season. Flamingos live on Inagua year-round, but the greatest concentrations come at these times. If you visit right after hatching, the scrambling flocks of fuzzy, gray baby flamingos—they can't fly until they're older—are quite entertaining. On the northwest side of the Park is the **Union Creek Reserve,** where BNT is working with the Caribbean Conservation Corporation on marine turtle research. To tour any part of the park or reserve, you must be accompanied by a BNT warden. Contact the Bahamas National Trust's Nassau office (☎ 242/393–1317 🖷 242/393–4978) to make reservations for your visit. BNT will send a visitor reservation form that you must fill out and return with your flight information, length of stay, and number of people in your party. You must also pay for your tour before arrival on Inagua.

From **Southwest Point,** a mile or so south of the capital, you can see Cuba's coast on a clear day, slightly more than 50 mi west, from atop the lighthouse (built in 1870 in response to a huge number of shipwrecks on offshore reefs). This is one of the last four hand-operated kerosene lighthouses in the Bahamas. Be sure to sign the guest book after your climb.

Inagua A to Z

AIR TRAVEL
Bahamasair has flights on Monday, Wednesday, and Friday from Nassau to Matthew Town Airport.
🛈 Airlines & Contacts **Bahamasair** ☎ 242/339-4415 or 800/222-4262.

AIRPORTS & TRANSFERS
Taxis sometimes meet incoming flights, though taxi service is not always reliable. It's best to make prior arrangements with your hotel to be picked up.
🛈 Airport Information **Matthew Town Airport** ☎ 242/339-1254.

BIKE TRAVEL
The Pour More Bar rents bikes for exploring the island.
🛈 Bike Rentals **Pour More Bar** ☎ 242/339-1232.

BOAT & FERRY TRAVEL

M/V *Trans Cargo II* makes weekly trips from Nassau to Matthew Town, also stopping at Abraham's Bay, Mayaguana. The cost is $70 one-way, and the trip takes approximately 24 hours. For information on specific schedules contact the Dockmaster's Office at Potter's Cay, Nassau.

🔒 Boat & Ferry Information **Dockmaster's Office** ☎ 242/393-1064.

BUSINESS HOURS

BANKS & OFFICES The Bank of the Bahamas in Matthew Town is open Monday through Thursday 9:30–2 and Friday 9:30–5:30.

🔒 **Bank of the Bahamas** ☎ 242/339-1815.

CAR RENTAL

Inagua Trading Ltd. has several cars for rent by the day. They are often difficult to contact by phone. BNT Warden Henry Nixon can also arrange for vehicle rentals.

🔒 Local Agency **Inagua Trading Ltd.** ☎ 242/339-1330. **Warden Henry Nixon** ☎ 242/339-1616.

EMERGENCIES

There is no general emergency number in Inagua—call the police or hospital directly in case of an emergency.

🔒 **Hospital** ☎ 242/339-1249. **Police** ☎ 242/339-1263.

SIGHTSEEING TOURS

Warden Henry Nixon leads most tours into Inagua National Park and to Union Creek Reserve. Mr. Nixon is also a certified birding tour guide. He can arrange for rental vehicles, and generally point you in the right direction for all activities on Inagua.

🔒 **Warden Henry Nixon** ☎ 242/339-1616.

LONG ISLAND

Never more than 4 mi wide but close to 80 mi long, Long Island truly lives up to its name. The Queen's Highway traverses its length, through the Tropic of Cancer and some 35 settlements and farming towns. The island is known for its astonishing contrasts in geography, with chalk-white limestone cliffs, forested hillsides, mangrove swamps, and stark flatlands where salt is produced. Exposed to the open Atlantic, the east coast consists of black iridescent reefs, protected coves, long strands of shelling beaches, and craggy bluffs that drop precipitously into the deep blue sea. The tranquil west coast is composed of powdery-white beaches, wide open sandy flats, and calm turquoise bays.

Long Island was one of Columbus's early stopping-off places. In 1790, American Loyalists from the Carolinas brought their slaves to the island, where they built plantations and planted over 4,000 acres of cotton. The rich soil made crop growing more successful here than on any other Out Island, but with the abolition of slavery, the plantations failed. Agriculture, however, remains a thriving part of the local economy, where pothole farming is the favored method of growing corn, peas, squash, pineapples, bananas, and other fruits.

The island has blossomed as an Out Island jewel, with the population growing to over 5,000 residents in 2003, and tourism on the rise. Resort, diving, and snorkeling services have been enhanced in recent years, and vast unexplored bonefish flats are drawing anglers who enjoy remote fishing. Sailing enthusiasts will find Joe's Sound, sandwiched between Cape Santa Maria beach and Glenton Sound, a sheltered haven to rival any in the Bahamas. A sheltered deep-water marina in Clarence Town with fuel and other services has created more convenient boating access to the southern islands.

Numbers in the margin correspond to points of interest on the Long Island map.

Cape Santa Maria & Stella Maris

★ ⑫ Columbus originally named the island's northern tip **Cape Santa Maria** in honor of one of his ships. He called the entire island Fernandina, out of respect for his Spanish sponsor. Cape Santa Maria is known for its irresistibly dazzling beaches, which are considered among the best in the country.

Take a side trip on the unpaved road out to **Columbus Cove,** 1½ mi north of the Cape Santa Maria resort. The monument and plaque that commemorate Columbus's landing are here, as well as tremendous views of the protected harbor he sailed into. Divers can explore the wreck of a ship, the M/V *Comberbach,* which lies just off the headland. The Stella Maris Resort sunk the leaky 103-foot freighter in 1985 to create an artificial reef and an excellent dive site nearly 100 feet under. The road to the cove is too rough for most vehicles, but it happens to be a fine walk. An easier way to reach the cove is by boat. Anglers can fish for bonefish and tarpon at the lower tidal stages.

⑬ **Stella Maris,** meaning Star of the Sea, lies about 12 mi south of Cape Santa Maria. It's home to the all-encompassing Stella Maris Resort Club, along with an airport. In a world of its own, the resort has a marina, yacht club, and tiny shopping complex, with a bank, a post office, and a general store. If you're interested in aquatic adventures, contact the resort, which runs numerous daily outings, including diving and fishing trips.

Shark Reef, about 4 mi west of Hog Cay, is easily reached by boaters from Cape Santa Maria and Joe's Sound. The water is startlingly clear, and the drop-off from the white-sand bottom to deep blue is a visual wonder. You can take a guided diving excursion and watch a scuba master safely feed groups of a dozen sharks at a time. Just north of Stella Maris, off Queen's Highway, are the ruins of the 19th-century **Adderley's Plantation.** Long Island was another Bahamian island where fleeing Loyalists attempted, with little success, to grow cotton. You can still see parts of the plantation's three buildings up to roof level. The remains of two other plantations, **Dunmore's** and **Gray's,** are also on the island.

Where to Stay & Eat

★ $$ ✕⊡ **Cape Santa Maria Beach Resort.** During the 1960s, the Du Ponts, Kelloggs, and Kennedys would hide out here in three lee "fishing cabins."

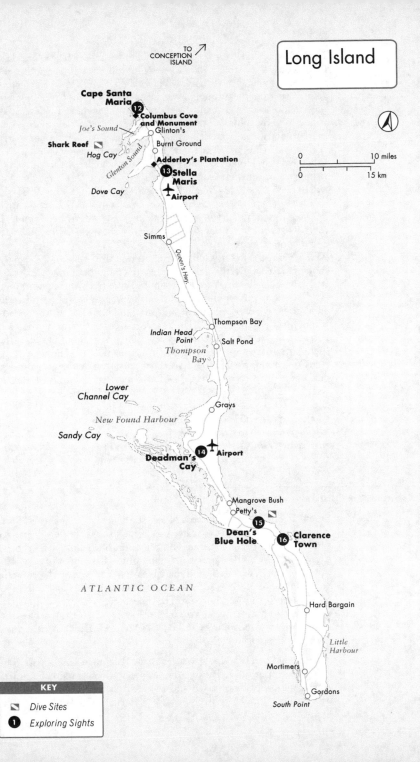

Now, this peaceful luxury resort has 10 colonial-style cottages spread along a gorgeous, 4-mi stretch of velvety white-sand beach. Spacious one- or two-bedroom units have their own large, fully furnished screened porches steps away from the turquoise water. The marble-floored reception building contains a small gym and TV room. A lovely mahogany staircase leads to the brightly colored dining room ($–$$), where you can dine on superb broiled lobster and delicious conch salads. Magenta sunsets are the trademark of the beachside bar. The fishing and watersports activities office arranges Hobie cat sailing, snorkeling, and deep-sea, reef, or bonefishing excursions. ⬡ *Oak Bay Marine Group, 1327 Beach Dr., Victoria, BC V8S 2N4* ☎ *242/338–5273 or 800/663–7090* 🖷 *242/338–6013 or 250/598–3366* ⊕ *www.capesantamaria.com* ⇲ *10 1- to 2-bedroom villas* ☖ *Restaurant, gym, beach, snorkeling, windsurfing, boating, waterskiing, fishing, bicycles, bar, shops, baby-sitting, laundry facilities; no room phones, no room TVs* ▭ *AE, D, MC, V.*

★ $ ✕▥ **Stella Maris Resort Club.** Sitting atop a hilly east-coast ridge overlooking the Atlantic, this sprawling resort's range of daily activities make it a Bahamian classic. You can swim in three freshwater pools, lounge on a series of private beaches, or explore sandy coves with excellent snorkeling. Dive, fish, hike, or take advantage of free morning and afternoon activity programs. The resort has colorful hillside rooms and cottages, and oceanfront houses, a few with private pools. Fresh seafood highlights the restaurant's ($–$$) rotating menus. The weekly cave party on Monday has buffet barbecue, music, and dancing set in a cavern on the property. ⬡ *1100 Lee Wagener Blvd., No. 310, Fort Lauderdale, FL 33315* ☎ *242/338–2051 or 800/426–0466* 🖷 *242/338–2052* ⊕ *www.stellamarisresort.com* ⇲ *20 rooms, 12 1-bedroom cottages, 7 2-bedroom cottages, 4 beach houses* ☖ *Restaurant, grocery, some kitchenettes, refrigerators, 3 pools, dive shop, snorkeling, boating, marina, waterskiing, fishing, bicycles, billiards, Ping-Pong, bar, recreation room, shop, complimentary weddings, laundry service; no room phones, no room TVs* ▭ *AE, D, MC, V.*

Simms & South

Simms is one of Long Island's oldest settlements, 8 mi south of Stella Maris past little pastel-color houses. Some of these homes display emblems to ward off evil spirits, an indication of the presence of obeah, the voodoolike culture found on many of the Bahamian islands. There are a few quirky eats to be had roadside on this stretch of Queen's Highway. On the road's east side, look for a small conch-salad stand that's intermittently open and prepares the snack right before your eyes. Immediately south of Simms, you may see rising smoke and tables out in the front yard of **Jeraldine's Jerk Pit** (☎ No phone). The barbecued chicken and pork are delectable.

The annual Long Island Regatta, featuring Bahamian-made boats, is held in **Salt Pond** every June. The regatta is the island's biggest event, attracting contestants from all over the islands. Three days of partying and pig roasts are sparked at night by lively local bands. Salt Pond is 10 mi south of Simms.

⑭ The town of **Deadman's Cay** is the island's largest settlement. Here you'll find a few shops, churches, and schools. Just east of Deadman's Cay, **Cartwright's Cave** has stalactites and stalagmites and eventually leads to the sea. The cave has apparently never been completely explored, although Arawak drawings were found on one wall. For guided cave tours, contact Leonard Cartwright (☎ 242/337–0235). There are several other caves, supposedly pirate-haunted, around Simms, Millers, and Salt Pond; a local should be able to point you in the right direction.

Between Deadman's Cay and Clarence Town, just past the settlement of Petty's, watch for the pink-and-white pillars that line the turnoff for
⑮ **Dean's Blue Hole.** At 660 feet, it's thought to be the world's second deepest blue hole. Curious divers will want to contact the dive shop at Stella Maris (☎ 242/338–2050).

⑯ **Clarence Town** has Long Island's most celebrated landmarks, **St. Paul's Church** (Anglican) and **St. Peter's Church** (Catholic). They were both built by Father Jerome, a priest who is buried in a tomb in the Hermitage atop Cat Island's Mt. Alvernia. As an Anglican named John Hawes, he constructed St. Paul's. Later, after converting to Catholicism, he built St. Peter's. The architecture of the two churches is similar to that of the missions established by the Spaniards in California in the late 18th century. Clarence Town is simply gorgeous, fringed by white-sand beaches, and fronted by a stunning oval-shape bay of clear aqua-blue water dotted with coral heads, sand bars, and small green cays. The harbor is also home to the local government headquarters and dock.

Where to Stay & Eat

¢–$ ✕ **Earlie's Tavern.** The Knowles family runs this dining room, bar, and pool room. Try the delicious lobster, grouper, or cracked conch. Burgers, sandwiches, and boxed fishing lunches are made to order. This is a lively night spot some weekends, and the place rocks on occasional special events, including the Long Island Regatta. ⊠ *Queen's Hwy., Mangrove Bush* ☎ *242/337–1628* ▤ *No credit cards.*

¢–$ ✕ **Kooters.** Grab a seat on the deck at this casual spot for a lovely view of Mangrove Bush Point and watch bonefish and tarpon cruise the adjacent shallow flat. Enjoy a conch burger, club sandwich with homemade fries, or a cold Kalik. Daily specials range from ribs to seafood. Save room for one of the many flavors of ice cream. ⊠ *Queen's Hwy., Mangrove Bush* ☎ *242/337–0340* ▤ *No credit cards* ✆ *Closed Sun.*

¢–$ ✕ **Max's Conch Grill and Bar.** If you sit all day on a stool at this pink-, green-, and yellow-striped roadside gazebo, nursing beers and nibbling on conch, you'll become a veritable expert on Long Island and the life of its residents. Such is the draw of this laid-back watering hole, open 9 to 9 daily, and sometimes later when the bar is hopping. Have a chat with Max while sampling his conch salad ($3.50 or $6), conch dumplings (6 for $1), or daily specials like baked ham and steamed pork. Pink conch shells line the free miniature golf course behind the gazebo; to the side is a general store. ⊠ *Deadman's Cay* ☎ *242/337–0056* ▤ *MC, V.*

★ $ ✕▦ **Chez Pierre Bahamas.** Six elevated cottages with generous bedrooms, bath, and airy screened porches line this secluded Millers Bay beach location, halfway between Stella Maris and Deadman's Cay.

Canadian owners Pierre and Anne deliver exceptional personalized service. Chef Pierre whips up fresh innovative dishes with homegrown ingredients and daily caught seafood in the relaxing oceanfront restaurant (¢–$$). Explore nearby cays in sea kayaks, wade the adjacent flats for bonefish, or schedule a diving adventure through the Stella Maris marina. Fishing guides, car rentals, and airport transfers can be arranged. *Box S-30811, Simms, Long Island* 🕾 *242/338–8809 or 242/464–2181* ⊕ *www.chezpierrebahamas.com* 🛏 *6 cottages* ⚭ *Restaurant, fans, beach, snorkeling, fishing, bicycles, bar, lounge, baby-sitting, Internet; no a/c, no room phones, no room TVs* 🖃 *AE, MC, V* ⦶ *MAP.*

¢ ✕⛶ **The Forest.** Just south of Clarence Town on the west side of the highway, this popular laid-back restaurant (¢–$$) serves spicy wings, potato skins, cracked conch, barbecued chicken, and grouper fingers in a large open room furnished with simple tables and chairs. Enjoy a drink at the bar—which is made of seashells embedded in glossy resin—and a game of pool. Every other weekend there's live music and dancing. Six spacious motel rooms are in a concrete building behind the bar. Each room has white-tile floors and bright wood furnishings, including two double beds, satellite TV, and a private bath. ⊠ *Queen's Hwy., Miley's* 🕾 *242/337–3287* 🖷 *242/337–3288* 🛏 *6 rooms* ⚭ *Restaurant, cable TV, bar; no room phones* 🖃 *No credit cards.*

$ ⛶ **Lochabar Beach Lodge.** Mellow and remote, the brightly painted two-story lodge consists of two thoughtfully constructed 600-square-foot guest studios downstairs that overlook a pristine beach and dramatic blue hole. There are dinette islands with stools, although you can also eat alfresco on your deck. The larger upstairs suite includes a full kitchen and private bedroom. At low tide, you can stroll the cove's entire beach and round the point into Clarence Town. You'll need to rent a car to stay here. Bonefishing guides and car rentals can be arranged by the management. ⊠ *1 mi south of Clarence Town.* *Box CB-13839, Nassau, Bahamas* 🕾 *242/337–3123 or 242/337–3124* 🖷 *242/337–6556* 🛏 *2 studios, 1 suite* ⚭ *Fans, kitchens/kitchenettes, snorkeling, fishing; no room a/c in upstairs suite* 🖃 *No credit cards.*

Nightlife

Just south of Clarence Town, **The Forest** (⊠ Queen's Hwy., Miley's 🕾 242/337–3287) has dancing and partying to live bands playing rock, Calypso, and reggae music every other weekend.

Shopping

Bonafide Tackle Shop and Cafe (⊠ Queen's Hwy., Stella Maris 🕾 242/338–2025) sells fly-fishing tackle and accessories, clothing, souvenirs, and snacks. You can book a fishing trip here, and arrange for fishing gear rental. Internet access is available.

Wild Tamarind (⊠ about ½ mi east of Queen's Hwy., Petty's 🕾 242/337–0262) is Denis Knight's ceramics studio. Stop in for a lovely bowl, vase, or sculpture, but call first in case he's out fishing.

Sports & the Outdoors

FISHING **Bonafide Bonefishing** (🕾 242/338–2025) is run by guide James "Docky"
★ Smith and his wife, Jill. Highly regarded as one of the best guides in the Bahamas, Docky conducts full- and half-day guided trips in his state-

of-the-art 16-foot Hewes flats skiffs, and also runs reef fishing trips. The operation is based out of Bonafide Tackle Shop and Cafe at Stella Maris, which rents conventional and fly-fishing gear, prepares snacks and box lunches, and sells a range of tackle, clothing, and flies.

The 15-slip **Flying Fish Marina** (✉ Lighthouse Point Road, Clarence Town ☎ 242/337–3430) in the northern corner of Clarence Town Harbour can take boats up to 130 feet. Bathrooms, showers, and laundry facilities are available to marina guests only. Bonefishing, reef, and off-shore guides can be arranged by the management with advance notice.

SCUBA DIVING For more information about these sites, or to arrange a dive, contact the Stella Maris Resort Club.

Dean's Blue Hole is lauded by locals as one of the world's deepest ocean holes. It's surrounded by a powder-beach cove. **Conception Island Wall** is an excellent wall dive, with hard and soft coral, plus interesting sponge formations. **Shark Reef** is the site of the Bahamas' first shark dive. The Stella Maris Resort has been running trips there for more than 25 years.

Long Island A to Z

AIR TRAVEL
Bahamasair flies most days from Nassau to Stella Maris and Deadman's Cay. Flights from Fort Lauderdale are available during the winter season. Stella Maris has charter flights from Exuma and Nassau to Stella Maris. If you're a pilot, the island is a great base for exploring other islands. Stella Maris rents well-maintained planes—a four-seat Piper Seneca and a six-seat Piper Navajo—for about $90 an hour. Island Wings, an air charter company owned by Captain Marty Fox, has charter flight service to and from any Bahamian island with a legal airstrip, and to and from Stella Maris or Deadman's Cay.

🛫 Airlines & Contacts **Bahamasair** ☎ 242/339–4415 or 800/222–4262. **Island Wings** ☎ 242/338–2022 or 242/357–1021. **Stella Maris** ☎ 800/426–0466, 954/359–8236, or 242/338–2051 ⊕ www.stellamarisresortairservice.com.

AIRPORTS & TRANSFERS
If you're a guest at Cape Santa Maria or Stella Maris, fly into the Stella Maris airport. Use the Deadman's Cay airport if you're staying in Clarence Town. Landing at the wrong airport will mean a $120 cab ride—in which case, renting a car will save you money. Guests staying at Chez Pierre pay $25 one-way for the taxi from Stella Maris, and $35 one-way for the taxi from Deadman's Cay.

TRANSFERS Taxis meet incoming flights at both airports. From the Stella Maris airport, the fare to Stella Maris Resort is $4; to Cape Santa Maria, it's $40.

BOAT & FERRY TRAVEL
M/V *Mia Dean* makes a 12-hour weekly trip from Nassau to Clarence Town, on the island's south end. The boat leaves Nassau on Tuesday and returns on Thursday; the fare is $45 one-way. The M/V *Sherice M* leaves Nassau on Tuesday with stops in Salt Pond, Deadman's Cay, and

Seymour's. The return trip is on Friday. Travel time is 15 hours; the fare is $45 one way. For more information, contact the Dockmaster's Office at Potter's Cay, Nassau.

☎ **Boat & Ferry Information Dockmaster's Office** ☎ 242/393-1064.

BUSINESS HOURS

At Stella Maris Resort Club, the Bank of Nova Scotia is open Tuesday and Thursday 9:30–2, Friday 9:30–5. Farther south, the Deadman's Cay branch is open Monday–Thursday 9–1 and Friday 9–5. Royal Bank of Canada has a branch on Deadman's Cay; hours are Monday–Thursday 9–1 and Friday 9–5.

☎ **Bank of Nova Scotia** ☎ 242/338-2057 Stella Maris, 242/338-2002 Deadman's Cay. **Royal Bank of Canada** ☎ 242/337-1044.

CAR RENTAL

Taylor's Rentals rents high-quality cars for the most reasonable rates on the island. Hotels and lodges will also arrange for guests' automobile rental.

☎ **Local Agency Taylor's Rentals** ☎ 242/338-7001.

EMERGENCIES

Clarence Town, Deadman's Cay, and Simms each have their own police departments.

☎ **Police** ☎ 242/337-0999 Clarence Town, 242/337-0444 Deadman's Cay, 242/338-8555 Simms.

SAN SALVADOR

On October 12, 1492, Christopher Columbus disrupted the lives of the peaceful Lucayan Indians by landing on the island of Guanahani, which he named San Salvador. Apparently he knelt on the beach and claimed the land for Spain. (Skeptics of this story point to a study published in a 1986 *National Geographic* article in which Samana Cay, 60 mi southeast, is identified as the exact point of the weary explorer's landing.) Three monuments on the island commemorate Columbus's arrival, and the 500th anniversary of the event was officially celebrated here.

A 17th-century pirate named George Watling, who frequently sought shelter on the island, changed San Salvador's name to Watling's Island. The Bahamian government switched the name back to San Salvador in 1926.

The island is 12 mi long—roughly the length of Manhattan—and about 5 mi wide along the lake-filled portion of its interior. The Queen's Highway forms an oval that skirts the coastline. Most visitors come for the peaceful isolation and the diving; there are about 950 residents and over 50 dive sites. There is also world-renowned offshore fishing and good bonefishing.

Numbers in the margin correspond to points of interest on the San Salvador map.

Fernandez Bay to Riding Rock Point

In 1492, the inspiring sight that greeted Christopher Columbus by moonlight at 2 AM was a terrain of gleaming beaches and far-reaching forest. The peripatetic traveler and his crews—"men from Heaven," the locals called them—steered the *Niña, Pinta,* and *Santa María* warily among the coral reefs and anchored, so it is recorded, in **Fernandez Bay**. A cross erected in 1956 by Columbus scholar Ruth C. Durlacher Wolper Malvin stands at his approximate landing spot. Ms. Malvin's **New World Museum** (☎ No phone), near North Victoria Hill on the east coast, contains artifacts from the era of the Lucayans. Admission to the museum is free; it's open by appointment only (your hotel can make arrangements). An underwater monument marks the place where the *Santa María* anchored. Nearby, another monument commemorates the Olympic flame's passage on its journey from Greece to Mexico City in 1968.

Fernandez Bay is just south of what is now the main community of **Cockburn Town,** mid-island on the western shore. Queen's Highway encircles the island from Cockburn Town, where the weekly mail boat docks. This small village's narrow streets contain two churches, a commissioner's office, a police station, a courthouse, a library, a clinic, a drugstore, and a telephone station.

Columbus first spotted and made a record of **Riding Rock Point.** The area now serves as the home for the Riding Rock Inn, a popular resort for divers. Just north of the point is the island's other resort, the Club Med–Columbus Isle, at the foot of a gorgeous 2-mi-long beach. Riding Rock Point is about a mile north of Cockburn Town.

Where to Stay & Eat

★ $$$–$$$$ ✕▥ **Club Med–Columbus Isle.** The 80-acre village is billed as one of Club Med's most luxurious resorts, with state-of-the-art dive facilities, including three custom-made 45-foot catamarans and a decompression chamber. The buildings are painted brilliant blues, greens, yellows, pinks, and purples. All rooms have patios or balconies and handcrafted furniture. Guided bike tours introduce vacationers to island life beyond the resort. Unlike some Club Meds, this one caters primarily to upscale couples, and the atmosphere is more low-key than at most. With advance notice, nonguests can partake of the sumptuous buffet lunches and dinners ($$$–$$$$). ✉ *3 mi north of Riding Rock Point* 🖊 *40 W. 57th St., New York, NY 10019* ☎ *242/331–2000, 888/722–0697, or 800/258–2633* 🖷 *242/331–2458* ⊕ *www.clubmed.com* 🛏 *288 rooms* 🍴 *3 restaurants, refrigerators, 9 tennis courts, pool, gym, hair salon, massage, beach, dive shop, bicycles, lounge, nightclub, theater, laundry service, Internet, car rental* ▭ *AE, D, MC, V* 🍽 *All-inclusive.*

$ ✕▥ **Riding Rock Resort and Marina.** A diver's paradise, this motel-style resort offers three dives per day to pristine offshore reefs and a drop-off wall teeming with life. It's also the only place to stay on San Salvador if you want to manage your own activities. The inn's three buildings house rooms facing either the ocean or the freshwater pool. All rooms have washed-oak furniture and a sitting area with a table and

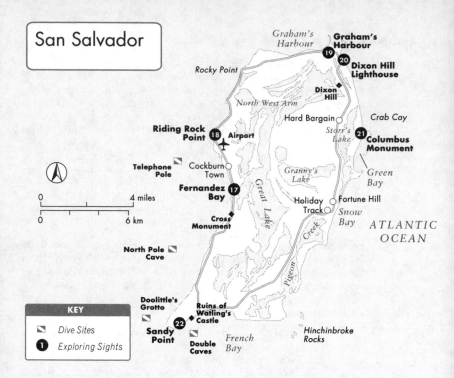

San Salvador

Graham's Harbour

Graham's Harbour

19

20 **Dixon Hill Lighthouse**

Rocky Point

Dixon Hill

North West Arm

Hard Bargain

Crab Cay

Riding Rock Point 18 **Airport**

Storr's Lake

21 **Columbus Monument**

Telephone Pole Cockburn Town

Granny's Lake

Green Bay

Fernandez Bay 17

Holiday Track

Fortune Hill

Snow Bay

ATLANTIC OCEAN

Cross Monument

Great Lake

North Pole Cave

Doolittle's Grotto

Ruins of Watling's Castle

22

Sandy Point

Double Caves

French Bay

Hinchinbroke Rocks

Pigeon Creek

0 — 4 miles

0 — 6 km

KEY

🗾 *Dive Sites*

❶ *Exploring Sights*

chairs; oceanside rooms have refrigerators and queen-size beds. The restaurant (¢–$$) serves grilled wahoo and tuna right off the boat as well as hearty pancake breakfasts. ⊠ *Riding Rock Point* 🕾 *1170 Lee Wagener Blvd., Suite 103, Fort Lauderdale, FL 33315* 🕿 *954/359–8353 or 800/272–1492* 🖷 *954/359–8254* ⊕ *www.ridingrock.com* ⇘ *42 rooms, 2 villas* ♿ *Restaurant, some refrigerators, cable TV, tennis court, pool, dive shop, fishing, bicycles, bar, Internet, car rental* ▭ *D, MC, V.*

Sports & the Outdoors

Club Med (🕿 242/331–2000) has dive boats and a decompression chamber. There is also tennis, sailing, and windsurfing, among other sports.

Riding Rock Inn (🕿 800/272–1492) is affiliated with Guanahani Dive Ltd., which uses mostly buoyed sites to avoid any damage caused to the marine environment by dropping anchor. It also offers resort and certification courses, and a modern underwater photographic facility. It rents all kinds of camera gear and does slide shows of divers' work. Riding Rock also rents bicycles and snorkel gear and will arrange fishing trips ($400 for a half day and $600 for a full day). The waters hold tuna, blue marlin, dorado, and, in the winter, wahoo.

Around San Salvador

19 Columbus describes **Graham's Harbour** in his diaries as large enough "to hold all the ships of Christendom." A complex of buildings near the harbor houses the **Bahamian Field Station,** a biological and geological research institution that attracts scientists and students from all over the world.

20 A couple of miles south of Graham's Harbour stands **Dixon Hill Lighthouse.** Built around 1856, it is still hand operated. The lighthouse keeper must wind the apparatus that projects the light, which beams out to sea every 15 seconds to a maximum distance of 19 mi, depending on visibility. A climb to the top of the 160-foot landmark offers a fabulous view of the island, which includes a series of inland lakes. The keeper is present 24 hours a day. Knock on his door, and he'll take you up to the top and explain the machinery. Drop $1 in the box when you sign the guest book on the way out.

21 No road leads to the **Columbus Monument** on Crab Cay; you have to make your way along a bushy path. This initial tribute to the explorer was erected by the *Chicago Herald* newspaper in 1892, far from the presumed site of Columbus's landing. A series of little villages—Polly Hill, Hard Bargain, Fortune Hill, Holiday Track—winds south of here for several miles along Storr's Lake. You can still see the ruins of several plantations, and the deserted white-sand beaches on this eastern shore are some of the most spectacular in the islands. A little farther along is Pigeon Creek, which is a prime spot for bonefishing.

22 **Sandy Point** anchors the island's southwestern end, overlooking French Bay. Here, on a hill, you'll find the **ruins of Watling's Castle,** named after the 17th-century pirate. The ruins are more likely the remains of a Loyalist plantation house than a castle from buccaneering days. A five- to ten-minute walk from Queen's Highway will take you to see what's left of the ruins, which are now engulfed in vegetation.

Sports & the Outdoors

SCUBA DIVING For more information about these and other sites, contact the Riding Rock Inn, or visit ⊕ www.ridingrock.com

Doolittle's Grotto is a popular site featuring a sandy slope down to 140 feet. There are lots of tunnels and crevices for exploring, and usually a large school of horse-eye jacks to keep you company. **Double Caves,** as the name implies, has two parallel caves leading out to a wall at 115 feet. There's typically quite a lot of fish activity along the top of the wall. **North Pole Cave** has a wall that drops sharply from 40 feet to more than 150 feet. Coral growth is extensive, and you might see a hammerhead or two. **Telephone Pole** is a stimulating wall dive where you can watch stingrays, grouper, snapper, and turtles in action.

San Salvador A to Z

AIR TRAVEL

Air Sunshine flies from Fort Lauderdale into Cockburn Town. Riding Rock Inn has charter flights every Saturday from Fort Lauderdale.

American Eagle flies from Miami on the weekends. Bahamasair flies into Cockburn Town from Nassau and also offers direct service from Miami three days a week.

🛪 **Airlines & Contacts Air Sunshine** ☎ 954/434-8900 or 800/327-8900. **American Eagle** ☎ 800/433-7300 ⊕ www.aa.com **Bahamasair** ☎ 242/339-4415 or 800/222-4262. **Riding Rock Inn** ☎ 800/272-1492 or 954/359-8353.

AIRPORTS & TRANSFERS

TRANSFERS Taxis meet arriving planes at Cockburn Town Airport. Club Med meets all guests at the airport (your account is charged $10 for the three-minute transfer). Riding Rock provides complimentary transportation for guests.

BIKE TRAVEL

🛪 **Bike Rentals Riding Rock Inn** ☎ 800/272-1492 or 954/359-8353 rents bicycles for $8 a day.

BOAT & FERRY TRAVEL

M/V *Lady Francis,* out of Nassau, leaves Tuesday for San Salvador and Rum Cay. The trip takes 12 hours, and the fare is $40 one-way. The return trip is on Sunday. For information on specific schedules and fares, contact the Dockmaster's Office at Potter's Cay, Nassau.

🛪 **Boat & Ferry Information Dockmaster's Office** ☎ 242/393-1064.

CAR RENTAL

🛪 **Riding Rock Inn** ☎ 800/272-1492 or 954/359-8353 rents cars for $85 a day.

EMERGENCIES

🛪 **Medical Clinic** ☎ 207. **Police** ☎ 218.

OUT ISLANDS A TO Z

To research prices, get advice from other travelers, and book travel arrangements, visit ⊕ *www.fodors.com.*

EMERGENCIES

There are health centers and clinics scattered throughout the islands, but in the event of emergency, illnesses, or accidents requiring fast transportation to the United States, AAPI Air Ambulance Services provides aero-medical services out of Fort Lauderdale Executive Airport. Its three jet aircraft are equipped with sophisticated medical equipment and a trained staff of nurses and flight medics.

🛪 **AAPI Air Ambulance Services** ☎ 954/491-0555 or 800/752-4195.

TOURS & PACKAGES

Florida Yacht Charters, at the high-tech Boat Harbour Marina in Marsh Harbour, offers an endless supply of boats (trawlers, sailboats, and catamarans with inflatable dinghies) and amenities, such as air-conditioning, refrigeration, and GPS. Licensed captains, instruction, and provisioning are also available. For captained yacht charters, contact The Moorings in Marsh Harbour. This is the Bahamas' division of one of the largest yacht-charter agencies in the world, which provides many services needed for yachties, from provisions to professional captains.

Swift Yacht Charters also has yacht charters. If you're looking for a guided kayak tour, call Ibis Tours.

Tour-Operator Recommendations In the United States: **Changes in L'Attitudes** 3080 East Bay Dr., Largo, FL 33771 727/573-3536 or 800/330-8272 www.changes.com. **Florida Yacht Charters** 305/532-8600 or 800/537-0050 www.floridayacht.com. **Future Vacations** 110 E. Broward Blvd., Box 1525, Fort Lauderdale, FL 33301 954/522-1440 or 800/456-2323 954/357-4687. **Ibis Tours** Box 208, Pelham, NY 10803 800/525-9411 www.ibistours.com. **The Moorings** Box AB-20469, Marsh Harbour, Abaco 242/367-4000 or 800/535-7289 www.go-abacos.com/conchinn/moorings. **Swift Yacht Charters** 209 S. Main St., Sherborn, MA 01770 800/866-8340 or 508/647-1554 www.swiftyachts.com. In Canada: **Americanada** 139 Sauve O, Montréal, Québec H3L LY4 514/384-6431 or 800/361-8242. **Holiday House** 110 Richmond St. E, Suite 304, Toronto, Ontario M5C 1P1 416/364-2433.

VISITOR INFORMATION

The Bahama Out Islands Promotion Board has a fantastic staff that provides information about lodging, travel, and activities in the islands and can book reservations at many of the hotels. On request, the board will send color brochures about island resorts.

The Bahamas Ministry of Tourism's Bahamas Tourist Office can assist with travel plans and information.

The best overall Web sites for information on all the islands are the Ministry of Tourism and the Out Island Promotion Board's Web sites. Also try www.bahamasvg.com and www.bahamasnet.com. The best site for planning a fishing vacation is www.bahamasflyfishingguide.com.

Tourist Information Bahama Out Islands Promotion Board 19495 Biscayne Blvd., Suite 809, Aventura, FL 33180 305/931-6612 or 800/688-4752 305/931-6867 www.bahama-out-islands.com. **Bahamas Tourist Office** Box N-3701, Market Plaza, Bay St., Nassau 242/322-7500 242/328-0945 www.bahamas.com.

TURKS &
CAICOS ISLANDS

REEL IN A WAHOO
in the waters off Provo ⇨*p.234*

DISCOVER UNSPOILED BEACHES
on Big Sand Cay ⇨*p.225*

SEE WHAT EXCLUSIVITY MEANS
at Parrot Cay Resort ⇨*p.238*

FIND UNDERWATER WONDERS
at Smith's Reef ⇨*p.234*

PLAY A FEW ROUNDS
at Provo Golf & Country Club ⇨*p.235*

GET AWAY FROM IT ALL
at Windmills Plantation ⇨*p.225*

Updated by
Kathy Borsuk

SPORTFISHERMEN, SCUBA DIVERS, and beach aficionados have long known about the Turks & Caicos (pronounced *kay*-kos). To them this British Crown colony of more than 40 islands and small cays (only 10 of which are inhabited) is a gem that offers dazzling turquoise seas, priceless stretches of fine ivory sand, and reefs rich in marine life. Whether you're swimming with the fishes or attempting to catch them from the surface, the Turks & Caicos won't disappoint. In an archipelago 575 mi (927 km) southeast of Miami and 90 mi (145 km) north of Haiti, the total landmass of these two groups of islands is 193 square mi (500 square km); the total population around 25,000.

Inhabited islands in the Turks chain include Grand Turk, which is the capital and seat of government, and Salt Cay. It's claimed that Columbus's first landfall was at Guanahani Beach on Grand Turk. Legend also has it that these islands were named by early settlers who thought the scarlet blossoms on the local cactus resembled the Turkish fez.

Approximately 22 mi (35½ km) west of Grand Turk, across the 7,000-foot-deep Columbus Passage, is the Caicos group: South, East, West, Middle, and North Caicos and Providenciales (nicknamed Provo). All but East Caicos are now inhabited, along with Pine, Parrot, and Ambergris Cays. "Caicos" is derived from *cayos,* the Spanish word for "cay" and is believed to mean, appropriately, "string of islands."

In the mid-1600s, Bermudians began to rake salt from the salinas on the Turks Islands, returning to Bermuda to sell their crop. Despite French and Spanish attacks and pirate raids, the Bermudians persisted and established a trade that became the bedrock of the islands' economy. In 1766 Andrew Symmers settled here to hold the islands for England. The American Declaration of Independence left British loyalists from South Carolina and Georgia without a country, causing many to take advantage of British Crown land grants in the Turks & Caicos. Cotton plantations were established and prospered for nearly 25 years until the boll weevil, soil exhaustion, and a terrible hurricane in 1813 devastated the land. Left behind to make their living off the land and sea were the former slaves, who remained to shape the islands' culture.

Today the Turks & Caicos are known as a reputable offshore tax haven whose company formation, banking, trusts, and insurance institutions lure investors from North America and beyond. Provo, in particular, is becoming a popular Caribbean tourist destination, and real-estate sales—especially for luxury beachfront condominiums—are booming. Mass tourism, however, shouldn't be in the cards; government guidelines promote a quality, not quantity policy, including conservation awareness. However, at this writing—and for the first time—regular cruise ship stops were scheduled to begin in Grand Turk in mid-2004. If proposed plans come to fruition, Grand Turk's quaint, quiet atmosphere is likely to change drastically.

WHAT IT COSTS In U.S. dollars				
$$$$	**$$$**	**$$**	**$**	**¢**
RESTAURANTS				
over $30	$20–$30	$12–$20	$8–$12	under $8
HOTELS				
EP, BP, AND CP over $350	$250–$350	$150–$250	$80–$150	under $80
AI, FAP over $450	$350–$450	$250–$350	$125–$250	under $125

Restaurant prices are for a main course at dinner and do not include 10% tax. EP, BP, and CP prices are per night for a standard double room in high season, excluding 10% tax, 10%–15% service charge, and meal plans. AI (all-inclusive) and FAP (full American plan) prices are per night for two people during high season, excluding 10% tax and 10%–15% service charges.

THE TURKS

Grand Turk

Bermudian colonial architecture abounds on this string bean of an island (just 7 mi [11 km] long and 1½ mi [2½ km] wide). Buildings have walled-in courtyards to keep wandering horses from nibbling on the foliage. The island caters to divers, and it's no wonder: the Wall, a slice of vertical coral mountain, is less than 300 yards from the beach.

Where to Stay

Throughout the islands, accommodations range from small (sometimes non-air-conditioned) inns to splashy resorts and hotels that are the ultimate in luxury. Most medium and large hotels offer a choice of EP and MAP. Almost all hotels offer dive packages, which are an excellent value.

$$ 🏨 **The Arches of Grand Turk.** If you're looking for a home away from home, these immaculate vacation town houses offer space, privacy, and a loving touch. Each of the four two-story suites is fully furnished in clean-cut country style. Kitchen–dining areas are on the lower levels, with two huge, air-conditioned bedrooms upstairs. Arched balconies front and back promise breathtaking sunrises and sunsets. Since the buildings sit atop the ridge northeast of town, steady breezes are refreshing, and there's an eagle's-eye view of the island. The new pool–patio with adjoining covered gazebo shares the view and is an ideal place to cook dinner on one of the grills. ⊠ *Lighthouse Rd., Box 226* 📞📞 *649/946–2941* ⊕ *www. grandturkarches.com* 🛏 *4 town houses* ⚴ *BBQs, fans, kitchens, cable TV with movies, pool, bicycles, laundry facilities* ☴ *D, MC, V* ⊙ *EP.*

$$ 🏨 **Island House.** Perched on a breezy hill overlooking North Creek, about 1 mi (1½ km) outside of town, this Mediterranean-style all-suites inn offers romantic comfort and panoramic views from large porches. Gas-powered golf carts are provided free of charge so you can get around easily. Relax in the expansive, palm-shaded pool–patio area with barbecue grill. Fishing from the dock and bird-watching are popular at this peaceful retreat, and kayaks, small sailboats, and dive packages are available for more active types. ⊠ *Lighthouse Rd., Box 36* ☎ *649/946–1519* 🖶 *649/946–2646* ⊕ *www.islandhouse-tci.com* ◆ *8 suites* ⚥ *BBQs, kitchenettes, cable TV with movies, pool, dock, fishing, bicycles, laundry facilities, Internet, some pets allowed* ▤ *AE, D, MC, V* ⍾ *EP.*

$–$$ ⊡ **Turks Head Hotel.** Although thoroughly modernized, the historical Turks Head Hotel has maintained its romantic charm and tranquil ambience—so much so that it has served as a filming location for several movies. The two-story structure, filled with antique furnishings, was built in 1823 as the home of a prosperous shipwright and has also served as the American consulate and governor's guest house. Rooms are a comfortable blend of old and new, with a coffeemaker and minibar beside the canopied four-poster bed. The hotel bar and Calico Jack's restaurant bustle at night; the beach is only a few strides away, and dive packages are available. ⊠ *Duke St., Box 58, Cockburn Town* ☎ *649/946–2466* 🖶 *649/946–1716* ⊕ *www.grand-turk.com* ◆ *7 rooms* ⚥ *Restaurant, some minibars, cable TV with movies, golf privileges, beach, bicycles, pub* ▤ *D, MC, V* ⍾ *CP.*

$ ⊡ **Salt Raker Inn.** Across a quaint, foliage-lined street from the beach, this inn—once the home of a Bermudian shipwright—was built in the early 19th century. The rooms are clean and comfortable, all with the original pine floors. Upstairs suites have balconies overlooking the ocean; lush tropical gardens at back envelop the Secret Garden restaurant. Hotel service is unpretentious and friendly. ⊠ *Duke St., Box 1, Cockburn Town* ☎ *649/946–2260* 🖶 *649/946–2263* ⊕ *www.saltraker.com* ◆ *10 rooms, 3 suites* ⚥ *Restaurant, refrigerators, cable TV, bicycles, bar, Internet, some pets allowed* ▤ *D, MC, V* ⍾ *EP.*

¢–$ ⊡ **Osprey Beach Hotel.** Rooms in this two-story oceanfront building open onto a private verandah overlooking the beach; there are airy cathedral ceilings on the top floors. Deluxe units have king-size four poster beds; suites include sitting rooms and full kitchens. The pool bar–restaurant serves drinks, tapas, and barbecue specials to the sound of breaking waves just steps away. A pleasant touch is the lush foliage lining the walkways. ⊠ *Duke St., Box 1, Cockburn Town* ☎ *649/946–2888* 🖶 *649/946–2817* ⊕ *www.ospreybeachhotel.com* ◆ *28 rooms* ⚥ *Restaurant, some kitchens, some kitchenettes, cable TV with movies, golf privileges, pool, beach, snorkeling, bar, meeting rooms, some pets allowed* ▤ *AE, MC, V* ⍾ *EP.*

Where to Eat

Like everything else on these islands, dining out is a very laid-back affair, which is not to say it's cheap. Because of the high cost of importing all edibles, the price of a meal is higher than in the United States. Reservations are generally not required, and dress tends to be casual.

AMERICAN   ✗ **Water's Edge.** This pleasantly rustic eatery would have to float to be
$$–$$$ any closer to the ocean. Here you'll find conch served in any way, shape, or form—conch salad, cracked conch, conch creole, curried conch, and even conch po'boys. Other choices include giant, juicy "Goo" burgers, grouper sandwiches, steak, local lobster, made-from-scratch pizza, and homemade pies. A two-story, shaded deck makes it even more comfortable

TO BAHAMAS

Caicos Passage

Three Mary's Cays

⑬

Parrot Cay

⑧

⑦

⑥

㊹ - ㊻

Spanish
Point

Highas
Cay

Platico
Point

Haulover Point

**Football
Fields** Fort George Cay

Northwest
Point

Pine Cay

Little Water Cay

**North
Caicos**

*Juniper
Hole*

㊼

⑨

Providenciales

Grace Bay

㊷

⑤ ③ ④

Southwest
Bluff

Juba Point

Middle Caicos

Long Bay

Joe Gran

⑭ - ㊸

*Ocean
Hole*

Vine Point

Toll Crawl
Point

East C

**West
Caicos**

C A I C O S   I S L A N D S

Big Southern
Bush

Big Cameron Cay

Southwest Reef

Sail Rock Isl

Horse

Molasses Reef

C A I C O S

Six Hill Cays

Long Cay

B A N K

Fish Cays

Little
Ambergris
Cay

Big Amberg

AMBERGRIS CAYS

SEAL CAYS

White Cay   Shot Cay   Bush Cay

0   15 miles

0   20 km

Turks & Caicos Islands

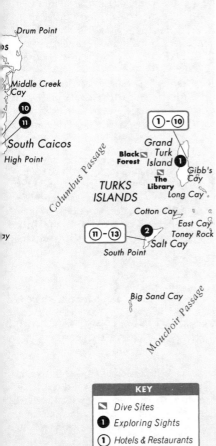

ATLANTIC OCEAN

Drum Point

Middle Creek Cay

10
11

South Caicos

High Point

Columbus Passage

TURKS ISLANDS

Black Forest

The Library

Grand Turk Island **1**

Gibb's Cay

Long Cay

Cotton Cay

①-⑬ **2**

East Cay
Toney Rock
Salt Cay

South Point

Big Sand Cay

Mouchoir Passage

KEY

◹ Dive Sites
1 Exploring Sights
① Hotels & Restaurants

to dine by the sea. ⊠ *Duke St., Cockburn Town* ☎ *649/946–1680* ⊟ *MC, V* ⊘ *Closed Sun.*

CAFÉS ✗ **Courtyard Café.** Homemade waffles with fresh fruit and whipped
¢–$ cream? Huge omelets and blueberry muffins? Submarine sandwiches and
pasta salad? It's all at this casual café, where you can enjoy your meal
in the cool shade of the garden courtyard. Prices are reasonable, and
daily specials range from lasagna and quiche to island-style beef pat-
ties. ⊠ *Duke St., Cockburn Town* ☎ *649/946–1453* ⊟ *AE, MC, V.*

ECLECTIC ✗ **Calico Jack's.** The menu changes daily at this lively restaurant—touted
$$–$$$ by many residents as the best on the island—in the Turks Head Hotel.
Look for lobster, steaks, chicken curry, lamb shanks, pizza, and homemade soups on the menu, as well as an excellent selection of wines. On
Friday nights there's a courtyard barbecue, with live music by local musicians. The English pub is usually abuzz with local gossip and mirth-
ful chatter. ⊠ *Turks Head Hotel, Duke St., Cockburn Town* ☎ *649/*
946–2466 ⊟ *D, MC, V.*

SEAFOOD ✗ **Secret Garden.** Menu highlights at the Salt Raker Inn's restaurant in-
$–$$$ clude local conch and fish dishes, grilled lobster tail, and a different in-
ternational specialty every night. For dessert try the Caribbean bread
pudding or key lime pie. Morning offerings include a full English break-
fast and an island favorite, fish-and-grits. ⊠ *Salt Raker Inn, Duke St.,*
Cockburn Town ☎ *649/946–2260* ⊟ *MC, V.*

¢–$ ✗ **Regal Begal.** Drop by this local eatery for island specialties such as
cracked conch, minced lobster, and fish-and-chips. It's a casual place with
unmemorable decor, but the portions are large and the prices easy on
your wallet. ⊠ *Hospital Rd., Cockburn Town* ☎ *649/946–2274* ⊟ *No*
credit cards.

Beaches

There are more than 230 mi (370 km) of beaches in the Turks & Caicos
Islands, ranging from secluded coves to miles-long stretches, and most
beaches are soft coralline sand. Tiny cays offer complete isolation for
nude sunbathing and skinny-dipping. Many are accessible only by boat.

★ **Governor's Beach,** a long white strip on the west coast of Grand Turk,
is one of the island's nicest, with plenty of sparkling, powder-soft sand
on which to stroll.

Sports & the Outdoors

CYCLING The island's flat terrain isn't very taxing, and most roads have hard sur-
faces. Take water with you: there are few places to stop for refreshment.
Most hotels in Cockburn Town, Grand Turk's only town, have bicycles
available, but you can also rent them for $10 to $15 a day from **Sea Eye**
Diving (⊠ Duke St., Cockburn Town ☎☎ 649/946–1407 ⊕ www.
seaeyediving.com).

DIVING & In these waters you can find undersea cathedrals, coral gardens, and count-
SNORKELING less tunnels, but note that you must carry and present a valid certificate
★ card before you'll be allowed to dive. As its name suggests, the **Black**
Forest offers staggering black-coral formations as well as the occasional
black-tip shark. In the **Library** you can study fish galore, including large

numbers of yellowtail snapper. At the Columbus Passage separating South Caicos from Grand Turk, each side of a 22-mi-wide (35-km-wide) channel drops more than 7,000 feet. From January through March, thousands of Atlantic humpback whales swim through en route to their winter breeding grounds.

Dive outfitters can all be found in Cockburn Town. Two-tank boat dives generally cost $60 to $75. **Blue Water Divers** (✉ Duke St., Cockburn Town 🕾 649/946–2432 ⊕ www.grandturkscuba.com) has been in operation on Grand Turk since 1983 and is the only PADI Gold Palm/5-Star Dive Center on the island. **Oasis Divers** (✉ Duke St., Cockburn Town 🕾 649/946–1128 ⊕ www.oasisdivers.com) specializes in complete gear handling and pampering treatment. It also supplies NITROX and rebreathers. Owner Everette Freites is a local authority on humpback whales and leads whale-watching trips in season. Besides daily dive trips to the Wall, **Sea Eye Diving** (✉ Duke St., Cockburn Town 🕾 649/946–1407 ⊕ www.seaeyediving.com) offers encounters with friendly stingrays on a popular snorkeling trip to nearby Gibbs Cay.

Nightlife

On weekends and holidays the younger crowd heads over to the **Nookie Hill Club** (✉ Nookie Hill 🕾 No phone) for late-night wining and dancing. There's folk and pop music at the **Osprey Beach Hotel** (✉ Duke St., Cockburn Town 🕾 649/946–2817) on Wednesday nights. A fun crowd gathers at **Turks Head Hotel** (✉ Duke St., Cockburn Town 🕾 649/946–2466) almost every night.

Exploring Grand Turk

Pristine beaches with vistas of turquoise waters, small local settlements, historic ruins, and native flora and fauna are among the sights on Grand Turk. Fewer than 5,000 people live on this 7½-square-mi (19-square-km) island, and it's hard to get lost, as there aren't many roads.

Numbers in the margin correspond to points of interest on the Turks & Caicos Islands map.

❶ **Cockburn Town.** The buildings in the colony's capital and seat of government reflect a 19th-century Bermudian style of architecture. Narrow streets are lined with low stone walls and old street lamps, now powered by electricity. The once-vital salinas have been restored, and covered benches along the sluices offer shady spots for observing wading birds, including flamingos that frequent the shallows. Be sure to pick up a copy of the Tourist Board's new Heritage Walk guide to discover Grand Turk's rich history.

In one of the oldest stone buildings on the islands, the **Turks & Caicos National Museum** houses the Molasses Reef wreck of 1513, the earliest shipwreck discovered in the Americas. The natural history exhibits include artifacts left by Taíno, African, North American, Bermudian, French, and Latin American settlers. An impressive addition to the museum is the coral-reef and sea-life exhibit, faithfully modeled on a popular dive site just off the island. ✉ *Duke St.* 🕾 *649/946–2160* 🖃 *$5* ☺ *Mon., Tues., Thurs., and Fri. 9–4, Wed. 9–5, Sat. 9–1.*

CloseUp
DIVING THE TURKS & CAICOS

S CUBA DIVING WAS THE ORIGINAL water sport to draw visitors to the Turks & Caicos Islands back in the early 1970s. The first dive operations were on South Caicos and through Art Pickering's fledgling operation on Provo. Aficionados were drawn by the abundant marine life, sparkling clean waters, warm and calm seas, and by the variety of walls and reefs around the Islands. Diving in the Turks & Caicos—especially off the out-islands of Grand Turk and Salt Cay—is still considered among the best in the world.

Off the most-visited island of Providenciales, dive sites are located along the barrier reef, which runs the length of the north shore and follows the curve of the island past West Caicos. Sites are anywhere from 2 to 15 mi out and take from 10 minutes to 1½ hours to reach. Dive sites in Grace Bay, which are within the Princess Alexandra National Park, feature spur and groove coral formations atop a coral-covered slope. Popular stops like Aquarium, Pinnacles, and Grouper Hole offer the opportunity to see large schools of fish, turtles, nurse sharks, and gray reef sharks. (There's a good chance you might encounter JoJo the dolphin here, as well. This national treasure has been swimming with visitors since the early 1980s.) Just east of Provo is Pine Cay, home to the Fort George Land & Sea Park. Two favorite sites here, the Football Field and Eagle Ray Pass, offer a diversity of sea life and corals.

Northwest Point Marine National Park is Provo's famous wall-diving area, where the spectacular wall starts at 40 feet and drops into the abyss that is 7,000 feet deep. Here, divers enjoy swim-throughs exiting at varying depths and a variety of formations including purple and yellow tube sponges and large fish.

From the south side of Provo, areas most commonly visited by dive boats are French Cay, West Caicos, South West Reef, and Northwest Point. Known for typically calm conditions and clear water, the West Caicos Marine National Park is a favorite stop. The area offers virgin diving, with dramatic walls and marine life including sharks, eagle rays, and octopus, with large stands of pillar coral and huge barrel sponges.

The island of Grand Turk is home to the Columbus Landfall National Park. Here, the wall drop-off is actually within swimming distance of the beach. Buoyed sites along the wall offer swim-through tunnels, cascading sand chutes, imposing coral pinnacles, dizzying vertical drops, and undercuts where the wall goes beyond the vertical and fades beneath the reef.

On nearby Salt Cay, the wall runs along the island's western shore, varying from a slope to a true precipice. Huge, deep water gorgonians grow along the wall, with stands of pillar coral erupting from the reef. A longer boat trip brings you to the shallow wreck site of the H.M.S. Endymion, a British warship that went down in 1790, with anchors, cannons, and ballast stones visible among a bright coral garden.

Each island is serviced by professional, experienced dive operators, all of whom have been in business for years. "Cattle boat" diving is virtually nonexistent among private operators; while a keen enthusiasm and desire to protect the Islands' environment are common.

Salt Cay

Fewer than 100 people live on this 2½-square-mi (6-square-km) dot of land, maintaining an unassuming lifestyle against a backdrop of quaint stucco cottages, stone ruins, and weathered wooden windmills standing sentry in the abandoned salinas. There's not much in the way of development, but there are splendid beaches on the north coast. The most spectacular sights are beneath the waves: 10 dive sites are just minutes from shore.

Where to Stay

For approximate costs, *see* the dining and lodging price chart at the beginning of this chapter.

★ **$$$$** ⊡ **Windmills Plantation.** The attraction here is the lack of distraction. The hotel resembles a romantic's version of a colonial-era plantation with over two miles of deserted beach. The greathouse has four suites, each with a sitting area, a four-poster bed, ceiling fans, and a verandah or balcony with a sea view. All are furnished in a mix of antique English and wicker furniture. Four other rooms are housed in adjacent buildings. Managers Jim and Sharon Shafer bring a sterling reputation as gracious hosts. ⊠ *North Beach Rd.* ☎ *649/946–6962or 800/225–4255* 🖷 *649/946–6930* ⊕ *www.windmillsplantation.com* 🛏 *4 rooms, 4 suites* 🖧 *Restaurant, pool, beach, snorkeling, fishing, hiking, horseback riding, bar, library; no a/c, no room phones, no room TVs, no kids, no smoking* 🖃 *AE, MC, V* ⦿ *AI.*

$–$$ ⊡ **Tradewinds Guest Suites.** A grove of whispering casaurina trees surrounds the single-story Tradewinds building, which houses large, bright, well-kept one-bedroom suites. Each includes a private screened patio overlooking the sea at Dean's Dock; a shared outdoor deck is the ideal spot for whale watching or sunbathing. All-inclusive meal–dive packages are available, although many guests enjoy cooking locally caught seafood in the well-equipped kitchens. You must pay extra to use the air-conditioning. ⊠ *Victoria St., Balfour Town* ☎ *649/946–6906* 🖷 *649/946–6940* ⊕ *www.tradewinds.tc* 🛏 *5 suites* 🖧 *Some kitchenettes, some kitchens, beach, snorkeling, fishing, bicycles; no room phones, no room TVs* 🖃 *MC, V* ⦿ *EP.*

$ ⊡ **Mount Pleasant Guest House.** This simple, somewhat rustic hotel was a former salt-plantation home, now serving as a guest house catering to divers. Rooms are bright, clean, and simply furnished. The premises are filled with memorabilia and artifacts, and the gazebo bar overlooks a cut-stone cistern pit converted into a palm grove for hammocks. Meals are superb, with dinners including whelk soup, grilled fresh fish and lobster, buttery cracked conch, and New York strip steaks. ⊠ *Balfour Town* ☎ *649/946–6927* ⊕ *www.turksandcaicos.tc/mtpleasant* 🛏 *7 rooms* 🖧 *Restaurant, fans, bicycles, horseback riding, bar, library; no a/c in some rooms, no room phones, no room TVs* 🖃 *MC, V* ⦿ *EP.*

Beaches

★ There are superb beaches on the north coast of **Salt Cay. Big Sand Cay,** 7 mi (11 km) south of Salt Cay, is also known for its long, unspoiled stretches of open sand.

Sports & the Outdoors

DIVING &
SNORKELING
Scuba divers can explore the *Endymion,* a 140-foot wooden-hull British warship that sank in 1790. It's off the southern point of Salt Cay. **Salt Cay Divers** (✉ Balfour Town ☎ 649/946–6906 ⊕ www.saltcaydivers. tc) conducts daily trips and rents all the necessary equipment. It costs around $80 for a two-tank dive.

Exploring Salt Cay

Numbers in the margin correspond to points of interest on the Turks & Caicos Islands map.

Salt sheds and salinas are silent reminders of the days when the island was a leading producer of salt. Island tours are often conducted by motorized golf cart. From January through March, whales pass by on the way to their winter breeding grounds.

 Balfour Town. What little development there is on Salt Cay is found here. It's home to several small hotels and a few stores that sell handwoven baskets, T-shirts, convenience foods, and beach items.

THE CAICOS

West Caicos

The 2003 dredging of the previously uninhabited island's natural harbor was the first step in the proposed "Isle of West Caicos" project. Construction is underway on a very exclusive island retreat centering around a harbor town (re-created with 18th-century atmosphere) and three coastal residential settlements. For many years the island was accessible only by boat, but developers have restored an old 3,000-foot airport runway.

Fortunately, offshore diving here remains among the most exotic in the islands. The "Wilds of West Caicos" encompass a pristine wall, about ¼ mi (½ km) from shore, which starts at 35 feet to 45 feet and cascades to 7,000 feet. Sharks, eagle rays, and turtles are commonly seen on the many dive sites. It's about an hour's boat ride from Provo, but well worth the trip. Most dive operators depart from satellite locations on the south side of Provo for the journey.

Providenciales

In the mid-18th century, so the story goes, a French ship was wrecked near here, and the survivors were washed ashore on an island they gratefully christened La Providentielle. Under the Spanish, the name was changed to Providenciales. Today about 18,000 people live on Provo (as everybody calls it); a considerable number are expatriate British, Canadian, and American businesspeople and retirees, or immigrants from nearby Haiti and the Dominican Republic. The island's 44 square mi (114 square km) are by far the most developed in the Turks and Caicos.

Along the beach-lined north shore there are no fewer than 18 high-end condominium hotels (some currently under construction) and three all-inclusive resorts. Shopping and business plazas in this area are also proliferating, as tourist activity concentrates in the popular Grace Bay "Gold Coast." Residential development is also booming, especially in the upscale Leeward and Chalk Sound areas. Although the long-awaited Leeward Highway expansion project is nearly finished, remaining roads are in desperate need of upgrading. Power, water, telecommunications, and cable TV utilities are modern and well serviced.

Where to Stay

For approximate costs, *see* the dining and lodging price chart at the beginning of this chapter.

VILLA RENTALS A popular option on Provo is renting a self-catering villa or private home. For the best villa selection, plan to make your reservations three to six months in advance.

Elliot Holdings & Management Company (🖂 Box 235 ☎ 649/946–5355 ⊕ www.elliotholdings.com) offers a wide selection of modest to magnificent villas in the Leeward, Grace Bay, and Turtle Cove areas of Providenciales. **T. C. Safari** (🖂 Box 64 ☎ 649/941–5043 ⊕ www.tcsafari. tc) has exclusive oceanfront properties in the beautiful and tranquil Sapodilla Bay–Chalk Sound neighborhood on Provo's southwest shores.

HOTELS & 🏨 **Beaches Turks & Caicos Resort & Spa.** There's plenty to satisfy fami-
RESORTS lies at this member of the Sandals chain, including a children's park com-
★ ☾ **$$$$** plete with a video-game center, water slides, a swim-up soda bar, a 1950s-style diner, and a teen disco. Nice rooms, lots of activities, extravagant meals, and many kinds of water sports (with scuba diving included in the price) make this beachfront all-inclusive resort an indulgent experience. Rooms range from quaint bungalow villas to chic French Village suites. Wedding packages are popular; honeymoon villas include a Jacuzzi in the bedroom. The full-service, European-style spa offers body wraps, massages, and facials. ⊠ *Lower Bight Rd., Grace Bay* ☎ *649/946–8000 or 800/726–3257* 🖷 *649/946–8001* ⊕ *www.beaches. com* ➷ *359 rooms, 103 suites* ☾ *9 restaurants, in-room safes, cable TV with movies, miniature golf, 4 tennis courts, 5 pools, 3 hot tubs, health club, hair salon, spa, beach, dive shop, snorkeling, windsurfing, boating, parasailing, fishing, bicycles, 12 bars, nightclub, recreation room, theater, video game room, shops, baby-sitting, children's programs (ages 0–5), concierge, meeting rooms, car rental* ▤ *AE, MC, V* ⊄⊙⊄ *AI.*

★ **$$$$** 🏨 **Grace Bay Club.** Every suite at the island's original luxury property has breathtaking views of stunning Grace Bay. Privacy and peaceful relaxation are encouraged throughout the foliage-rich grounds. Rooms, freshly upgraded in 2003, have Spanish tiles, rich woods, textured fabrics, and decorative pottery in keeping with the look of the gracious, Mediterranean-style resort. Due to be completed by 2005 are 30 ultraluxurious, beachfront condominiums. Activities range from diving to golf to catered picnics on surrounding islands, but relaxing remains the major pastime. Elegant European–Caribbean meals are served in the Anacaona restaurant with cocktails and tapas offered in the new oceanfront lounge. ⊠ *Grace Bay, Box 128* ☎ *649/946–5050 or 800/946–5757* 🖷 *649/946–5758* ⊕ *www.gracebayclub.com* ➷ *21 suites* ☾ *Restaurant, room service, in-room data ports, in-room fax, in-room safes, kitchens,* *cable TV with movies, in-room VCRs, 2 tennis courts, 2 pools, hot tub, spa, beach, snorkeling, windsurfing, boating, parasailing, bicycles, bar, shop, laundry service, concierge, Internet, business services; no kids under 12 ⊟ AE, D, MC, V ⊗ Closed Sept. ⌐◯∣ CP.*

★ **$$$$**   ⊞ **Point Grace.** This boutique hotel raises the bar for luxury resorts on the islands. Majestically designed in British colonial style, two ocean-front buildings house magnificent two- and three-bedroom suites. All have expansive terraces overlooking Grace Bay and are furnished with Indonesian hardwood and teak. Hand-painted tiles line the bathrooms, and Frette linens cover the king-size four-poster beds. The four-bedroom penthouse suite has a separate massage room and rooftop Jacuzzi. Spa services, including thalassotherapy, are offered in private cottages on the dunes overlooking the sea. ⊠ *Grace Bay, Box 700* ☎ *888/924–7223 or 649/946–5096* ☒ *649/946–5097* ⊕ *www.pointgrace.com* ⥽ *23 suites, 9 cottages, 2 villas* ⌂ *2 restaurants, room service, in-room fax, in-room safes, some in-room hot tubs, kitchenettes, microwaves, cable TV with movies, in-room VCRs, pool, spa, beach, snorkeling, windsurfing, boating, parasailing, fishing, bicycles, 2 bars, library, baby-sitting, laundry service, concierge, Internet, business services, car rental* ⊟ *AE, D, MC, V* ⊗ *Closed Sept.* ⌐◯∣ *CP.*

★ **$$$$**   ⊞ **Turks & Caicos Club.** Although its name and striking appearance conjure images of pretension, this luxury resort combines the intimacy of a private club with a comfortable atmosphere and warm hospitality. At the western end of Grace Bay, the wide, sandy beach here usually sees only the footprints of club guests. One- and two-bedroom suites occupy two colonial-style buildings sheltering a petal-shape pool; each has a spacious private verandah. The spotless rooms are elegantly designed in a safari theme, with raised four-poster beds swathed in wisps of mosquito netting. The gated property has already attracted high-powered guests and hosted magazine shoots. ⊠ *West Grace Bay Beach, Box 687, West Grace Bay* ☎ *800/269–0966 or 649/946–5800* ☒ *649/946–5858* ⊕ *www.turksandcaicosclub.com* ⥽ *21 suites* ⌂ *Restaurant, fans, in-room data ports, in-room safes, kitchens, cable TV, in-room VCRs, pool, gym, beach, snorkeling, windsurfing, bicycles, bar, laundry facilities* ⊟ *AE, D, MC, V* ⌐◯∣ *CP.*

$$$–$$$$ ⊞ **Club Med Turkoise.** This village is a major water-sports center, with scuba diving, windsurfing, sailing, and waterskiing on the turquoise waters at its doorstep. Two-story bungalows line a 1-mi (1½-km) beach, and all the usual sybaritic pleasures are here. The vibrant party atmosphere at this all-inclusive club is geared toward adults—whether couples of singles—and divers. There are also a flying trapeze, nightly entertainment, dive packages, and excursions offered to sites in the Turks & Caicos. ⊠ *Grace Bay* ☎ *649/946–5500 or 888/932–2582* ☒ *649/946–5497* ⊕ *www.clubmed.com* ⥽ *293 rooms* ⌂ *2 restaurants, cable TV with movies, 8 tennis courts, pool, health club, hot tub, massage, beach, dive shop, snorkeling, windsurfing, boating, fishing, bicycles, billiards, soccer, volleyball, 3 bars, dance club, theater, shops, laundry service; no kids* ⊟ *AE, D, MC, V* ⌐◯∣ *AI.*

★ **$$$–$$$$**   ⊞ **Coral Gardens.** This intimate beachfront resort fronts one of Provo's most popular snorkeling reefs and is in a tranquil area well west of bustling

Grace Bay. The deluxe suites have terraces and floor-to-ceiling walls of sliding glass. Gourmet kitchens open into the dining areas, and bedrooms and baths overlook the luxurious gardens. Fine dining alfresco is offered at Coyaba Restaurant, with creatively casual fare served at the Beach Café. The European-style Serenity Spa specializes in tropical indulgence. Other pluses include an on-site dive shop and car rental. At this writing, expansion plans for 2004 included 24 additional one-bedroom condominiums. ⊠ *Penn's Rd., Box 281, The Bight* ☎ *649/941–3713 or 800/532–8536* 🖳 *649/941–5171* ⊕ *www.coralgardens.com* 🛏 *30 suites* ⚒ *2 restaurants, room service, in-room data ports, in-room safes, kitchens, cable TV with movies, in-room VCRs, 2 pools, fitness classes, spa, beach, dive shop, snorkeling, boating, fishing, boccie, 2 bars, laundry facilities, concierge, Internet, car rental* ▭ *AE, MC, V* ⦿ *EP.*

★ **$$–$$$$** 🖭 **Ocean Club.** These luxury all-suites condominiums are on a 12-mi (19-km) stretch of pristine beach, a short walk from Provo's only golf course. Units range from efficiency studios with kitchenettes to three-bedroom suites with living rooms, dining rooms, kitchens, and screened balconies. Management and service are consistently superb. You can take a free shuttle to use the facilities of sister property Ocean Club West. The on-site Gecko Grille serves creative island dishes. ⊠ *Grace Bay, Box 240* ☎ *649/946–5880 or 800/457–8787* 🖳 *649/946–5845* ⊕ *www. oceanclubresorts.com* 🛏 *86 suites* ⚒ *2 restaurants, in-room data ports, in-room safes, some kitchens, some kitchenettes, cable TV with movies, in-room VCRs, golf privileges, tennis court, 2 pools, gym, spa, beach, dive shop, snorkeling, boating, 2 bars, shops, laundry facilities, concierge, Internet, meeting room, car rental* ▭ *AE, D, MC, V* ⦿ *EP.*

★ **$$–$$$$** 🖭 **Ocean Club West.** This sister property to the Ocean Club maintains signature details of the original—breathtaking seascapes, large balconies, and exquisite landscaping—while expanding the oceanfront central courtyard area to include a gazebo-capped island, winding free-form pool with a swim-up bar, and a seaside café. Interiors are decorated in subdued sophistication, utilizing whites, light woods, and wicker. Junior one-bedrooms and get-away packages are especially good values. ⊠ *Grace Bay, Box 640* ☎ *649/946–5880 or 800/457–8787* 🖳 *649/946–5845* ⊕ *www.oceanclubresorts.com* 🛏 *90 suites* ⚒ *1 restaurant, in-room data ports, in-room safes, some kitchens, some kitchenettes, cable TV with movies, in-room VCRs, golf privileges, tennis court, 2 pools, gym, spa, beach, dive shop, snorkeling, boating, bar, laundry facilities, concierge, Internet, meeting room, car rental* ▭ *AE, D, MC, V* ⦿ *EP.*

★ **$$–$$$$** 🖭 **Royal West Indies Resort.** Distinctive British colonial architecture and extensive gardens highlight this well-run luxury condominium resort. All condos have private balconies to make the most of the sea views; interiors are an eclectic blend of wood and fabrics from Central and South America. Although the beach is steps away, the 80-foot pool surrounded by tropical fruit trees is a peaceful place to relax and sip a drink from the superb on-site Mango Reef restaurant and bar. ⊠ *Grace Bay, Box 482* ☎ *649/946–5004 or 800/332–4203* 🖳 *649/946–5008* ⊕ *www. royalwestindies.com* 🛏 *99 suites* ⚒ *Restaurant, fans, in-room data ports, in-room safes, kitchenettes, cable TV with movies, 2 pools, beach,* *snorkeling, boating, fishing, bar, baby-sitting, laundry facilities, laundry service, car rental* ☰ *AE, MC, V* ⌾ *EP.*

★ **$$–$$$$** ⊡ **The Sands at Grace Bay.** "Simply breathtaking" describes the sparkling ocean views from the huge screened patios and floor-to-ceiling windows of units at this beach lover's haven. The upscale condominium resort offers accommodations ranging from studios to three-bedroom suites; larger suites have two TVs, extra sleeper sofas, and washer-dryers. Contemporary furnishings combine Indonesian wood, wrought iron, and wicker with seaside-tone fabrics to emphasize the resort's theme of sophisticated simplicity. Hemingway's, an excellent oceanfront cabana restaurant and bar, is on site. Look for senior discounts in May, June, September, and October. ✉ *Grace Bay, Box 681* ☎ *649/941–5199 or 877/777–2637* ⊟ *649/946–5198* ⊕ *www.thesandsresort.com* ✍ *118 suites* ⚹ *Restaurant, in-room data ports, in-room safes, some kitchens, some kitchenettes, microwaves, refrigerators, cable TV with movies, tennis court, 3 pools, gym, spa, beach, snorkeling, boating, bicycles, bar, shop, baby-sitting, laundry facilities, laundry service, concierge, car rental* ☰ *AE, MC, V* ⌾ *EP.*

$$ ⊡ **Harbour Club Villas.** Well off the beaten path, this tranquil enclave includes six individual 650-square-foot villas surrounded by beautiful natural landscaping. The site straddles peaceful Flamingo Lake and the ocean at the south-central shore's Discovery Bay, affording outstanding views and refreshing breezes. Many guests come to bonefish in the lake and nearby flats, or scuba dive from the adjoining marina. The cottages are cheerful and homelike with an open-plan living area, dining alcove, and fully equipped kitchen; separate bedrooms are air-conditioned. Owners Barry and Marta Morton are personable hosts, who will even drive guests on errands around the island. ✉ *Venetian Rd., Box 77, Discovery Bay* ☎☎ *649/941–5748* ⊕ *www.harbourclubvillas.com* ✍ *6 villas* ⚹ *Kitchens, cable TV, pool, dock, scuba diving, snorkeling, boating, fishing* ☰ *AE, MC, V* ⌾ *CP.*

$$ ⊡ **Sibonné.** Just steps from the peaceful waters and soft sand of Grace Bay Beach, this small, quiet "boutique hotel" is especially popular with honeymooners and older couples. Each comfortable room has a patio or balcony. They are built around a lush courtyard, where you'll find hammocks nestled among the trees. A circular pool overlooks the beach. Oceanfront Bay Bistro is known for its creative international cuisine, including tapas-style entrées and luscious chocolate desserts. With longtime island aficionados Ken and Sandra McLeod at the helm, hospitality is superb. ✉ *Grace Bay, Box 144* ☎ *649/946–5547 or 800/528–1905* ⊟ *649/946–5770* ⊕ *www.sibonne.com* ✍ *26 rooms, 1 apartment* ⚹ *Restaurant, in-room data ports, in-room safes, cable TV, pool, beach, snorkeling, boating, bicycles, bar, laundry service* ☰ *AE, MC, V* ⌾ *CP.*

$$ ⊡ **Comfort Suites.** Although Comfort Suites is the island's only "franchise" hotel, the property's exceptional hospitality makes it anything but standard. Suites are in two three-story buildings built around a landscaped pool and patio area; drinks are served at the tiki bar. Like the rest of the hotel, rooms are spotless and furnished in bright Caribbean colors. Grace Bay's pearly white beach is just across the street. The hotel flanks the Ports of Call shopping village. ✉ *Grace Bay, Box 590* ☎ *649/*

946–8888 or 888/678–3483 🖷 *649/946–5444* ⊕ *www.comfortsuitestci. com* ⇆ *100 suites* ⚇ *Fans, in-room data ports, in-room safes, refrigerators, cable TV with movies, pool, bar, shops, travel services* ☰ *AE, D, MC, V* ⧖ *CP.*

$ 🖼 **Turtle Cove Inn.** This pleasant two-story inn offers affordable and comfortable lodging. Next to Turtle Cove Marina, it's popular with divers, boaters, and fishing enthusiasts. All rooms include a private balcony or patio overlooking either the courtyard's lush tropical gardens and pool or the marina. Besides the dockside Aqua Bar & Terrace, the inn has a souvenir shop, liquor store, and local artisan's gallery. You can readily stroll to the snorkeling at Smith's Reef, and access the remaining miles of north shore beach from there. ⊠ *Turtle Cove Marina, Box 131, Turtle Cove* ☎ *649/946–4203 or 800/887–0477* 🖷 *649/946–4141* ⊕ *www. turtlecoveinn.com* ⇆ *28 rooms, 2 suites* ⚇ *Restaurant, in-room safes, refrigerators, cable TV with movies, pool, marina, fishing, bicycles, bar, shops, car rental, no-smoking rooms* ☰ *AE, D, MC, V* ⧖ *EP.*

Where to Eat

There are more than 50 restaurants on Provo, ranging from casual to elegant, with cuisine from Continental to Asian (and everything in between). You can spot the islands' own Caribbean influence no matter where you go, exhibited in fresh seafood specials, colorful presentations, and a tangy dose of spice.

For approximate costs, *see* the dining and lodging price chart at the beginning of this chapter.

CARIBBEAN ✕ **Mango Reef.** Third-generation restaurateur Doug Camozzi (of Tiki Hut
$$–$$$ fame) was determined to spotlight Caribbean ingredients when he created the menu for his newest venture, in the Royal West Indies Resort. The end result is a marvelous medley of flavors, colors, and textures made by marinating meats and seafood prior to grilling and pairing them with inventive fruit- and vegetable-based chutneys and salsas. Meals are served throughout the day, and the separate bar area is a popular evening spot for residents. ⊠ *Royal West Indies Resort, Grace Bay* ☎ *649/946– 8200* ☰ *AE, MC, V.*

¢–$ ✕ **Macky's Café.** This is where the locals go for their favorite fare, served hot and tasty from the impossibly small kitchen. Daily specials include steamed grouper, cracked conch, minced lobster, and barbecued ribs, all hearty helpings complete with peas 'n' rice, coleslaw, and fried plantains. You can enjoy a cold beer or soda along with your meal at the outdoor seating in the courtyard of a small shopping plaza. ⊠ *Leeward Hwy., The Market Place* ☎ *649/941–3640* ☰ No credit cards.

DELI ✕ **Top o' the Cove New York Style Delicatessen.** Order breakfast, deli
¢–$ sandwiches, salads, and enticingly rich desserts and freshly baked goods at this newly expanded island institution on Leeward Highway, just south of Turtle Cove. From the deli case you can buy the fixings for a picnic; the shop's shelves are stocked with an eclectic selection of fancy foodstuffs, as well as beer and wine. It's open at 6:30 AM for a busy trade in coffees, cappucinos, and frappacinos. ⊠ *Leeward Hwy., Turtle Cove* 🖷 *649/946–4694* ☰ No credit cards ⊗ No dinner.

ECLECTIC ✕ **Anacaona.** At the Grace Bay Club, this *palapa*-style restaurant (with
★ **$$$–$$$$** tables clustered under large thatched-roof structures) offers a memorable
dining experience minus the tie, the air-conditioning, and the attitude.
Start with a bottle of fine wine and then enjoy the chef's light and
healthy Mediterranean cuisine, which utilizes the island's bountiful
seafood and fresh produce. Oil lamps on the tables, gently circulating
ceiling fans, and the murmur of the trade winds add to the Eden-like
environment. The elegant atmosphere, entrancing ocean view, and care-
ful service make it an ideal choice when you want to be pampered.
⊠ *Grace Bay Club, Grace Bay* ☎ *649/946–5050* ⌔ *Reservations es-*
sential ▭ *AE, D, MC, V* ☞ *No kids under 12.*

★ **$$$–$$$$** ✕ **Coyaba Restaurant.** Chef Paul Newman's talents soar at Coral Gar-
dens' elegantly appointed, terrace-style restaurant. A typical meal (served
on Royal Doulton china, no less) might start with tuna ceviche, followed
by sweet ancho chili-marinated duck breast, and finish with coconut pud-
ding with rum toffee sauce, all complemented by wines from the out-
standing list. The careful attention to detail makes an evening here live
up to its name's translation from the Arawak Indian tongue, "heavenly."
Very popular is the seven-course tasting menu. ⊠ *Penn's Rd., The Bight*
☎ *649/946–5186* ▭ *AE, MC, V* ☾ *Closed Tues.*

$$–$$$$ ✕ **Gecko Grille.** At this Ocean Club resort restaurant, you can eat indoors surrounded by tropical murals or out on the garden patio, where
the trees are interwoven with tiny twinkling lights. Creative "Floribbean"
fare combines native specialties with exotic fruits and zesty island spices
and includes Black Angus steaks grilled to order. Pecan-encrusted grouper
is a long-time menu favorite. ⊠ *Ocean Club, Grace Bay* ☎ *649/946–*
5885 ▭ *AE, D, MC, V* ☾ *Closed Mon. and Tues.*

$$$ ✕ **Caicos Café Bar & Grill.** There's a pervasive air of celebration in the
tree-shaded outdoor dining terrace of this popular eatery across from
the Allegro Resort. Choose from grilled seafood, steak, lamb, and
chicken served hot off the outdoor barbecue. Owner-chef Pierrik Marziou
adds a French accent to his appetizers, salads, and homemade desserts,
along with an outstanding collection of fine French wines. ⊠ *Grace Bay*
☎ *649/946–5278* ▭ *AE, MC, V.*

★ **$$$** ✕ **Magnolia Wine Bar & Restaurant.** With nearly a decade of experience
in the challenging Provo restaurant business, hands-on owners Gianni
and Tracey Caporuscio make success seem simple here. Expect well-pre-
pared, uncomplicated choices that range from French to Asian to Italian and Caribbean. The atmosphere is romantic, the presentations
picture-perfect, and the service careful. It's easy to see why the Capor-
uscios have a following of loyal admirers. The adjoining wine bar includes
a hand-picked list of specialty wines, which can be ordered by the glass.
⊠ *Miramar Resort, Turtle Cove* ☎ *649/941–5108* ▭ *AE, D, MC, V.*

$–$$ ✕ **Barefoot Café.** This lively indoor–outdoor café is always bustling,
drawing residents and tourists with hearty, affordable fare. Fresh-roasted
gourmet coffee, homemade muffins and pastries, and breakfast sandwiches start the day. Huge burgers, grinders, and savory pizzas are popular lunchtime options, along with fresh fruit smoothies and ice cream.
Dinner fare always includes fresh island seafood and farm-raised baby
conch in daily specials. Look for value-priced evening specials, such as

the popular $15 Caribbean Tuesday dinner. Centrally located on the lower level of Ports of Call shopping plaza, it's a great place to people-watch, as well. ⊠ *Ports of Call, Grace Bay* ☎ 649/946–5282 ⊟ *AE, MC, V.*

$–$$ ✕ **Tiki Hut.** From its location overlooking the marina, the ever-popular Tiki Hut continues to serve consistently tasty, value-priced meals in a fun atmosphere. Locals take advantage of the Wednesday night $10 chicken-and-rib special, and the lively bar is a good place to sample local Turks Head brew. There's a special family-style menu and kid's seating. Don't miss pizzas made with their signature white sauce. ⊠ *Turtle Cove Marina, Turtle Cove* ☎ 649/941–5341 ⊟ *AE, D, MC, V.*

ITALIAN ✕ **Baci Ristoranté.** Aromas redolent of the Mediterranean waft from the **$$–$$$** open kitchen as you walk into this intimate eatery east of Turtle Cove. Outdoor seating is on a romantic canal-front patio. The menu offers a small, varied selection of Italian delights. Veal is prominent on the menu, but main courses also include pasta, chicken, fresh fish, and brick-oven pizza. House wines are personally selected by the owners and complement the tasteful wine list. Try the tiramisu for dessert with a flavored coffee drink. ⊠ *Harbour Town, Turtle Cove* ☎ 649/941–3044 ⊟ *AE, MC, V.*

SEAFOOD ✕ **Aqua Bar & Terrace.** This popular restaurant on the grounds of the Tur-**$$–$$$$** tle Cove Inn has an inviting waterfront dining deck. Specializing in locally caught seafood and farm-raised conch, the menu includes long-time favorites like wahoo sushi, conch fillets encrusted with ground pecans, and grilled fish served with flavorful sauces. A selection of more casual entrées, including salads and burgers, appeals to the budget-conscious. Top it all off with a scoop of homemade ice cream. ⊠ *Turtle Cove Inn, Turtle Cove Marina, Turtle Cove* ☎ 649/946–4763 ⊟ *AE, MC, V.*

$–$$ ✕ **Banana Boat.** Buoys and other sea relics deck the walls of this lively restaurant–bar on the wharf. Grilled grouper, lobster salad sandwiches, conch fritters, and conch salad are among the options. Tropical drinks include the rum-filled Banana Breeze—a house specialty. ⊠ *Turtle Cove Marina, Turtle Cove* ☎ 649/941–5706 ⊟ *AE, D, MC, V.*

TEX-MEX ✕ **Hey Jose's Caribbean Cantina.** Frequented by locals, this restaurant, **$–$$$** just south of Turtle Cove, claims to serve the island's best margaritas. Customers also return for the tasty Tex-Mex treats: tacos, tostadas, nachos, burritos, fajitas, and special-recipe hot chicken wings. Thick, hearty pizzas are another favorite—especially the Kitchen Sink, with a little bit of everything thrown in. ⊠ *Leeward Hwy., Central Square* ☎ 649/946–4812 ⊟ *D, MC, V* ☽ *Closed Sun.*

Beaches

There are good beaches at **Sapodilla Bay** and **Malcolm Roads,** at North West Point, which is accessible only by four-wheel-drive vehicles. A fine ★ white-sand beach stretches 12 mi (19 km) along Provo's **north coast,** where most of the hotels are.

Sports & the Outdoors

BICYCLING Provo has a few steep grades to conquer, but they're short. Unfortunately, traffic on Leeward Highway and rugged road edges make pedaling here a less than relaxing experience. Instead, try the less-traveled roads through the settlements of Blue Hills, the Bight, and Five Cays. Most hotels have bikes available. You can rent mountain bikes at **Scooter Bob's** (⊠ Turtle Cove Marina, Turtle Cove ☎ 649/946–4684) for $15 a day.

BOATING &   Provo's calm, reef-protected turquoise seas combine with constant east-
SAILING   erly trade winds for excellent sailing conditions. Several multihull ves-
sels offer charters with snorkeling stops, food and beverage service, and sunset vistas. Prices range from $39 for group trips to $600 or more for private charters. *Atabeyra* is a retired rum runner and the choice of res-idents for special events. It's owned by **Sun Charters** (☎ 649/941–5363 ⊕ www.seatrek.tc). **Sail Provo** (☎ 649/946–4783 ⊕ www.sailprovo. com) runs 52-foot and 48-foot catamarans on scheduled half-day, full-day, and sunset cruises.

For sightseeing below the waves, try the new semi-submarine *Undersea Explorer* operated by **Caicos Tours** (⊠ Turtle Cove Marina, Turtle Cove ☎ 649/231–0006 ⊕ www.caicostours.com). You can stay dry within the lower observatory as it glides along on a one-hour tour of the reef, with large viewing windows on either side. The trip costs $39.

DIVING &   The island's many shallow reefs offer excellent and exciting snorkel-
SNORKELING   ing relatively close to shore. Try **Smith's Reef**, over Bridge Road east of
Fodor'sChoice   Turtle Cove.
★

Scuba diving in the crystalline waters surrounding the islands ranks among the best in the Caribbean. The reef and wall drop-offs thrive with bright, unbroken coral formations and lavish numbers of fish and marine life. Mimicking the idyllic climate, waters are warm all year, averaging 76°F to 78°F in winter and 82°F to 84°F in summer. With minimal rainfall and soil runoff, visibility is naturally good and frequently superb, rang-ing from 60 feet to more than 150 feet. An extensive system of marine national parks and boat moorings, combined with an ecoconscious mindset among dive operators, contributes to an uncommonly pristine underwater environment.

Dive operators in Provo regularly visit sites at **Grace Bay** and **Pine Cay** for spur-and-groove coral formations and bustling reef diving. They make the longer journey to the dramatic walls at **North West Point** and **West Caicos** depending on weather conditions. Instruction from the major div-ing agencies is available for all levels and certifications. An average one-tank dive costs $45; a two-tank dive, $90. There are also two live-aboard dive boats available for charter working out of Provo.

Art Pickering's Provo Turtle Divers (⊠ Turtle Cove Marina, Turtle Cove ☎ 649/946–4232 or 800/833–1341 ⊕ www.provoturtledivers.com), which also operates satellite locations at the Ocean Club and Ocean Club West, has been on Provo for more than 30 years. The staff is friendly, knowledgeable, and unpretentious. **Big Blue Unlimited** (⊠ Leeward Ma-rina, Leeward ☎ 649/946–5034 ⊕ www.bigblue.tc) specializes in eco-diving adventures, with a certified marine biologist on staff. It also offers Nitrox, Trimix, and rebreathers. **Caicos Adventures** (⊠ La Petite Pl., Grace Bay ☎☎ 649/941–3346 ⊕ www.tcidiving.com) is run by friendly Frenchman Fifi Kuntz, and offers daily trips to West Caicos, French Cay, and Molasses Reef. **Dive Provo** (⊠ Ports of Call, Grace Bay ☎ 649/946–5040 or 800/234–7768 ⊕ www.diveprovo.com) is a resort-based, PADI five-star operation that runs daily one- and two-tank dives to popular Grace Bay sites. **Flamingo Divers** (⊠ Provo Marine Biology Centre, Discovery Bay ☎ 649/946–4193 or 800/204–9282 ⊕ www.flamingodivers. com) focuses on small groups and personalized service for the discerning diver. **The Turks and Caicos Aggressor II** (☎ 800/348–2628 ⊕ www. turksandcaicosaggressor.com), a live-aboard dive boat, plies the islands' pristine sites with weekly charters from Turtle Cove Marina.

FISHING   The island's fertile waters are great for angling—anything from bottom- and reef fishing (most likely to produce plenty of bites and a large catch) to bonefishing and deep-sea fishing (among the finest in the Caribbean). You're required to purchase a $15 visitor's fishing license; operators generally furnish all equipment, drinks, and snacks. Prices range from $100 to $375, depending on the length of trip and size of boat. For deep-sea fishing trips in search of marlin, sailfish, wahoo, tuna, barracuda, and shark, look up **Gwendolyn Fishing Charters** (⊠ Turtle Cove Marina, Turtle Cove ☎ 649/946–5321 ⊕ www.fishingtci.com). You can rent a boat with a captain for a half- or full day of bottom- or bonefishing through **J&B Tours** (⊠ Leeward Marina, Leeward ☎ 649/946–5047 ⊕ www.jbtours.com). Captain Arthur Dean at **Silver Deep** (⊠ Leeward Marina, Leeward ☎ 649/946–5612 ⊕ www.silverdeep.com) is said to be among the Caribbean's finest bonefishing guides.

GOLF   The par-72, 18-hole championship course at **Provo Golf & Country Club**
Fodor'sChoice   (⊠ Governor's Rd., Grace Bay ☎ 649/946–5991), is a combination of
★   lush greens and fairways, rugged limestone outcroppings, and freshwater lakes and is ranked among the Caribbean's top courses. Fees are $130 for 18 holes with shared cart. Premium golf clubs can be rented.

HORSEBACK   Provo's long beaches and secluded lanes are ideal for trail rides on
RIDING   horseback. **Provo Ponies** (☎ 649/946–5252 ⊕ www.provo.net/ ProvoPonies) offer morning and afternoon rides for all levels of experience. A 45-minute ride costs $45; an 80-minute ride is $65.

PARASAILING   A 15-minute parasailing flight over Grace Bay is available for $70 (single) or $120 (tandem) from **Captain Marvin's Watersports** (☎ 649/231–0643 ⊕ www.captainmarvinsparasail.com), who will pick you up at your hotel for your flight.

TENNIS   You can rent equipment at **Provo Golf and Country Club** (⊠ Grace Bay ☎ 649/946–5991) and play on their two lighted courts, which has some of the island's best courts.

WINDSURFING   Windsurfers find the calm, turquoise water of Grace Bay ideal. **Windsurfing Provo** (⊠ Ocean Club, Grace Bay ☎ 649/946–5649 ⊕ www. windsurfingprovo.tc ⊠ Ocean Club W, Grace Bay ☎ 649/231–1687) rents Windsurfers, kayaks, motorboats, and Hobie Cats and offers windsurfing instruction.

Shopping

With the opening of two new retail plazas in the Grace Bay area in 2003, the selection of goods offered has expanded, but is still not on par with more developed Caribbean island destinations. There are several main shopping areas in Provo: Market Place and Central Square, on the Leeward Highway about ½ mi to 1 mi (1 to 1½ km) east of downtown, and Grace Bay, which has the new Saltmills complex and La Petite Place retail plaza and the original Ports of Call shopping village. Hand-woven straw baskets and hats, polished conch-shell crafts, paintings, wood carvings, model sailboats, handmade dolls, and metalwork are crafts native to the area.

ArtProvo (⊠ Ocean Club Plaza Grace Bay ☎ 649/941–4545) is the island's largest gallery of designer wall art; also shown are native crafts, jewelry, hand-blown glass, candles and other gift items. **Bamboo Gallery** (⊠ Leeward Hwy., The Market Place ☎☎ 649/946–4748) sells Caribbean art, from vivid Haitian paintings to wood carvings and local metal sculptures. **Caicos Wear Boutique** (⊠ La Petite Pl., Grace Bay Rd., Grace Bay ☎ 649/941–3346) is wall to wall with unique beach and casual resort wear, including Caribbean-print shirts, swim suits from Brazil, sandals, beach jewelry, and gifts. **Greensleeves** (⊠ Central Sq., Leeward Hwy., Turtle Cove ☎☎ 649/946–4147) offers paintings and pottery by local artists, baskets, jewelry, and sisal mats and bags. **Marilyn's Craft** (⊠ Ports of Call, Grace Bay ☎ No phone) sells handmade dolls, rag rugs, and wood carvings, plus tropical clothing and knickknacks. **Royal Jewels** (⊠ Providenciales International Airport ☎ 649/941–4513 ⊠ Arch Plaza ☎ 649/946–4699 ⊠ Beaches Turks & Caicos Resort & Spa, Grace Bay ☎ 649/946–8285 ⊠ Club Med Turkoise, Grace Bay ☎ 649/946–5602) sells gold and jewelry, designer watches, perfumes, fine leather goods and cameras—all duty-free—at several outlets. Termed "the best little water-sports shop in Provo," **Seatopia** (⊠ Ports of Call, Grace Bay ☎ 649/941–3355) sells reasonably priced scuba and snorkeling equipment, swimwear, beachwear, sandals, hats, and related water gear and swim toys. **The Tourist Shoppe** (⊠ Central Sq., Leeward Hwy., Turtle Cove ☎ 649/946–4627) has a large selection of souvenirs, including quality T-shirts, CDs, cards and postcards, beach toys, and sunglasses. If you need to supplement your beach-reading stock or are looking for island-specific materials, visit **The Unicorn Bookstore** (⊠ In front of Graceway IGA Mall, Leeward Hwy., Grace Bay ☎ 649/941–5458) for a wide assortment of books and magazines, including a large children's section with crafts, games, and art supplies.

For a large selection of duty-free liquor, visit **Discount Liquors** (⊠ Leeward Hwy., east of Suzie Turn Rd. ☎ 649/946–4536). Newly expanded in 2003 and including a large fresh produce section, a bakery, gourmet deli, and extensive meat counter, **Graceway IGA Supermarket** (⊠ Leeward Hwy., Grace Bay ☎ 649/941–5000), Provo's largest, is likely to have what you're looking for. Be prepared: prices are much higher than you would expect at home. Besides having a licensed pharmacist on duty, **Lockland Trading Co.** (⊠ Neptune Plaza, Grace Bay ☎ 649/946–8242), sells flavored coffees, snacks, ice cream, and a selection of T-shirts and souvenirs.

Nightlife
On Friday nights you can find a local band and lively crowd at **Calico Jack's Restaurant & Bar** (⊠ Ports of Call, Grace Bay ☎ 649/946–5129).

A popular gathering spot for locals to shoot pool, play darts, slam dominoes, and catch up on gossip is **Club Sodax Sports Bar & Grill** (✉ Leeward Hwy., Grace Bay ☎ 649/941–4540). You won't go hungry with snacks such as conch and fish fingers, jerk pork, and typical native dishes. Residents and tourists flock to **Stardust & Ashes Night Club** (✉ Leeward Hwy., Grace Bay ☎ 649/941–5745) to let their hair down.

Exploring Providenciales

Numbers in the margin correspond to points of interest on the Turks & Caicos Islands map.

3 **Downtown Providenciales.** Near Providenciales International Airport, downtown Provo is really an extended strip mall that houses a grocery store, car-rental and travel agencies, law offices, banks, and other businesses.

4 **Caicos Conch Farm.** On the northeast tip of Provo, this is a major mariculture operation where mollusks are farmed commercially (more than 3 million conch are here). Guided tours are available; call to confirm times. The small gift shop sells conch-related souvenirs. ✉ *Leeward-Going-Through, Leeward* ☎ *649/946–5330* 💲 *$6* ☉ *Mon.–Sat. 9–4.*

5 **Cheshire Hall.** Standing eerily just west of downtown Provo are the remains of a circa-1700 cotton plantation owned by Loyalist Thomas Stubbs. A trail weaves through the ruins, where interpretive signs tell the story of the island's doomed cotton industry. A variety of local plants are also identified. To visit, you must arrange for a tour through the Turks & Caicos National Trust. ✉ *Near downtown Providenciales* ☎ *649/941–5710 for National Trust* ⊕ *www.turksandcaicos.tc/NationalTrust* 💲 *$5* ☉ *Daily by appointment only.*

Little Water Cay

This small, uninhabited cay is a protected area under the Turks & Caicos National Trust. On these 150 acres are two trails, small lakes, red mangroves, and an abundance of native plants. Boardwalks protect the ground and interpretive signs explain the habitat. The cay is home to about 2,000 rare, endangered rock iguanas. They say the iguanas are shy, but these creatures actually seem rather curious. They waddle right up to you, as if posing for a picture. Several water-sports operators from Provo or North Caicos include a stop on the island as a part of their snorkel or sailing excursions, and your fee for the trip will include the $5 fee for a permit to visit.

Parrot Cay

Once said to be a hideout for pirate Calico Jack Rackham and his lady cohorts Mary Reid and Anne Bonny, the 1,000-acre cay, between Fort George Cay and North Caicos, is now the site of an ultraexclusive hideaway resort, a holistic health spa, and upscale homesites. Bordered by a wild stretch of pristine beach to the north and mangrove-lined wetlands to the south, tiny Parrot Cay is a natural wonder.

Where to Stay

For approximate costs, *see* the dining and lodging price chart at the beginning of this chapter.

$$$$
Fodor'sChoice
★

Parrot Cay Resort. Frequented by celebrities and international jet-setters, this exclusive resort combines natural beauty and elegant simplicity to create a rarified, tranquil atmosphere. Mediterranean-style hillside structures house the rooms and one-bedroom suites, all with private terraces. Seaside villas—some with private pools—have butler service and fully equipped kitchens, complete with staff on request. Three new villas on a private bay offer the ultimate in seclusion for $4,800 per night. International cuisine is served in the main dining room, while the poolside restaurant specializes in authentic Asian dishes. The Shambhala Spa—expanding at this writing for the 2005 season—ranks among the world's finest. The resort can only be accessed by private boat from Leeward Marina. ⊠ *Parrot Cay* ⬧ *Box 164, Providenciales* ☎ *649/946–7788* 🖷 *649/946–7789* ⊕ *www.parrot-cay.com* ⥯ *42 rooms, 4 suites, 14 villas* ⟡ *2 restaurants, room service, in-room data ports, in-room safes, some kitchens, some kitchenettes, minibars, cable TV with movies, in-room VCRs, 2 tennis courts, pool, gym, hot tub, Japanese baths, sauna, spa, Turkish bath, beach, snorkeling, windsurfing, boating, waterskiing, fishing, mountain bikes, 2 bars, library, baby-sitting, laundry service* ▤ *AE, D, MC, V* ⟲ *BP.*

Pine Cay

One of a chain of small cays linking North Caicos and Provo, 800-acre Pine Cay is where you'll find the Meridian Club—a retreat for people seeking peaceful seclusion. Its 2½-mi (4-km) beach is among the most beautiful in the archipelago. The island has a 3,800-foot airstrip and electric golf carts for getting around. Offshore is the **Football Fields** dive site, which has been called the Grand Central Station of the fish world.

Where to Stay

For approximate costs, *see* the dining and lodging price chart at the beginning of this chapter.

★ **$$$$**
Meridian Club. Here you can enjoy an unspoiled cay with vast stretches of soft, white sand and a 500-acre nature reserve that lures bird-watchers and botanists. A stay here is truly getting away from it all, as there are no air-conditioners, phones, or TVs. Accommodations are in spacious rooms with king-size beds and patios, as well as cottages that range from rustic to well appointed. Meals and activities are included in the room rate, as is your boat or air-taxi trip from Provo. Children under six are allowed only during the month of June. ⊠ *Pine Cay* ☎ *866/746–3229 or 770/500–1134* 🖷 *649/941–7010 direct to hotel, 203/602–2265 U.S. reservations number* ⊕ *www.meridianclub.com* ⥯ *12 rooms, 38 cottages* ⟡ *Restaurant, fans, tennis court, pool, beach, snorkeling, windsurfing, boating, fishing, bicycles, hiking, bar, library, airstrip; no a/c, no room phones, no room TVs, no kids under 12* ▤ *No credit cards* ⟲ *AI* ⊗ *Closed July–Oct.*

North Caicos

Thanks to abundant rainfall, this 41-square-mi (106-square-km) island is the lushest of the Turks and Caicos. Bird lovers can see a large flock of flamingos here, fishermen can find shallow creeks full of bonefish and history buffs can visit the ruins of a Loyalist plantation. Although there's no traffic, almost all the roads are paved, so bicycling is an excellent way to sightsee.

Where to Stay

For approximate costs, *see* the dining and lodging price chart at the beginning of this chapter.

$$$ ▦ **Prospect of Whitby Hotel.** This secluded, all-inclusive retreat is run by an Italian resort chain, Club Vacanze. Miles of beach are yours for sunbathing, windsurfing, or snorkeling. Spacious rooms have elegant Tuscan floor tiles and pastel pink paneling; in true chic getaway fashion, rooms lack TVs but include minibars. The restaurant, on a verandah overlooking the sea, is excellent, with a selection of local, Italian, and international dishes served buffet style. Scuba diving and daily excursions to nearby natural wonders are available. ⊠ *Whitby* ☎ *649/946–7119* 🖷 *649/946–7114* ⊕ *www.prospectofwhitby.com* 🛏 *24 rooms, 4 suites* ♤ *Restaurant, in-room safes, minibars, tennis court, pool, beach, dive shop, snorkeling, windsurfing, boating, fishing, bicycles, bar, piano bar; no room TVs* ▤ *AE, D, MC, V* ❘◍❘ *AI.*

$-$$ ▦ **Ocean Beach Hotel Condominiums.** This unpretentious place provides family-style accommodations on a 10-mi (16-km) stretch of sheltered beach. The spacious units, with full kitchens, face the ocean and are cooled by the constant trade winds. You can learn about local plants from the botanical walk encircling the premises. Tasty meals, featuring local seafood and homemade breads and desserts, are served in the common dining room. Diving, snorkeling, and exploring trips are arranged through Beach Cruiser Charters, at the hotel. ⊠ *Whitby* ☎ *649/946–7113 or 800/710–5204, 905/690–3817 in Canada* 🖷 *649/946–7386* ⊕ *www.turksandcaicos.tc/oceanbeach* 🛏 *3 rooms, 7 suites* ♤ *Restaurant, fans, kitchenettes, pool, beach, dive shop, snorkeling, boating, fishing, bicycles, bar, car rental; no a/c, no room TVs* ▤ *AE, D, MC, V* ☉ *Closed June–Oct.* ❘◍❘ *EP.*

$ ▦ **Pelican Beach Hotel.** Built and operated by Clifford Gardiner (the Islands' first licensed solo pilot) and his family, this laid-back hotel is on a beautiful expanse of deserted, windswept beach. Large rooms are done in pastels and dark-wood trim; the sound of breaking waves will soothe you in the first-floor beachfront units. Excellent local dishes and homemade bread are served in the airy dining room shaded by a grove of whispering casuarina pines. ⊠ *Whitby* ☎ *649/946–7112* 🖷 *649/946–7139* ⊕ *www.pelicanbeach.tc* 🛏 *14 rooms, 2 suites* ♤ *Restaurant, beach, snorkeling, fishing, bicycles, bar; no room TVs* ▤ *D, MC, V* ❘◍❘ *EP.*

Beaches

The beaches of North Caicos are superb for shelling and lolling, and the waters offshore have excellent snorkeling and scuba diving.

Exploring North Caicos

Numbers in the margin correspond to points of interest on the Turks & Caicos Island map.

6 **Flamingo Pond.** This is a regular nesting place for the beautiful pink birds. They tend to wander out in the middle of the pond, so bring binoculars.

7 **Kew.** This settlement has a small post office, a school, a church, and ruins of old plantations—all set among lush tropical trees bearing limes, papayas, and custard apples. Visiting Kew will give you a better understanding of the daily life of many islanders.

8 **Wades Green.** Visitors can view well-preserved ruins of the great house, overseer's house, and surrounding walls of one of the most successful plantations of the loyalist era. A lookout tower provides views for miles. Contact the National Trust for tour details. ⊠ *Kew* 🕾 *649/941–5710 for National Trust* 🖃 *$5* ⊙ *Daily, by appointment only.*

Middle Caicos

At 48 square mi (124 square km) and with fewer than 300 residents, this is the largest and least developed of the inhabited Turks & Caicos. A limestone ridge runs to about 125 feet above sea level, creating dramatic cliffs on the north shore and a cave system farther inland. Middle Caicos is best suited to those looking to unwind and who enjoy nature.

Where to Stay

For approximate costs, *see* the dining and lodging price chart at the beginning of this chapter.

$$ 🏨 **Blue Horizon Resort.** Breathtaking scenery and sweet seclusion abound in this 50-acre retreat. Cottages (and two villas) come in several sizes; all have screened-in porches, bleached-wood furniture, comfortable beds, and spectacular views of the beachfront cliff, where there's a hillside cave and private swimming cove. Fax a (basic) grocery list ahead of time, and management will stock your refrigerator. Activities by request include spelunking, fishing, and snorkeling with local guides. ⊠ *Mudjin Harbor, Conch Bar* 🕾 *649/946–6141* 🖷 *649/946–6139* ⊕ *www.bhresort.com* ⇨ *5 cottages, 2 villas* ♨ *Fans, some kitchenettes, refrigerators, cable TV with movies, beach, snorkeling, fishing, bicycles, hiking, laundry service; no a/c in some rooms, no phones in some rooms, no TV in some rooms* ▤ *AE, MC, V* ⅋ *EP.*

Exploring Middle Caicos

Numbers in the margin correspond to points of interest on the Turks & Caicos Island map.

9 **Conch Bar Caves.** These limestone caves have eerie underground lakes and milky-white stalactites and stalagmites. Archaeologists have discovered Lucayan Indian artifacts in the caves and the surrounding area. It's an easy walk through the main part of the cave, but wear sturdy shoes to avoid slipping. You'll hear, see, and smell some bats, but they don't bother visitors. J&B Tours in Providenciales offers boat trips to the caves from Provo (*see* Sightseeing Tours *in* Turks & Caicos A to Z).

South Caicos

This 8½-square-mi (21-square-km) island was once an important salt producer; today it's the heart of the fishing industry. Nature prevails, with long, white beaches, jagged bluffs, quiet backwater bays, and salt flats. Diving and snorkeling on the pristine wall and reefs are a treat enjoyed by only a few.

Beaches

Due south of South Caicos is **Big Ambergris Cay,** an uninhabited cay about 14 mi (23 km) beyond the Fish Cays, with a magnificent beach at Long Bay. To the north of South Caicos, uninhabited **East Caicos** has a beautiful 17-mi (27-km) beach on its north coast. The island was once a cattle range and the site of a major sisal-growing industry. Both places are accessible only by boat.

Exploring South Caicos

Numbers in the margin correspond to points of interest on the Turks & Caicos Island map.

At the northern end of the island are fine white-sand beaches; the south coast is great for scuba diving along the drop-off; and there's excellent snorkeling off the windward (east) coast, where large stands of elkhorn and staghorn coral shelter several varieties of small tropical fish. Spiny lobster and queen conch are found in the shallow Caicos Bank to the west, and are harvested for export by local processing plants. The bonefishing here is some of the best in the West Indies. **Beyond the Blue** (✉ Cockburn Harbour ☎ 649/231–1703 ⊕ www.beyondtheblue.com) offers bonefishing charters on a specialized airboat, which can operate in less than a foot of water.

⑩ Boiling Hole. Abandoned salinas make up the center of this island—the largest, across from the downtown ballpark, receives its water directly from an underground source connected to the ocean through this boiling hole.

⑪ Cockburn Harbour. The best natural harbor in the Caicos chain hosts the South Caicos Regatta, held each year in May.

TURKS & CAICOS A TO Z

To research prices, get advice from other travelers, and book travel arrangements, visit www.fodors.com.

AIR TRAVEL

Although carriers and schedules can vary according to season, American Airlines flies nonstop to Provo from Miami, JFK, and Boston, either daily or several times a week. US Airways flies daily between Charlotte and Provo. Delta Air Lines travels on Saturdays between Atlanta and Provo. British Airways connects London/Heathrow and Provo on Sundays. Air Canada flies between Toronto and Provo on Saturdays. Bahamasair flies between Nassau and Provo several times a week. Air Jamaica Express travels between Provo and Montego Bay several times a week. Turks & Caicos Airways offers regularly scheduled flights between Provo and the outer Caicos Islands. SkyKing connects Provo with Grand Turk and South Caicos several times daily and also offers flights to the Bahamas, Cuba, Jamaica, the Dominican Republic, and Haiti. Additionally, in season there are weekly charter flights from a number of North American cities, including Boston, Chicago, Detroit, New York, Philadelphia, and Toronto.

🛪 **Air Canada** ☎ 888/247-2262. **Air Jamaica Express** ☎ 800/523-5585. **American Airlines** ☎ 649/946-4948 or 800/433-7300. **Bahamasair** ☎ 649/946-4999 or 800/222-4262. **British Airways** ☎ 649/941-3352 or 800/247-9297. **Delta Air Lines** ☎ 800/241-4141. **SkyKing** ☎ 649/941-5464. **Turks & Caicos Airways** ☎ 649/946-4255. **US Airways** ☎ 800/622-1015.

AIRPORTS

All international flights arrive at Providenciales International Airport. Then you use domestic carriers to fly on to airports in Grand Turk and the out-islands of North Caicos, Middle Caicos, South Caicos, and Salt Cay. All have paved runways in good condition. Providenciales International Airport has modern, secure arrival and check-in services. You'll find taxis at the airports, and most resorts provide pickup service. A trip between Provo's airport and most major hotels runs about $15. On Grand Turk a trip from the airport to Cockburn Town is about $5; it's $5 to $8 to hotels outside town.

For private planes, Provo Air Center is a full service FBO (Fixed Base Operator) offering refueling, maintenance, and short-term storage, as well as on-site customs and immigration clearance, a lounge, and concierge services.

🛪 **Grand Turk International Airport** ☎ 649/946-2233. **Providenciales International Airport** ☎ 649/941-5670. **Provo Air Center** ☎ 649/946-4181 ⊕ www.provoaircenter.com.

BIKE & MOPED TRAVEL

Although scooters and bicycles are available for rental on Provo, the option has dwindled in popularity with the deteriorating condition of the side roads and an increase in auto traffic. Provo Fun Cycles in Providenciales rents double-seater scooters and bicycles (as well as jeeps, SUVs, vans, and cars). Rates are $32 to $44 per day for scooters and $16 per day for bicycles.

🛪 Bike & Moped Rentals **Provo Fun Cycles** ✉ Ports of Call, Providenciales ☎ 649/946-5868 ⊕ www.provo.net/provofuncycles.

BOAT & FERRY TRAVEL

Surprisingly, there's no scheduled boat or ferry service between Provo and the other Turks and Caicos Islands. Instead, islanders tend to catch rides leaving from the marina at Leeward-Going-Through.

BUSINESS HOURS

BANKS   Banks are open Monday through Thursday from 9 to 3, Friday 9 to 5.

POST OFFICES   Post offices are open weekdays from 8 to 4.

SHOPS   Shops are generally open weekdays from 8 or 8:30 to 5.

CAR RENTALS

Car- and jeep-rental rates average $35 to $80 per day, plus a $15-per-rental-agreement government tax. Reserve well ahead of time during the peak winter season. Most agencies offer free mileage and airport pickup service. Tony's Car Rental is the only player on Grand Turk. Several agencies, including Avis, Budget, Provo Rent-a-Car, Rent a Buggy, and Tropical Auto Rentals, operate on Provo.

Avis ☎ 649/946-4705 ⊕ www.AvisTCI.com. **Budget** ☎ 649/946-4079 ⊕ www.provo.net/budget. **Provo Rent-a-Car** ☎ 649/946-4404 ⊕ www.provo.net/rentacar. **Rent a Buggy** ☎ 649/946-4158 ⊕ www.rentabuggy.tc. **Tony's Car Rental** ☎ 649/231-1806. **Tropical Auto Rentals** ☎ 649/946-5300 ⊕ www.provo.net/tropicalauto.

CAR TRAVEL

GASOLINE   Gasoline is expensive, running around $3.25 per gallon.

ROAD CONDITIONS   Major reconstruction of Leeward Highway on Providenciales has been completed and most of the road is now a four-lane divided highway complete with roundabouts. However, the paved two-lane roads through the settlements on Providenciales are still pocked with potholes and have steep shoulder drop-offs. Dusty, rutted side roads are in worse condition. Ironically, the little-traveled roads in Grand Turk and the out-islands are, in general, smooth and paved.

RULES OF THE ROAD   Driving here is on the left side of the road, British style; when pulling out into traffic, remember to look to your right. Give way to anyone entering a roundabout, even if you are on what appears to be the primary road. The maximum speed is 40 mph, 20 mph through settlements, and limits, as well as the use of seat belts, are enforced.

ELECTRICITY

Electricity is fairly stable throughout the islands, and the current is suitable for all U.S. appliances (120/240 volts, 60 Hz).

EMERGENCIES

Ambulance & Fire Ambulance and Fire ☎ 999 or 911.

Hospitals Associated Medical Practices ⊠ Leeward Hwy., Glass Shack, Providenciales ☎ 649/946-4242. **Grand Turk Hospital** ⊠ Hospital Rd., Grand Turk ☎ 649/946-2040.

Pharmacies Grand Turk Hospital ⊠ Grand Turk Hospital, Grand Turk ☎ 649/946-2040. **Grace Bay Medical Center** ⊠ Neptune Plaza, Grace Bay, Providenciales ☎ 649/941-5252.

Police Police Emergencies ☎ 649/946-2499 in Grand Turk, 649/946-7116 in North Caicos, 649/946-4259 in Provo, 649/946-3299 in South Caicos.

Scuba Diving Emergencies Associated Medical Practices ⊠ Leeward Hwy., Glass Shack, Providenciales ☎ 649/946-4242.

HOLIDAYS

Public holidays are: New Year's Day, Commonwealth Day (2nd Mon. in Mar.), Good Friday, Easter Monday, National Heroes Day (last Mon. in May), Queen's Birthday (3rd Mon. in June), Emancipation Day (1st Mon. in Aug.), National Youth Day (last Mon. in Sept.), Columbus Day (2nd Mon. in Oct.), International Human Rights Day (last Mon. in Oct.), Christmas Day, and Boxing Day (Dec. 26).

LANGUAGE

The official language of the Turks and Caicos is English. Native islanders (termed "Belongers") are of African descent, though the population—especially on cosmopolitan Provo—also consists of Canadian, British, American, European, Haitian, and Dominican expats.

MAIL & SHIPPING

The post office is in downtown Provo at the corner of Airport Road. Collectors will be interested in the wide selection of stamps sold by the Philatelic Bureau. It costs 50¢ to send a postcard to the United States, 60¢ to Canada and the United Kingdom, and $1.25 to Australia and New Zealand; letters, per ½ ounce, cost 60¢ to the United States, 80¢ to Canada and the United Kingdom, and $1.40 to Australia and New Zealand. When writing to the Turks and Caicos Islands, be sure to include the specific island and "Turks and Caicos Islands, BWI" (British West Indies). Delivery service is provided by FedEx, with offices in Provo and Grand Turk.

🚩 **FedEx** ☎ 649/946–2542 on Grand Turk, 649/946–4682 on Provo. **Philatelic Bureau** ☎ 649/946–1534.

MONEY MATTERS

Prices quoted in this chapter are in U.S. dollars. Scotiabank and First-Caribbean have offices on Provo, with branches on Grand Turk. Many larger hotels and the casino can take care of your money requests. Bring small denominations to the less-populated islands.

🚩 **FirstCaribbean** ☎ 649/946–5303. **Scotiabank** ☎ 649/946–4750.

ATMS   There are few ATMs on the islands, primarily at the banks and in the casino on Providenciales.

CREDIT CARDS   Major credit cards and traveler's checks are accepted at many establishments.

CURRENCY   The unit of currency is the U.S. dollar.

PASSPORTS & VISAS

U.S. and Canadian citizens need some proof of citizenship, such as a birth certificate (original or certified copy), plus a photo I.D. or a current passport. All other travelers, including those from the United Kingdom, Australia, and New Zealand, require a current passport. Everyone must have an ongoing or return ticket. We strongly urge all travelers going to the Caribbean to carry a valid passport, whether or not it is an absolute requirement.

SAFETY

Although crime is not a major concern in the Turks & Caicos Islands, petty theft does occur here, and you're advised to leave your valuables in the hotel safe-deposit box and lock doors in cars and rooms when unattended.

SIGHTSEEING TOURS

Whether by taxi, boat, or plane, you should try to venture beyond your resort's grounds and beach. Big Blue Unlimited specializes in ecoadventures to the out-islands and cays. Global Airways specializes in trips to North Caicos. If you want to island-hop on your own schedule, air charters are available through Inter-Island Airways. Nell's Taxi offers taxi tours of the islands, priced between $25 and $30 for the first hour and $25 for each additional hour. J&B Tours offers sea and land tours, including trips to Middle Caicos, the largest of the islands, for a visit to the caves, or to North Caicos to see flamingos and plantation ruins.

🔢 **Big Blue Unlimited** ☎ 649/946-5034 ⊕ www.bigblue.tc. **Global Airways** ☎ 649/941-3222 ⊕ www.globalairways.org. **Inter-Island Airways** ☎ 649/941-5481 ⊕ www.interislandairways.com. **J&B Tours** ☎ 649/946-5047 ⊕ www.jbtours.com. **Nell's Taxi** ☎ 649/231-0051.

TAXES & SERVICE CHARGES

DEPARTURE TAX   The departure tax is $23, payable only in cash or traveler's checks, although it's now built into the cost of most tickets.

SALES TAX   Restaurants and hotels add a 10% government tax. Hotels also add 10% to 15% for service.

TAXIS

Cabs (actually large vans) are now metered, and rates are regulated by the government at $2 per person per mile traveled. In Provo call the Provo Taxi and Bus Group for more information. Many resorts and car-rental agencies offer complimentary airport transfers. Ask ahead of time.

🔢 **Provo Taxi & Bus Group** ☎ 649/946-5481.

TELEPHONES

All telephone service is provided by Cable & Wireless. Many U.S.–based cell phones work on the islands; use your own or rent one from Cable & Wireless. Internet access is available via hotel-room phone connections or Internet kiosks on Provo and Grand Turk. You can also connect to the World Wide Web from any telephone line by dialing C-O-N-N-E-C-T to call Cable & Wireless and using the user name *easy* and the password *access*. Calls from the islands are expensive, and many hotels add steep surcharges for long-distance. Talk fast.

🔢 **Cable & Wireless** ☎ 649/946-2200, 800/744-7777 for long distance, 649/266-6328 for Internet access, 811 for mobile service ⊕ www.tcimall.tc.

AREA CODE   The area code for the Turks and Caicos is 649. Just dial 1 plus the 10-digit number, including area code, from the United States.

INTERNATIONAL CALLS   To make calls from the Turks and Caicos, dial 0, then 1, the area code, and the number.

LOCAL CALLS   To make local calls, dial the seven-digit number.

TIPPING

At restaurants, tip 15% if service isn't included in the bill. Taxi drivers also expect a token tip, about 10% of your fare.

VISITOR INFORMATION

The Turks and Caicos Islands Tourist Board maintains a comprehensive Web site covering each of the islands. Another excellent source of information is TCISearch, which—besides all the basics and information about resorts, restaurants, and activities—includes weather information, maps, a business directory, downloadable postcards, and video clips and a helpful "chat" forum of island-related topics. Times Publications publishes a quarterly magazine on all aspects of life in the islands.

🖪Before You Leave **Turks & Caicos Islands Tourist Board** ⊕www.turksandcaicostourism. com ✉ 2715 E. Oakland Park Blvd., #101, Fort Lauderdale, FL 33316 ☎ 954/568-6588 or 800/241-0824. **TCISearch** ⊕ www.tcisearch.com.

🖪 In Turks & Caicos Islands **Turks & Caicos Islands Tourist Board** ✉ Front St., Cockburn Town, Grand Turk ☎ 649/946-2321 ✉ Stubbs Diamond Plaza, The Bight, Providenciales ☎ 649/946-4970. **Times Publications** ⊕ www.timespub.tc.

WEDDINGS

Beautiful oceanfront backdrops, endless starlit nights, and a bevy of romantic accommodations make the islands an ideal wedding destination. The residency requirement is only 24 hours, after which you can apply for a marriage license to the Registrar in Grand Turk; the ceremony can take place at any time after the application has been granted, generally within two to three days. You must present a passport, original birth certificate, and proof of current marital status, as well as a letter stating both parties' occupations, ages, addresses, and fathers' full names. No blood tests are required, and the license fee is $50. The ceremony is conducted by a local minister, Justice of the Peace, or the Registrar. The marriage certificate is filed in the islands, although copies can be sent to your home. There are a number of wedding coordinators on-island, and many resorts offer special wedding packages, which include handling all the details.

🖪 Wedding Planners **Nila Destinations Wedding Planning** ☎ 649/941-4375 ⊕ www. nilavacations.com.

UNDERSTANDING
THE BAHAMAS

BAHAMAS AT A GLANCE

Fast Facts

Type of government: Constitutional parliamentary democracy
Capital: Nassau
Administrative divisions: 21 districts: Acklins and Crooked Islands, Bimini, Cat Island, Exuma, Freeport, Fresh Creek, Governor's Harbour, Green Turtle Cary, Harbour Island, High Rock, Inagua, Kemps, Long Island, Marsh Harbour, Mayaguana, New Providence, Nichollstown, Berry Islands, Ragged Island, Rock Sound, Sandy Point, San Salvador, and Rum Cay
Independence: July 10, 1973 (from the United Kingdom)
Legal system: Based on English common law; Supreme Court, Court of Appeal, magistrates courts
Legislature: Bicameral parliament: upper house: 16-member appointed Senate; lower house: 40-member elected Assembly
Population: 297,477
Birth Rate: 18.57 births per 1,000 population

Infant Mortality: 26.21 deaths per 1,000 live births; female: 19.83; male: 32.45
Language: English, Creole (among Haitian immigrants), and strong Bahamian dialect
Ethnic groups: Bahamians are mainly of African descent—85% black, 12% white, and 3% Asian and Latino
Life expectancy: Male, 62.3; female, 69.18
Literacy: Total population: 95.6%; male: 94.7%; female, 96.5%
Religion: Dominant religion: Christianity; largest three denominations: Baptist, 32%; Anglican, 20%; and Roman Catholic, 19% Other denominations and religions represented: Assembly of God, Ba'hai faith, Brethren, Christian and Missionary Alliance, Christian Science, Church of God of Prophecy, Greek Orthodox, Jehovah's Witnesses, Jewish, Latter-day Saints (Mormon), Lutheran, Methodist, Presbyterian, and Seventh Day Adventist

Geography

Location: The archipelago of the islands of the Bahamas is in the Atlantic Ocean, extending more than 650 miles from the eastern coast of Florida to the southeastern tip of Cuba. Of the some 700 islands and almost 2,500 small islets of cays, approximately 30 are inhabited.
Coastline: 2,201 mi
Area: Total: 8,664 square mi; land, 6,259 square mi; water, 2,405 square mi; slightly larger than the state of Connecticut in the U.S.
Climate: Tropical marine moderated by warm waters of the Gulf Stream
Terrain: Long, flat coral formations with some low, rounded hills

Islands: New Providence Island, home to the capital Nassau; Grand Bahama Island; and other inhabited islands officially called the Family Islands but commonly known as the Out Islands, including The Abacos, Andros, Cat Island, The Biminis, The Berries, Eleuthera, The Exumas, and Long Island
Natural resources: Salt, aragonite, timber, arable land
Natural hazards: Hurricanes and other tropical storms that cause extensive flooding and wind damage

Economy

Annual growth: 0.1% (2002)
Inflation: 1.8%
Unemployment: 6.9%
GDP per capita: $17,000 (2002)
GDP: $5.2 billion (2002)
Agriculture: Citrus, vegetables, and poultry
Industry: Tourism, banking, e-commerce, oil refining, cement, salt, rum, transshipment, aragonite, pharmaceuticals, and spiral-welded steel pipe
Work force: Tourism, 50%; other services, 40%; industry, 5%; agriculture, 5%
Currency: Bahamian dollar (U.S. dollar widely accepted)

Exchange rate: One Bahamian dollar per U.S. dollar
Debt (external): $371.6 million (2001)
Economic aid: $9.8 million (1995)
Major industries: Tourism, 80%; financial services, 20%
Major export products: Fish and crawfish, rum, salt, chemicals, fruit and vegetables
Export partners U.S., 20%; France, 16.5%; Germany, 14.1%; U.K., 12.9%
Imports: Machinery and transport equipment, manufactures, chemicals, mineral fuels, food, and live animals
Import partners: U.K., 6.3%; U.S., 6.0%; Belgium, 5.7%; Japan, 3.5%; Germany 3.5%

Environment

Environmental issues: Coral reef decay, solid waste disposal

Did You Know?

- The Bahamas is a stable, developing nation; its economy is predominantly dependent on tourism and offshore banking.

- Tourism accounts for 60% of the GDP and employs about half of the labor force.

- Arawak Indians inhabited the islands when Christopher Columbus first landed in the New World on San Salvador in 1492.

- British settlement of the islands began in 1647; they became a colony in 1783.

- Since attaining independence from the U.K. in 1973, the Bahamas has prospered through tourism, international banking, and investment management.

- Because of its geography, the country is a major transshipment point for illegal drugs, particularly shipments to the U.S., and its territory is used for smuggling illegal migrants into the U.S.

IN THE WAKE OF COLUMBUS: A SHORT HISTORY OF THE BAHAMAS

YOU MIGHT CALL CHRISTOPHER COLUM-BUS the first tourist to hit the Bahamas, although he was actually trying to find a route to the East Indies with his *Niña, Pinta,* and *Santa María.* Columbus is popularly believed to have made his first landfall in the New World on October 12, 1492, at San Salvador, in the southern part of the Bahamas. Researchers of the National Geographic Society, however, have come up with the theory that he may first have set foot ashore Samana Cay, some 60 mi southeast of San Salvador. The Bahamians have taken this new theory under consideration, if not too seriously; tradition dies hard in the islands, and they are hardly likely to tear down the New World landfall monument on San Salvador.

The people who met Columbus on his landing day were Arawak Indians, said to have fled from the Caribbean to the Bahamas to escape the depredations of the murderous Caribs around the turn of the 9th century. The Arawaks were a shy, gentle people who offered Columbus and his men their hospitality. He was impressed with their kindness and more than slightly intrigued by the gold ornaments they wore. But the voracious Spaniards who followed in Columbus's footsteps a few years later repaid the Indians' kindness by forcing them to work in the conquistadors' gold and silver mines in Cuba and Haiti; the Bahamas' indigenous peoples were virtually wiped out in the next 30 years, despite the fact that the Spaniards never settled their land.

In 1513 another well-known seafarer stumbled upon the westernmost Bahamian islands. Juan Ponce de León had been a passenger on Columbus's second voyage, in 1493. He conquered Puerto Rico in 1508 and then began searching thirstily for the Fountain of Youth. He thought he had found it on South Bimini, but he changed his mind and moved on to visit the site of St. Augustine, on the northeast coast of Florida.

In 1629 King Charles I claimed the Bahamas for England, though his edict was not implemented until the arrival of English pilgrims in 1648. Having fled the religious repression and political dissension then rocking their country, they settled on the Bahamian island they christened Eleuthera, the Greek word for freedom. Other English immigrants followed, and in 1656 another group of pilgrims, from Bermuda, took over a Bahamian island to the west and named it New Providence because of their links with Providence, Rhode Island. By the last part of the 17th century, some 1,100 settlers were trying to eke out a living, supplemented by the cargoes they salvaged from Spanish galleons that ran aground on the reefs. Many settlers were inclined to give nature a hand by enticing these ships onto the reefs with lights.

Inevitably, the British settlers were joined by a more nefarious subset of humanity, pirates and buccaneers like Edward Teach (better known as Blackbeard, he was said to have had 14 wives), Henry Morgan, and Calico Jack Rackham. Rackham numbered among his crew two violent, cutlass-wielding female members, Anne Bonney and Mary Read, who are said to have disconcerted enemies by swinging aboard their vessels topless. Bonney and Read escaped hanging in Jamaica by feigning pregnancy.

For some 40 years until 1718, pirates in the Bahamas constantly raided the Spanish galleons that carried booty home from the New World. During this period, the Spanish government, furious at the raids, sent ships and troops to destroy the New Providence city of Charles Town, which was later rebuilt and renamed Nassau, in

1695, in honor of King William III, formerly William of Orange-Nassau.

In 1718 King George I appointed Captain Woodes Rogers the first royal governor of the Bahamas, with orders to clean up the place. Why the king chose Rogers for this particular job is unclear—his thinking may well have been that it takes a pirate to know one, for Woodes Rogers had been a privateer. But he did take control of Nassau, hanging eight pirates from trees on the site of what was to become the British Colonial Hotel. Today, a statue of the former governor stands at the hotel entrance, and the street that runs along the waterfront is named after him. Rogers also inspired the saying *Expulsis piratis, restitua commercia* (Piracy expelled, commerce restored), which remained the country's motto until Prime Minister Lynden O. Pindling replaced it with the more appropriate and optimistic Forward, Upward, Onward Together, on the occasion of independence from Britain in 1973.

Although the Bahamas enjoyed a certain measure of tranquillity, thanks to Rogers and the governors who followed him, the British colonies in America at the same time were seething with a desire for independence. The peace of the islanders' lives was to be shattered during the Revolutionary War by a raid in 1778 on Nassau by the American navy, which purloined the city's arms and ammunition without even firing a shot. Next, in 1782, the Spanish came to occupy the Bahamas until the following year. Under the Treaty of Versailles of 1783, Spain took possession of Florida, and the Bahamas reverted to British rule.

* * *

THE BAHAMAS WERE ONCE AGAIN OVERRUN, between 1784 and 1789, this time by merchants from New England and plantation owners from Virginia and the Carolinas who had been loyal to the British and were fleeing the wrath of the American revolutionaries. Seeking asylum under the British flag, the Southerners brought their families and slaves with them. Many set up new plantations in the islands, but frustrated by the islands' arid soil, they soon opted for greener pastures in the Caribbean. The slaves they left behind were set free in 1834, but many retained the names of their former masters. That is why you'll find many a Johnson, Saunders, and Thompson in the towns and villages throughout the Bahamas.

The land may have been less than fertile, but New Providence Island's almost perfect climate, marred only by the potential for hurricanes during the fall, attracted other interest. Tourism was foreseen as far back as 1861, when the legislature approved the building of the first hotel, the Royal Victoria. Though it was to reign as the grande dame of the island's hotels for more than a century, its early days saw it involved in an entirely different profit-making venture. During the U.S. Civil War, the Northern forces blockaded the main Southern ports, and the leaders of the Confederacy turned to Nassau, the closest neutral port to the south. The Royal Victoria became the headquarters of the blockade-running industry, which reaped huge profits for the British colonial government from the duties it imposed on arms supplies. (In October 1990, the Royal Victoria Hotel burned down.)

A similar bonanza, also at the expense of the United States, was to come in the 1920s, after Prohibition was signed into U.S. law in 1919. Booze brought into the Bahamas from Europe was funneled into a thirsty United States by rumrunners operating out of Nassau, Bimini, and West End, the community on Grand Bahama Island east of Palm Beach. Racing against, and often exchanging gunfire with, Coast Guard patrol boats, the rumrunners dropped off their supplies in Miami, the Florida Keys, and other Florida destinations, making their contribution to the era known as the Roaring '20s.

Even then, tourists were beginning to trickle into the Bahamas, many in opulent yachts belonging to the likes of Whitney, Vanderbilt, and Astor. In 1929 a new airline, Pan American, started to make daily flights from Miami to Nassau. The Royal Victoria, shedding its shady past, and two new hotels, the Colonial (now the British Colonial Hilton Nassau) and the Fort Montagu Beach, were all in full operation. Nassau even had instant communication with the outside world: A few miles northwest of the Colonial, a subterranean telegraph cable had been laid linking New Providence with Jupiter, Florida. It took no flash of inspiration to name the area Cable Beach.

One of the most colorful and enigmatic characters of the era, Sir Harry Oakes, came to Nassau in the 1930s from Canada. He built the Bahamas Country Club and the Cable Beach Golf Course; he also built Nassau's first airport in the late '30s to lure the well-heeled and to make commuting easier for the wealthy residents. Oakes Field can still be seen on the ride from Nassau International Airport to Cable Beach.

Oakes was to die in an atmosphere of eerie and mysterious intrigue. Only his good friend, the late Sir Harold Christie, a powerful real-estate tycoon, was in the house at the time that Oakes' body was found, battered and burned. This was a period when all of the news that was fit to print was coming out of the war theaters in Europe and the Far East, but the Miami newspapers and wire services had a field day with the society murder.

Although a gruff, unlikable character, Oakes had no known enemies, but there was speculation that mob hit men from Miami had come over and taken care of him because of his unyielding opposition to the introduction of gambling casinos to the Bahamas. Finally, two detectives brought from Miami pinned the murder on Oakes' son-in-law, Count Alfred de Marigny, for whom the Canadian was known to have a strong dislike. De Marigny was tried and acquitted in an overcrowded Nassau court. Much of the detectives' research and testimony was later discredited. For many years afterward, however, the mysterious and still unsolved crime was a sore point with New Providence residents.

During World War II, New Providence also played host to a noble, if unlikely, couple. In 1936 the Duke of Windsor had forsaken the British throne in favor of "the woman I love," an American divorcée named Wallis Warfield Simpson, and the couple temporarily found a carefree life in Paris and the French Riviera. When the Nazis overran France, they fled to neutral Portugal. Secret papers revealed after the war suggest that the Germans had plans to use the duke and duchess, by kidnapping if necessary, as pawns in the German war against Britain. This would have taken the form of declaring them king and queen in exile, and seating them on the throne when Hitler's assumed victory was accomplished.

Word of the plot might have reached the ears of Britain's wartime prime minister, Winston Churchill, who encouraged King George VI, the duke's younger brother and his successor, to send the couple as far away as possible out of harm's way. In 1939 the duke had briefly returned to England, offering his services to his brother in the war effort. He was given a position of perhaps less import than he had expected, for he and Wallis suddenly found themselves in the Bahamas, with the duke as governor and commander in chief.

***

CHANGES IN THE BAHAMAS' POLITICAL CLIMATE had to wait for the war's end. For more than 300 years, the country had been ruled by whites; members of the United Bahamian Party (UBP) were known as the Bay Street Boys, after Nassau's main business thoroughfare, because they controlled the islands' commerce. But the voice of the overwhelmingly black majority was making itself heard. In 1953 a London-educated black barrister named Lynden O. Pindling joined the opposition Progressive Liberal Party (PLP); in 1956 he was elected to Parliament.

Pindling continued to stir the growing resentment most Bahamians now had for the Bay Street Boys, and his parliamentary behavior became more and more defiant. In 1965, during one parliamentary session, he picked up the speaker's mace and threw it out the window. Because this mace has to be present and in sight at all sessions, deliberations had to be suspended; meanwhile, Pindling continued his harangue to an enthusiastic throng in the street below. Two years later, Bahamian voters threw the UBP out, and Pindling led the PLP into power.

Pindling's magnetism kept him in power through independence from Britain in 1973 (though loyalty to the mother country led the Bahamians to choose to remain within the Commonwealth of Nations, recognize Queen Elizabeth II as their sovereign, and retain a governor-general appointed by the queen). For his services to his nation, the prime minister was knighted by the queen in 1983. His deputy prime minister Clement Maynard received the same accolade in 1989.

In August 1992 there came the biggest political upset since Pindling took power in 1967. His Progressive Liberal Party was defeated in a general election by the Free National Movement party, headed by lawyer Hubert Alexander Ingraham. The 45-year-old former chairman of the PLP and Cabinet member under Pindling had been expelled from the party by Pindling in 1986 because of his outspoken comments on alleged corruption inside the government. Ingraham's continued emphasis on this issue during the 1992 campaign did much to lead to Pindling's defeat and Ingraham's taking over as prime minister. Ingraham was reelected for another five-year term in 1996. In May 2002, the PLP again took the reigns with the election of the Right Honourable Perry G. Christie.

Residents, for the most part, are proud of their country and are actively involved in bettering their own lot—the last complete census showed about 27% of the population was attending school at one level or another. And in the spirit of their national motto—Forward, Upward, Onward Together—they graciously welcome the ever-increasing numbers of outsiders who have discovered their little piece of paradise.

— Ian Glass

IN SEARCH OF COLUMBUS

I FIRST HEARD THE SINGING toward the middle of the night, as the mail boat M/V *Maxine* plowed southward between Eleuthera and the Exumas. The sound drifted faintly to where I lay doubled up on a bench in the main cabin with my head on a cardboard crate of pears and a copy of the *Bahama Journal* shielding my eyes from a yellow bug light.

It was a two-part chant, almost African in its rhythm. I looked down the dim corridor to the bridge, where the crewman at the wheel was singing softly in harmony with his companion on the midnight-to-four watch. The second man was shuffling back and forth, keeping time. It was a scene out of Conrad, and a reminder that this is still what transportation is like in much of the world: pitching through the waters of a dark archipelago, sleeping with your head on a box of fruit, while guys sing and dance on the bridge.

The *Maxine* was 14 hours out of Potter's Cay, Nassau, the Bahamas, on the 22-hour run to the island of San Salvador. I had long since abandoned my claustrophobic upper bunk in the boat's only passenger compartment and had stayed out on deck until dark, sprawling over a tarp that covered bags of cement, taking shallow breaths to ration the stench of diesel fuel. Finally, half soaked from the waves constantly breaching the port rail, I had retreated to the last remotely habitable place on board—the big common room with its table and benches and its clutter of cargo for the islands. Four dozen eggs, the cartons taped together. An oscillating fan. Gallon jars of mayonnaise, their future owners' names written on the labels. Two galvanized tubs. Homemade sound equipment for the band that plays in the bar on San Salvador. My pillow of pears, consigned to Francita Gardiner of Rum Cay. Bags, boxes, crates—and, secured somehow on

the opposite bench, with ears alert and bright, eager eyes, a life-size ceramic German shepherd, soon to be a boon companion to someone in a place where a real German shepherd probably would die of heat prostration. Every time I woke to shift positions during that endless night, I would glance across the cabin, and there would be the good dog, looking as if he were waiting for a biscuit.

It is altogether possible to fly from Nassau to San Salvador in an hour and a half, but I had cast my lot with the mayonnaise and the galvanized tubs because I wanted to reach the island by water. San Salvador is arguably the most famous landfall in history: In 1992 the New World and the Old celebrated (or lamented, depending on one's politics) the 500th anniversary of the arrival of the *Niña, Pinta,* and *Santa María* at this coral-gilt outcrop. Anticipation of the tourism the quincentennial would inspire is no doubt the reason why the creaking and malodorous *Maxine* was eventually replaced by a new 110-foot mail boat with air-conditioned cabins. Fruit-box pillows are finally going out of style in the Bahamas.

My plan was to retrace, by whatever transportation was available, the route Christopher Columbus followed through Bahamian waters after his landing at San Salvador on October 12, 1492. On the face of it, this seems a simple enough task: The log of the first voyage, lost in the original but substantially transcribed by the near-contemporary chronicler Bartolome de Las Casas, describes the fleet's circuitous route through the archipelago and the series of island landfalls it made. The problem is, the island names given are those that Columbus coined with each new discovery. From San Salvador he sailed to what he called "Santa María de la Concepción," then to "Fernandina," then to "Isabela," then to the southwest and out of the Bahamian archipelago on his way to Cuba. With the exception of San Salvador, which was called Watling Island until 1926, none of these islands bears its Columbus name today. And the distances, directions, and descriptions of terrain given in the surviving version of the log are just ambiguous enough, at crucial junctures, to have inspired nine major theories as to exactly which sequence of island landfalls was followed. Some of the theories are more than a bit tenuous, depending heavily on a blithe disregard of their own weak points and an amplification of everyone else's departures from the log or from common sense. You begin to wonder, after a while, if someone couldn't take the Las Casas translation and use it to prove that Columbus landed on Chincoteague and sailed into the Tidal Basin by way of Annapolis.

But two plausible theories stand out. One, championed by the late historian and Columbus biographer Admiral Samuel Eliot Morison, is based on a first landing at today's San Salvador. The other says the first landing was at Samana Cay, a smaller, uninhabited island on the eastern fringes of the chain. Samana Cay's most recent proponent has been Joseph Judge of the National Geographic Society; in 1986 he published an exhaustive defense of his position, based in part on a computer's estimation of where Columbus should have ended up after the Atlantic crossing. The jury is still out on both major theories, as it is on the less commonly held ones. It probably always will be. For the purposes of my trip, though, I had to choose one version and stick with it. On the basis of my layman's reading of the log, I decided to go with Morison.

In this version, San Salvador is San Salvador, Santa María de la Concepción is today's Rum Cay, Fernandina is Long Island, and Isabela is Crooked Island.

This was the sequence I planned to follow as the *Maxine* approached San Salvador's Fernandez Bay at 9 o'clock in the morning.

This island is fairly large and very flat. It is green, with many trees and several bodies of water. There is a very large lagoon in the middle of the island and there are no mountains. It is a pleasure to gaze upon this place because it is all so green, and the weather is delightful.

— Christopher Columbus's log,
October 13, 1492

We docked at Cockburn Town, the only settlement of any size on San Salvador. Cockburn Town, population several hundred souls, was the type and model of the Bahamian Out Island communities I would see along the Columbus track over the next few days: three or four streets of cinder-block-and-stucco houses, some brightly painted; a grocery store and a bar—the Harlem Square Club, site of a big dominoes tournament that week; a post office/radiophone station; and a couple of churches. On the facade of the Catholic church, Holy Savior, there was a peeling relief portrait of Christopher Columbus.

In the late morning heat I walked the half mile of blacktop—scrub brush on one side and ocean views on the other—that separates Cockburn Town from the Riding Rock Inn.

The latter is a handful of cottages, a short block of plain but cheerful motel units, and a restaurant-bar, all right on the water; up at the bar most of the talk you hear has to do with skin diving. Divers are the principal clientele here. When I arrived, the place was securely in the hands of a California club called the Flipperdippers. At the poolside cookout just after I pulled in, the first snippet of conversation I caught was a tyro Flipperdipper asking an

Excerpted from The Log of Christopher Columbus, *by Robert H. Fuson, courtesy of* International Marine Publishing, © 1987.

old hand if a basket starfish would eat until it exploded. The answer was no, and without waiting around to find out why the questioner suspected such a thing I got up for more rice and crabs. That's when the *maîtresse de barbecue* hove into my path and told me about the dance that night: "If you don't dance, you don't get breakfast."

With the assistance of a Flipperdipper or two, I earned my breakfast. The band was a Cockburn Town outfit of indeterminate numerical strength. Guitarists and conga drummers came and went, and everyone kept commenting that things were really supposed to start jumping when the Kiwanis meeting at the Harlem Square Club let out. Shortly after 10, the band did get a transfusion of new talent, all wearing white cabana shirts patterned with yellow-and-black Kiwanis emblems. They played a couple of good sets, but they did an even better job of exemplifying the phenomenon scholars call the "Columbian Exchange," that cross-pollination of peoples, cultures, flora and fauna, foodstuffs, and microorganisms that followed in the wake of the admiral's fleet and has been transmogrifying the Eastern and Western hemispheres ever since. Here were six descendants of African slaves, wearing the insignia of an American fraternal organization, playing music written by a Jamaican who thought Haile Selassie was God, for a merry throng of skin-diving orthodontists from California on an island discovered by an Italian working for Spain but settled along with the rest of the archipelago by British and American planters who imported the slaves to begin with.

About all that was missing were the Lucayans, the native Bahamians extirpated by the Spaniards—who worked them to death in the mines of Hispaniola—within a generation after Columbus's arrival. It was the Lucayans' island I set off to see the following morning, by motor scooter and on foot.

The people here call this island Guanahani in their language, and their speech is very fluent, although I do not understand any of it. They are friendly and well-dispositioned people who bear no arms except for small spears, and they have no iron. I showed one my sword, and through ignorance he grabbed it by the blade and cut himself.

— October 12

The San Salvador of the Lucayans is but a memory, as they are. When Columbus arrived, there were tall trees on the island, but the planters of the late 18th and early 19th centuries deforested the place so that now virtually the only vegetation is the dense, stickery brush called "haulback." The island's interior, though, still conveys the same sense of impenetrability and desolation that it must have to the first Europeans who came here, and no doubt to the Lucayans themselves. Fishermen as well as cultivators must have stayed close to shore, except to travel from one end of San Salvador to the other by dugout canoe across a system of brackish lakes that covers nearly half of the interior. From a crude concrete-and-wood observation platform on a rise near the airport, you can take in the sprawl of these lakes and the lonely, thicketed hills (the terrain isn't all as flat as Columbus described it) that break them into crazy patterns. No one lives there; it's hard to imagine that anyone ever goes there.

I drove the scooter the length of the island's circuit road, past crescent beaches with white sand so fine it coats your feet like flour, past ruined plantation buildings, past "Ed's First and Last Bar," a homey little joint out in the sticks that would be beerless until the cases made it up from the mail boat dock, past four monuments to Columbus's landing at four different places (a fifth marker is underwater, where somebody decided his anchor hit bottom), and past the Dixon Hill Lighthouse ("Imperial Lighthouse Service"), billed as one of 10 left in the world that run on kerosene.

Past, and then back again—I bullied the scooter up Dixon Hill, because you don't get to climb to the top of a lighthouse every day.

I went looking for the light keeper, but instead I found my ride to Rum Cay, according to Morison the second of Columbus's landfalls on his first voyage. It was a family of blue-water sailors—an American named Kent, his German wife, Britta, and their two-month-old baby, Luke, who had cruised to San Salvador from St. Thomas in their 32-foot sailboat. Having hitchhiked up from Cockburn Town, the baby in a shaded basket, they too were waiting for the light keeper to show up; after she did, and took us to the top, the sailing couple offered to let me hitch with them the next day on the 30-mi run to Rum Cay. I soon learned I would be in good hands: Later that day, Kent asked a local if he knew anything about Rum Cay.

"What do you want to know?" the man responded.

"What's the anchorage like in a southeast wind?"

I'd have asked where to eat, or if the Kiwanis had a band.

I made sail and saw so many islands that I could not decide where to go first . . . Finally, I looked for the largest island and decided to go there.

— October 14

Christopher Columbus left San Salvador on October 11, 1492, and later that day arrived at the island he named Santa María de la Concepción. My adopted family and I weighed anchor at Cockburn Town and sailed out of Fernandez Bay early in the morning of a bright June day, flying fish scudding around our bows and cottony trade clouds riding briskly above. Luke, already a veteran mariner, slept in his basket below. We sighted Rum Cay when we were 10 mi out from San Salvador—Columbus had a much higher mast to

climb—but the distant shoreline was to loom for a long time before we could draw very close to it. The east shore and much of the south shore of Rum Cay are girded with lethal reefs, and both the charts and the *Yachtsman's Guide to the Bahamas* go to great pains to point out so precise a route to the anchorage that it might as well have been the directions to a parking space in George Town. Six other boats had negotiated the coral gauntlet that day, including one whose captain gave us half of a blackfin tuna he'd just caught. How Columbus safely pulled it off (his anchorage was at a point west of ours) is beyond imagining.

Rum Cay, which once made a living selling sea salt to Nova Scotia's cod packers, has shriveled in population until barely 60 people today inhabit its sole settlement of Port Nelson. An American, David Melville, opened a small skin-diving resort called the Rum Cay Club a mile from town a few years back: When I arrived, the place was closed for renovations. There were no Flipperdippers here—just Melville, a couple of handymen, and the locals down the road. Rum Cay was, for the moment, almost out of things to do and people to do them.

Almost, but not quite. There's always Kay's Bar, where proprietor Dolores Wilson turns out lovely baked chicken and coconut bread to wash down with the Out Islands' requisite gallons of beer and rum in an atmosphere dominated by a satellite TV, an antique space-age jukebox, turtle shells with colored lightbulbs in them, and a giant poster of Bob Marley wearing a beatific grin and knitted hat that looks like a Rasta halo. People who sailed to the Bahamas years ago have told me that Dolores was once something of a hellraiser, but she seems to have settled into sweet grandmotherliness by now. For ethyl-powered amusement, I had to rely on an expatriate Oklahoman named Billy. Billy, whose personal style ran to the pirate-biker look, was Melville's mechanical factotum at the

Rum Cay Club. His avocation, as I discovered when I took a Jeep ride with him to the other side of the island, is nonstop talking. In the space of an hour, Billy went chapter and verse on everything from his archery prowess in Oklahoma, to how he could build an ammonia-powered icehouse like the one in *The Mosquito Coast*, to his deepest feelings about the universe: "You know, I like everything and I hate everything."

"That's called having a lover's quarrel with the world," I told him, remembering Frost.

"Oh, they have a name for it now?"

I decided not to linger very long at Santa María de la Concepción, for I saw that there was no gold there and the wind freshened to a SE crosswind. I departed the island for the ship after a two hours' stay.

— October 16

It was Billy who drove me to catch a plane to Long Island—Columbus's Fernandina, his third landfall—on the following afternoon. Back on San Salvador, I'd been told that the ticket to getting off Rum Cay without waiting for the next mail boat was to "ask for Bobby with the plane." But there was no plane on the island's crushed-coral landing strip. Bobby had flown somewhere, so rather than spend another night I asked Melville to radio the Stella Maris Inn on Long Island for a plane. They sent a Cessna four-seater, which landed just as Billy was pouring me a rum-and-powdered-lemonade at his house—he insisted on this hospitable stopover, since it was a whole mile between Kay's Bar and the airstrip. Besides, his own much-loved blue plastic cup was empty.

Long Island: a day's sail from Rum Cay for the *Niña*, *Pinta*, and *Santa María* on October 17, 1492; 15 minutes in the Cessna. As we approached the landing strip, I looked down to see territory that looked almost like a manicured suburb compared with the trackless scrub forests of Rum Cay and San Salvador. Here were roads, trees, villas, broad beaches, swimming pools . . . in short, a modest but complete resort, and run by Germans to boot. This last fact is worthy of remark because of the concept known as "Bahamian time," best defined as a devil-may-care approach to the minute hand. Somehow, the Germans and Bahamians had arrived at a compromise: The shuttle to the beach leaves more or less on time, but you don't have to eat breakfast at 7:23 AM.

I wanted to follow Columbus up and down this island. Near its northern tip is a shallow cove outside of which he anchored while several of his men went ashore for water. If local legend can be trusted, they filled their casks at a deep natural well in the coral rock, which a Stella Maris driver showed me. He had drawn water there as a small boy, just 450 years after the Spanish expedition.

A couple of miles from the well was the cove, a harbor with "two entrances," according to the 1492 log, which the admiral sounded in his ships' boats. At least it seemed to me to be the place, and "Where Was Columbus?" is a game that anyone with a copy of the log can play. I explored the cove and, while snorkeling, was reminded of the entry for October 17: "Here the fishes are so unlike ours that it is amazing."

To reach Columbus's final Long Island anchorage, at a place called Little Harbour in a village with the pretty name of Roses, was not such an easy job. I rented a VW bug and drove south for nearly 80 mi to the tip of this 2-mi-wide island. The road passed through one little town after another, each with its neat cinder-block school and tiny Protestant church. At Roses I found a storekeeper who knew the road to Little Harbour. It ended at a dump a mile into the bush. I walked nearly another mile—had I been heading due east I would have been in the water. I wasn't going to find Little Harbour, not in this pounding sun on a trail narrowing to the width of an iguana, any more than Columbus was going to find Japan.

Columbus got farther than I did, though. He wandered southeast from Long Island to Crooked Island, then southwest to the southernmost of the Ragged Islands, where the tiny outpost called Duncan Town now stands. This was his last Bahamas anchorage before he sailed off to Cuba, Hispaniola, and immortality.

The odd thing is, Columbus had an easier time pressing ahead than I would have had. Although it's true that he was not only lost in the Caribbean but stuck in the 15th century, at least his fleet was self-contained, and one island was as good as another. For me, the Cessnas were too expensive, the mail boats too infrequent, the lodgings from Long Island south, on Crooked Island, and at Duncan Town, nonexistent. These places are as far away as they ever were. They are, in fact, parts of the New World that haven't really been discovered yet.

— William G. Scheller

A resident of Newbury, Massachusetts, William G. Scheller contributes travel pieces regularly to National Geographic, Condé Nast Traveler, and the Washington Post Magazine.

CASHING IN: A CASINO GAMBLING PRIMER

For a short-form handbook on the rules, the plays, the odds, and the strategies for the most popular casino games—or to decide on the kind of action that's for you and suits your style—read on. You must be 18 to gamble; Bahamians and permanent residents are not permitted to indulge.

The Good Bets

The first part of any viable casino strategy is to risk the most money on wagers that present the lowest edge for the house. Blackjack, craps, video poker, and baccarat are the most advantageous to the bettor in this regard. The two types of bets at baccarat have a house advantage of a little more than 1%. The basic line bets at craps, if backed up with full odds, can be as low as ½%. Blackjack and video poker, at times, can not only put you even with the house (a true 50–50 proposition), but actually give you a slight long-term advantage.

How can a casino possibly provide you with a 50–50 or even a positive expectation at some of its games? First, because a vast number of suckers make the bad bets (those with a house advantage of 5%–35%, such as roulette, keno, and slots) day in and day out. Second, because the casino knows that very few people are aware of the opportunities to beat the odds. Third, because it takes skill—requiring study and practice—to be in a position to exploit these opportunities the casino presents. However, a mere hour or two spent learning strategies for the beatable games will put you light years ahead of the vast majority of visitors who give the gambling industry an average 12% to 15% profit margin.

Baccarat

The most "glamorous" game in the casino, baccarat (pronounced *bah*-kuh-rah) is a version of *chemin de fer,* popular in European gambling halls, and is a favorite with high rollers, because thousands of dollars are often staked on one hand. The Italian word *baccara* means "zero"; this refers to the point value of 10s and picture cards. The game is run by four pit personnel. Two dealers sit side by side in the middle of the table; they handle the winning and losing bets and keep track of each player's "commission" (explained below). The "caller" stands in the middle of the other side of the table and dictates the action. The ladderman supervises the game and acts as final judge if any disputes arise.

How to Play. Baccarat is played with eight decks of cards dealt from a large "shoe" (or cardholder). Each player is offered a turn at handling the shoe and dealing the cards. Two two-card hands are dealt, the "player" and the "bank" hands. The player who deals the cards is called the banker, though the house, of course, banks both hands. The players bet on which hand, player or banker, will come closest to adding up to 9 (a "natural"). The cards are totaled as follows: ace through 9 retain face value, while 10s and picture cards are worth zero. If you have a hand adding up to more than 10, the number 10 is subtracted from the total. For example, if one hand contains a 10 and a 4, the hand adds up to 4. If the other holds an ace and 6, it adds up to 7. If a hand has a 7 and 9, it adds up to 6.

Depending on the two hands, the caller either declares a winner and loser (if either hand actually adds up to 8 or 9), or calls for another card for the player hand (if it totals 1, 2, 3, 4, 5, or 10). The bank hand then either stands pat or draws a card, determined by a complex series of rules depending on what the player's total is and dictated by the caller. When one or the other hand is declared a winner, the dealers go into action to pay off the winning wagers, collect the losing wagers, and add up the commission (usually 5%) that the house collects on the bank hand. Both bets have a house advantage of slightly more than 1%.

The player-dealer (or banker) continues to hold the shoe as long as the bank hand wins. As soon as the player hand wins, the shoe moves counterclockwise around the table. Players are not required to deal; they can refuse the shoe and pass it to the next player. Because the caller dictates the action, the player responsibilities are minimal. It's not necessary to know any of the card-drawing rules, even if you're the banker.

Baccarat Strategy. Making a bet at baccarat is very simple. All you have to do is place your money in either the bank, player, or tie box on the layout, which appears directly in front of where you sit at the table. If you're betting that the bank hand will win, you put your chips in the bank box; bets for the player hand go in the player box. (Only real suckers bet on the tie.) Most players bet on the bank hand when they deal, since they "represent" the bank, and to do otherwise would seem as if they were betting "against" themselves. This isn't really true, but it seems that way. In the end, playing baccarat is a simple matter of guessing whether the player or banker hand will come closest to 9, and deciding how much to bet on the outcome.

Blackjack

How to Play. Basically, here's how it works: You play blackjack against a dealer, and whichever of you comes closest to a card total of 21 is the winner. Number cards are worth their face value, picture cards are worth 10, and aces are worth either 1 or 11. (Hands with aces in them are known as "soft" hands. Always count the ace first as an 11; if you also have a 10, your total will be 21, not 11.) If the dealer has a 17 and you have a 16, you lose. If you have an 18 against a dealer's 17, you win (even money). If both you and the dealer have a 17, it's a tie (or "push") and no money changes hands. If you go over a total of 21 (or "bust"), you lose immedi-

ately, even if the dealer also busts later in the hand. If your first two cards add up to 21 (a "natural"), you're paid 3 to 2. However, if the dealer also has a natural, it's a push. A natural beats a total of 21 achieved with more than two cards.

You're dealt two cards, either face down or face up, depending on the custom of the particular casino. The dealer also gives herself two cards, one face down and one face up (except in double-exposure blackjack, where both the dealer's cards are visible). Depending on your first two cards and the dealer's up card, you can **stand**, or refuse to take another card. You can **hit**, or take as many cards as you need until you stand or bust. You can **double down**, or double your bet and take one card. You can **split** a like pair; if you're dealt two 8s, for example, you can double your bet and play the 8s as if they're two hands. You can **buy insurance** if the dealer is showing an ace. Here you're wagering half your initial bet that the dealer *does* have a natural; if so, you lose your initial bet, but are paid 2 to 1 on the insurance (which means the whole thing is a push). You can **surrender** half your initial bet if you're holding a bad hand (known as a "stiff") such as a 15 or 16 against a high-up card like a 9 or 10.

Blackjack Strategy. Playing blackjack is not only knowing the rules—it's also knowing *how* to play. Many people devote a great deal of time to learning complicated statistical schemes. However, if you don't have the time, energy, or inclination to get that seriously involved, the following basic strategies, which cover more than half the situations you'll face, should allow you to play the game with a modicum of skill and a paucity of humiliation:

- When your hand is a stiff (a total of 12, 13, 14, 15, or 16) and the dealer shows a 2, 3, 4, 5, or 6, always stand.

- When your hand is a stiff and the dealer shows a 7, 8, 9, 10, or ace, always hit.

- When you hold 17, 18, 19, or 20, always stand.

- When you hold a 10 or 11 and the dealer shows a 2, 3, 4, 5, 6, 7, 8, or 9, always double down.

- When you hold a pair of aces or a pair of 8s, always split.

- Never buy insurance.

Craps

Craps is a dice game played at a large rectangular table with rounded corners. Up to 12 players can crowd around the table, all standing. The layout is mounted at the bottom of a surrounding "rail," which prevents the dice from being thrown off the table and provides an opposite wall against which to bounce the dice. It can require up to four pit personnel to run an action-packed, fast-paced game of craps. Two dealers handle the bets made on either side of the layout. A "stickman" wields the long wooden "stick," curved at one end, which is used to move the dice around the table; the stickman also calls the number that's rolled and books the proposition bets made in the middle of the layout. The "boxman" sits between the two dealers and oversees the game; he settles any disputes about rules, payoffs, mistakes, and so on.

How to Play. To play, just stand at the table wherever you can find an open space. You can start betting casino chips immediately, but you have to wait your turn to be the shooter. The dice move around the table in a clockwise fashion: The person to your right shoots before you, the one to the left after (the stickman will give you the dice at the appropriate time). It's important, when you're the "shooter," to roll the dice hard enough so they bounce off the end wall of the table; this ensures a random bounce and shows that you're not trying to control the dice with a "soft roll."

Craps Strategy. Playing craps is fairly straightforward; it's the betting that's complicated. The basic concepts are as follows: If, the first time the shooter rolls the dice, he or she turns up a 7 or 11, that's called a "natural"—an automatic win. If a 2, 3, or 12 comes up on the first throw (called the "come-out roll"), that's termed "craps"—an automatic lose. Each of the numbers 4, 5, 6, 8, 9, or 10 on a first roll is known as a "point": The shooter keeps rolling the dice until the point comes up again. If a 7 turns up before the point does, that's another loser. When either the point or a losing 7 is rolled, this is known as a "decision," which happens on average every 3.3 rolls.

But "winning" and "losing" rolls of the dice are entirely relative in this game, because there are two ways you can bet at craps: "for" the shooter or "against" the shooter. Betting for means that the shooter will "make his point" (win). Betting against means that the shooter will "seven out" (lose). (Either way, you're actually betting against the house, which books all wagers.) If you're betting "for" on the come-out, you'd place your chips on the layout's "pass line." If a 7 or 11 is rolled, you win even money. If a 2, 3, or 12 (craps) is rolled, you lose your bet. If you're betting "against" on the come-out, you place your chips in the "don't pass bar." A 7 or 11 loses, a 2, 3, or 12 wins. A shooter can bet for or against himself or herself, as well as for or against the other players.

There are also roughly two dozen wagers you can make on any single specific roll of the dice. Craps strategy books can give you the details on Come/Don't Come, Odds, Place, Buy, Big Six, Field, and Proposition bets.

Roulette

Roulette is a casino game that utilizes a perfectly balanced wheel with 38 numbers (0, 00, and 1 through 36), a small white ball, a large layout with 11 different betting options, and special "wheel chips." The layout organizes 11 different bets into six "inside bets" (the single numbers, or those closest to the dealer) and five "outside bets" (the grouped bets, or those closest to the players).

The dealer spins the wheel clockwise and the ball counterclockwise. When the ball slows, the dealer announces, "No more bets." The ball drops from the "back track" to the "bottom track," caroming off built-in brass barriers and bouncing in and out of the different cups in the wheel before settling into the cup of the winning number. Then the dealer places a marker on the number and scoops all the losing chips into her corner. Depending on how crowded the game is, the casino can count on roughly 50 spins of the wheel per hour.

How to Play. To buy in, place your cash on the layout near the wheel. Inform the dealer of the denomination of the individual unit you intend to play (usually 25¢ or $1, but it can go up as high as $500). Know the table limits (displayed on a sign in the dealer area)—don't ask for a 25¢ denomination if the minimum is $1. The dealer gives you a stack of wheel chips of a different color from those of all the other players, and places a chip marker atop one of your wheel chips on the rim of the wheel to identify its denomination. Note that you must cash in your wheel chips at the roulette table before you leave the game. Only the dealer can verify how much they're worth.

Roulette Strategy. With **inside bets,** you can lay any number of chips (depending on the table limits) on a single number, 1 through 36 or 0 or 00. If the number hits, your payoff is 35 to 1, for a return of $36. You could, conceivably, place a $1 chip on all 38 numbers, but the return of $36 would leave you $2 short, which divides out to 5.26%, the house advantage. If you place a chip on the line between two numbers and one of those numbers hits, you're paid 17 to 1 for a return of $18 (again, $2 short of the true odds). Betting on three numbers returns 11 to 1, four numbers returns 8 to 1, five numbers pays 6 to 1 (this is the worst

bet at roulette, with a 7.89% disadvantage), and six numbers pays 5 to 1.

To place an **outside bet,** lay a chip on one of three "columns" at the lower end of the layout next to numbers 34, 35, and 36; this pays 2 to 1. A bet placed in the first 12, second 12, or third 12 boxes also pays 2 to 1. A bet on red or black, odd or even, and 1 through 18 or 19 through 36 pays off at even money, 1 to 1. If you think you can bet on red *and* black, or odd *and* even, in order to play roulette and drink for free all night, think again. The green 0 or 00, which fall outside these two basic categories, will come up on average once every 19 spins of the wheel.

Slot Machines

Around the turn of the century, Charlie Fey built the first mechanical slot in his San Francisco basement. Slot-machine technology has exploded in the past 20 years, and now there are hundreds of different models, which accept everything from pennies to specially minted $500 tokens. The major advance in the game, however, is the progressive jackpot. Banks of slots within a particular casino are connected by computer, and the jackpot total is displayed on a digital meter above the machines. Generally, the total increases by 5% of the wager. If you're playing a dollar machine, each time you pull the handle (or press the spin button), a nickel is added to the jackpot.

How to Play. To play, insert your penny, nickel, quarter, silver dollar, or dollar token into the slot at the far right edge of the machine. Pull the handle or press the spin button, then wait for the reels to spin and stop one by one, and for the machine to determine whether you're a winner (occasionally) or a loser (the rest of the time). It's pretty simple—but because there are so many different types of machines nowadays, be sure you know exactly how the one you're playing operates.

Slot-Machine Strategy. The house advantage on slots varies widely from machine to machine, between 3% and 25%. Casinos that advertise a 97% payback are telling you that at least one of their slot machines has a house advantage of 3%. Which one? There's really no way of knowing. Generally, $1 machines pay back at a higher percentage than quarter or nickel machines. On the other hand, machines with smaller jackpots pay back more money more frequently, meaning that you'll be playing with more of your winnings.

One of the all-time great myths about slot machines is that they're "due" for a jackpot. Slots, like roulette, craps, keno, and Big Six, are subject to the Law of Independent Trials, which means the odds are permanently and unalterably fixed. If the odds of lining up three sevens on a 25¢ slot machine have been set by the casino at 1 in 10,000, then those odds remain 1 in 10,000 whether the three 7s have been hit three times in a row or not hit for 90,000 plays. Don't waste a lot of time playing a machine that you suspect is "ready," and don't think if someone hits a jackpot on a particular machine only minutes after you've finished playing on it that it was "yours."

Video Poker

Like blackjack, video poker is a game of strategy and skill, and at select times on select machines, the player actually holds the advantage, however slight, over the house. Unlike slot machines, you can determine the exact edge of video poker machines. Like slots, however, video poker machines are often tied into a progressive meter; when the jackpot total reaches high enough, you can beat the casino at its own game. The variety of video poker machines is already large, and it's growing steadily larger. All of the different machines are played in similar fashion, but the strategies are different. This section deals only with straight-draw video poker.

How to Play. The schedule for the payback on winning hands is posted on the machine, usually above the screen. It lists the returns for a high pair (generally jacks or better), two pair, three of a kind, a flush, full house, straight flush, four of a kind, and royal flush, depending on the number of coins played—usually 1, 2, 3, 4, or 5. Look for machines that pay with a single coin played: one coin for "jacks or better" (meaning a pair of jacks, queens, kings, or aces; any other pair is a stiff), two coins for two pairs, three for three of a kind, six for a flush, nine for a full house, 50 for a straight flush, 100 for four of a kind, and 250 for a royal flush. This is known as a 9/6 machine—one that gives a nine-coin payback for the full house and a six-coin payback for the flush with one coin played. Other machines are known as 8/5 (8 for the full house, 5 for the flush), 7/5, and 6/5.

You want a 9/6 machine because it gives you the best odds: The return from a standard 9/6 straight-draw machine is 99.5%; you give up only a half percent to the house. An 8/5 machine returns 97.3%. On 6/5 machines, the figure drops to 95.1%, slightly less than roulette. Machines with varying paybacks are scattered throughout the casinos. In some you'll see an 8/5 machine right next to a 9/6, and someone will be blithely playing the 8/5 machine!

As with slot machines, it's always optimum to play the maximum number of coins to qualify for the jackpot. You insert five coins into the slot and press the "deal" button. Five cards appear on the screen—say, 5, J, Q, 5, 9. To hold the pair of 5s, you press the hold buttons under the first and fourth cards. The word "hold" appears underneath the two 5s. You then press the "draw" button (often the same button as "deal") and three new cards appear on the screen—say, 10, J, 5. You have three 5s; with five coins bet, the machine will give you 15 credits. Now you can press the "max bet" button: five units will be removed from your number of credits, and five new cards will appear on the screen. You repeat the hold and draw process; if you hit a winning hand, the proper payback will be added to your credits. Those who want coins rather than credit can hit the "cash out" button at any time. Some machines don't have credit counters and automatically dispense coins for a winning hand.

Video-Poker Strategy. Like blackjack, video poker has a basic strategy that's been formulated by the computer simulation of hundreds of millions of hands. The most effective way to learn it is with a video poker computer program that deals the cards on your screen, then tutors you in how to play each hand properly. If you don't want to devote that much time to the study of video poker, memorizing these six rules will help you make the right decision for more than half the hands you'll be dealt:

- If you're dealt a completely "stiff" hand (no like cards and no picture cards), draw five new cards.

- If you're dealt a hand with no like cards but with one jack, queen, king, or ace, always hold on to the picture card; if you're dealt two different picture cards, hold both. But if you're dealt three different picture cards, only hold two (the two of the same suit, if that's an option).

- If you're dealt a pair, always hold it, no matter what the face value.

- Never hold a picture card with a pair of 2s through 10s.

- Never draw two cards to try for a straight or a flush.

- Never draw one card to try for an inside straight.

INDEX

NOTES

NOTES

NOTES

NOTES

NOTES

NOTES

FODOR'S KEY TO THE GUIDES

America's guidebook leader publishes guides for every kind of traveler. Check out our many series and find your perfect match.

FODOR'S GOLD GUIDES

America's favorite travel-guide series offers the most detailed insider reviews of hotels, restaurants, and attractions in all price ranges, plus great background information, smart tips, and useful maps.

COMPASS AMERICAN GUIDES

Stunning guides from top local writers and photographers, with gorgeous photos, literary excerpts, and colorful anecdotes. A must-have for culture mavens, history buffs, and new residents.

FODOR'S CITYPACKS

Concise city coverage in a guide plus a foldout map. The right choice for urban travelers who want everything under one cover.

FODOR'S EXPLORING GUIDES

Hundreds of color photos bring your destination to life. Lively stories lend insight into the culture, history, and people.

FODOR'S TRAVEL HISTORIC AMERICA

For travelers who want to experience history firsthand, this series gives in-depth coverage of historic sights, plus nearby restaurants and hotels. Themes include the Thirteen Colonies, the Old West, and the Lewis and Clark Trail.

FODOR'S POCKET GUIDES

For travelers who need only the essentials. The best of Fodor's in pocket-size packages for just $9.95.

FODOR'S FLASHMAPS

Every resident's map guide, with dozens of easy-to-follow maps of public transit, restaurants, shopping, museums, and more.

FODOR'S CITYGUIDES

Sourcebooks for living in the city: thousands of in-the-know listings for restaurants, shops, sports, nightlife, and other city resources.

FODOR'S AROUND THE CITY WITH KIDS

Up to 68 great ideas for family days, recommended by resident parents. Perfect for exploring in your own backyard or on the road.

FODOR'S HOW TO GUIDES

Get tips from the pros on planning the perfect trip. Learn how to pack, fly hassle-free, plan a honeymoon or cruise, stay healthy on the road, and travel with your baby.

FODOR'S LANGUAGES FOR TRAVELERS

Practice the local language before you hit the road. Available in phrase books, cassette sets, and CD sets.

KAREN BROWN'S GUIDES

Engaging guides—many with easy-to-follow inn-to-inn itineraries—to the most charming inns and B&Bs in the U.S.A. and Europe.

BAEDEKER'S GUIDES

Comprehensive guides, trusted since 1829, packed with A–Z reviews and star ratings.

OTHER GREAT TITLES FROM FODOR'S

Baseball Vacations, The Complete Guide to the National Parks, Family Vacations, Golf Digest's Places to Play, Great American Drives of the East, Great American Drives of the West, Great American Vacations, Healthy Escapes, National Parks of the West, Skiing USA.